Lecture Notes in Artificial Intelligence   9858

Subseries of Lecture Notes in Computer Science

LNAI Series Editors

Randy Goebel
University of Alberta, Edmonton, Canada
Yuzuru Tanaka
Hokkaido University, Sapporo, Japan
Wolfgang Wahlster
DFKI and Saarland University, Saarbrücken, Germany

LNAI Founding Series Editor

Joerg Siekmann
DFKI and Saarland University, Saarbrücken, Germany

More information about this series at http://www.springer.com/series/1244

Steven Schockaert · Pierre Senellart (Eds.)

Scalable Uncertainty Management

10th International Conference, SUM 2016
Nice, France, September 21–23, 2016
Proceedings

 Springer

Editors
Steven Schockaert
Cardiff University
Cardiff
UK

Pierre Senellart
Télécom ParisTech
Paris
France

ISSN 0302-9743   ISSN 1611-3349   (electronic)
Lecture Notes in Artificial Intelligence
ISBN 978-3-319-45855-7   ISBN 978-3-319-45856-4   (eBook)
DOI 10.1007/978-3-319-45856-4

Library of Congress Control Number: 2016949633

LNCS Sublibrary: SL7 – Artificial Intelligence

Printed on acid-free paper

This Springer imprint is published by Springer Nature
The registered company is Springer International Publishing AG Switzerland

Preface

Research areas such as Artificial Intelligence and Databases increasingly rely on principled methods for representing and manipulating large amounts of uncertain information. To meet this challenge, researchers in these fields are drawing from a wide range of different methodologies and uncertainty models. While Bayesian methods remain the default choice in most disciplines, sometimes there is a need for more cautious approaches, relying for instance on imprecise probabilities, ordinal uncertainty representations, or even purely qualitative models.

The International Conference on Scalable Uncertainty Management (SUM) aims to provide a forum for researchers who are working on uncertainty management, in different communities and with different uncertainty models, to meet and exchange ideas. Previous SUM conferences have been held in Washington DC (2007), Naples (2008), Washington DC (2009), Toulouse (2010), Dayton (2011), Marburg (2012), Washington DC (2013), Oxford (2014), and Québec City (2015).

This volume contains contributions from the 10th SUM conference, which was held in Nice, France on September 21–23, 2016. The conference attracted 25 submissions of long papers and 5 submissions of short papers, of which respectively 18 and 5 were accepted for publication and presentation at the conference, based on three rigorous reviews by members of the Program Committee or external reviewers. In addition, we received 5 extended abstracts, which were accepted for presentation at the conference but are not included in this volume.

An important aim of the SUM conference is to build bridges between different communities. This aim is reflected in the choice of the three keynote speakers, who are all active in more than one community, using a diverse set of approaches to uncertainty management: Guy Van den Broeck, Jonathan Lawry, and Eyke Hüllermeier. To further embrace the aim of facilitating interdisciplinary collaboration and cross-fertilization of ideas, and building on the tradition of invited discussants at SUM, the conference featured 11 tutorials, covering a broad set of topics related to uncertainty management. A companion paper for 3 of these tutorials is present in this volume.

We would like to thank all authors and invited speakers for their valuable contributions, and the members of the Program Committee and external reviewers for their detailed and critical assessment of the submissions. We are also very grateful to Andrea Tettamanzi and his team for hosting the conference in Nice.

July 2016

Pierre Senellart
Steven Schockaert

Organization

Program Committee

Antoine Amarilli	Télécom ParisTech, France
Chitta Baral	Arizona State University, USA
Salem Benferhat	CRIL, CNRS, Université d'Artois, France
Laure Berti-Equille	Qatar Computing Research Institute, Hamad Bin Khalifa University, Qatar
Richard Booth	Cardiff University, UK
Stephane Bressan	National University of Singapore, Singapore
T-H. Hubert Chan	The University of Hong Kong, Hong Kong, China
Olivier Colot	Université Lille 1, France
Fabio Cozman	Universidade de Sao Paulo, Brazil
Jesse Davis	KU Leuven, Belgium
Thierry Denoeux	Université de Technologie de Compiègne, France
Didier Dubois	IRIT, CNRS, France
Thomas Eiter	Vienna University of Technology, Austria
Wolfgang Gatterbauer	Carnegie Mellon University, USA
Lluis Godo	Artificial Intelligence Research Institute, IIIA - CSIC, Spain
Anthony Hunter	University College London, UK
Gabriele Kern-Isberner	Technische Universität Dortmund, Germany
Evgeny Kharlamov	University of Oxford, UK
Benny Kimelfeld	Technion - Israel Institute of Technology, Israel
Andrey Kolobov	Microsoft Research, USA
Sébastien Konieczny	CRIL, CNRS, France
Sanjiang Li	University of Technology Sydney, Australia
Thomas Lukasiewicz	University of Oxford, UK
Zongmin Ma	Nanjing University of Aeronautics and Astronautics, China
Silviu Maniu	Université Paris-Sud, France
Serafin Moral	University of Granada, Spain
Wilfred Ng	HKUST, Hong Kong, China
Rafael Peñaloza	Free University of Bozen-Bolzano, Italy
Olivier Pivert	IRISA-ENSSAT, France
Sunil Prabhakar	Purdue University, USA
Henri Prade	IRIT, CNRS, France
Steven Schockaert	Cardiff University, UK
Pierre Senellart	Télécom ParisTech, France

Guillermo Simari	Universidad Nacional del Sur in Bahia Blanca, Argentina
Umberto Straccia	ISTI-CNR, Italy
Guy Van den Broeck	UCLA, USA
Maurice Van Keulen	University of Twente, Netherlands
Andreas Zuefle	George Mason University, USA

Additional Reviewers

Bouraoui, Zied
Kuzelka, Ondrej
Weinzierl, Antonius
Zheleznyakov, Dmitriy

Contents

Short Papers

Invited Surveys

Combinatorial Games: From Theoretical Solving to AI Algorithms

Eric Duchêne[(✉)]

Université de Lyon, CNRS Université Lyon 1, LIRIS, UMR5205, 69622 Lyon, France
eric.duchene@univ-lyon1.fr

Abstract. Combinatorial game solving is a research field that is frequently highlighted each time a program defeats the best human player: Deep Blue (IBM) vs Kasparov for Chess in 1997, and Alpha Go (Google) vs Lee Sedol for the game of Go in 2016. But what is hidden behind these success stories? First of all, I will consider combinatorial games from a theoretical point of view. We will see how to proceed to properly define and deal with the concepts of outcome, value, and winning strategy. Are there some games for which an exact winning strategy can be expected? Unfortunately, the answer is no in many cases (including some of the most famous ones like Go, Othello, Chess or Checkers), as exact game solving belongs to the problems of highest complexity. Therefore, finding out an effective approximate strategy has highly motivated the community of AI researchers. In the current survey, the basics of the best AI programs will be presented, and in particular the well-known *Minimax* and *Monte-Carlo Tree Search* approaches.

1 Combinatorial Games

1.1 Introduction

Playing combinatorial games is a common activity for the general public. Indeed, the games of Go, Chess or Checkers are rather familiar to all of us. However, the underlying mathematical theory that enables to compute the winner of a given game, or more generally, to build a sequence of winning moves, is rather recent. It was settled by Berlekamp, Conway and Guy only in the late 70s [2,8]. The current section will present the highlights of this beautiful theory.

In order to avoid any confusion, first note that *combinatorial game theory* (here shortened as *CGT*) is very different from the so-called "economic" game theory introduced by Von Neumann and Morgenstern. I often consider that a preliminary activity to tackle CGT issues is the reading of Siegel's book [31] which gives a strong and formal background on CGT. Strictly speaking, a combinatorial game must satisfy the following criteria:

Definition 1 (Combinatorial Game). *In a combinatorial game, the following constraints are satisfied:*

Supported by the ANR-14-CE25-0006 project of the French National Research Agency and the CNRS PICS-07315 project.

S. Schockaert and P. Senellart (Eds.): SUM 2016, LNAI 9858, pp. 3–17, 2016.
DOI: 10.1007/978-3-319-45856-4_1

- *There are exactly two players, called "Left" and "Right", who alternate moves. Nobody can miss his turn.*
- *There is no hidden information: all possible moves are known to both players.*
- *There are no chance moves such as rolling dice or shuffling cards.*
- *The rules are defined in such a way that play will always come to an end.*
- *The last move determines the winner: in the* normal play convention, *the first player unable to move loses. In the* misère play convention, *the last player to move loses.*

Examples of such games are NIM [6] or DOMINEERING [20]. In the first one, game positions are tuples of non-negative integers $(a_1, \ldots, a_n)$. A move consists in strictly decreasing exactly one of the values a_i for some $1 \leq i \leq n$, provided the resulting position remains valid. The first player unable to move loses. In other words, reaching the position $(0, \ldots, 0)$ is a winning move. The game DOMINEERING is played on a rectangular grid. The two players alternately place a domino on the grid under the following condition: Left must place his dominoes vertically and Right horizontally. Once again, the first player unable to place a domino loses. Figure 1 illustrates a position for this game, where Left started and wins, since Right cannot place any additional horizontal domino.

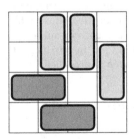

Fig. 1. Playing DOMINEERING: right cannot play and loses

A useful property derived from Definition 1 is that any combinatorial game can be played indifferently on a particular (finite) tree. This tree is built as described in Definition 2.

Definition 2 (Game Tree). *Given a game $\mathcal{G}$ with starting position S, the game tree associated to $(\mathcal{G}, S)$ is a semi-ordered rooted tree defined as follows:*

- *The vertex root correspond to the starting position S.*
- *All the game positions reachable for Left (resp. Right) in a single move from S are set as left (resp. right) children of the root.*
- *Apply the previous rule recursively for each child.*

Figure 2 gives an example of such a game tree for DOMINEERING with starting position ⌐ . For more convenience, note that only the top three levels of the tree are depicted (there is one additional level when fully expanded).

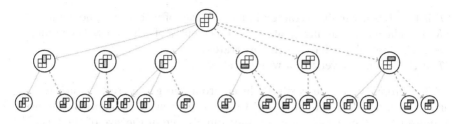

Fig. 2. Game tree of a DOMINEERING position

Now, playing any game on its game tree consists is moving alternately a token from the root to a leaf. Each player must follow an edge corresponding to his direction (i.e., full edges for Left and dashed ones for Right). In the normal play convention, the first player who moves the token on a leaf of the tree is the winner. We will see later on that this tree representation is very useful, both to compute exact and approximate strategies.

In view of Definition 1, one can remark that the specified conditions are too strong to cover some of the well-known abstract 2-player games. For example, Chess and Checkers may have draw outcomes, which is not allowed in a combinatorial game. This is due to the fact that some game positions can be visited several times during the play. Such games are called *loopy*. In games like Go, Dots and Boxes or Othello, the winner is determined with a score and not according to the player making the last move. However, such games remain very close to combinatorial games. Some keys can be found in the literature to deal with their resolution ([31], chap. 6 for loopy games, and [24] for an overview on scoring game theory). In addition, first attempts to built an "absolute" theory that would cover normal and misère play conventions, loopy and scoring games have been recently made [23]. Note that the concepts and issues that will be introduced in the current survey make also sense in this extended framework.

1.2 Main Issues in CGT

Given a game, researchers in CGT are generally concerned with the following three issues:

- Who is the winner?
- What is the value of a game (in the sense of Conway)?
- Can one provide a winning strategy, i.e., a sequence of optimal moves for the winner whatever his opponent's moves are?

For each of the above questions, I will give some parts of answer relative to the known theory.

The first problem is the determination of the winner of a given game, also called *outcome*. In a strict combinatorial game (i.e., a game satisfying the conditions of Definition 1), there are only four possible outcomes [31]:

- $\mathcal{L}$ if Left has a winning strategy independently of who starts the game,
- $\mathcal{R}$ if Right has a winning strategy independently of who starts the game,
- $\mathcal{N}$ if the first player has a winning strategy,
- $\mathcal{P}$ if the second player has a winning strategy.

This property can be easily deduced from the game tree, by labeling the vertices from the leaves to the root. Consequently, such an algorithm allows to compute the outcome of a game in polynomial time in the size of the tree. Yet, a game position has often a smaller input size than the size of its corresponding game tree. For example, a position $(a_1, \ldots, a_n)$ of NIM has an input size $\mathcal{O}(\sum_{i=1}^{n} \log_2(a_i))$, which is far smaller than the number of positions in the game tree. Hence, computing the whole game tree is generally not the good key to determine effectively the answer to Problem 1 below.

Problem 1 (Outcome). Given a game $\mathcal{G}$ with a starting position S, compute the complexity of deciding whether $(\mathcal{G}, S)$ is $\mathcal{P}$, $\mathcal{N}$, $\mathcal{L}$ or $\mathcal{R}$?

Note that for loopy games, the outcome *Draw* is added to the list of the possible outcomes.

Example 1. *The game* DOMINEERING *played on a 3×1 grid is clearly $\mathcal{L}$ since there is no available (horizontal) move for Right. On a 3×2 and 3×3 grids, one can quickly check that the first player has a winning strategy. Such positions are thus $\mathcal{N}$. When $n > 3$, it can also be easily proved that $3 \times n$ grids are $\mathcal{R}$, since placing an horizontal domino in the middle row allows two free moves for Right, whereas a vertical move do not constraint further moves of Left.*

We now present a second major issue in CGT that can be considered as a refinement of the previous one.

Problem 2 (Value). Given a game $\mathcal{G}$ with a starting position S, compute its Conway's value.

The concept of game value was first defined by Conway in [8]. In his theory, each game position is assigned a numeric value among the set of *surreal numbers*. Roughly speaking, it corresponds to the number of moves ahead that Left has towards his opponent. For instance, position ⬚⬚⬚⬚ of DOMINEERING has value -2 since Right can place two more dominoes than Left before being blocked. A more formal definition can be found in [31]. Just note that Conway's values are defined recursively and can also be computed from the game tree.

Knowing the value of a game allows to deduce its outcome. For example, all games having a strictly positive value are $\mathcal{L}$ and all games having a zero value are $\mathcal{P}$. Moreover, its knowledge is even more paramount when the game splits in sums: it means that a game $\mathcal{G}$ can be considered as a set of independent smaller games whose values allows to compute the overall value of $\mathcal{G}$. Consider the example depicted by Fig. 3. This game position can be considered as a sum of the three components ⬚, ⬚ and ⬚⬚⬚ of respective outcomes $\mathcal{L}$, $\mathcal{L}$ and $\mathcal{R}$, and respective Conway's values $1/2$, $1/2$ and -1. From this decomposition, there is no way to compute the outcome of the general position from the outcomes of each component. Indeed, the sum of three components having outcomes $\mathcal{L}$, $\mathcal{L}$, and $\mathcal{R}$can either be $\mathcal{L}$, $\mathcal{R}$, $\mathcal{P}$ or $\mathcal{N}$. However, the sum of the three values can be easily computed and equals 0: we can conclude that the overall position of Fig. 3 is $\mathcal{P}$.

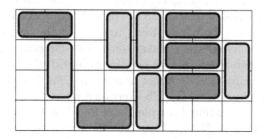

Fig. 3. Sum of DOMINEERING positions

Example 2. *Computing Conway's values of* DOMINEERING *is not easy even for small grids and there is no known formula to get them. On the other hand, the case of the game of* NIM *is better known. Indeed, Conway's value of any position* $(a_1, \ldots, a_n)$ *is an infinitesimal surreal number equal to* $a_1 \oplus \ldots \oplus a_n$, *where* $\oplus$ *is the bitwise XOR operator.*

The last problem is generally considered once (at least) the first one is solved.

Problem 3 (Winning Strategy). Given a game $\mathcal{G}$ and a starting position S, give a winning move from S for the player having a winning strategy. Do it recursively whatever the answer of the other player is.

There are really few games for which this question can be solved with a polynomial time algorithm. The game of NIM is one of them.

Example 3. *A winning strategy is known for the game of* NIM: *from any position* $(a_1, \ldots, a_n)$ *of outcome* $\mathcal{N}$, *there always exists a greedy algorithm that yields to a position* $(a_1', \ldots, a_n')$ *whose bitwise sum* $a_1' \oplus \ldots \oplus a_n'$ *equals 0 (meaning that it will be losing for the other player).*

2   Complexity of Combinatorial Games

The complexity of combinatorial games is correlated to the computational complexity of the above problems. First of all, one can notice that all these problems are decidable, since it suffices to consider a simple algorithm on the game tree to have an answer. Of course, the size of the game tree remains an obstacle compared with the size of a game position. In [18], Fraenkel claims a game $\mathcal{G}$ is *polynomial* if:

- Problems 1 and 3 can be solved in polynomial time for any starting position S of $\mathcal{G}$.
- Winning strategies in $\mathcal{G}$ can be consumed in at most an exponential number of moves.
- These two properties remain valid for any sum of two game positions of $\mathcal{G}$.

If this definition is not always considered as a standard by the CGT community, there is a general agreement to say that the computational complexities of Problems 1 and 3 are the main criteria to evaluate the overall complexity of a game. Of course, this question makes sense only for games whose positions depends on some parameters such as the size of a grid, the values in a tuple... This explains why many famous games have been defined in the literature in a generalized version (e.g. Chess, Go, Checkers on a $n \times n$ board...). For almost all of them, even the computational complexity of Problem 1 is very high, as shown by Table 1 (extracted from [5,21]). Note that the belonging to class PSPACE or EXPTIME depends on the length of the play (exponential for EXPTIME and polynomial for PSPACE).

Table 1. Complexity of well-known games in their generalized versions

Game	Complexity
Tic Tac Toe	PSPACE-complete
Othello	PSPACE-complete
Hex	PSPACE-complete
Amazons	PSPACE-complete
Checkers	EXPTIME-complete
Chess	EXPTIME-complete
Go	EXPTIME-complete

In addition to these well-known games, there are many other combinatorial games that have been proved to be at least PSPACE-hard: NODE-KAYLES and SNORT [28], many variations on GEOGRAPHY [25] or many other games on graphs. In 2009, Demaine and Hearn wrote a rich book about the complexity of many combinatorial games and puzzles [16]. If this list confirms that games belong to decision problems of highest complexity, some of them admit a lower one. The game of NIM is one of them and is luckily not the only one. For example, many games played on tuples of integers admit a polynomial winning strategy derived from tools arising from arithmetic, algebra or combinatorics on words. See the recent survey [11] which summarizes some of these games. Moreover, some games on graphs proved to be PSPACE-complete have a more affordable complexity on particular families of graphs. For example, NODE KAYLES is proved to be polynomial on paths and cographs [4]. This is also the case for GEOGRAPHY played on undirected graphs [19]. Finally, note that the complexity of DOMINEERING is still an open problem.

If the computational complexity of many games is often very high, it makes no sense to consider it when the game positions have a constant size. It is in particular the case for well-known board games such as Chess on a 8×8 board, the game of Go on a 19×19 board, or standard Hex. Solving them is often a question a computational performance and algorithmic optimization on the game tree. In this context, these games can be classified according to the status of their resolution. For that purpose, Allis [1] defined three levels of resolution for a game:

- *ultra-weakly solved*: the answer of Problem 1 is known, but Problem 3 remains open. This is for instance the case of Hex, that is winning for the first player, but no winning strategy has been computed yet.
- *weakly solved*: Problems 1 and 3 are solved for the standard starting position (e.g., standard initial position of Checkers, empty board of Tic Tac Toe). As a consequence, the known winning strategy is not improved if the opponent does not play optimally.
- *strongly solved*: Problems 1 and 3 are solved for any starting position.

According to this definition, Table 2 summarizes the current knowledge about the resolution of some games.

Table 2. Status of the resolutions of several well-known games

Game	Size of the board	Resolution status
Tic Tac Toe	3×3	Strong
Connect Four	6×7	Strong
Checkers	8×8	Weak
Hex	11×11	Ultra-Weak
Go	19×19	Open
Chess	8×8	Open
Othello	8×8	Open

A natural question arises when reading the above table. What makes a game harder than another one? If there is obviously no universal answer, Fraenkel suggests several relevant criteria in [17].

- The average *branching factor*, i.e., the average number of available moves from a position (around 35 for Chess and 250 for the game of Go).
- The total number of game positions (10^{18} for Checkers, 10^{171} for the game of Go).
- The existence of cycles. In other words, loopy games are harder than non loopy ones.

- *Impartial* or *Partizan*. A game is said *impartial* if both players always have the same available moves. It implies the game tree to be symmetric. NIM is an example of an impartial game, whereas DOMINEERING and all the games mentioned in Table 2 are not. Such games are called partizan. Impartial games are in general easier to solve since their Conway's values are more "controlled".
- The fact that the game can be decomposed into sums of smaller independent games (as it is the case for DOMINEERING).
- The number of final positions.

Based on these considerations, how to deal with games whose complexity is too high - either theoretically, or simply in view of their empirical hardness? Approximate resolutions (especially for Problem 3) must be considered and artificial intelligence algorithms were introduced to this end.

3   AI Algorithms to Deal with the Hardest Games

In the previous section, we have seen that Problem 1 remains unsolved for games having a huge number of positions. If the recent work of Schaeffer et al. [29] on Checkers was a real breakthrough (they found the exact outcome, which is a Draw), getting a similar result for games like Chess, Othello or Go seems currently out of reach. Moreover, researchers generally feel more concerned by finding a good way to play these games rather than computing the exact outcome. In the 50s, this interest led to the beginnings of artificial intelligence [30] and the construction of the first programs to play Chess [3]. For more information about computer game history, see [27]. Before going into more details on AI programs for games, note that in general, these algorithms work on a slight variation of the game tree given in Definition 2, where Left is always supposed to be the first player, and only the moves of one player are represented on a level of the tree. For example, the children of the root correspond exclusively to the moves available for Left, their children to the possible answers for Right...

3.1   MiniMax Algorithms

The first steps in combinatorial game programming were made for Chess. The so-called *MiniMax* approach is due to Shannon and Turing in the 50 s and has been widely considered in many other AI programs. Its main objective is to minimize the maximum loss of each player. This algorithm requires some expert knowledge of the game, as it uses an evaluation function of the values of game positions.

Roughly speaking, in a MiniMax algorithm, the game tree is built up to a certain depth. Then each leaf of this partial game tree is evaluated thanks to an evaluation function. This function is the key of the algorithm and is based on heuristic considerations. For example, the Chess computer *Deep Blue* (who first defeated a human world champion in 1996) had an evaluation function based on hundreds of parameters (e.g. compare the power of a non-blocked tower versus a protected king). These parameters were tuned after an fine analyze of 700,000 master games. Each parent node of a leaf is then assigned a value equals to the minimum value of its children (wlog, we here assume that the depth is even - then the last moves correspond to moves for Right, whose goal is to minimize the game value). The next parent nodes are evaluated by taking the maximum value among their children (it corresponds to moves for Left). Then recursively each parent node is evaluate according to the values of its children, by taking alternately the minimum or the maximum according to whether it is Left or Right's turn. Figure 4 illustrates this algorithm on a tree of depth 4. In this example, assume an evaluation function provides the values located on the leaves of the tree. Then MiniMax ensures that Left can force a win with a score equals to 4. Red nodes are those for which the maximum of the children is taken, i.e., positions from which Left has to play.

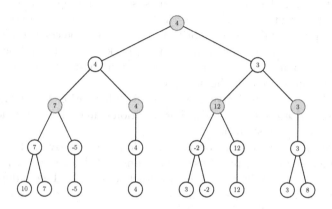

Fig. 4. MinMax algorithm on a tree of depth 4

In addition to an expert tuning of the evaluation function, another significant enhancement was made with the introduction of *Alpha-Beta pruning* [12]. It consists in a very effective selective cut-off of the Minimax algorithm without loss of information. Indeed, if after having computed the values of the first branches, it turns out that the overall value of the root is at least v, then one can prune all the unexplored branches whose values are guaranteed to be less than v. The ordering of the branches in the game tree then turns out to be paramount, as it can considerably increase the efficiency of the algorithm. In addition to this technique, one can also mention the use of *transposition tables* (adjoined to alpha-beta pruning) to speed up the search in the game tree.

Nowadays, the MiniMax algorithm (together with its improving techniques) is still used by the best algorithms to solve games admitting a relevant evaluation function. This is for example the case for Chess, Checkers, Connect Four or Othello. Yet, we will see that for other games, some probabilistic approaches turn out to be more efficient.

3.2   Monte-Carlo Approaches

In 2006, Coulom [9] suggested to combine the principle of the MiniMax algorithm with Monte Carlo methods. These methods were formalized in the 40s to deal with hard problems by taking a random sampling. For example, they can be used to estimate the value of π. Of course, the quality of the approximated solution partially depends on the size of the sample. In our case, their application will consist in simulating many random games.

The combination of both MiniMax and Monte Carlo methods is called MCTS, which stands for *Monte Carlo Tree Search*. Since its introduction, it has been considered by much research on AI for games. This success is mainly explained by the significant improvements made by computer Go programs that are using this technique. Moreover, it has also shown very good performances for problems for which other techniques had poor ones (e.g. some problems in combinatorial optimization, puzzles, multi-player games, scheduling, operation research...). Another great advantage of MCTS is that there is no need of a strong expert knowledge to implement a good algorithm. Hence it can be considered for problems for which humans do not have a strong background. In addition, MCTS can be stopped at any time to provide the current best solution and the tree built so far can be reused for the next step.

In what follows, we will give the necessary information to understand the essence of MCTS applied to games. For additional material, the reader could refer to the more exhaustive survey [7].

The basic MCTS algorithm consists in building progressively the game tree, guided by the results of the previous explorations of it. Unlike the standard MiniMax algorithm, the tree is built in an asymmetric manner. The in-depth search is considered only for the most promising branches that are chosen according to a tuned selection policy. This policy relies on the values of each node of the tree. Roughly speaking, the value of a node v_i corresponds to the percentage of winning random simulations when v_i is played. Of course this value become more and more accurate when the tree grows.

Description. As illustrated in Fig. 5, each iteration of MCTS is organized around 4 steps called *descent, growth, roll-out* and *update*. Numbers in grey correspond to the estimate values of each node (a function of the pourcentage of win). Here are their main description:

- Descent: starting from the root of the game tree, a child is recursively selected according to the selection policy. As seen on the figure, a MiniMax selection is used to descend the tree, according to the values of each node (here, $B1$ is the most promising move for Left, then $E1$ for Right). This descent stops when it lands on a node that needs to be expanded (also given by the policy). In our example, the node $E1$ is such a node.
- Growth: Add one or more children to this expandable node in the tree. On Fig. 5, Node $B4$ is added to the tree.

– Rollout: From an added node, make a simulation by playing random moves until the end of the game. In our example, the random simulation from $B4$ leads to a loss for Left.
– Update: the result of the simulation is backpropagated to the moves of the tree that have been selected. Their values are thus updated.

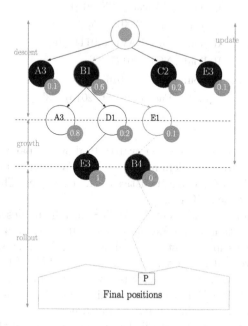

Fig. 5. The four stages of the MCTS algorithm

Improvements. In general, MCTS is not used in a raw version and is frequently combined with additional features. As detailed in [36], there is a very rich literature on the improvements brought to MCTS. They can be organized according to the stage they impact. Table 3 summarizes the most important enhancements brought to MCTS.

One of the most important feature of the algorithm is the node selection policy during the descent. At each step of this stage, MCTS chooses the node that maximizes (or minimizes, according to whether it is Left or Right's turn) some quantity. A formula that is frequently used is called *Upper Confidence Bounds* (UCB). It associates to each node v_i of the tree the following value:

$$V(v_i) + C \times \sqrt{\frac{\ln N}{n_i}},$$

where $V(v_i)$ is the percentage of winning simulations involving v_i, n_i is the total number of simulations involving v_i, N is the number of times its parent has been visited, and C is a tunable parameter. This formula is well-known in the context of bandit problems (choose sequentially amongst n actions the best one

Table 3. Main improvements brought to MCTS

Stage	Improvement
Descent	UCT (2006) [22]
Descent	RAVE (2007) [15]
Descent	Criticality (2009) [10]
Growth	FPU (2007) [35]
Rollout	Pool-RAVE (2011), [26]
Rollout	NST (2012) [33]
Rollout	BHRF (2016) [14]
Update	Fuego reward (2010) [13]

in order to maximize the cumulative reward). It allows in particular to deal with the exploration-exploitation dilemma, i.e., to find a balance between exploring unvisited nodes and reinforce the statistics of the best ones. The combination of MCTS and UCB is called UCT [22].

A second common enhancement for MCTS during the descent is the RAVE estimator (Rapide Action-Value Estimator [15]). It consists in considering each move of the rollout as important as the first move. In other words, the moves visited during the rollout stage will also affect the values of the same moves in the tree. On Fig. 5, imagine the move $E3$ is played during the simulation depicted with dashed line. Then RAVE will thus modify the UCB value of the node $E3$ of the tree (the RAVE formula will not be given here).

MCTS has also been widely studied in order to increase the quality of the random simulations. A first way to mimic the strategy of a good player is to consider evaluations functions based on expert knowledge. In [34], moves are categorized according to several criteria: location on the board, capturing or blocking potential and proximity to the last move. Then the approach is to evaluate the probability that a move belonging to a category will be played by a real player. This probability is determined by analyzing a huge sample of real games played by either humans or computers. Of course this strategy is fully specific to the game on which MCTS is applied. More generic approaches were considered such as *NST* [33], *BHRF* [14] or *Pool RAVE* [26]. In the first two ones, good sequences of moves are kept in memory. Indeed, it is rather frequent that given successive attacking moves of a player, there is an usual sequence of answers of the opponent to defend himself. In the second one, the random rollout policy is biased by the values in the game tree, i.e., good moves visited in the tree are likely to be played during a simulation.

In addition to the enhancements applied to the different stages of MCTS, one can also mention several studies to parallelize the algorithm that perform very good results [36].

We cannot conclude this survey without mentioning the outstanding performances of Google's program *Alpha Go* [32]. Like *Deep Blue* for Chess, Alpha

Go is the first AI to defeat the best human player in Go. This program runs an MCTS algorithm combined with two deep neural networks. The first one is called the *Policy network* and is used during the descent phase to find out the most promising moves. It was bootstrapped from many games of human experts (around 30 million moves analyzed during three weeks on 50 GPU). The reinforcement learning was then enhanced by many games of self-play. The second neural network is called *Value network* and can be considered as the first powerful evaluation function for Go that is used to bias the rollout policy. If Alpha Go's performances show a real breakthrough in AI programs for games, the last day of this research field has not yet come. In particular, the need of expert knowledge to bootstrap the networks cannot be considered when dealing with problems for which humans have a poor expertise.

4   Perspectives

Working on problems as hard as combinatorial games is a real challenge, both for CGT and AI researchers. The major results obtained in the past years are very stimulating and encourage many people to strengthen the overall effort on the topic. Hence, from a theoretical point of view, the next step for CGT is the construction of a general framework to cope with scoring games. In particular, the question of the sum of two scoring games is paramount, as it is radically different from the sum games in normal play convention (one cannot simply add the values of each game). First attempts have been recently made in that sense to consider Conway's values as waiting moves in scoring games.

Concerning AI algorithms for games, as said in the above paragraph, Alpha Go has been a breakthrough for the area but very exciting issues remain. More precisely, the neural network approach proposed by Google requires a wide set of expert knowledge and needs computer power for a long time. However, there are some games for which both are not available. In particular, the example of *General Game Playing* is a real challenge for AI algorithms, as the rules of the game are given at the latest 20 minutes before running the program. Supervised learning techniques like those of Alpha Go are thus almost impossible to set up, and standard MCTS enhancements are currently the most effective ones for this kind of problem. In addition, one can also look for adapting MCTS to problems of higher uncertainty such as multi-player games or games having randomness in their rules (use of dices for example). First results have already been made in that direction [36].

References

1. Allis, L.V.: Searching for solutions in games an artificial intelligence. Ph.D. Maastricht, Limburg University, Netherland (1994)
2. Berlekamp, E., Conway, J.H., Guy, R.K.: Winning ways for your mathematical plays, vol. 1, 2nd edn. A K Peters Ltd., Natick (2001)
3. Bernstein, A., Roberts, M.: Computer V. Chess player. Sci. Am. **198**, 96–105 (1958)

4. Bodlaender, H.L., Kratsch, D.: Kayles and numbers. J. Algorithms **43**, 106–119 (2002)
5. Bonnet, E., Saffidine, A.: Complexit des Jeux (in french). Bulletin de la ROADEF **31**, 9–12 (2014)
6. Bouton, C.L.: Nim, a game with a complete mathematical theory. Ann. Math. **3**, 35–39 (1905)
7. Browne, C., Powley, E., Whitehouse, D., Lucas, S., Cowling, P.I., Rohlfshagen, P., Tavener, S., Perez, D., Samothrakis, S., Colton, S.: A survey of monte carlo tree search methods. IEEE Trans. Comput. Intell. AI Games **4**(1), 1–43 (2012)
8. Conway, J.H.: On Number and Games. Academic Press Inc., Cambridge (1976)
9. Coulom, R.: Efficient selectivity and backup operators in Monte-Carlo tree search. In: Proceedings of the 5th International Conference on Computers and Games, Turin, Italy, pp. 72–83 (2006)
10. Coulom, R.: Criticality: a Monte-Carlo Heuristic for Go Programs. Invited talk in University of Electro-Communication, Tokyo (2009)
11. Duchêne, E., Fraenkel, A.S., Gurvich, V., Ho, N.B., Kimberling, C., Larsson, U.: Wythoff Wisdom (preprint)
12. Edwards, D.J., Hart, T.P.: The $\alpha - \beta$ heuristic. In: Artificial intelligence project RLE and MIT Computation Centre, Memo 30 (1963)
13. Enzenberger, M., Muller, M., Arneson, B., Segal, R.: Fuego an open-source framework for board games and Go engine based on Monte Carlo tree search. IEEE Trans. Comput. Intell. AI Games **2**(4), 259–270 (2010)
14. Fabbri, A., Armetta, F., Duchne, E., Hassas, S.: A self-acquiring knowledge process for MCTS. Int. J. Artif. Intell. Tools **25**(1), 1660007 (2016)
15. Gelly, S., Silver, D.: Combining online and offline knowledge in UCT. In: Ghahramani, Z. (ed.) Proceedings of the International Conference on Machine Learning (ICML), pp. 273–280. ACM, New York (2007)
16. Hearn, R.A., Demaine, E.D.: Games, Puzzles, and Computation. A K Peters (2009)
17. Fraenkel, A.S.: Nim is easy, chess is hard - but why? J. Int. Comput. Games Assoc. **29**, 203–206 (2006)
18. Fraenkel, A.S.: Complexity, appeal and challenges of combinatorial games. Theor. Comput. Sci. **313**, 393–415 (2004)
19. Fraenkel, A.S., Simonson, S.: Geography. Theor. Comput. Sci. **110**, 197–214 (1993)
20. Gardner, M.: Mathematical games: cram, crosscram and quadraphage: new games having elusive winning strategies. Sci. Am. **230**, 106–108 (1974)
21. Junghanns, A., Schaeffer, J.: Sokoban: enhancing general single-agent search methods using domain knowledge. Artif. Intell. **129**(1), 219–251 (2001)
22. Kocsis, L., Szepesvári, C.: Bandit based Monte-Carlo planning. In: Fürnkranz, J., Scheffer, T., Spiliopoulou, M. (eds.) ECML 2006. LNCS (LNAI), vol. 4212, pp. 282–293. Springer, Heidelberg (2006)
23. Larsson, U., Nowakowski, R.J., Santos, C.: Theory, Absolute Combinatorial Game. arXiv:1606.01975 (2016)
24. Larsson, U., Nowakowski, R.J., Santos, C.: When waiting moves you in scoring combinatorial games. arXiv:1505.01907 (2015)
25. Renault, G., Schmidt, S.: On the complexity of the misre version of three games played on graphs (preprint)
26. Rimmel, A., Teytaud, F., Teytaud, O.: Biasing Monte-Carlo simulations through RAVE values. In: van den Herik, H.J., Iida, H., Plaat, A. (eds.) CG 2010. LNCS, vol. 6515, pp. 59–68. Springer, Heidelberg (2011)

27. Rougetet, L.: Combinatorial games and machines. In: Pisano, R. (ed.) A Bridge between Conceptual Frameworks, Sciences, Society and Technology Studies, Pisano, vol. 27, pp. 475–494. Springer, Dordrecht (2015)
28. Schaeffer, T.J.: On the complexity of some two-person perfect-information games. J. Comput. Syst. Sci. **16**, 185–225 (1978)
29. Schaeffer, J., Burch, N., Bjrnsson, Y., Kishimoto, A., Mller, M., Lake, R., Lu, P., Sutphen, S.: Checkers is solved. Science **317**(5844), 1518–1522 (2007)
30. Shannon, C.: Programming a computer for playing chess. Philos. Mag. Ser. 7 **41**(314), 256–275 (1950)
31. Siegel, A.N.: Combinatorial Game Theory. American Mathematical Society, San Francisco (2013)
32. Silver, D., Huang, A., Maddison, C.J., Guez, A., Sifre, L., Van Den Driessche, G., Schrittwieser, J., Antonoglou, I., Panneershelvam, V., Lanctot, M., et al.: Mastering the game of Go with deep neural networks and tree search. Nature **529**(7587), 484–489 (2016)
33. Tak, M.J.W., Winands, M.H.M., Bjornsson, Y.: N-grams and the last-good-reply policy applied in general game playing. IEEE Trans. Comput. Intell. AI Games **4**(2), 73–83 (2012)
34. Tsuruoka, Y., Yokoyama, D., Chikayama, T.: Game-tree search algorithm based on realization probability. ICGA J. **25**(3), 132–144 (2002)
35. Wang, Y., Gelly, S.: Modifications of UCT and sequence-like simulations for Monte-Carlo Go. In: IEEE Symposium on Computational Intelligence and Games, Honolulu, Hawai, pp. 175–182 (2007)
36. Winands, M.: Monte-Carlo tree search in board games. In: Nakatsu, R., Rauterberg, M., Ciancarini, P. (eds.) Handbook of Digital Games and Entertainment Technologies, pp. 1–30. Springer, Heidelberg (2015)

A Gentle Introduction to Reinforcement Learning

Ann Nowé[✉] and Tim Brys

Vrije Universiteit Brussel, Pleinlaan 2, Brussels, Belgium
{anowe,timbrys}@vub.ac.be

Abstract. This paper provides a gentle introduction to some of the basics of reinforcement learning, as well as pointers to more advanced topics within the field.

Keywords: Reinforcement learning · Heuristic information · Multi-objective · Multi-agent

1 Introduction

AI is quickly developing. Every year, the boundaries of what is possible are being pushed further and further. Since 2015, computers can play our video games from the 80's at a level comparable to that of an experienced gamer [20]. In 2016, they first beat the world champion of Go, the holy grail of board games, pulling moves that are inhuman, but "so beautiful" (*dixit Fan Hui*, reigning European champion). Fully self-driving cars have been around for at least a couple of years [15], and in a few more years Amazon drones will be whizzing around delivering packages to anybody and everybody [2].

One of the strengths of many of these systems is their ability to learn from data. The rules they follow, the behaviour they exhibit, is not exclusively programmed by some smart engineer. Rather, the engineer implements a learning algorithm, which is then fed data relevant for the task at hand. The learning algorithm then finds patterns in the data, discovers what are 'good' decisions for which situations, and an 'intelligent' system emerges.

This is *Machine Learning*.

2 Reinforcement Learning

Some of the examples cited above use a specific Machine Learning approach called reinforcement learning. This approach to learning is inspired by behaviourist psychology, where human and animal behaviour is studied from a reward and punishment perspective. A small illustrative example conveys the main principle of this learning theory:

Example 1. Say you want to train your dog to sit.
You take your dog outside and shout 'sit'.

© Springer International Publishing Switzerland 2016
S. Schockaert and P. Senellart (Eds.): SUM 2016, LNAI 9858, pp. 18–32, 2016.
DOI: 10.1007/978-3-319-45856-4_2

The dog realizes it needs to do something (you shouting and pointing to the ground is a definite clue), but it doesn't know what to do.
It barks, but nothing happens...
It gives a paw (something it learned before), but nothing happens...
It sits on the ground, and lo and behold, a dog cookie appears!

If you repeat this process many times, your dog will probably learn to associate the situation (you shouting 'sit') and its own action (sitting down), with the positive stimulus (a tasty cookie) and will repeat this behaviour on future occasions.

In essence, the learner is considered to crave 'something' that it receives depending on its behaviour; it receives more of it when it exhibits desirable behaviour, and less (or even something opposite) when it does not. Whether this 'something' be cookies for a dog, or dopamine in the human brain, or a simple numerical value, an increase of it tells the learner that it has done something right, and an intelligent learner will repeat that behaviour when it encounters a similar situation in the future.

This same principle was successfully used in the examples cited above to train AIs to play video games and play Go.[1] The former using the score in the game as reward, the latter the win or loss as reward or punishment.

3   The Reinforcement Learning Problem

In this section, we describe reinforcement learning (RL) more formally. We set the stage with the classic RL diagram, displayed in Fig. 1. It shows how an RL *agent* interacts with its *environment*. First, to say what an agent exactly is, is surprisingly difficult; definitions abound in AI literature. In this article, we adopt the following simple definition [25]:

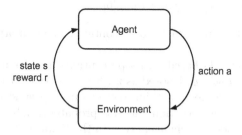

Fig. 1. The reinforcement learning agent-environment interaction loop.

---

[1] Do not dismiss these results as only academically interesting due to the 'game' nature of the problems: the complexity of these problems approaches and surpasses that of many more useful applications [28]. Furthermore, the past has shown that breakthrough advances in games have lead to breakthroughs in other fields. Monte Carlo Tree Search, initially developed for Go, is one example [8].

Definition 1 (An Agent.) *An agent is just something that perceives and acts.*

What the agent perceives and acts upon, we call the environment. This environment typically changes due to the agent's actions and possibly other factors outside the agent's influence. The agent perceives the state (s) of the environment (a potentially incomplete observation), and must decide which action (a) to take based on that information, such that the accumulation of rewards (r) it receives from the environment is maximized.

This agent-environment interaction process is most commonly formulated as a Markov Decision Process (MDP):

Definition 2 (Markov Decision Process). *A Markov Decision Process is a tuple $\langle S, A, T, \gamma, R \rangle$.*

- *$S = \{s_1, s_2, \ldots\}$ is the possibly infinite set of states the environment can be in.*
- *$A = \{a_1, a_2, \ldots\}$ is the possibly infinite set of actions the agent can take.*
- *$T(s'|s, a)$ defines the probability of ending up in environment state s' after taking action a in state s.*
- *$\gamma \in [0, 1]$ is the discount factor, which defines how important future rewards are.*
- *$R(s, a, s')$ is the possibly stochastic reward given for a state transition from s to s' through taking action a. It defines the goal of an agent interacting with the MDP, as it indicates the immediate quality of what the agent is doing.*

It is called a *Markov* Decision Process, since the state signal is assumed to have the Markov property:

Definition 3 (Markov Property). *A stochastic process has the Markov property if the conditional probability distribution of future states of the process (conditional on both past and present states) depends only upon the present state, not on the sequence of events that preceded it [6].*

In other words, the state signal should contain enough information to reliably predict future states.

The way an agent acts based on its perceptions, i.e., its behaviour, is commonly referred to as a *policy*, denoted as $\pi : S \times A \rightarrow [0, 1]$. It formally describes how likely an agent is to do something (action) in a given situation (state), by mapping state-action pairs to action selection probabilities. In this article, we use this notation for policies interchangeably with the following notation $\pi : S \rightarrow A$, which is a reformulation where not the action selection probabilities are output for a given state-action pair, but given a state and these probabilities, $\pi(s)$ outputs a probabilistically selected action.

The goal of an agent interacting with an MDP is to learn behaviour, a policy, that maximizes the discounted accumulation of rewards collected during its lifetime in the environment. This accumulation of reward up to a given time horizon or into infinity is called the return:

$$\mathcal{R}_t = R(s_t, a_t, s_{t+1}) + \gamma R(s_{t+1}, a_{t+1}, s_{t+2}) + \gamma^2 R(s_{t+2}, a_{t+2}, s_{t+3}) + \ldots$$

$$= \sum_{k=0}^{\infty} \gamma^k R(s_{t+k}, a_{t+k}, s_{t+k+1})$$

The discount factor γ determines the current value of future rewards. As $\gamma \to 1$, the agent becomes more farsighted, and will prefer large future rewards over smaller short-term rewards.

Given a state s and a policy π, we can express the return an agent can expect when starting from that state and following that policy as follows:

$$V^\pi(s) = E \left\{ \sum_{k=0}^{\infty} \gamma^k R(s_{t+k}, a_{t+k}, s_{t+k+1}) | s_t = s \right\}$$

This *value function* expresses the quality of being in state s when following policy π, given the MDP to-be-solved that generates state transitions and rewards for these transitions. The expectation $E\{\}$ accounts for the stochasticity in these transition and reward functions, as well as in the policy that generates the action sequence.

Similarly, we can define the quality of being in state s, taking action a, and subsequently following policy π. This is called the action-value function:

$$Q^\pi(s, a) = E \left\{ \sum_{k=0}^{\infty} \gamma^k R(s_{t+k}, a_{t+k}, s_{t+k+1}) | s_t = s, a_t = a \right\}$$

The expected returns encoded in these value functions yield a way to evaluate the quality of policies. A policy π is better than another policy π' if it has higher expected returns. A reinforcement learning agent needs to learn a policy that maximizes the expected return $\forall s \in S, a \in A$:

$$\pi^* = \arg \max_{\pi} Q^\pi(s, a)$$

π^* is called an optimal policy,[2] as it represents the behaviour that gets the highest return in expectation, thus solving the task encoded in the reward function.

4 Reinforcement Learning Algorithms

If the MDP's transition and reward functions are known, Dynamic Programming techniques can be used to optimally solve the problem [5]. Yet, it is uncommon to have a full specification of a system's dynamics or the reward function, and thus the use of techniques that can work with only knowledge of state and action spaces is necessary. These techniques must generate policies that maximize the expected return in environments with unknown dynamics and goals through trial-and-error. Learning a model of the environment may be part of

---

[2] There may be many, although their (action-)value functions will all be the same.

this process, but it is not necessary and many techniques are successful without this component.

As is the case in Dynamic Programming, there are basically two paradigms for reinforcement learning: policy iteration and value iteration. Both methods can be considered as on-line versions of their dynamic programming counterparts. In policy iteration, the learning agent contains two units, the evaluation unit and the action unit. The former is the internal evaluator, while the latter is responsible for determining the actions which look most promising according to the internal evaluator [4]. Policy gradient (PG) methods [34] are closely related to this policy iteration approach, with the internal evaluator usually replaced by sampled returns. These methods assume a parametric representation of the policy and the parameters are updated following a gradient in policy space. As they make assumptions on smoothness, these reinforcement learning techniques can naturally cope with continuous states and actions and uncertain state information. Exploration is typically achieved the same way as in policy iteration, i.e. by applying some noise on the action proposed by the current policy. Alternatively, exploration can also be realised by assuming a probability distribution (typically a Gaussian distribution) over the parameters involved in the policy. This approach is named Policy Gradients with Parameter-based Exploration (PGPE) [27]. Each time an action needs to be sampled, the parameters of the policy are drawn according to the distribution, resulting a policy instantiation that prescribes the action. The parameters of the policy are then updated based on the reward received using again a gradient approach. More advanced methods allow this idea to be applied to non-differential policies and also reduce the risk of getting stuck in a local optimum through a multi-modal approach [26].

In contrast, value iteration methods do not store a policy explicitly, but learn a value function from which they derive a policy. In the remainder of this section, we introduce and elaborate on temporal difference (TD) learning algorithms, a popular type of value iteration algorithms.

Definition 4 (TD Learning). *Temporal difference learning is an approach to reinforcement learning that keeps estimates of expected return and updates these estimates based on experiences and differences in estimates over successive time-steps.*

In other words, in TD learning, the agent incrementally updates estimates of a value function, using observed rewards and the previous estimates of that value function. One of the best known and simplest temporal difference learning algorithms is Q-learning [44]. It estimates the optimal Q-function Q^* by iteratively updating its estimates $\hat{Q}$ after each state-action-reward-next state (s, a, r, s') interaction with the environment:

$$\hat{Q}(s, a) \leftarrow \hat{Q}(s, a) + \alpha \delta$$

$0 \leq \alpha \leq 1$ is the stepsize, controlling how much the value function is updated in the direction of the temporal difference error δ. The temporal difference error δ is the difference between the previous estimate and the observed sample:

$$\delta = r + \gamma \max_{a'} \hat{Q}(s', a') - \hat{Q}(s, a)$$

Q-learning performs *off-policy* learning. This means that it learns about a different policy than the one generating the interactions with the environment, which is called the behaviour policy. In the case of Q-learning, the policy being learned about is the optimal policy. The *on-policy* variant of Q-learning is called SARSA. It modifies the temporal difference error in such a way that the algorithm learns about the behaviour policy, using the action a' actually executed in next state s', instead of using the action with the highest estimate in that state:

$$\delta = r + \gamma \hat{Q}(s', a') - \hat{Q}(s, a)$$

If all state-action pairs are visited infinitely often, given some boundary conditions, Q-learning and SARSA are guaranteed to converge to the true Q-values [29, 37]. In practice, a finite number of experiences is usually sufficient to generate near-optimal behaviour.

From an estimated Q-function, an agent can easily derive a greedy deterministic policy π:

$$\pi(s) = \arg\max_a \hat{Q}(s, a)$$

If the estimates have converged to the optimal Q-values Q^*, then this formula generates an optimal policy.

Since an agent typically needs to sufficiently explore the state-action space in order to find optimal behaviour (infinitely often in the case of Q-learning), it is in most cases insufficient to just use the greedy policy derived from the agent's estimates to generate interactions with the environment. That is because initial underestimation of the quality of actions might lead the agent to always select the first action it tries, because it yielded a higher return than expected and than estimated for the other actions. This results in the agent ceasing exploration prematurely, and the value function converging to a local optimum. Instead of always using the greedy policy with respect to the estimates to select actions, it is therefore often advisable to inject stochasticity into the policy to generate the necessary exploration. One way is to take a random action at every timestep with probability ϵ. This ensures that every reachable state-action pair has a non-zero visitation probability, irrespective of the estimated Q-values at that time. Let $\xi \in [0, 1]$ be a randomly drawn real number:

$$\pi(s) = \begin{cases} \text{a random action} & \textit{if } \xi < \epsilon \\ \arg\max_a \hat{Q}(s, a) & \textit{otherwise} \end{cases}$$

This is called ϵ-greedy action selection.

Another popular approach is softmax action selection, which determines the probability of every action based on the relative magnitude of the actions' estimates:

$$\pi(s, a) = \frac{e^{\frac{Q(s,a)}{\tau}}}{\sum_{a'} e^{\frac{Q(s,a')}{\tau}}}$$

The 'temperature' parameter τ determines how random (high τ) or greedy (low τ) action selection is. Actions with higher estimated Q-values will have relatively higher probabilities of being selected, and actions with lower estimated Q-values will have proportionally lower probabilities.

Defining a reward function requires some experience, however coming up with a reward function is often quite straightforward. Consider for example the case where we want an RL agent to find its way in unknown maze. Then we can give a reward of say +100 when it reaches its goal and 0 otherwise. Similarly, it we want the agent to learn to play chess, then we reward it with, e.g. +100 when it enters a winning state, −100 when it losses and 0 for all other states. Reward functions are not unique, consider for example the well known cart-pole problem. We can give the agent a reward of +1 at each time step it keeps the system under control, as such the agent will try to keep the system under control as long as possible, in order to collect as many +1's as possible. Another way to express the same goals, is to reward the agent with a 0 and only when it fails, punishing it with a −1, combined with a discount factor γ strictly smaller than 1, this results in a reward of $-1 \times \gamma^t$, with t the time step of failure.

5   Function Approximation and Eligibility Traces

The basic versions of the algorithms described above are defined for discrete state-action spaces. They use a simple table to store the Q estimates: one entry for every possible state-action pair. Since many practical reinforcement learning problems have very large and/or continuous state spaces,[3] basic tabular learning methods are impractical, due to the sheer size of storage required, or even unusable, due to a table's inherent inability to faithfully represent continuous spaces. Therefore, function approximation techniques are required to render the learning problem tractable. Many different approximators exist, with deep neural networks being currently very much in vogue [20,28]. We introduce here a more basic and common function approximator, called tile-coding [1]. It is a linear approximator which overlays the state space with multiple randomly-offset, axis-parallel tilings. See Fig. 2 for an illustration. This allows for a discretization of the state-space, while the overlapping tilings guarantee a certain degree of generalization. The Q-function can be approximated by learning weights that map the tiles activated by the current state s and action a to an estimated Q-value:

$$\hat{Q}(s,a) = \theta^T \phi(s,a)$$

$\phi(s,a)$ is the feature vector representing state-action pair (s,a), i.e., a binary vector indicating the tiles activated by this state and the action, and θ is the parameter vector that needs to be learned to approximate the actual Q-function. This weight vector is updated using an update-rule similar to the one used in the tabular case:

$$\theta \leftarrow \theta + \alpha\delta$$

---

[3] Not to speak of continuous action spaces. That is not considered in this paper.

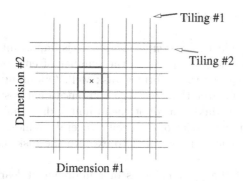

Fig. 2. An illustration of tile-coding function approximation on a two-dimensional state space, with two tilings. Figure taken from [35].

Alternatively, instead of discrete tilings, concepts from fuzzy set theory can be used, with fuzzy sets defined over the state space, and the membership operator $\mu(s)$ used as follows [14, 22]:

$$\theta \leftarrow \theta + \alpha \mu(s)\delta$$

This update rule expresses that the more the state belongs to the fuzzy region described the fuzzy set, the more that sample is relevant for updating the Q-value associated to that region. Action selection techniques as described above can still be applied by combining the selected actions for each of the regions by weighting them according to the state membership.

A last commonly used mechanism in temporal difference reinforcement learning is called eligibility traces. Eligibility traces [17] are records of past occurrences of state-action pairs. These give a sense of how 'long ago' a given action was taken in a given state. They can be used to propagate reward further into the past (n-step) than the algorithms discussed until now do (one step). Using eligibility traces, not only the Q-value of the currently observed state-action pair is updated, but also those of past state-action pairs, inversely proportional to the time since they were experienced. Concretely, a (replacing) eligibility trace $e(s, a)$ for state s and action a is updated as follows [30]:

$$e(s, a) \leftarrow \begin{cases} 1 & s = s_t, a = a_t \\ \gamma \lambda e(s, a) & otherwise \end{cases}$$

It is set to 1 if (s, a) is currently observed, and otherwise it is decayed by $\gamma\lambda$, with $0 \le \lambda \le 1$ the eligibility trace decay parameter. Higher λ results in rewards being propagated further into the past. This eligibility trace update is performed at every step, thus making traces decay over time. The eligibility traces are included as a vector e in the Q update rule as follows:

$$\theta \leftarrow \theta + \alpha e \delta$$

6   Sample Complexity

As in general machine learning, *sample complexity* is important in reinforcement learning. Sample complexity represents the number of environment (s, a, s', r) samples an agent requires to perform a task well. Obtaining samples usually carries a cost, often greater than just the computational cost associated with processing the sample. Making a robot spend hours, days and weeks to learn a task is very costly. It takes a lot of electricity, several engineers to attend to the robot, and physical space for the robot to execute the task, none of which are cheap to obtain.

Therefore, one of the primary goals of reinforcement learning algorithms, besides convergence and (near-) optimality, is an efficient use of samples. The less samples an algorithm requires to achieve some desirable level of behaviour, the better. In general, there is an interplay between, setting of the learning rate, the value of the discount factor, the exploration strategy and the initialisation of e.g. the Q-values. Also the state description and the kind of function approximator plays a role in the learning performance. While the theoretical frame work for RL is the Markov decision processes, one can state that there is a graceful degradation, meaning the less Markovian the problem is (as perceived by the agent), the more carefully the exploration needs to be. This is especially the case in Multi-agent settings see Sect. 9.

Broadly speaking, researchers take either one of two approaches to reduce the number of samples an agent requires. They either build algorithms and techniques that inherently require less samples (one of the first algorithms of this kind was Dyna-Q [33][4], or they use some prior/external knowledge to bias the agent. Some argue that the former is superior to the latter, as it is the more general approach [32]. Yet, we believe that both will always be intertwined. One can see this for example in the success of AlphaGo [28], which definitely is a great example of new algorithms using their samples in a better way, yet still it required a great deal of human demonstrations to work well. One of the popular ways to include such external knowledge is through reward shaping.

7   Reward Shaping

The modern version of reward shaping, a technique with roots in behavioural psychology [31], provides a learning agent with extra intermediate rewards, much like a dog trainer would reward a dog for completing part of a task. This extra reward can enrich a sparse base reward signal (for example a signal that only gives a non-zero feedback when the agent reaches the goal), providing the agent with useful gradient information. This shaping reward F is added to the environment's reward R to create a new composite reward signal that the agent uses for learning:

---

[4] Dyna-Q combines Q-learning with learning a transition model. This (approximate) model is then used generated simulated samples for the Q-learner. Real life sample and simulated samples can be arbitrarily inter-twined. This principled is also referred to as planning in an RL context.

$$R_F(s, a, s') = R(s, a, s') + F(s, a, s')$$

Of course, since the reward function defines the task, modifying the reward function may modify the total order over policies, and make the agent converge to suboptimal policies (with respect to the environment's original reward).

If we define a potential function $\Phi : S \rightarrow \mathbb{R}$ over the state space, and take F as the difference between the new and old states' potential, Ng et al. proved that the total order over policies remains unchanged, and convergence guarantees are preserved [21]:

$$F(s, a, s') = \gamma\Phi(s') - \Phi(s) \tag{1}$$

Prior knowledge can be incorporated by defining the potential function Φ accordingly.

The definition of F and Φ was extended by [11,16,46] to include actions and timesteps, allowing for the incorporation of behavioural knowledge that reflects the quality of actions as well as states, and allowing the shaping to change over time:

$$F(s, a, t, s', a', t') = \gamma\Phi(s', a', t') - \Phi(s, a, t)$$

This extension also preserves the total order over policies and therefore does not change the task, given Ng's original assumptions. Harutyunyan et al. [16] use this result to show how any reward function $R^\dagger$ can be transformed into a potential-based shaping function, by learning a secondary Q-function $\Phi^\dagger$ in parallel on the negation of $R^\dagger$, and using that to perform dynamic shaping on the main reward R.

Many different types of knowledge can be used to bias a learning agent, ranging from expert knowledge [12] and human demonstrations [9] to knowledge transferred from a previous task [36] and on-line teacher advice [18].

How this different techniques relate to each other is discussed in the Ph.D. of Tim Brys[5]

8   Multi-objective Reinforcement Learning

Multi-objective reinforcement learning [24] (MORL) is a generalization of standard single-objective reinforcement learning, with the environment formulated as a multi-objective MDP, or MOMDP $\langle S, A, T, \gamma, \mathbf{R}\rangle$. The difference with the single-objective case is the reward function. Instead of returning a scalar value, it returns a vector of scalars, one for each of the m objectives:

$$\mathbf{R}(s, a, s') = [R_1(s, a, s'), \ldots, R_m(s, a, s')]$$

Policies are in this case evaluated by their expected vector returns $\mathbf{Q}^\pi$:

$$\mathbf{Q}^\pi(s, a) = [Q_1^\pi(s, a), \ldots, Q_m^\pi(s, a)]$$

$$= \left[E\left\{\textstyle\sum_{k=0}^{\infty} \gamma^k R_1(s_{t+k}, a_{t+k}, s_{t+k+1}) | s_t = s, a_t = a\right\}, \ldots, \right.$$

$$\left. E\left\{\textstyle\sum_{k=0}^{\infty} \gamma^k R_m(s_{t+k}, a_{t+k}, s_{t+k+1}) | s_t = s, a_t = a\right\} \right]$$

---

[5] To appear, will be available online at ai.vub.ac.be.

Since there are multiple (possibly conflicting) signals to optimize, there is typically no total order over policies. Policies may be incomparable, i.e., the first is better on one objective while the second is better according to another objective, and thus the notion of optimality has to be redefined. A policy π_1 is said to strictly Pareto dominate another policy π_2, i.e., $\pi_1 \succ \pi_2$, if for each objective, π_1 performs at least as well as π_2, and it performs strictly better on at least one objective. The set of non-dominated policies is referred to as the *Pareto optimal set* or *Pareto front*. The goal in multi-objective reinforcement learning, and multi-objective optimization in general, is either to find a Pareto optimal solution, or to approximate the whole set of Pareto optimal solutions.

With a multi-objective variant of Q-learning, Q-values for each objective can be learned in parallel, stored as Q-vectors [13,41]:

$$\hat{\mathbf{Q}}(s,a) \leftarrow \hat{\mathbf{Q}}(s,a) + \alpha \boldsymbol{\delta}$$

$$\boldsymbol{\delta}_i = \mathbf{R}_i(s,a,s') + \gamma \max_{a'} \hat{\mathbf{Q}}_i(s',a') - \hat{\mathbf{Q}}_i(s,a)$$

The most common approach to derive a policy from these estimates is to calculate a linear scalarization, or weighted sum based on the estimated Q-vectors and a weight vector w [24,38,41]:

$$\pi(s) = \arg\max_a w^T \hat{\mathbf{Q}}(s,a)$$

The weight vector determines which trade-off solutions are preferred, although setting these weights *a priori* to achieve a particular trade-off is hard and non-intuitive [10], often requiring significant amounts of parameter tuning. Furthermore, because linear scalarization is a convex combination method, only solutions on convex parts of the Pareto-front can be found [39].

Algorithms that learn multiple trade-offs at the same time (multi-policy), and use operators that ensure access to both convex and concave parts of the Pareto-front are therefore very important. Only a restricted number of multi-policy MORL algorithms have been proposed so far. For instance, Barrett and Narayanan [3] propose the Convex Hull Value Iteration (CHVI) algorithm. From batch data, CHVI extracts and computes every linear combination of the objectives in order to obtain all deterministic optimal policies. As the algorithm relies on linear combinations, only policies on the convex hull are learned. The most computationally expensive operator is the procedure to compute and combine the convex hulls in the convex-hull version of the Bellman equation. Lizotte et al. [19] reduce the asymptotic space and time complexity of the bootstrapping rule by learning several value functions corresponding to different weight vectors using a piecewise linear spline representation. Wang and Sebag [43] propose a multi-objective Monte Carlo Tree Search (MO-MCTS) method to learn a set of solutions. The algorithm performs tree traversals by selecting the most promising actions. The upper confidence bounds of these actions are scalarized by applying the hypervolume indicator on the combination of their estimates and the set of Pareto optimal policies computed so far. Hence, a scalarized multi-objective value function is constructed that eases the process of selecting an action with vectorial estimates. Finally, Pareto Q-Learning is to the best of our knowledge the only temporal-difference based multi-policy MORL algorithm [42]. It uses the Pareto dominance operator to selection actions, thus allowing for policies in concave areas of the Pareto front, and learns sets of Q-values by separately learning immediate rewards and expected future discounted rewards. It has been shown to be more sample efficient compared to for example MO-MCTS on a typical benchmark problem [40].

9   Multi-agent Reinforcement Learning

So far we have discussed approaches for single agent settings. However, when multiple learners simultaneously apply reinforcement learning in a shared environment, the traditional approaches often fail.

In a multi-agent setting, the assumptions that are needed to guarantee convergence, are often violated. Already in the most basic case where agents share a stationary environment and need to learn a strategy for a single interaction, many new complexities arise. These are mainly due to the fact that the agents are learning simultaneously and therefore the non-determinism in the reward signal might not only be due to the stochasticity of the environment, but also due to the actions taken by the other agents. Despite the added complexity, a real need for multi-agent systems exists. Often systems are inherently decentralized, and a central, single agent learning approach is not feasible because that would require too many resources or communication overhead. Examples of such systems are multi-robot set-ups, decentralized network routing, distributed load-balancing, electronic auctions, smart grids and traffic control. Depending on the characteristics of the system different multi-agent RL techniques might be more appropriate. The settings characteristics are for instance, whether the agents can observe each others actions or whether these actions are not observable by the other agents or only partially, whether the agents take their actions synchronously at fixed time steps or if they act asynchronously, whether the interactions are frequent or sparse, whether the rewards follow the actions instantaneously or are delayed (as for instance in queueing systems) and whether the agents have common or conflicting interests. In general, one can state that in a multi-agent setting, exploration is a very crucial aspect to make the reinforcement learning approach perform well. More precisely, exploration should be limited to allow the agent to differ some how between noise due to the environment and noise due the presence of other agents. Because of this, policy iteration techniques are interesting candidates in a Multi-agent Reinforcement Learning (MARL) setting, however value-iteration methods with specific exploration strategies have also been successfully applied. In case the agents have conflicting interests, the additional problem of the solution concept arises. As the agents have conflicting goals, it is no longer obvious what the solution of the system should be and where Game Theory becomes relevant. We refer the reader to [23] for a more in depth discussion on MARL. A recent paper by Bloembergen et al. [7], provides an overview of the dynamics of MORL techniques based on evolutionary game theory.

10 Conclusion

This paper gave a brief introduction to reinforcement learning basics, and some more recent extensions such as Multi-agent reinforcement learning and Multi-criteria reinforcement learning. We also gave some pointers to approaches to reduce the sample complexity, where reward shaping is a safe way to incorporated domain knowledge which recently received quite a lot of attention. We refer the reader to [33] for learning more about the basics of reinforcement learning and to [45] for an overview of some more advanced reinforcement learning algorithms.

References

1. Albus, J.S.: Brains, Behavior, and Robotics. Byte Books, Peterborough (1981)
2. Amazon: Amazon prime air (2016). http://www.amazon.com/b?node=8037720011. Accessed 20 Apr 2016
3. Barrett, L., Narayanan, S.: Learning all optimal policies with multiple criteria. In: Proceedings of the 25th International Conference on Machine Learning, pp. 41–47. ACM (2008)
4. Barto, A.G., Sutton, R.S., Anderson, C.W.: Neuronlike adaptive elements that can solve difficult learning control problems. IEEE Trans. Syst. Man Cybern. **5**, 834–846 (1983)
5. Bertsekas, D.P.: Dynamic Programming and Optimal Control, vol. 1. Athena Scientific, Belmont (1995)
6. Bhattacharya, R., Waymire, E.C.: A Basic Course in Probability Theory. Springer, New York (2007)
7. Bloembergen, D., Tuyls, K., Hennes, D., Kaisers, M.: Evolutionary dynamics of multi-agent learning: a survey. J. Artif. Intell. Res. **53**, 659–697 (2015)
8. Browne, C.B., Powley, E., Whitehouse, D., Lucas, S.M., Cowling, P.I., Rohlfshagen, P., Tavener, S., Perez, D., Samothrakis, S., Colton, S.: A survey of monte carlo tree search methods. IEEE Trans. Comput. Intell. AI Games **4**(1), 1–43 (2012)
9. Brys, T., Harutyunyan, A., Suay, H.B., Chernova, S., Taylor, M.E., Nowé, A.: Reinforcement learning from demonstration through shaping. In: Proceedings of the International Joint Conference on Artificial Intelligence (IJCAI), pp. 3352–3358 (2015)
10. Das, I., Dennis, J.E.: A closer look at drawbacks of minimizing weighted sums of objectives for Pareto set generation in multicriteria optimization problems. Struct. Optim. **14**(1), 63–69 (1997)
11. Devlin, S., Kudenko, D.: Dynamic potential-based reward shaping. In: Proceedings of the 11th International Conference on Autonomous Agents and Multiagent Systems, vol. 1, pp. 433–440. International Foundation for Autonomous Agents and Multiagent Systems (2012)
12. Devlin, S., Kudenko, D., Grześ, M.: An empirical study of potential-based reward shaping and advice in complex, multi-agent systems. Adv. Complex Syst. **14**(02), 251–278 (2011)
13. Gábor, Z., Kalmár, Z., Szepesvári, C.: Multi-criteria reinforcement learning. In: ICML, vol. 98, pp. 197–205 (1998)
14. Glorennec, P.Y.: Fuzzy q-learning and evolutionary strategy for adaptive fuzzy control. EUFIT **94**(1521), 35–40 (1994)

15. Google: Google self-driving car project. Accessed 20 Apr 2016
16. Harutyunyan, A., Devlin, S., Vrancx, P., Nowé, A.: Expressing arbitrary reward functions as potential-based advice. In: Proceedings of the Twenty-Ninth AAAI Conference on Artificial Intelligence (2015)
17. Klopf, A.H.: Brain function, adaptive systems: a heterostatic theory. Technical report AFCRL-72-0164, Air Force Cambridge Research Laboratories, Bedford, MA (1972)
18. Knox, W.B., Stone, P.: Combining manual feedback with subsequent MDP reward signals for reinforcement learning. In: Proceedings of the 9th International Conference on Autonomous Agents and Multiagent Systems, pp. 5–12 (2010)
19. Lizotte, D.J., Bowling, M.H., Murphy, S.A.: Efficient reinforcement learning with multiple reward functions for randomized controlled trial analysis. In: Proceedings of the 27th International Conference on Machine Learning (ICML-2010), pp. 695–702 (2010)
20. Mnih, V., Kavukcuoglu, K., Silver, D., Rusu, A.A., Veness, J., Bellemare, M.G., Graves, A., Riedmiller, M., Fidjeland, A.K., Ostrovski, G., et al.: Human-level control through deep reinforcement learning. Nature **518**(7540), 529–533 (2015)
21. Ng, A.Y., Harada, D., Russell, S.: Policy invariance under reward transformations: theory and application to reward shaping. In: Proceedings of the Sixteenth International Conference on Machine Learning, vol. 99, pp. 278–287 (1999)
22. Nowé, A.: Fuzzy reinforcement learning: an overview. In: Advances in Fuzzy Theory and Technology (1995)
23. Nowé, A., Vrancx, P., De Hauwere, Y.-M.: Game theory and multi-agent reinforcement learning. In: Wiering, M., van Otterlo, M. (eds.) Reinforcement Learning. ALO, vol. 12, pp. 441–470. Springer, Heidelberg (2012)
24. Roijers, D.M., Vamplew, P., Whiteson, S., Dazeley, R.: A survey of multi-objective sequential decision-making. J. Artif. Intell. Res. **48**, 67–113 (2013)
25. Russell, S., Norvig, P.: Artificial Intelligence: A Modern Approach. Artificial Intelligence, vol. 25, p. 27. Prentice-Hall, Egnlewood Cliffs (1995)
26. Sehnke, F., Graves, A., Osendorfer, C., Schmidhuber, J.: Multimodal parameter-exploring policy gradients. In: Ninth International Conference on Machine Learning and Applications (ICMLA), pp. 113–118. IEEE (2010)
27. Sehnke, F., Osendorfer, C., Rückstieß, T., Graves, A., Peters, J., Schmidhuber, J.: Parameter-exploring policy gradients. Neural Netw. **23**(4), 551–559 (2010)
28. Silver, D., Huang, A., Maddison, C.J., Guez, A., Sifre, L., van den Driessche, G., Schrittwieser, J., Antonoglou, I., Panneershelvam, V., Lanctot, M., et al.: Mastering the game of go with deep neural networks and tree search. Nature **529**(7587), 484–489 (2016)
29. Singh, S., Jaakkola, T., Littman, M.L., Szepesvári, C.: Convergence results for single-step on-policy reinforcement-learning algorithms. Mach. Learn. **38**(3), 287–308 (2000)
30. Singh, S.P., Sutton, R.S.: Reinforcement learning with replacing eligibility traces. Mach. Learn. **22**(1–3), 123–158 (1996)
31. Skinner, B.F.: The Behavior of Organisms: An Experimental Analysis. Appleton-Century, New York (1938)
32. Sutton, R.: The future of AI (2006). https://www.youtube.com/watch?v=pD-FWetbvN8. Accessed 28 June 2016
33. Sutton, R., Barto, A.: Reinforcement Learning: An Introduction, vol. 1. Cambridge University Press, Cambridge (1998)

34. Sutton, R.S., McAllester, D.A., Singh, S.P., Mansour, Y., et al.: Policy gradient methods for reinforcement learning with function approximation. In: NIPS, vol. 99, pp. 1057–1063 (1999)
35. Taylor, M.E.: Autonomous Inter-Task Transfer in Reinforcement Learning Domains. ProQuest, Ann Arbor (2008)
36. Taylor, M.E., Stone, P.: Transfer learning for reinforcement learning domains: a survey. J. Mach. Learn. Res. **10**, 1633–1685 (2009)
37. Tsitsiklis, J.N.: Asynchronous stochastic approximation and Q-learning. Mach. Learn. **16**(3), 185–202 (1994)
38. Vamplew, P., Dazeley, R., Berry, A., Issabekov, R., Dekker, E.: Empirical evaluation methods for multiobjective reinforcement learning algorithms. Mach. Learn. **84**(1–2), 51–80 (2010)
39. Vamplew, P., Yearwood, J., Dazeley, R., Berry, A.: On the limitations of scalarisation for multi-objective reinforcement learning of Pareto fronts. In: Wobcke, W., Zhang, M. (eds.) AI 2008. LNCS (LNAI), vol. 5360, pp. 372–378. Springer, Heidelberg (2008)
40. Van Moffaert, K.: Multi-criteria reinforcement learning for sequential decision making problems. Ph.D. thesis, Vrije Universiteit Brussel (2016)
41. Van Moffaert, K., Drugan, M.M., Nowé, A.: Scalarized multi-objective reinforcement learning: novel design techniques. In: IEEE International Symposium on Approximate Dynamic Programming and Reinforcement Learning. IEEE (2013)
42. Van Moffaert, K., Nowé, A.: Multi-objective reinforcement learning using sets of pareto dominating policies. J. Mach. Learn. Res. **15**(1), 3483–3512 (2014)
43. Wang, W., Sebag, M., et al.: Multi-objective monte-carlo tree search. In: ACML, pp. 507–522 (2012)
44. Watkins, C.J.C.H.: Learning from delayed rewards. Ph.D. thesis, University of Cambridge (1989)
45. Wiering, M., Otterlo, M.: Reinforcement Learning: State-of-the-Art (Adaptation, Learning, and Optimization). Springer, Berlin (2012)
46. Wiewiora, E., Cottrell, G., Elkan, C.: Principled methods for advising reinforcement learning agents. In: International Conference on Machine Learning, pp. 792–799 (2003)

Possibilistic Graphical Models for Uncertainty Modeling

Karim Tabia[1,2]([✉])

[1] University of Lille Nord de France, 59000 Lille, France
[2] CRIL University of Artois & CNRS, 62300 Lens, France
tabia@cril.univ-artois.fr

Abstract. Belief graphical models, especially the probabilistic ones, have now a long history and they are successfully used in a wide range of tasks and applications. Thanks to independence relations, they allow a compact representation of complex and uncertain information and they greatly simplify the critical tasks of information elicitation, representation and inference. Many alternative belief graphical models have been proposed to overcome the limits of probability theory and take advantage of the decomposability property. This paper surveys most of the works dealing with belief graphical models based on possibility theory, an alternative uncertainty theory particularly suited for dealing with incomplete and qualitative uncertain knowledge.

Keywords: Belief graphical models · Possibility theory · Modeling and reasoning under uncertainty

1 Introduction

Since the classical probability theory, many uncertainty frameworks have been developed, essentially since the sixties. Such alternative uncertainty theories, often generalizing probability theory, allow to model and reason with different forms of uncertain information such as qualitative information, imprecise knowledge and so on. However, in order to use such settings in real world applications, many issues have to be solved such as the compactness of the representation, the easiness of elicitation from an expert, learning from empirical data, the computational efficiency of the reasoning tasks, etc. Among the compact representations of uncertain information, we mention in particular two categories. The first one is the family of *weighted logics* such as possibilistic logic [35,49] and probabilistic logic [53] where formulas (sets of interpretations) are attached with weights assessing their certainty/priority. The other popular category of compact representations of uncertain information is *belief graphical models*. These latter are widely used in practice and popularized especially in academia with the development of several software platforms dedicated to modeling and reasoning with Bayesian networks and influence diagrams.

The key idea of belief graphical models is to rely on the concept of *independence* to factorize a large joint uncertain representation over a set of variables in

© Springer International Publishing Switzerland 2016
S. Schockaert and P. Senellart (Eds.): SUM 2016, LNAI 9858, pp. 33–48, 2016.
DOI: 10.1007/978-3-319-45856-4_3

the form of a combination of smaller size local representations. Such a factorization brings many advantages in terms of compactness, elicitation and inference. A graphical model is first of all a graph displaying the independence relations existing among the variables. It is also a modular representation making it easier to elicit and draw inferences. Possibilistic networks attempt to combine the advantages of graphical representations and possibility theory, better suited for modeling qualitative and partial knowledge.

This paper surveys the main works on possibilistic networks since their beginning. It focuses on the main contributions and attempts to highlight the similarities but also and especially the main differences between possibilistic networks and probabilistic models from which they are mainly inspired. The paper presents in Sect. 2 the fundamental concept of independence which is tightly linked with the notion of conditioning. The paper then presents the syntax and semantics of possibilistic networks in Sect. 3. Section 4 is devoted to reasoning tasks and inference issues. Learning and elicitation of possibilistic networks are reviewed in Sect. 5. The main extensions of possibilistic networks are presented in Sect. 6 while Sect. 7 presents few applications based on possibilistic networks.

2   Independence Relations and Conditioning

Independence relations are fundamental as they allow to factorize joint uncertainty distributions. Such relations are also heavily exploited by inference algorithms to efficiently answer queries. As stressed in the following, the concept of event and variable independence is closely related to the one of conditioning.

2.1   Conditioning in a Possibilistic Setting

By conditioning, it is meant updating the current knowledge encoded by a possibility distribution π over a universe of discourse Ω when a completely sure event $\phi \subseteq \Omega$ (evidence or observation for instance) is obtained. In the possibilistic setting, there are several definitions of conditioning [32,38,45,51]. This is due to the different views of the possibilistic scale [0, 1] used to asses the uncertainty. Hence, different interpretations result in different conjunction operators that are used to perform the conditioning task (eg. *product, min, Lukasiewicz t-norm*). Two major definitions of possibilistic conditioning are however used in the literature. The first one is called *product-based conditioning* (also known as possibilistic Dempster rule of conditioning [57]) stems from a quantitative view of the possibilistic scale. This semantics views a possibility distribution as a special plausibility function in the context of Dempster-Shafer theory. More precisely, a possibility distribution π corresponds to a consonant (nested) belief function. Hence, the underlying conditioning meets Dempster rule of conditioning [57] and it is formally defined as follows (it is assumed that $\Pi(\phi) > 0$):

$$\pi(w|_p \phi) = \begin{cases} \frac{\pi(w)}{\Pi(\phi)} & \text{if } w \in \phi; \\ 0 & \text{otherwise.} \end{cases} \tag{1}$$

In the qualitative setting, the possibilistic scale is ordinal and only the relative order of events matters. Hisdal [45] argued that a conditioning operator in such a qualitative setting should satisfy the condition:

$$\forall \omega \in \phi, \pi(\omega) = \min(\pi(\omega|\phi), \Pi(\phi)).$$

In [33], the authors proposed to select the least specific conditional possibility distribution satisfying this condition, leading to the well-known min-based conditioning operator, defined as follows:

$$\pi(w|_m \phi) = \begin{cases} 1 & \text{if } \pi(w) = \Pi(\phi) \text{ and } w \in \phi; \\ \pi(w) & \text{if } \pi(w) < \Pi(\phi) \text{ and } w \in \phi; \\ 0 & \text{otherwise.} \end{cases} \qquad (2)$$

While there are many similarities between the quantitative possibilistic and the probabilistic frameworks, the qualitative one is significantly different. Note that the two above definitions of conditioning satisfy the condition: $\forall \omega \in \phi, \pi(\omega) = \pi(\omega|\phi) \otimes \Pi(\phi)$ where $\otimes$ is the used conjunction operator and can be either the product or min-based operator.

2.2 Independence in a Possibilistic Setting

Intuitively, an event $\phi \subseteq \Omega$ is said to be independent of the event $\psi \subseteq \Omega$ in the context of $\varphi \subseteq \Omega$ if given φ, knowing ψ is irrelevant and does not provide any extra information about ϕ (namely, if we know φ, further learning ψ does not change what we think about ϕ). Let us denote in the rest of this paper such a relation by $\phi \perp \psi|\varphi$. This definition can be straightforwardly extended to finite sets of variables as follows: Let X, Y and Z be three disjoint sets of variables and having the finite domains D_X, D_Y and D_Z respectively. X is said to be *independent* of Y *conditionally* to Z denoted $X \perp Y|Z$ iff $\forall x_i \in D_X, \forall y_j \in D_Y, \forall z_k \in D_Z$ the statement $x_i \perp y_j|z_k$ holds. The main properties of conditional independence relations are (here X, Y, Z and W are disjoints sets of variables):

- **Symmetry:** $X \perp Y|Z$ iff $Y \perp X|Z$.
- **Decomposition:** $X \perp Y \cup W|Z$ if $X \perp Y|Z$ and $X \perp W|Z$.
- **Weak union:** $X \perp Y \cup W|Z$ if $X \perp W|Z \cup Y$.
- **Contraction:** $X \perp Y|Z$ and $X \perp W|Z \cup Y$ if $X \perp W \cup Y|Z$.
- **Intersection:** $X \perp Y|Z \cup W$ and $X \perp W|Z \cup Y$ if $X \perp W \cup Y|Z$.

Independence relations fulfilling *Symmetry, Decomposition, Weak union* and *Contraction* properties are called *semi-graphoids*. If in addition the independence relation satisfies the *Intersection* property, then it is said *graphoid*. Note that probabilistic independence relationships are graphoids and they can be encoded by means of directed acyclic graphs [55]. Of course, the notions of independence, stochastic correlation and causality are strongly related. For instance, independence relations imply lack of causality but lack of independence does not mean causality. The independence notion along with conditioning in the possibilistic setting have been addressed in many works [2,3,22,33,37,38,45,51]. The main definitions of possibilistic independence are:

– **No-interactivity:** This concept proposed by Zadeh [59] can be stated as follows:

Definition 1. *Let* X, Y *and* Z *be three disjoint sets of variables and having the domains* D_X, D_Y *and* D_Z *respectively.* X *is said to* not interact *with* Y *conditionally to* Z *and denoted* $X \perp Y | Z$ *iff* $\forall x_i \in D_X, y_j \in D_Y, z_k \in D_Z,$

$$\Pi(X = x_i, Y = y_j | Z = z_k) = \min(\Pi(X = x_i | Z = z_k), \Pi(Y = y_j | Z = z_k)).$$

– **Conditional independence:** Proposed in [38], this definition of independence can be stated as follows:

Definition 2. *Let* X, Y *and* Z *be three disjoint sets of variables and having the domains* D_X, D_Y *and* D_Z *respectively.* X *is said to be* independent *of* Y *conditionally to* Z *iff* $\forall x_i \in D_X, y_j \in D_Y, z_k \in D_Z,$

$$\Pi(X = x_i | Y = y_j, Z = z_k) = \Pi(X = x_i | Z = z_k) \; and$$
$$\Pi(Y = y_j | X = x_i, Z = z_k) = \Pi(Y = y_j | Z = z_k)$$

Note that in Definition 2, the statement $\Pi(X = x_i | Y = y_j, Z = z_k) = \Pi(X = x_i | Z = z_k)$ does not imply $\Pi(Y = y_j | X = x_i, Z = z_k) = \Pi(Y = y_j | Z = z_k)$ in a min-based possibilistic setting. The conditional independence relations of Definition 2 are graphoids [37,38]. Note also that conditional independence relations of Definition 2 are stronger than *no-interactivity* relations of Definition 1, namely conditional independence implies no-interactivity but the converse is not guaranteed.

3   Possibilistic Networks: Syntax and Semantics

From a representation point of view, possibilistic graphical models share most of their concepts with probabilistic graphical models and differ only regarding the assessment of uncertainty which is based on possibility theory instead of probability theory.

Definition 3. *A possibilistic network* $\mathcal{PN} = < \mathcal{G}, \Theta >$ *is specified by:*

(i) *A graphical component* $G = < V, E >$ *consisting of a directed acyclic graph (DAG) where vertices* V *represent the variables and edges* E *encode conditional independence relationships between variables. Each variable* $A_i \in V$ *is associated with a finite domain* D_{A_i} *containing the values* a_i *taken by a variable* A_i.

(ii) *A numerical component* $\Theta = \{\theta_1, \dots, \theta_n\}$ *consisting in a set of local possibility tables* $\theta_i = \pi(A_i | par(A_i))$ *for each variable* A_i *in the context of its parents* $par(A_i)$.

Note that all the local possibility distributions must be normalized, namely $\forall i = 1 \dots n$, for each parent context $par(a_i)$, $\max_{a_i \in D_{A_i}} (\pi(a_i \mid par(a_i))) = 1$.

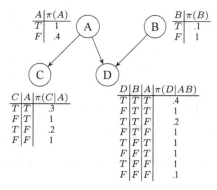

A	$\pi(A)$
T	1
F	.4

B	$\pi(B)$
T	.1
F	1

C	A	$\pi(C\|A)$
T	T	.3
F	T	1
T	F	.2
F	F	1

D	B	A	$\pi(D\|AB)$
T	T	T	.4
F	T	T	1
T	T	F	.2
F	T	F	1
T	F	T	1
F	F	T	1
T	F	F	1
F	F	F	.1

Fig. 1. Example of a possibilistic network

Example 1. Figure 1 gives an example of a possibilistic network over four Boolean variables A, B, C and D. The structure of G encodes a set of independence relationships. For example, variable C is independent of B and D in the context of A.

In the possibilistic setting, the joint possibility distribution is factorized using the following possibilistic counterpart of the chain rule:

$$\pi(a_1, a_2, \ldots, a_n) = \otimes_{i=1}^{n} (\pi(a_i | par(a_i))). \tag{3}$$

where $\otimes$ denotes the product or the min-based operator depending on the quantitative or the qualitative interpretation of the possibilistic scale.

Example 2 (Example 1 cont'd). In the network of Fig. 1, the joint possibility distribution factorizes as follows:

$$\pi(A, B, C, D) = \otimes(\pi(A), \pi(B), \pi(C|A), \pi(D|AB)).$$

While the size of a joint possibility distribution is exponential in the number of variables, the size of a possibilistic network is exponential in its *treewidth* which denotes the largest number of parents of the variables in the network. Indeed, the size of the network depends on the size of local distributions which is exponential in the *treewidth*. According to the topology of the DAG, we distinguish three main possibilistic networks:

- **Trees:** In a tree, (i) there is at most one (undirected) path between each pair of nodes and (ii) a node can have at most one parent.
- **Polytrees:** In a polytree, (i) there is at most one (undirected) path between each pair of nodes and (ii) a node can have more than one parent.
- **Multiply Connected**: Many paths are allowed between pairs of variables as long as the structured remains a DAG (Fig. 2).

As mentioned in the following sections, the topology of a network (which encodes the independence relations) is fundamental for the propagation process in inference algorithms.

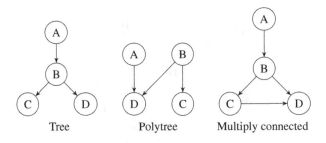

Fig. 2. Main topologies of belief graphical models

4   Possibilistic Networks: Reasoning and Inference

A possibilistic network models the available information regarding the problem under study. Once the model built, it can be used for answering queries and performing different types of reasoning tasks.

4.1   Main Reasoning Tasks

A belief graphical model, be it possibilistic or not, provides two kinds of information: (i) graphical qualitative information allowing to answer any query regarding the independence of a set of variables $X \subseteq V$ with $Y \subseteq V$ conditionally to $Z \subseteq V$. In order to answer such queries, a generalized notion of conditional independence, called *d-separation* allows to determine for each subset of variables X the subset of variables Z which renders it independent of all the remaining variables. This notion of *d-separation* is dealt with in a possibilistic setting for instance in [16]. Regarding the numerical information encoded by a possibilistic network, there are three main query types:

- Compute the possibility/necessity degree of an event q of interest given an evidence o (o is an instance of observation variables $O \subseteq V$ while q is an instance of query variables $Q \subseteq V$).
- Compute the most plausible explanation (MPE). Given an observation o of a subset of variables $O \subseteq V$, the objective is to compute the most plausible instantiation q of all the remaining (unobserved) query variables $Q \subseteq V$. Note that here $O \cup Q = V$ and $Q \cap O = \emptyset$.
- Compute the maximum a posteriori (MAP). Given some observations o of the values of some variables $O \subseteq V$, the objective is to compute the most plausible instantiation q of the query variables $Q \subseteq V$. In MAP queries, $Q \cap O = \emptyset$. Note that MPE queries are a special case of MAP ones.

It is important to note that while the complexity results regarding inference in probabilistic networks are well-established [27], there is to the best of our knowledge no systematic study of such issues for possibilistic networks (except a study of complexity in possibilistic influence diagrams [39]). Indeed, there is a kind of tacit assumption that the same complexity results hold in the possibilistic setting but there this is not yet formally demonstrated. Actually, some probabilistic network inference algorithms have been adapted from the probabilistic setting and seem to show the same complexity.

4.2 Inference Algorithms

Inference in probabilistic models is a hard task in the general case. For instance, in multiply connected networks, the problem of computing the probability of an event is PP-Complete, computing MPE queries is NP-complete while computing MAP queries is NP^{PP}-Complete [27]. Among the first works on inference in possibilistic graphical models we mention [34] dealing with inference in hypergraphs. Most of the works are more or less direct adaptations of probabilistic networks inference algorithms.

- **Variable elimination:** This category of algorithms are direct adaptations of the probabilistic versions. Given a query, the general approach is to eliminate variables through marginalization and combination operations until reaching the query variables, then answer the query. Examples of possibilistic elimination variable algorithms can be found in [16] in the context of possibilistic network classifiers. Such algorithms are efficient only on networks with bounded treewidth like trees.
- **Message passing-like algorithms:** Such algorithms, also called *sum-product algorithms* are developed for tree-like networks and proceed by a series of message passing procedures to compute the probability degree of interest [54]. In [19], a possibilistic counterpart of this algorithm is presented.
- **Junction tree algorithm:** The junction tree algorithm is a well-known and widely used inference algorithm in Bayesian networks with general structures [50]. The main idea of the algorithm is to decompose the joint belief distribution into a combination of local potentials (local joint distributions). The algorithm consists in (i) A set of graphical transformations (moralization and triangulation) transforming the initial DAG into an undirected graph (tree) composed of cliques and clusters and (ii) numerical operations (initialization and stabilization) allowing to integrate the initial local distributions into the new structure then perform stabilization operation consisting in propagating marginals in order to guarantee that the marginal distribution relative to a given variable appearing in two adjacent clusters are the same. A direct adaptation of this algorithm in the possibilistic setting can be found in [18]. In [11], an extension of the junction tree algorithm to the interval-based possibilistic setting and to three-valued possibilistic setting [8] are proposed.
- **Compilation-based algorithms:** Inference based on compilation-based algorithms consists in first encoding the uncertain information represented by the graphical model into a target language then perform inference in the target language. For inference with Bayesian networks, the graphical model is first encoded in the form of a logical knowledge base, then this latter is encoded in an appropriate encoding accepting the requests that are made for

the initial probabilistic model. Probabilistic compilation-based methods are proposed in [26] and some possibilistic counterparts are studied in [5].

In addition to the above works, an anytime algorithm for inference in min-based possibilistic networks is proposed in [7]. Unlike the junction tree approach which transforms the initial graph, the proposed algorithm in [7] only propagates the information present in each node to ensure that the information present in each local table is coherent with the information at the parents of that node. An approximate inference algorithm for qualitative possibilistic networks in proposed in [1]. This algorithm is based on a possibilistic adaptation of the probabilistic loopy belief propagation algorithm. In [9], possibilistic networks are encoded in the form of possibilistic logics bases (the two representations are semantically equivalent and encode a possibility distribution) and inferences could be achieved using possibilistic logic inference rules and mechanisms. Possibilistic networks could be seen as approximate models of some imprecise probabilistic models. In [13], an approach based on probability-possibility transformations is proposed to perform approximate MAP inference in credal networks where MAP inference is very hard [27]. Reasoning under uncertain inputs in possibilistic networks is dealt with in [17] where possibilistic counterparts of Pearl's methods of virtual evidence are discussed. In [15], the authors dealt with handling interventions in causal possibilistic networks.

5   Possibilistic Networks: Learning and Elicitation

As probabilistic graphical models, possibilistic ones either model the subjective knowledge of an agent or represent the knowledge learnt from empirical data or a combination of subjective beliefs and empirical data.

5.1   Elicitation of Possibilistic Networks

When modeling the epistemic uncertainty of an agent about a given problem, the process starts with defining the variables of interest. Then the second step consists in eliciting the graphical structure of the model. This is usually dealt with as eliciting direct cause-effect relationships or simply eliciting possibilistic independence relations. More generally, this task requires to list the conditional independence relationships then to encode them by a directed acyclic graph as in probabilistic models. The approaches developed in the probabilistic setting [29] can as well suit the possibilistic one.

Once the graph fixed, there comes the tricky and sometimes tedious step of filling local tables. In fact, there is need to assign for each value of each variable in every context of its parents a possibility degree in agreement with the quantitative or qualitative semantics of the possibilistic scale. In the literature, different methods for building possibility distributions can be used [36]. In an ordinal setting, the expert could only provide an ordering of the values of the variables to be elicited in each context of its parents. Then such an ordering is encoded numerically using values within the scale [0,1]. Note that encoding numerically ordinal information can yield different encodings hence different joint distributions especially if the variables have different domain sizes. This problem is due to the fact that when modeling with qualitative possibilistic networks, the information elicitation process proceeds locally (for each variable conditionally to its parents) but the use of the same unit scale *implies* some commensurability. Approaches based on symbolic uncertainty weights could help solving this issue [25]. For eliciting causal possibilistic networks, an elicitation approach is proposed in [31]. This approach offers noisy gates that better capture the insights and intuitions of the expert. Indeed, an expert is often more comfortable when specifying a relative order on the possible causes that when he has to precisely quantify the causal strength of cause-effect relationships.

5.2   Learning Possibilistic Networks from Data

As for learning Bayesian networks from data, learning possibilistic ones comes down to derive the structure and the local possibility tables of each variable from a dataset. Learning possibilistic networks makes sense within quantitative interpretations of possibility distributions and it is suitable especially in case of learning with imprecise data, scarce datasets and learning from datasets with missing values.

Structure Learning. Structure learning aims to infer from the data the *best* DAG encoding the conditional independences. Similar to learning the structure of Bayesian networks, two main approaches are used for possibilistic networks structure learning:

- *Constraint-based methods:* The principle of this approach is to detect conditional independence relations I by performing a set of tests on the training dataset then try to find a DAG that satisfies I seen as a set of constraints. A constraint-based possibilistic network structure learning algorithm called *POSSCAUSE* is proposed in [56]. This algorithm is based on a similarity measure between possibility distributions to check conditional independences. The main disadvantage of constraint-based methods is that the search space is very large even for a small number of variables.
- *Score-based methods:* Such methods don't explore the whole search space to find the best structure fitting the data. They are based on heuristics that start with a completely disconnected (or completely connected) DAG. At each iteration, the heuristic adds (or removes) an arc and evaluates the quality of the new DAGs with respect to the training dataset. The best DAG at each iteration is selected using a score function. The key issues of *score-based methods* are the scoring functions and the heuristics used to search the DAG space. For the heuristics, one can make use of the ones defined for Bayesian networks (eg. K2 algorithm, simulated annealing, etc.). However, for the score functions, they are assumed to assess how much a given structure captures the independence relations in the training sample. Examples of possibility

theory-based scoring functions are *possibilistic network non-specificity* [20] and *specificity gain* [56].

Some structure learning approaches [40], called *hybrid*, attempt to combine the constraint-based and the score-based approaches for instance to make use of the conditional independence tests in the heuristics used in score-based approaches.

Parameter Learning. Parameter learning is needed to fill the local tables once the structure is learnt from data or elicited by an expert. For possibilistic networks, parameter learning from data consists basically in deriving conditional local possibility distributions from data. There are two main approaches for learning the parameters [43]:

(i) *Transformation-based approach:* It consists in first learning probability distributions from data then transforming them into possibilistic ones [12,43,58]. Many probability-possibility transformations exist [30,48,59]. Among these transformations, the optimal transformation [30] transforms a probability distribution p into a possibilistic one π and guarantees that π is the most specific one that is consistent and preserving the order of interpretations in p. In case of imprecise probability distributions (generally learnt from imprecise data or datasets with missing data), one can also use probability - possibility transformations turning for instance an interval-based probability distribution into a possibilistic one. The transformation proposed in [52] allows to find a possibility distribution dominating all the probability measures defined by probability intervals. In [28], the authors show that any upper generalized cumulative distribution built from one linear extension is a possibility distribution dominating all the probability distributions that are compatible with the interval-based probability distribution.

(ii) *Possibilistic-based approach:* Such approaches stem from some quantitative interpretations of possibility distributions. For instance, a possibility distribution is viewed as a contour function of a consonant belief function [57]. In [41], possibility distributions are derived from data samples using the non-specificity concept. In [47], the author propose a method for computing possibility distributions from imprecise datasets (namely datasets containing some set-valued outcomes) based on the frequencies of the values. For a recent survey on possibilistic network parameter learning, please refer to [43].

It is clear that learning a possibilistic network by first learning a Bayesian network then turning it into a possibilistic network by transforming the local probability tables into possibilistic ones (as done in [12,13,58]) may be questionable regarding the fact that possibilistic independence and probabilistic one do not capture exactly the same information. A software for inducing possibilistic networks called INeS is available at http://www.borgelt.net/ines.html.

6   Possibilistic Networks: Main Extensions

In this section, we briefly present the main extensions of possibilistic graphical models.

- **Possibilistic Influence diagrams:** Influence diagrams [46] are probabilistic models for modeling and decision making under uncertainty. They have three kinds of nodes: chance nodes (corresponding to the variables as in Bayesian networks), decision nodes (representing the decisions and actions that can be chosen) and utility nodes (assessing the gain or satisfaction provided by each taken decision). Possibilistic influence diagrams are proposed [39,42]. They depart from the probabilistic models regarding the ordinal uncertain information and ordinal preferences instead of additive utilities.
- **Hybrid possibilistic networks:** The main difference of this formalism [14] with standard possibilistic networks relies on the use of possibilistic logic to compactly encode local possibility distributions. In addition to a more compact representation, an inference algorithm adapting the junction tree approach is proposed for hybrid networks and it is shown to be more efficient than standard propagation algorithms.
- **Interval-based possibilistic networks:** Possibilistic networks have been extended to the interval-based setting in [11] in order to associate intervals of possible values instead of single values to assess uncertainty. This allows to compactly encode and reason with epistemic uncertainty and imprecise beliefs as well as with multiple expert knowledge. Interestingly enough, computing the uncertainty bounds of any event can be computed without extra computational cost with respect to standard possibilistic networks.
- **Three-valued possibilistic networks:** This extension [8] uses only three possibility levels to encode uncertain information: 1 for fully possible events, 0 for impossible events while a third value is used to encode imprecise or conflicting information. A direct adaptation of the junction tree algorithm for such networks is also proposed.
- **Possibilistic preference networks:** Encoding preferences with graphical formalisms is very popular both in quantitative and qualitative settings. In [4], a new setting based on possibilistic networks for modeling and reasoning with conditional preference statements is introduced. While allowing to encode and reason with conditional preferences, this setting overcomes some of the limitations of the CP-net formalism. An approach combining preferential possibilistic networks and ontological knowledge for preference-based query answering is proposed in [21].

  Other extensions and variants of possibilistic networks are developed for modeling some specific kinds of information such as dynamic possibilistic networks [44], negated possibilistic networks [10], etc.

7   Possibilistic Networks: Applications

In this section, we briefly describe two applications based on possibilistic networks.

- **Classification:** It is one of the early applications of possibilistic networks. Classification consists in predicting the value of a (discrete) variable on the basis of some observations. In terms of inference queries, it is a special case of MAP queries consisting in computing the most plausible value of the class variable given the observations. This task has been dealt with in many works (see for instance [16] for inference issues and [24] for learning possibilistic network classifiers from data). Possibilistic network-based classifiers could provide an efficient alternative for problems with imprecise and scarce datasets and datasets with missing values [24]. A software based on naive possibilistic classifiers in available at http://www.borgelt.net/nposs.html.

- **Information retrieval:** In [23], an application of possibilistic networks in an information retrieval application is presented. The particularity of this approach compared with those based on Bayesian networks for instance, is the use of two measures (possibility and necessity) to model the relations *documents-terms* and *query-terms*. Using these two measures, the approach aims to distinguish between *informative* and *non-informative* terms in a document. Given a query, a given document is considered relevant with respect to its plausibility (assessed by a conditional possibility degree) and the certainty (assessed by a conditional necessity degree) that the document is relevant for the query. The authors provide experimental results carried out on the TREC benchmarks showing the effectiveness of their approach. A similar approach in language processing based on possibilistic networks in proposed in [6].

8   Concluding Remarks

This survey attempted to highlight the most important aspects of possibilistic networks: representation, reasoning and applications. Despite the obvious similarities and the many direct adaptations of probabilistic approaches, it is clear that possibilistic graphical models offer some advantages over the probabilistic models especially for modeling and reasoning with qualitative and incomplete uncertainty. Extensions have been proposed for some types of information such as conditional preference statements. Some possibility theory particularities may offer interesting gains in inference algorithms. For example, in the ordinal possibilistic setting, there may be meaningful differences as stressed in [34] where the idempotence property of min and max operators benefit to inference algorithms. To promote the use of possibilistic graphical models, there is a clear need to develop software tools for modeling and reasoning that can be used by the scientific community and beyond. Moreover, many competitions and challenges have been organized last years to assess the efficiency of learning and inference algorithms in probabilistic graphical models. Similar events devoted to possibilistic approaches may help promoting possibilistic graphical models. Other issues need to be addressed to provide evidence showing that possibilistic networks could be successfully used in real applications. For instance, a systematic study of complexity issues in possibilistic networks needs to be done. Dealing with continuous variables which are common in real problems is another issue requiring effective solutions [24].

References

1. Ajroud, A., Benferhat, S.: An approximate algorithm for min-based possibilistic networks. Int. J. Intell. Syst. **29**, 615–633 (2014)
2. Amor, N.B., Benferhat, S.: Graphoid properties of qualitative possibilistic independence relations. Int. J. Uncertain. Fuzziness Knowl.-Based Syst. **13**(1), 59–96 (2005)
3. Amor, N.B., Benferhat, S., Dubois, D., Geffner, H., Prade, H.: Independence in qualitative uncertainty frameworks. In: KR 2000, Principles of Knowledge Representation and Reasoning Proceedings of the Seventh International Conference, Breckenridge, Colorado, USA, 11–15 April 2000, pp. 235–246 (2000)
4. Amor, N.B., Dubois, D., Gouider, H., Prade, H.: Possibilistic conditional preference networks. In: Destercke, S., Denoeux, T. (eds.) ECSQARU 2015. LNCS, vol. 9161, pp. 36–46. Springer, Heidelberg (2015)
5. Ayachi, R., Amor, N.B., Benferhat, S.: Inference using compiled min-based possibilistic causal networks in the presence of interventions. Fuzzy Sets Syst. **239**, 104–136 (2014)
6. Ayed, R., Bounhas, I., Elayeb, B., Evrard, F., Bellamine-Bensaoud, N.: A possibilistic approach for the automatic morphological disambiguation of Arabic texts. In: International Conference on Software Engineering, Artificial Intelligence, Networking and Parallel/Distributed Computing, Kyoto, Japan. IEEE Computer Society (2012)
7. Ben Amor, N., Benferhat, S., Mellouli, K.: Anytime propagation algorithm for min-based possibilistic graphs. Soft Comput. **8**, 150–161 (2003)
8. Benferhat, S., Delobelle, J., Tabia, K.: Three-valued possibilistic networks: semantics & inference. In: 2013 IEEE 25th International Conference on Tools with Artificial Intelligence, Herndon, VA, USA, 4–6 November 2013, pp. 38–45 (2013)
9. Benferhat, S., Dubois, D., Garcia, L., Prade, H.: On the transformation between possibilistic logic bases and possibilistic causal networks. Int. J. Approximate Reasoning **29**(2), 135–173 (2002)
10. Benferhat, S., Khellaf, F., Zeddigha, I.: Negated min-based possibilistic networks. In: Florida Artificial Intelligence Research Society Conference (2016)
11. Benferhat, S., Lagrue, S., Tabia, K.: Interval-based possibilistic networks. In: Straccia, U., Calì, A. (eds.) SUM 2014. LNCS, vol. 8720, pp. 37–50. Springer, Heidelberg (2014)
12. Benferhat, S., Levray, A., Tabia, K.: On the analysis of probability-possibility transformations: changing operations and graphical models. In: Destercke, S., Denoeux, T. (eds.) ECSQARU 2015. LNCS, vol. 9161, pp. 279–289. Springer, Heidelberg (2015)
13. Benferhat, S., Levray, A., Tabia, K.: Probability-possibility transformations: application to credal networks. In: Beierle, C., Dekhtyar, A. (eds.) SUM 2015. LNCS, vol. 9310, pp. 203–219. Springer, Heidelberg (2015)
14. Benferhat, S., Smaoui, S.: Hybrid possibilistic networks. Int. J. Approx. Reasoning **44**(3), 224–243 (2007)
15. Benferhat, S., Smaoui, S.: Inferring interventions in product-based possibilistic causal networks. Fuzzy Sets Syst. **169**(1), 26–50 (2011)
16. Benferhat, S., Tabia, K.: Inference in possibilistic network classifiers under uncertain observations. Ann. Math. Artif. Intell. **64**(2–3), 269–309 (2012)
17. Benferhat, S., Tabia, K.: Reasoning with uncertain inputs in possibilistic networks. In: Principles of Knowledge Representation, Reasoning: Proceedings of the Fourteenth International Conference, KR 2014, Vienna, Austria, 20–24 July 2014 (2014)

18. Borgelt, C., Gebhardt, J., Kruse, R.: Graphical models. In: Proceedings of International School for the Synthesis of Expert Knowledge (ISSEK 98), pp. 51–68. Wiley (2002)
19. Borgelt, C., Kruse, R.: Graphical Models - Methods for Data Analysis and Mining. Wiley, New York (2002)
20. Borgelt, C., Kruse, R.: Learning possibilistic graphical models from data. IEEE Trans. Fuzzy Syst. 11(2), 159–172 (2003)
21. Borgwardt, S., Fazzinga, B., Lukasiewicz, T., Shrivastava, A., Tifrea-Marciuska, O.: Preferential query answering over the semantic web with possibilistic networks. In: Kambhampati, S. (ed.) Proceedings of the 25th International Joint Conference on Artificial Intelligence, IJCAI 2016, New York, NY, USA, 9–15 July 2016. AAAI Press (2016)
22. Bouchon-Meunier, B., Coletti, G., Marsala, C.: Independence and possibilistic conditioning. Ann. Math. Artif. Intell. 35(1–4), 107–123 (2002)
23. Boughanem, M., Brini, A., Dubois, D.: Possibilistic networks for information retrieval. Int. J. Approx. Reasoning 50(7), 957–968 (2009)
24. Bounhas, M., Hamed, M.G., Prade, H., Serrurier, M., Mellouli, K.: Naive possibilistic classifiers for imprecise or uncertain numerical data. Fuzzy Sets Syst. 239, 137–156 (2014)
25. Cayrol, C., Dubois, D., Touazi, F.: Symbolic possibilistic logic: completeness and inference methods. In: Destercke, S., Denoeux, T. (eds.) ECSQARU 2015. LNCS, vol. 9161, pp. 485–495. Springer, Berlin (2015)
26. Chavira, M., Darwiche, A.: Compiling bayesian networks with local structure. In: Proceedings of the 19th International Joint Conference on Artificial Intelligence (IJCAI), pp. 1306–1312 (2005)
27. De Campos, C.P.: New complexity results for map in bayesian networks. In: Proceedings of the Twenty-Second International Joint Conference on Artificial Intelligence, IJCAI 2011, vol. 3, pp. 2100–2106. AAAI Press (2011)
28. Destercke, S., Dubois, D., Chojnacki, E.: Transforming probability intervals into other uncertainty models. In: EUSFLAT 2007 Proceedings, vol. 2, pp. 367–373. Universitas Ostraviensis, Ostrava (2007)
29. Druzdzel, M.J., Van Der Gaag, L.C.: Elicitation of probabilities for belief networks: combining qualitative and quantitative information. In: Proceedings of the Eleventh Conference on Uncertainty in Artificial Intelligence, UAI 1995, pp. 141–148. Morgan Kaufmann Publishers Inc., San Francisco (1995)
30. Dubois, D., Foulloy, L., Mauris, G., Prade, H.: Probability-possibility transformations, triangular fuzzy sets, and probabilistic inequalities. Reliable Comput. 10(4), 273–297 (2004)
31. Dubois, D., Fusco, G., Prade, H., Tettamanzi, A.: Uncertain logical gates in possibilistic networks. An application to human geography. In: Beierle, C., Dekhtyar, A. (eds.) SUM 2015. LNCS, vol. 9310, pp. 249–263. Springer, Heidelberg (2015)
32. Dubois, D., Prade, H., Theory, P.: An Approach to Computerized Processing of Uncertainty. Plenum Press, New York (1988)
33. Dubois, D., Prade, H.: The logical view of conditioning and its application to possibility and evidence theories. Int. J. Approx. Reasoning 4(1), 23–46 (1990)
34. Dubois, D., Prade, H.: Inference in possibilistic hypergraphs. In: Bouchon-Meunier, B., Zadeh, L.A., Yager, R.R. (eds.) IPMU 1990. LNCS, vol. 521, pp. 250–259. Springer, Heidelberg (1991)
35. Dubois, D., Prade, H.: Possibilistic logic: a retrospective and prospective view. Fuzzy Sets Syst. 144(1), 3–23 (2004)

36. Dubois, D., Prade, H.: Practical methods for constructing possibility distributions. Int. J. Intell. Syst. **31**(3), 215–239 (2016)
37. Fonck, P.: Conditional independence in possibility theory. In: Proceedings of the Tenth International Conference on Uncertainty in Artificial Intelligence, UAI 1994, pp. 221–226. Morgan Kaufmann Publishers Inc., San Francisco (1994)
38. Fonck, P.: A comparative study of possibilistic conditional independence and lack of interaction. Int. J. Approximate Reasoning **16**(2), 149–171 (1997)
39. Garcia, L., Sabbadin, R.: Complexity results and algorithms for possibilistic influence diagrams. Artif. Intell. **172**(8), 1018–1044 (2008)
40. Gasse, M., Aussem, A., Elghazel, H.: A hybrid algorithm for bayesian network structure learning with application to multi-label learning. Expert Syst. Appl. **41**(15), 6755–6772 (2014)
41. Gebhardt, J., Kruse, R.: Learning possibilistic networks from data. In: Proceedings 5th International Workshop on Artificial Intelligence and Statistics, Fort Lauderdale, pp. 233–244 (1996)
42. Guezguez, W., Amor, N.B., Mellouli, K.: Qualitative possibilistic influence diagrams based on qualitative possibilistic utilities. Eur. J. Oper. Res. **195**(1), 223–238 (2009)
43. Haddad, M., Leray, P., Amor, N.B.: Learning possibilistic networks from data: a survey. In: 2015 Conference of the International Fuzzy Systems Association and the European Society for Fuzzy Logic and Technology (IFSA-EUSFLAT-15), Gijón, Spain, 30 June 2015 (2015)
44. Heni, A., Amor, N.B., Benferhat, S., Alimi, A.: Dynamic possibilistic networks: representation and exact inference. In: 2007 IEEE International Conference on Computational Intelligence for Measurement Systems and Applications, pp. 1–8, June 2007
45. Hisdal, E.: Conditional possibilities independence and non interaction. Fuzzy Sets Syst. **1**(4), 283–297 (1978)
46. Howard, R.A., Matheson, J.E.: Influence diagrams. Principles Appl. Decis. Anal. **2**, 720–761 (1984)
47. Joslyn, C.: Towards an empirical semantics of possibility through maximum uncertainty. In: Fourth World Congress of the International Fuzzy Systems Association: Artificial Intelligence, pp. 86–89 (1991)
48. Klir, G.J., Geer, J.F.: Information-preserving probability-possibility transformations: recent developments. In: Lowen, R., Roubens, M. (eds.) Fuzzy Logic, pp. 417–428. Kluwer Academic Publishers, Dordrecht (1993)
49. Lang, J.: Possibilistic logic: complexity and algorithms. In: Kohlas, J., Moral, S. (eds.) Algorithms for Uncertainty and Defeasible Reasoning, vol. 5, pp. 179–220. Kluwer Academic Publishers (2001)
50. Lauritzen, S.L., Spiegelhalter, D.J.: Local computations with probabilities on graphical structures and their application to expert systems. In: Readings in Uncertain Reasoning, pp. 415–448. Morgan Kaufmann Publishers Inc., San Francisco (1990)
51. De Campos, L.M., Huete, J.F., Moral, S.: Possibilistic independence. In: Proceedings of EUFIT 1995, vol. 1, pp. 69–73 (1995)
52. Masson, M.-H., Denoeux, T.: Inferring a possibility distribution from empirical data. Fuzzy Sets Syst. **157**(3), 319–340 (2006)
53. Nilsson, N.J.: Probabilistic logic. Artif. Intell. **28**(1), 71–88 (1986)
54. Pearl, J.: Reverend bayes on inference engines: a distributed hierarchical approach. In: Proceedings of the American Association of Artificial Intelligence National Conference on AI, Pittsburgh, PA, pp. 133–136 (1982)

55. Pearl, J.: Probabilistic Reasoning in Intelligent Systems: Networks of Plausible Inference. Morgan Kaufmann Publishers Inc., San Francisco (1988)
56. Sangesa, R., Cabs, J., Corts, U.: Possibilistic conditional independence: a similarity-based measure and its application to causal network learning. Int. J. Approximate Reasoning 18(1), 145–167 (1998)
57. Shafer, G.: A Mathematical Theory of Evidence. Princeton University Press, Princeton (1976)
58. Slimen, Y.B., Ayachi, R., Amor, N.B.: Probability-possibility transformation: application to Bayesian and possibilistic networks. In: Masulli, F. (ed.) WILF 2013. LNCS, vol. 8256, pp. 122–130. Springer, Heidelberg (2013)
59. Zadeh, L.A.: Fuzzy sets as a basis for a theory of possibility. Fuzzy Sets Syst. 100, 9–34 (1999)

Regular Papers

On the Explanation of SameAs Statements Using Argumentation

Abdallah Arioua[1], Madalina Croitoru[2(✉)], Laura Papaleo[4,5],
Nathalie Pernelle[3], and Swan Rocher[2]

[1] GraphIK, INRA, Montpellier, France
[2] GraphIK, University of Montpellier, Montpellier, France
croitoru@lirmm.fr
[3] LaHDAK, LRI, University of Paris Sud, Orsay, France
[4] ICT Department, Metropolitan City of Genoa, Italy
[5] Tetherless World Constellation, Rensselaer Polytechnic Institute, Troy, USA

Abstract. Due to the impressive growing of the LOD graph in the last years, assuring the quality of its content is becoming a very important issue. Thus, it is crucial to design techniques for supporting experts in validating facts and links in complex data sources. Here, we focus on identity links (*sameAs*) and apply argumentation semantics to (*i*) detect inconsistencies in sameAs statements and to (*ii*) explain them to the experts using dialogues. We formalize the framework, explaining its purposes. Finally we provide a promising preliminary evaluation and discuss on some interesting future directions we foresee.

1 Introduction

Today, we are experiencing an unprecedented production of resources, published as *Linked Open Data* (LOD). This is leading to the creation of a *global data space* with billions of assertions [9]. RDF [24] provides formal ways to build these assertions. Most of the RDF links, connecting resources coming from different data sources, are *identity links*, also called *sameAs statements*. They are defined using the *owl:sameAs* property, expressing that two URIs actually refer to the same thing [1]. Unfortunately, many existing identity links do not reflect genuine real identity [15,16] and therefore might lead to inconsistencies. Over the years, inconsistency-tolerant semantics (e.g. [7,8,26,27]) have been proposed for query answering over potentially inconsistent existing data (and thus overcoming inconsistencies within the data).

In this work, we formalize *explanation dialogues* that use *argument-based explanation* based on inconsistency tolerant semantics. Our explanation dialogue supports a domain expert in discovering inconsistencies as in (eventually) performing corrections on erroneous data, or in revising the logical rules used for the invalidation or even in deciding the (potential) redesign of the initial linking strategy.

© Springer International Publishing Switzerland 2016
S. Schockaert and P. Senellart (Eds.): SUM 2016, LNAI 9858, pp. 51–66, 2016.
DOI: 10.1007/978-3-319-45856-4_4

The *explanation dialogue* relies on a method for invalidating the sameAs that computes *repairs* so that, when a sameAs is *not entailed by the defined semantics*, an explanation of the reasons against this entailment is provided.

This is the first work that uses argumentation for sameAs links invalidation together with a formalization of a general explanation framework supporting the dialogue between user and reasoner. The salient point of this paper is to show how inconsistency-tolerant semantics can represent a first step in the direction of the design of new interactive paradigms for assessing the quality of sameAs statements.

The paper is organized as follows. Section 2 argues on related works while in Sect. 3 we provide background notions for argumentation theory. Section 4 is devoted to the presentation of our argumentation problem for sameAs invalidation. Section 5 formally introduces the novel *Explanation Dialogue* and Sect. 6 provides an example of the overall strategy implemented in a prototype. Finally, Sect. 7 draws some concluding remarks and possible future directions.

2   Related Work

To the extent of our knowledge the work presented here is the first attempt to combine argumentation theory, identity links evaluation and explanation dialogues, however, related works can be found in the context of sameAs evaluation and in general approaches which use argumentation in the Semantic Web.

For what concern the sameAs validation problem, it is very recent and few methods exist. In [17] an approach is presented where the structural properties of large graphs of sameAs links are analyzed, without analyzing the quality. In [22] a framework dedicated to the assessment of sameAs using network metrics is described, while in [23] the authors reported on the quality of sameAs links in the LOD using a manual method. In [15], the author illustrates how to assess the quality of sameAs, using a constraint-based method which, in the end, consider only one property (name of the entity), while in [29] an ontology-based logical invalidation method is presented which discovers invalid sameAs by the use of contextual graphs build around the resources, thus using more properties. Finally, the recent work presented in [14] evaluate a sameAs by using position and relevance of each resource involved with regards to the associated DBpedia categories, modeled through two probabilistic category distribution and selection functions. We need to recall that there exist a lot of linking methods (see [21] as survey) that, during their process of sameAs discovery, include a strategy for evaluating the reliability of the sameAs just computed.

Regarding argumentation in the Semantic Web, several works exist that mainly address ontologies alignment agreement based on argumentation theory (e.g. [18,19,25]). Basically, all of them use argumentation to provide a final agreement (or a final answer), and do not exploit the argumentation as a form of explanation of the answer to a query. Recently, in [10] the problem of *data fusion* in Linked Data is addressed, by adopting a bipolar argumentation theory (with fuzzy labeling) to reason over inconsistent information sets, and to provide a unique answer.

This last method has common points with our line of work, namely the use of argumentation theory to detect inconsistencies, but the scenarios in which the approach is exploited are different as its general aim is. This obviously leads to different addressed issues and proposed solutions.

3 Background Notions

There exist two major approaches for representing an ontology for the OBDA (Ontology-Based Data Access) problem: (i) *Description Logics* (DL) (such as $\mathcal{EL}$ [4] and DL_{Lite} [12] families) and (ii) *Rule-based Languages* (such as Datalog$_{+/-}$ [11] language). Despite its undecidability when answering conjunctive queries, different decidable fragments of Datalog$_{+/-}$ have been studied in the literature [6]. They overcome their limitations allowing n-arity for predicates and cyclic structures. We consider *the positive existential* conjunctive fragment of first-order logic, denoted by $\text{FOL}(\wedge, \exists)$, which is composed of formulas built with the connectors $(\wedge, \rightarrow)$ and the quantifiers $(\exists, \forall)$.

We consider first-order vocabularies with constants but no other function symbol. A term t is a constant or a variable. Different constants represent different values (unique name assumption), an atomic formula (or atom) is of the form $p(t_1, \ldots, t_n)$ where p is an n-ary predicate, and $t_1, \ldots, t_n$ are terms. A *ground* atom is an atom with no variables. A variable in a formula is *free* if it is not in the scope of a quantifier. A formula is *closed* if it has not free variable. We denote by $\mathbf{X}$ (bold font) sequences of variables $X_1, \ldots, X_k$ with $k \geq 1$. A *conjunct* $C[\mathbf{X}]$ is a finite conjunction of atoms, where $\mathbf{X}$ is the sequence of variables occurring in C. Given an atom or a set of atoms A, $vars(A)$, $consts(A)$ and $terms(A)$ denote its set of variables, constants and terms, respectively.

An *existential rule* is a first-order formula of the form $R = \forall \mathbf{X} \forall \mathbf{Y} (H[\mathbf{X}, \mathbf{Y}]) \rightarrow \exists \mathbf{Z} C[\mathbf{Z}, \mathbf{Y}]$, with $vars(H) = \mathbf{X} \cup \mathbf{Y}$, and $vars(C) = \mathbf{Z} \cup \mathbf{Y}$ where H and C are *conjuncts* (hypothesis and conclusion of R), respectively. $R = (H, C)$ is a contracted form for R. An existential rule with an empty hypothesis is called a *fact*. A *fact* is an existentially closed (with no free variable) conjunct. A *rule* $r = (H, C)$ is *applicable* to a set of facts F iff there exists $F' \subseteq F$ such that there is a homomorphism π from H to the conjunction of elements of F'. If a rule r is applicable to a set F, its application according to π produces a set $F \cup \{\pi(C)\}$. The new set $F \cup \{\pi(C)\}$, denoted also by $r(F)$, is called *immediate derivation* of F by r. Finally, we say that a set of facts $F \subseteq \mathcal{F}$ and a set of rules $\mathcal{R}$ entail a fact f (and we write $F, \mathcal{R} \models f$) iff the closure of F by all the rules entails f (i.e. $\text{Cl}_{\mathcal{R}}(F) \models f$). A *negative constraint* is a first-order formula $n = \forall \mathbf{X} \, H[\mathbf{X}] \rightarrow \bot$ where $H[\mathbf{X}]$ is a conjunct called hypothesis of n and $\mathbf{X}$ sequence of variables appearing in the hypothesis. A *knowledge base* $\mathcal{K} = (\mathcal{F}, \mathcal{R}, \mathcal{N})$ is composed of, a finite set of facts $\mathcal{F}$, a finite set of existential rules $\mathcal{R}$ and a finite set of negative constraints $\mathcal{N}$. Given a knowledge base $\mathcal{K} = (\mathcal{F}, \mathcal{R}, \mathcal{N})$, a set $F \subseteq \mathcal{F}$ is said to be *inconsistent* iff there exists a constraint $n \in \mathcal{N}$ such that $F \models H_n$, where H_n is the hypothesis of the constraint n. A set of facts is consistent iff it is not inconsistent. A *conjunctive query* (CQ) has the form $Q(\mathbf{X}) = \exists \mathbf{Y} \Phi[\mathbf{X}, \mathbf{Y}]$ where $\Phi[\mathbf{X}, \mathbf{Y}]$ is a conjunct such that $\mathbf{X}$ and $\mathbf{Y}$ are variables in Φ. A *Boolean* CQ (BCQ) is a CQ with *yes* or *no* as answer.

Inconsistency Handling. If a knowledge base $\mathcal{K} = (\mathcal{F}, \mathcal{R}, \mathcal{N})$ is inconsistent, then everything is entailed from it. A common way to face inconsistency [7,26] is to construct maximal (with respect to set inclusion) consistent subsets of $\mathcal{F}$, called *repairs*, denoted by $\mathcal{R}epair(\mathcal{K})$. In this paper, we consider a fragment of our language where the deduction method (the chase) halts, thus the closure $\mathtt{Cl}_{\mathcal{R}}(F)$ of any set of facts F is *finite*. Once the repairs are computed, different semantics can be used for query answering over the knowledge base. Here we focus on *brave-semantics* [26] and *ICR-semantics* [7].

The brave-semantics accepts a query if it is entailed from at least one repair. This kind of semantics has been criticized because it allows conflicting answers. Let $\mathcal{K} = (\mathcal{F}, \mathcal{R}, \mathcal{N})$ be a knowledge base and let Q be a query. Q is brave-entailed from $\mathcal{K}$, written $\mathcal{K} \models_{brave} Q$ if and only if: $\exists \mathcal{A} \in \mathcal{R}epair(\mathcal{K})$ such that $\mathtt{Cl}_{\mathcal{R}}(\mathcal{A}) \models Q$. A prudent and more preservative semantics has been proposed in [7]. Let $\mathcal{K} = (\mathcal{F}, \mathcal{R}, \mathcal{N})$ be a knowledge base and let Q be a query. Q is ICR-entailed from $\mathcal{K}$, written $\mathcal{K} \models_{ICR} Q$ if: $\bigcap_{\mathcal{A} \in \mathcal{R}epair(\mathcal{K})} \mathtt{Cl}_{\mathcal{R}}(\mathcal{A}) \models Q$.

An alternative method for handling inconsistency is the use of **argumentation**. Given a knowledge base $\mathcal{K} = (\mathcal{F}, \mathcal{R}, \mathcal{N})$, the *corresponding argumentation framework* $\mathcal{AF}_{\mathcal{K}}$ is a pair $(\mathtt{Arg}, \mathtt{Att})$ where $\mathtt{Arg}$ is the set of arguments that can be constructed from $\mathcal{F}$ and $\mathtt{Att}$ is an asymmetric binary relation called *attack* defined over $\mathtt{Arg} \times \mathtt{Arg}$ (as defined in [13]). Given a knowledge base $\mathcal{K} = (\mathcal{F}, \mathcal{R}, \mathcal{N})$, an argument $\mathbf{a}$ is a tuple $\mathbf{a} = (F_0, F_1, \ldots, F_n, C)$ where: $(F_0, \ldots, F_n)$ is an $\mathcal{R}$-derivation of F_0 in $\mathcal{K}$, such that (i) F_0 is $\mathcal{R}$-consistent and (ii) C is an atom, a conjunction of atoms, the existential closure of an atom or the existential closure of a conjunction of atoms such that $F_n \models C$. F_0 is the support of the argument $\mathbf{a}$ ($\mathtt{Supp}(\mathbf{a})$) and C is its conclusion ($\mathtt{Conc}(\mathbf{a})$).

An argument $\mathbf{a}$ *supports* a query Q if $\mathtt{Conc}(\mathbf{a})$ entails Q and $\mathbf{a}$ is *against* Q if it attacks at least one argument that supports Q. An attack between two arguments $\mathbf{a}$ and $\mathbf{b}$ expresses the **conflict** between their conclusions and supports. Thus, $\mathbf{a}$ attacks $\mathbf{b}$ iff there exists $f \in \mathtt{Supp}(\mathbf{a})$ (f is a fact) such that the set $\{\mathtt{Conc}(\mathbf{b}), f\}$ is $\mathcal{R}$-inconsistent.

Let $\mathcal{K} = (\mathcal{F}, \mathcal{R}, \mathcal{N})$ be a knowledge base and $\mathcal{AF}_{\mathcal{K}}$ be its *corresponding argumentation framework*. Let $E \subseteq \mathtt{Arg}$ be a set of arguments. We say that E is *conflict free* iff there exist no arguments $a, b \in E$ such that $(a, b) \in \mathtt{Att}$. E *defends* an argument a iff for every argument $b \in \mathtt{Arg}$, if we have $(b, a) \in \mathtt{Att}$ then there exists $c \in E$ such that $(c, b) \in \mathtt{Att}$. E is *admissible* iff it is conflict free and defends all its arguments. E is a *preferred extension* iff it is maximal (with respect to set inclusion) admissible set (please see [20] for other types of semantics). We denote by $\mathtt{Ext}(\mathcal{AF}_{\mathcal{K}})$ the set of all extensions of $\mathcal{AF}_{\mathcal{K}}$. a is *sceptically accepted* if it is in all extensions, *credulously accepted* if it is in at least one extension and *not accepted* if not in any extension.

In [13] has been proved the equivalence between *skeptical acceptance under preferred semantics* and *ICR-entailment*. This allows us to use the argumentation approach in our explanation dialogue (Sect. 5) as to ensure its correctness and completeness w.r.t. ICR query explanation and failure.

Given a knowledge base $\mathcal{K}$ and a query Q, the general problem is to explain if Q is entailed by $\mathcal{K}$ or not. Let $\mathcal{K}$ be an inconsistent knowledge base, Q a Boolean conjunctive query. $\Pi = \langle \mathcal{K}, Q \rangle$ is a query result explanation problem (QREP) iff (i) $\mathcal{K}$ is inconsistent, and (ii) $\mathcal{K} \models_{brave} Q$. [3]. Using ICR semantics we distinguish:

1. The *Query Failure Explanation Problem* (QFEP). In the ICR setting, a QREP Π is defined to be a QFEP iff $\mathcal{K} \not\models_{ICR} Q$.
2. The *Query Acceptance Explanation Problem* (QAEP): In the ICR setting, a QREP Π is a QAEP iff $\mathcal{K} \models_{ICR} Q$.

The first one refers to the case when the query fails (*no* answer) due to contradictions; the second refers to the case when the query is accepted, so a *yes* answer is obtained.

4   QFEP for SameAs Invalidation

Let $\mathcal{K} = (\mathcal{F}, \mathcal{R}, \mathcal{N})$ be a knowledge base and $\mathcal{AF}_{\mathcal{K}}$ its *corresponding argumentation framework*. We define now the main components of $\mathcal{K}$ for a QFEP in case of a sameAs invalidation.

Defining the Facts, the Rules and the Negative Constraints. $\mathcal{F}$ is a set of facts including (*i*) RDF triples, coming from RDF graphs representing the knowledge described in (possibly) different inter-connected datasets, and (*ii*) facts asserting similarity values between specific literals. These second type of facts are in the form of

$$is[\text{prop}]Diff[\text{SimFunction}](x, y, \sigma)$$

where (*i*) [*prop*] is the name of a datatype (inverse-functional) functional property, (*ii*) [*SimFunction*] is a similarity measure (e.g. Jaccard, Levenshtein, ...), (*iii*) x, y are literals and (*iv*) σ is a similarity value between x and y. These facts are considered when σ is less than a given threshold ϵ, defined for the similarity measure [*SimFunction*] of a given property [*prop*].

There are several kind of logical rules that we consider. There are rules defined by the W3C standards: for instance, we exploit the OWL2 RL rules which define the $owl : sameAs$ predicate as being reflexive, symmetric, and transitive, and the rules that axiomatize the standard replacement properties. We also use rules declared or discovered using mining techniques on RDF triples. For these kind of rules, here, we consider two types of properties: functional and inverse-functional properties [1].

When a property p is a **datatype functional property**, it can be expressed via the following logical rule: $p(r, v) \wedge p(r, v') \rightarrow isEquiv(v, v')$, where $isEquiv$

expresses equivalence of two literals. If the property p is an **object functional property**, the following logical rule can be used: $p(r, v) \wedge p(r, v') \rightarrow sameAs(v, v')$. Instead, when p is an **inverse-functional property**, the logical rule is $p(w_1, x) \wedge p(w_2, x) \rightarrow sameAs(w_1, w_2)$.

We also add the set of rules which have all the following form:

$$is[\text{prop}]Diff[\text{SimFunction}](x, y, \sigma) \rightarrow isDiff(x, y)$$

A rule like this basically asserts that, when two literals x and y have a low similarity value σ for a specific property $[prop]$, they are declared as different (thus the fact $isDiff(x, y)$ is added to $\mathscr{F}$).

In our setting, the negative constraints are very simple. The only necessary negative constraints are in the following form: $isEquiv(x, y) \wedge isDiff(x, y) \rightarrow \bot$, where $isEquiv(x, y)$ are predicates coming from the rules defined for the datatype functional properties and $isDiff(x, y)$ comes from the similarity value between the literals. Note that all the other negative constraints, meaningful for discovering inconsistencies for a given $sameAs$, can be logically derived from the rules defined before. In case of a datatype functional property *title* the following leads to an inconsistency:

$$sameAs(s, o) \wedge title(s, w) \wedge title(o, w_1) \wedge isDiff(w, w_1) \rightarrow \bot$$

This can be derived from one rule and a negative constraint, namely:

1. $sameAs(s, o) \wedge title(s, w) \wedge title(o, w_1) \rightarrow isEquiv(w, w_1)$
2. $isEquiv(w, w_1) \wedge isDiff(w, w_1) \rightarrow \bot$

The problem $QFEP$. For completing the components and thus the instantiation of the QFEP, using ICR semantics, in the setting of sameAs invalidation, we need to define the query Q which is basically a $sameAs(x, y)$. The problem becomes:

Query Failure Explanation Problem ($QFEP_{sameAs}$). Given a knowledge base $\mathscr{K} = (\mathscr{F}, \mathscr{R}, \mathscr{N})$ with $\mathscr{F}$, $\mathscr{R}$, $\mathscr{N}$ defined above and the query Q as a $sameAs(x, y)$ statement. The $QFEP_{sameAs}$, in the ICR setting (which is equivalent to $\mathscr{AF}_{\mathscr{K}}$ as *argumentation framework*) is a QREP where $\mathscr{K} \not\models_{ICR} Q$.

At this point, we formally instantiated a QFEP as a *sameAs invalidation problem*. Given a sameAs statement (as query), by the use of facts, rules and negative constraints as described above, we are able to discover if the sameAs is not entailed with respect to the given knowledge base (in ICR semantics). This proves that a sameAs invalidation method can be seen as a instantiation of QFEP in ICR. By itself, this represents an interesting result when searching for effective methods for evaluating the quality of sameAs statements. But, we also need interactions with the domain experts to explain the problems encountered and to support the corrective actions. In the following, we define our explanation framework (and dialogues) which provides these interactive functionalities.

5   The Explanation Framework

It is clear that if a *sameAs* has problems, it makes sense to show to the experts what kind of actions and negative conditions lead to this answer. Here we introduce our explanation framework that is custom-tailored for the problem of *Query Failure Explanation Problem* under ICR-semantics in inconsistent knowledge bases.

Example 1 (Motivating Example). Let us consider the case of a QFEP $\Pi = \langle \mathcal{K}, Q \rangle$ with a query as $Q = worksIn(Linda, Statistics)$. The dialogue we would like is similar to the following:

Actor	Dialogue expression
User	Why not $worksIn(Linda, Statistics)$?
Reasoner	Because Linda works in Accounting.
User	Clarify?
Reasoner	Because Linda uses office o_1 and o_1 is located in Accounting, so Linda works in Accounting.
User	How's that a problem?
Reasoner	The following negative constraint is violated $$\forall x \forall y \forall z \; (worksIn(x, y) \land worksIn(x, z) \land y \neq z) \rightarrow \bot.$$
User	Understood.

This simple example (not explicitly related to SameAs) is only to clarify that, in our ideal explanation framework, each iteration need to respect certain rules and some predefined locutions must be used (like *understood, clarify, why,* etc.). In addition, all the information must be represented as *arguments* and/or *elaboration of arguments*. Finally, our dialogue will use a *turn taking mechanism* where the User and the Reasoner switch turn at each stage.

In the following, we formalize the dialogue system and a legal dialogue for our explanation framework and, for doing this, we define the necessary syntax and semantics. The formalization is based on a very preliminary work [3], where the idea of dialogue was firstly introduced. The novelty here is the full formalization of the dialogue with specific references and custom definitions to the problem at hand.

5.1   Syntax

Definition 1 (Dialogue System). *Given a QFEP $\Pi = \langle \mathcal{K}, Q \rangle$. A dialogue system for Π is a tuple $\mathscr{D} = (\Pi, \mathscr{P}r, \mathscr{U}, \mathbb{R})$, where Π is the **topic**, $\mathscr{P}r$ is the set of **participants**, $\mathscr{U}$ is a finite set of the allowed **utterances**, $\mathbb{R}$ is an irreflexive binary relation defined over $\mathscr{U}$ called the **reply** relation.*

The definition above is intentionally general, the reader should note that, in the case of this work, the **topic** of the dialogue is a discussion that aims to get the User understand the refusal of a query Q ($sameAs(x,y)$) in the $\mathscr{K} = (\mathscr{F}, \mathscr{R}, \mathscr{N})$ with $\mathscr{F}, \mathscr{R}, \mathscr{N}$ defined in the previous section. The **participants** $\mathscr{P}r = \{\text{Reasoner}, \text{User}\}$ are *(i)* the User, namely the domain expert who is analysing the quality of a set of sameAs, *(ii)* and the Reasoner, who represents an agent providing explanations in case of refusal.

The set of allowed **utterances** $\mathscr{U}$ and the **reply** relation $\mathbb{R}$ for our dialogue system $\mathscr{D}$ is given in Table 1. Note that a, a', t, t' and Q in the table represent metavariables of arbitrary well-formed syntactical objects (e.g. queries, arguments, integers, etc.) of an arbitrary formal language.

Table 1. The set of allowed utterances $\mathscr{U}$. In the table **U** is User and **R** is Reasoner.

Utterances	Description	Reply
EXPLAIN$(t,\mathbf{U},Q)$	User requests an explanation for a query Q	ATTEMPT$(t',\mathbf{R},a')$
ATTEMPT$(t,\mathbf{R},a)$	Reasoner provides an explanation a	CLARIFY $(t',\mathbf{U},a)$ or NEGATIVE $(t',\mathbf{U},a')$
CLARIFY$(t,\mathbf{U},a)$	User requests a clarification regarding the explanation a	CLARIFICATION$(t',\mathbf{R},a')$
CLARIFICATION$(t,\mathbf{R},a)$	Reasoner clarifies by advancing a	DEEPEN $(t',\mathbf{U},a)$ or NEGATIVE $(t',\mathbf{U},a)$
DEEPEN$(t,\mathbf{U},a)$	User requests a deepening regarding the explanation a	DEEPENING$(t',\mathbf{R},a')$
DEEPENING$(t,\mathbf{R},a)$	Reasoner deepens by advancing a	NEGATIVE $(t',\mathbf{U},a)$
POSITIVE$(t,\mathbf{U},Q)$	User acknowledges understanding of Q	no reply
NEGATIVE $(t,\mathbf{U},a)$	User disacknowledges understanding of Q and present the argument a that supports the query Q	ATTEMPT$(t',\mathbf{R},a')$

A dialogue D has a potential infinite sequence of legal utterances. An utterance is considered a **legal reply** for another utterance iff it is a correct reply with respect to the reply relation $\mathbb{R}$ and it is the turn of the participant x to talk. We provide here a simple explanatory example.

Example 2 (Legal/Illegal Reply). Consider the dialogue: ⟨EXPLAIN$(1, \text{User}, Q)$, ATTEMPT$(2, \text{Reasoner}, a)$, CLARIFY$(3, \text{User}, a)$, NEGATIVE$(4, \text{User}, a')$⟩ As one may notice, the reply NEGATIVE to CLARIFY is illegal because it is not in $\mathbb{R}$. A legal reply would be CLARIFICATION$(4, \text{Reasoner}, a')$.

At this point, it is necessary to define the protocol which will decide if a dialogue is legal or not. We introduce the following definition for a Legal Dialogue.

Definition 2 (Legal Dialogues). *Given a dialogue D_n at stage n, $n \geq 0$. The dialogue D_n is legal iff:*

Empty dialogue rule: *if $n = 0$ then D_0 is legal.*
Commencement rule: *if $n = 1$ then $D_1 = \langle u_1 \rangle$ is legal iff $u_1 =$ EXPLAIN$(1, \text{User}, Q)$.*
Dialogue rules: *if $n > 1$ then D_n is legal iff D_{n-1} is legal and u_n is a legal reply to u_{n-1} and there is no $u_i \in D_{n-1}$, $i < n$ and u_n equals u_i.*

Our definition indicates that an empty dialogue is legal. Furthermore, a legal dialogue always starts with an explanation request made by the User. Also, the protocol defines a legal dialogue as a sequence of utterances which legally replies to each other and no utterance is repeated twice.

5.2   Semantics

Now we shift to the semantic aspect of the dialogue where we deal with the content of the utterances. For instance, the utterance EXPLAIN$(2, \text{User}, Q)$ is legal (syntactically correct) but it will not be semantically legal if $\Pi = \langle \mathcal{K}, Q \rangle$ is not a query result explanation problem (or, in our more specific case a QFEP). The same applies to the utterance ATTEMPT$(2, \text{Reasoner}, a)$ if a is not an argument or a combination of arguments in our argumentation framework.

In Table 2 we put the conditions under which a given utterance or a reply is considered semantically legal in our setting. Here a *deepening* of an argument a explains the conflict between a and another argument b by showing the set of violated constraints. A *clarification*, instead, intends to unfold the knowledge (rules) used in the argument a to exhibit the line of reasoning that drives the conclusion.

Table 2. The utterances and their semantical conditions. $\mathcal{K}$ is an inconsistent knowledge base defined as in Sect. 4 and $\mathcal{AF}_{\mathcal{K}}$ is the corresponding argumentation framework.

Utterances	Conditions
EXPLAIN(t, User, Q)	$\Pi = \langle \mathcal{K}, Q \rangle$ is a QFEP
ATTEMPT$(t, \text{Reasoner}, a)$	a is an argument in $\mathcal{AF}_{\mathcal{K}}$
CLARIFY(t, User, a) or DEEPEN(t, User, a)	a is an argument in $\mathcal{AF}_{\mathcal{K}}$
CLARIFICATION$(t, \text{Reasoner}, a)$	a is a clarification of an arbitrary argument in $\mathcal{AF}_{\mathcal{K}}$
DEEPENING$(t, \text{Reasoner}, a)$	a is a deepening of an arbitrary argument in $\mathcal{AF}_{\mathcal{K}}$
POSITIVE(t, User, Q)	$\Pi = \langle \mathcal{K}, Q \rangle$ is the topic of the dialogue
NEGATIVE(t, User, a)	a is an argument in $\mathcal{AF}_{\mathcal{K}}$

The semantical legality must also be considered within a context where replies are taken into account. Table 3 indicates the conditions under which a reply is semantically legal. For instance, a reply by the utterance ATTEMPT$(2, \text{Reasoner}, a)$ to the utterance EXPLAIN$(1, \text{User}, Q)$ is legal but it will not be semantically legal if a is not a proponent (opponent) argument of the query Q.

Table 3. The replies and their semantical conditions. Here U is for User and R is for Reasoner.

Utterances	Replies	Conditions
EXPLAIN(t, U, Q)	ATTEMPT(t', R, a')	a' either supports or is against Q
ATTEMPT(t, R, a)	CLARIFY(t', U, a')	$a' = a$
ATTEMPT(t, R, a)	NEGATIVE(t', U, a')	a' supports or is against Q
CLARIFY(t, U, a)	CLARIFICATION(t', R, a')	if a' is a clarification of a
DEEPEN(t, U, a)	DEEPENING(t', R, a')	if a' is a deepening of a
CLARIFICATION(t, R, a)	DEEPEN(t', U, a')	$a' = a$
CLARIFICATION(t, R, a) or DEEPENING(t, R, a)	NEGATIVE(t', U, a')	a' is empty or a' supports or is against Q
POSITIVE(t, U, Q)	no reply	no condition
NEGATIVE(t, U, a)	ATTEMPT(t', R, a')	$a' \neq a$ and a' either supports or is against Q

The dialogue is defined as a finite set of semantically legal moves. An explanation dialogues is typed, depending on its topic. Here, the topic is a QFEP, thus our explanation dialogue D_n is called a *Query Failure Explanation Dialogue* QFED: the `Reasoner` will show, by presenting opponent arguments, why a query Q has failed.

6   First Results and Discussion

To verify our strategy, we have implemented a prototype of the explanation dialogue that communicates with a Datalog$_{+/-}$ rule-based reasoner called *Graal* [5]. For the knowledge base, we considered facts from the CORA dataset [28] and sameAs computed using the SILK framework [2]. We provide an example of sameAs invalidation explaining what has been obtained while running dialogues and we discuss over these results. Due to space limitations, here we present a single example and we provide only a meaningful portion of the set of facts, rules and negative constraints (only those related to the sameAs used in the query or in the dialogue).

Let us consider a query Q as $sameAs(r_1, r_2)$, where r_1, r_2 are URIs describing two resources in CORA. We show our explanation framework in the form of a QFED, where the `User` and the `Reasoner` interact in order to explain why Q is invalid. In Table 4 we report a subset of the knowledge base $\mathcal{K} = (\mathcal{F}, \mathcal{R}, \mathcal{N})$ we used. This subset provides sufficient details to discuss over the results.

Table 4. A portion of the facts $\mathcal{F}$, rules $\mathcal{R}$ and negative constraints $\mathcal{N}$ used to build our knowledge base $\mathcal{K} = (\mathcal{F}, \mathcal{R}, \mathcal{N})$.

Facts (portion of $\mathcal{F}$)
$sameAs(r_3, r_2)$, $sameAs(r_2, r_4)$, $sameAs(a_1, a_2)$, $sameAs(r_1, r_2)$
$confName(r_1, \text{'proceedings aaai-98'})$
$confName(r_3, \text{'in proceedings aaai-98'})$
$confName(r_2, \text{'in proceedings of aaai'})$
$confName(r_4, \text{'in proc. aaai'})$
$isconfNameDiffLevenshtein(\text{'proceedings aaai-98'}, \text{'in proceedings of aaai'}, 0.73)$
$isconfNameDiffLevenshtein(\text{'proceedings aaai-98'}, \text{'in proceedings aaai-98'}, 0.73)$
$isconfNameDiffLevenshtein(\text{'in proceedings aaai-98'}, \text{'in proc. aaai'}, 0.73)$
$isconfNameDiffLevenshtein(\text{'proceedings aaai-98'}, \text{'in proc. aaai'}, 0.41)$
$ispageFromDiffJaccard(30, 15, 0)$
$published(a_1, r_1)$, $published(a_2, r_3)$
$pageFrom(a_2, 15)$, $pageFrom(a_1, 30)$

Rules (portion of $\mathcal{R}$)
$sameAs(x, y) \wedge published(x, w_1) \wedge published(y, w_2) \rightarrow sameAs(w_1, w_2)$
$sameAs(x, y) \wedge pageFrom(x, w_1) \wedge pageFrom(y, w_2) \rightarrow isEquiv(w_1, w_2)$
$sameAs(x, y) \wedge confName(x, w_1) \wedge confName(x, w_1) \rightarrow isEquiv(w_1, w_2)$
$sameAs(x, y) \wedge sameAs(y, z) \rightarrow sameAs(x, z)$
$sameAs(y, x) \rightarrow sameAs(x, y)$
$isDiff(y, x) \rightarrow isDiff(x, y)$
$isconfNameDiffLevenshtein(x, y, \sigma) \rightarrow isDiff(x, y)$
$ispageFromDiffJaccard(x, y, \sigma) \rightarrow isDiff(x, y)$

Negative Constraints (portion of $\mathcal{N}$ and implicitly derivable)
$isEquiv(x, y) \wedge isDiff(x, y) \rightarrow \perp$
[derivable negative constraints]
$sameAs(x, y) \wedge pageFrom(x, w_1) \wedge pageFrom(x, w_1) \wedge isDiff(w_1, w_2) \rightarrow \perp$
$sameAs(x, y) \wedge confName(x, w_1) \wedge confName(x, w_1) \wedge isDiff(w_1, w_2) \rightarrow \perp$

To be more clear, the query $Q = sameAs(r_1, r_2)$ involves two resources which describe two 'conferences' with title $(confName)$ 'proceedings aaai-98' and 'in proceedings of aaai', respectively. The query Q is *not entailed*, according to the inconsistency-tolerant semantics $\mathscr{AF}_\mathscr{H}$: the two conferences are *not the same*. In Table 5 we show our explanation dialogue providing details on the reasons *why* Q is not entailed.

Table 5. A query failure explanation dialogue for a sameAs query involving the resources r_1 and r_2. For each dialogue we outline the formalism and the utterances involved.

1. User: Why r_1 and r_2 are not the same?   • *formalism:* $Q = sameAs(r_1, r_2)$?   • *explanation:* This is an **explanation request** made by the User (EXPLAIN).
2. Reasoner: Because r_1 is the same as r_4.   • *formalism:* $\langle\{sameAs(r_1,r_2), sameAs(r_2,r_4)\}, sameAs(r_1,r_4)\rangle$.   • *explanation:* Reasoner provides an **attempt** with an argument **against** Q (ATTEMPT).
3. User: clarify?   • *explanation:* The User asks for a **clarification**, meaning the *rule* relying the support and the conclusion of the argument before. (CLARIFY)
4. Reasoner: r_1 is the same of r_2, r_2 is the same of r_4 *and by transitivity* r_1 is the same of r_4   • *formalism:* $\langle\{sameAs(r_1,r_2), sameAs(r_2,r_4)\}, \{sameAs(x,y) \wedge sameAs(y,z) \rightarrow sameAs(x,z)\}, \{sameAs(r_1,r_4)\}\rangle$.   • *explanation:* The Reasoner provides the **clarification**. In this case, the rule of transitivity for *sameAs* (CLARIFICATION)
5. User: Why is this a problem?   • *explanation:* the User wants to know more about the logic behind the attack (DEEPEN)
6. Reasoner: $confName_{r_1}$ is **'proceedings aaai-98'** (a) and $confName_{r_4}$ is **'in proc. aaai'** (b). a, b have Levenshtein similarity of 0.41. It is **impossible** that r_1 and r_4 are the same thing and they have dissimilar conference names ($confName$ is *functional*).   • *formalism:*   - $sameAs(r_1,r_4), confName(r_4,b), confName(r_1,a)$ - $isconfNameDiffLevenshtein(a,b,0.41) \rightarrow isDiff(a,b)$ - $sameAs(x,y) \wedge confName(x,w_1) \wedge confName(x,w_1) \wedge isDiff(w_1,w_2) \rightarrow \perp$.   • *explanation:* The Reasoner provides the facts, the rules and the negative constraints that triggers the attack. (DEEPENING)
7. User: Understood.   • *explanation:* the User ends the dialogue (POSITIVE)

As mentioned in the formal specification of the dialogue in Sect. 5, utterances succession respects certain constraints: in step **1.** the User is the one who is allowed to make the opening *move* (EXPLAIN), not the Reasoner. At step **2.** the Reasoner responds providing an argument against the query (ATTEMPT) and the request for clarification (CLARIFY) at step **3.** made by the User is followed by a response made by the Reasoner (CLARIFICATION). Note that, after this clarification, the possible utterances can be: (i) a deepening request (DEEPEN), followed immediately by a deepening response (DEEPENING) or (ii) a NEGATIVE (understanding dis-acknowledgment) since, according to the semantical conditions we provided in Table 3, another deepening request is prohibited.

Another interesting property of our explanation dialogue is that it provides to the domain expert (User) the possibility to ask additional *follow-ups*. In the portion of dialogue described in Table 6, we report an extension of the previous dialogue (Table 5), where the User inputs additional arguments supporting her

Table 6. A new portion of the failure explanation dialogue for an invalid sameAs involving the resources r_1 and r_2. In this case, the user asks for further explanations by providing an argument against the reasoner conclusion.

7. User: *sameAs*(a_1,a_2), a_1 **is published in** r_1, a_2 **is published in** r_3, *sameAs*(r_3,r_2), **thus** r_1 **is the same as** r_2. *(published is functional.)*
• *formalism:*
- *sameAs*(a_1,a_2), *published*(a_1,r_1), *published*(a_2,r_3), *sameAs*(r_3,r_2)
- *sameAs*$(a_1,a_2) \land published(a_1,r_1) \land published(a_2,r_3) \to sameAs(r_1,r_3)$
- *sameAs*$(r_1,r_3) \land sameAs(r_3,r_2) \to sameAs(r_1,r_2)$.
• *explanation:* The User gives disacknowledges and presents an argument that supports her query Q (NEGATIVE).
8. Reasoner: But a_1 **has** *pageFrom* **value 30,** a_2 **has** *pagefrom* **value 15 and 30 and 15 are different**
• *formalism:*
- *sameAs*(a_1,a_2), *pageFrom*$(a_1,30)$, *pageFrom*$(a_2,15)$
- *ispageFromDiffJaccard*$(30,15,0) \to isDiff(30,15)$
- *sameAs*$(x,y) \land pageFrom(x,w_1) \land pageFrom(x,w_1) \land isDiff(w_1,w_2) \to \bot$.
• *explanation:* Reasoner provides an **attempt** with an argument **against** the previous argument (ATTEMPT).
9. User: Understood.
• *explanation:* the User ends the dialogue (POSITIVE)

query Q and thus she asks for further explanations. We continue from step 7 of Table 5 and, instead of declaring 'understood' (POSITIVE), we disacknowledge the dialogue by providing a feedback in form of an argument.

Finally, to better illustrate the explanation dialogue, we present here the sequence of utterances, in terms of the formal model we formalized before. The dialogue D_i ($i = 7$) depicted in Table 5 is the following, where a is an argument and C_a, D_a are clarification and deepening of a, respectively.

$\langle$EXPLAIN$(1, \textbf{User}, Q)$, ATTEMPT$(2, \textbf{Reasoner}, a)$, CLARIFY$(3, \textbf{User}, a)$,
CLARIFICATION$(4, \textbf{User}, C_a)$, DEEPEN$(5, \textbf{User}, a)$, DEEPENING$(6, \textbf{User}, D_a)$,
POSITIVE$(7, \textbf{User}, Q)\rangle$

The second dialogue (Table 6) is composed by 9 steps. Its formal representation as sequence of utterances is:

$\langle$EXPLAIN$(1, \textbf{User}, Q)$, ATTEMPT$(2, \textbf{Reasoner}, a)$, CLARIFY$(3, \textbf{User}, a)$,
CLARIFICATION$(4, \textbf{User}, C_a)$, DEEPEN$(5, \textbf{User}, a)$, DEEPENING$(6, \textbf{User}, D_a)$,
NEGATIVE$(7, \textbf{User}, a')$, ATTEMPT$(8, \textbf{Reasoner}, a'')$, POSITIVE$(9, \textbf{User}, Q)\rangle$

It is worthy to make a consideration on the semantics of the utterance NEGATIVE, which has two goals. First, it declares that the **User** has not understood the last explanation; second, it provides to the **Reasoner** a feedback. This feedback is in form of an argument a'. Thus, if the **User** has an expectation about a query and her expectation is endorsed by an argument then, she can present this argument in this utterance. Henceforth, NEGATIVE$(7, \textbf{User}, a')$ can be read as "*I do not understand why Q is not entailed **given that** the argument a' supports it*". When a' is empty, the user has no argument to propose.

6.1   Discussion

Our tests on the prototype have shown that, running dialogues on various sameAs statements (computed externally and considered potentially problematic[1]) was a support for different corrective actions. In some cases, errors in the data have been found (e.g. resource 100001135 has *confYear* property value 0, while its correct sameAs resources are conferences of the year 1995, or resource 100000021 has *pageFrom* to 24.1 which is again an error since it should be 24). Thanks to the dialogues with the reasoner, the expert has easily located these problems. In some other tests, the explanation dialogue supported the expert to understand that an update of some similarity functions used in specific properties was necessary (e.g. Levensthein instead of Jaccard for *confName*), or that the threshold ϵ to determine "dissimilar literals" had to be lowered for some properties (e.g. *title*). Finally, at the very first running, we used a set of sameAs links computed loosely (full of erroneous links). Thanks to the explanation dialogue it was clear that every sameAs query had strong inconsistencies over fundamental properties and values, thus this supported the idea to redo the linking process with a different strategy (in our case using composite keys in the linkage phase).

An important question may occur at this point, *"what happens if the* Reasoner *has multiple explanations (several potential arguments against/for the query)?"*.

In this case, we adapt a selection strategy: we choose each time which argument must be presented. In this work we aim at providing a general account for such process, thus we use the concept of a *selection function* $\mathbb{S}$ over a set of arguments. Note that $\mathbb{S}$ can be instantiated to express preferences with respect to some criteria that can possibly be defined by the expert User, such as "the property *confName* is very important (high weight $w_{confName}$)" or "the property *year* may contain errors, thus it has lower importance (low weight w_{year})". To order the sameAs presented to the expert, we used *Graal* to compute all the conflicts in the knowledge base. Then, we highlighted those sameAs statements that were more involved in conflicts (and sub-sequentially more present in attacks in the corresponding argumentation framework). These sameAs have been compared with the gold standard of the CORA dataset, and they have been used to define the order by which the dialogue should propose the sameAs links to the User. The sameAs links with most attacks, thus the most debatable ones, were showed first. The procedure we used to compute the conflicts is expensive from a computational point of view[2]. Such approach can be further improved in future work, by suitably adapting the conflict computation in order to obtain an incremental any-time algorithm with better computational properties.

7   Concluding Remarks

In this paper we presented an *explanation dialogue* based on argumentation theory where a domain expert can interact with the reasoner regarding a problematic sameAs statement.

---

[1] Experiment, at this moment, with one domain expert.

[2] Exponential in the size of the facts in the knowledge base.

The paper demonstrates the significance of the explanation framework by the use of a real world example. All the dialogue moves are detailed, so that the reader can comprehend the types of interactions allowed. To the extent of our knowledge, the work presented in this paper, is the first attempt to use argumentation for sameAs links invalidation and for providing an explanation framework.

The results we obtained with the first prototype are very promising, motivating us in the continuation of the research activity. In these days, we are working on conducting tests using different (in size and quality) synthetic datasets (e.g. OAEI) and, in the immediate future, we are planning to analyze and evaluate sameAs coming directly from the LOD. In parallel, we are studying suitable improvements and strategies in order to ensure scalability of the approach when dealing with big datasets.

Different interesting long-term research directions can be exploited. For example, it could be interesting to study how to design innovative methods for modeling and combining *contextual weights* associated to each property used in the QFEP. Such weights could depend on different factors such as the *reliability* (automatically acquired or computed) of each property in the initial dataset. In addition, these weights could include suggestions (or restrictions) provided directly from the expert/user (something like '*I trust this data, please consider it true over all the other computations*'), and so on.

Another interesting future research direction could be also to study suitable user interfaces (by the use of innovative interactive systems) in the explanation of the inconsistencies and the properties involved, such that the type of interactions as the way in which the arguments are presented could be more 'user-friendly' and supported by graphical representations.

Acknowledgments. The authors acknowledge the support of ANR grants ASPIQ (ANR-12- BS02-0003), QUALINCA (ANR-12-0012) and DURDUR (ANR-13-ALID-0002). The work of the second author has been carried out in a part of the research delegation at INRA MISTEA Montpellier and INRA IATE CEPIA Axe 5 Montpellier.

References

1. OWL 2 Web Ontology Language: Primer. www.w3.org/TR/owl2-primer
2. Silk - The Linked Data Integration Framework. http://silk-framework.com/
3. Arioua, A., Tamani, N., Croitoru, M., Buche, P.: Query failure explanation in inconsistent knowledge bases: a dialogical approach. In: Bramer, M., Petridis, M. (eds.) Research and Development in Intelligent Systems XXXI. Springer, Heidelberg (2014)
4. Baader, F., Brandt, S., Lutz, C.: Pushing the EL envelope. In: Proceedings of IJCAI 2005 (2005)
5. Baget, J.-F., Leclère, M., Mugnier, M.-L., Rocher, S., Sipieter, C.: Graal: a toolkit for query answering with existential rules. In: Bassiliades, N., Gottlob, G., Sadri, F., Paschke, A., Roman, D. (eds.) RuleML 2015. LNCS, vol. 9202, pp. 328–344. Springer, Heidelberg (2015)

6. Baget, J.-F., Mugnier, M.-L., Rudolph, S., Thomazo, M.: Walking the complexity lines for generalized guarded existential rules. In: Proceedings of IJCAI 2011 (2011)
7. Bienvenu, M.: On the complexity of consistent query answering in the presence of simple ontologies. In: Proceedings of AAAI (2012)
8. Bienvenu, M., Rosati, R.: Tractable approximations of consistent query answering for robust ontology-based data access. In: Proceedings of IJCAI 2013. AAAI Press (2013)
9. Bizer, C., Heath, T., Berners-Lee, T.: Linked data - the story so far. Int. J. Semant. Web Inf. Syst. **5**(3) (2009)
10. Cabrio, E., Cojan, J., Villata, S., Gandon, F.: Argumentation-based inconsistencies detection for question-answering over dbpedia. In: Proceedings of the NLP&DBpedia Workshop (2013)
11. Calì, A., Gottlob, G., Lukasiewicz, T.: A general datalog-based framework for tractable query answering over ontologies. Web Semant. Sci. Serv. Agents World Wide Web **14**, 57–83 (2012)
12. Calvanese, D., De Giacomo, G., Lembo, D., Lenzerini, M., Rosati, R.: Tractable reasoning and efficient query answering in description logics: the DL-Lite family. J. Autom. Reasoning **39**(3), 385–429 (2007)
13. Croitoru, M., Vesic, S.: What can argumentation do for inconsistent ontology query answering? In: Liu, W., Subrahmanian, V.S., Wijsen, J. (eds.) SUM 2013. LNCS, vol. 8078, pp. 15–29. Springer, Heidelberg (2013)
14. Cuzzola, J., Bagheri, E., Jovanovic, J.: Filtering inaccurate entity co-references on the linked open data. In: Chen, Q., Hameurlain, A., Toumani, F., Wagner, R., Decker, H. (eds.) DEXA 2015. LNCS, vol. 9261, pp. 128–143. Springer, Heidelberg (2015)
15. de Melo, G.: Not quite the same: Identity constraints for the web of linked data. In: Proceedings of the Conference on Artificial Intelligence. AAAI Press (2013)
16. Ding, L., Shinavier, J., Finin, T., McGuinness, D.: owl: sameAs and linked data: an empirical study. In: International Web Science Conference (2010)
17. Ding, L., Shinavier, J., Shangguan, Z., McGuinness, D.L.: SameAs networks and beyond: analyzing deployment status and implications of owl:sameAs in linked data. In: Patel-Schneider, P.F., Pan, Y., Hitzler, P., Mika, P., Zhang, L., Pan, J.Z., Horrocks, I., Glimm, B. (eds.) ISWC 2010, Part I. LNCS, vol. 6496, pp. 145–160. Springer, Heidelberg (2010)
18. Doran, P., Tamma, V., Palmisano, I., Payne, T.: Efficient argumentation over ontology correspondences. In: International Conference on AAMAS (2009)
19. dos Santos, C., Euzenat, J.: Consistency-driven argumentation for alignment agreement. In: International Workshop on Ontology Matching (OM-2010) (2010)
20. Dung, P.M.: On the acceptability of arguments and its fundamental role in non-monotonic reasoning, logic programming and n-person games. AI **77**(2), 321–357 (1995)
21. Ferrara, A., Nikolov, A., Scharffe, F.: Data linking. J. Web Semant. **23** (2013)
22. Guéret, C., Groth, P., Stadler, C., Lehmann, J.: Assessing linked data mappings using network measures. In: Simperl, E., Cimiano, P., Polleres, A., Corcho, O., Presutti, V. (eds.) ESWC 2012. LNCS, vol. 7295, pp. 87–102. Springer, Heidelberg (2012)
23. Halpin, H., Hayes, P., Thompson, H.: When owl: sameAs isn't the same: a preliminary theory of identity and inference on the semantic web. In: International Workshop LHD (2011)
24. Heath, T., Bizer, C.: Linked Data: Evolving the Web into a Global Data Space, 1st edn. Morgan & Claypool, Palo Alto (2011)

25. Laera, L., Blacoe, I., Tamma, V., Payne, T., Euzenat, J., Bench-Capon, T.: Argumentation over ontology correspondences in MAS. In: International Conference on AAMAS (2007)
26. Lembo, D., Lenzerini, M., Rosati, R., Ruzzi, M., Savo, D.: Inconsistency-tolerant semantics for description logics. In: Proceedings of International Conference on Web Reasoning Rule Systems (2010)
27. Lukasiewicz, T., Martinez, M.V., Simari, G.I.: Complexity of inconsistency-tolerant query answering in datalog+/−. In: Meersman, R., Panetto, H., Dillon, T., Eder, J., Bellahsene, Z., Ritter, N., De Leenheer, P., Dou, D. (eds.) ODBASE 2013. LNCS, vol. 8185, pp. 488–500. Springer, Heidelberg (2013)
28. McCallum, A. (ed.): Cora Research Paper Dataset. http://people.cs.umass.edu/~mccallum/data.html
29. Papaleo, L., Pernelle, N., Saïs, F., Dumont, C.: Logical detection of invalid SameAs statements in RDF data. In: Janowicz, K., Schlobach, S., Lambrix, P., Hyvönen, E. (eds.) EKAW 2014. LNCS, vol. 8876, pp. 373–384. Springer, Heidelberg (2014)

Reasoning with Multiple-Agent Possibilistic Logic

Asma Belhadi[1], Didier Dubois[2], Faiza Khellaf-Haned[1], and Henri Prade[2(✉)]

[1] RIIMA, Université des Sciences et de la Technologie Houari Boumediene,
BP 32, El Alia, 16111 Bab Ezzouar, Algeria
{abelhadi,fkhellaf}@usthb.dz
[2] IRIT Université Paul Sabatier,
118 route de Narbonne, 31062 Toulouse Cedex 09, France
{dubois,prade}@irit.fr

Abstract. In multiple-agent logic, a formula is in the form of (a, A) where a is a propositional formula and A is a subset of agents. It states that at least all agents in A believe that a is true. This paper presents a method of refutation for this logic, based on a general resolution principle and using a linear strategy, which is sound and complete. This strategy is then extended so as to deal with certainty levels. It manipulates formulas in the form $(a, \alpha/A)$ expressing that all agents in set A believe at least at some level α that a is true. Finally, an experimental study is provided with the aim to estimate the performance of the proposed algorithms.

Keywords: Possibilistic logic · Multiple-agent logic · Multiple-agent possibilistic logic · Possibility theory · Refutation · Uncertainty

1 Introduction

A piece of information can be generally associated with a source or an agent. In multiple-agent logic, a logical formula is associated with a *group* of agents that hold it for true. Then one can reason both on the information contents of a multiple-agent logic base and on the attitudes of groups of agents with respect to different sets of beliefs, and consider queries of the type "who believes what?".

A multiple-agent logic was initially proposed in [10,11] and developed in [1]. In this logic, formulas are pairs of the form of (a, A), made of a proposition a and a subset of agents A. The formula (a, A) is intended to mean "at least all agents in A believe that a is true". The semantics of the set of multiple-agent logic formulas is expressed by a mapping which associates a subset of agents with each interpretation. In the graded extension of multiple-agent logic, propositions are associated with both a set of agents and a certainty level. A formula $(a, \alpha/A)$ expresses that "at least all agents in set A believe at least at some level α (in the sense of a necessity measure) that a is true". The semantics is given in terms of fuzzy sets of agents. When all the logical formulas are associated with the same set of agents (e.g., a singleton), one retrieves possibilistic logic [9]. The

© Springer International Publishing Switzerland 2016
S. Schockaert and P. Senellart (Eds.): SUM 2016, LNAI 9858, pp. 67–80, 2016.
DOI: 10.1007/978-3-319-45856-4_5

paper investigates the reasoning mechanism of the proposed logic based on the refutation method using a linear strategy. Namely, we propose an extension of the classical refutation method adapting the search algorithm A*.

The paper is organized in the following way. The next section provides a refresher on multiple-agent logic and its possibilistic extension. It also establishes soundness and completeness of the multiple-agent possibilistic logic. Section 3 presents the refutation method, based on a generalized resolution principle using a linear strategy, and then its generalization to multiple-agent possibilistic logic. Section 4 discusses the experimental study pertaining to the refutation method applied to both investigated logics. The concluding section briefly mentions potential applications. Preliminary versions of Sect. 3 appeared in French [3,4], while Sect. 4 is brand new.

2   Multiple-Agent Logic and Its Possibilistic Extension

We present a background on multiple-agent logic by describing its syntax and its semantics in terms of generalized possibility distributions and then the syntax and the semantics of its extension with graded certainty levels.

2.1   A Multiple-Agent Logic

Let $\mathcal{L}$ denote a propositional logical language. The set of all agents is denoted by All. A subset of agents is denoted by capital letters A, B, or by indexed letters A_i. The set of subsets of agents is equipped with the usual set operations, i.e., $(2^{All}, \cap, \cup, \overline{}, \subseteq)$ is a Boolean algebra. Thus, only a partial order exists between subsets of agents.

Syntax. A multiple agent propositional formula is a pair (a, A), where a is a classical propositional formula of $\mathcal{L}$ and A is a non empty subset of All, i.e., $A \subseteq All$. (a, A) represents the piece of information: at least all agents in A believe that a is true. The subset A may be given in extension or in intension.

A multiple-agent knowledge base is a finite set $\Gamma = \{(a_i, A_i), i = 1, \ldots, n\}$, viewed as the conjunction of multiple agent propositional formulas. Multiple agent logic has two inference rules:

- if $B \subseteq A$ then $(a, A) \vdash (a, B)$ (subset weakening)
- $(\neg a \vee b, A), (a, A) \vdash (b, A), \forall A \in 2^{All} \setminus \emptyset$ (subset modus ponens)

The axioms of multiple-agent logic [1] are those of propositional logic where each axiom schema is associated with subset All.

Using subset weakening, the following inference rule is valid:

$$(\neg a \vee b, A), (a \vee c, B) \vdash (b \vee c, A \cap B) \text{ (A-B-resolution)}$$

The subset of inconsistent agents for Γ can be defined as:

$$inc\text{-}s(\Gamma) = \bigcup \{A \subseteq All \mid \Gamma \vdash (\bot, A)\} \text{ and } inc\text{-}s(\Gamma) = \emptyset \text{ if } \nexists A \text{ s.t. } \Gamma \vdash (\bot, A).$$

Let Γ° denote the set of classical formulas obtained from Γ by ignoring the sets of agents: $\Gamma^\circ = \{a_i \mid (a_i, A_i) \in \Gamma, i = 1, \ldots, n\}$. The consistency of Γ does not necessarily imply that Γ° is consistent too. Indeed, if we take for example $\Gamma = \{(a, A), (\neg a, \overline{A})\}$, then $inc\text{-}s(\Gamma) = A \cap \overline{A} = \emptyset$ whereas Γ° is inconsistent. This is because there is nothing anomalous with agents that contradict each other.

Semantics. A multiple-agent possibility distribution is a function π from a set of interpretations Ω to 2^{All}. $\pi(\omega)$ represents the subset of agents in *All* who find ω possible. A multiple-agent possibility distribution is said *multiple-agent-normalized* if $\exists \omega \in \Omega, \pi(\omega) = All$. This means that there is at least one interpretation that all agents find possible.

From π, a function from $\mathcal{L}$ to 2^{All} called multiple-agent possibility measure is defined:

$$\mathbf{\Pi}(a) = \bigcup_{\omega \in \Omega} \{\pi(\omega), \omega \models a\}$$

It is the set of agents for whom a is possibly true.

By duality, a multiple-agent necessity measure $\mathbf{N}$, from $\mathcal{L}$ to 2^{All} is defined:

$$\mathbf{N}(a) = \overline{\mathbf{\Pi}(\neg a)} = \bigcap_{\omega \in \Omega} \{\overline{\pi(\omega)}, \omega \models \neg a\}$$

$\mathbf{N}(a)$ represents the subset of agents who are sure that a is true (it is the complement of the subset of agents who find $\neg a$ possible).

Since the multiple agent propositional formula (a, A) represents the piece of information "at least all agents in A believe a", the agents in A find all interpretations of $\neg a$ impossible. This means that the maximal set of agents who think that $\neg a$ is possible is $\overline{A}$. Besides, the agents in $\overline{A}$ remain free to find the interpretations of a possible or not. Thus the maximal set of agents who may think that the interpretations that make a true are possible is *All* itself. This leads to the following semantical representation of formula (a, A) by the multiple-agent possibility distribution $\pi_{\{(a,A)\}}$:

$$\forall \omega \in \Omega, \pi_{\{(a,A)\}}(\omega) = \begin{cases} All & \text{if } \omega \models a \\ \overline{A} & \text{if } \omega \models \neg a \end{cases}$$

where Ω is the set of interpretations associated with $\mathcal{L}$.

More generally, the multiple-agent possibility distribution π_Γ semantically associated with a set of multiple agent formulas $\Gamma = \{(a_i, A_i), i = 1, \ldots, n\}$ is given by:

$$\pi_\Gamma(\omega) = \begin{cases} All & \text{if } \forall (a_i, A_i) \in \Gamma, \omega \models a_i \\ \bigcap \{\overline{A_i} : (a_i, A_i) \in \Gamma, \omega \models \neg a_i\} & \text{otherwise} \end{cases}$$

Thus, the "value" $\pi_\Gamma(\omega)$ of the multiple agent possibility distribution for ω is obtained as the intersection of the different subsets $\overline{A_i}$ of agents that still find ω possible according to the different formulas (a_i, A_i) violated by this interpretation.

2.2   A Multiple-Agent Possibilistic Logic

A natural generalization of multiple-agent logic stems from extending multiple-agent possibility distributions from 2^{All} to $[0,1]^{All}$.

Syntax. In the following, the distributive lattice $L = [0,1]^{All}$ is considered. This lattice is equipped with fuzzy set intersection $\cap$, fuzzy set union $\cup$ and fuzzy set complementation $\overline{}$ defined by means of operators: min, max, and $1 - (.)$ respectively. Then, the order becomes a fuzzy set inclusion defined by the inequality between membership functions.

A multiple-agent possibilistic formula (a, F) is built by attaching to a classical propositional formula a a nonempty fuzzy set of agents F belonging to All. The membership grade $\mu_F(k)$ is understood as a lower bound on the degree of certainty (in the sense of a necessity measure) of a for agent k. In the following, the fuzzy set $F = \alpha/A$ is defined by: $\mu_{\alpha/A}(k) = \alpha$ if $k \in A$, and $\mu_{\alpha/A}(k) = 0$ if $k \in \overline{A}$. Given that any fuzzy set F of agents can be written as a disjunction $\bigcup_{i=1}^{\ell} \alpha_i/A_i$ where A_i is the α_i-cut of F, the formula (a, F) can be assumed to encode the set of formulas $\{(a, \alpha_i/A_i) \mid i = 1, \cdots, \ell\}$.

Henceforth, the language is limited to formulas of the form (α/A) that expresses the information that at least all agents in A believe at least at level α that a is true. Indeed, the possibilistic multiple agent formula $(a, \alpha/A)$ is the syntactic expression of the semantic constraint $N(a) \supseteq \alpha/A$ where N is a graded multiple-agent necessity measure, defined later on. Formulas of the form $(a, 0/A)$ or $(a, \alpha/\emptyset)$ are trivial since they do not provide any information, and thus they do not belong to the syntax (as $\forall a$, $N(a) \supseteq 0/A$ with $A \neq \emptyset$, and $N(a) \supseteq \alpha/\emptyset$). A multiple-agent possibilistic knowledge base may be viewed as the conjunction of multiple-agent possibilistic formulas.

Let $\Sigma = \{(a_1, \alpha_1/A_1), ..., (a_n, \alpha_n/A_n)\}$ be a multiple-agent possibilistic knowledge base. It can be viewed as a stratified set of multiple-agent knowledge bases:

$$\Sigma_\alpha = \{(a_i, A_i) | (a_i, \alpha_i/A_i) \in \Sigma \text{ and } \alpha_i \geq \alpha\}$$

In the same way, a possibilistic knowledge base Σ_A can be defined for every non empty set $A \subseteq All$ of agents:

$$\Sigma_A = \{(a_i, \alpha_i) | (a_i, \alpha_i/A_i) \in \Sigma \text{ and } A_i \supseteq A\}$$

and if the A_i's are given in extension, the projection of Σ on each agent k of All is defined by:

$$\Sigma_k = \{(a_i, \alpha_i) | (a_i, \alpha_i/A_i) \in \Sigma \text{ and } k \in A_i\}$$

Furthermore, if subsets of agents in Σ are ignored, the possibilistic knowledge base $\Sigma^{All} = \{(a_i, \alpha_i), i = 1, ..., n\}$ is obtained. This possibilistic knowledge base represents beliefs of agents in All. Symmetrically, $\Sigma^{(0,1]} = \{(a_i, A_i), i = 1, ..., n\}$ is the multiple agent knowledge base where groups of agents are somewhat certain of propositions in Σ (since for all i such that $(a_i, \alpha_i/A_i) \in \Sigma$, $\alpha_i > 0$). Finally by ignoring fuzzy sets of agents associated with formulas of Σ, a propositional knowledge base Σ° is obtained: $\Sigma^\circ = \{a_i, i = 1, ..., n\}$. It expresses the set of all beliefs a_i possessed by some groups of agents in All at some degree.

Fuzzy sets of agents are only partially ordered. Thus, a restriction of Σ by a fuzzy subset of agents α/A can be defined as:

$$\Sigma^{\alpha/A} = \{(a_i, \alpha_i/A_i)|A_i \cap A \neq \emptyset \text{ and } \alpha_i \geq \alpha \text{ and } (a_i, \alpha_i/A_i) \in \Sigma\}$$

$\Sigma^{\alpha/A}$ contain all formulas believed at least at level α by some agents in A.

Multiple agent possibilistic logic has the following inference rules:

- If $A \cap B \neq \emptyset$ then $(c, \alpha/A), (c', \beta/B) \vdash (c'', \min(\alpha, \beta)/(A \cap B))$ (gradual subset resolution), where c'' is the resolvent of c, c'.
- If $\beta/B \subseteq \alpha/A$ then $(c, \alpha/A) \vdash (c, \beta/B)$ (gradual subset weakening),
- $(c, \alpha/A), (c, \beta/B) \vdash (c, \alpha/A \cup \beta/B)$ (fusion).

Moreover, the axioms of multiple-agent possibilistic logic are those of propositional logic weighted by $(1/All)$.

The fuzzy subset of individually inconsistent agents of Σ is defined by:

$$inc\text{-}\Sigma = \bigcup\{\alpha/A|\Sigma \vdash (\bot, \alpha/A)\}$$

It should be noted that the consistency of the multiple-agent possibilistic knowledge base Σ does not entail necessarily the consistency of its classical projection Σ°. Again, agents may contradict each other.

Semantics. A graded multiple-agent possibility distribution is a function π from a set of interpretations Ω to $[0, 1]^{All}$, the set of all fuzzy subsets of agents. The fuzzy subset $\pi(\omega)$ collects agents k in All who find ω possible at degree $\mu_{\pi(\omega)}(k)$. In the following, (α/A) will be the fuzzy subset of agents $k \in All$ such that $\mu_{\alpha/A}(k) = \alpha$ if $k \in A$ and 0 otherwise. By convention, $\pi(\omega) = 1/All$ means that all agents find ω completely possible, while $\pi(\omega) = 0/All$ means that all agents find ω impossible. If $\exists \omega$ such that $\pi(\omega) = 1/All$ then the graded multiple-agent possibility distribution π is again said to be multiple-agent normalized. This property reflects collective consistency since there exists at least one interpretation that all agents find completely possible. Associated with the graded multiple-agent possibility distribution π, a function, from $\mathcal{L}$ to $[0, 1]^{All}$ called graded multiple-agent possibility measure is defined:

$$\Pi(a) = \bigcup_{\omega \models a} \pi(\omega)$$

$\Pi(a)$ is the fuzzy set of agents who think that it is possible to some extent that a is true.

In a dual manner, $N(a)$ is the fuzzy set of agents who are certain to some extent that a is true. It defines the graded multiple-agent necessity measure N:

$$N(a) = \overline{\Pi}(\neg a) = \bigcap_{\omega \models \neg a} \overline{\pi(\omega)}$$

In multiple-agent possibilistic logic, the satisfiability of a formula is defined in terms of graded multiple-agent possibility distributions. The formula $(a, \alpha/A)$

expresses the piece of information: "at least all agents in A believe at least at level α that a is true". So agents in A find any interpretation of a completely possible. Furthermore, other agents in $\overline{A}$ are free to find the interpretation of a completely possible or not. So, the maximal set of agents who find any interpretation of a completely possible is again $A \cup \overline{A} = All$. Besides, the maximal set of agents who find all interpretations of $\neg a$ possible at least at level $1 - \alpha$ are agents in A, and agents in $\overline{A}$ find $\neg a$ possible at least at level 1. So, the semantics representation of the formula $(a, \alpha/A)$ is as follows:

$$\pi_{\{(a,\alpha/A)\}}(\omega) = \begin{cases} 1/All & if \ \omega \models a \\ \{(1 - \alpha)/A \cup 1/\overline{A}\} & if \ \omega \models \neg a \end{cases}$$

More generally, the graded multiple-agent possibility distribution π semantically associated with the set $\Sigma = \{(a_1, \alpha_1/A_1, ..., a_n, \alpha_n/A_n)\}$ of multiple agents possibilistic formulas is defined by:

$$\pi_\Sigma(\omega) = \begin{cases} 1/All \ \text{if} \ \forall (a_i,\alpha_i/A_i) \in \Sigma, \omega \models a_i \\ \bigcap_{(a_i,\alpha_i/A_i) \in \Sigma, \omega \models \neg a_i} (1 - \alpha_i)/A_i \cup 1/\overline{A_i} \ \text{otherwise.} \end{cases}$$

Since $N(a \wedge b) = N(a) \cap N(b)$, $\{(a \wedge b, \alpha/A)\}$ is equivalent to $\{(a, \alpha/A), (b, \alpha/A)\}$, and a possibilistic multiple-agent formula can always be put under a clausal form. The knowledge base Σ can be interpreted as a set of constraints of the form:

$$N_\Sigma(a_i) \supseteq \alpha_i/A_i \ \text{for} \ i = 1, ..., n.$$

For any graded multiple-agent possibility distribution π, π satisfies Σ (denoted by $\pi \models \Sigma$) if and only if $\pi \subseteq \pi_\Sigma$ (namely $\forall \omega, \pi(\omega) \subseteq \pi_\Sigma(\omega)$). Thus, $(b, \beta/B)$ is a logical consequence of Σ if and only if $\pi_\Sigma(\omega)$ is included into $\pi_{\{(b,\beta/B)\}}(\omega)$. Formally:

$$\Sigma \models (b, \beta/B) \Leftrightarrow \forall \omega, \pi_\Sigma(\omega) \subseteq \pi_{\{(b,\beta/B)\}}(\omega).$$

2.3   Soundness/Completeness of Multiple-Agent Possibilistic Logic

In [8], soundness and completeness of possibilistic logic have been established in the following way:

$$\Sigma = \{(a_i, \alpha_i)|i = 1, ..., n\} \vdash (a, \alpha) \Leftrightarrow \Sigma \models (a, \alpha) \Leftrightarrow \forall \omega, \pi_\Sigma(\omega) \leq \pi_{(a,\alpha)}(\omega).$$

In a similar manner, authors in [1], have proved the soundness and completeness of multiple-agent logic as follows:

$$\Sigma = \{(a_i, A_i)|i = 1, ..., n\} \vdash (a, A) \Leftrightarrow \Sigma \models (a, A) \Leftrightarrow \forall \omega, \pi_\Sigma(\omega) \subseteq \pi_{(a,A)}(\omega)$$

The multiple-agent possibilistic logic is also sound and complete. Indeed, using previous results and with notations Σ_k and $\Sigma^{\alpha/A}$ introduced in Sect. 2, we have:

$\Sigma \vdash (a, \alpha/A) \Leftrightarrow \forall k \in A, \Sigma_k \vdash (a, \alpha)$ (by definition)
$\Leftrightarrow \forall k \in A, \Sigma_k \models (a, \alpha)$ (completeness of possibilistic logic)
$\Leftrightarrow \Sigma^{\alpha/A} \models (a, \alpha/A)$ (by definition, keeping only formulas in Σ
         which may play a role in the inference of $(a, \alpha/A)$)
$\Leftrightarrow \Sigma \models (a, \alpha/A)$ (inference monotony)

3   A Refutation Method by Linear Multiple Agent Resolution

In possibilistic logic, the linear resolution strategy for the procedure of refutation by resolution, defined in [7], works in the same way as in classical logic, and thanks to an A*-like search method (changing the sum of the costs into their minimum), one can obtain the refutation having the strongest weight first, this weight being the one of the formula we want to prove. Here, the (fuzzy) subsets of agents play the role of weights, but they are not totally ordered, while the weights in possibilistic logic are; this makes the problem more tricky (since the costs in the A*-like algorithm will be computed from these weights). However, the procedure can be adapted to multiple-agent logic.

3.1   Refutation by Linear Multiple Agent Resolution

Let Γ be a knowledge base composed of multiple agent formulas. Proving (a, A) from Γ comes down to adding $(\neg a, All)$, in clausal form, to Γ and applying the resolution rule repeatedly until producing $(\bot, A)$. Clearly, it comes down to getting the empty clause with the greatest subset of agents $set(a, \Gamma)$. Formally:

$$set(a, \Gamma) = \cup \{A | \Gamma \models (a, A)\}$$

Refutation by resolution using a linear strategy can be expressed in terms of tree search in a state space. A state $(C_0 C_1, ..., C_i)$ is defined by a central clause C_i and the sequence $(C_0 C_1, ..., C_{i-1})$ of central clauses ancestors of C_i. For each state of the search tree, a subset of agents is associated, playing the role of a cost. It corresponds to the subset of agents of the latest generated central clause s.t. $set(C_i)$ (short for $set(C_i, \Gamma)$) is associated with state $(C_0 C_1, ..., C_i)$. The goal is to find the states ending with the empty clause with the greatest subsets of agents. An analogy with the search in the state space with costs is established in the following way:

- The initial state S_0 is defined by the initial central clause C_0 with a cost equal to $set(C_0)$,
- The cost associated with the arc $(C_0 C_1, ..., C_i) \rightarrow (C_0 C_1, ..., C_i C_{i+1})$ is the set associated with C_{i+1},
- The global cost of the path $C_0 \rightarrow C_1 \rightarrow ... \rightarrow C_i$ is the intersection of (set-valued) costs of the elementary arcs,
- The objective states are states $(C_0 C_1, ..., C_i)$ such that $C_i = (\bot, A_i)$ with $A_i \neq \emptyset$,
- The state $(C_0 C_1, ..., C_n)$ is expanded by generating all resolvents of C_n authorized by the linear strategy.

Searching for a refutation with the greatest subsets of agents is then equivalent to searching for a path with maximal cost from the initial state to the objective states. However, many differences exist:

- costs here are to be maximized not to be minimized. Indeed, the goal is to find the greatest subset of agents who believe a formula.
- costs are not additive but they are combined using the intersection operator.
- since only partial order can be defined between subsets, several objective states exist. The latter are then combined by the union operator.
- if an order exists between subsets, the greatest subset is considered and the other path is never explored, unlike search in space states.

As for heuristic search in space states, the ordered search is guided by an evaluation function f calculated as follows: for each state S of the search tree, $f(S) = g(S) \cap h(S)$ where $g(S)$ is the path cost from the initial state to S, and $h(S)$ a cost estimation from S to an objective state.

The different steps of the refutation by resolution using a linear strategy, presented by Algorithm 1, can be summarized in the following way:

Let $R(\Gamma)$ be the set of clauses that has been produced (using resolution) from Γ. For each refutation using the clause C, for each literal l of C and in order to obtain $\bot$, the use of a clause C' containing the literal $\neg l$ is required. A refutation expanded from C will have a cost less than or equal to:

$$H(l) = \bigcup\{set(C'), C' \in R(\Gamma), \neg l \in C'\}$$

The cost of the path until the contradiction developed from the clause C is then:

$$h_1(C) = \bigcap\{H(l), l \in C\} = \bigcap_{l \in C} \bigcup\{set(C'), C' \in R(\Gamma), \neg l \in C'\}$$

with $S = (C_0, ..., C)$. An admissible evaluation function is obtained $f_1(S) = set(C) \cap h_1(S)$. $h_1(S)$ depends only on C. A sequence of evaluation functions can be defined as follows:

$$h_0(C) = All;$$

$$f_p(C) = set(C) \cap h_p(C); p \geq 0$$

$$h_{p+1}(C) = \bigcap_{l \in C} \bigcup\{f_p(C'), C' \in R(\Gamma), \neg l \in C'\}; p \geq 0$$

Example 1. Let Γ be a multiple-agent clausal knowledge base:

$C_1 : (\neg a \vee b, All);$ $C_2 : (a \vee d, All);$
$C_3 : (a \vee \neg c, A);$ $C_4 : (\neg d, A);$
$C_5 : (\neg d, B).$

Let us to consider the search of the greatest subset of agents who believe b. Let then Γ' be the set of clauses equivalent to $\Gamma' = \Gamma \cup \{(\neg b, All)\}$. $C_0 = (\neg b, All)$ as $\Gamma' - \{C_0\}$ is coherent. The only clause which contains the literal b is C_1 (see Fig. 1). The next state is then $S_1 = (C_0 C_6)$ with $C_6 : (\neg a, All)$ and cost equal to $set(C_0) \cap set(C_1) = set(C_6) = All$. Different paths with C_2 and C_3 exist from this state. The evaluation function then will be calculated. The greatest set that maximizes the evaluation function is All, because $A \subset All$. Effectively, taking

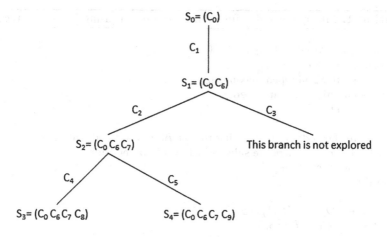

Fig. 1. Refutation tree of Example 1

into account this inclusion order, the path with the clause C_3 is not explored. The next state is then $S_2 = (C_0 C_6 C_7)$ and has a cost $set(C_6) \cap set(C_2) = set(C_7) = All$, with $C_7 : (d, All)$.

Several paths exist from this state. Those paths will be all explored because they have incomparable evaluation functions, due to the partial order of subsets. Let $S_3 = (C_0 C_6 C_7 C_8)$ be the next state. Its associated cost is $set(C_7) \cap set(C_4) = set(C_8) = A$. The clause C_8 is a contradiction. So, the first objective state is reached.

When dealing with the clause C_5, the next state is then $S_4 = (C_0 C_6 C_7 C_9)$ having the cost $set(C_7) \cap set(C_5) = set(C_9) = B$. The clause C_9 is a contradiction. The last objective state is then reached. Thus $\Gamma \models (b, A \cup B)$.

3.2   Refutation by Linear Possibilistic Multiple Agent Resolution

In multiple-agent possibilistic logic, the gradual subset weakening states that if $\beta/B \subseteq \alpha/A$ then $(c, \alpha/A) \vdash (c, \beta/B)$. The inclusion $F \subseteq G$ between two fuzzy subsets F and G of a referential U is classically defined by $\forall u \in U, F(u) \leq G(u)$. In particular, if $U = All$, then $\alpha/A \supseteq \beta/B$ if and only if $A \supseteq B$ and $\alpha \geq \beta$.

The goal is then to find a given formula with the greatest subset of agents with the greatest certainty degree. Obviously, the union of two partial results $(\bot, \alpha/A)$ and $(\bot, \beta/B)$ should be taken if $\alpha > \beta$ and $A \subset B$. These observations are used to directly extend the procedure of the previous section.

Example 2. Let Σ be a multiple-agent possibilistic knowledge base composed by the following clauses:

$C_1 : (\neg a \vee b, 0.8/All)$
$C_2 : (a \vee d, 0.7/All)$
$C_3 : (a \vee \neg c, 0.9/A)$

Algorithm 1. Multiple agent refutation by resolution using linear strategy

```
begin
    Open ← {S₀}; Closed ← {S₀}; bset = ∅
    while Open ≠ ∅ do
        Select a state Sₙ in Open maximizing f
        if Sₙ is an objective state then
            bset = bset ∪ Sₙ
        else
            Explore the node Sₙ by creating the set E'ₙ of produced states.
            if In the set E'ₙ there are subsets included in other then
                remove them from E'ₙ
            end if
            Eₙ ← E'ₙ \ Closed
            Open ← (Open − {Sₙ}) ∪ Eₙ
            Closed ← Closed ∪ {Sₙ}
            calculate f for each new state of Open
        end if
    end while
    if Open = ∅ then
        failure
    else
        display bset
    end if
End.
```

$$C_4 : (\neg d, 0.4/A)$$
$$C_5 : (\neg d, 0.3/B)$$

Note that the propositional knowledge base Σ° coincides with Γ° in the example of Sect. 3. The problem is to find the greatest subset of agents who believe b with the greatest certainty degree.

Let then Σ' be the set of clauses equivalent to $\Sigma' = \Sigma \cup \{(\neg b, 1/All)\}$. As depicted in Fig. 2, let us take $C_0 = (\neg b, 1/All)$ because $\Sigma' - \{C_0\}$ is coherent. As the classical projection of Σ is the same as Γ, the next state is then $S_1 = (C_0 C_6)$ and the associated cost is $fset(C_0) \cap fset(C_1) = fset(C_6) = 0.8/All$. Different paths starting with C_2 and C_3 exist from this state. However, unlike in the previous example, both paths will be explored because the fuzzy set $0.9/A$ is not included in the fuzzy set $0.7/All$. Using C_2, let $S_2 = (C_0 C_6 C_7)$ be the next state with cost $fset(C_6) \cap fset(C_2) = fset(C_7) = 0.7/All$.

Several paths exist from this state using C_4 or C_5. Let $S_3 = (C_0 C_6 C_7 C_8)$ be the next state using C_4. Its associated cost is $fset(C_7) \cap fset(C_4) = fset(C_8) = 0.4/A$. The clause C_8 is a contradiction. The first objective state is then reached. With the path using the clause C_5, the next state is then $S_4 = (C_0 C_6 C_7 C_9)$ with the cost $fset(C_7) \cap fset(C_5) = fset(C_9) = 0.3/B$. The clause C_9 is a contradiction. An objective state is then reached.

The development of the path with the clause C_3 induces the next state $S_5 = (C_0 C_6 C_{10})$ with the cost $fset(C_6) \cap fset(C_3) = fset(C_{10}) = 0.8/A$. The clause

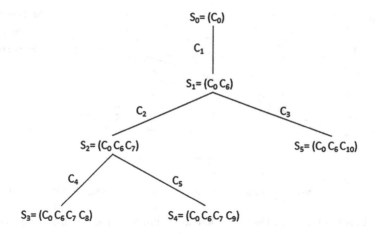

Fig. 2. Refutation tree of Example 2

C_{10} is not a contradiction and there is no clause containing a literal c so no objective state is reached here. Thus $\Sigma \models (b, 0.4/A \cup 0.3/B)$.

4   Experimental Study

In order to analyse the behaviour of the proposed approach, the proposed algorithms were implemented with Java and intensive experiments have been performed. For this purpose, several consistent knowledge bases, including multiple-agent knowledge bases and possibilistic multiple-agent knowledge bases, have been generated by varying the number of clauses. For each case of the following experiments, the execution time of the algorithm is evaluated in seconds. The number of Booleanvariables is set to 30 and the number of groups of agents is set respectively to 5, 10 and 15 by setting to 20 the number of agents.

1. **Results with multiple-agent knowledge bases:**
   Figure 3 shows the behaviour of refutation algorithm by varying the number of clauses from 5000 to 50000. According to the obtained results, we notice that the execution time increase proportionally to the number of clauses.
2. **Results with multiple-agent possibilistic knowledge bases:**
   Figure 4 shows the behaviour of refutation algorithm by varying the number of clauses from 5000 to 50000. According to Fig. 4, we notice also that the execution time is increased by rising the number of clauses.
3. **Comparison between refutations by linear multiple agent resolution and by linear possibilistic multiple agent resolution:**
   In order to compare both approaches, other experiments have been carried out, using large bases containing 50000 clauses, 30 variables and 15 groups of agents. By varying the number of agents from 25 to 200, Fig. 4 reveals us that the execution time of refutation by linear possibilistic multiple agent resolution is only slightly greater than the execution time of refutation by linear multiple agent resolution.

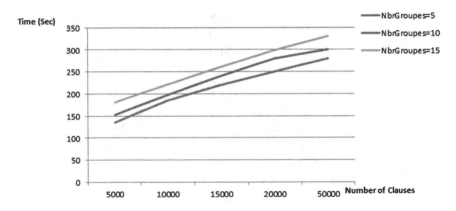

Fig. 3. Execution time of the refutation algorithm for large multiple agent bases.

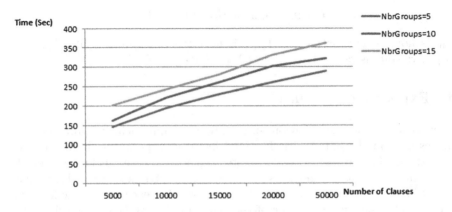

Fig. 4. Execution time of the algorithm for large *possibilistic* multiple-agent bases

Discussion. The obtained results allow us to estimate the performance of the proposed approach, which depends on the number of agent groups. Indeed, the execution time linearly increases with the number of clauses, but it increases exponentially with the number of variables. Whereas, when the number of group of agents increases, the execution time increases exponentially (but it linearly increases with the number of agents if their subsets are given in extension)[1]. This can be explained by the way of the refutation tree is constructed, which is based on the suitable clauses. Moreover, each branch of the tree represents one suitable clause for the literal to be deduced. The results also confirm that the execution time of the refutation algorithm for possibilistic multiple-agent knowledge bases

---

[1] It should be noticed that a base $\Sigma = \{(a_1, \alpha_1/A_1), ..., (a_n, \alpha_n/A_n)\}$ can be equivalently rewritten as a collection of at most 2^n possibilistic logic bases, each of them associated with an element of the partition of *All* induced by the A_i's. However, it is in generally computationally better to handle the initial base in a global way using the procedure described in this paper.

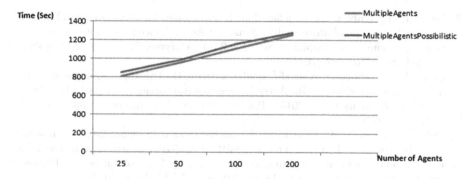

Fig. 5. Comparison between multiple-agent logic and possibilistic multiple-agent logic in terms of computational time

is slightly greater than the one obtained for multiple-agent knowledge bases. This is due to the fact that the construction of the refutation tree with fuzzy sets of agents consumes more time than the construction of refutation trees with crisp groups of agents.

5 Conclusion

This paper has investigated a multiple-agent logic. From a representation point of view, this multiple-agent logic allows us to represent beliefs of groups of agents and its possibilistic extension handles fuzzy subsets of agents, thus integrating certainty levels associated with agent beliefs. From a reasoning point of view, we proposed a refutation resolution based on linear strategy for the multiple logic and its possibilistic extension. An experimental study was conducted to evaluate the proposed algorithms. It shows the tractability of the approach.

One may think of several extensions. On the one hand, the multiple agent extension of the Boolean generalized possibilistic logic [5] would allow us to consider the disjunction and the negation of formulas like (p, A), and to express quantifiers in propositions such as "*at most* the agents in subset A believe p". On the other hand, one might also take into account trust data about information transmitted between agents [6,12]. For instance, assume agent a trusts agent b at level θ, which might be written $(b, \theta/a)$, assimilating a, b to propositions. Then together with $(p, \alpha/b)$ (agent b is certain at level α that p is true), it would enable us to infer $(p, \min(\alpha, \theta)/a)$ [2].

References

1. Belhadi, A., Dubois, D., Khellaf-Haned, F., Prade, H.: Multiple agent possibilistic logic. J. Appl. Non-Class. Logics **23**(4), 299–320 (2013)
2. Belhadi, A., Dubois, D., Khellaf-Haned, F., Prade, H.: Reasoning about the opinions of groups of agents. In: 11th Europe Workshop on Multi-Agent Systems (EUMAS 2013), Toulouse, France, 12–13 December (2013). https://www.irit.fr/EUMAS2013/Papers/eumas2013_submission_68.pdf

3. Belhadi, A., Dubois, D., Khellaf-Haned, F., Prade, H.: Algorithme d'infrence pour la logique possibiliste multi-agents. In: Actes Rencontres francophones sur la logique floue et ses applications (LFA 2014), Cargese, France, 22–24 October, pp. 259–266. Cépaduès (2014)
4. Belhadi, A., Dubois, D., Khellaf-Haned, F., Prade, H.: Lalogique possibiliste multi-agents: Une introduction. In: Actes Rencontres francophones sur la logique floue et ses applications (LFA 2015), Poitiers, France, 5-6 November, pp. 271–278. Cépaduès (2015)
5. Dubois, D., Prade, H., Schockaert, S.: Stable models in generalized possibilistic logic. In: Brewka, G., Eiter, Th., McIlraith, S.A. (eds.) Proceedings of the 13th International Conference on Principles of Knowledge Representation and Reasoning (KR 2012), Roma, June 10–14, pp. 519–529. AAAI Press (2012)
6. Cholvy, L.: How strong can an agent believe reported information? In: Liu, W. (ed.) ECSQARU 2011. LNCS, vol. 6717, pp. 386–397. Springer, Heidelberg (2011)
7. Dubois, D., Lang, J., Prade, H.: Theorem proving under uncertainty - a possibility theory-based approach. In: McDermott, J.P. (ed.) Proceedings of the 10th International Joint Conference on Artificial Intelligence (IJCAI 1987), Milan, August, pp. 984–986. Morgan Kaufmann (1987)
8. Dubois D., Lang J., Prade H.: Possibilistic logic. In: Gabbay, D.M., Hogger, C.J., Robinson, J.A., Nute, D. (eds.) Handbook of Logic in Artificial Intelligence and Logic Programming, vol. 3, pp. 439–513. Oxford University Press (1994)
9. Dubois, D., Prade, H.: Possibilistic logic: a retrospective and prospective view. Fuzzy Sets Syst. **144**, 3–23 (2004)
10. Dubois D., Prade H.: Extensions multi-agents de la logique possibiliste. In: Proceedings of the Rencontres Francophones sur la Logique Floue et ses Applications (LFA 2006), Toulouse, 19–20 October, pp. 137–144. Cépaduès (2006)
11. Dubois, D., Prade, H.: Toward multiple-agent extensions of possibilistic logic. In: Proceedings of the IEEE International Conference on Fuzzy Systems (FUZZ-IEEE 2007), London, 23–26 July, pp. 187–192 (2007)
12. Gutscher, A.: Reasoning with uncertain and conflicting opinions in open reputation systems. Electron. Notes Theor. Comput. Sci. **244**, 67–79 (2009)

Incremental Preference Elicitation in Multi-attribute Domains for Choice and Ranking with the Borda Count

Nawal Benabbou[1(✉)], Serena Di Sabatino Di Diodoro[1,2], Patrice Perny[1], and Paolo Viappiani[1]

[1] Sorbonne Universités, UPMC Univ Paris 06 and CNRS,
LIP6, UMR 7606, Paris, France
{nawal.benabbou,serena.disabatinodidiodoro,
patrice.perny,paolo.viappiani}@lip6.fr
[2] Department of Electronics and Information (DEIB),
Politecnico di Milano, Milan, Italy

Abstract. In this paper, we propose an interactive version of the Borda method for collective decision-making (social choice) when the alternatives are described with respect to multiple attributes and the individual preferences are unknown. More precisely, assuming that individual preferences are representable by linear multi-attribute utility functions, we propose an incremental elicitation method aiming to determine the Borda winner while minimizing the communication effort with the agents. This approach follows the recent work of Lu and Boutilier [8] relying on the minimax regret as a criterion for dealing with uncertainty in the preferences. We show that, when preferences are expressed on a multi-attribute domain and are additively separable over attributes, regret-based incremental elicitation methods can be made more efficient to determine or approximate the Borda winner. Our approach relies on the representation of incomplete preferences using convex polyhedra of possible utilities and is based on linear programming both for minimizing regrets and selecting informative preference queries. It enables to incrementally collect preference judgements from the agents until the Borda winner can be identified. Moreover, we provide an incremental technique for eliciting a collective ranking instead of a single winner.

1 Introduction

Voting is an effective method for collective decision-making, used in political elections, technical committees, academic institutions. Recently, interest in voting has increased in computer science, given the possibility offered by online web systems to support voting protocols, or protocols inspired by voting, for group decision-making (for example, for scheduling a meeting). In many real situations, however, it may be necessary to reason with partial preferences, as some preferences are not available and too expensive to obtain (with respect to a cognitive or economic cost). This observation has motivated a number of recent works on

© Springer International Publishing Switzerland 2016
S. Schockaert and P. Senellart (Eds.): SUM 2016, LNAI 9858, pp. 81–95, 2016.
DOI: 10.1007/978-3-319-45856-4_6

social choice with partial preferences, e.g., [2–6,8,9,12]. In this research stream, typical questions concern the determination of possible and necessary winners, the selection of preference queries to ask to the agents for further eliciting preferences, the approximation of optimal solutions or the determination of robust recommendations based on the available preference information.

Acquiring agents' preferences is expensive (with respect to time and cognitive cost). It is therefore essential to provide techniques that allow to reason with partial preference information, and that can effectively elicit the most relevant part of preferences to make a decision. Adaptive utility elicitation [1,10,11] tackles the challenges posed by preference elicitation by representing the system knowledge about the agents' preferences in the form of a set of admissible utility functions. This set includes all functions compatible with the preferences collected so far, and is updated following agents' responses. In this way, one can often make good (or even optimal) recommendations with sparse knowledge of the users' utility functions.

The aim of this paper is to introduce an adaptive utility elicitation procedure in the context of voting, for the fast determination of a Borda winner or a social ranking based on the Borda score, and to test the practical efficiency of this procedure. In particular, we extend the work of [8] to the multi-attribute case. Multiple attributes may appear in well-known collective decision problems such as committee elections or voting in multi-issue domains [7]. In these cases, attributes are boolean and represent elementary decisions on candidates or issues. More generally, the multi-attribute case occurs when the alternatives of a collective decision problem are described by different features, non-necessarily boolean. Individual preferences are assumed here to be representable by a linear function of the attribute values. Since utilities are decomposable over attributes, a set of preference statements formulated by an agent on some pairs of alternatives will possibly allow to infer other preference statements with respect to other pairs, without asking them explicitly. We show in the paper how this type of inference mechanism can be implemented using mathematical programming to reduce the number of queries and speed-up the determination of a necessary Borda winner.

The paper is organized as follows: in Sect. 2, we introduce the basic framework for voting on multi-attribute domains. Then, we present the minimax regret decision criterion as a useful tool for decision under uncertainty and preference elicitation. In Sect. 3, we introduce a new method based on mathematical programming to minimize regrets based on the Borda count. Section 4 deals with preference elicitation for the Borda count; we introduce different strategies for generating preference queries and compare them experimentally. Finally, in Sect. 5, we extend the approach to ranking problems based on the Borda score and provide additional numerical tests to evaluate the efficiency of our approach in ranking.

2 Social Choice in Multi-attribute Domains with Incomplete Preferences

We consider a set of n voters or agents and a set X of m alternatives (candidates, options, items), characterized by a finite set of q attributes or criteria; an alternative is associated to a vector $x = (x_1, \ldots, x_q)$ where each x_k represents the value of an attribute k or a performance with respect to a given point of view.

Individual preferences are assumed here to be represented by linear utilities of the form $u^i(x) = \sum_{k=1}^{q} \omega_k^i x_k$, where $\omega^i = (\omega_1^i, \ldots, \omega_q^i)$ is a vector of weights characterizing the preferences of agent i. Hence, an alternative x is as least as good as y for agent i whenever $\sum_{k=1}^{q} \omega_k^i x_k \geq \sum_{k=1}^{q} \omega_k^i y_k$. Our framework can be used to address two different cases: a multi-criteria decision setting or a multi-attribute utility where the utility is defined as the weighted sum of attribute values. Formally, these preferences are defined by the following relation $\succsim_i$:

$$x \succsim_i y \quad \text{iff} \quad \sum_{k=1}^{q} \omega_k^i (x_k - y_k) \geq 0$$

A preference profile $\langle \succsim_1, \ldots, \succsim_n \rangle$ of an election is therefore completely characterized by the weight vectors $\omega^1, \ldots, \omega^n$ (each associated with an agent). We can now define the Borda score in our multi-attribute settings, where preferences are defined by the utility weights. Given $\omega = \langle \omega^1, \ldots, \omega^n \rangle$, the Borda score $s(x, \omega)$ of an alternative x is

$$s(x, \omega) = \sum_{i=1}^{n} s^i(x, \omega^i)$$

where $s^i(x, \omega^i) = |\{y \in X \mid x \succ_i y\}|$ counts the number of alternatives that are strictly beaten by x according to the preference relation induced from ω^i, where $\succ_i$ is the asymmetric part of $\succsim_i$: $x \succ_i y$ iff $\succsim_i$ and $\neg(y \succsim_i x)$. Our definition allows for ties in each ranking. When using only linear orders (i.e. the ω^is are such that there are no ties) we get the usual Borda count.

When the weights of the agents are not known to the system with certainty, we need to reason about partially specified preferences. This is done by assuming a vector $\Omega = \langle \Omega^1, \ldots, \Omega^n \rangle$ where each Ω^i is the set of feasible ω^i that are consistent with the available preference information on agent i. Later, we will use Ω (that represents our uncertainty about the weights associated with the agents) in order to provide a recommendation based on minimax regret. At the level of a single agent i, we can check whether pairs of alternatives are in a necessary preference relation given Ω^i.

Definition 1. *Alternative x is necessarily weakly preferred to y for agent i, written $x \succsim_i^N y$, iff $\forall \omega^i \in \Omega^i, \sum_{k=1}^{q} \omega_k^i (x_k - y_k) \geq 0$. Similarly, x is necessarily strictly preferred to y for agent i, written $x \succ_i^N y$, iff $\forall \omega^i \in \Omega^i, \sum_{k=1}^{q} \omega_k^i (x_k - y_k) > 0$.*

The necessarily strictly preferred relation $\succ_i^N$ should not be confused with the asymmetric part[1] of the necessarily weakly preferred relation $\succsim_i^N$.

At the level of the community of the agents, a possible Borda winner is an alternative such that there exists a feasible instantiation of the weights that makes it a Borda winner; a necessary Borda winner is a Borda winner for all feasible instantiations of the weights.

In general the sets $\Omega^1, \ldots, \Omega^n$ are not given directly but are inferred by available preference statements. Any preference statement of type $x \succsim_i y$ for agent i is indeed interpreted as a linear constraint $\omega^i \cdot (x - y) \geq 0$. Therefore, after collecting several preferences of this type, Ω^i is a convex polyhedron in the space of weights.

When the utility weights are known and characterized by $\omega = \langle \omega^1, \ldots, \omega^n \rangle$, the actual loss or *real regret* of an alternative x is the shortfall in Borda score that occurs by choosing x instead of the optimal choice x_ω^*; more formally:

$$\text{Regret}(x, \omega) = \max_{y \in X}\{s(y, \omega)\} - s(x, \omega) = s(x_\omega^*, \omega) - s(x, \omega).$$

Instead, when the actual weights $\omega = \langle \omega^1, \ldots, \omega^n \rangle$ are not known, but some preferences are available, we are interested in quantifying how "bad" a choice can be with respect to the current uncertainty about the weights, encoded by $\Omega = \langle \Omega^1, \ldots, \Omega^n \rangle$. To this end, we first define pairwise max regret, then max regret and finally minimax regret as proposed in [8,10]. The *pairwise max regret* $\text{PMR}(x, y, \Omega)$ of alternative x relative to y under Ω is the worst-case loss, in terms of Borda score, of selecting the alternative x instead of y. The *max regret* $\text{MR}(x, \Omega)$ is the worst-case loss of choosing x: this can be viewed as an adversarial selection of the instantiation of the weights ω to maximize the loss between x and the true winner under ω. We want to choose the alternative x minimizing max regret: the *minimax regret* $\text{MMR}(\Omega)$ represents the smallest max regret under Ω. These concepts are formalized below:

$$\text{PMR}(x, y, \Omega) = \max_{\omega \in \Omega}\left[s(y, \omega) - s(x, \omega) \right],$$

$$\text{MR}(x, \Omega) = \max_{y \in X} \text{PMR}(x, y, \Omega), \tag{1}$$

$$\text{MMR}(\Omega) = \min_{x \in X} \text{MR}(x, \Omega). \tag{2}$$

Finally the *minimax optimal alternative* x_Ω^* is any alternative x minimizing regret MR over Ω (i.e. $x_\Omega^* \in \arg\min_{x \in X} \text{MR}(x, \Omega)$). Solution x_Ω^* is an approximate winner of the current election according to the minimax regret criterion; it gives us the safest choice with respect to the uncertainty on the preference weights attached to the agents; this will be suggested as a recommendation for the social choice problem given the available preference information. We recall from [8] the observation that the regret-minimizing alternative may not be a possible winner. Another important property is that, if $\text{MMR}(\Omega) = 0$, then x_Ω^* is a necessary winner.

---

[1] The asymmetric part $\rhd_i^N$ of $\succsim_i^N$ is defined as $x \rhd_i^N y$ iff $(x \succsim_i^N y) \wedge \neg(y \succsim_i^N x)$.

3 Minimax Regret Computation for Borda

We are now interested in the computation of minimax regret, given the uncertainty sets $\langle \Omega^1, \ldots, \Omega^n \rangle$, when using Borda count as voting rule on a multi-attribute domain. Note that the computation of the pairwise max-regret values PMR is the cornerstone of the problem: once we have computed $\mathrm{PMR}(x, y, \Omega)$ for all $x, y \in X$, max regret $\mathrm{MR}(x, \Omega)$ for all x and then minimax regret $\mathrm{MMR}(\Omega)$ can be computed directly from the definitions (Eqs. 1 and 2).

The main intuition for computing minimax regrets comes from [8]; however, in our multi-attribute settings, computing PMR is more involved as we need to deal with the multi-attribute structure of the domain. The key idea is to exploit the decomposition of PMR with respect to the different agents:

$$\mathrm{PMR}(x, y, \Omega) = \sum_{i=1}^{n} \max_{\omega^i \in \Omega^i} \left[s^i(y, \omega^i) - s^i(x, \omega^i) \right]$$

This decomposition allows to decompose the PMR maximization problem into a series of simpler maximization problems. For each agent i, we maximise the contribution to PMR separately, which is defined as follows:

$$\mathrm{PMR}_i(x, y, \Omega^i) = \max_{\omega^i \in \Omega^i} \left[s^i(y, \omega^i) - s^i(x, \omega^i) \right]$$

This optimization problem gives the maximal difference between the number of alternatives strictly less preferred than y and the number of alternatives strictly less preferred than x (according to the ith-agent's preferences); note that, if there is no tie, this corresponds to maximizing the difference between their rank. Let ω^i be the weighted vector maximizing this value and $\succsim_i$ be the preference relation induced by ω^i. From the definition of the scores, we have:

$$s^i(y, \omega^i) - s^i(x, \omega^i) = \begin{cases} - |\{z \in X,\ x \succ_i z \succsim_i y\}| & \text{if } x \succsim_i y \\ |\{z \in X,\ y \succ_i z \succsim_i x\}| & \text{otherwise} \end{cases}$$

However, since we do not know in which case we are (ω^i is not known), we make use of the necessarily preferred relation $\succsim_i^N$ in order to check whether some conclusions can be drawn from the available information about the preference between x and y. More precisely, we distinguish whether it is known that x is necessarily weakly preferred to y or not. Then, we deduce the weighting vector that maximizes the contribution to regret of agent i. Note that checking whether $x \succsim_i^N y$ can be simply performed using a linear program, by testing the condition $\min_{\omega^i \in \Omega^i} \{(x - y) \cdot \omega^i\} \geq 0$. We now express two mutually exclusive cases using the necessary preference relation.

(1) case $x \succsim_i^N y$: in that case, we have $s^i(y, \omega^i) - s^i(x, \omega^i) \leq 0$ for all $\omega^i \in \Omega^i$ by definition of $\succsim_i^N$. This induces that the contribution to $\mathrm{PMR}(x, y, \Omega)$ is non-positive and more precisely, we have $\mathrm{PMR}_i(x, y, \Omega^i) = -\min_{\omega^i \in \Omega^i} |\{z \in X,\ x \succ_i z \succsim_i y\}|$. Hence, to maximize the pairwise max regret $\mathrm{PMR}(x, y, \Omega)$, we need to minimize over Ω^i the cardinality of the set $\{z \in X,\ x \succ_i z \succsim_i y\}$ as much as possible.

(2) case $\neg(x \succsim_i^N y)$: there exists $\omega^i \in \Omega^i$ such that $s^i(y, \omega^i) - s^i(x, \omega^i) \geq 0$ by definition of $\succsim_i^N$. Therefore, we know that the contribution to $\mathrm{PMR}(x, y, \Omega)$ is non-negative here. More precisely, we have $\mathrm{PMR}_i(x, y, \Omega^i) = \max_{\omega^i \in \Omega^i} |\{z \in X, y \succ_i z \succsim_i x\}|$. Hence, we need to maximize the cardinality of the set $\{z \in X, y \succ_i z \succsim_i x\}$ to maximize the pairwise max regret $\mathrm{PMR}(x, y, \Omega)$.

In the following, we consider the problem of computing $\mathrm{PMR}_i(x, y, \Omega^i)$ for any x, y and i. First of all, we need to define the following sets for any $a \in \{x, y\}$:

$$U^a = \{z \in X \setminus \{a\}, z \succsim_i^N a\}, \quad L^a = \{z \in X, a \succ_i^N z\}, \quad V^a = X \setminus (\{a\} \cup U^a \cup L^a)$$

and for any pair of alternatives $(a, b) \in \{(x, y), (y, x)\}$:

$$M^{a,b} = L^a \cap U^b, \quad Z_1^{a,b} = L^a \cap V^b, \quad Z_2^{b,a} = U^b \cap V^a, \quad Z_3^{a,b} = V^a \cap V^b$$

These sets are computed for each user i using linear programming (repeatedly testing $\succsim_i^N$ or $\succ_i^N$ on pairs of alternatives) and allow us to partition the set X for the computation of $\mathrm{PMR}_i(x, y, \Omega^i)$. We refer the reader to Fig. 1 where the different cases are visualized; for simplicity, we only show the transitive reduction of the preference relation and we distinguish whether it is known that y is necessarily weakly preferred to x or not (if not, set $M^{y,x}$ is empty). Note that, in the following, we may write Z_1, Z_2 and Z_3 (dropping the superscripts) when the case considered is clear from the context.

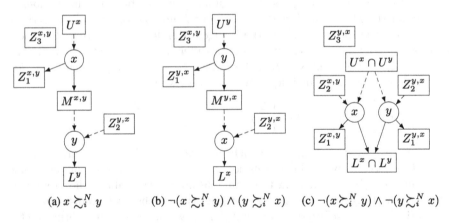

(a) $x \succsim_i^N y$ (b) $\neg(x \succsim_i^N y) \wedge (y \succsim_i^N x)$ (c) $\neg(x \succsim_i^N y) \wedge \neg(y \succsim_i^N x)$

Fig. 1. Partition of set X with respect to the value of $\succsim_i^N$ with x and y for agent i. The solid (resp. dashed) arcs represent necessary strict (resp. weak) preferences.

(1) case $x \succsim_i^N y$ *(Fig. 1a):* We want to compute $\mathrm{PMR}_i(x, y, \Omega^i)$. Recall that, in this case, $\mathrm{PMR}_i(x, y, \Omega^i) = -\min_{\omega^i \in \Omega^i} |\{z \in X, x \succ_i z \succsim_i y\}|$. Hence, we want to find a feasible $\omega^i \in \Omega^i$ such that as few of the alternatives $z \in X$ are such that $x \succ_i z \succsim_i y$. First, let us note that none of the alternatives z in $U^x \cup L^y$ verify $x \succ_i z \succsim_i y$ for some $\omega^i \in \Omega^i$ (by definition of U^x and L^y). Moreover, $x \succ_i z \succsim_i y$ for all alternatives $z \in M^{x,y}$ and all $\omega^i \in \Omega^i$ (by definition of $M^{x,y}$). Therefore, we have:

$$\mathrm{PMR}_i(x, y, \Omega^i) = -|M^{x,y}| - \min_{\omega^i \in \Omega^i} |\{z \in Z_1 \cup Z_2 \cup Z_3 \cup \{y\}, \ x \succ_i z \succsim_i y\}|$$

Thus, we need to compute $\min_{\omega^i \in \Omega^i} |\{z \in Z_1 \cup Z_2 \cup Z_3 \cup \{y\}, \ x \succ_i z \succsim_i y\}|$ to determine $\mathrm{PMR}_i(x, y, \Omega^i)$. We propose now a mixed-integer programming formulation (named $\mathrm{MIP}_{x,y}$) to solve the latter optimization problem:

$$(\mathrm{MIP}_{x,y}): \quad \min \ b_0 + \sum_{z \in Z_1} b_1^z + \sum_{z \in Z_2} b_2^z + \sum_{z \in Z_3} b_3^z$$

$$\text{s.t.} \quad \sum_{j=1}^{q} \omega_j^i = 1 \tag{3}$$

$$\omega^i \cdot (a - b) \geq 0, \quad \forall (a, b) \in \mathcal{P}_{\geq}^i \tag{4}$$

$$\omega^i \cdot (a - b) \geq \varepsilon, \quad \forall (a, b) \in \mathcal{P}_{>}^i \tag{5}$$

$$\omega^i \cdot (y - x) + C b_0 \geq 0 \tag{6}$$

$$\omega^i \cdot (y - z) + C b_1^z \geq \varepsilon, \quad \forall z \in Z_1 \cup Z_3 \tag{7}$$

$$\omega^i \cdot (z - x) + C b_2^z \geq 0, \quad \forall z \in Z_2 \cup Z_3 \tag{8}$$

$$b_3^z \geq b_1^z + b_2^z - 1, \quad \forall z \in Z_3 \tag{9}$$

$$\omega_j^i \geq 0, \ \forall j \in \{1, \ldots, q\}; \ b_0 \in \{0, 1\}; \ b_3^z \in \{0, 1\}, \ \forall z \in Z_3$$

$$b_1^z \in \{0, 1\}, \ \forall z \in Z_1 \cup Z_3; \ b_2^z \in \{0, 1\}, \ \forall z \in Z_2 \cup Z_3$$

In this program, the variables are $\omega^i = (\omega_1^i, \ldots, \omega_q^i)$, a vector of q positive real numbers, binary variable b_0 and binary variables b_1^z for each $z \in Z_1 \cup Z_3$, b_2^z for each $z \in Z_2 \cup Z_3$, and b_3^z for each $z \in Z_3$ (we therefore have $q + |Z_1| + |Z_2| + 3|Z_3| + 1$ variables). C is an arbitrary large constant value and ε is an arbitrary small and positive constant modelling strict inequalities. Constraint 3 simply states that the weights should be normalized to add up to 1. Constraints 4 and 5 model the fact that weight ω^i should satisfy both the weak preference statements in $\mathcal{P}_{\geq}^i$ and the strict preference statements in $\mathcal{P}_{>}^i$ obtained from agent i; indeed, set Ω^i is defined by these preference statements.

Proposition 1. *If* $x \succsim_i^N y$, *then* $\mathrm{PMR}_i(x, y, \Omega^i) = -|M^{x,y}| - OPT$, *where* OPT *is the optimum of mixed-integer program* $MIP_{x,y}$.

Proof. We want to prove that $\min_{\omega^i \in \Omega^i} |\{z \in Z_1 \cup Z_2 \cup Z_3 \cup \{y\}, \ x \succ_i z \succsim_i y\}|$ is the optimum of $\mathrm{MIP}_{x,y}$, i.e. we want to show that the objective function counts the cardinality of $\{z \in Z_1 \cup Z_2 \cup Z_3 \cup \{y\}, \ x \succ_i z \succsim_i y\}$. In this program, we use a set of binary variables b_1^z, b_2^z and b_3^z to represent the condition $x \succ_i z \succsim_i y$ for alternatives z in Z_1, Z_2 and Z_3 respectively. Binary variable b_0 represents whether x is strictly preferred to y (otherwise the contribution to PMR is null). The objective function sums up over all variables b_0, b_1^z, b_2^z and b_3^z, so that we count the cardinality of $\{z \in Z_1 \cup Z_2 \cup Z_3 \cup \{y\}, \ x \succ_i z \succsim_i y\}$. We now prove that each binary variable is equal to one iff the corresponding constraint is satisfied. Since the objective is a minimization, the values of the binary variables b_0, b_1^z, b_2^z and b_3^z (that appear in the objective function), will be 0 unless forced to 1.

The binary variable b_1^z, for $z \in Z_1$, represents whether alternative z verifies $x \succ_i z \succsim_i y$. Equation 7 indeed enforces $b_1^z = 1$ when $\omega^i \cdot (z - y) \geq 0$, i.e. when $z \succsim_i y$; otherwise, variable b_1^z is set to zero since we are minimizing the objective function. Then, since $x \succ_i z$ (by definition of Z_1), we have that $b_1^z = 1$ iff $x \succ_i z \succsim_i y$.

For all alternatives $z \in Z_2$, we know that $z \succsim_i y$ by definition. Therefore, z will be such that $x \succ_i z \succsim_i y$ iff $x \succ_i z$. The binary variable b_2^z will take value 1 in this case. This is indeed guaranteed by Constraint 8 enforcing $b_2^z = 1$ when $\omega^i \cdot (z - x) < 0$, i.e. if x is strictly preferred to z. If instead z is preferred to x, then the value $\omega^i \cdot (z - x)$ is positive and Constraint 8 is vacuous; in this case, b_2^z will take value 0, as desired, because we are minimizing.

For all alternatives $z \in Z_3$, the two previous conditions need to be satisfied in order for z to contribute to the score difference. Constraint 9 implements an *and* between these two conditions ($b_3^z = 1$ iff $x \succ_i z$ and $z \succsim_i y$).

Finally, while we know that y cannot be strictly preferred to x (since $x \succsim_i^N y$), it might be the case that they are equally preferred. The binary variable b_0 represents whether x is strictly preferred to y; more precisely, Constraint 6 enforces that $b_0 = 1$ whenever $\omega^i \cdot (y - x) < 0$.   □

(2) case $\neg(x \succ_i^N y)$ (Figs. 1b and c)*:* Recall that, in this case, $\text{PMR}_i(x, y, \Omega^i) = \max_{\omega^i \in \Omega^i} |\{z \in X, \ y \succ_i z \succsim_i x\}|$. Therefore, we aim to find a feasible $\omega^i \in \Omega^i$ so that as many of the alternatives $z \in X$ are such that $y \succ_i z \succsim_i x$. Since we are maximizing, the optimal $\omega^i \in \Omega^i$ will be such that $y \succsim_i x$; thus, the case represented in Fig. 1c reduces to the one depicted in Fig. 1b. We now focus on the optimization of $\text{PMR}_i(x, y, \Omega^i)$ for Fig. 1b. Similarly to the first case, note that none of the alternatives z in $U^y \cup L^x$ verifies $y \succ_i z \succsim_i x$ for some $\omega^i \in \Omega^i$. Moreover, all alternatives $z \in M^{y,x}$ are such that $y \succ_i z \succsim_i x$ for all $\omega^i \in \Omega^i$. Therefore:

$$\text{PMR}_i(x, y, \Omega^i) = |M^{y,x}| + \max_{\omega^i \in \Omega^i} |\{z \in Z_1 \cup Z_2 \cup Z_3 \cup \{x\}, \ y \succ_i z \succsim_i x\}|$$

Thus, we need to compute $\max_{\omega^i \in \Omega^i} |\{z \in Z_1 \cup Z_2 \cup Z_3 \cup \{x\}, \ y \succ_i z \succsim_i x\}|$. This can be performed by solving the following program (named $\text{MIP}_{y,x}$ hereafter):

$$(\text{MIP}_{y,x}): \quad \max \ b_0 + \sum_{z \in Z_1} b_1^z + \sum_{z \in Z_2} b_2^z + \sum_{z \in Z_3} b_3^z$$

$$\text{s.t.} \quad \sum_{j=1}^{q} \omega_j^i = 1$$

$$\omega^i \cdot (a - b) \geq 0, \quad \forall (a, b) \in \mathcal{P}_{\geq}^i$$

$$\omega^i \cdot (a - b) \geq \varepsilon, \quad \forall (a, b) \in \mathcal{P}_{>}^i$$

$$\omega^i \cdot (y - x) + (1 - b_0)C \geq \varepsilon \tag{10}$$

$$\omega^i \cdot (z - x) + (1 - b_1^z)C \geq 0, \quad \forall z \in Z_1 \cup Z_3 \tag{11}$$

$$\omega^i \cdot (y - z) + (1 - b_2^z)C \geq \varepsilon, \quad \forall z \in Z_2 \cup Z_3 \tag{12}$$

$$b_3^z \leq b_1^z, \quad \forall z \in Z_3 \tag{13}$$
$$b_3^z \leq b_2^z, \quad \forall z \in Z_3 \tag{14}$$
$$\omega_j^i \geq 0, \ \forall j \in \{1, \ldots, q\}; \ b_0 \in \{0, 1\}; \ b_3^z \in \{0, 1\}, \ \forall z \in Z_3$$
$$b_1^z \in \{0, 1\}, \ \forall z \in Z_1 \cup Z_3; \ b_2^z \in \{0, 1\}, \ \forall z \in Z_2 \cup Z_3$$

Proposition 2. *If* $\neg(x \succsim_i^N y)$, *then* $\text{PMR}_i(x, y, \Omega^i) = |M^{y,x}| + OPT$, *where* OPT *is the optimum of mixed-integer program* $MIP_{y,x}$.

The proof is similar to that of the previous condition, however since the objective is a maximization, the values of the binary variables b_0, b_1^z (for $z \in Z_1$), b_2^z (for $z \in Z_2$) and b_3^z (for $z \in Z_3$) will be 1 unless forced to be 0. Constraints 10–14 formalize the required behaviour: the value of each binary variable, relative to a specific z, will be set to 1 unless ω^i is chosen in a way such that $y \succ_i z \succsim_i x$.

   Note that the MIP formulations might be too computationally demanding for problems involving a large number of alternatives (since there are one or more integer variables per alternative). For this reason, we will consider the linear programming relaxation of these programs, i.e., the linear programs obtained by replacing boolean variables b_0, b_1^z, b_2^z, b_3^z by continuous variables belonging to the unit interval. The resulting optimization problems are solvable in polynomial time using linear programming; however the solution gives an upper bound on pairwise max regret values (instead of the exact value). The relaxed values for PMR are then aggregated giving a relaxed MMR value. Note that, since optimizing the relaxed problem gives an upper bound, the result can still be used in order to provide a robust recommendation with worst-case guarantees; the guarantee is less strong than if pairwise max regret values were computed exactly, but computation times are significantly improved as shown in Subsect. 4.2.

4   Incremental Elicitation

Given the available preference information, the worst-case loss ensured by the minimax regret might be at unacceptable level. In order to approximate the Borda winner with the desired guarantee (expressed by the minimax regret value), we may ask additional preference information to the agents. By incorporating the responses to additional questions, we can indeed refine the uncertainty sets and therefore reduce this loss.

4.1   Elicitation Strategies

We adopt an incremental setting where preference queries are selected incrementally according to the current available information until the minimax regret is zero; at that point, we know that alternative x_Ω^* is a necessary Borda winner. We allow asking queries that may induce either weak or strict preference statements. In order to limit the cognitive effort of the agents, it is important to ask queries that are informative (roughly, a query is informative if it significantly reduces regrets whatever the answer); in particular, the computation of minimax regret can suggest queries that may be able to impose a significant reduction of regrets. One common technique, also known as the *Current Solution Strategy* (CSS), is to consider one of the current "best challenger" y_Ω^* of the approximate winner: $y_\Omega^* \in \arg\max_{y \in X} \mathrm{PMR}(x_\Omega^*, y, \Omega)$. New preference information involving the pair (x_Ω^*, y_Ω^*) is indeed often useful to reduce the minimax regret efficiently, which is equal to $\mathrm{PMR}(x_\Omega^*, y_\Omega^*, \Omega)$. We propose now two elicitation strategies of different complexity, that are aimed to reduce $\mathrm{PMR}(x_\Omega^*, y_\Omega^*, \Omega)$.

Multi-attribute-CSS0 *(MA-CSS0).* This strategy selects a pair (agent, query) such that the answer may reduce the agent's contribution to $\mathrm{PMR}(x_\Omega^*, y_\Omega^*, \Omega)$. More precisely, an agent i is selected at random and the strategy proceeds as follows:

(1) case $x_\Omega^* \succsim_i^N y_\Omega^*$: recall that, in this case, $\mathrm{PMR}_i(x_\Omega^*, y_\Omega^*, \Omega^i) = -|M^{x_\Omega^*, y_\Omega^*}| - \min_{w^i \in \Omega^i} |\{z \in Z_1 \cup Z_2 \cup Z_3 \cup \{y\}, x_\Omega^* \succ_i z \succsim_i y_\Omega^*\}|$. We distinguish two cases:

- *case* $Z_1 \cup Z_2 \cup Z_3 = \emptyset$: if $\neg(x_\Omega^* \succ_i^N y_\Omega^*)$, then we ask the agent whether x_Ω^* is strictly preferred to y_Ω^*. If, instead, $x_\Omega^* \succ_i^N y_\Omega^*$, we know precisely the difference of scores between x_Ω^* and y_Ω^* for agent i, that is $-|M^{x_\Omega^*, y_\Omega^*}| - 1$. In this case, asking a query to agent i is useless (since his/her contribution to $\mathrm{PMR}(x_\Omega^*, y_\Omega^*, \Omega)$ cannot be decreased) and so the strategy selects another agent at random.
- *case* $\neg(Z_1 \cup Z_2 \cup Z_3 = \emptyset)$: an alternative z in $Z_1 \cup Z_2 \cup Z_3$ is selected at random. For each $z \in Z_1 \cup Z_2 \cup Z_3$, our current knowledge about the agent's preferences is not sufficient to conclude on whether $x_\Omega^* \succ_i z \succsim_i y_\Omega^*$ is satisfied or not. More precisely, if $z \in Z_1$, then we know that x_Ω^* is strictly preferred to z by definition, but there exists $w^i \in \Omega^i$ such that $\neg(z \succsim_i y_\Omega^*)$. Therefore, we ask the agent whether z is (weakly) preferred to y_Ω^* so as to obtain the missing information. Similarly, if $z \in Z_2$, then we know that z is preferred to y_Ω^*, and so the agent is asked whether x_Ω^* is strictly preferred to z. Finally, if $z \in Z_3$, then we ask one of the two previous questions, the choice between the two questions being randomly made.

(2) case $\neg(x_\Omega^* \succsim_i^N y_\Omega^*)$: recall that, in this case, $\mathrm{PMR}_i(x_\Omega^*, y_\Omega^*, \Omega^i) = |M^{y_\Omega^*, x_\Omega^*}| + \max_{w^i \in \Omega^i} |\{z \in Z_1 \cup Z_2 \cup Z_3 \cup \{x\}, y_\Omega^* \succ_i z \succsim_i x_\Omega^*\}|$. We distinguish three cases:

- *case* $\neg(y_\Omega^* \succsim_i^N x_\Omega^*)$: in this case, x_Ω^* and y_Ω^* are incomparable for the system, and so we ask the agent to compare them directly.
- *case* $(y_\Omega^* \succsim_i^N x_\Omega^*) \wedge (Z_1 \cup Z_2 \cup Z_3 = \emptyset)$: if $\neg(y_\Omega^* \succ_i^N x_\Omega^*)$, then the agent is asked whether y_Ω^* is strictly preferred to x_Ω^*. If, instead, $y_\Omega^* \succ_i^N x_\Omega^*$, then the difference of scores between x_Ω^* and y_Ω^* for this agent is equal to $|M^{y_\Omega^*, x_\Omega^*}| + 1$. In this case, asking a query to agent i is useless and another agent is selected at random.
- *case* $(y_\Omega^* \succsim_i^N x_\Omega^*) \wedge \neg(Z_1 \cup Z_2 \cup Z_3 = \emptyset)$: an alternative z in $Z_1 \cup Z_2 \cup Z_3$ is selected at random and we want to know whether $y_\Omega^* \succ_i z \succsim_i x_\Omega^*$. More

precisely, if $z \in Z_1$, then we ask the agent whether z is (weakly) preferred to x_Ω^*. Instead, if $z \in Z_2$, then we ask the agent if y_Ω^* is strictly preferred to z. Finally, if $z \in Z_3$, then we ask one of the two previous questions.

Multi-attribute-CSS1 *(MA-CSS1)*. This strategy is based on the heuristics proposed by Lu and Boutilier [8] but adapted to our multi-attribute setting. The aim is to choose the query with the highest potential of reducing $PMR(x^*, y^*, \Omega)$. More precisely, instead of choosing the agent and the alternative $z \in Z_1 \cup Z_2 \cup Z_3$ at random (as in MA-CSS0), strategy MA-CSS1 selects the pair (agent, query) that maximizes the minimax regret reduction in the most optimistic scenario; it therefore requires the computation of the resulting minimax regret for each pair (agent, query).

4.2   Numerical Tests

We performed a number of numerical experiments in order to evaluate the proposed elicitation procedures for determining the Borda winner in an incremental process. In these experiments, the attribute values for each alternative are randomly sampled in $[0,1]^q$. Starting from an empty set of preference statements, we repeatedly compute minimax regret and we ask a new question to one of the agent according to an elicitation strategy. We simulate answers to queries according to randomly generated vectors $\omega^1, \ldots, \omega^n$ (one vector per agent). Optimizations are performed using the Gurobi solver; the simulation environment is implemented in Java.

In the first experiment, we evaluate the impact of exploiting the fact that the domain is multi-attribute. We implemented the elicitation procedure proposed in [8] (named CSS1 hereafter) where no assumption is made about the "structure" of the agents preferences, and compare it with our strategies MA-CSS0 and MA-CSS1.[2] In Fig. 2a, we report the minimax regret, computed at each step of the incremental elicitation procedure. Regret values are expressed on a normalized scale, with 1 corresponding to the initial MMR (computed before acquiring any preference information). Note that a value of 0 for MMR implies identification of a Borda winner. We observe that the MMR reduces much more slowly with CSS1 than with its multi-attribute version MA-CSS1; after 20 queries, the MMR is still above 40 % of the initial value with CSS1, while it is under 10 % with MA-CSS1. Moreover, after 30 queries per agent on average, the MMR is still around 40 % of the initial regret with CSS1 while MA-CSS1 has identified the Borda winner. Then, we observe (somewhat surprisingly) that the heuristics used by MA-CSS1 is less effective than MA-CSS0. Since MA-CSS1 is much more computational demanding than MA-CSS0, in the following experiments, we use MA-CSS0.

---

[2] Note that CSS1 and MA-CSS1 adopt the same heuristics for choosing the pair (agent, query); the difference is that MA-CSS1 makes use of the multi-attribute structure (using linear programming) for identifying the sets Z_1, Z_2, etc., and computing regrets, while CSS1 does not.

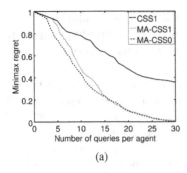
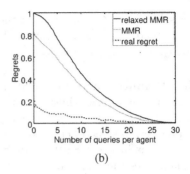

(a)   (b)

Fig. 2. Evaluation of the elicitation strategies; regret reduction is plotted as a function of the average number of queries per agent (30 alternatives, 5 criteria and 10 agents; results averaged over 30 runs). In (a) we plot the reduction of minimax regret obtained by different elicitation strategies; in (b) we compare the upper bound of MMR obtained with the relaxed optimization, the exact computation of MMR and the real regret.

The second experiment evaluates the quality of the upper bound obtained when using the linear programming relaxation of the MMR optimization. Figure 2b shows the minimax regret, the upper bound obtained by linear programming relaxation and the real regret (the actual loss in terms of Borda score) at each iteration step of the elicitation procedure. We can see that the linear programming relaxation gives us a relatively tight upper bound on the minimax regret and its quality improves with the number of preference statements. Recall that the relaxed version is significantly faster than the exact version, as the former solves linear programming problems instead of mixed integer linear problems. For instance, when no preferences are given, the relaxed optimization takes about $1s$ on average while the exact method needs $30s$ to compute the value of initial minimax regret. The determination of the next query is also faster when using the relaxed optimization ($2s$ againsts $12s$). Even if, by optimizing the relaxed problem, we are potentially ignoring some valuable information, the experiment shows that the elicitation performs well. The recommended choice is the alternative whose "relaxed" MMR is lowest; the real regret associated to this choice is small and quickly decreases to zero. Note that the fact that real regret is much smaller than minimax regret in practice has already been observed [10].

The third experiment aims to evaluate the performance of MA-CSS0, using the relaxed optimization of regrets, when increasing the size of the problem (number of agents, number of alternatives and number of criteria). Figure 3 shows that, with 5 attributes, our incremental elicitation procedure determines a necessary Borda winner in about 30–35 queries asked to each agent; however, with 7 attributes, slightly more than 50 queries are needed. In all cases, the real regret is low even after a few queries.

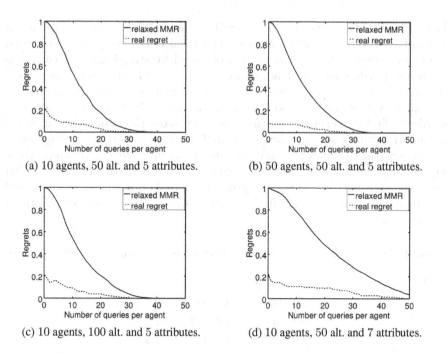

(a) 10 agents, 50 alt. and 5 attributes.

(b) 50 agents, 50 alt. and 5 attributes.

(c) 10 agents, 100 alt. and 5 attributes.

(d) 10 agents, 50 alt. and 7 attributes.

Fig. 3. Performance of MA-CSS0 with the relaxed version of minimax regret (30 runs).

5 Determination of the Social Ranking Induced by Borda Scores

There are many decision situations where knowing the top-k alternatives is the desirable output. When the preference profile is fully known, ranking alternatives with a scoring rule is straightforward. However, when preferences are incomplete, incremental elicitation methods need to be adapted to efficiently focus the elicitation effort on the determination of the top-k alternatives. We address here the problem of ranking as one of repeated choices, assuming that we want to incrementally rank alternatives from best to worst; we can generate preference queries until the minimax regret drops to 0, meaning that the Borda winner has been identified. Then, this alternative is put aside[3] and the selection process is iterated on the remaining set of alternatives. The alternative selected in the second stage will be the second best alternative in the ranking induced by Borda scores and so forth.

Numerical Tests. We perform an experiment that evaluates the performance of our incremental assessment of ranking (when used with MA-CSS0) in comparison to approaches that are more systematic. We consider the following two

---

[3] It may still be associated with a binary variable b^z in the optimization problems for computing regrets (as it can impact the Borda score of other alternatives).

elicitation procedures: strategy *S1* determines the preference order of each agent by adapting a standard sorting algorithm (it requires $O(m \log_2(m))$ comparison queries per agent); the ranking is then obtained by straightforward computation of the Borda scores. Instead, strategy *S2* iteratively applies a regret-based incremental elicitation procedure for the determination of the best alternative in terms of a linear utility model *for a single agent*. The procedure is repeated in order to find the second item, the third, and so on; this is done for all agents and finally Borda scores are computed. In Table 1, we report the average number of comparison queries per agent required to identify the top-10 alternatives, varying n the number of agents, m the number of alternatives and q the number of criteria. Our incremental ranking procedure based on Borda scores is referred to as Incremental Ranking Elicitation (IRE); overall, IRE outperforms both S1 and S2.

Table 1. Average number of queries per agent for determining the top-10 (30 runs)

n	m	q	IRE	S1	S2
10	30	5	43.3	147.2	58.7
10	50	5	43.7	282.2	67.4
100	30	5	51.1	147.2	87.2
10	30	10	93.3	147.2	178.2

We now present some experimental results about our incremental ranking method (when used with MA-CSS0). Figure 4 shows the average number of queries needed to determine the top-k alternatives in domains with 20 agents and 5 criteria. We observe that the marginal amount of queries needed to determine the next best alternative decreases as the rank of the alternatives increases. Actually, most of the elicitation "cost" in terms of queries occurs when determining the top alternative.

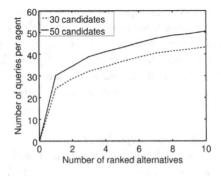

Fig. 4. Performance of top-k elicitation with MA-CSS0 (30 runs).

6 Conclusions

This paper dealt with social choice in a context where preferences are dictated by a latent (linear) utility function. We provided algorithms for the computation of an approximate winner and elicitation strategies based on minimax regret, extending previous work [8] to multi-attribute domains. We also provided an iterative procedure for top-k ranking and compared our results with full elicitation procedures. Possible directions for future research include: dealing with other voting rules in multi-attribute domains, considering different kinds of queries, and addressing combinatorial domains.

Acknowledgements. This work is supported by the ANR project 14-CE24-0007-01-Cocorico-CoDec.

References

1. Braziunas, D., Boutilier, C.: Elicitation of factored utilities. AI Mag. **29**(4), 79–92 (2008)
2. Dery, L.N., Kalech, M., Rokach, L., Shapira, B.: Reaching a joint decision with minimal elicitation of voter preferences. Inf. Sci. **278**, 466–487 (2014)
3. Ding, N., Lin, F.: Voting with partial information: what questions to ask? In: Proceedings of AAMAS 2013, pp. 1237–1238 (2013)
4. Kalech, M., Kraus, S., Kaminka, G.A.: Practical voting rules with partial information. Auton. Agent. Multi-agent Syst. **22**(1), 151–182 (2010)
5. Konczak, K., Lang, J.: Voting procedures with incomplete preferences. In: Proceedings of IJCAI 2005 Multidisciplinary Workshop on Advances in Preference Handling, vol. 20 (2005)
6. Lang, J., Pini, M.S., Rossi, F., Salvagnin, D., Venable, K.B., Walsh, T.: Winner determination in voting trees with incomplete preferences and weighted votes. Auton. Agent. Multi-agent Syst. **25**(1), 130–157 (2012)
7. Lang, J., Xia, L.: Sequential composition of voting rules in multi-issue domains. Math. Soc. Sci. **57**(3), 304–324 (2009)
8. Tyler, L., Boutilier, C.: Robust approximation and incremental elicitation in voting protocols. In: Proceedings of the IJCAI 2011, pp. 287–293 (2011)
9. Lu, T., Boutilier, C.: Vote elicitation with probabilistic preference models: empirical estimation and cost tradeoffs. In: Brafman, R. (ed.) ADT 2011. LNCS, vol. 6992, pp. 135–149. Springer, Heidelberg (2011)
10. Wang, T., Boutilier, C.: Incremental utility elicitation with the minimax regret decision criterion. In: Proceedings of IJCAI, Acapulco, pp. 309–316 (2003)
11. White III, C.C., Sage, A.P., Dozono, S.: A model of multiattribute decision-making and trade-off weight determination under uncertainty. IEEE Trans. Syst. Man Cybern. **14**(2), 223–229 (1984)
12. Xia, L., Conitzer, V.: Determining possible and necessary winners given partial orders. J. Artif. Intell. Res. (JAIR) **41**, 25–67 (2011)

Graphical Models for Preference Representation: An Overview

Nahla Ben Amor[1], Didier Dubois[2], Héla Gouider[1(✉)], and Henri Prade[2]

[1] LARODEC Laboratory, ISG de Tunis, 41 rue de la Liberté, 2000 Le Bardo, Tunisia
nahla.benamor@gmx.fr, gouider.hela@gmail.com
[2] IRIT – CNRS, 118, route de Narbonne, 31062 Toulouse Cedex 09, France
{dubois,prade}@irit.fr

Abstract. Representing preferences into a compact structure has become an important research topic. Graphical models are of special interest. Indeed, they facilitate elicitation, exhibit some form of independence, and serve as a basis for solving optimization and dominance queries about choices. The expressiveness of the representation setting and the complexity of answering queries are then central issues for each approach. This paper proposes an extensive overview of the main graphical models for preference representation and provides a comparative survey by emphasizing their main characteristics. We also indicate possible transformations between some of these models. We contrast qualitative models such as CP-nets and TCP-nets with quantitative ones such as GAI networks, UCP-nets, and Marginal utility nets, and advocate π-Pref nets, recently introduced by the authors, as an interesting compromise between the two types of models.

1 Introduction

Modeling preferences is essential in any decision analysis task. However, getting these preferences becomes non trivial as soon as alternatives are described by a Cartesian product of multiple features. Indeed, the direct assessment of a preference relation between these alternatives is usually not feasible due to its combinatorial nature. Fortunately, the decision maker can express *contextual* preferences that exhibit some independence relations, which allows us to be represent her/his preferences in a compact manner. Moreover, graphical representations facilitate preference elicitation, as well as the construction of an ordering from these contextual local preferences. This use of graphical preference representations has been inspired by the success of Bayesian networks as a computationally tractable uncertainty management device [23].

Various graphical models have been proposed in the literature in order to capture preferences in an intuitive manner. We may roughly distinguish two classes: (i) qualitative models where preferences are contextually expressed by comparisons between attributes values. Within these models, CP-nets [6] are the most popular and well-developed compact representation setting for preferences; (ii) quantitative models, where a numerical value function can be computed for

© Springer International Publishing Switzerland 2016
S. Schockaert and P. Senellart (Eds.): SUM 2016, LNAI 9858, pp. 96–111, 2016.
DOI: 10.1007/978-3-319-45856-4_7

comparing all possible choices, such as GAI networks [19], UCP-nets [4], or marginal utility nets [9]. In general, these models are mostly motivated by the easiness of elicitation. However, some of them still suffer from various limitations: their expressive power may be somehow restricted, elicitation may be complex, or answering queries may require costly reasoning algorithms.

This paper surveys most graphical models for preference representation. It enlarges the only existing past overview [21]. For each model, we emphasize the independence relation underlying it, study how it operates for defining an order between the choices from the expressed preferences, and we recall the computational complexity of dominance and optimization algorithms. The paper is organized as follows. Sections 2 and 3 provide a presentation of the major qualitative or quantitative graphical models respectively, allowing for a local processing of elementary preferences by exploiting some structural independence relations carried by their graphical components. Section 4 presents a symbolic graphical model for preferences based on possibility theory and possibilistic networks. This approach recently introduced by the authors, is halfway between qualitative and quantitative models. Section 5 concludes with a summary and a thorough comparative discussion.

2   Graphical Preferential Qualitative Models

Let $V = \{A_1, \ldots A_N\}$ be a set of N variables. Each variable A_i has a domain $D(A_i)$; a_i denotes any value of A_i. $\Omega = \{\omega_1, \ldots, \omega_{|\Omega|}\}$ denotes the universe of discourse, which is the Cartesian product of domains all variables in V. Each element $\omega_i \in \Omega$ is called a *configuration*. It corresponds to a complete instantiation of the variables in V. If $X \subseteq V$, let $D(X)$ refer to the Cartesian product of the domains of variables in X and $\omega[X]$ denotes the restriction of variable ω to variables in X.

Semantically, preferences are defined by an order between the configurations (or choices). Let $\succeq$ be a binary relation on Ω such that $x \succeq y$ means that "x is at least as preferred as y". Other relations can be derived from $\succeq$ as usual: $\omega_i \sim \omega_j$ iff $\omega_i \succeq \omega_j$ and $\omega_j \succeq \omega_i$; $\omega_i \succ \omega_j$ iff $\omega_i \succeq \omega_j$ but not $\omega_j \succeq \omega_i$; $\omega_i \pm \omega_j$ iff neither $\omega_i \succeq \omega_j$ nor $\omega_j \succeq \omega_i$ (non comparability). Ordering relations may be complete (i.e. we can compare any two configurations) or partial, strict (i.e. asymmetric) or weak. Preference relations between different configurations $\omega_i \in \Omega$ can be expressed via some preference relations over subsets of variables, taking advantage of (in)dependencies that exist between the variables or subsets of variables. We denote by $Pa(A_i)$ the set of parents of A_i, p_i any instantiation of $Pa(A_i)$ and $\mathcal{Y}(A_i) = \{Y_1, \ldots, Y_n\}$ the set of its children. $Dn(A_i)$ denotes its descendants and $Co(A_i) = V \setminus (Dn(A_i) \cup Pa(A_i) \cup A_i)$ denotes the set of non-descendants. We will use these notations for the rest of the paper.

In a preference model, two types of queries are commonly used: namely, optimization queries for finding the optimal configuration(s) (i.e. those which are not dominated by others) and dominance queries for comparing configurations. Besides, another important task is the elicitation of the model which corresponds to constructing the graph and collecting the user preferences. Most of practically used preferential graphical models are qualitative since they are easy to elicit. In the sequel, we detail two of the most important ones, namely, Conditional Preference networks (CP-nets) and their extension Tradeoffs-enhanced CP-nets.

2.1 Conditional Preference Networks (CP-Nets)

CP-nets, initially introduced in [6], are considered as an efficient model to manage qualitative preferences. They are based on a preferential independence property often referred to as a Ceteris Paribus assumption such that a partial configuration is preferred to another everything else being equal. Formally, it is defined as follows:

Definition 1 (Preferential Independence). *Let V be a set of variables and W be a subset of V. W is said to be preferentially independent from its complement $Z = V \setminus W$ iff for any instantiations, z, z', w, w', $(w, z) \succ (w', z) \Leftrightarrow (w, z') \succ (w', z')$.*

Preferential independence is asymmetric. Indeed, it might happen, e.g., for disjoint sets X, Y and Z of variables that X is preferentially independent (Definition 1) from Y given Z without having Y preferentially independent from X. This independence is at a work in the graphical structure underlying CP-nets.

Definition 2 (CP-Nets). *A CP-net consists of a directed graph $\mathcal{G} = (\mathcal{V}, \mathcal{E})$ where $\mathcal{V}$ denotes the set of nodes and $\mathcal{E}$ denotes the set of edges. A node corresponds to a variable. Edges represent the preference dependencies between the variables. To each variable A_i we associate a conditional preference table that corresponds to a strict total order between the values of A_i, for all instantiations p_i of parent variables.*

Here, preferences over values of a variable depend only on the parent(s) context, and are preferentially independent from the rest of variables. In contrast with Bayesian nets, CP-nets may be cyclic (without necessarily encoding inconsistent preferences). Using the information in the CP-Tables and applying the *Ceteris Paribus* principle, when *flipping* one variable value in a configuration one may obtain either an improved configuration, or a worsened one. These swap pairs can be organized into a collection of worsening (directed) paths with a unique root corresponding to the best configuration and where the other path extremities are the worst ones. A CP-net is said to be satisfiable if there exists at least one partial order of configurations that satisfies it. Note that every acyclic CP-net is satisfiable.

Example 1. Let us consider the simple CP-Net of Fig. 1(a), with 3 variables. The building of the worsening flips graph (Fig. 1(b)) leads to the partial ordering: $abc \succ_{CP} ab\neg c \succ_{CP} \neg ab\neg c \succ_{CP} \neg abc \succ_{CP} \neg a\neg bc \succ_{CP} \neg a\neg b\neg c$, $ab\neg c \succ_{CP} a\neg b\neg c \succ_{CP} \neg a\neg b\neg c$, $abc \succ_{CP} a\neg bc \succ_{CP} \neg a\neg bc$. The best configuration is abc.

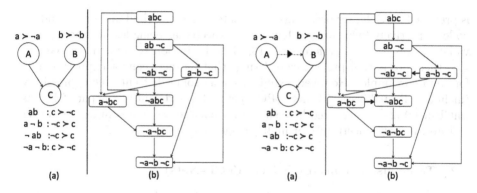

Fig. 1. An example of a CP-net (a) and its worsening flips graph (b)

Fig. 2. An example of a TCP-net (a) and its worsening flips graph (b)

Acyclic CP-nets have a unique optimal configuration. Finding it amounts to looking for a configuration where all the conditional preferences are best satisfied. It can be done by a simple forward sweeping procedure where, for each node, we assign the most preferred value according to the parents context. For acyclic CP-nets, this procedure is linear w.r.t. the number of variables [6]. In contrast, for cyclic ones answering this query needs an NP-hard algorithm and may lead to more than one optimal configuration [17]. Dominance queries are more complex. Using the information in the CP-Tables and applying the *Ceteris Paribus* principle, when one *flips* one variable value in a configuration one may obtain either an improved configuration, or a worsened one. These swap pairs can be organized into a collection of worsening (directed) paths with a unique root corresponding to the best configuration and where the other path extremities are the worst ones. Thus, a configuration is preferred to another if there exists a chain (directed path) of worsening flips between them [5]. Note that if for any variable $A_i \in V$, A_i is preferentially independent from $V \setminus A_i$, then the CP-net graph is disconnected and many configurations cannot be compared. Testing dominance is PSPACE-complete for unrestricted CP-nets, NP-hard for acyclic ones, and quadratic for tree-structures [17]. In general, the ordering induced by a CP-net is strict and partial, since several configurations may remain non comparable (i.e. no worsening flips chain exists between them). Clearly, acyclic CP-nets cannot exhibit any ties. *Ceteris Paribus* makes the preference elicitation simple for CP-nets; the elicitation complexity is equal to $O(N^k)$ such that N is the number of nodes and k is the maximal number of parents [22].

However, in CP-nets, a parent preference tends to be more important than a child one [5]. In other words, violating a preference associated with a father node is more important than violating a preference associated with a child one; this priority *implicitly* given by the application of *Ceteris Paribus* may be debatable. For instance, in the previous example, configuration $ab\neg c$ is preferred to configuration $\neg abc$. Moreover, this kind of priority is not transitive in the sense that CP-nets cannot always decide whether violating preferences of two children nodes is preferred to violating preferences associated with one child and one grandson node respectively (which might have been expected as being less damaging than violating two children preferences) [13]. This limitation is problematic. Generally, there are partial preference orderings that CP-nets cannot express, see [3] for counterexamples. However, extensions may somewhat enhance expressivity (including Probabilistic CP-nets (PCP-nets) [12] and Multiple agents CP-nets (mCP-nets) [24] not covered here since they enlarge the representation to other features, namely uncertainty or multiple agents).

2.2 Tradeoffs-Enhanced CP-Nets (TCP-Nets)

As mentioned above, the expressive power of CP-nets is limited. In particular, we are unable to specify importance relations between variables, beside those implicitly imposed between parents and children. Tradeoffs-enhanced CP-nets (TCP-nets) [7] are an extension of CP-nets that adds a notion of importance between the variables by enriching the network with new arcs. These arcs express importance relations for stating the priority of a node over another (i.e., "preference about the values of X is more important than preference about the values of Y"). Such priority statements may be conditioned on the values of other variables, e.g., "if the variable Z has value z, the preference about values of X is more important than the preference about the values of Y." Formally, TCP-nets are annotated graphs with three types of edges and are defined as below.

Definition 3 (TCP-Nets). *A TCP-net $\mathcal{G}'$ over a set V of variables is a CP-net $\mathcal{G} = (\mathcal{V}, \mathcal{E})$ augmented with two types of arcs:*

1. *A set of directed i-arcs (where i stands for importance). An i-arc$\langle \overrightarrow{A_i, A_j} \rangle$ belongs to $\mathcal{G}'$ iff A_i is more important than A_j, which is denoted by $A_i \triangleright A_j$.*
2. *A set of undirected ci-arcs (where ci stands for conditional importance). A ci-arc (A_i, A_j) belongs to $\mathcal{G}'$ iff the relative importance of A_i and A_j is conditioned on Z s.t. $Z \subseteq V \backslash \{A_i, A_j\}$. Each ci-arc (A_i, A_j) is associated with a mapping from a subset of $D(Z)$ to strict total orders over the set $\{A_i, A_j\}$.*

Let us turn to the expressive power of TCP-nets. TCP-nets obey the preference statements induced by *Ceteris Paribus*, since the ordering obtained is a refinement of the CP-nets ordering. In fact, the refinement brought by TCP-nets cannot override the implicit priority in favor of parents nodes. Indeed, in case one would add a $i-$, or a $ci-$ arc yielding a preference in favor of a son with respect to a parent (at least in some context), one would face an inconsistency between a worsening I-flip and a worsening CP-flip that act in opposite directions, thus we would have inconsistent TCP-nets.

The main issue for TCP-nets is the challenge of performing queries with this representation. Some first proposals are presented in [8]. For consistent TCP-nets, the optimization procedure works like CP-nets. Indeed, the relative importance relations do not play a role in this case. The dominance problem can be also be treated as a search for an improving flipping sequence, where the notion of flipping sequence is extended. In fact, a flip corresponds either to a CP-flip like CP-nets or to an I-flip ("importance flip"). Let ω and ω' be two configurations, such that ω differs from ω' in the value of exactly two variables A_j and A_k, and such that $\omega[A_j] \succ \omega'[A_j]$ and $\omega[A_k] \prec \omega'[A_k]$ (given the same values of $Pa(A_j)$ and $Pa(A_k)$ in ω and ω'). Then, a worsening I-flip from ω to ω' takes place when there is a priority of A_j over A_k conditional (or not) on a subset of variables Z such that Z takes the same values in ω and ω'. However, no general algorithm is known for dominance query since results in the context of CP-nets do not seem to be immediately adaptable to TCP-nets.

Example 2. Let us consider the TCP-net in Fig. 2(a). An unconditioned importance $a \rhd b$ is added. Indeed, a new arc $i\text{-}arc\langle \overrightarrow{A, B} \rangle$ is added with respect to the CP-net in Fig. 1(a). The ordering given by the worsening flips graph in Fig. 2(b) is refined, compared to the CP-net. Indeed, $a \neg b \neg c \succ_{TCP-net} \neg a b \neg c$ and $a \neg bc \succ_{TCP-net} \neg abc$, while these configurations comparable by I-flips, are not comparable in the CP-net, see Fig. 1(b). In place of the previous unconditioned importance statement, one may exhibit an example of $ci\text{-}arc\,(A, B)$ by stating that A is more important than B if $C = c$, and B is more important than A if $C = \neg c$. Then, we would have $a \neg b \neg c \prec_{TCP-net} \neg a b \neg c$ and $a \neg bc \succ_{TCP-net} \neg abc$.

TCP-nets also yield partial orderings that, from the same CP-net preference statements, are refinements of the ordering induced by the corresponding CP-nets.

Example 3. Let us consider the following preferences over variables A and B with $D(A) = \{a, \neg a\}$ and $D(B) = \{b, \neg b\}$: (i) In all cases a is preferred to $\neg a$; (ii) b is preferred to $\neg b$. The CP-net view yields the order: $ab \succ_{CP} a \neg b \pm_{CP} \neg ab \succ_{CP} \neg a \neg b$. No CP-net yields the refined order $ab \succ a \neg b \succ \neg ab \succ \neg a \neg b$, while it can be represented with a TCP-net, with the additional information "A is more important than B".

3   Graphical Preferential Quantitative Models

It is often convenient to have preferences expressed in numerical terms, since it enables an easy comparison of possible choices. It is therefore interesting to consider quantitative graphical models for preferences. These latter are generally based on utility functions corresponding to a mapping from the Cartesian product of variables domains to numerical values, namely $u : \Omega \mapsto \mathbb{R}$. These utilities correspond to a total ordering s.t., for two configurations ω and ω', $\omega \succ \omega'$ (respectively $\omega \sim \omega'$) if and only if $u(\omega) > u(\omega')$ (respectively $u(\omega) = u(\omega')$). In this section, we review the most important quantitative graphical models based on these utilities.

3.1   Generalized Additive Independence Networks (GAI-Nets)

GAI-networks [19] are one of the first graphical quantitative preference models. They rely on generalized additive independence decomposition (GAI decomposition, for short) [16]. This independence allows to represent the preferences by a utility function separable into a sum of local functions. Each local function pertains to a subset of variables and represents a total ordering between their possible instantiations. Moreover, there may be some interactions between these local utilities since the subsets of variables pertaining to them can be non disjoint. Thus, these GAI-decompositions can express some general interactions between attributes while preserving some decomposability of the model.

Definition 4 (GAI Decomposition). *Let $C_1, \ldots, C_k$ be subsets of V s.t. $V = \bigcup_{j=1}^{k} C_j$. A utility function $u(\cdot)$ representing $\succeq$ over Ω is GAI-decomposable w.r.t. $C_1, \ldots, C_k$ iff $\forall\, j \in [1,k]$, there exists a function $u_j \colon D(C_j) \mapsto \mathbb{R}$ s.t., $\forall\, \omega \in \Omega$:*

$$u(\omega) = \sum_{j=1}^{k} u_j(\omega[C_j]) \tag{1}$$

These GAI decompositions can be represented by graphical structures called GAI networks. They are undirected graphs where each clique consists of a subset of variables. Between two cliques having some variables in common there exists a path linking them. Each edge in the network is labeled by the intersection between the nodes.

Definition 5 (GAI-Nets). *A GAI network is an undirected graph $\mathcal{G} = (\mathcal{C}, \mathcal{E})$ where $\mathcal{C}$ denotes the set of cliques and $\mathcal{E}$ denotes the set of edges. $\mathcal{G}$ has two components:*

- *Graphical component: Each clique $C_j \in \mathcal{C}$, is a set of variables such that $C_j \subseteq V$ and $\bigcup_{i=1}^{k} C_i = V$; For each edge $(C_i, C_j) \in \mathcal{E}$, $C_i \cap C_j \neq \emptyset$. Each edge is labeled by $C_i \cap Cj$;*
- *Numerical component: To each clique C_j we associate a local utility function u_j that defines a complete preorder between the configurations in $D(C_j)$.*

The graphical structure of GAI-nets is similar to the notion of junction tree used for Bayesian networks [20,23]. Indeed, even for a GAI-net with a more general graph structure, we can always construct a tree-structured network based on the triangulation of the Markov network corresponding to it [18] (This transformation is NP-complete [1]). Optimization queries look for the configurations having the maximal global utility value. A standard algorithm for finding the optimal configurations has been proposed for tree structured GAI networks. However, as mentioned above, this is not restrictive. Optimization for GAI-nets corresponds to an adaptation of the belief propagation algorithm used in Bayesian networks and its complexity is exponential with the number of variables of the biggest clique. To compare two configurations ω and ω' by a GAI-net, we compute their corresponding utilities and compare them. Thus, the dominance test for GAI is linear in the number of the cliques which is considered as an advantage compared to the other models.

Example 4. Let $\omega_1 = abcde$ and $\omega_2 = a\neg bc\neg d\neg e$. From the GAI-network $\mathcal{G}$ of Fig. 3, we can compute the utilities of the configurations: $u_{\mathcal{G}}(\omega_1) = u_1(ab) + u_3(ac) + u_2(ade) = 0.7 + 1.5 + 0 = 2.2$, $u_{\mathcal{G}}(\omega_2) = u_1(a\neg b) + u_3(ac) + u_2(a\neg d\neg e) = 1.2 + 1.5 + 0 = 2.7$. Thus $u_{\mathcal{G}}(\omega_2) > u_{\mathcal{G}}(\omega_1)$, and $\omega_2 \succ_{GAI} \omega_1$.

AB		A		ADE		A		AC

	$u_1(.)$		$u_2(.)$		$u_2(.)$		$u_3(.)$
ab	0.7	ade	0	$\neg ade$	2	ac	1.5
$a\neg b$	1.2	$ad\neg e$	1	$\neg ad\neg e$	1.2	$a\neg c$	1
$\neg ab$	1.8	$a\neg de$	0.5	$\neg a\neg de$	1.8	$\neg ac$	1.2
$\neg a\neg b$	0.5	$a\neg d\neg e$	0	$\neg a\neg d\neg e$	0.4	$\neg a\neg c$	0.2

Fig. 3. An example of GAI network

GAI-nets rely on a weak form of symmetric independence which make the model flexible enough to be applied to many situations. GAI-nets are not limited to the expression of *Ceteris Paribus* preferences as CP-nets, TCP-nets, or their numerical counterpart, UCP-nets. Still there are cases of numerical preferences that are not representable by a GAI-net [15]. With regard to elicitation, there is no method to construct the GAI decompositions. In practice it is always assumed that an expert provided the GAI decomposition and only the utilities are elicited. One may take advantage of the GAI structure for designing an elicitation method based on "local" utility queries rather than global queries over full configurations [11].

Another graphical model for numerical preferences, called CUI-nets, based on conditional utility independence (CUI) was proposed in [15]. It is motivated by the use of a weaker *asymmetric* independence relation. This independence is not additive and may represent preferences that cannot be factored using strong additive independence conditions [15]. However, this kind of independence does not lead to decompositions that are as easy to handle as those given under additive independence.

3.2   Utility CP-Nets (UCP-Nets)

Utility CP-nets (UCP-nets), introduced in [4], are an extension of CP-nets that replaces the ordinal preference relations of CP-nets by utility factors. In fact, UCP-nets combine the aspects of two preference models, namely, CP-nets and GAI-nets. Like GAI-nets, utility is obtained from the sum of functions associated to groups of variables, defined here by a variable and its parents. Similarly to CP-nets, UCP-nets are directed and arcs reflect the *Ceteris Paribus* independence.

Definition 6 (UCP-Nets). *A UCP-net is a directed graph* $\mathcal{G} = (\mathcal{V}, \mathcal{E})$, *where the graphical component is the same as for CP-nets and the conditional preference tables are replaced by a set of numerical factors* $f_i(a_i, p_i)$, *for all* $a_i \in D(A_i)$

and parents instantiations p_i, such that the global utility of a configuration is defined by:

$$u_{\mathcal{G}}(a_1, ..., a_N) = \sum_{i=1}^{N} f_i(a_i, p_i) \tag{2}$$

Example 5. The UCP-net $\mathcal{G}$ presented in Fig. 4 has 3 variables $V = \{A, B, C\}$. For instance, we can check that the configuration $a \neg b \neg c$ is preferred to abc since $u_{\mathcal{G}}(abc) = 5 + 2 + 2 = 9 < u_{\mathcal{G}}(a \neg b \neg c) = 5 + 10 + 6 = 21$.

The UCP-net formalism has a number of computational advantages. In particular, dominance queries can be answered trivially since they amount to computing the global utilities and compare them, as in the above example. This can be done in linear time in the number of variables (this contrasts with CP-nets where dominance testing is computationally difficult). Optimization queries can also be answered directly, taking linear time in the network size, where each node is instantiated to its maximal value given the instantiation of it parents. This procedure, inherited from CP-nets, exploits the considerable power of *Ceteris Paribus* semantics. Thus, CP-nets are endowed with quantitative utility information, and then the expressive power is enhanced and dominance queries become computationally efficient. Moreover, when introducing directionality and the *Ceteris Paribus* semantics to GAI relations, we allow utility functions to be expressed more naturally and optimization queries to be answered more easily.

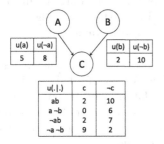

Fig. 4. An example of a UCP-net

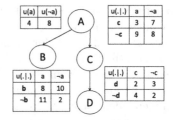

Fig. 5. An example of a marginal utility net

This model is intuitive to assess since, as CP-nets, it captures preference statements that are naturally expressed by the user. However, in order to remain consistent with CP-nets, utilities should be subject to constraints expressing the priority of father nodes over child nodes. More precisely, let A be a variable with parents $Pa(A)$ and children $\mathcal{Y}(A) = \{Y_1, \ldots, Y_n\}$ and let $\mathcal{Z}_i$ be the subset of parents of Y_i excluding A and any of its parents in $Pa(A)$. Let $\mathcal{Z} = \bigcup \mathcal{Z}_i$ and P_i be the subset of variables in $Pa(A)$ that are parents of Y_i and where p_i is an instantiation of P_i. The fact that the node corresponding to variable A dominates its children given any instantiation u of $Pa(A)$ is expressed by the requirement $\forall\ a_1, a_2 \in D(A)$ such that $f_A(a_1, u) \geq f_A(a_2, u)$, we should have $\forall$ z an instantiation of $\mathcal{Z}$ and $\forall y_i$ an instantiation of $\mathcal{Y}(A)$, $f_A(a_1, u) - f_A(a_2, u) \geq$

$\sum_i f_{Y_i}(y_i, (a_2, p_i, z_i)) - f_{Y_i}(y_i, (a_1, p_i, z_i))$. This expresses that for any variable A, given an instantiation of its parents, the utility gain in choosing a_1 rather than a_2 in this context, should be more important than the maximum value of the sum of the possible utility loss for its children over all possible instantiations of the other related variables.

This means that not every GAI decomposition can be represented by a UCP-net. Thus, beside the difficulty encountered for learning utilities, added constraints should be taken into account in order to remain consistent with the *Ceteris Paribus* principle.

3.3 Marginal Utility Networks

With the aim to define preference networks that resemble Bayesian networks, Brafman and Engel [9,10] introduce a notion of conditional independence (denoted CDI_r) using an arbitrarily fixed reference instantiation ω^r. Indeed utility functions differ from probability distributions in the fact there is no obvious analogue of marginalization for utility; to cope with this difficulty, the authors propose to use reference instantiation for fixing the values of the independent variables. Then, the utility satisfies additive analogues of the Bayes and chain rules of Bayesian networks. Variables A_i and A_j are CDI_r if any difference in values among instantiations to A_i does not depend on the current instantiation of A_j, for any possible instantiation to the rest of the variables.

Definition 7 (Reference Configuration and the Reference Utility). *Let $\omega^r = a_1^r, \ldots, a_N^r \in \Omega$ be a predetermined configuration and, X and Y be subsets of V. The reference utility function u_r is defined by $u_r(x) = u(x\bar{x}^r)$, s.t. $\bar{X} = V \backslash X$ is fixed on the values of the reference configuration ω^r. Its conditional form is defined by $u_r(X|Y) = u_r(XY) - u_r(Y)$.*

Definition 8 (Difference Utility Independence). *Let Z and W be two subsets of V, s.t. $Z \cap W = \emptyset$. Z and W are CDI_r given $X \subseteq V \setminus (Z \cup W)$, denoted by $CDI_r(Z, W|X)$, if for all assignments x, z', z'', w', w'' we have: $u_r(z'w') - u_r(z''w') = u_r(z'w'') - u_r(z''w'')$.*

This type of independence (CDI_r) satisfies the properties of graphoids [10], that is, each variable is independent from its non descendants in the context of its parents as for Bayesian nets. This leads to a preference representation by directed graphs.

Definition 9 (Marginal Utility Network). *A marginal utility network is a directed graph $\mathcal{G} = (\mathcal{V}, \mathcal{E})$ where $\mathcal{V}$ is the set of nodes and $\mathcal{E}$ is the set of edges. $\mathcal{G}$ has two components:*

- *Graphical component: A node for each variable and edges correspond to conditional (in)dependencies between variables such that, given a fixed configuration $\omega^r \in \Omega$, for any $A_i \in V$, $CDI_r(A_i, Co(A_i)|Pa(A_i))$.*

– *Numerical component: Each node A_i is associated to a conditional utility table (CUT) corresponding to the function $u_r(a_i|p_i)$ such that p_i is an instantiation of the parents $Pa(A_i)$ of A_i. Containing $\forall a_i \in D(A_i)$, $\forall p_i$, $u_r(a_i \mid p_i)$.*

The utility of a configuration is then computed as $u_{\mathcal{G}}(a_1, ..., a_N) = \sum_{i=1}^{N} u_r(a_i|p_i)$ where p_i is an instantiation of $P(A_i)$. This is now exemplified.

Example 6. Let us consider preferences over four binary variables A, B, C and D represented by the marginal utility network of Fig. 5. Assume that $\omega_r = abc\neg d$ is the reference configuration. Then, $u_r(abc) - u_r(a\neg bc) = u_r(ab\neg c) - u_r(a\neg b\neg c)$. In fact, $(4 + 8 + 3 + 4) - (4 + 11 + 3 + 4) = (4 + 8 + 9 + 4) - (4 + 11 + 9 + 4)$. Thus, $CDI_r(B, D|A)$. The utility of a configuration is the summation of all the local utilities. For instance, $u_{\mathcal{G}}(abcd) = u_r(a) + u_r(b|a) + u_r(c|a) + u_r(d|c) = 4 + 8 + 3 + 2 = 17$ and $u_{\mathcal{G}}(a\neg b\neg c\neg d) = 4 + 11 + 9 + 2 = 26$. Therefore, we have $abcd \prec_{MU} a\neg b\neg c\neg d$ since $u_{\mathcal{G}}(abcd) < u_{\mathcal{G}}(a\neg b\neg c\neg d)$.

Thanks to the strong similarity between Bayesian nets and marginal utility nets, adaptations of algorithms are possible. The authors in [10] briefly mention two of them. First, an optimization query for finding the optimal configuration is like finding the most probable explanation. Second, finding the best configuration when particular combinations between the variables are impossible is like constraint belief propagation. No method to answer dominance queries has been proposed, however the algorithm used in GAI nets seems to be applicable in this case. Elicitation may be inspired from Bayesian nets [9].

Following also the idea of keeping close to Bayesian nets, it has been recently proposed to use *Ordinal Conditional Function* networks (they are like Bayesian nets with infinitesimal probabilities: the value n of the OCF is like the probability 10^{-n}) for describing preferences [14]. OCF-nets satisfy the local directed independence property of Markov networks. By enforcing the priority of father nodes over child nodes by suitable constraints, it is possible to build an OCF-net that induces a total order compatible with the partial order of a given CP-net [14]. Besides, note that UCP-nets can be viewed as particular cases of marginal utility nets where constraints should be added in order to make them consistent with *Ceteris Paribus*.

4   Conditional Preference Possibilistic Networks

Marginal networks are inspired from Bayesian networks. Similarly, one may use possibilistic networks [2], a possibility theory counterpart to Bayes nets, for modeling preferences rather than uncertainty (understanding the possibility degrees as satisfaction levels). Possibility theory uses possibility distribution π, which are mapping from a universe of discourse Ω to the unit interval $[0, 1]$, or to any bounded totally ordered scale. Two forms of conditioning, respectively based on minimum and product, make sense in possibility theory, leading to two types of chain rules. We may then compute satisfaction values for configurations, taking advantage of Markov property, and obtain a total order between configurations in both cases. In the absence of available quantitative values, one may think of keeping the possibility degrees unspecified (which also preserves the ability of representing partial orders). This led us to propose a new graphical preference model based on possibilistic networks [3], called π-Pref nets. In a π-Pref net, for each variable $A_i \in V$, for each instantiation p_i of $Pa(A_i)$, the preference order between the values of variable A_i is encoded by a local conditional possibility distribution expressed by symbolic weights. A symbolic weight means a symbol representing a real number whose value is unspecified.

Definition 10 (π-Pref Nets). *A possibilistic preference network (π-Pref net) over a set of variables V is a possibilistic network, i.e., a directed graph $\mathcal{G} = (\mathcal{V}, \mathcal{E})$, where each node A_i is associated with symbolic conditional possibility distributions. It encodes the ordering between values a_i and a_i' in $D(A_i)$ in each context p_i:*

- *If $a_i \prec a_i'$ then $\pi(a_i|p_i) = \alpha, \pi(a_i'|p_i) = \beta$ where α and β are non-instantiated weights on (0, 1] called symbolic weights, and $\alpha < \beta \leq 1$;*
- *If $a_i \sim a_i'$ then $\pi(a_i|p_i) = \pi(a_i'|p_i) = \alpha$ where $\alpha \leq 1$;*
- *$\forall p_i, \exists\ a_i \in D(A_i)$ such that $\pi(a_i|p_i) = 1$.*

In *addition* to the preferences encoded by a π-Pref net, *additional* a set $\mathcal{C}$ of equality or inequality constraints between symbolic weights can be taken into account. Such constraints may represent, for instance, the relative strength of preferences associated to different instantiations of parent variables of the same variable. The satisfaction value of each configuration is computed as the product of symbolic weights using the chain rule associated with product-based conditioning, namely $\pi(a_1, ..., a_N) = \prod_{i=1}^{N} \pi(a_i|p_i)$ where p_i is an instantiation of $Pa(A_i)$. In spite of the symbolic nature of expressions just obtained, one may still compare some configurations thanks to properties of product and constraints (e.g., $\alpha < 1$, $\alpha \times \beta < \alpha$, or, if $\beta < \gamma \in \mathcal{C}, \alpha \times \beta < \alpha \times \gamma$). Obviously, some expressions may remain incomparable, then only a partial order is obtained.

Example 7. Let Fig. 6 represent a π-Pref net over 3 variables $V = \{A, B, C\}$ and $\mathcal{C} = \{\delta_3 < \delta_1\}$ represent the set of constraints. Consider two configurations $ab\neg c$ and $\neg abc$. Using the chain rule, we obtain their corresponding symbolic joint possibility expressions: $\pi(ab\neg c) = 1 \times 1 \times \delta_1, \pi(\neg abc) = \alpha_1 \times 1 \times \delta_3$. Since $\delta_3 < \delta_1$, we can deduce that $ab\neg c \succ_{\pi Pref} \neg abc$. However, $ab\neg c \pm \neg ab\neg c$ since no constraint exists between δ_1 and α. These two configurations remain non compared.

Each configuration $\omega = a_1 ... a_N$ can be associated with a vector $\overrightarrow{\omega} = (\alpha_1, ..., \alpha_N)$, where $\alpha_i = \pi(a_i|p_i)$ and $p_i = \omega[Pa(A_i)]$, e.g., $\overrightarrow{\neg abc} = (\alpha, 1, \delta_3)$. Symbolic vectors can be equivalently compared by the symmetric Pareto ordering [3], which amounts to reordering them so as to exploit the constraints between weights as much as possible. The resulting partial order is indeed the same as the one obtained by the comparison of the product expressions.

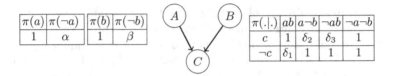

$\pi(a)$	$\pi(\neg a)$	$\pi(b)$	$\pi(\neg b)$
1	α	1	β

$\pi(.\|.)$	ab	$a\neg b$	$\neg ab$	$\neg a\neg b$
c	1	δ_2	δ_3	1
$\neg c$	δ_1	1	1	1

Fig. 6. An example of a π-Pref net

In π-Pref nets, it is clear that the best configurations are those having a joint possibility degree equal to 1, due to the normalization of conditional possibility distributions. We can always find an optimal configuration, starting from the root nodes where we choose each time the most or one of the most preferred value(s). At the end of the procedure, we get one or several configurations having a possibility equal to 1. This procedure is linear in the size of the network (using a forward sweep algorithm). Dominance queries are answered by comparing the symbolic vectors. The complexity of dominance queries is at worst $O(N!)$.

π-Pref nets may be considered as being halfway between qualitative and quantitative models. This is due to the use of symbolic weights. Indeed, π-Pref nets can be used in two ways: symbolically, or in an instantiated manner. The use of product, even in the symbolic case, adds a quantitative flavor. Moreover, symbolic possibilistic networks, using a logarithmic transformation, may be equivalently represented as symbolic OCF-nets [3]. Instantiated π-Pref nets and OCF-nets share the same type of (Markovian) independence, and lead exactly to the same orderings.

Lastly, a π-Pref net can be equivalently represented by a possibilistic logic base [3]. In [13], attempts at representing a CP-net ordering using a possibilistic logic framework are reported. But, it may not be possible to build an exact logical representation due to the particular behavior of CP-nets (see Sect. 2.1). [13] suggests that symmetric Pareto and leximin orderings respectively lower and upper bound the CP-net ordering. It may have counterparts in other graphical models based on the Markov property as OCF-nets.

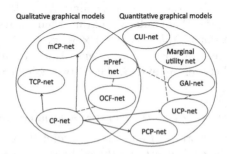

Fig. 7. Classification of preferential graphical models (continuous arrows point to extensions of CP-nets and dashed lines are discussed later in the section)

5   Discussion and Concluding Remarks

Figure 7 presents a classification of the preferential graphical models surveyed. Roughly speaking, there are three classes: qualitative, quantitative and models that are halfway. A summary of the main differences and similarities between the models is given below. These models can be further compared in terms of the underlying independence relation (and expressiveness), and the ease of elicitation. Regarding the first issue, we distinguish three situations: (i) *Ceteris Paribus* independence is shared by CP-nets, and its extensions. Models based on it are unable to express all possible orderings between configurations. UCP-nets can represent some total orderings, at the expense of constraints added on utilities; (ii) Generalized additive independence used in GAI-nets, is a weaker form of independence leading to an improved expressive power; (iii) Markov independence is used by π-Pref nets, OCF-nets and marginal utility nets. In contrast with GAI, this kind of independence does not allow mutual dependencies between variables due to the acyclicity constraint. *Ceteris Paribus* and Markov independence lead to different completion principles. With *Ceteris Paribus*, pairs of compared partial configurations are completed with the same instantiation of the rest of the variables, while with Markov-based nets, first we choose the best instantiation for all dependent variables, and next, instantiate the other variables in the same manner in all possible ways.

Properties	Model					
	CP-nets	TCP-nets	GAI-nets	UCP-nets	Marginal utility nets	π Pref-nets
Graphical component						
Node	Variable	Variable	Cliques	Variable	Variable	Variable
Edges	Directed	Directed	Undirected	Directed	Directed	Directed
Preference table	Conditional pref. relation on variables	Cond. pref. relation + Importance relation	Utility functions	Conditional utility distribution	Conditional utility distribution	Conditional symbolic possibility distributions
Independence relation	*Ceteris Paribus*	*Ceteris Paribus*	Generalized Additive	*Ceteris Paribus* + GAI	Markovian	Markovian
Ordering	Partial	Partial	Total	Total	Total	Partial/Total
Queries complexity						
Optimization	Linear	Linear	Exponential	Linear	Unknown	Linear
Dominance	NP-complete to PSPACE	Unknown	Linear	Linear	Unknown	Linear to O(N!)

Regarding elicitation, although quantitative models are convenient since providing total orderings, they are not easy to assess (any difference in values may lead to different orderings). In contrast, eliciting qualitative models is easier since it suffices to provide contextual preference ordering. π-Pref nets enable a progressive elicitation since we may add constraints between symbolic weights, or completely instantiate them.

Thanks to some resemblances between those models many transformations can be considered and are depicted by dashed lines in Fig. 7. UCP-nets are a restriction of GAI-nets and a generalization of CP-nets. Indeed, a UCP-net structure can be transformed into a junction tree such that for each clique we sum up the local utilities of the variables belonging to it, just leading to a GAI net. However, due to the acyclic restriction of UCP-nets and the necessary, commitment with *Ceteris Paribus*, not any GAI-net can be represented by a UCP-net. Besides, when handled symbolically, π-Pref nets and marginal utility nets lead to the same orderings. Indeed comparing configurations using product or addition makes no difference on symbolic weights. Transformation from π-Pref nets to GAI-nets might also be considered since, as for Bayesian nets, possibilistic nets can be translated into junction trees. However, an important difference between these two settings lies in the meaning of values. Both utilities and possibility degrees express levels of satisfaction, but the latter are bounded. In GAI-nets, what really matters is the difference between utilities. Thus, representing the same information in π-Pref nets is not possible; one may only try to induce the same qualitative order between the configurations. The opposite transformation requires two steps. First, translating utilities to possibility degrees. Second, moving from a junction tree to a possibilistic network. Such a procedure has never been studied in the literature.

As can be seen, the advantages of the different models are a matter of trade-off. One may prefer one or another depending on the level of information available, the expressiveness needed for the situation at hand, and the time available for eliciting preferences. From a computational viewpoint, UCP-nets, instantiated π-Pref nets and OCF-nets are the less demanding. On the other hand, elicitation and construction might be onerous for UCP-nets, GAI-nets and TCP-nets, while CP-nets and π-pref nets are easy to elicit. Getting a total order may also be considered as important. Thus, one may prefer models such as GAI-nets, OCF-nets and instantiated π-Pref nets in that respect.

References

1. Arnborg, S., Corneil, D.G., Proskurowski, A.: Complexity of finding embeddings in ak-tree. J. Algebr. Discret. Methods **8**(2), 277–284 (1987)
2. Amor, N.B., Benferhat, S.: Graphoid properties of qualitative possibilistic independence relations. Int. J. Uncertain. Fuzziness Knowl. Based Syst. **13**(1), 59–96 (2005)
3. Amor, N.B., Dubois, D., Gouider, H., Prade, H.: Possibilistic conditional preference networks. In: Siegel, P., Kruse, R. (eds.) ECSQARU 2015. LNCS, vol. 9161, pp. 36–46. Springer, Heidelberg (2015)
4. Boutilier, C., Bacchus, F., Brafman, R.I.: UCP-networks: a directed graphical representation of conditional utilities. In: Proceedings of UAI, pp. 56–64. Morgan Kaufmann Publishers Inc. (2001)
5. Boutilier, C., Brafman, R. I., Hoos, H., Poole, D.: Reasoning with conditional ceteris paribus preference statements. In: Proceedings of UAI, pp. 71–80 (1999)
6. Boutilier, C., Brafman, R., Domshlak, C., Hoos, H., Poole, D.: CP-nets: a tool for representing and reasoning with conditional ceteris paribus preference statements. J. Artif. Intell. Res. **21**, 135–191 (2004)

7. Brafman, R.I., Domshlak, C.: TCP-nets for preference-based product configuration. In: The Forth Workshop on Configuration (ECAI), pp. 101–106 (2002)
8. Brafman, R.I., Domshlak, C., Shimonyl, S.: On graphical modeling of preference and importance. J. Artif. Intell. Res. **25**, 389–424 (2006)
9. Brafman, R.I., Engel, Y.: Directional decomposition of multiattribute utility functions. In: Rossi, F., Tsoukias, A. (eds.) ADT 2009. LNCS, vol. 5783, pp. 192–202. Springer, Heidelberg (2009)
10. Brafman, R.I., Engel, Y.: Decomposed utility functions and graphical models for reasoning about preferences. In: Proceedings of 24th AAAI Conference on Artificial Intelligence, pp. 267–272 (2010)
11. Braziunas, D., Boutilier, C.: Local utility elicitation in GAI models. In: Proceedings of 21st Conference on Uncertainty in Artificial Intelligence, pp. 42–49 (2005)
12. Bigot, D., Zanuttini, B., H.F., Mengin, J.: Probabilistic conditional preference networks. In: Proceedings of 29th Conference on Uncertainty in Artificial Intelligence (2013)
13. Dubois, D., Prade, H., Touazi, F.: Conditional preference-nets, possibilistic logic, and the transitivity of priorities. In: Bramer, M., Petridis, M. (eds.) Research and Development in Intelligent Systems XXX, pp. 175–184. Springer, Switzerland (2013)
14. Eichhorn, C., Fey, M., Kern-Isberner, G.: CP-and OCF-networks-a comparison. Fuzzy Sets Syst. **298**, 109–127 (2016)
15. Engel, Y., Wellman, M.P.: CUI networks: a graphical representation for conditional utility independence. J. Artif. Intell. Res. **31**, 83–112 (2008)
16. Fishburn, P.C.: Utility theory for decision making. Technical report, DTIC Document (1970)
17. Goldsmith, J., Lang, J., Truszczynski, M., Wilson, N.: The computational complexity of dominance and consistency in CP-nets. J. Artif. Intell. Res. **33**, 403–432 (2008)
18. Gonzales, C., Perny, P.: GAI networks for utility elicitation. In: Proceedings of 9th International Conference on Principles of Knowledge Representation and Reasoning, pp. 224–234 (2004)
19. Gonzales, C., Perny, P.: GAI networks for decision making under certainty. In: IJCAI-Workshop on Advances in Preference Handling (2005)
20. Jensen, F.V., Lauritzen, S.L., Olesen, K.G.: Bayesian updating in causal probabilistic networks by local computations. Proc. Comput. Stat. Q. **4**, 269–282 (1990)
21. Kaci, S., Lang, J., Perny, P.: Représentation des préférences. In: Panorama de l'Intelligence Artificielle, vol. 1, pp. 181–214. Cépaduès éditions (2014)
22. Koriche, F., Zanuttini, B.: Learning conditional preference networks. Artif. Intell. **174**(11), 685–703 (2010)
23. Pearl, J.: Probabilistic Reasoning in Intelligent Systems: Networks of Plausible Inference. Morgan Kaufmann, California (1988)
24. Rossi, F., Venable, K., Walsh, T.: mCP-nets: representing and reasoning with preferences of multiple agents. In: Proceedings of 19th AAAI National Conference on Artificial Intelligence, pp. 729–734 (2004)

Diffusion of Opinion and Influence

Laurence Cholvy[(✉)]

ONERA, Toulouse, France
laurence.cholvy@onera.fr

Abstract. In this paper, we present a formal model of opinion diffusion among agents which influence each other. Opinions are modelled as propositional formulas or equivalently, as sets of logical interpretations, which allows us to express some kind of uncertainty. Any agent changes its opinion by merging the opinions of its influencers, from the most influential one to the least one. Then we generalize this model by taking topics of opinion into account.

1 Introduction

Understanding the dynamics of opinion among agents is an important question which has recently received large attention in the community of autonomous agents and multi-agent systems [1,2,4–6,10–12]. This question depends on several parameters.

The first important parameter is the population of agents. This population may be unstructured, in such a case, agents interact randomly [1,8]. But generally, some relations exist between agents. The population of agents may be divided in communities modelling neighborhood relations between agents [2,4,7]. The population may also be structured via an influence relation which relates two agents, the opinion of one of these agents being influenced by the opinion of the other [11]. Graphs are widely used to model the structured population: nodes are agents and links are the relations between agents. Links are symmetrical or not, depending on the type of relations and they may also be labelled with probabilities [13].

The second parameter is the model of opinion. Here again, several options exist. Most of the works previously cited consider only one opinion and model it as a real number in $[0, 1]$. For instance, if the question is to evaluate the opinion of people about the fact that Canada will host the Winter Olympics in 2026, then an opinion which is close to 1 means that the agent is quite confident in Canada candidature or that according to this agent, the probability that Canada will host the Olympics is high. An opinion which is close to 0 means that the agent thinks that Canada candidature will be rejected or that according to this agent, the probability that Canada will host the Olympics is low. Some other works are based on formal logic and model opinions as propositional formulas or, more precisely, as the sets of their models. In [6], an opinion is a single interpretation, called ballot. For instance, an agent whose opinion is $CAN\_2026 \wedge acroski$, thinks that Canada should organize the Winter Olympics in 2026 and that there should be acroski trials. Another agent whose opinion is $\neg CAN\_2026 \wedge acroski$, thinks

© Springer International Publishing Switzerland 2016
S. Schockaert and P. Senellart (Eds.): SUM 2016, LNAI 9858, pp. 112–125, 2016.
DOI: 10.1007/978-3-319-45856-4_8

that 2026 Winter Games should not be hosted by Canada but there should be acroski trials. More generally, [10] considers that an opinion is any propositional formula, thus modelled by a set of interpretations which is not necessarily a singleton. For instance, an agent opinion is $(CAN\_2026 \lor Norway\_2026) \land acroski$ if it thinks that the 2026 Winter Olympics will be hosted by Canada or by Norway and that there will be acroski trials.

The last parameter is the model of opinion dynamics. Many works in the field of opinion dynamics in multi-agent systems are based on a theory introduced in the field of Social Psychology called *Social Judgment Theory (SJT)*. The basic idea of *SJT* is that individual opinion changing is a judgmental process: if an agent considers that a presented opinion is close to its current opinion, then it is likely to shift in the direction of this opinion (*assimilation*); if it considers that the presented opinion is distant to its current opinion, then it is likely to shift away from this opinion (*contrast*); otherwise, the agent does not change its opinion (*non-commitment*). This general idea has led to different formal models [1,5,8] in which the thresholds agents use to characterize what are close and distant opinions are identical or not, universal or agent dependent. Some other works, like [11], are based on the theory of *motivated cognition*, defined in Cognitive Psychology, and which also says that agents are skeptical of another agent when their opinions diverge, but are more receptive to persuasion when their opinions better align. Some other works in the field of diffusion in multi agent systems claim to be based on models provided by the Network Science community. For instance, [2] is based on the *SIR model* which says that the value of an agent's feature evolves according to the values of its neighbors feature values. For instance an agent is infected if one of its neighbor is. Or an agent may say that it believes something if its neighbors said that they also do.

In the present paper, we extend a work presented recently in a short paper [3]. We model opinions by propositional formulas. As a consequence, some kind of uncertainty may be expressed: $(CAN\_2026 \lor Norway\_2026) \land acroski$ is an uncertain opinion because of the disjunctive term: the agent does not know exactly who, between Canada and Norway, will host the games. We also assume that the population of agents is structured by a binary relation of influence which relates two agents when one influences the other. In a first step, we assume that any agent orders its influencers (i.e. agents which influence it) according to the strength of the influence relation. Then, any agent changes its opinion by merging the opinions of its influencers (who may be contradictory) from the most influential one to the least. In a second step, we consider that agents order their influencers according to the topics of opinions. Then, any agent changes its opinions by merging the opinions of its influencers, topic by topic. This will allow us to model the fact that, when forming your opinion, you are influenced more by your friend *Paul* than by your friend *Mary* about *winter sport events* but you are influenced more by *Mary* than by *Paul* about *literature*. Moreover, the merging operator used by any agent in both cases, takes into account some consistent formula (called *integrity constraint*) which expresses something true in the world.

This paper is organized as follows. Section 2 presents the notion of Importance-Based Merging Operators and provides some original properties of these operators. Section 3 presents the notion of Influence-Based Belief Revision Games (IBRG) used to model opinion diffusion. Section 4 presents some properties of (IBRG). Section 5 extends (IBRG) so that influencers may be ordered according to several orders of influence, depending on the topics of opinions. It also studies some of their properties. Finally, Sect. 6 presents some perspectives.

2   Importance-Based Merging Operators

Consider a finite propositional language L. If φ is a formula of L, $Mod(\varphi)$ denotes the set of models of φ i.e., the set of interpretations in which φ is true. A multi-set of formulas $\{\varphi_1, ..., \varphi_n\}$ equipped with a total order $\prec$ s.t. $\varphi_i \prec \varphi_{i+1}$ ($i = 1...n - 1$) is called *an ordered multi-set of formulas* and denoted $\varphi_1 \prec ... \prec \varphi_n$.

Definition 1 (Importance-Based Merging Operator). *An Importance-Based Merging Operator is a function Δ which associates a formula μ and a non empty ordered multi-set of consistent formulas $\varphi_1 \prec ... \prec \varphi_n$ with a formula denoted $\Delta_\mu(\varphi_1 \prec ... \prec \varphi_n)$ so that: $Mod(\Delta_\mu(\varphi_1 \prec ... \prec \varphi_n)) = Min_{\leq_{d,\varphi_1 \prec ... \prec \varphi_n}} Mod(\mu)$ with:*

- *$w \leq_{d,\varphi_1 \prec ... \prec \varphi_n} w'$ iff*
  $[D(w, \varphi_1), ..., D(w, \varphi_n)] \leq_{lex} [D(w', \varphi_1), ..., D(w', \varphi_n)]$
- *$[D(w, \varphi_1), ..., D(w, \varphi_n)]$ is a vector whose k^{th} element is $D(w, \varphi_k)$*
- *$D(w, \varphi) = min_{w' \in Mod(\varphi)} d(w, w')$, w and w' being two interpretations and d is a pseudo-distance[1] between interpretations.*
- *$\leq_{lex}$ is a lexicographic comparison of vectors of reals defined by: $[v_1, ...v_n] \leq_{lex} [v'_1, ...v'_n]$ iff (i) $\forall k\ v_k = v'_k$ or (ii) $\exists k\ v_k < v'_k$ and $\forall j < k\ v_j = v'_j$.*

Some simple distances d which can be used for instanciating the previous definition are: d_D, the drastic distance, ($d_D(w, w') = 0$ iff $w = w'$, 1 otherwise); d_H, the Hamming distance ($d_H(w, w') = m$ iff w and w' differ on m variables).

Example 1. Let μ be a tautology. $\varphi_1 = a \vee b$, $\varphi_2 = \neg a$, $\varphi_3 = \neg b \wedge c$. The eight interpretations[2] are $w_1 = (a, b, c)$, $w_2 = (a, b, \neg c)$, $w_3 = (a, \neg b, c)$, $w_4 = (a, \neg b, \neg c)$, $w_5 = (\neg a, b, c)$, $w_6 = (\neg a, b, \neg c)$, $w_7(\neg a, \neg b, c)$, $w_8 = (\neg a, \neg b, \neg c)$, and $Mod(\Delta_\mu(\varphi_1 \prec \varphi_2 \prec \varphi_3)) = Min_{\leq_{d, a \vee b \prec \neg a \prec \neg b \wedge c}}(\{w_1, ...w_8\})$. With $d = d_H$ we get: $Mod(\Delta_\mu(\varphi_1 \prec \varphi_2 \prec \varphi_3)) = \{w_5\}$ thus $\Delta_\mu(\varphi_1 \prec \varphi_2 \prec \varphi_3)) = \neg a \wedge b \wedge c$. With $d = d_D$ we get: $Mod(\Delta_\mu(\varphi_1 \prec \varphi_2 \prec \varphi_3)) = \{w_5, w_6\}$ thus $\Delta_\mu(\varphi_1 \prec \varphi_2 \prec \varphi_3)) = \neg a \wedge b$.

Let's now consider the postulates that merging operators should satisfy according to [9]. We reformulate them within our context where formulas to be merged are ordered and we check whether Importance-Based Merging Operators satisfy them or not.

---

[1] $\forall w \forall w'\ d(w, w') = d(w', w)$ and $d(w, w') = 0 \implies w = w'$.

[2] By convention, a propositional letter is positive in an interpretation if it is satisfied, negative if it is not satisfied.

Proposition 1. [3] *All the postulates but* **(IC4)** *are satisfied by Importance-Based Merging Operators, i.e.*

- **(IC0)** $\Delta_\mu(\varphi_1 \prec ... \prec \varphi_n) \models \mu$
- **(IC1)** *If* μ *is consistent then* $\Delta_\mu(\varphi_1 \prec ... \prec \varphi_n)$ *is consistent*
- **(IC2)** *If* $\bigwedge_{i=1}^{n} \varphi_i \wedge \mu$ *is consistent then* $\models \Delta_\mu(\varphi_1 \prec ... \prec \varphi_n) \leftrightarrow \bigwedge_{i=1}^{n} \varphi_i \wedge \mu$
- **(IC3)** *If* $\models \mu \leftrightarrow \mu'$ *and* $\forall i = 1...n,$ $\models \varphi_i \leftrightarrow \varphi_i'$ *then* $\models \Delta_\mu(\varphi_1 \prec ... \prec \varphi_n) \leftrightarrow \Delta_{\mu'}(\varphi_1' \prec ... \prec \varphi_n')$
- **(IC4)** *is not satisfied i.e. it is not necessarly the case that if* $\varphi_1 \models \mu$ *and* $\varphi_2 \models \mu$ *then* $\Delta_\mu(\varphi_1 \prec \varphi_2) \wedge \varphi_1$ *is consistent if f* $\Delta_\mu(\varphi_1 \prec \varphi_2) \wedge \varphi_2$ *is consistent*
- **(IC5)** $\Delta_\mu(\varphi_1 \prec ... \prec \varphi_n) \wedge \Delta_\mu(\varphi_{n+1} \prec ... \prec \varphi_m) \models \Delta_\mu(\varphi_1 \prec ... \prec \varphi_m)$
- **(IC6)** *If* $\Delta_\mu(\varphi_1 \prec ... \prec \varphi_n) \wedge \Delta_\mu(\varphi_{n+1} \prec ... \prec \varphi_m)$ *is consistent then* $\Delta_\mu(\varphi_1 \prec ... \prec \varphi_m) \models \Delta_\mu(\varphi_1 \prec ... \prec \varphi_n) \wedge \Delta_\mu(\varphi_{n+1} \prec ... \prec \varphi_m)$
- **(IC7)** $\Delta_\mu(\varphi_1 \prec ... \prec \varphi_n) \wedge \mu' \models \Delta_{\mu \wedge \mu'}(\varphi_1 \prec ... \prec \varphi_n)$
- **(IC8)** *If* $\Delta_{\mu_1}(\varphi_1 \prec ... \prec \varphi_n) \wedge \mu_2$ *is consistent then* $\Delta_{\mu_1 \wedge \mu_2}(\varphi_1 \prec ... \prec \varphi_n) \models \Delta_{\mu_1}(\varphi_1 \prec ... \prec \varphi_n)$

We can also prove the following:

Proposition 2.

$$Mod(\Delta_\mu(\varphi_1 \prec ... \varphi_j ... \prec \varphi_n)) = Mod(\Delta_\mu(\varphi_1 \prec ... \Delta_\mu(\varphi_1 \prec ... \prec \varphi_n) ... \prec \varphi_n))$$

This means that the result of merging different formulas with Δ_μ, does not change when one formula, whatever its strength, is replaced by the merged formula. This property is called *ballot-monotonicity* in [6].

3   Influence-Based Belief Revision Games (IBRG)

In the following, we present the notions of Influence-Based Belief Revision Games and Influence-Based Belief Sequences which are adapted from [10].

Definition 2 (Influence-Based Belief Revision Game). *An Influence-Based Belief Revision Game (IBRG) is a quadruplet* $G = (A, \mu, B, Inf)$ *where:*

- $A = \{1, ..., n\}$ *is a finite set of agents.*
- μ *is a consistent formula of* L.
- B *is a function which associates any agent* i *of* A *with a consistent formula of* L *denoted for short* B_i *such that* $B_i \models \mu$.
- Inf *is a function which associates any agent* i *of* A *with a non-empty set of agents* $\{i_1, ... i_{n_i}\}$ *equipped with a total order* $\prec_i$ *s.t.* $i_k \prec_i i_{k+1}$ *for* $i = 1...(n_i - 1)$. *For short, we denote* $Inf(i) = \{i_1 \prec_i ... \prec_i i_{n_i}\}$.

A is the finite set of agents. The formula μ represents the information which is true in the world. It is called *integrity constraint*. For any agent i, the formula B_i represents its initial beliefs. It is called the *initial belief state of* i. We assume that agents are rational and thus that B_i is consistent and satisfies the integrity

---

[3] Proofs are omitted due to paper length limitation.

constraint μ. For any agent i, $Inf(i)$ is the non-empty set of agents i considers as influent i.e., i considers that its own opinion is influenced by the opinions of agents in $Inf(i)$. With the total order $\prec_i$, i ranks these influential agents according to their degree of influence: for any agents j and k in $Inf(i)$, $j \prec_i k$ means that, according to i, it own opinion is more influenced by j's opinion than by k's opinion. Notice that $Inf(i) = \{i\}$ is allowed and represents the fact that agent i is not influenced by some other agent but itself.

Definition 3 (Influence-Based Belief Sequence). *Consider $G = (A, \mu, B, Inf)$ and $i \in A$ with $Inf(i) = \{i_1 \prec_i ... \prec_i i_{n_i}\}$. The Influence-Based Belief Sequence of i, denoted $(B_i^s)_{s \in \mathbb{N}}$, is defined by:*

(i) $B_i^0 = B_i$
(ii) $\forall s \in \mathbb{N}$, $B_i^{s+1} = \Delta_\mu(B_{i_1}^s \prec ... \prec B_{i_{n_i}}^s)$

The Influence-Based Belief Sequence (or Belief Sequence for short) of agent i, $(B_i^s)_{s \in \mathbb{N}}$, represents i's belief state all along the game: B_i^0 is the initial belief state of i; B_i^s is the belief state of i after s moves i.e., the opinion of i after s steps. The evolution of i's opinion is done according to the importance-Based merging operator Δ_μ: i's opinion at step s is the result of Δ_μ applied to the ordered multi-set of opinions: $B_{i_1}^s \prec ... \prec B_{i_{n_i}}^s$.

The definition of (IBRG) is inspired by the definition of Belief Revision Games (BRG), given in [10], which is generic: each agent is associated with a generic revision policy R_i which defines how an agent's opinion evolves according to its acquaintance opinions. In (IBRG), the set of agents which influence a given agent i, $Inf(i)$, (which corresponds to the acquaintances of i in (BRG)) is equipped with a total order expressing the relative strength of influence of these agents. The definition of Influence-Based Belief Sequence shows that opinions evolve according to this order. Thus, an (IBRG) can be seen as an instantiation of a (BRG) in which acquaintances are ordered according to their influence and in which the opinion revision operator is based on this influence order. Notice also that, like (BRG), (IBRG) offers the possibility of expressing integrity constraints. This allows to consider that opinions and their evolution are constrained by information which are true in the world and that agents are rational. For instance, if $a \rightarrow b$ is the integrity constraint, any agent who believes a also believes b. In particular, any agent who revises its opinion with a will also believe b. It is important to notice that i may belong to $Inf(i)$ i.e., we do not require that i's opinion is only influenced by other agents opinion: i may take it own opinion into account in the process of opinion changing. Consequently, i may rank itself in $Inf(i)$. For instance, $i \prec_i j$, for any $j \in Inf(i)$ and $j \neq i$ when i considers that, even if it is influenced by other influential agents, its own opinion will only be strengthened by their opinions. At the opposite, $j \prec_i i$, for any $j \in Inf(i)$ and $j \neq i$ when i is keen to modify its opinion according to the influential agent opinions.

Proposition 3. *In an (IBRG), the belief sequence of any agent is cyclic i.e., the belief sequence of any agent i is characterized by an initial segment $B_i^0...B_i^{b-1}$ and a belief cycle $B_i^b...B_i^e$ which will be repeated ad infinitum.*

If the belief cycle of the belief sequence of i is $B_i^b...B_i^e$, then the size of the cycle is defined by: $\mid Cyc(B_i) \mid = e - b + 1$.

Example 2. Consider the (IBRG) $G = (A, \mu, B, Inf)$ with: $A = \{1, 2, 3\}$. μ is a tautology. $B_1 = a \vee b$, $B_2 = \neg a \wedge \neg b$, $B_3 = a \vee \neg a$. $Inf_1 = \{1\}$, $Inf_2 = \{2 \prec_2 1\}$, $Inf_3 = \{1 \prec_3 2\}$. The three agents are called $1, 2, 3$. Agent 1 is its own and only influential agent. Agent 2 is influenced by 1 and by itself, but more influenced by itself than by 1. Agent 3 is influenced by 1 and by 2, 1 being the agent who influences it the most. 1 initially believes $a \vee b$, 2 initially believes $\neg a \wedge \neg b$, and 3 has initially no opinion. Table 1 shows the evolution of agent opinions when the distance used is d_H. Agent 1 is not influenced by anyone except itself, so its opinion remains $a \vee b$. Agent 2 is keen to change its opinion by integrating opinion of 1 if possible. But here, 2 has a complete opinion which is inconsistent with 1's opinion. Consequently, 2's opinion remains $\neg a \wedge \neg b$. Finally, 3 who had intially no opinion, is keen to form its own opinion by integrating 1's opinion and 2's opinion by giving preference to the first one. Here it gets: $(a \wedge \neg b) \vee (b \wedge \neg a)$ Here, $\mid Cyc(B_1) \mid = \mid Cyc(B_2) \mid = \mid Cyc(B_3) \mid = 1$.

Table 1. Opinion evolution in Example 2

	$s = 0$	$s \geq 1$
$i = 1$	$a \vee b$	$a \vee b$
$i = 2$	$\neg a \wedge \neg b$	$\neg a \wedge \neg b$
$i = 3$	$a \vee \neg a$	$(a \wedge \neg b) \vee (b \wedge \neg a)$

The following example shows a case where lengths of cycles are greater than 1.

Example 3. Consider $G = (A, \mu, B, Inf)$ with: $A = \{1, 2\}$, μ being a tautology, $Inf_1 = \{2\}$, $Inf_2 = \{1\}$, $B_1 = a$, $B_2 = \neg a$. G represents a network of two agents each one being influenced by the other one only. Agent 1 initially believes a and agent 2 initially believes $\neg a$. Assume that μ is a tautology. Table 2 shows the evolution of opinions (for distance d_H and d_D as well). By definition, agent 1 adopts 2's opinion and agent 2 adopts 1's opinion in the same time. Since their initial opinions contradict, the agents change opinion recursively. Here, $\mid Cyc(B_1) \mid = \mid Cyc(B_2) \mid = 2$.

Table 2. Opinion evolution in Example 3

	$s = 0$	$s = 1$	$s = 0 \bmod 2$	$s = 1 \bmod 2$
$i = 1$	a	$\neg a$	a	$\neg a$
$i = 2$	$\neg a$	a	$\neg a$	a

Finally, let us introduce three more definitions on (IBRG) which will be useful for the next section. The following adapts the definition provided in [6] and defines some type of IBRG in which only some particular loops are permitted in the relation of influence.

Definition 4 (DAG with Self-loops). *From $G = (A, \mu, B, Inf)$, we can build a graph whose nodes are agents of A and edges are $i \to j$ iff $i \in Inf(j)$. We say that G is a DAG with self-loops if this graph is a directed graph where the only permitted cycles are of type $i \to i$.*

The following definition introduces *dogmatic agents*. An agent is dogmatic when it is not influenced by other agents. As a consequence, a dogmatic agent i will never change its opinion i.e., $\forall s \geq 0$ $B_i^s = B_i^0$.

Definition 5 (Dogmatic Agent). *Consider the (IBRG) $G = (A, \mu, B, Inf)$ and $i \in A$. i is a dogmatic agent iff $Inf(i) = \{i\}$.*

The next definition introduces the notion of *sphere of influence*.

Definition 6 (Sphere of Influence of an Agent). *Let $G = (A, \mu, B, Inf)$ and $i \in A$. $Sphere(i) = \{j : Inf(j) = \{i \prec ...\}\} \cup \{j_k : \exists j_0...j_{k-1} \ \forall m = 1...(k-1) \ Inf(j_m) = \{j_{m-1} \prec ...\} \ and \ j_0 = i\}$.*

The sphere of influence of an agent is thus defined as the set of agents which are directly or indirectly mostly influenced by i. Notice that i may belong to $Sphere(i)$. For instance in Example 2 and in Example 4, $1 \in Sphere(1)$.

Finally, we introduce the notion of *leader*.

Definition 7 (Leader). *Let $G = (A, \mu, B, Inf)$ an IBRG. Consider $i \in A$ and $S \subseteq A$. i is the leader of S iff i is dogmatic and $S \subseteq Sphere(i)$.*

I.e., for being the leader of a set of agents S, an agent i must not be influenced by no other agent and any agent of S must be directly or indirectly mostly influenced by i.

4   Properties of IBRG

In this section, we consider some properties, many of them being introduced in [10], and we check whether (IBRG) satisfy them or not.

Proposition 4. *Let $G = (A, \mu, B, Inf)$ be an (IBRG). Then, $\forall i \in A \ \forall s \in \mathbb{N} \ B_i^s \models \mu$.*

This proposition shows that agents take integrity constraints into account to revise their opinion.

Proposition 5. *Let $G = (A, \mu, B, Inf)$ be an (IBRG). Then, $\forall i \in A \ \forall s \in \mathbb{N}$ B_i^s is consistent.*

This property corresponds to the property of (BRG) called *Consistency Preservation* (**CP**) defined in [10] as: $\forall i \in A$, *if* B_i *is consistent then* $\forall s \in \mathbb{N}$ B_i^s *is consistent*. In the case of (IBRG), the premisse is omitted because the initial belief states are consistent.

Proposition 6. *Let* $G = (A, \mu, B, Inf)$ *be an (IBRG) and a consistent formula* φ *of L. Then, if* $\forall i \in A, \varphi \models B_i$ *then* $\forall i \in A$ $\forall s \in \mathbb{N}, \varphi \models B_i^s$.

This proves that (IBRG) satisfy the property called *Agreement Preservation* (**AP**) defined in [10]: if all agents initially agrees on some alternatives then they will not change their mind about them.

Proposition 7. *Let* $G = (A, \mu, B, Inf)$ *be an (IBRG) and let* φ *be a formula of L. Then, if* $\forall i \in A$, $B_i \models \varphi$ *then* $\forall i \in A, \forall s \in \mathbb{N}$, $B_i^s \models \varphi$.

This proposition proves that (IBRG) satisfy the property called *Unanimity Preservation* (**UP**) defined in [10]: every formula which is a logical consequence of the initial belief states remains so after opinion diffusion. I.e, any opinion initially shared by the agents remains so after opinion diffusion.

The property of *Responsiveness* (**Resp**) introduced in [10] states that an agent should take into account the opinions of the agents who influence it whenever (i) its beliefs are inconsistent with the beliefs of its acquaintances (but itself) and (ii) its acquaintances (but itself) agree on some alternatives. It is adapted here as follows:

Definition 8 (Resp). $G = (A, \mu, B, Inf)$ *satisfies* (**Resp**) *iff* $\forall i \in A$ $\forall s \in \mathbb{N}$, *if* $\forall j \in Inf(i) \setminus \{i\}$ $B_j^s \wedge B_i^s$ *is inconsistent and if* $\wedge_{j \in Inf(i) \setminus \{i\}} B_j^s$ *is consistent, then* $B_i^{s+1} \not\models B_i^s$.

(**Resp**) is not necessarily satisfied in (IBRG). As a counterexample, consider an (IBRG) in which $A = \{1, 2, 3\}$, $Inf(1) = \{1\}$, $Inf(2) = \{2\}$, $Inf(3) = \{3 \prec 1 \prec 2\}$, $B_1 = a \wedge b$, $B_2 = a$, $B_3 = \neg a$ and μ is a tautology. Then $\forall s \geq 1$, $B_3^s = \neg a \wedge b$. Consequently, $B_3^s \models B_3$.

Let us now focus on the property of *Convergence* (**Conv**) introduced in [10] and in [6] as well, which states that there is a step in the game when all opinions stop evolving.

Definition 9 (Conv). *An (IBRG)* $G = (A, \mu, B, Inf)$ *satisfies (**Conv**) iff* $\forall i \in A$ $| Cyc(B_i) | = 1$.

Some (IBRG) satisfy (**Conv**) and some don't. In example 2, G converges: the stable opinions of 1, 2 and 3 are respectively $a \wedge b$, $\neg a \wedge b$ and $a \wedge b$. In example 5, G does not converge. The following proposition identifies a case where IBRG converge.

Proposition 8. *DAG with self-loops satisfy (**Conv**).*

Let us finally consider the property of *Acceptability* given in [10]. We extend it for (IBRG) as follows:

Definition 10 (Acceptability). *Let* $G = (A, \mu, B, Inf)$ *be an (IBRG) and* φ *a formula of L.* φ *is accepted by agent* i *of* A *iff for all* $B_i^s \in Cyc(B_i)$, *we have* $B_i^s \models \varphi$. φ *is unanimously accepted in* G *iff* φ *is accepted by all* i *in* A. φ *is majoritary accepted if the number of agents who accept it is strictly greater than the number of agents who do not.*

In Example 3, for instance, a is majoritary accepted and b is unanimously accepted. The following proposition identifies cases in which an IBRG satisfies Acceptability.

Proposition 9. *Let* G *be an IBRG and* i *the leader of a set of agents* S. *Then* B_i *is accepted by any agent in* S.

This means that the opinion of the leader of a group is accepted by any agent in this group.

Proposition 10. *Let* G *be an IBRG and* i *a dogmatic agent. Then:*
   (i) If $Sphere(i) = A$ *then* B_i *is unanimously accepted.*
   (ii) If $| Sphere(i) | > \frac{|A|}{2}$ *then* B_i *is majoritary accepted.*

Obviously, if a dogmatic agent is the most infuential one for any agent in the population, then its opinion is unanimously accepted. If a dogmatic agent is the most infuential one for more than a half population, then its opinion is majoritary accepted.

5   Taking Topics into Account

In this section, we extend (IBRG) in order to take topics of opinions into account.

5.1   Topics

Definition 11 (Topics). *Topics* $T_1, ..., T_m$ *of L are sets of propositional literals[4] of L so that: (i) any literal of L belongs to a topic; (ii) for any proposition letter* p *of L, for any topic* T_i *in* $\{T_1, ... T_n\}$, *we have:* $p \in T_i \iff \neg p \in T_i$.

Definition 12 (Topic Compatible Orders). *Consider* m *topics* $T_1 ... T_m$ *and* n *formulas* $\{\varphi_1 ... \varphi_n\}$. *Let* $\prec_1 .... \prec_m$ *be* m *total orders on* $\{\varphi_1 ... \varphi_n\}$. *We say that* $\prec_1 .... \prec_m$ *are topic-compatible iff for any two topics* T_i *and* T_j, *if* $T_i \cap T_j \neq \emptyset$ *then* $\prec_i$ *and* $\prec_j$ *are identical.*

---

[4] A literal is a propositional letter or the negation of a propositional letter.

According to this definition, if an agent is preferred to another one regarding a topic then it is also preferred to this one regarding any topic which is not disjoint. For instance, consider the two topics *skiing* and *ballets* (i.e. choreographic disciplines). They are not disjoint because *acroski* is a kind of skiing with a choreography. Consider two agents *Paul* and *Mary* providing information related to these topics. If you assume that *Paul* influences you strictly more than *Mary* regarding *skiing* and that *Mary* influences you strictly more than *Paul* regarding *ballets*, then you can conclude that, regarding *acroski*, *Paul* influences you strictly more than *Mary* and *Mary* influences you strictly more tha *Paul*, which is nonsense. In the same way, according to Definition 12, if an agent is preferred to another one regarding a topic, then it is also preferred to this one regarding any sub-topic (topic which is included in it) or any super-topic (topic which includes it). For instance, consider the two topics *winter sports* and *skiing*. The latter is included in the former. Consider two agents *Paul* and *Mary* providing information related to *winter sports*. It is not realistic to assume that *Paul* influences you strictly more than *Mary* regarding *winter sports* and that *Mary* influences you strictly more than *Paul* regarding *skiing* since *skiing* is a special case of *winter sport*.

5.2   Topic-Dependent Importance Based Merging Operators

We now extend the notion of Importance-Based Merging Operator for taking topics into account. Before, we introduce the following:

Definition 13. *Let* φ *a formula and* T_i *a topic.* $\prod_i \varphi$ *is the formula defined by:* $Mod(\prod_i \varphi) = \{w \cap T_i : w \in Mod(\varphi)\}$.

Definition 14 (Topic-Dependent Importance-Based Merging Operator). *A topic dependent Importance-Based Merging Operator, is a function* Θ *which, given a formula* μ, *given a multi-set of consistent formulas of* L *and* m *topic-compatible orders on this multi-set denoted* $\prec_1 \ldots \prec_m$, *produces a formula denoted* $\Theta_\mu(\prec_1 \ldots \prec_m)$ *so that:*

$$Mod(\Theta_\mu(\prec_1 \ldots \prec_m)) = \bigoplus_{i=1\ldots m} Mod(\Delta_{\prod_i \mu}(\prec_i))$$

with

- Δ *an importance-based merging operator as defined in Definition 1.*
- $\bigoplus_{i=1\ldots m} M_i = \{w : w \in Mod(\mu) \text{ and } \forall i \ w \cap T_i \in M_i\}$ *if not empty;* $\bigoplus_{i=1\ldots m} M_i = Mod(\mu)$ *else.*

Θ first merges formulas topic by topic and computes $Mod(\Delta_{\prod_i \mu}(\prec_i))$. Then it agregates the results with operator $\bigoplus$. This agregation operator aims to select models of μ whose projections on all topics are results of independent mergings (i.e., belong to $Mod(\Delta_{\prod_i \mu}(\prec_i))$). But it may happen that no model of μ satisfies this condition, even if each initial formula satisfies μ as shown in Example 4. In such a case, the operator selects all the models of μ i.e., the merging is vacuous and the resulting formula is nothing else than μ. Notice that, when μ is consistent, $Mod(\Delta_\mu(\prec_1 \ldots \prec_m))$ is not empty.

Example 4. Consider a language with two letters a, b and two topics: $T_1 = \{a, \neg a\}$, $T_2 = \{b, \neg b\}$. Consider $\varphi_1 = a \wedge b$ and $\varphi_2 = \neg a \wedge \neg b$ and $\mu = a \rightarrow b$. Notice that $\varphi_1 \models \mu$ and $\varphi_2 \models \mu$. Consider two orders, $\{\varphi_1 \prec_{T_1} \varphi_2, \varphi_2 \prec_{T_2} \varphi_1\}$. Then $Mod(\Delta_{\prod_{T_1} \mu}(\prec_{T_1})) = \{\{a\}\}$ and $Mod((\Delta_{\prod_{T_2} \mu}(\prec_{T_2}) = \{\{\neg b\}\}$. But $\{a, \neg b\} \notin Mod(\mu)$. In this case $Mod(\Theta_\mu(\prec_{T_1} \prec_{T_2}) = Mod(\mu)$ i.e., $\Theta_\mu(\prec_{T_1} \prec_{T_2}) = a \rightarrow b$.

Notice that Definition 1 is a special case of Definition 14 i.e., if there is only one topic and only one order on a multi-set of formulas, then $\Theta_\mu(\prec)$ as defined in Definition 14 is identical to $\Delta_\mu(\prec)$ as defined in Definition 1.

Again, we consider the different postulates that merging operators should satisfy according to [9]. Here, we focus on the first four, we reformulate them within our context where we have several orders in parameters and we check whether Topic-dependent Importance-Based Merging Operators satisfy them or not. Results are shown below.

Proposition 11. *Topic-dependent Importance-Based Merging Operators satisfy postulates* **(IC0)-(IC3)** *and do not satisfy postulate* **(IC4)** *i.e.*

- **(IC0)** $\Theta_\mu(\prec_1 ... \prec_m) \models \mu$
- **(IC1)** *If μ is consistent then $\Theta_\mu(\prec_1 ... \prec_m)$ is consistent*
- **(IC2)** *If $\bigwedge_{i=1}^{n} \varphi_i \wedge \mu$ is consistent then $\models \Theta_\mu(\prec_1 ... \prec_m) \leftrightarrow \bigwedge_{i=1}^{n} \varphi_i \wedge \mu$*
- **(IC3)** *If $\models \mu \leftrightarrow \mu'$ and $\forall i = 1...n$, $\models \varphi_i \leftrightarrow \varphi_i'$ then $\models \Theta_\mu(\varphi_1 \prec ... \prec \varphi_n) \leftrightarrow \Theta_{\mu'}(\varphi_1' \prec ... \prec \varphi_n')$*
- **(IC4)** *is not satisfied i.e. it is not necessarly the case that if $\varphi_1 \models \mu$ and $\varphi_2 \models \mu$ then $\Theta_\mu(\prec_1 ... \prec_m) \wedge \varphi_1$ is consistent iff $\Theta_\mu(\prec_1 ... \prec_m) \wedge \varphi_2$ is consistent (each $\prec_k$ being an order on $\{\varphi_1, \varphi_2\}$).*

5.3 Topic-Dependent Influence-Based Belief Revision Game (TIBRG)

Let us here extend the notion of Influence-Based Belief Revision Game to take topics into account.

Definition 15 (Topic-Dependent Influence-Based Belief Revision Game). *A Topic dependent Influence-Based Belief Revision Game (TIBRG) is a quadruplet $G = (A, \mu, B, Inf)$ where:*

- *$A = \{1, ..., n\}$ is a finite set of agents.*
- *μ is a consistent formula of L.*
- *B is a function which associates any agent i of A with a consistent formula of L denoted B_i such that $B_i \models \mu$.*
- *For any agent i of A, $Inf(i) = \{\prec_1, ..., \prec_m\}$ where $\prec_1, ... \prec_m$ are m total topic-compatible orders on a single set of agents $\{i_{i_1}...i_{n_i}\}$.*

A, μ, B_i are defined as before. $Inf(i)$ is here defined by m orders on the set of i's influencers. Each order corresponds to a topic. Given a topic T_k and $\prec_k \in Inf(i)$, $i_1 \prec_k i_2$ means that i's opinion is more influenced by i_1's opinion than by i_2's opinion regarding the topic T_k.

Definition 16 (Topic-Dependent Influence-Based Belief Sequence). *Consider a (TIBRG) $G = (A, \mu, B, Inf)$. Let $i \in A$ with $Inf(i) = \{\prec_1, \dots \prec_m\}$ m orders on the set $\{i_{i_1} \dots i_{n_i}\}$. The Topic-dependent Influence-Based Belief Sequence of i, denoted $(B_i^s)_{s \in \mathbb{N}}$, is defined as follows:*

- *$B_i^0 = B_i$*
- *$\forall s \in \mathbb{N}$, $B_i^{s+1} = \Theta_\mu(\prec_1^s \dots \prec_m^s)$ where each $\prec_k^s$ is defined from $\prec_k$ by: $B_{i_1}^s \prec_k^s B_{i_2}^s$ iff $i_1 \prec_k i_2$.*

As before, the Belief Sequence of agent i, $(B_i^s)_{s \in \mathbb{N}}$, represents i's belief state along the game: B_i^0 is the initial belief state of i; B_i^s is the opinion of i after s steps. Here, i's opinion is revised according to the topic-importance-Based merging operator Θ_μ: i's opinion at step s is the result of Θ_μ applied to the multi-set of opinions: $B_{i_1}^s \dots B_{i_{n_i}}^s$ ordered topic by topic by $\prec_1 \dots \prec_m$.

Proposition 12. *In a (TIBRG), the belief sequence of any agent is cyclic i.e., the belief sequence of any agent i is characterized by an initial segment $B_i^0 \dots B_i^{b-1}$ and a belief cycle $B_i^b \dots B_i^e$ which will be repeated ad infinitum.*

Example 5. Consider a language whose topics are $T_1 = \{a, \neg a\}$ and $T_2 = \{b, \neg b\}$ and a (TIBRG) $G = (A, \mu, B, Inf)$ with: $A = \{1, 2\}$, μ is a tautology, $Inf_1 = \{1\}$, $Inf_2 = \{1 \prec_{T_1} 2, 2 \prec_{T_1} 1\}$, $B_1 = a$, $B_2 = \neg a \wedge b$. In other terms, we consider two agents 1 and 2. 1 is its own and only influencer. Regarding topic T_1, 2 is influenced by 1 and by itself, but more by 1 than by itself; regarding topic T_2, 2 is influenced by 1 and by itself, but more by itself than by 1. Initially, 1 believes a and 2 believes $\neg a \wedge b$. Table 3 shows the evolution of opinions (for distance d_H and d_D as well).

Table 3. Opinion evolution in Example 5

	$s = 0$	$s \geq 1$
$i = 1$	a	a
$i = 2$	$\neg a \wedge b$	$a \wedge b$

5.4   Some Properties of (TIBRG)

We present here some results about (TIBRG). Mainly, we prove that in (TIBRG), agents always agree with integrity constraint, that (TIBRG) satisfy *Consistency Preservation* and *Agreement Preservation* but do not satisfy *Unanimity Preservation*.

Proposition 13. *Let $G = (A, \mu, B, Inf)$ be a (TIBRG). Then $\forall i \in A \ \forall s \in \mathbb{N} \ B_i^s \models \mu$.*

Proposition 14. *Let $G = (A, \mu, B, Inf)$ be a (TIBRG). Then $\forall i \in A \ \forall s \in \mathbb{N}$ B_i^s is consistent.*

Proposition 15. *Let* $G = (A, \mu, B, Inf)$ *be a (TIBRG) and* φ *a consistent formula of L. If* $\forall i \in A, \varphi \models B_i$ *then* $\forall i \in A$ $\forall s \in \mathbb{N}, \varphi \models B_i^s$.

Proposition 16. *Let* $G = (A, \mu, B, Inf)$ *be a (TIBRG) and* φ *a consistent formula of L. Then the implication "if* $\forall i \in A, B_i \models \varphi$ *then* $\forall i \in A, \forall s \in \mathbb{N}, B_i^s \models \varphi$" *is not always true.*

This means that an opinion initially shared by all the agents may be rejected by one agent after opinion diffusion. This is illustrated by the following example.

Example 6. Consider a language with two letters a, b and two topics: $T_1 = \{a, \neg a\}$, $T_2 = \{b, \neg b\}$. Consider $A = \{1, 2, 3\}$ so that $Inf(1) = \{1\}$, $Inf(2) = \{2\}$ and $Inf(3) = \{1 \prec_{T_1} 2, 2 \prec_{T_2} 1\}$ i.e., agent 3 is more influenced by agent 1 than by agent 2 regarding topic T_1 but it is more influenced by agent 2 than by agent 1 regarding topic T_2. Suppose that μ is a tautology, $B_1^0 = a \wedge b$, $B_2^0 = \neg a \wedge \neg b$, $B_3^0 = a \rightarrow b$. We have: $\forall i \in A, B_i^0 \models a \rightarrow b$. But $B_3^1 = a \wedge \neg b$ and thus $B_3^1 \not\models a \rightarrow b$.

6   Concluding Remarks

In a first part of this paper, we have presented a formal model of opinion diffusion among agents assuming that each agent revises its opinion by merging the opinions of its influencers, from the most influential to the least one. We have made some analysis on this model and found some sufficient conditions for convergence or acceptability. In a second part of the paper, we have extended this model in order to take into account the notion of topic. More precisely, the model has been extended so that an agent may order its influencers topic by topic. Again, some analysis on this model has been made.

As far as we know, such models have never been studied before and topic-dependent Importance-Based merging operators are quite original. Hovever, many open questions remain. Let us cite some of them.

First of all, as it has been done for the first model, it could be interesting to find sufficient conditions which ensure convergence or acceptability in the second model. For instance, for convergence, the notion of DAG with self-loops must be extended to take into account several influence relations. The question is to check wether such extended DAG with self-loops converge.

Secondly, it could be interesting to change our assumption about the way agents orders their influencers. In this present work, we have assumed that agents order their influencers according to a strict order (or according to several strict orders if many topics). Thus, two agents cannot be considered as equally influential for a given agent. Changing this assumption will lead us to consider pre-orders instead of orders. Defining a merging operator which takes into account preorders is an open question. More, in this present work, an agent has got a single set of influencers, which are ordered differently depending on the topics. But it would be interesting to consider that the sets of influencers are themselves topic-dependent.

A third perspective concerns the dynamicity of the influence relation. In this present work, agents do not change their influencers, nor the relative influence of their influencers. What if, during the opinion diffusion process, an agent change its mind about who are its influencers and how strong they influence it?

Finally, an interesting extension is to consider that there is no global integrity constraint but only some local ones, shared by the agents who, in some way, belong to a commn community. Studying the acceptability in such a context is challenging.

Acknowledgements. This work was supported by ONERA under grant number 25348.01F (project ROSARIO).

References

1. Crawford, C., Brooks, L., Sen, S.: Opposites repel: the effect of incorporating repulsion on opinion dynamics in the bounded confidence model. In: Proceedings of the 12th International Conference on Autonomous Agents and Multi-agent Systems (AAMAS 2013), Saint Paul, Minnesota, USA, 6–10 May 2013
2. Christoff, Z., Hansen, J.U.: A logic for diffusion in social networks. J. Appl. Logic **13**, 48–77 (2015)
3. Cholvy, L.: Influence-based opinion diffusion (extended abstract). In: Proceedings of the 15th International Conference on Autonomous Agents and Multi-agent Systems (AAMAS 2016), Singapur (2016)
4. Chatterjee, S., Hafizoglu, F.M., Sen, S.: Predicting migration and opinion adoption patterns in agent communities. In: Proceedings of the 12th International Conference on Autonomous Agents and Multi-agent Systems (AAMAS 2013), Saint Paul, Minnesota, USA, 6–10 May 2013
5. Chau, H.F., Wong, C.Y., Xhow, F.K., Fung, C.F.: Social judgment theory based model on opinion formation, polarization and evolution. Physica A **415**, 133–140 (2014). Elsevier
6. Grandi, U., Lorini, E., Perrussel, L.: Propositional opinion diffusion. In: Proceedings of the 14th International Conference on Autonomous Agents and Multi-agent Systems (AAMAS 2015), Istanbul, Turkey, 4–8 May 2015
7. Hafızoğlu, F.M., Sen, S.: Analysis of opinion spread through migration and adoption in agent communities. In: Rahwan, I., Wobcke, W., Sen, S., Sugawara, T. (eds.) PRIMA 2012. LNCS, vol. 7455, pp. 153–167. Springer, Heidelberg (2012)
8. Jager, W., Amblard, F.: A dynamical perspective on attitude change. Presented to NAACSOS (North American Association for Computational Social and Organizational Science) Conference, Pittsburgh, 22–25 June 2004
9. Konieczny, S., Pino Pérez, R.: Merging information under constraints: a logical framework. J. Logic Comput. **12**(5), 773–808 (2002)
10. Schwind, N., Inoue, K., Bourgne, G., Konieczny, S., Marquis, P.: Belief revision games. In: Proceedings of AAAI 2015, pp. 1590–1596 (2015)
11. Tsang, A., Larson, K.: Opinion dynamics of skeptical agents. In: Proceedings of the 13th International Conference on Autonomous Agents and Multi-agent Systems (AAMAS 2014), Paris, France, 5–9 May 2014
12. Yan, F., Li, Z., Jiang, Y.: Noised diffusion dynamics with individual biased opinion. In: Proceedings of ECAI 2014, pp. 1129–1130 (2014)
13. Wang, Z., Chen, E., Liu, Q., Yang, Y., Ge, Y., Chang, B.: Maximizing the coverage of information propagation in social networks. In: Proceedings of IJCAI 2015, pp. 2104–2110 (2015)

Fuzzy Labeling for Abstract Argumentation: An Empirical Evaluation

Célia da Costa Pereira[1], Mauro Dragoni[2], Andrea G.B. Tettamanzi[1]([⊠]), and Serena Villata[1]

[1] Université Côte d'Azur, CNRS, Inria, I3S, Nice, France
{celia.pereira,andrea.tettamanzi,serena.villata}@unice.fr
[2] Fondazione Bruno Kessler, Trento, Italy
dragoni@fbk.eu

Abstract. Argumentation frameworks have to be evaluated with respect to argumentation semantics to compute the set(s) of accepted arguments. In a previous approach, we proposed a fuzzy labeling algorithm for computing the (fuzzy) set of acceptable arguments, when the sources of the arguments in the argumentation framework are only partially trusted. The convergence of the algorithm was proved, and the convergence speed was estimated to be linear, as it is generally the case with iterative methods. In this paper, we provide an experimental validation of this algorithm with the aim of carrying out an empirical evaluation of its performance on a benchmark of argumentation graphs. Results show the satisfactory performance of our algorithm, even on complex graph structures as those present in our benchmark.

1 Introduction

In crisp argumentation, arguments are evaluated, following a specific semantics, as being acceptable or not acceptable, as shown by Dung [9]. Roughly, accepted arguments are those arguments which are not attacked by other accepted arguments, and rejected arguments are those attacked by accepted arguments. The set of accepted arguments, called *extensions*, represent consistent set(s) of arguments that can be accepted together. However, in many applications, such as decision making and agent-based recommendation systems, such a crisp evaluation of the arguments is not suitable to represent the complexity of the considered scenario. To address this issue, we [8] proposed to perform a *fuzzy* evaluation of the arguments of an argumentation framework. Such a fuzzy evaluation of the arguments is originated by the observation that some arguments may come from only partially trusted sources. To represent the degrees of trust, we rethink the usual crisp argument evaluation [6,9] by evaluating arguments in terms of fuzzy degrees of acceptability. In our previous contribution [8], we proved that the fuzzy labeling algorithm used to assign to the arguments fuzzy degrees of acceptability converges, and we discussed its convergence speed. However, no empirical evaluation was addressed to support this discussion.

© Springer International Publishing Switzerland 2016
S. Schockaert and P. Senellart (Eds.): SUM 2016, LNAI 9858, pp. 126–139, 2016.
DOI: 10.1007/978-3-319-45856-4_9

In this paper, we face this issue by providing an extensive evaluation of the performance and scalability of the fuzzy labeling algorithm with respect to a benchmark of abstract argumentation frameworks. We first select three existing datasets for abstract argumentation tasks used in the literature, namely the datasets created by Bistarelli et al. [3], by Cerutti et al. [7], and by Vallati et al. [12]. Moreover, we generate our own dataset of abstract argumentation frameworks by randomly combining some well known *graph patterns* in argumentation theory into 20,000 bigger argumentation frameworks. Second, we study the behaviour of the algorithm with respect to the frameworks in the benchmark, to check whether its performance are satisfiable even considering huge and complex networks as those represented in the datasets, e.g., presenting an increasing number of strongly connected components.

The reminder of the paper is as follows. In Sect. 2, we provide the basics of abstract argumentation theory and fuzzy set theory. Section 3 firstly recalls the main concepts behind the definition of the fuzzy labeling algorithm presented in [8], and secondly, describes its current implementation. In Sect. 4, we describe the four datasets which compose the bechmark used to evaluate our algorithm, and we report about the obtained results. Conclusions end the paper.

2 Preliminaries

In this section, we provide some insights about abstract argumentation theory and fuzzy sets.

2.1 Abstract Argumentation Theory

We provide the basics of Dung's abstract argumentation [9].

Definition 1. *(Abstract Argumentation Framework) An abstract argumentation framework is a pair* $\langle \mathcal{A}, \rightarrow \rangle$ *where* $\mathcal{A}$ *is a set of elements called arguments and* $\rightarrow \subseteq \mathcal{A} \times \mathcal{A}$ *is a binary relation called attack. We say that an argument* A_i *attacks an argument* A_j *if and only if* $(A_i, A_j) \in \rightarrow$.

Dung [9] presents several acceptability semantics which produce zero, one, or several sets of accepted arguments. These semantics are grounded on two main concepts, called conflict-freeness and defence.

Definition 2. *(Conflict-Free, Defence) Let* $C \subseteq \mathcal{A}$. *A set* C *is conflict-free if and only if there exist no* $A_i, A_j \in C$ *such that* $A_i \rightarrow A_j$. *A set* C *defends an argument* A_i *if and only if for each argument* $A_j \in A$ *if* A_j *attacks* A_i *then there exists* $A_k \in C$ *such that* A_k *attacks* A_j.

Definition 3. *(Acceptability Semantics) Let* C *be a conflict-free set of arguments, and let* $\mathcal{D} : 2^{\mathcal{A}} \mapsto 2^{\mathcal{A}}$ *be a function such that* $\mathcal{D}(C) = \{A | C \ defends \ A\}$.

- *C is admissible if and only if* $C \subseteq \mathcal{D}(C)$.
- *C is a complete extension if and only if* $C = \mathcal{D}(C)$.

- C is a grounded extension if and only if it is the smallest (w.r.t. set inclusion) complete extension.
- C is a preferred extension if and only if it is a maximal (w.r.t. set inclusion) complete extension.
- C is a stable extension if and only if it is a preferred extension that attacks all arguments in $\mathcal{A} \setminus C$.

The concepts of Dung's semantics are originally stated in terms of sets of arguments. It is equal to express these concepts using argument *labeling* [6,10,13] In a reinstatement labeling [6], an argument is labeled "in" if all its attackers are labeled "out" and it is labeled "out" if it has at least an attacker which is labeled "in".

Definition 4. *(AF-Labeling [6]) Let $\langle \mathcal{A}, \rightarrow \rangle$ be an abstract argumentation framework. An AF-labeling is a total function $lab : \mathcal{A} \rightarrow \{in, out, undec\}$. We define $in(lab) = \{A_i \in \mathcal{A} | lab(A_i) = in\}$, $out(lab) = \{A_i \in \mathcal{A} | lab(A_i) = out\}$, $undec(lab) = \{A_i \in \mathcal{A} | lab(A_i) = undec\}$.*

Definition 5. *(Reinstatement Labeling [6]) Let lab be an AF-labeling.*

- *a in-labeled argument is said to be legally in iff all its attackers are labeled out.*
- *a out-labeled argument is said to be legally out iff it has at least one attacker that is labeled in.*
- *an undec-labelled argument is said to be legally undec iff not all its attackers are labelled out and it does not have an attacker that is labelled in.*

Definition 6. *An admissible labelling is a labelling lab where each in-labelled argument is legally in and each out-labelled argument is legally out. lab is a complete labeling if there are no arguments illegally in and illegally out and illegally undec. We say that lab is a*

- grounded, *iff $in(lab)$ is minimal (w.r.t. set inclusion);*
- preferred, *iff $in(lab)$ is maximal (w.r.t. set inclusion);*
- stable, *iff $undec(lab) = \emptyset$*

2.2 Fuzzy Sets

Fuzzy sets [14] are a generalization of classical (crisp) sets obtained by replacing the characteristic function of a set A, χ_A, which takes up values in $\{0, 1\}$ ($\chi_A(x) = 1$ iff $x \in A$, $\chi_A(x) = 0$ otherwise) with a *membership function* μ_A, which can take up any value in $[0, 1]$. The value $\mu_A(x)$ or, more simply, $A(x)$ is the membership degree of element x in A, i.e., the degree to which x belongs in A.

A fuzzy set is completely defined by its membership function. Therefore, it is useful to define a few terms describing various features of this function. Given a fuzzy set A, its *core* is the (conventional) set of all elements x such that $A(x) = 1$; its *support*, supp(A), is the set of all x such that $A(x) > 0$. A fuzzy set is *normal* if its core is nonempty. The set of all elements x of A such that $A(x) \geq \alpha$, for a given $\alpha \in (0, 1]$, is called the α-cut of A, denoted A_α.

The usual set-theoretic operations of union, intersection, and complement can be defined as a generalization of their counterparts on classical sets by introducing two families of operators, called triangular norms and triangular co-norms. In practice, it is usual to employ the min norm for intersection and the max co-norm for union. Given two fuzzy sets A and B, and an element x,

$$(A \cup B)(x) = \max\{A(x), B(x)\}; \tag{1}$$
$$(A \cap B)(x) = \min\{A(x), B(x)\}; \tag{2}$$
$$\bar{A}(x) = 1 - A(x). \tag{3}$$

Finally, given two fuzzy sets A and B, $A \subseteq B$ if and only if, for every element x, $A(x) \leq B(x)$.

3 Fuzzy Labeling for Abstract Argumentation

In this section, we recall the fuzzy labeling algorithm for abstract argumentation [8] we want to empirically evaluate over the available datasets for abstract argumentation to study its performance. For a complete description of the algorithm and its convergence theorem as well as the comparison with the related approaches we remind the reader to [8]. Moreover, we report about the implementation we develop to test the perfomances of the algorithm.

3.1 Algorithm

In order to account for the fact that arguments may originate from sources that are trusted only to a certain degree, the (crisp) abstract argumentation structure described in Sect. 2 may be extended by allowing gradual membership of arguments in the set of arguments $\mathcal{A}$. We have that $\mathcal{A}$ is a fuzzy set of trustworthy arguments, and $\mathcal{A}(A)$, the membership degree of argument A in $\mathcal{A}$, is given by the trust degree of the most reliable (i.e., trusted) source that offers argument A,[1]

$$\mathcal{A}(A) = \max_{s \in \mathrm{src}(A)} \tau_s, \tag{4}$$

where $\mathrm{src}(A)$ is the set of sources proposing argument A and τ_s is the degree to which source $s \in \mathrm{src}(A)$ is trusted. We do not make any further assumptions on the trust model, as it is out of the scope of this paper. However, we refer the interested reader to [11], where a more detailed description of how the source trustworthiness degree can be computed starting from elements, like the source sincerity and expertise, is provided.

---

[1] Here, we suppose that the agent is optimistic. To represent a pessimistic behaviour, we should use the min operator, for example.

Definition 7. *(Fuzzy AF-Labeling) Let $\langle \mathcal{A}, \rightarrow \rangle$ be an abstract argumentation framework. A fuzzy AF-labeling is a total function $\alpha : \mathcal{A} \rightarrow [0,1]$.*

Such an α may also be regarded as (the membership function of) the fuzzy set of acceptable arguments: $\alpha(A) = 0$ means the argument is outright unacceptable, $\alpha(A) = 1$ means the argument is fully acceptable, and all cases inbetween are provided for.

Definition 8. *(Fuzzy Reinstatement Labeling) Let α be a fuzzy AF-labeling. We say that α is a fuzzy reinstatement labeling iff, for all arguments A,*

$$\alpha(A) = \min\{\mathcal{A}(A), 1 - \max_{B:B \rightarrow A} \alpha(B)\}. \tag{5}$$

The above definition combines two intuitive postulates of fuzzy labeling: (1) the acceptability of an argument should not be greater than the degree to which the arguments attacking it are unacceptable and (2) an argument cannot be more acceptable than the degree to which its sources are trusted: $\alpha(A) \leq \mathcal{A}(A)$.

We can verify that the fuzzy reinstatement labeling is a generalization of the crisp reinstatement labeling of Definition 5, whose *in* and *out* labels are particular cases corresponding, respectively, to $\alpha(A) = 1$ and $\alpha(A) = 0$. The intermediate cases, $0 < \alpha(A) < 1$ correspond to a continuum of degrees of "undecidedness", of which 0.5 is but the most undecided representative.

We denote by $\alpha_0 = \mathcal{A}$ the initial labeling, and by α_t the labeling obtained after the tth iteration of the labeling algorithm.

Definition 9. *Let α_t be a fuzzy labeling. An iteration in α_t is carried out by computing a new labeling α_{t+1} for all arguments A as follows:*

$$\alpha_{t+1}(A) = \frac{1}{2}\alpha_t(A) + \frac{1}{2}\min\{\mathcal{A}(A), 1 - \max_{B:B \rightarrow A} \alpha_t(B)\}. \tag{6}$$

This defines a sequence $\{\alpha_t\}_{t=0,1,...}$ of labelings which always converges to a limit fuzzy labeling, as proven in [8]. Moreover, the convergence speed is linear: in practice, a small number of iterations is enough to compute the limit up to the desired precision. The fuzzy labeling of a fuzzy argumentation framework is thus the limit of $\{\alpha_t\}_{t=0,1,...}$.

Definition 10. *Let $\langle \mathcal{A}, \rightarrow \rangle$ be a fuzzy argumentation framework. A fuzzy reinstatement labeling for such argumentation framework is, for all arguments A,*

$$\alpha(A) = \lim_{t \rightarrow \infty} \alpha_t(A). \tag{7}$$

3.2   Implementation

The fuzzy labeling algorithm has been implemented by using the Java language without using any specific library. The first version of the algorithm was developed with the support of multi-threading where the update of each node was parallelized. However, preliminary tests run in multi-threading mode reported some computational overhead that make the observation of algorithm performance not consistent. For this reason and for measuring performance values easing the comparison with the obtained results, we opted for running all tests in a single-thread mode.

Each run was performed on a server equipped with a Xeon E5-2609 v2 @ 2.50 GHz. According to official user-based benchmarks,[2] the single thread mark of the CPU is 1229 points. This value can be used as reference for normalizing results concerning the timing of each run obtained on other machines.

4   Evaluation

In this section, we study the behaviour and the performances of the fuzzy-labeling algorithm over a benchmark for abstract argumentation, and then we report about the obtained results.

The aim of our experimental analysis is to assess the scalability of the fuzzy-labeling algorithm concerning two perspectives:

- the number of iterations needed for convergence with respect to the number of the nodes in the graph, and
- the time needed for convergence with respect to the number of the nodes in the graph.

It must be stressed that the time needed for convergence depends on (i) the time needed for computing each iteration, (ii) the time needed to update the α of each single argument, and (iii) the number of iterations required for the labeling to converge.

4.1   Benchmark

The benchmark we used to evaluate the performances of the fuzzy labeling algorithm is composed of different datasets for abstract argumentation tasks used in the literature. More precisely, we have considered the following datasets:

- The Perugia dataset [2–4]:[3] the dataset is composed of randomly generated directed-graphs. To generate random graphs, they adopted two different libraries. The first one is the Java Universal Network/Graph Framework (JUNG), a Java software library for the modeling, generation, analysis and visualization of graphs. The second library they used is NetworkX, a Python software package for the creation, manipulation, and study of the structure, dynamics, and functions of complex networks. Three kinds of networks are generated:

---

[2] https://www.cpubenchmark.net/CPU_mega_page.html.

[3] The dataset is available at http://www.dmi.unipg.it/conarg/dwl/networks.tgz.

- In the Erdős-Rényi graph model, the graph is constructed by randomly connecting n nodes. Each edge is included in the graph with probability p independent from every other edge. For the generation of these argumentation graphs, they adopted $p = c \log n / n$ (with c empirically set to 2.5), which ensures the connectedness of such graphs.
- The Kleinberg graph model adds a number of directed long-range random links to an $n \times n$ lattice network, where vertices are the nodes of a grid with undirected edges between any two adjacent nodes. Links have a non-uniform distribution that favors edges to close nodes over more distant ones.
- In the Barabási-Albert graph model, at each time step, a new vertex is created and connected to existing vertices according to the principle of "preferential attachment", such that vertices with higher degree have a higher probability of being selected for attachment.

For more details about the generation of these networks as well as the graph models, we refer the reader to [2–4].

- The dataset used by Cerutti *et al.* in their KR 2014 paper [7] (which we will call the KR dataset): the dataset has been generated to evaluate a meta-algorithm for the computation of preferred labelings, based on the general recursive schema for argumentation semantics called SCC-Recursiveness. The dataset is composed of three sets of argumentation frameworks, namely:
  - 790 randomly generated argumentation frameworks where the number of strongly connected components (SCC) is 1, varying the number of arguments between 25 and 250 with a step of 25.
  - 720 randomly generated argumentation frameworks where the number of strongly connected components varies between 5 and 45 with a step of 5. The size of the SCCs is determined by normal distributions with means between 20 and 40 with a step of 5, and with a fixed standard deviation of 5. They similarly varied the probability of having attacks between arguments among SCCs.
  - 2800 randomly generated argumentation frameworks where the number of strongly connected components is between 50 and 80 with a step of 5.
- The dataset presented by Vallati *et al.* at ECAI 2014 [12] (which we will call the ECAI dataset): the dataset was produced to study the features of argumentation frameworks. More precisely, it is composed of 10,000 argumentation frameworks generated using a parametric random approach allowing to select (probabilistically average, standard deviation) the density of attacks for each strongly connected component, and how many arguments (probabilistically) in each SCC attack how many arguments (probabilistically) in how many (probabilistically) other SCCs. The number of arguments ranges between 10 and 40,000, and they exploited a 10-fold cross-validation approach on a uniform random permutation of the instances.

The availability of real-world benchmarks for argumentation problems is quite limited, with some few exceptions like [5] or AIFdb.[4] However, these

---

[4] http://corpora.aifdb.org.

$a \to b, b \to a$
$a \to b, b \to a, b \to c$
$a \to b, b \to a, b \to c, c \to d, d \to c$
$a \to b, b \to c, c \to d, d \to e, e \to f, f \to e$
$a \to b, b \to c, c \to d, d \to c$
$a \to b, b \to c, c \to a$
$a \to b, b \to a, b \to c, c \to c$
$a \to b, b \to a, b \to c, c \to c, d \to d$
$a \to b, b \to a, b \to c, a \to c, c \to d, d \to c$
$a \to b, b \to a, b \to c, a \to c, c \to d$
$a \to b, b \to c, c \to a, b \to d, a \to d, c \to d, d \to e, e \to d$
$a \to b, b \to c, e \to c, c \to d$
$a \to b, b \to a, b \to c, c \to d, d \to e, e \to c$
$a \to b, b \to c, c \to c$
$a \to b, b \to c, c \to a, a \to d, b \to d, c \to d$
$a \to b, a \to c, c \to a, c \to d, d \to c, d \to a, a \to d, c \to e, d \to f$

Fig. 1. The "patterns" used for constructing the Sophia Antipolis dataset.

benchmarks are tailored towards problems of argument mining and their representation as abstract argumentation frameworks usually leads to topologically simple graphs, such as cycle-free graphs. These kinds of graphs are not suitable for evaluating the computational performance of solvers for abstract argumentation problems. For this reason, we decided to use artificially generated graphs as benchmarks, in line with the preliminary performance evaluation of Bistarelli *et al.* [2].

In order to ensure the consideration of all kinds of interesting "patterns" that could appear in argumentation frameworks (e.g., the abstract argumentation frameworks used to exemplify the behaviour of the semantics in [1]), we have generated further graphs by composing these basic well-known examples of *interesting* argumentation patterns (shown in Fig. 1) into bigger frameworks.

Our generated dataset (which we will call the Sophia Antipolis dataset)[5] consists of 20,000 argumentation graphs created through a random aggregation of the patterns shown above. This process has been executed with different settings in order to obtain complex graphs of specific sizes. In particular, a set of 1,000 argumentation graphs is generated for graph sizes from 5,000 to 100,000 nodes, with incremental steps of 5,000 nodes each. The aggregation of patterns has been done incrementally, and the connections (edges) between single patterns were generated randomly. The number of created graphs and their different sizes should support the evaluation of argumentation reasoning algorithms under a broad number of scenarios.

4.2 Results

Figures 2, 3, 4, 5, 6, 7, 8, 9, 10 and 11 summarize the behavior of the fuzzy-labeling algorithm on the four datasets we considered. For each dataset, we applied the algorithm to the argumentation graphs with all argument weights set to 1 (i.e., arguments coming from fully trusted sources) and with random

---

[5] The Sophia Antipolis dataset is available at https://goo.gl/pN1M9r.

weights (i.e., arguments coming from a variety of more or less trusted sources as it may be the case in application scenarios like multiagent systems). From a first inspection of the figures, it is clear that certain graph types are harder than others: the Sophia Antipolis appears to be the hardest, followed by the Erdős-Rényi, the Barabási-Albert, and the KR + EKAI datasets. The Kleinberg dataset appears to be the easiest. Furthermore, for all datasets, the graphs with random weights never require a smaller number of iterations for convergence than their counterparts with all weights fixed to 1.

Figures 2 and 3 show the behaviour of the fuzzy labeling algorithm when applied to the Barabási-Albert dataset. In particular, Fig. 2 (left-hand side) illustrates the evolution of the number of iterations needed to reach convergence when all the weights are equal to 1. We can notice that the curve follows a

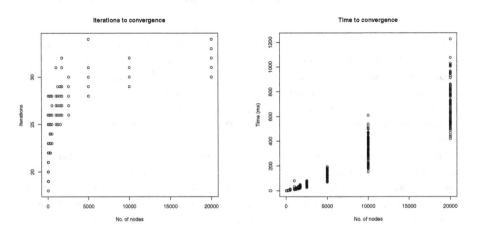

Fig. 2. Barabási-Albert dataset of the Perugia benchmark with all weights equal to 1.0.

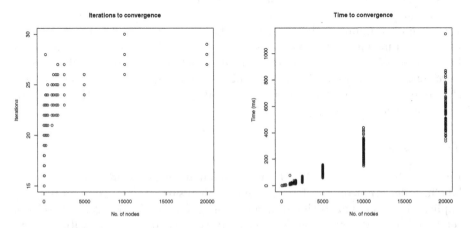

Fig. 3. Barabási-Albert dataset of the Perugia benchmark with random weights.

logarithmic rise with the increasing of the number of nodes. The figure illustrated through the (right-hand side) curve represents the evolution of the time needed to reach the convergence. It shows a behaviour rather linear. However, we can notice that the slope of the curve decreases with the increasing of the number of nodes. A similar behaviour is depicted in Fig. 3 which illustrates the evolution of the quantity of time (in ms) needed to reach the convergence when the weights are assigned randomly. These two illustrations clearly show the capability of the fuzzy labeling algorithm to handle a growing amount of data.

In Figs. 4 and 5, we present the behaviour of the fuzzy labeling algorithm when applied to the Erdős-Rényi dataset. We can notice that when all the weights are equal to 1, the convergence is reached very quickly both when considering the number of iterations, and the quantity of time needed for convergence.

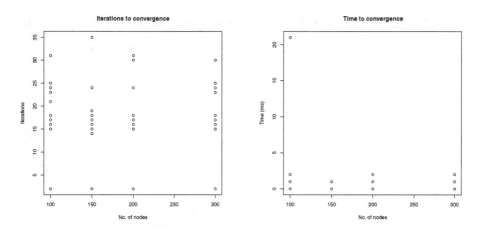

Fig. 4. The Erdős-Rényi dataset of the Perugia benchmark with all weights equal to 1.0.

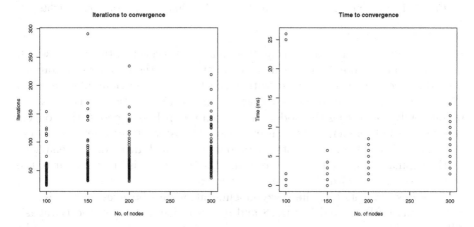

Fig. 5. The Erdős-Rényi dataset of the Perugia benchmark with random weights.

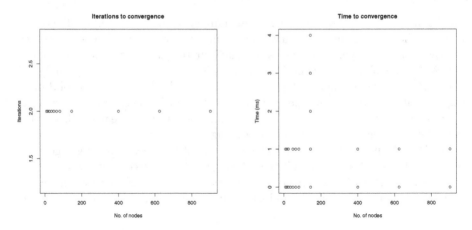

Fig. 6. The Kleinberg dataset of the Perugia benchmark with all weights equal to 1.0.

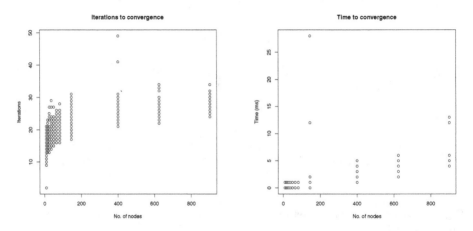

Fig. 7. The Kleinberg dataset of the Perugia benchmark with random weights.

However, while such a quantity is quite similar with respect to the case in which the weights are randomly assigned, we can notice that the number of iterations needed for convergence is higher with respect to the behaviour illustrated in Fig. 4. This can be due to the fact that the Erdős-Rényi dataset is constructed by randomly connecting the nodes. As we can see in Figs. 6 and 7, the convergence with the Kleinberg dataset is even globally faster, either when all weights are equal to 1 or when the weights are randomly assigned. Instead, the behaviour on the Sophia Antipolis dataset, shown in Figs. 10 and 11, is quite similar to the behaviors obtained with the Barabási-Albert dataset.

It is less evident, but the fuzzy-labeling algorithm behaves on the KR + ECAI dataset (illustrated in Figs. 8 and 9) much like it does on the Barabási-Albert and Sophia Antipolis datasets, with the exception of a few small graphs which are outliers and which demand a relatively large number of iterations to

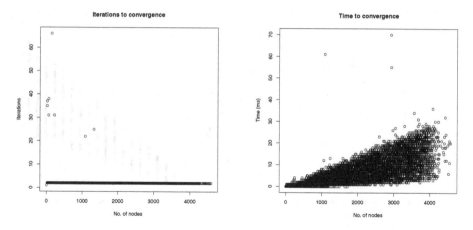

Fig. 8. The benchmark consisting of the KR + ECAI dataset with all weights equal to 1.0.

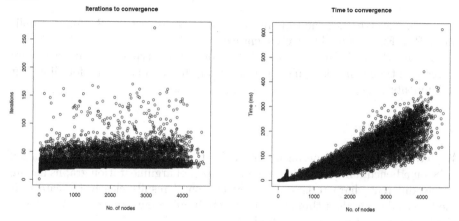

Fig. 9. The benchmark consisting of the KR + ECAI dataset with random weights.

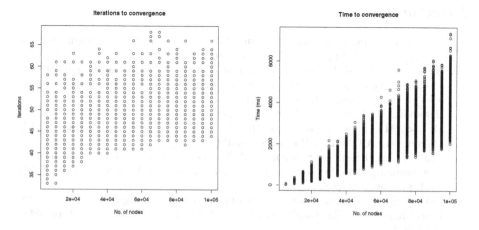

Fig. 10. The Sophia Antipolis benchmark with all weights equal to 1.0.

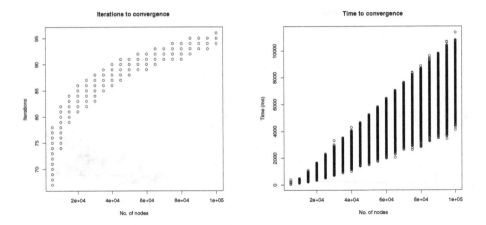

Fig. 11. The Sophia Antipolis benchmark with random weights.

converge. Nevertheless, the time behavior of Barabási-Albert, Sophia Antipolis and KR + ECAI is qualitatively identical.

Despite the differences among the various graph types, we have a rate of increase in time which is at most log-linear for all graph types and for all weight assignments.

5   Conclusions

We have evaluated the performance of the fuzzy labeling algorithm proposed in [8] on a benchmark consisting of four datasets of argumentation graphs having widely different characteristics. The experimental results clearly indicate that the fuzzy labeling algorithm scales up nicely in all circumstances, and is thus a viable argumentation reasoning tool.

References

1. Baroni, P., Caminada, M., Giacomin, M.: An introduction to argumentation semantics. Knowl. Eng. Rev. **26**(4), 365–410 (2011)
2. Bistarelli, S., Rossi, F., Santini, F.: A first comparison of abstract argumentation systems: a computational perspective. In: Proceedings of the 28th Italian Conference on Computational Logic, pp. 241–245 (2013)
3. Bistarelli, S., Rossi, F., Santini, F.: Benchmarking hard problems in random abstract AFs: the stable semantics. In: Proceedings of the Computational Models of Argument, COMMA 2014, pp. 153–160 (2014)
4. Bistarelli, S., Rossi, F., Santini, F.: A first comparison of abstract argumentation reasoning-tools. In: 21st European Conference on Artificial Intelligence, ECAI 2014, pp. 969–970 (2014)
5. Cabrio, E., Villata, S.: NoDE: a benchmark of natural language arguments. In: Proceedings of the Computational Models of Argument, COMMA 2014, pp. 449–450 (2014)

6. Caminada, M.: On the issue of reinstatement in argumentation. In: Fisher, M., van der Hoek, W., Konev, B., Lisitsa, A. (eds.) JELIA 2006. LNCS (LNAI), vol. 4160, pp. 111–123. Springer, Heidelberg (2006)
7. Cerutti, F., Giacomin, M., Vallati, M., Zanella, M.: An SCC recursive meta-algorithm for computing preferred labellings in abstract argumentation. In: Proceedings of the Fourteenth International Conference Principles of Knowledge Representation and Reasoning, KR 2014 (2014)
8. da Costa Pereira, C., Tettamanzi, A., Villata, S.: Changing one's mind: erase or rewind? In: Proceedings of the 22nd International Joint Conference on Artificial Intelligence, IJCAI 2011, pp. 164–171 (2011)
9. Dung, P.M.: On the acceptability of arguments and its fundamental role in non-monotonic reasoning, logic programming and n-person games. Artif. Intell. **77**(2), 321–358 (1995)
10. Jakobovits, H., Vermeir, D.: Robust semantics for argumentation frameworks. J. Log. Comput. **9**(2), 215–261 (1999)
11. Paglieri, F., Castelfranchi, C., da Costa Pereira, C., Falcone, R., Tettamanzi, A., Villata, S.: Trusting the messenger because of the message: feedback dynamics from information quality to source evaluation. Comput. Math. Organ. Theor. **20**(2), 176–194 (2014)
12. Vallati, M., Cerutti, F., Giacomin, M.: Argumentation frameworks features: an initial study. In: 21st European Conference on Artificial Intelligence, ECAI 2014, pp. 1117–1118 (2014)
13. Verheij, B.: Artificial argument assistants for defeasible argumentation. Artif. Intell. **150**(1–2), 291–324 (2003)
14. Zadeh, L.A.: Fuzzy sets. Inf. Control **8**, 338–353 (1965)

A Belief-Based Approach to Measuring Message Acceptability

Célia da Costa Pereira, Andrea G.B. Tettamanzi$^{(\boxtimes)}$, and Serena Villata

Université Côte d'Azur, CNRS, Inria, I3S, Nice, France
{celia.pereira,andrea.tettamanzi,serena.villata}@unice.fr

Abstract. We propose a formal framework to support belief revision based on a cognitive model of credibility and trust. In this framework, the acceptance of information coming from a source depends on *(i)* the agent's goals and beliefs about the source's goals, *(ii)* the credibility, for the agent, of incoming information, and *(iii)* the agent's beliefs about the context in which it operates. This makes it possible to approach belief revision in a setting where new incoming information is associated with an acceptance degree. In particular, such degree may be used as input weight for any possibilistic conditioning operator with uncertain input (i.e., weighted belief revision operator).

1 Introduction

Fulfilling its goals is an important concern for an agent. The agent's perceptions about its environment highly influences this process. Such perceptions dynamically enrich the agent's beliefs, namely thanks to new more or less credible/trusted information. According to the principle of *primacy update*, in belief revision new information is generally accepted. However, as pointed out by several authors [10,11,13], in real-world situations it is often the case that new information is not fully considered or simply not accepted due to an insufficient amount of plausibility [5]. The extent to which new information will be accepted (i.e., really considered) by the agent directly depends on these credibility and trust values. A key factor for the agent's success in fulfilling its goals is then its ability to compute both the *credibility* of new information and its *trust* in the source providing information. Recently, Adali [1] has proposed to define information trust as a computational concept whose value depends on the trustworthiness of the information source,[1] and on the credibility of the information content. Adali's approach also agrees with the one proposed by Sparks [26]. However, to the best of our knowledge, a formal framework for measuring the acceptability of a message which takes into account the agent's goals and the agent's beliefs about the source's goals, the credibility of the message with respect to its content and with respect to both the agent's competence and the source's competence, and the agent's beliefs about the source's nature (malicious or not) is still missing.

---

[1] In the rest of the paper we will also refer to the "trustworthiness of an information source" for an agent as the agent's "trust in a source".

S. Schockaert and P. Senellart (Eds.): SUM 2016, LNAI 9858, pp. 140–154, 2016.
DOI: 10.1007/978-3-319-45856-4_10

The research question of how to provide such a framework breaks down into the following subquestions:

- How do we take the *nature* of the information source into account?
- How do we take the agent's and source's goals into account?
- How do we measure the credibility of information based on the agent's and the source's competences?

We answer these questions by proposing a possibilistic model whereby the cognitive notions of trust and credibility can be formalized and the acceptability of the pieces of information can be computed. Our framework makes it possible to:

- represent the fact that the agent's beliefs may include the "nature" of a source, which may be categorized as malicious, rational, etc.—each evaluation of a component of trust should consider this fact;
- somehow measure the source's willingness to cooperate thanks to the agent's perceptions about the source's goals—a source sharing my goals should (implicitly or explicitly) act/help for the achievement of these goals, unless, perhaps, it is not rational;
- compute the credibility of information coming from a given source with respect to:
    - the agent's competence—the agent may be able to evaluate the information content regardless of how trustworthy it considers the information source;
    - the source's competence—we suppose that (1) each piece of information belongs to a domain of competence and (2) the agent has beliefs about the domains of competence of the sources. It is then possible to evaluate the credibility of such a new piece of information with respect to the source's competence;

Our approach is cast within the framework of possibility theory in order to cover cases when not enough data to compute probabilities are available.

The paper is organized as follows: first, we present some related work and we compare them to the proposed approach. Then, we provide some basic notions of possibility theory, upon which our model is built. Our proposal is put forth in Sect. 4, and its formal properties are discussed. Conclusions end the paper.

2   Related Work

In multi-agent systems, representing and making possible the evaluation of the credibility associated with a piece of information is important especially when the agents have their own beliefs and can obtain new information from other sources. In this case, assessing to which extent such new information should be integrated with the agents' beliefs depends on its credibility and on the trustworthiness of its source. Tamargo *et al.* [27] address this problem in a collaborative multi-agent system in which agents can receive new information from informant agents through communication. The authors consider a credibility order among the informant agents. A belief is then revised when new contradictory incoming information arrives from an informant that is highly credible. Unlike in Tamargo's approach, where credibility is associated to agents, here we propose to associate a (computed) credibility degree to the new piece of information.

Krümpelmann et al. [14] propose to attach an agent identifier to each piece of information, representing the credibility of the transferred information. But still, credibility is associated to an agent. Besides, while our value of credibility together with the trust value will determine the extent to which the new piece of information will be accepted, in the above-mentioned approaches the aim of the credibility order is to help in the choice of which, of the old belief and the new piece of information, will be adopted/maintained.

On the other hand, there exist several works about trust in the literature and in different disciplines [19,20,26,31]. Among the numerous and interesting contributions by Falcone et al., we can underline [12], in which the authors claim that an agent's decision about trusting an information source or not depends on the agent's representation of the source's nature. The principle according to which "only an agent endowed with goals and beliefs can trust another agent" has been pointed out by Castelfranchi and Falcone [7]. Trust is thus considered as a matter of utility and a context-sensitive concept. All the above proposals lead us to argue that trust is a multidimensional concept. Sabater et al. [23] share this point of view. Indeed, they proposed a model which deals with three dimensions of trust or reputation. The first dimension is based on an agent's own experiences. The second dimension is based on third-party information obtained thanks to the agent's social relationships, and the third dimension, also called the ontological dimension, helps to transfer trust information between related contexts. Sierra and Debenham [25] propose a trust-based decision model to be used in the context of negotiation. They propose a probabilistic method to represent and define trust as depending on the information gain caused by a piece of evidence—the more information an agent has about an event, the smaller its (probabilistic) uncertainty about that event. Probability theory is also used by Teacy et al. [28] to represent trust by taking past interactions with other agents into account while possibility theory is used in [2] for proposing an interval-based representations of trust and distrust based on past performances by considering the fact that data are not necessarily numerous in practice.

3   Background

In this section, we provide basic notions of possibility theory and define how beliefs and goals are formalized in our framework to model cognitive agents. Finally, we propose a way to associate the information content of a message to domains of competence, by adopting implication in logical Information Retrieval models.

3.1 Language and Interpretations

A classical propositional language may be used to represent information for manipulation by a cognitive agent.

Definition 1. *(Language) Let* Prop *be a finite set of atomic propositions and let $\mathcal{L}$ be the propositional language such that* $\text{Prop} \cup \{\top, \bot\} \subseteq \mathcal{L}$, *and,* $\forall \phi, \psi \in \mathcal{L}$, $\neg \phi \in \mathcal{L}$, $\phi \wedge \psi \in \mathcal{L}$, $\phi \vee \psi \in \mathcal{L}$.

As usual, one may define additional logical connectives and consider them as useful shorthands for combinations of connectives of $\mathcal{L}$, e.g., $\phi \supset \psi \equiv \neg \phi \vee \psi$. We will denote by $\Omega = \{0,1\}^{\text{Prop}}$ the set of all interpretations on Prop. An interpretation $\mathcal{I} \in \Omega$ is a function $\mathcal{I} : \text{Prop} \to \{0,1\}$ assigning a truth value $p^{\mathcal{I}}$ to every atomic proposition $p \in \text{Prop}$ and, by extension, a truth value $\phi^{\mathcal{I}}$ to all formulas $\phi \in \mathcal{L}$.[2] We will denote by $[\phi]$ the set of all models of ϕ, $[\phi] = \{\mathcal{I} : \mathcal{I} \models \phi\}$.

3.2 Possibility Theory

Fuzzy sets [32] are sets whose elements have degrees of membership in $[0,1]$. Possibility theory is a mathematical theory of uncertainty that relies upon fuzzy set theory, in that the (fuzzy) set of possible values for a variable of interest is used to describe the uncertainty as to its precise value. At the semantic level, the membership function of such set, π, is called a *possibility distribution* and its range is $[0,1]$. A possibility distribution can represent the beliefs of an agent: $\pi(\mathcal{I})$ represents the degree of compatibility of the interpretation $\mathcal{I}$ with the available evidence about the real world if we are representing uncertain beliefs. By convention, $\pi(\mathcal{I}) = 1$ means that it is totally possible for $\mathcal{I}$ to be the real world, $1 > \pi(\mathcal{I}) > 0$ means that $\mathcal{I}$ is only somehow possible, while $\pi(\mathcal{I}) = 0$ means that $\mathcal{I}$ is certainly not the real world.

A possibility distribution π is said to be normalized if there exists at least one interpretation $\mathcal{I}_0$ s.t. $\pi(\mathcal{I}_0) = 1$, i.e., there exists at least one possible situation which is consistent with the available knowledge.

Definition 2 (Fuzzy Measure). *Let Ω be a universe of discourse; a function $f : 2^{\Omega} \to [0,1]$ is a* fuzzy measure *if*

1. $f(\emptyset) = 0$;
2. *for all* $A, B \subseteq \Omega$, $A \subseteq B \Rightarrow f(A) \le f(B)$.

A fuzzy measure f is normalized *if $f(\Omega) = 1$.*

Definition 3 (Possibility and Necessity Measures). *A possibility distribution π induces a* possibility measure *and its dual* necessity measure, *denoted*

---

[2] When $\phi^{\mathcal{I}} = 1$, i.e., $\mathcal{I}$ satisfies formula ϕ, in symbols $\mathcal{I} \models \phi$, $\mathcal{I}$ is called a model of ϕ.

by Π and N respectively. Both measures apply to a classical set $S \subseteq \Omega$ and are defined as follows:

$$\Pi(S) = \max_{\mathcal{I} \in S} \pi(\mathcal{I}); \tag{1}$$

$$N(S) = 1 - \Pi(\bar{S}) = \min_{\mathcal{I} \in \bar{S}}\{1 - \pi(\mathcal{I})\}. \tag{2}$$

A few properties of Π and N induced by a normalized possibility distribution on a finite universe of discourse Ω are the following. For all subsets $S \subseteq \Omega$:

1. $\Pi(A \cup B) = \max\{\Pi(A), \Pi(B)\}$; $N(A \cap B) = \min\{N(A), N(B)\}$;
2. $\Pi(A \cap B) \leq \min\{\Pi(A), \Pi(B)\}$; $N(A \cup B) \geq \max\{N(A), N(B)\}$;
3. $\Pi(\emptyset) = N(\emptyset) = 0$; $\Pi(\Omega) = N(\Omega) = 1$;
4. $\Pi(S) = 1 - N(\bar{S})$ (duality);
5. $N(S) > 0 \Rightarrow \Pi(S) = 1$; $\Pi(S) < 1 \Rightarrow N(S) = 0$;

In case of complete ignorance on S, $\Pi(S) = \Pi(\bar{S}) = 1$ and $N(S) = N(\bar{S}) = 0$.

3.3   Beliefs

We assume a possibilistic BDI model of agency like the one proposed in [9]. In that model, the epistemic state of an agent is represented by a normalized possibility distribution $\pi : \Omega \rightarrow [0,1]$. The degree to which a given arbitrary formula $\phi \in \mathcal{L}$ is believed can, therefore, be calculated from it as

$$\mathbf{B}(\phi) = N([\phi]) = 1 - \max_{\mathcal{I} \not\models \phi}\{\pi(\mathcal{I})\}. \tag{3}$$

Straightforward consequences of the properties of possibility and necessity measures are that $\mathbf{B}(\phi) > 0 \Rightarrow \mathbf{B}(\neg\phi) = 0$, i.e., if the agent somehow believes ϕ then it cannot believe $\neg\phi$ at all; $\mathbf{B}(\phi \wedge \psi) = \min\{\mathbf{B}(\phi), \mathbf{B}(\psi)\}$ and $\mathbf{B}(\phi \vee \psi) \geq \max\{\mathbf{B}(\phi), \mathbf{B}(\psi)\}$. Notice that $\mathbf{B}(\top) = 1$ and $\mathbf{B}(\bot) = 0$.

The rationale for choosing possibility theory to represent beliefs is its ability to capture epistemic uncertainty. It is well known that possibility theory is suited to represent uncertainty by only using a notion of order (much easier to have with few data) between the possible outcomes. A viable alternative would be the Dempster-Shafer theory of evidence [24]; however, the use of that theory would be computationally much heavier, due to the need to maintain a probability mass assignment to every element of 2^{Ω}, as compared to a possibility assignment to every interpretation of Ω in possibility theory.

3.4   Goals

The goals of an agent may be represented as a set G of formulas from the same language $\mathcal{L}$. The meaning of saying that $\psi \in G$ is a goal for the agent is that the agent would be happy with any state of the world $\mathcal{I} \in \Omega$ such that $\mathcal{I} \models \psi$.

3.5   Domains of Competence

We propose to associate formulas to domains of competence. This is in line with what has been proposed by Paglieri et al. [18], except that they referred to arguments instead of just formulas and they defined domains based on the propositions their truth depends on. We propose a more general definition inspired by the use of implication in logical Information Retrieval models [30]. More precisely, given a domain d described by a formula χ_d (like a query in (fuzzy) set-based models of information retrieval) and a formula ϕ (like a document), we use implication to determine if ϕ is relevant to d i.e., if $\chi_d \models \phi$. The intuitive meaning of this is that incoming information is relevant to a domain if the models of the formula describing the domain are included in the models of the formula describing incoming information. However, because entailment is too rigid a relation and cannot express partial relevance [15], what we propose is in line with fuzzy set-based models in Information retrieval [29], where one resorts to a fuzzy measure of the $\chi_d \models \phi$ entailment. We define one such measure based on possibilistic conditioning [4] of ϕ by χ_d.

Definition 4. *Given language $\mathcal{L}$ and D the set of domains of competence, such that every $d \in D$ is defined by a formula $\chi_d \in \mathcal{L}$, the association between formulas and domains is represented by a fuzzy relation $R : \mathcal{L} \times D \to [0,1]$ such that, given $\phi \in \mathcal{L}, d \in D$, the membership degree of formula ϕ in domain d is*

$$R(\phi,d) = \begin{cases} 1, & if \chi_d \models \phi, \\ \Pi([\phi \wedge \chi_d]), & otherwise. \end{cases}$$

In addition, we may require that the domains D form a partition of the universe of discourse, i.e., that

$$\bigvee_{d \in D} \chi_d = \top, \quad \forall d_1, d_2 \in D, \chi_{d_1} \wedge \chi_{d_2} = \bot.$$

Proposition 1. *Let $\phi, \psi \in \mathcal{L}$. For all domain $d \in D$, if $\phi \models \psi$, $R(\phi,d) \leq R(\psi,d)$.*

Proof. Given a domain d, we may distinguish three cases:

1. $\chi_d \models \phi$; in this case, it must also be that $\chi_d \models \psi$ and, as a consequence, $R(\phi,d) = R(\psi,d) = 1$, and the thesis holds;
2. $\chi_d \not\models \phi$ and $\chi_d \models \psi$; in this case, $R(\phi,d) = \Pi([\phi \wedge \chi_d]) \leq 1$ and $R(\psi,d) = 1$, and the thesis holds;
3. $\chi_d \not\models \phi$ and $\chi_d \not\models \psi$; in this case, $R(\phi,d) = \Pi([\phi \wedge \chi_d])$ and $R(\psi,d) = \Pi([\psi \wedge \chi_d])$; now, $\phi \models \psi$ means $[\phi] \subseteq [\psi]$; therefore, $[\phi] \cap [\chi_d] \subseteq [\psi] \cap [\chi_d]$, hence $\Pi([\phi \wedge \chi_d]) \leq \Pi([\psi \wedge \chi_d])$, and the thesis holds. $\square$

4   A Formal Framework of Cognitive Trust

We are now ready to formalize the notion of trust, the nature of an information source, the relation between beliefs and goals, and credibility.

4.1   Trust as Belief

Some pieces of information can contribute to increase or decrease the trust that an agent has in a source, and others can contribute to increase or decrease distrust. Trust is also a matter of competences.[3] Indeed, we can have different evaluations of trust (distrust) in the same source relevant to different domains of competence.

Like in [17], we suppose that trust and distrust are not the opposite ends of a single continuum, but linked dimensions that can coexist and have different antecedents and consequences [20]. We consider the social-cognitive model of trust [7,22], in which trust is defined as beliefs: an agent trusts a source s, in a domain d, if and only if it somehow believes that s will be able to somehow help it fulfill its goals. We will also define distrust as a belief: an agent distrusts a source s with respect to a domain of competence d if and only if it somehow believes that s might try to prevent it to reach its goals. Although in the next sections we will show how to compute trust and distrust in a source s, we should always keep in mind that trust and distrust in s are to be construed conceptually as if they were defined as follows:

$$\text{trust}(s) \equiv \mathbf{B}(\text{``}s \text{ is trustworthy''}), \tag{4}$$

$$\text{distrust}(s) \equiv \mathbf{B}(\text{``}s \text{ is untrustworthy''}). \tag{5}$$

Notice that proposition "s is untrustworthy" is the logical negation of "s is trustworthy".

Some authors treat "distrust" as if it were defined as $\neg\mathbf{B}(\text{``}s \text{ is trustworthy''})$, in which case $\text{distrust}(s) = 1 - \text{trust}(s)$: trust is considered as the complement of distrust [31]. Here, we give distrust a stronger meaning: we distrust someone if we have valid reasons to believe he is lying, not if we do not have valid reasons to believe he is telling the truth. In other words, distrust is not the complement of trust.

A consequence of Eqs. 4 and 5, together with the properties of Π and N, is that trust and distrust, wrt a given domain, obey the following mutual constraints:

$$\text{trust}(s) > 0 \Rightarrow \text{distrust}(s) = 0, \tag{6}$$

$$\text{distrust}(s) > 0 \Rightarrow \text{trust}(s) = 0. \tag{7}$$

In case of total ignorance, we have that $\text{trust}(s) = \text{distrust}(s) = 0$. Notice that if we consider trust as the complement of distrust, we cannot represent the situations of total ignorance in which the agent does not know anything which could lead it to trust or distrust the source; $\text{distrust}(s) = 1 - \text{trust}(s) = 0.5$ would not mean ignorance!

4.2   The Nature of a Source

Any judgment about the competence or willingness of a source to provide useful information must be, implicitly or explicitly, based on an agent's judgment (i.e.,

---

[3] Here, we name such a competence-based trust *credibility*.

beliefs) about the source according to past interactions as well as recommendations or the source's reputations. We will refer to such assessment as the source's *nature*.

Without any claim of exhaustiveness and just to ground our presentation on an intuitive setting, we draw inspiration from the abstract model of a human agent's social behavior proposed by Italian economist Carlo Cipolla [8] as the backdrop on which his theory of human stupidity is expounded.

According to Cipolla's model, an agent's behavior may be summarized by two coordinates:

x the average gain (or loss) that an agent obtains as a result of his or her actions;

y the average gain (or loss) that an agent produces to other agents or groups of agents.

As a result, agents can be plotted as points on a diagram like the one shown in Fig. 1 based on their $\langle x, y \rangle$ behavior. Such a diagram divides the two-dimensional plane into four quadrants or eight sectors, corresponding to different natures of the agents.

For the sake of simplicity, let us represent an agent's position in one of the eight sectors by means of three propositional variables: r if agent s is *rational* $(x > 0)$; m if agent s is *malicious* $(y < 0)$; and e if $|y| < |x|$.

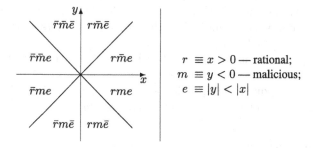

Fig. 1. The correspondence between the eight sectors of the source nature diagram and the truth assignments to the propositional variables r, m, and e.

It is worth mentioning that this concept of *source nature* allows us to model the two kinds of beliefs, namely "willingness belief" and "persistence belief", proposed by Ramchurn [21] to ensure that a certain task can be delegated by an agent to another one. More precisely, the eight sectors we identify are used by the agent to decide when it needs to maintain a suspicious attitude in dealing with malicious or irrational agents.

4.3   Trust and (Shareable) Goals

We make the assumption that the agent's beliefs about the source's goals may also influence its trust in the source. Indeed, regardless of the content of

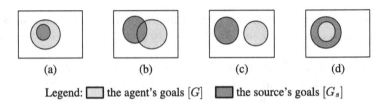

Legend: ▢ the agent's goals $[G]$ ◼ the source's goals $[G_s]$

Fig. 2. A schematic illustration of the four cases of agent's goal-source'goals relationships.

information, if, for example, a source s shares the same goal g with the agent, we may suppose that s will act to fulfill g. This should, at least in case of rational sources, prevent s from taking actions that could negatively influence the satisfaction of g.

The way beliefs about the source's goals, G_s are taken into account is by comparing them with the agent's own goals, G. We distinguish four cases, which represent three possible situations. The four cases are schematically illustrated in Fig. 2.

(a) $[G_s] \subseteq [G]$ or, equivalently, $G_s \models G$: if the source achieves its goals, the agent does too (*necessary help*).

(b) $[G_s] \cap [G] \neq \emptyset$ and $\overline{[G_s]} \cap \overline{[G]} \neq \emptyset$: the agent's and the source's goals are independent: the fact that either of the two achieves its goals does not necessarily imply or exclude that the other does; there is thus room for cooperation (*compatibility*).

(c) $[G_s] \cap [G] = \emptyset$: there is an overt conflict between the agent's and the source's goals (*conflict*).

(d) $[G] \subset [G_s]$ or, equivalently, $G \models G_s$: if the agent achieves its goals, the source does too, but not *vice versa* (*compatibility*).

4.4   Trust in a Source

We assume that an agent has an internal reasoning mechanism allowing it to compute the trust/distrust, τ_z / δ_z, with $z \in \{(a), (b), (c), (d)\}$ (the four cases in Sect. 4.3). Such degrees depend on the agent's beliefs about the source's position in the nature diagram and its beliefs about the source's goals with respect to its own goals. Figure 3 shows a minimal such mechanism based on look-up tables.

Computing trust can be seen as a set of material implications. Given a source's position in the nature diagram, "if the source's goals configuration is z, then the agent will associate a trust τ_z to that source". However, the agent may not know precisely the source's position and it can just have a notion of order about which among the eight possible sectors the source could be in, some of them being more possible than others. If we consider a source s, the uncertainty is captured in our formalism trough the possibility distribution on the worlds (i.e., interpretations) $\mathcal{I}$ which are consistent with $\{0,1\}^{\{r_s, m_s, e_s\}}$. The

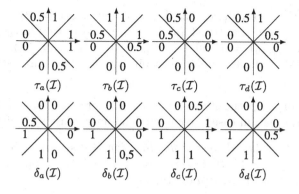

Fig. 3. A definition of functions $\tau_z(\mathcal{I})$ and $\delta_z(\mathcal{I})$, for $z \in \{a, b, c, d\}$ and $\mathcal{I} \in \{0, 1\}^{\{r, m, s\}}$.

above implication is then represented as a fuzzy implication. Among the existing definitions of fuzzy implications (see for example [16] for a survey) we adopt the Kleene-Dienes fuzzy implication. Other definitions might be used as well. The truth value of the fuzzy implication "If a source is somehow compatible with situation $\mathcal{I}$, then the agent trusts that source to degree $\tau_z(\mathcal{I})$" quantifies to what extent "the agent trusts that source to degree $\tau_z(\mathcal{I})$" is at least as true as "that source is somehow compatible with situation $\mathcal{I}$". Let us recall that we consider eight possible positions and that we have a possibility distribution on these positions. We have then eight fuzzy implications with their respective truth values. Therefore, for each goal configuration z, we define the trust and distrust that the agent has in source s as follows:[4]

$$\text{trust}_z(s) = \min_{\mathcal{I} \in \{0,1\}^{\{r_s, m_s, e_s\}}} \max\{\tau_z(\mathcal{I}), 1 - \pi(\mathcal{I})\}, \tag{8}$$

$$\text{distrust}_z(s) = \min_{\mathcal{I} \in \{0,1\}^{\{r_s, m_s, e_s\}}} \max\{\delta_z(\mathcal{I}), 1 - \pi(\mathcal{I})\}. \tag{9}$$

Besides, we can also have uncertainty about the configuration of the source's goals. The overall trust/distrust of an agent in a source s depends then on *(i)* its judgment about a source defined by τ_z/δ_z, *(ii)* the uncertainty about the source's real nature, and *(iii)* the uncertainty about the source's goals. We thus define these trust and distrust values based on goals and nature as follows:

$$\text{trust}(s) = \min_{z \in \{a,b,c,d\}} \max\{\text{trust}_z(s), 1 - \pi(z)\}, \tag{10}$$

$$\text{distrust}(s) = \min_{z \in \{a,b,c,d\}} \max\{\text{distrust}_z(s), 1 - \pi(z)\}. \tag{11}$$

Proposition 2. *If the two functions $\tau_z(\mathcal{I})$ and $\delta_z(\mathcal{I})$ are such that, for all z and $\mathcal{I}$, $\tau_z(\mathcal{I}) > 0 \Rightarrow \delta_z(\mathcal{I}) = 0$ and $\delta_z(\mathcal{I}) > 0 \Rightarrow \tau_z(\mathcal{I}) = 0$, then, for all source s, trust(s) and distrust(s) satisfy the bipolar conditions of Eqs. 6 and 7.*

---

[4] For the the sake of readability, we restrict the interpretations $\mathcal{I}$ as if the language were built on atomic propositions r_s, m_s, and e_s only.

Proof. Since π is normalized, $\exists z_0, \mathcal{I}_0$ such that $\pi(z_0) = \pi(\mathcal{I}_0) = 1$. Then, $\mathrm{trust}(s) > 0 \Rightarrow \forall z \; \max\{\mathrm{trust}_z(s), 1 - \pi(z)\} > 0 \Rightarrow \mathrm{trust}_{z_0}(s) > 0 \Rightarrow \tau_{z_0}(\mathcal{I}_0) > 0 \Rightarrow \delta_{z_0}(\mathcal{I}_0) = 0$ and $1 - \pi(\mathcal{I}_0) = 0 \Rightarrow \max\{\delta_{z_0}(\mathcal{I}_0), 1 - \pi(\mathcal{I}_0)\} = 0 \Rightarrow \mathrm{distrust}(s) = 0$. A similar reasoning proves that $\mathrm{distrust}(s) > 0 \Rightarrow \mathrm{trust}(s) = 0$. □

A corollary of this proposition is that, for all source s, $\mathrm{trust}(s) + \mathrm{distrust}(s) \leq 1$. We can notice that, in case of complete ignorance, $\mathrm{trust}(s) = \mathrm{distrust}(s) = 0$.

Definition 5. *(Trustworthiness Order Relation) Let s_1 and s_2 be two information sources. We consider that s_1 is less trustworthy than s_2, $s_1 \preceq s_2$, if and only if $\mathrm{trust}(s_1) \leq \mathrm{trust}(s_2)$ and $\mathrm{distrust}(s_1) \geq \mathrm{distrust}(s_2)$.*

Proposition 3. *(Total Order) The relation $\preceq$ is a total order.*

Proof. The thesis is a direct consequence of Eqs. 6 and 7. □

4.5   Credibility and Competence

Let D be the set of domains of competence considered for the agent and the sources. The agent's competences are represented through a vector κ, whose component κ_d represents the extent to which the agent is competent with respect to domain $d \in D$. Moreover, we suppose that the agent may have beliefs about the competences of a source. To this aim, we assume that Prop contains propositions c_d^s, meaning "source s is competent about domain d"; $\mathbf{B}(c_d^s)$ will thus be the extent to which the agent believes s is competent about d.

Definition 6. *Let $\phi \not\equiv \perp$ be new information provided by s. The extent to which the agent deems ϕ credible, given that ϕ is reported by source s, is*

$$\mathrm{cr}(\phi, s) = \max\{\mathbf{B}(\phi), \max_{d \in D} \min\{\mathrm{cr}_d(\phi, s), R(\phi, d)\}\}, \quad (12)$$

where

$$\mathrm{cr}_d(\phi, s) = \begin{cases} \min\{\mathbf{B}(c_d^s), 1 - \kappa_d, \Pi([\phi])\}, & \textit{if } \kappa_d > \mathbf{B}(c_d^s); \\ \mathbf{B}(c_d^s), & \textit{otherwise.} \end{cases} \quad (13)$$

For the sake of completeness, $\forall s, \mathrm{cr}(\perp, s) = 0$.

Equation 12 may be paraphrased as "ϕ being reported by s is credible if there exists a domain to which ϕ is related and with respect to which it is credible". Taking a max with $\mathbf{B}(\phi)$ accounts for the fact that the extent to which something is believable cannot be less than it is already believed, no matter which source is reporting it, since credibility is the quality of being believable. Besides, a message is believable if we deem it possible. Formally, for all formula ϕ provided by a source s we have $\mathbf{B}(\phi) \leq \mathrm{cr}(\phi, s) \leq \Pi([\phi])$. This definition of credibility allows us to capture the notion of "competence belief" proposed in [21], going even further by using both the receiving agent's own competence and the source's expected competences to assess the credibility of the information item.

Equation 13 involves two cases:

- if the agent is not more competent about d than the source is ($\kappa_d \leq \mathbf{B}(c_d^s)$, second case of Eq. 13), then it will not try to filter the incoming message according to its own beliefs; this is a mandatory assumption if an agent is to be capable of learning from sources it believes to be more knowledgeable than it is;
- if, however, the agent believes to be more competent about d than the source ($\kappa_d > \mathbf{B}(c_d^s)$, first case of Eq. 13), information supplied by the source should be evaluated by its internal credibility; in addition, the resulting credibility of supplied information should not be greater than the competence of the source providing it, otherwise an agent scarcely competent about a domain would incur the risk of accepting acritically anything that a source just a little more competent than it about that domain would say, which is not in conflict with its (admittedly very incomplete) beliefs.

Furthermore, the first case in Eq. 13 refers to an "internal" credibility of ϕ, which satisfies the following two intuitive properties:

1. if ϕ is completely relevant to d, $\mathrm{cr}_d(\phi) \leq 1 - \mathbf{B}(\neg\phi)$;
2. the more the agent's knowledge is complete on domain d (i.e., the agent is competent), the more $\mathrm{cr}_d(\phi)$ will approach its lower bound $\mathbf{B}(\phi)$ and, *vice versa*, the more the agent is ignorant about d, the more it must be keen on heeding a ϕ that does not contradict its current beliefs.

Like in [6], for example, the idea here is to capture the fact that a piece of information is accepted by the agent if and only if it is "credible" for the agent. "Our definition" of credibility is nevertheless different from the one used by Booth *et al.* They consider the set of credible formulas as "an (explicit) part of an epistemic state, since it defines how easily an agent can accept very implausible new pieces of information". In our setting, the credibility of a piece of information represents the capability of the agent to evaluate the tenability of the piece of information with respect to its own competences and the ones of the sources. Obviously, if the agent is less competent or not competent at all with respect to a domain, this credibility degree must depend (be weighted), in a sense, by the source's competence.

Proposition 4. *Given a source s, $\mathrm{cr}(\cdot, s)$ is a normalized fuzzy measure.*

Proof. We must prove that $\mathrm{cr}(\bot, s) = 0$; $\mathrm{cr}(\top, s) = 1$; and $\forall \phi, \psi \in \mathcal{L}$, $\phi \models \psi \Rightarrow \mathrm{cr}(\phi, s) \leq \mathrm{cr}(\psi, s)$ (monotonicity). Now, $\mathrm{cr}(\bot, s) = 0$ holds by definition; $\mathrm{cr}(\top, s) = 1$ holds because $\mathrm{cr}(\top, s) = \max\{\mathbf{B}(\top), \max_{d \in D} \min\{\mathrm{cr}_d(\top, s), R(\top, d)\}\} \geq \mathbf{B}(\top) = 1$. To prove monotonicity, we observe that, for every domain $d \in D$,

- $\mathbf{B}(\phi) \leq \mathbf{B}(\psi)$, because $\mathbf{B}$ is a fuzzy measure;
- $R(\phi, d) \leq R(\psi, d)$ by Proposition 1;
- $\Pi([\phi]) \leq \Pi([\psi])$, because Π is a fuzzy measure;
- $\mathbf{B}(c_d^s)$ and κ_d do not depend on ϕ or ψ.

Therefore, since $\max\{a, b\} \leq \max\{c, d\}$ and $\min\{a, b\} \leq \min\{c, d\}$ if $a \leq c$ and $b \leq d$, $\mathrm{cr}(\phi, s) \leq \mathrm{cr}(\psi, s)$. $\square$

Being the credibility $\mathrm{cr}(\cdot, s)$ in an information content provided by a certain source a fuzzy measure, the following two properties hold:

Proposition 5. *Given a source* s, $\forall \phi, \psi \in \mathcal{L}$, $\mathrm{cr}(\phi \vee \psi, s) \geq \max(\mathrm{cr}(\psi, s), and$ $\mathrm{cr}(\psi, s))$ $\mathrm{cr}(\phi \wedge \psi, s) \leq \min(\mathrm{cr}(\psi, s), \mathrm{cr}(\psi, s))$.

Proof. $\forall \phi, \psi \in \mathcal{L}$, (a) $\phi \models \phi \vee \psi$, and $\psi \models \phi \vee \psi$; therefore, $\mathrm{cr}(\phi, s) \leq \mathrm{cr}(\phi \vee \psi, s)$ and $\mathrm{cr}(\psi, s) \leq \mathrm{cr}(\phi \vee \psi, s)$; (b) $\phi \wedge \psi \models \phi$ and $\phi \wedge \psi \models \psi$; therefore, $\mathrm{cr}(\phi \wedge \psi, s) \leq \mathrm{cr}(\phi, s)$ and $\mathrm{cr}(\phi \wedge \psi, s) \leq \mathrm{cr}(\psi, s)$. $\square$

4.6 Accepting Information

The extent to which a piece of information ϕ (provided by a source s) is accepted by an agent depends on the trust and distrust computed on the basis of the source's goals and nature (Eqs. 10 and 11) and the credibility of ϕ for the agent (Eq. 12) which depends on the competences of the agent and the sources. We may be combined these values using the minimum triangular norm, to yield the extent to which ϕ provided by s is accepted by the agent:

$$\mathrm{acc}(\phi, s) = \min\{\mathrm{cr}(\phi, s), \mathrm{trust}(s)\}. \tag{14}$$

The choice of min as the aggregation operator is motivated by the fact that an agent should accept information ϕ provided by source s to the extent to which it deems ϕ credible and s trustworthy according to its goals and nature.

Proposition 6. $\forall s$, $\mathrm{acc}(\cdot, s)$ *is a fuzzy measure. It is normalized if* $\mathrm{trust}(s) = 1$.

Proof. Since $\mathrm{acc}(\cdot, s)$ is the min of a normalized fuzzy measure and $\mathrm{trust}(s)$, which is a constant for a fixed s, $\mathrm{acc}(\cdot, s)$ is a fuzzy measure, i.e., $\mathrm{acc}(\bot, s) = 0$ and, for $\phi, \psi \in \mathcal{L}$ such that $\phi \models \psi$,

$$\mathrm{acc}(\phi, s) = \min\{\mathrm{cr}(\phi, s), \mathrm{trust}(s)\} \leq \min\{\mathrm{cr}(\psi, s), \mathrm{trust}(s)\} = \mathrm{acc}(\psi, s).$$

Finally, if $\mathrm{trust}(s) = 1$, $\mathrm{acc}(\top, s) = \min\{\mathrm{cr}(\top, s), 1\} = \min\{1, 1\} = 1$. $\square$

A piece of information ϕ may be provided by more sources. In this case, the extent to which ϕ is accepted by the agent, $\mathrm{accepted}(\phi)$ may be defined as

$$\mathrm{accepted}(\phi) = \max_{s \in \mathrm{src}(\phi)} \{\mathrm{acc}(\phi, s)\}, \tag{15}$$

where $\mathrm{src}(\phi)$ denotes the sources of ϕ. Operators other than max might be used, e.g., operators with cumulative effects. The value $\mathrm{accepted}(\phi)$ may be used as input weight for any weighted belief revision operator, like the ones studied in [3].

Experimental results obtained by Sparks in [26] shows that when untrustworthy sources provide non-credible information, individuals are less likely to revise their initial beliefs. Our formalism also captures the fact that the initial beliefs of an agent are not revised if new information is non-credible or is provided by untrustworthy sources.

5 Conclusion

The goal of this paper is to shed some light on a few fundamental formal aspects of credibility and trust as used by humans in view of their implementation on computers. More precisely, our contribution consists in providing a model for computing the acceptance of information provided by a source taking into account both trust in the source and credibility of the message.

Our model encompasses, but is not limited to, the four "kinds" of beliefs needed by an agent before delegating a task to another agent [21], where the task is "to provide useful information". In particular,

- "competence belief" is captured by "our" definition of credibility that goes even further by using also the receiving agent's own competence to assess information provided by another agent;
- "willingness belief" and "persistence belief" are captured thanks to the concept of "source nature": we should always adopt and maintain a suspicious attitude with respect to an agent we believe to be irrational for example; and
- "motivation belief" is captured by taking into account both the goals of the agent and the ones of the source: the agent believes that a source sharing its goals has some motivation to help it.

As for future work, we plan to apply our formalism towards a cognitive view of *adversarial reasoning*, and to analyze and reason over *irrational* behavior (i.e., stupid agents are dangerous because they act irrationally).

References

1. Adali, S.: Modeling Trust Context in Networks. Springer Briefs. Springer, Heidelberg (2013)
2. Ben-Naim, J., Prade, H.: Evaluating trustworthiness from past performances: interval-based approaches. In: Greco, S., Lukasiewicz, T. (eds.) SUM 2008. LNCS (LNAI), vol. 5291, pp. 33–46. Springer, Heidelberg (2008)
3. Benferhat, S., da Costa Pereira, C., Tettamanzi, A.: Syntactic computation of hybrid possibilistic conditioning under uncertain inputs. In: IJCAI (2013)
4. Benferhat, S., Dubois, D., Prade, H., Williams, M.-A.: A practical approach to revising prioritized knowledge bases. Stud. Logica **70**(1), 105–130 (2002)
5. Booth, R., Fermé, E., Konieczny, S., Pino Pérez, R.: Credibility-limited revision operators in propositional logic. In: KR 2012 (2012)
6. Booth, R., Fermé, E., Konieczny, S., Pino Pérez, R.: Credibility-limited improvement operators. In: ECAI 2014, pp. 123–128 (2014)
7. Castelfranchi, C., Falcone, R.: Social trust: a cognitive approach. In: Castelfranchi, C., Tan, Y.-H. (eds.) Trust and Deception in Virtual Societies, pp. 55–90. Springer, Heidelberg (2001)
8. Cipolla, C.M.: The Basic Laws of Human Stupidity. il Mulino, Bologna (2011)
9. da Costa Pereira, C., Tettamanzi, A.: Belief-goal relationships in possibilistic goal generation. In: ECAI 2010, pp. 641–646 (2010)
10. Delgrande, J., Dubois, D., Lang, J.: Iterated revision as prioritized merging. In: KR, pp. 210–220 (2006)

11. Dragoni, A., Giorgini, P.: Belief revision through the belief-function formalism in a multi-agent environment. In: ATAL, pp. 103–115 (1996)

12. Falcone, R., Piunti, M., Venanzi, M., Castelfranchi, C.: From manifesta to krypta: the relevance of categories for trusting others. ACM Trans. Intell. Syst. Technol. **4**(2), 27:1–27:24 (2013)

13. Gabbay, D., Pigozzi, G., Woods, J.: Controlled revision–an algorithmic approach for belief revision. J. Log. Comput. **13**(1), 3–22 (2003)

14. Krümpelmann, P., Tamargo, L.H., García, A.J., Falappa, M.A.: Forwarding credible information in multi-agent systems. In: Karagiannis, D., Jin, Z. (eds.) KSEM 2009. LNCS, vol. 5914, pp. 41–53. Springer, Heidelberg (2009)

15. Lalmas, M.: Logical models in information retrieval: introduction and overview. Inf. Process. Manage. **34**(1), 19–33 (1998)

16. Mas, M., Monserrat, M., Torrens, J., Trillas, E.: A survey on fuzzy implication functions. Trans. Fuzzy Syst. **15**(6), 1107–1121 (2007)

17. McKnight, D.H., Chervany, N.L.: Trust and distrust definitions: one bite at a time. In: Falcone, R., Singh, M., Tan, Y.-H. (eds.) AA-WS 2000. LNCS (LNAI), vol. 2246, pp. 27–54. Springer, Heidelberg (2001)

18. Paglieri, F., Castelfranchi, C., da Costa Pereira, C., Falcone, R., Tettamanzi, A., Villata, S.: Trusting the messenger because of the message: feedback dynamics from information quality to source evaluation. Comput. Math. Organ. Theor. **20**(2), 176–194 (2014)

19. Pinyol, I., Sabater-Mir, J.: Computational trust and reputation models for open multi-agent systems: a review. Artif. Intell. Rev. **40**(1), 1–25 (2013)

20. Bies, R.J., Lewicki, R.J., Mcallister, D.J.: Trust and distrust: new relationships and realities. Acad. Manage. Rev. **23**(3), 438–458 (1998)

21. Ramchurn, S.D., Huynh, D., Jennings, N.R.: Trust in multi-agent systems. Knowl. Eng. Rev. **19**(1), 1–25 (2004)

22. Robinson, J.P., Shaver, P.R., Wrightsman, L.S.: Measures of Personality and Social Psychological Attitudes. Measures of Social Psychological Attitudes. Academic Press, Cambridge (1991)

23. Sabater, J., Sierra, C.: Regret: reputation in gregarious societies. In: Proceedings of the Fifth International Conference on Autonomous Agents, AGENTS 2001, pp. 194–195 (2001)

24. Shafer, G.: A Mathematical Theory of Evidence. Princeton University Press, Princeton (1976)

25. Sierra, C., Debenham, J.: An information-based model for trust. In: AAMAS, pp. 497–504. ACM (2005)

26. Sparks, J.R., Rapp, D.N.: Unreliable and anomalous: how the credibility of data affects belief revision. In: Annual Conference of the Cognitive Science Society, pp. 741–746 (2011)

27. Tamargo, L., García, A., Falappa, M., Simari, G.: Modeling knowledge dynamics in multi-agent systems based on informants. Knowl. Eng. Rev. **27**(1), 87–114 (2012)

28. Teacy, L., Patel, J., Jennings, N., Luck, M.: TRAVOS: trust and reputation in the context of inaccurate information sources. JAAMAS **12**, 183–198 (2006)

29. Ughetto, L., Claveau, V.: Different interpretations of fuzzy gradual-inclusion-based IR models. In: EUSFLAT, pp. 431–438 (2011)

30. Ughetto, L., Pasi, G., Claveau, V., Pivert, O., Bosc, P.: Implication in information retrieval systems. In: RIAO, pp. 61–64 (2010)

31. Ullmann-Margalit, E.: Trust out of distrust. J. Philos. **99**(10), 532–548 (2002)

32. Zadeh, L.A.: Fuzzy sets. Inf. Control **8**, 338–353 (1965)

Intertranslatability of Labeling-Based Argumentation Semantics

Sarah Alice Gaggl$^{(\boxtimes)}$ and Umer Mushtaq

Faculty of Informatics, Technische Universität Dresden, Dresden, Germany
omarmalizai@gmail.com

Abstract. Abstract Argumentation is a simple yet powerful formalism for modeling the human reasoning and argumentation process. Various semantics have been suggested with a view of arriving at coherent outcomes of the argumentation process. Two categories of semantics are well-known, extension-based semantics and labeling-based semantics. Translations between semantics are an important area of interest that enhance our understanding of the dynamics of various semantics and their structural and semantic interrelationship. The application of translations to extension-based semantics has been investigated in detail in the literature, however for labeling-based semantics which provide a more fine grained notion of acceptability such translations have not yet been studied. In this work, we fill this gab by investigating intertranslatability of labeling-based semantics. We show in which cases the existing results from the extension-based setting carry over to the labeling-based setting and we investigate intertranslatability between the three unique status semantics *grounded, ideal* and *eager*.

Keywords: Argumentation · Labeling-based semantics · Translations

1 Introduction

Argumentation theory and in particular abstract argumentation frameworks have become a popular field in artificial intelligence. In an abstract argumentation framework (AF) as introduced by Dung in 1995 [6], one can model scenarios with conflicting knowledge by considering only abstract entities called *arguments* and a binary relation between them the so-called *attack relation*. The inherent conflicts are solved on a semantical level usually by selecting sets of arguments, so-called *extensions* which can be accepted together. An alternative view on the semantics is in terms of labeling functions, where one assigns a label to each argument, depending on the specific semantics, denoting if it should be accepted (*in*), rejected (*out*) or undecided (*undec*) [5,13]. Thus, labeling-based semantics give a more fine grained notion of the status of each argument.

The notion of intertranslatability for the extension-based semantics has been investigated in much detail for most of the prominent semantics [8,9]. For two semantics σ, σ', intertranslatability involves translating an AF F to another AF

© Springer International Publishing Switzerland 2016
S. Schockaert and P. Senellart (Eds.): SUM 2016, LNAI 9858, pp. 155–169, 2016.
DOI: 10.1007/978-3-319-45856-4_11

F' through new arguments and new attacks between arguments such that the σ-extensions of F are in a certain relation to the σ'-extensions of F'. In case of extensions one just needs to compare the sets of accepted arguments, however when one considers labelings one needs to compare the status of each argument, as the transformation of the AF might also change the status of the *out* and *undec* labeled arguments.

Knowing about intertranslatability might become more and more important when it comes to the use of argumentation systems for the evaluation. In particular if one has an efficient system for semantics σ but one wants to evaluate an AF F w.r.t. semantics τ where no good implementations exits. Then, one would be interested in translating F into F' such that the σ-labelings of F are in a certain relation to the τ-labelings of F'.

The development of efficient systems to evaluate argumentation frameworks became a major topic. This is also reflected by the newly founded International Competition on Computational Models of Argumentation (ICCMA) which took place in 2015 for the first time [11]. Several argumentation systems use labeling-based algorithms in their computation [10,13], thus knowing about intertranslatability for labeling-based semantics can contribute to the development for such systems, or in the use of such systems.

The main contributions of this article are (i) the definition of *exact, faithful* and *weakly* translations for the labeling-based semantics, according to the intuition from [8,9]; (ii) we show under which conditions the results from the extension-based setting carry over to the labeling-based setting, in particular for the results on faithful translations we need to introduce an additional restriction on the translation to preserve the status of arguments labeled with *undec*; and (iii) we investigate intertranslatability between the unique-status semantics *grounded, ideal* and *eager* [3,7].

This article is organized as follows. In Sect. 2 we introduce the necessary background on abstract argumentation frameworks and the semantics in terms of extensions and labelings. In Sect. 3 we define the different types of translations for the labeling-based semantics, and in Sect. 4 we show which results from the extension-based setting carry over to the labeling-based one. Then, in Sect. 5 we analyze intertranslatability between the unique-status semantics grounded, ideal and eager. Finally, in Sect. 6 we conclude and discuss future directions.

2 Preliminaries

In this chapter we introduce argumentation frameworks. We then define various extension and labeling-based semantics. We also recall some results from other works which shall prove useful in our investigations.

Argumentation Frameworks were introduced by Dung [6]. Formally, an argumentation framework is a pair (A, R) where A is a set of arguments and $R \subseteq A \times A$ is the attack relation. The relation $(a, b) \in R$ means argument a attacks argument b. Similarly, a set of arguments $S \subseteq A$ attacks an argument $a \in A$ if and only if, $\exists b \in S$ such that $(b, a) \in R$.

Additionally, for a set $S \subseteq A$ of arguments, we denote by S^-, the set of all arguments that attack S, i.e., $S^- = \{b \mid \exists a \in S : (b, a) \in R\}$. For a set $S \subseteq A$ of arguments, we denote by S^+ the set of all arguments which are attacked by S, i.e., $S^+ = \{b \mid \exists a \in S : (a, b) \in R\}$. For $S \subseteq A$ and $a \in A$, we write $S \rightarrow a$, if there exists an argument $b \in S$ such that $(b, a) \in R$. Furthermore, an argument a is defended in an AF F by a set $S \subseteq A$ if for every $b \in A$, such that $(b, a) \in R$, $S \rightarrow b$. Lastly, the range of a set $S \subseteq A$, denoted by S_R^+, is defined as $S_R^+ = S \cup \{b \mid S \rightarrow b\}$. Argumentation frameworks can be represented as directed graphs with nodes representing arguments and edges representing attacks. We now define extension-based semantics drawing upon the works [1,2,6,12].

Let $F = (A_F, R_F)$ be an AF. A set $S \subseteq A$ is *conflict-free* in F, if there are no $a, b \in S$ such that $(a, b) \in R$. For a conflict-free set S:

- $S \in adm(F)$, if each $a \in S$ is defended by S;
- $S \in prf(F)$, if $S \in adm(F)$ and there is no $T \in adm(F)$ with $S \subset T$;
- $S \in com(F)$, if $S \in adm(F)$ and for each $a \in A$ that is defended by S, $a \in S$;
- $S \in grd(F)$, if $S \in com(F)$ and there is no $T \in com(F)$ with $T \subset S$;
- $S \in sem(F)$, if $S \in adm(F)$ and there is no $T \in adm(F)$ with $S_R^+ \subset T_R^+$;
- $S \in stb(F)$, if for each $a \in A \setminus S$, $S \rightarrow a$;
- $S \in stg(F)$, if there is no conflict-free set T in F, such that $T_R^+ \subset S_R^+$;
- $S \in idl(F)$, if $S \in adm(F)$ and S is the biggest set (w.r.t. set inclusion) such that for all $T \in prf(F)$, $S \subseteq T$;
- $S \in eag(F)$, if $S \in adm(F)$ and S is the biggest set (w.r.t. set inclusion) such that for all $T \in com(F)$, $S \subseteq T$.

Where *adm, prf, com, grd, sem, stb, stg, idl* and *eag* stand for admissible, preferred, complete, grounded, semi-stable, stable, stage, ideal and eager semantics.

Labeling-based semantics start by assigning a label from a set of labels $\Lambda = \{in, out, undec\}$ to every argument in an AF F. The set of labels, Λ, stands for accepted, rejected and undecided arguments respectively. The semantics then selects labelings from the set of all possible labelings which it sees as representing a coherent outcome of the conflicts in the AF. Another important notion is that of *'legally'* labeled.

- An *in*-labeled argument is said to be legally *in* if and only if all it's attackers are labeled *out*;
- An *out*-labeled argument is said to be legally *out* if and only if at least one of it's attackers is labeled *in*;
- An *undec*-labeled argument is said to be legally *undec* if and only if not all it's attackers are labeled *out* and it does not have an attacker that is labeled *in*.

In this work, we will denote by L, possibly indexed, a single labeling and $\mathcal{L}_\sigma(F)$ will represent the set of labelings for an AF F under a semantics σ.

We represent a labeling L for an AF F as a triple $L = (in(L), out(L), undec(L))$ where $in(L) = \{a \in A \mid L(a) = in\}$; $out(L) = \{a \in A \mid L(a) = out\}$; $undec(L) = \{a \in A \mid L(a) = undec\}$. For the set of *in*-labeled arguments of a labeling L, $in(L)$, we define $in(L) \downarrow_S$, the reduction of $in(L)$ to a set $S \subseteq A_F$ of arguments as: $in(L) \downarrow_S = \{in(L) \cap S\}$. $out(L) \downarrow_S$ and $undec(L) \downarrow_S$ are defined similarly. For a set of labelings of an AF F under the semantics σ, $\mathcal{L}_\sigma(F)$, the reduction of this set of labelings to a set of arguments S, $\mathcal{L}_\sigma(F) \downarrow_S$, is defined as: $\mathcal{L}_\sigma(F) \downarrow_S = \{(in(L) \cap S, out(L) \cap S, undec(L) \cap S) \mid L \in \mathcal{L}_\sigma(F)\}$.

Let L_1, L_2 be two labelings for an argumentation framework F. We say that L_2 is more or equally committed than $L_1(L_1 \sqsubseteq L_2)$ iff $in(L_1) \subseteq in(L_2)$ and $out(L_1) \subseteq out(L_2)$. We can then characterize a labeling as being bigger or smaller than another labeling with respect to $\sqsubseteq$ which is a partial order.

We now introduce certain specific labeling-based semantics. A labeling L for an argumentation framework is said to be:

- **Admissible** if every *in*-labeled argument is legally in and every *out*-labeled argument is legally out.
- **Complete** if for all arguments $a \in A$: a is labeled *in* iff it is legally *in*; a is labeled *out* iff it is legally *out*; a is labeled *undec* iff it is legally *undecided*.
- **Grounded** if L is a complete labeling and $in(L)$ is minimal (w.r.t. set inclusion) among all complete labelings.
- **Preferred** if L is a complete labeling and $in(L)$ is maximal (with respect to set inclusion) among all complete labelings.
- **Semi-stable** if L is a complete labeling and $undec(L)$ is minimal (w.r.t set inclusion) among all complete labelings.
- **Stable** if it is a complete labeling with $undec(L) = \emptyset$.
- **Stage** if it is a conflict-free labeling where $undec(L)$ is minimal (w.r.t. set inclusion) among all conflict-free labelings.
- **Ideal** if it is the biggest admissible labeling (with respect to the partial order $\sqsubseteq$) that is smaller than or equal to each preferred labeling.
- **Eager** if it is the biggest admissible labeling (with respect to the partial order $\sqsubseteq$) that is smaller than or equal to each semi-stable labeling.

Among these semantics, *grounded*, *ideal* and *eager* labelings are unique status semantics in that they return a single, unique labeling for every AF. All other semantics are multiple status semantics which return possibly multiple labelings for every AF. *Stable* semantics is the only semantics that is not universally defined.

We now briefly recall some results from previous works which will help us in our investigations. From Caminada and Gabbay [5], we have that there is a bijective correspondence between complete extensions and complete labelings. It follows that for all completeness-based semantics, there is a bijective correspondence between the extension(s) and the labeling(s) for that semantics. All the semantics we consider in this work except *admissible* and *stage* semantics are completeness-based. We also recall from Caminada [4] that stage extensions and stage labelings are in a bijective correspondence. From Caminada [3], we have that the ideal and eager extensions (and hence the ideal and eager labelings) are also complete extensions (labelings). The proofs of these results are omitted here.

3   Translation Properties

By a translation, we mean an expansion of the source argumentation framework with further arguments and attacks, giving rise to the target argumentation framework. Formally, a translation Tr is defined as: $Tr = (A^*, R^*)$ where A^* is a set of additional arguments and R^* is the set of additional attack relations between arguments.

In this section, we first recall exactness and faithfulness properties of translations in the extension-based settings as defined in [9]. We then proceed to define exactness and faithfulness properties for translations in labeling-based semantics.

For two AFs $F = (A, R)$ and $F' = (A', R'), F \subseteq F'$ if and only if $A \subseteq A'$ and $R \subseteq R'$. A translation Tr is called *covering* if for every AF F, $F \subseteq Tr(F)$. A translation Tr is called *embedding* if for every AF F, $A_F \subseteq A_{Tr(F)}$ and $R_F = R_{Tr(F)} \cap (A_F \times A_F)$. We now recall the definitions of exactness and faithfulness properties of translations in the extension-based setting from [9]. For two extension-based semantics σ and σ', a translation Tr is called:

- **Exact:** if for every AF F, $\sigma(F) = \sigma'(Tr(F))$.
- **Weakly Exact:** if there exists S a given finite collection of (remainder) sets of arguments that are exclusively occurring in translated AFs, $\sigma(F) = \sigma'(Tr(F)) \setminus S$.
- **Faithful:** if for every AF F, $\sigma(F) = \{E \cap A_F \mid E \in \sigma'(Tr(F))\}$ and $|\sigma(F)| = |\sigma'(Tr(F))|$.
- **Weakly Faithful:** if there exists S a given finite collection of (remainder) sets of arguments that are exclusively occurring in translated AFs, $\sigma(F) = \{E \cap A_F \mid E \in \sigma'(Tr(F)) \setminus S\}$ and $|\sigma(F)| = |\sigma'(Tr(F)) \setminus S|$.

We now define *exactness* and *faithfulness* for labeling-based semantics. Intuitively, by exactness we mean that the labelings of the source AF under the semantics σ and those of the target framework under the semantics σ' coincide. Formally:

Definition 1. *A translation Tr is called **exact** for semantics $\sigma \Rightarrow \sigma'$ if for every AF F:*

1. $\forall L \in \mathcal{L}_\sigma(F)$: $\exists L' \in \mathcal{L}_{\sigma'}(Tr(F))$: $in(L) = in(L'), out(L) = out(L')\downarrow_{A_F}$, $undec(L) = undec(L')\downarrow_{A_F}$.
2. $|\mathcal{L}_\sigma(F)| = |\mathcal{L}_{\sigma'}(Tr(F))|$.

Definition 2. *A translation Tr is called **weakly exact** for semantics $\sigma \Rightarrow \sigma'$ if there exists a set of arguments A_p that are exclusively occurring in the translated AFs and a finite set of partial labelings $\mathcal{L}_p$ of A_p such that for every AF F and the remainder set $\mathcal{L}' = \{L \in \mathcal{L}_{\sigma'}(Tr(F)) \mid \exists L_p \in \mathcal{L}_p : L\downarrow_{(A_p \cap A_{Tr(F)})} = L_p\}$:*

1. $\forall L \in \mathcal{L}_\sigma(F) : \exists L' \in \mathcal{L}_{\sigma'}(Tr(F)) \setminus \mathcal{L}' : in(L) = in(L'), out(L) = out(L')\downarrow_{A_F}, undec(L) = undec(L')\downarrow_{A_F}$.
2. $|\mathcal{L}_\sigma(F)| = |\mathcal{L}_{\sigma'}(Tr(F)) \setminus \mathcal{L}'|$.

Intuitively, by faithful translations we mean translations that retain the original labelings of the source AF under the initial semantics. Formally:

Definition 3. *A translation Tr is called **faithful** for semantics $\sigma \Rightarrow \sigma'$ if for every AF F, $\mathcal{L}_\sigma(F) = \mathcal{L}_{\sigma'}(Tr(F))\downarrow_{A_F}$ and $|\mathcal{L}_\sigma(F)| = |\mathcal{L}_{\sigma'}(Tr(F))|$.*

Definition 4. *A translation Tr is called **weakly faithful** for semantics $\sigma \Rightarrow \sigma'$ if there exists a finite set of arguments A_p that are exclusively occurring in the translated AFs and a finite set of partial labelings $\mathcal{L}_p$ of labelings A_p such that for every AF F and the remainder set $\mathcal{L}' = \{L \in \mathcal{L}_{\sigma'}(Tr(F)) \mid \exists L_p \in \mathcal{L}_p : L\downarrow_{(A_p \cap A_{Tr(F)})} = L_p\}$: $\mathcal{L}_\sigma(F) = (\mathcal{L}_{\sigma'}(Tr(F)) \setminus \mathcal{L}') \downarrow_{A_F}$ and $|\mathcal{L}_\sigma(F)| = |\mathcal{L}'_\sigma(Tr(F)) \setminus \mathcal{L}'|$.*

Example 1. We now present an example to demonstrate the workings of a *weakly faithful* translation. Let $F = (\{a,b,c\}, \{(a,b),(b,c),(c,b)\})$ be an AF. The translation Tr_3 [9] is defined as: $Tr_3(F) = (A^*, R^*)$ where $A^* = A_F \cup \{t\}$ and $R^* = R_F \cup \{(a,t),(t,a) \mid a \in A_F\}$. The F target framework obtained from applying Tr_3 to F is depicted in Fig. 1.

We have that $\mathcal{L}_{stb}(F) = \{\{a,c\}, \{b\}, \emptyset\}$ and that $\mathcal{L}_{stg}(Tr_3(F)) = \{(\{a,c\}, \{b\}, \emptyset), (\{t\}, \{a,b,c\}, \emptyset)\}$. It is proven in [9] that Tr_3 is weakly exact for $stb \Rightarrow stg$ in the extension-based setting. By Theorem 2, we have that Tr_3 is embedding and weakly exact for $stb \Rightarrow stg$ in the labeling-based setting with $A_p = \{t\}$ and $\mathcal{L}' = \{(\{t\}, \{a,b,c\}, \emptyset)\}$.

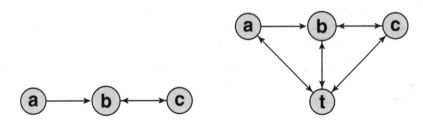

Fig. 1. The source AF F (left) and the target AF $Tr_3(F)$ (right)

4 Extension-Based and Labeling-Based Semantics Translation Comparison

Dvořák and Woltran [9] investigated intertranslatability between extension-based semantics and defined the notions of exactness and faithfulness for extension-based semantics. Having defined exactness and faithfulness for labeling-based semantics, in this section we investigate the relationship between the exactness and faithfulness of translations in extension-based setting to that in labeling-based setting.

First, we define a class of translations called *reserved translations* which will help simplify our investigations. We need the notion of reserved translations in order to be able to establish equivalence between faithfulness in extension-based and labeling-based setting since a translation which is faithful in extension-based setting maybe not be faithful in labeling-based because new arguments in the translation may attack arguments which were *undec* in the original framework and cause them to be *out* in the target framework. We say that a set of arguments in an AF F constitutes a cycle iff every argument in the set is reachable via the attack relation from every other argument in the set. The set of cycles of an AF is denoted by $cyc(F)$. The length of a cycle C is denoted by l_c. We define the function $\Psi(F)$ as:

$$\Psi(F) = \{C \in cyc(F) \mid \forall c \in A \setminus C, b \in C, (c, b) \in R : \{c\}^- \neq \emptyset\}$$

An argument $a \in A$ is *cycle-reachable* in F i.e. $a \in cr(F)$ iff one of the following conditions holds true:

1. $\exists C \in \Psi(F) : a \in C$
2. $\exists C \in \Psi(F)$ s.t. there exists a path from an argument $b \in C$ to a and no argument in the path is attacked by an argument which has no attackers.

The set of cycle-reachable arguments of an AF F is denoted by $cr(F)$.

Then *reserved translations* are translations where new arguments that attack cycle-reachable arguments in the original AF cannot be labeled *in* under any completeness-based semantics. For an AF F and a translation $Tr = (A^*, R^*)$ we define the function $\Omega(Tr(F))$ as:

$$\Omega(Tr(F)) = \{a \in A^* \mid \exists b \in cr(F) : (a, b) \in R^*\}$$

A translation Tr is called *reserved* iff one of the following conditions holds:

1. $\forall a \in \Omega(Tr(F)) : (a, a) \in R^*$
2. $\forall a \in \Omega(Tr(F)) : \exists c \in A' : (c, a) \in R^*, \{c\}^- = \emptyset$
3. $\forall a \in \Omega(Tr(F)) : a$ is cycle-reachable in $Tr(F)$.

Lemma 1. *Let $F = (A_F, R)$ be an AF and let σ be a completeness-based semantics. Then: $\forall a \in A_F : \exists L \in \mathcal{L}_\sigma(F) : L(a) = undec$ only if a is cycle-reachable in F.*

Proof. We do a proof by contradiction. Let $a \in A_F$ be an argument in F and for a labeling L under a completeness-based semantics σ, let $L(a) = undec$ and let a be non cycle-reachable.

Since $L(a) = undec$, by definition we have that there exists an argument $b \in A$ such that $(b, a) \in R$ and $L(b) = undec$. Now we have that either a attacks b or b has an attacker c and $L(c) = undec$. In the first case we get that (a, b) is a cycle and we have a contradiction. In the second case, we have that either b attacks c or c has an attacker d and $L(d) = undec$. Again, in the first case we have that (b, c) constitutes a cycle and we have a contradiction. In the second case, we have that either c attacks d or d has another undecided attacker. By the same token, we have that either there exists an infinite chain of undecided arguments or their exists an undecided argument x_i which is attacked by an undecided argument x_{i-1} which it also attacks. Since we confine ourselves to finite AFs, we have that (x_i, x_{i-1}) constitutes a cycle and hence that a is cycle-reachable which is a contradiction and this completes our proof. $\qquad\qquad\square$

4.1   Exactness Comparison

We now derive the equivalences between translation properties in the extension-based and labeling-based settings.

Theorem 1. *Let σ, $\sigma' \in \{com, grd, prf, sem, stb, idl, eag\}$. A embedding translation Tr is exact for $\sigma \Rightarrow \sigma'$ in the extension-based setting, if and only if Tr is exact for $\sigma \Rightarrow \sigma'$ in the labeling-based setting.*

Proof. $\Rightarrow$: Let a translation Tr be exact for $\sigma \Rightarrow \sigma'$ in the extension-based setting. Then, by definition, we have that for all AFs F, $\sigma(F) = \sigma'(Tr(F))$. Let $in(\mathcal{L}_\sigma(F))$ be the set of in-labeled arguments (extensions) of F under the semantics σ, i.e., $in(\mathcal{L}_\sigma(F)) = \{in(L) \mid L \in \mathcal{L}_\sigma(F)\}$. Let $in(\mathcal{L}_{\sigma'}(Tr(F))) = \{in(L) \mid L \in \mathcal{L}_{\sigma'}(Tr(F))\}$ be the same for the AF $Tr(F)$ and the semantics σ'. Since $\sigma(F) = \sigma'(Tr(F))$, we have that $in(\mathcal{L}_\sigma(F)) = in(\mathcal{L}_{\sigma'}(Tr(F)))$. Hence we have that $\forall L \in \mathcal{L}_\sigma(F) : \exists L' \in \mathcal{L}_{\sigma'}(Tr(F)) : in(L) = in(L')$. We note that since both σ, σ' are completeness-based and that it is proven in [5] that there is a bijective correspondence between complete extensions and complete labelings, we can conclude that

$$\forall L \in \mathcal{L}_\sigma(F) : \exists L' \in \mathcal{L}_{\sigma'}(Tr(F)) : (in(L) = in(L'), out(L) = out(L')\!\downarrow_{A_F},$$
$$undec(L) = undec(L')\!\downarrow_{A_F}) \; and \; |\mathcal{L}_\sigma(F))| = |\mathcal{L}_{\sigma'}(Tr(F))|$$

which completes our proof.

$\Leftarrow$: We know from Caminada and Gabbay [5] that there is a bijective correspondence between complete extensions and complete labelings and we have by definition that σ, σ' are completeness-based. Since $\sigma(F) = \{in(L) \mid L \in \mathcal{L}_\sigma(F)\}$ and $\sigma'(F) = \{in(L) \mid L \in \mathcal{L}_{\sigma'}(Tr(F))\}$ and since Tr is exact for $\sigma \Rightarrow \sigma'$ in the labeling-based setting, it follows that Tr is exact for $\sigma \Rightarrow \sigma'$ in the extension-based setting as well. $\qquad\square$

Theorem 2. *Let σ, $\sigma' \in \{com, grd, prf, sem, stb, idl, eag\}$. If an embedding translation Tr is weakly exact for $\sigma \Rightarrow \sigma'$ in the extension-based setting, then Tr is weakly exact for $\sigma \Rightarrow \sigma'$ in the labeling-based setting.*

Proof. Let Tr be a weakly exact translation in extension-based setting. By definition we have that there exists a set S of arguments (remainder sets) occurring exclusively in $Tr(F)$ such that $\sigma(F) = \sigma'(Tr(F)) \setminus S$. By the fact that there is a bijective correspondence between complete and stage extensions and stage and complete labelings we have that $|\mathcal{L}_\sigma(F)| = |\mathcal{L}_{\sigma'}(Tr(F)) \setminus \mathcal{L}'|$ where

$\mathcal{L}'$ is the set of labelings in $Tr(F)$ corresponding to the set of extensions S. By the fact that Tr is weakly exact in extension-based setting, we get that $in(\mathcal{L}_\sigma(F)) = in(\mathcal{L}_{\sigma'}(Tr(F)) \setminus \mathcal{L}')$. Since $in(\mathcal{L}_{\sigma'}(Tr(F)) \setminus \mathcal{L}')$ only contains original arguments from F and Tr is embedding (i.e. that no additional arguments between the original set of arguments are added) we get that $out(\mathcal{L}_\sigma(F)) = out(\mathcal{L}_{\sigma'}(Tr(F)) \setminus \mathcal{L}')\downarrow_{A_F}$ and that $undec(\mathcal{L}_\sigma(F)) = undec(\mathcal{L}_{\sigma'}(Tr(F)) \setminus \mathcal{L}')\downarrow_{A_F}$ which completes our proof. $\qquad\square$

4.2 Faithfulness Comparison

Theorem 3. *Let σ, $\sigma' \in \{com, grd, prf, sem, stb, idl, eag\}$. If a reserved translation Tr is faithful for $\sigma \Rightarrow \sigma'$ in the extension-based setting then Tr is faithful for $\sigma \Rightarrow \sigma'$ in the labeling-based setting.*

Proof. Let a translation Tr be faithful for $\sigma \Rightarrow \sigma'$ in the extension-based setting. Then, by definition, we have that for all AFs F, $\sigma(F) = \sigma'(Tr(F))\downarrow_{A_F}$ and $|\sigma(F)| = |\sigma'(Tr)|$. We note that since σ, σ' are both completeness-based and that it is proven in [5] that there is a bijective correspondence between complete extensions and complete labelings and between stage extensions and stage labelings, we get that $|\mathcal{L}_\sigma(F)| = |\mathcal{L}_{\sigma'}(Tr(F))|$. By definition of faithfulness in extension-based semantics, we have that $in(\mathcal{L}_\sigma(F)) = in(\mathcal{L}_{\sigma'}(Tr(F)))\downarrow_{A_F}$. By definition of a reserved translation we have that new arguments in the translation which attack cycle-reachable arguments in the original AF cannot be labeled *in* under any completeness-based semantics. In other words, we get that the new arguments added in $Tr(F)$ do not cause a potentially undecided argument in F to become *out* in $Tr(F)$. By definition we have that $out(\mathcal{L}_\sigma(F)) = \{x \in F \mid (a,x) \in R, a \in in(\mathcal{L}_\sigma(F))\}$ and $out(\mathcal{L}_{\sigma'}(Tr(F))) = \{x' \in Tr(F) \mid (a',x') \in R^*, a' \in in(\mathcal{L}_{\sigma'}(Tr(F)))\}$. Since $in(\mathcal{L}_\sigma(F)) = in(\mathcal{L}_{\sigma'}(Tr(F)))\downarrow_{A_F}$, we have that

$$out(\mathcal{L}_\sigma(F)) = out(\mathcal{L}_{\sigma'}(Tr(F)))\downarrow_{A_F}, undec(\mathcal{L}_\sigma(F)) = undec(\mathcal{L}_{\sigma'}(Tr(F)))\downarrow_{A_F}$$

which completes our proof. $\qquad\square$

Theorem 4. *If a translation Tr is faithful for $\sigma \Rightarrow \sigma'$ in the labeling-based setting then Tr is faithful for $\sigma \Rightarrow \sigma'$ in the extension-based setting.*

Proof. Let a translation Tr be faithful for $\sigma \Rightarrow \sigma'$ in the labeling-based setting. Then, by definition, we have that:
$\mathcal{L}_\sigma(F) = \mathcal{L}_{\sigma'}(Tr(F)) \downarrow_{A_F}$ and $|\mathcal{L}_\sigma(F)| = |\mathcal{L}_{\sigma'}(Tr(F))|$. Reasoning from [5] and [4], we have that $\sigma(F) = in(\mathcal{L}_\sigma(F))$ and $\sigma'(Tr(F)) = in(\mathcal{L}_{\sigma'}(Tr(F)))$ and hence that $\mathcal{L}_{\sigma'}(Tr(F)) \downarrow_{A_F} = \sigma'(Tr(F)) \downarrow_{A_F}$. It follows that $\sigma(F) = \sigma'(Tr(F)) \downarrow_{A_F}$ and $|\sigma(F)| = |\sigma'(Tr(F)) \downarrow_{A_F}|$ which completes our proof. $\qquad\square$

Theorem 5. *Let σ, $\sigma' \in \{com, grd, prf, sem, stb, idl, eag\}$. If an embedding and reserved translation Tr is weakly faithful for $\sigma \Rightarrow \sigma'$ in the extension-based setting, then Tr is weakly faithful for $\sigma \Rightarrow \sigma'$ in the labeling-based setting.*

Proof. Let a translation Tr be weakly faithful for $\sigma \Rightarrow \sigma'$ in the extension-based setting. Then, by definition we have that for all AFs F, there exists a set of extensions S such that $\sigma(F) = \sigma'(Tr(F)) \setminus S)\downarrow_{A_F}$ and that $|\sigma(F)| = |\sigma'(Tr) \setminus S|$. By the fact that there is a bijective correspondence between complete extensions and complete labelings and between stage extensions and stage labelings, we get that $|\mathcal{L}_\sigma(F)| = |\mathcal{L}_{\sigma'}(Tr(F)) \setminus \mathcal{L}'|$ where $\mathcal{L}'$ is the set of labelings corresponding to the extensions in S.

Since Tr is an embedded reserved translation, from the reasoning in proof of Theorem 3 and the fact that Tr is exact for $\sigma \Rightarrow \sigma'$ in the extension-based setting, we get that

$$in(\mathcal{L}_\sigma(F)) = in(\mathcal{L}_{\sigma'}(Tr(F)) \setminus \mathcal{L}')\downarrow_{A_F}, out(\mathcal{L}_\sigma(F)) = out(\mathcal{L}_{\sigma'}(Tr(F)) \setminus \mathcal{L}')\downarrow_{A_F}$$
$$undec(\mathcal{L}_\sigma(F)) = undec(\mathcal{L}_{\sigma'}(Tr(F)) \setminus \mathcal{L}')\downarrow_{A_F}$$

which completes our proof.   □

4.3   Equivalence Theorem Results

Having established equivalences between translation properties in extension-based and labeling-based settings, we combine the equivalence theorems and the results about extension-based translations in [9] and in [8] to arrive at results about labeling-based translations. We present these results in table in Fig. 2. For example, we have from [9] that Tr_8 is exact for $grd \Rightarrow prf$ in the extension-based setting. By Theorem 1 we get that Tr_8 is exact for $grd \Rightarrow prf$ in the labeling-based setting as well. The naming and the numbering of translations follows the scheme used in the original works mentioned above. Translations 3.7, 3.8, 3.9 and 3.12 are from [8] and the rest are from [9].

	grd	adm	stb	com	prf	sem	stg
grd	id	$Tr_4 \cup Tr_8$/-	Tr_8/-	Tr_8/3.8	Tr_8/3.8	Tr_8/3.8	Tr_8/3.7
adm	-	id	-/-	Tr_1	-/-	-/-	-/-
stb	-	Tr_4	id	Tr_4	Tr_4	Tr_4	Tr_3
com	-	-/-	-/-	id	-	-/-	-/-
prf	-	-	-	-	id	Tr_1	3.9/-
sem	-	-	-	-	3.12	id	3.9/-
stg	-	-	-	-	-	Tr_2	id

Fig. 2. Summary of exact/faithful translations for labeling-based semantics obtained from equivalence theorems and results in [9] and [8]

5   Translations: Unique Status Semantics

We now introduce some translations related to the three unique status semantics whose intertranslatability has not been studied: *ideal*, *ground* and *eager*.

The first translation relates to *ideal* and *eager* semantics. For an AF $F = (A_F, R_F)$, Tr_1 is defined as: $Tr_1 = (A^*, R^*)$, where $A^* = A_F \cup \{a' \mid a \in A_F\}$ and $R^* = R_F \cup \{(a, a'), (a', a), (a', a') \mid a \in A_F\}$. It is proven in [9] that Tr_1 is an embedding and exact translation for $prf \Rightarrow sem$ and $adm \Rightarrow com$ in the extension-based setting.

Theorem 6. *The translation Tr_1 is exact for the semantics $idl \Rightarrow eag$.*

Proof. Recall the definition of exactness in labeling-based semantics from *Page 4*. Since both *ideal* and *eager* are unique status semantics by definition, i.e., that for every AF F both return one unique labeling. Hence we have that $|\mathcal{L}_{idl}(F)| = |\mathcal{L}_{eag}(Tr_1(F))| = 1$ and *Condition 2* is proven.

To prove *Condition 1*, let L be the ideal labeling of F and L' be the eager labeling of $Tr_1(F)$. Since all the additional arguments in Tr_1 are self-attacking, they do not appear *in*-labeled in any labeling of the AF $Tr_1(F)$. Hence $Tr_1(F)$ is essentially reduced to F. Let $in(L)$ be the set of *in*-labeled arguments of L and $in(L')$ be the same for L'. We have by definition [3] that: $in(L) \subseteq in(L')$. We now identify two cases:

1. $in(L) = in(L')$: Then we have that $out(L) = out(L') \cap A_F$ and that $undec(L) = undec(L') \cap A_F$ and hence, *Condition 1* is proven.
2. $in(L) \subset in(L')$: Assume $in(L) \subset in(L')$. Then there exists an argument $a \in A_F$ such that $a \in in(L) \subset in(L'))$ but $a \notin in(L)$. Since $a \in in(L')$, by the definition of *eager* semantics it follows that $a \in \bigcap_{i=1}^{i=n} in(L_i) : L_i \in \mathcal{L}_{sem}(Tr_1(F))$. Since the translation $Tr_1(F)$ is exact for $prf \Rightarrow sem$, it follows that

$$\bigcap_{i=1}^{i=n} in(L_i) : L_i \in \mathcal{L}_{sem}(Tr_1(F)) = \bigcap_{i=1}^{i=n} in(L_i) : L_i \in \mathcal{L}_{prf}(Tr_1(F))$$

Hence we get that $a \in \bigcap_{i=1}^{i=n} in(L_i) : L_i \in \mathcal{L}_{prf}(Tr_1(F))$ and hence $a \in in(L)$, which is a contradiction to our assumption. Hence we get that $in(L) = in(L')$ and by the reasoning in *case 1* (above), we complete our proof. □

The next three results present negative results about translatability in unique status semantics.

Theorem 7. *There does not exist a covering, embedding and exact translation for $eag \Rightarrow grd$ in the labeling-based setting.*

Proof. We do a proof by counter example. We provide an AF for which no covering, embedding and exact translation exists for $eag \Rightarrow grd$. Consider the AF $F = (A, R)$ where: $A = \{a, b\}$ and $R = \{(a, b), (b, a), (b, b)\}$.

Since we consider covering and embedding translations, we assume that the original attacks between the original arguments are retained and no additional attacks between them are added. Since $\mathcal{L}_{eag}(F) = (\{a\}, \{b\}, \emptyset)$, to prove that no exact translation exists it suffices to prove that for all covering and embedding translations Tr':

$$L_1 = (\emptyset, \emptyset, A^*) \notin \mathcal{L}_{com}(Tr'(F)) \longrightarrow L_2 = (\{a\}, \{b...\}, ...) \notin \mathcal{L}_{com}(Tr'(F))$$

This follows from that fact that if L_1 *is* a complete labeling of $Tr'(F)$, then by definition it is also the grounded labeling and our proof is complete. On the other hand, if L_1 *is not* a complete labeling of $Tr'(F)$, then we need to prove that a labeling of the form L_2 is not a complete labeling and hence cannot be a grounded labeling of $Tr'(F)$, which would complete our proof. Assume $L_2 = (\{a\}, \{b...\}, \{...\}) \in \mathcal{L}_{com}(Tr'(F))$. Since $L_2(a) = in$ and knowing that the translation is covering and embedding, we identify three cases:

1. the translation $Tr'(F)$ does not add any additional arguments that attack a. Since $Tr'(F)$ is covering and embedding, the original attack relations between a and b are retained. Since $in(L_2) = \{a\}$, we get that b does not have any in-labeled attackers. Since a and b have a mutual attack, we have that $L_1 = (\emptyset, \emptyset, A^*) \in \mathcal{L}_{com}(Tr'(F))$ which contradicts our assumption.
2. the translation $Tr'(F)$ adds additional arguments that attack a, but those arguments are labeled *out*. Then it follows that $\forall x \in a^-, \exists t \in A^*$ such that $(t, x) \in R^*$ and $L_2(t) = in$ and hence $in(L_2) \neq \{a\}$, which is a contradiction.
3. the translation $Tr'(F)$ adds additional arguments with mutual attacks to a, i.e., $\forall x \in a^-, (a, x) \in R^*$. Then it follows that $L_1 = (\emptyset, \emptyset, A^*) \in \mathcal{L}_{com}(Tr'(F))$ which contradicts our assumption. $\square$

Theorem 8. *There does not exist a covering, embedding and exact translation for eag$\Rightarrow$idl semantics.*

Proof. We do a proof by counter example. We provide an AF for which no covering, embedding and exact translation exists for $eag \Rightarrow idl$ in the labeling-based setting. Consider the AF $F = (A, R)$ where: $A = \{a, b, c, d, e\}$ and $R = \{(a, b), (b, a), (b, c), (c, d), (d, e), (e, c)\}$ [3].

We have that $\mathcal{L}_{eag}(F) = (\{b, d\}, \{a, c, e\}, \emptyset)$ and that $in(\mathcal{L}_{eag}(F)) = \{b, d\}$. Since by definition we have that for every AF F $|\mathcal{L}_{eag}(F))| = |\mathcal{L}_{idl}(F))| = 1$, in order to prove that there does not exist a covering, embedding and exact translation of F for $eag \Rightarrow idl$, we need to prove that for all covering and embedding translations $Tr'(F)$: $in(\mathcal{L}_{eag}(F)) \neq in(\mathcal{L}_{idl}(Tr'(F)))$. It suffices to prove that for all covering and embedding translations $Tr'(F)$:

$$\exists L' \in \mathcal{L}_{idl}(Tr'(F)) \ s.t. \ b \notin in(L') \ and \ d \notin in(L')$$

Let $Tr'(F)$ be a covering and embedding translation and $L = (\{b, d\}, \{a, c, e...\}, \{...\}) \in \mathcal{L}_{idl}(Tr'(F))$. Then by definition of *Preferred* semantics, we have that there does not exist a labeling $L' \in \mathcal{L}_{prf}(Tr'(F))$ such that $in(L) \subseteq in(L')$. Since $L(\{a, c, e\}) = out$, the construction of F and the covering and embedding properties of $Tr'(F)$, we deduce that none of the additional arguments that attack the original arguments may be have been added by $Tr'(F)$ can be labeled *in* or *undec*. We now see that $L'' = (\{a\}, \{b, ..\}, \{...\})$ is a complete labeling of $Tr'(F)$ and since $in(L'') \not\subseteq in(L')$, L'' is a preferred labeling of $Tr'(F)$. As $in(L'') \cap in(L') \neq \{b, d\}$, we have that $L = (\{b, d\}, \{a, c, e...\}, \{...\})$ is not the ideal labeling of $Tr'(F)$, which completes our proof. □

Theorem 9. *There does not exist a covering, embedding and exact translation for idl$\Rightarrow$grd.*

Proof (Proof Sketch). We provide a proof sketch. We present the AF $F = (A, R)$ where: $A = \{a, b\}$ and $R = \{(a, b), (b, a), (b, b)\}$ as a counter-example. Since $\mathcal{L}_{idl}(F) = (\{a\}, \{b\}, \emptyset)$, by the same reasoning as in the previous proof we now need to prove that: for every translation $Tr' = (A^*, R^*)$:

$$L_1 = (\emptyset, \emptyset, A^*) \notin \mathcal{L}_{com}(Tr'(F)) \longrightarrow L_2 = (\{a\}, \{...\}, \{...\}) \notin \mathcal{L}_{com}(Tr'(F))$$

The truth of the premise presents two cases: (1) there is an argument $x \in Tr'(F)$ such that $(x, a) \in R^*$ and x does not have any attackers and (2) all arguments $c \in a^-$ are labeled *out*; both of which lead to the conclusion. □

The next result relates to translatability between *grounded* and the other two unique status semantics. We recall translation $Tr_{3.8}$ [8] as $Tr_{3.8} = (A^*, R^*)$ where:

$$A^* = A_F \cup \{\tilde{F}_i \mid F_i \subseteq F\}$$
$$R^* = R_F \cup \{(\tilde{F}_i, \tilde{F}_i), (\tilde{F}_i, a) \mid F_i \subseteq (A, R), a \in A_{F_i} \setminus in(\mathcal{L}_{grd}(F_i))\}$$

It is proven in [8] that $Tr_{3.8}$ is an embedding and exact translation for $grd \Rightarrow \{prf, com, sem\}$ in extension-based setting. The target AF obtained by applying $Tr_{3.8}$ to the AF $F = (\{a, b\}, \{a, b\})$ is depicted in Fig. 3.

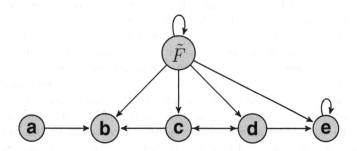

Fig. 3. The AF $Tr_{3.8}(F)$

Theorem 10. *The translation $Tr_{3.8}$ is exact for grd$\Rightarrow$\{idl, eag\}.*

Proof. We know from [9] that $Tr_{3.8}$ is exact for $grd \Rightarrow \{com, prf, sem\}$ in the extension-based setting. Since *grounded* is a unique status semantics, we have that, for every AF F, $|grd(F)| = |com(Tr_{3.8}(F))| = 1$ and $grd(F) =$

$com(Tr_{3.8}(F))$. By definition, we have that $com(Tr_{3.8}(F)) = prf(Tr_{3.8}(F)) = sem(Tr_{3.8}(F))$ and hence $com(Tr_{3.8}(F)) = idl(Tr_{3.8}(F)) = eag(Tr_{3.8}(F))$. We get that, for all AFs F, $grd(F) = idl(Tr_{3.8}(F)) = eag(Tr_{3.8}(F))$. Hence, we have that, for all AFs F,

$$in(\mathcal{L}_{grd}(F)) = in(\mathcal{L}_{idl}(Tr_{3.8}(F))) = in(\mathcal{L}_{eag}(Tr_{3.8}(F)))$$

and consequently that

$$out(\mathcal{L}_{grd}(F)) = out(\mathcal{L}_{idl}(Tr_{3.8}(F)))\!\downarrow_{A_F} = out(\mathcal{L}_{eag}(Tr_{3.8}(F)))\!\downarrow_{A_F}$$

and

$$undec(\mathcal{L}_{grd}(F)) = undec(\mathcal{L}_{idl}(Tr_{3.8}(F)))\!\downarrow_{A_F} = undec(\mathcal{L}_{eag}(Tr_{3.8}(F)))\!\downarrow_{A_F}$$

which completes our proof. □

Since *ideal*, *eager* and *grounded* are unique status semantics the notions of weakly exact and weakly faithful are not applicable to intertranslatability between these semantics.

6   Conclusion and Future Work

In this work, we built upon the investigations of Dvořák and Woltran [9] into the inter-translatability of extension-based semantics. We began our investigations by defining exactness and faithfulness of translations in the labeling-based setting. In order to establish faithfulness equivalence we defined a class of translations called reserved translations. We found that reserved translations which are exact or faithful in the extension-based setting are also exact or faithful in the labeling-based setting. This holds for all completeness based semantics. We also took into account the relatively new unique status semantics such as *ideal* and *eager*. We investigated and present results concerning the mutual inter-translatability of these three unique status semantics, *ideal*, *grounded* and *eager*.

There are promising directions for further research regarding translatability. One area of interest could be to examine the translatability of semantics in other classes of argumentation frameworks such as Abstract Dialectic Frameworks (ADF) especially the relationship between acceptance conditions of statements and AF semantics and translations between these semantics. Secondly, it would be interesting to explore translations between current semantics and various newly suggested semantics such as *cf2-semantics* and resolution based semantics in labeling-based setting.

Acknowledgments. We appreciate the valuable input and feedback of Mr Wolfgang Dvořák throughout this work. The authors were supported by the International MSc Program in Computational Logic (MCL) at TU Dresden.

References

1. Baroni, P., Caminada, M., Giacomin, M.: An introduction to argumentation semantics. Knowl. Eng. Rev. **26**(4), 365–410 (2011)
2. Caminada, M.: Semi-stable semantics. In: Dunne, P.E., Bench-Capon, T.J.M. (eds.) Proceedings of the 1st Conference on Computational Models of Argument (COMMA). Frontiers in Artificial Intelligence and Applications, vol. 144, pp. 121–130. IOS Press (2006)
3. Caminada, M.: Comparing two unique extension semantics for formal argumentation: ideal and eager. In: Proceedings of the 19th Belgian-Dutch Conference on Artificial Intelligence (BNIAC), pp. 81–87 (2007)
4. Caminada, M.: A labelling approach for ideal and stage semantics. Argument Comput. **2**(1), 1–21 (2011)
5. Caminada, M., Gabbay, D.: A logical account of formal argumentation. Stud. Log. (Spec. Issue: New Ideas Argumentation Theory) **93**(2–3), 64–102 (2009)
6. Dung, P.M.: On the acceptability of arguments and its fundamental role in non-monotonic reasoning, logic programming and n-person games. Artif. Intell. **77**(2)(10), 321–358 (1995)
7. Dung, P.M., Mancarella, P., Toni, F.: Computing ideal sceptical argumentation. Artif. Intell. **171**(10–15), 642–674 (2007)
8. Dvořák, W., Spanring, C.: Comparing the expressiveness of argumentation semantics. J. Logic Comput. exw008 (2016)
9. Dvořák, W., Woltran, S.: On the intertranslatability of argumentation semantics. J. Artif. Intell. Res. **41**(10), 445–475 (2011)
10. Nofal, S., Atkinson, K., Dunne, P.E.: Algorithms for decision problems in argument systems under preferred semantics. Artif. Intell. **207**, 23–51 (2014)
11. Thimm, M., Villata, S., Cerutti, F., Oren, N., Strass, H., Vallati, M.: Summary report of the first international competition on computational models of argumentation. AI Mag. **37**(1), 102 (2016)
12. Verheij, B.: Two approaches to dialectical argumentation: admissible sets and argumentation stages. In: Meyer, J., van der Gaag, L. (eds.) Proceedings of the 8th Dutch Conference on Artificial Intelligence (NAIC 1996), pp. 357–368 (1996)
13. Verheij, B.: A labeling approach to the computation of credulous acceptance in argumentation. In: Veloso, M.M. (ed.) Proceedings of the 20th International Joint Conference on Artificial Intelligence (IJCAI), pp. 623–628 (2007)

Preference Inference Based on Pareto Models

Anne-Marie George$^{(\boxtimes)}$ and Nic Wilson

Insight Centre for Data Analytics, University College Cork, Cork, Ireland
{annemarie.george,nic.wilson}@insight-centre.org
https://www.insight-centre.org

Abstract. In this paper, we consider Preference Inference based on a generalised form of Pareto order. Preference Inference aims at reasoning over an incomplete specification of user preferences. We focus on two problems. The Preference Deduction Problem (PDP) asks if another preference statement can be deduced (with certainty) from a set of given preference statements. The Preference Consistency Problem (PCP) asks if a set of given preference statements is consistent, i.e., the statements are not contradicting each other. Here, preference statements are direct comparisons between alternatives (strict and non-strict). It is assumed that a set of evaluation functions is known by which all alternatives can be rated. We consider Pareto models which induce order relations on the set of alternatives in a Pareto manner, i.e., one alternative is preferred to another only if it is preferred on every component of the model.

We describe characterisations for deduction and consistency based on an analysis of the set of evaluation functions, and present algorithmic solutions and complexity results for PDP and PCP, based on Pareto models in general and for a special case. Furthermore, a comparison shows that the inference based on Pareto models is less cautious than some other types of well-known preference model.

Keywords: Preference inference · Pareto models · Incomplete preference specifications · Uncertain user preferences

1 Introduction

Preference deduction can be valuable in many fields like recommender systems [3,9] and multi-objective optimization [8], where one wants to reason over user preferences. It is often difficult or excessively time-consuming to elicit all user preferences. Thus, only an incomplete picture of the user's preferences is given and there is therefore uncertainty regarding the user's preferences. In the Preference Deduction Problem (PDP), the idea is to elicit only a few preferences from the user and infer other preferences; this might then be used in a conversational recommender system, for example, to help choose which items to show to the user next. Here, it is important to check if the given user statements are consistent. Otherwise, it would be possible to deduce any arbitrary preference statement. The Preference Consistency Problem (PCP) decides if a

© Springer International Publishing Switzerland 2016
S. Schockaert and P. Senellart (Eds.): SUM 2016, LNAI 9858, pp. 170–183, 2016.
DOI: 10.1007/978-3-319-45856-4_12

set of given user preference statements is consistent, i.e., the statements do not contradict each other. PDP and PCP have been studied under different order relations such as lexicographic orders [9,11,12], hierarchical orders [5,13] and weighted sums [3,4,8]. Under these order relations PDP and PCP are mutually expressive, i.e., PDP can be solved using algorithms for PCP and vice versa. For Pareto models, PDP and PCP are not mutually expressive. While Pareto orders are widely studied in fields like voting theory [10] (unanimity), allocation problems [1] (Pareto optimality), decision making, database queries [2,7] (skyline operator) and economics (Pareto efficiency), there exists no general study of PDP or PCP based on Pareto orders so far. Pareto orders give a natural way of comparing alternatives; one alternative is better than another if it is better on all relevant evaluation functions (different criteria by which the alternatives can be evaluated). In recommender systems and multi-objective decision making frameworks as well as the other aforementioned fields it is a reasonable assumption, that the user expresses her preferences (direct comparisons of two alternatives) in a Pareto manner. Here, one tries to find a set of optimal alternatives, i.e., alternatives that are undominated w.r.t. Pareto order.

This form of order relation leaves no room for compromises or tradeoffs between evaluation functions. Consider different holiday packages which include travel and hotel. We can evaluate the different alternatives by four criteria; the distance from the hotel to the city center, the distance from the hotel to the beach, the costs for the hotel and the travel costs. One user could consider the distance from the hotel to the beach and the costs for the hotel as the only relevant aspects. Then she prefers a package α to another package β, if α is closer or equidistant to the beach than β and the costs of the hotel for α are lower or equal to the costs of the hotel for β. There is no compromise possible of, e.g., paying a little bit more in order to get a hotel closer to the beach. We generalise this type of order relation by considering groups of evaluation functions; only between the evaluation functions within the same group tradeoffs are possible. Consider different holiday packages again. One user could divide the four criteria into the aspects location and costs, such that one alternative is better than another if it is better in both the location and the costs. To evaluate the location, the two values for distance are combined by some operator $\oplus$ (e.g., addition). Similarly, the cost of the hotel and the travel costs are combined by $\oplus$ to evaluate the costs in total. This comparison allows tradeoffs between the distances from the hotel to the beach and to the city center, and between the costs for travel and for the hotel. Another user might want to divide the criteria into the aspects hotel and travel. The only allowed tradeoffs are between the hotel costs and the distance from the hotel to the beach and to the city center.

Since only partial information on the user preferences is known, we must consider the set of all Pareto models that satisfy the given preferences, i.e., that are possible candidates for the user's true preference model. Only if there exists such a model, is the given set of preference statements consistent. Only if all these Pareto models satisfy another statement φ, can we deduce φ with certainty.

In the next section we give basic definitions of Pareto models and the two problems of Preference Deduction and Preference Consistency. In Sect. 3, we first describe properties for the special case of consistency and deduction based on Pareto models that don't allow tradeoffs between evaluation functions. These properties are exploited to formulate polynomial time algorithms for PDP and PCP. We then develop similar properties for the case of consistency and deduction based on the general form of Pareto models, and show that PCP and PDP based on general Pareto models are NP-complete and coNP-complete, respectively. In the fourth section, we compare the cautiousness of the inference based on Pareto models with other types of order relations. The last section concludes. A longer version of this paper including further proves and examples can be found under http://ucc.insight-centre.org/nwilson/ParetoInferenceProofs.pdf.

2   Preference Consistency and Deduction

To formally define the problems PDP and PCP in a Pareto context, we first define preference structures and Pareto models. Furthermore, we describe the language in which preference statements are expressed.

Definition 1 (Preference Structure). *A preference structure is a tuple $\langle \mathcal{A},$ $\mathcal{C}, \oplus \rangle$. Here, $\mathcal{A}$ is a (finite) set of* alternatives *and $\mathcal{C}$ is a (finite) set of* evaluation functions *$c : \mathcal{A} \longrightarrow \mathbb{Q}^{\geq 0}$ by which the alternatives can be rated with non-negative rational numbers (the lower, the better; 0 is the best possible rating). The evaluation functions can be combined by the associative, commutative and strictly monotonic operation $\oplus$ on $\mathbb{Q}^{\geq 0}$, where strict monotonicity means $x \oplus y < z \oplus y$ if and only if $x < z$. Here, e is the neutral element such that $e \oplus x = x$ for all $x \in \mathbb{Q}^{\geq 0}$.*

Note, that $\oplus$ has been defined in a similar context to be only monotonic (not strictly monotonic) [13]. However, the strict monotonicity property is needed to establish some important theoretical results in Sect. 3. This excludes operators like maximum or minimum, but still allows interesting operators like addition with neutral element 0 which is a natural for combining, e.g., costs, distances, etc. In the special case of strictly positive evaluation functions $\mathcal{A} \longrightarrow \mathbb{Q}^{>0}$ multiplication can also be used as operator with neutral element 1. For computational and complexity results, we assume that $x \oplus y$ can be computed in logarithmic time for $x, y \in \mathbb{Q}^{\geq 0}$.

Example 1. *Consider the choice of holiday packages α, β and γ. We rate the holiday packages by the distance from the hotel to the city center d_c, the distance to the beach d_b, the costs for the hotel c_h and the travel costs c_t. The distances are categorised into far (2), medium (1) and near (0). The costs are categorised into high (2), medium (1) and low (0). The values of the four criteria for the alternatives α, β and γ are given by the table on the right.*

	α	β	γ
d_c	0	2	1
d_b	1	1	2
c_h	2	1	0
c_t	2	1	1

To combine evaluation functions, consider the operator $\oplus$ that is the standard addition on the natural numbers. Then $\langle \mathcal{A}, \mathcal{C}, \oplus \rangle$ is a preference structure, where $\mathcal{A} = \{\alpha, \beta, \gamma\}$ is the set of alternatives and $\mathcal{C} = \{d_c, d_b, c_h, c_t\}$ is the set of evaluation functions.

Let $\mathcal{L}_{\leq}^{\mathcal{A}}$ be the set of *non-strict preference statements* $\alpha \leq \beta$, and $\mathcal{L}_{<}^{\mathcal{A}}$ be the set of *strict preference statements* $\alpha < \beta$, over all $\alpha, \beta \in \mathcal{A}$. Let $\mathcal{L}^{\mathcal{A}} = \mathcal{L}_{\leq}^{\mathcal{A}} \cup \mathcal{L}_{<}^{\mathcal{A}}$. We write $\varphi \in \mathcal{L}^{\mathcal{A}}$ as $\alpha_\varphi < \beta_\varphi$, if φ is strict, and as $\alpha_\varphi \leq \beta_\varphi$, if φ is non-strict. For a set Γ of strict and non-strict preference statements in $\mathcal{L}^{\mathcal{A}}$, define $\Gamma^{(\leq)}$ to be the non-strict version of Γ, i.e., $\Gamma^{(\leq)} = \{\alpha_\varphi \leq \beta_\varphi \mid \varphi \in \Gamma\}$. Furthermore, define $\overline{\varphi}$ for a preference statement φ to be the statement $\alpha_\varphi > \beta_\varphi$ if φ is the non-strict statement $\alpha_\varphi \leq \beta_\varphi$, and $\alpha_\varphi \geq \beta_\varphi$ if φ is the strict statement $\alpha_\varphi < \beta_\varphi$.

Definition 2 (Pareto Model). *For a preference structure $\langle \mathcal{A}, \mathcal{C}, \oplus \rangle$, a Pareto model M is a set of pairwise disjoint subsets of evaluations. More specifically, $M = \{C_1, \ldots, C_r\}$ with $r \geq 0$ and pairwise disjoint sets $C_i \subseteq \mathcal{C}$ for $i = 1, \ldots, r$.*

Let $\mathcal{P}_\mathcal{C}$ denote the set of all Pareto models over the set $\mathcal{C}$ of evaluations. We will abbreviate this notation to $\mathcal{P}$, when the set of evaluations $\mathcal{C}$ is clear from the context. Informally, a Pareto model corresponds to a grouping of evaluation functions. In the context of votes, one can interpret each evaluation function to express the preferences from one individual. In a Pareto model, the individuals form groups in which they come to a decision together (by applying the operator to their preference functions). The collective prefers one alternative α over another alternative β, if all groups agree that α is at least as good as β. So, each Pareto model $M = \{C_1, \ldots, C_r\}$ induces an order relation on the set of alternatives $\mathcal{A}$ by comparing the combination of evaluations in the sets (by operator $\oplus$) in a Pareto manner. Formally, we define:

- $\alpha \leq_M \beta$ if $\bigoplus_{c \in C_i} c(\alpha) \leq \bigoplus_{c \in C_i} c(\beta)$ for all $i = 1, \ldots, r$. *(M satisfies $\alpha \leq \beta$, written $M \vDash_\mathcal{P} \alpha \leq \beta$.)*
- $\alpha <_M \beta$ if $\alpha \leq_M \beta$ and there exists $j \in \{1, \ldots, r\}$ such that $\bigoplus_{c \in C_j} c(\alpha) < \bigoplus_{c \in C_j} c(\beta)$. *($M$ satisfies $\alpha < \beta$ / M strictly satisfies $\alpha \leq \beta$, written $M \vDash_\mathcal{P} \alpha < \beta$.)*
- $\alpha \equiv_M \beta$ if $\alpha \leq_M \beta$ and $\beta \leq_M \alpha$. *(M satisfies $\alpha \equiv \beta$, written $M \vDash_\mathcal{P} \alpha \equiv \beta$.)*

Example 2 (Continued). *Consider the preference structure described in Example 1. The Pareto model $M = \{\{d_c, d_b\}, \{c_h, c_t\}\}$ describes the situation in which a user allows tradeoffs between the distance to the city center and the distance to the beach, and tradeoffs between the cost of the hotel and the travel costs. This Pareto model satisfies $\gamma <_M \beta$ since $d_c(\gamma) \oplus d_b(\gamma) = 1 + 2 = 2 + 1 = d_c(\beta) \oplus d_b(\beta)$ and $c_h(\gamma) \oplus c_t(\gamma) = 0 + 1 < 1 + 1 = c_h(\beta) \oplus c_t(\beta)$. Furthermore, the induced order relation of M leaves the pairs of alternatives α, β and α, γ incomparable. A user that considers Pareto model $M' = \{\{d_b, c_h\}, \{c_t\}\}$ to describe her preferences allows tradeoffs between the distance to the beach and the costs of the hotel. Here, the user considers the travel costs separately and disregards the distance of the hotel to the city completely. This Pareto model satisfies $\gamma \equiv_{M'} \beta <_{M'} \alpha$.*

Let $\mathcal{M}$ be a set of some preference models, e.g., $\mathcal{M} = \mathcal{P}$. In the following we define $\mathcal{M}$-PDP and $\mathcal{M}$-PCP.

$\mathcal{M}$-**Preference Deduction Problem** ($\mathcal{M}$-**PDP**): Given a preference structure $\langle \mathcal{A}, \mathcal{C}, \oplus \rangle$, a set of preference statements $\Gamma \subseteq \mathcal{L}^{\mathcal{A}}$ and a preference statement $\varphi \in \mathcal{L}^{\mathcal{A}} \setminus \Gamma$, the Preference Deduction Problem asks whether all preference models in $\mathcal{M}$ that satisfy all statements in Γ also satisfy φ, written $\Gamma \vDash_{\mathcal{M}} \varphi$.

Definition 3 ($\mathcal{M}$-**Consistency**). *For a preference structure* $\langle \mathcal{A}, \mathcal{C}, \oplus \rangle$ *and a set of preference models* $\mathcal{M}$*, the preference statements* $\Gamma \subseteq \mathcal{L}^{\mathcal{A}}$ *are* $\mathcal{M}$*-consistent if there exists a preference model in* $\mathcal{M}$ *that satisfies all statements in* Γ.

$\mathcal{M}$-**Preference Consistency Problem** ($\mathcal{M}$-**PCP**): Given a preference structure $\langle \mathcal{A}, \mathcal{C}, \oplus \rangle$ and a set of preference statements $\Gamma \subseteq \mathcal{L}^{\mathcal{A}}$, the Preference Consistency Problem asks whether there exists a preference model in $\mathcal{M}$ that satisfies all given statements Γ.

In Sect. 3, we consider properties and complexity of the problems PCP and PDP based on Pareto models $\mathcal{P}_{\mathcal{C}}$ in general and based on the special classes of Pareto models $\mathcal{P}_{\mathcal{C}}(1)$ and $\mathcal{P}_{\mathcal{C}}^{s}$ defined as follows. The class $\mathcal{P}_{\mathcal{C}}(1)$ consists of Pareto models with only singleton sets, i.e., $\mathcal{P}_{\mathcal{C}}(1) = \{\{C_1, \ldots, C_r\} \in \mathcal{P}_{\mathcal{C}} \mid |C_i| = 1 \text{ for all } i = 1, \ldots, r\}$. The class $\mathcal{P}_{\mathcal{C}}^{s}$ consists of Pareto models that contain only a single set, i.e., $\mathcal{P}_{\mathcal{C}}^{s} = \{\{C\} \in \mathcal{P}_{\mathcal{C}} \mid C \subset \mathcal{C}\}$. We adjust the notation where Pareto models in $\mathcal{P}_{\mathcal{C}}(1)$ or $\mathcal{P}_{\mathcal{C}}^{s}$ are considered to avoid confusion, and omit the set of evaluations $\mathcal{C}$ when this is clear from the context.

Example 3 (Continued). *Consider the preference structure described in Example 1 and the set of preference statements* $\Gamma = \{\alpha < \beta, \alpha \leq \gamma\}$*. The set* Γ *is consistent (for* $\mathcal{P}$ *in general and in particular for* $\mathcal{P}(1)$ *and for* $\mathcal{P}^{s}$*) and the following Pareto models satisfy* $\alpha < \beta$ *and* $\alpha \leq \gamma$:
$\{\{d_c\}\}$, $\{\{d_c, d_b\}\}$, $\{\{d_c, c_t\}\}$, $\{\{d_c, d_b, c_h\}\}$, $\{\{d_c, d_b, c_t\}\}$, $\{\{d_c\}, \{d_b\}\}$, $\{\{d_c, c_t\}, \{d_b\}\}$*. Furthermore,* $\Gamma \nvDash_{\mathcal{P}} \gamma \leq \beta$ *and* $\Gamma \nvDash_{\mathcal{P}(1)} \gamma \leq \beta$ *since the Pareto model* $\{\{d_c\}, \{d_b\}\} \in \mathcal{P}(1) \subseteq \mathcal{P}$ *satisfies* Γ *but not* $\gamma \leq \beta$*. However,* $\Gamma \vDash_{\mathcal{P}^{s}} \gamma \leq \beta$ *since the Pareto models* $\{\{d_c\}\}$, $\{\{d_c, d_b\}\}$, $\{\{d_c, c_t\}\}$, $\{\{d_c, d_b, c_h\}\}$ *and* $\{\{d_c, d_b, c_t\}\}$ *in* $\mathcal{P}^{s}$ *all satisfy* Γ *and satisfy* $\gamma \leq \beta$*.*

3 Properties and Solutions for PCP and PDP

For many order relations like lexicographic orders, hierarchical models and weighted sums, PDP and PCP are mutually expressive [4,13]. More specifically, for $\mathcal{M}$ being the set of all feasible preference models due to one of the aforementioned order relations, $\Gamma \vDash_{\mathcal{M}} \varphi$ if and only if $\Gamma \cup \{\overline{\varphi}\}$ is $\mathcal{M}$-inconsistent (i.e., there exists no model in $\mathcal{M}$ that satisfies all statements in $\Gamma \cup \{\overline{\varphi}\}$). The following example shows that the "$\Leftarrow$"-direction does not hold for Pareto models. Thus, we need to find algorithms to solve PCP and PDP separately.

Example 4. *Let the operator $\oplus$ be the standard addition on $\mathbb{Q}^{\geq 0}$. Consider the table on the right of values for evaluation functions c_1, c_2, c_3 evaluated at alternatives α, β, γ. Let the set of given preference statements be $\Gamma = \{\beta < \gamma\}$ and let φ be the strict statement $\alpha < \beta$, so that $\overline{\varphi}$ is $\alpha \geq \beta$. The following Pareto models satisfy Γ:* $\{\{c_2\}\}$, $\{\{c_3\}\}$, $\{\{c_2\}, \{c_3\}\}$, $\{\{c_2, c_3\}\}$, $\{\{c_1, c_2\}, \{c_3\}\}$, $\{\{c_1, c_2, c_3\}\}$. *However, none of the Γ-satisfying models satisfies $\alpha \geq \beta$. Thus, the set $\Gamma \cup \{\overline{\varphi}\} = \{\alpha \geq \beta, \beta < \gamma\}$ is $\mathcal{P}$-inconsistent. Also, $\Gamma \not\vDash_{\mathcal{P}} \varphi$, as the Pareto model $\{\{c_1, c_2\}, \{c_3\}\}$ satisfies Γ but not φ.*

	α	β	γ
c_1	5	3	1
c_2	0	1	3
c_3	1	3	4

However, we can show that $\Gamma \vDash_{\mathcal{P}} \varphi$ implies $\Gamma \cup \{\overline{\varphi}\}$ is $\mathcal{P}$-inconsistent.

Proposition 1. *Let $\Gamma \subseteq \mathcal{L}^{\mathcal{A}}$ and $\varphi \in \mathcal{L}^{\mathcal{A}} \setminus \Gamma$ be preference statements. If $\Gamma \vDash_{\mathcal{P}} \varphi$, then $\Gamma \cup \{\overline{\varphi}\}$ is $\mathcal{P}$-inconsistent.*

Proof. Suppose $\Gamma \cup \{\overline{\varphi}\}$ is $\mathcal{P}$-consistent, i.e., there exists a Pareto model $M = \{C_1, \ldots, C_m\}$ that satisfies Γ and $M \vDash_{\mathcal{P}} \overline{\varphi}$. Suppose φ is the strict statement $\alpha < \beta$. Since $M \vDash_{\mathcal{P}} \overline{\varphi}$, for all $i = 1, \ldots, m$, $\bigoplus_{c \in C_i} c(\alpha) \geq \bigoplus_{c \in C_i} c(\beta)$. Thus, $M \not\vDash_{\mathcal{P}} \varphi$, and $\Gamma \not\vDash_{\mathcal{P}} \varphi$. Analogously, we can show $\Gamma \not\vDash_{\mathcal{P}} \varphi$ for non-strict φ.   □

3.1 Singleton Models

In this section, we find a simpler representation of the Pareto inference restricted to the class $\mathcal{P}(1)$ by using set relations on sets of evaluation functions. We define the set $C_{\alpha \leq \beta} = \{c \in \mathcal{C} \mid c(\alpha) \leq c(\beta)\}$ of evaluations that satisfy $\alpha \leq \beta$. Similarly, $C_{\alpha < \beta} = \{c \in \mathcal{C} \mid c(\alpha) < c(\beta)\}$ and $C_{\alpha = \beta} = \{c \in \mathcal{C} \mid c(\alpha) = c(\beta)\}$. For better readability we abbreviate the notation of a model $M = \{\{c_1\}, \ldots, \{c_r\}\}$ in $\mathcal{P}_{\mathcal{C}}(1)$ to $\{c_1, \ldots, c_r\}$.

Note, that the empty Pareto model $\{\}$ always satisfies non-strict statements, i.e., a set $\Gamma \subseteq \mathcal{L}_{\leq}^{\mathcal{A}}$ is always $\mathcal{P}(1)$-consistent. We can prove the following characterisation of $\mathcal{P}(1)$-consistency.

Proposition 2. *Let $\Gamma \subseteq \mathcal{L}^{\mathcal{A}}$ be a set of preference statements that includes at least one strict statements. Γ is $\mathcal{P}(1)$-consistent if and only if for all $\varphi' \in \Gamma \cap \mathcal{L}_{<}^{\mathcal{A}}$ there exists an evaluation c that satisfies $\Gamma^{(\leq)}$ and strictly satisfies φ', i.e., $C_{\varphi'} \cap \bigcap_{\varphi \in \Gamma^{(\leq)}} C_\varphi \neq \emptyset$.*

Proof. Suppose, Γ is $\mathcal{P}(1)$-consistent and let $M = \{c_1, \ldots, c_k\}$ be a Γ-satisfying model in $\mathcal{P}(1)$. Since M satisfies every statement $\varphi \in \Gamma$, $c(\alpha_\varphi) \leq c(\beta_\varphi)$ for every $c \in M$, i.e., $c \in \bigcap_{\varphi \in \Gamma^{(\leq)}} C_\varphi$. Furthermore, for every strict statement $\varphi' \in \Gamma \cap \mathcal{L}_{<}^{\mathcal{A}}$ there exists a $c \in M$ such that $c(\alpha_{\varphi'}) < c(\beta_{\varphi'})$, i.e., $c \in C_{\varphi'} \cap \bigcap_{\varphi \in \Gamma^{(\leq)}} C_\varphi \neq \emptyset$. Conversely, suppose $C_{\varphi'} \cap \bigcap_{\varphi \in \Gamma^{(\leq)}} C_\varphi \neq \emptyset$ for all $\varphi' \in \Gamma \cap \mathcal{L}_{<}^{\mathcal{A}}$. Consider the set $M = \bigcup_{\varphi' \in \Gamma \cap \mathcal{L}_{<}^{\mathcal{A}}} (C_{\varphi'} \cap \bigcap_{\varphi \in \Gamma^{(\leq)}} C_\varphi)$. For every evaluation $c \in M$ and every statement $\varphi \in \Gamma$, $c \in \bigcap_{\varphi \in \Gamma^{(\leq)}} C_\varphi$, i.e., $c(\alpha_\varphi) \leq c(\beta_\varphi)$. Furthermore, for every strict statement $\varphi' \in \Gamma \cap \mathcal{L}_{<}^{\mathcal{A}}$ there exists a $c \in M$ such that $c \in C_{\varphi'} \cap \bigcap_{\varphi \in \Gamma^{(\leq)}} C_\varphi$, i.e., $c(\alpha_{\varphi'}) < c(\beta_{\varphi'})$. Thus M is a Pareto model in $\mathcal{P}(1)$ that satisfies Γ, i.e., Γ is $\mathcal{P}(1)$-consistent.   □

Following Proposition 2, we formulate the algorithm Singleton-Pareto-Consistency that solves $\mathcal{P}(1)$-PCP in polynomial time $O(|\Gamma||\mathcal{C}|)$.

Algorithm: Singleton-Pareto-Consistency($\Gamma,\mathcal{C}$)
Let $G = \Gamma \cap \mathcal{L}_{\leq}^{\mathcal{A}}$.
for all $c \in \mathcal{C}$ **do**
  if $c(\alpha_\varphi) \leq c(\beta_\varphi)$ for all $\varphi \in \Gamma$ **then** $G = G \setminus \{\varphi \in \Gamma \mid c(\alpha_\varphi) < c(\beta_\varphi)\}$.
  if $G = \emptyset$ **then return** $\mathcal{P}(1)$-*consistent* **else return** $\mathcal{P}(1)$-*inconsistent*.

We can prove criteria for strict and non-strict Pareto inferences based on $\mathcal{P}(1)$ models by utilising the following lemma.

Lemma 1. *Let $\Gamma \subseteq \mathcal{L}^{\mathcal{A}}$ be a set of $\mathcal{P}(1)$-consistent preference statements over preference structure $\langle \mathcal{A}, \mathcal{C}, \oplus \rangle$. For every evaluation $c \in \bigcap_{\varphi \in \Gamma^{(\leq)}} C_\varphi$ there exists a Γ-satisfying Pareto model in $\mathcal{P}(1)$ that contains c. Furthermore, for every Γ-satisfying Pareto model M in $\mathcal{P}(1)$, $M \subseteq \bigcap_{\varphi \in \Gamma^{(\leq)}} C_\varphi$.*

Proof. Let M be a Γ-satisfying Pareto model in $\mathcal{P}(1)$ that does not contain some $c \in \bigcap_{\varphi \in \Gamma^{(\leq)}} C_\varphi$. Since $c(\alpha_\varphi) \leq c(\beta_\varphi)$ for all $\varphi \in \Gamma$, $M \cup \{c\}$ is a Γ-satisfying Pareto model in $\mathcal{P}(1)$. Thus, for every evaluation $c \in \bigcap_{\varphi \in \Gamma^{(\leq)}} C_\varphi$ there exists a Γ-satisfying Pareto model in $\mathcal{P}(1)$ that contains c. Furthermore, for every evaluation c' in M and every $\varphi \in \Gamma$, $c'(\alpha_\varphi) \leq c'(\beta_\varphi)$, i.e., $c \in C_{\alpha_\varphi \leq \beta_\varphi}$. Thus, $M \subseteq \bigcap_{\varphi \in \Gamma^{(\leq)}} C_\varphi$ for every Γ-satisfying Pareto model M in $\mathcal{P}(1)$. $\square$

Proposition 3. *Let $\Gamma \subseteq \mathcal{L}^{\mathcal{A}}$ be a set of $\mathcal{P}_{\mathcal{C}}(1)$-consistent preference statements over preference structure $\langle \mathcal{A}, \mathcal{C}, \oplus \rangle$. We can deduce a preference statement $\alpha \leq \beta$ from Γ ($\Gamma \vDash_{\mathcal{P}_{\mathcal{C}}(1)} \alpha \leq \beta$) if and only if all evaluation functions $c \in \mathcal{C}$ that satisfy $\Gamma^{(\leq)}$ also satisfy $c(\alpha) \leq c(\beta)$, i.e., $\bigcap_{\varphi \in \Gamma^{(\leq)}} C_\varphi \subseteq C_{\alpha \leq \beta}$. Also, $\Gamma \vDash_{\mathcal{P}_{\mathcal{C}}(1)} \alpha < \beta$ if and only if $\bigcap_{\varphi \in \Gamma^{(\leq)}} C_\varphi \subseteq C_{\alpha \leq \beta}$ and Γ is $\mathcal{P}_{C_{\alpha=\beta}}(1)$-inconsistent for the set $\mathcal{P}_{C_{\alpha=\beta}}(1)$ of $\mathcal{P}(1)$ models on evaluations $C_{\alpha=\beta}$, i.e., no Γ-satisfying model satisfies $\alpha \equiv \beta$.*

Proof. Consider the case of non-strict inference. For every evaluation c involved in a Γ-satisfying Pareto model in $\mathcal{P}_{\mathcal{C}}(1)$, $c(\alpha) \leq c(\beta)$. By Lemma 1, the set of evaluations involved in a Γ-satisfying Pareto model in $\mathcal{P}_{\mathcal{C}}(1)$ is $\bigcap_{\varphi \in \Gamma^{(\leq)}} C_\varphi$. Thus, $\Gamma \vDash_{\mathcal{P}_{\mathcal{C}}(1)} \alpha \leq \beta$ is equivalent to $c \in C_{\alpha \leq \beta}$ for all $c \in \bigcap_{\varphi \in \Gamma^{(\leq)}} C_\varphi$, i.e., $\bigcap_{\varphi \in \Gamma^{(\leq)}} C_\varphi \subseteq C_{\alpha \leq \beta}$.

Now, consider the case of strict inference. For every evaluation c involved in a Γ-satisfying Pareto model in $\mathcal{P}_{\mathcal{C}}(1)$, $c(\alpha) \leq c(\beta)$, and there exists no Γ-satisfying Pareto model M such that $M \vDash_{\mathcal{P}_{\mathcal{C}}(1)} \alpha \equiv \beta$. Thus, $\Gamma \vDash_{\mathcal{P}_{\mathcal{C}}(1)} \alpha < \beta$ is equivalent to $\bigcap_{\varphi \in \Gamma^{(\leq)}} C_\varphi \subseteq C_{\alpha \leq \beta}$ and there exists no Γ-satisfying Pareto model $M \in \mathcal{P}_{\mathcal{C}}(1)$ with $M \subseteq C_{\alpha=\beta}$, i.e., Γ is $\mathcal{P}_{C_{\alpha=\beta}}(1)$-inconsistent for the set $\mathcal{P}_{C_{\alpha=\beta}}(1)$ of $\mathcal{P}(1)$ models on evaluations $C_{\alpha=\beta}$. $\square$

Following Proposition 3 and using the algorithm Singleton-Pareto-Consistency we formulate the algorithm Singleton-Pareto-Deduction that solves $\mathcal{P}_{\mathcal{C}}(1)$-PDP in polynomial time $O(|\Gamma||\mathcal{C}|)$.

Algorithm: Singleton-Pareto-Deduction(Γ,$\mathcal{C}$,φ)
if Singleton-Pareto-Consistency(Γ,$\mathcal{C}$) = $\mathcal{P}(1)$-*inconsistent* **then**
 return $\Gamma \vDash_{\mathcal{P}(1)} \varphi$.
Let $N = \emptyset$.
for all $c \in \mathcal{C}$ such that $c(\alpha_\rho) \leq c(\beta_\rho)$ for all $\rho \in \Gamma$ **do**
 if $c(\alpha_\varphi) > c(\beta_\varphi)$ **then return** $\Gamma \nvDash_{\mathcal{P}(1)} \varphi$.
 else if $c(\alpha_\varphi) = c(\beta_\varphi)$ **then** $N = N \cup \{c\}$.
if $\varphi \in \mathcal{L}_{\leq}^{\mathcal{A}}$ and Singleton-Pareto-Consistency(Γ,N) = $\mathcal{P}(1)$-*consistent* **then**
 return $\Gamma \nvDash_{\mathcal{P}(1)} \varphi$ **else return** $\Gamma \vDash_{\mathcal{P}(1)} \varphi$.

3.2 Pareto Inference

In this section, we want to find characterisations for Pareto inference in general by using set relations similar to those in the previous section. We define the set $\mathcal{C}_{\alpha \leq \beta} = \{B \subseteq \mathcal{C} \mid \bigoplus_{c \in B} c(\alpha) \leq \bigoplus_{c \in B} c(\beta)\}$ of sets of evaluations that satisfy $\alpha \leq \beta$. Similarly, $\mathcal{C}_{\alpha < \beta} = \{B \subseteq \mathcal{C} \mid \bigoplus_{c \in B} c(\alpha) < \bigoplus_{c \in B} c(\beta)\}$ and $\mathcal{C}_{\alpha = \beta} = \{B \subseteq \mathcal{C} \mid \bigoplus_{c \in B} c(\alpha) = \bigoplus_{c \in B} c(\beta)\}$.

As mentioned previous section before Proposition 2, a set $\Gamma \subseteq \mathcal{L}_{\leq}^{\mathcal{A}}$ is always $\mathcal{P}(1)$-consistent and thus $\mathcal{P}$-consistent. We can prove the following characterisation of $\mathcal{P}$-consistency.

Proposition 4. *Let* $\Gamma \subseteq \mathcal{L}^{\mathcal{A}}$. *$\Gamma$ is $\mathcal{P}$-consistent if and only if* $\bigcap_{\varphi \in \Gamma} \mathcal{C}_\varphi \neq \emptyset$.

Proof. Suppose, $\bigcap_{\varphi \in \Gamma} \mathcal{C}_\varphi \neq \emptyset$. Then any set in $\bigcap_{\varphi \in \Gamma} \mathcal{C}_\varphi$ is a Γ-satisfying Pareto model. Now suppose that Γ is $\mathcal{P}$-consistent, i.e., there exists a Γ-satisfying Pareto model $M = \{C_1, \ldots, C_r\}$. For every set $C_i \in M$ and every $\varphi \in \Gamma$, $\bigoplus_{c \in C_i} c(\alpha_\varphi) \leq \bigoplus_{c \in C_i} c(\beta_\varphi)$, and for all $\varphi \in \Gamma \cap \mathcal{L}_{<}^{\mathcal{A}}$ there exists $C_j \in M$ with $\bigoplus_{c \in C_j} c(\alpha_\varphi) < \bigoplus_{c \in C_j} c(\beta_\varphi)$. Let $C' = \bigcup_{i=1,\ldots,r} C_i$. By strict monotonicity of $\oplus$, $\bigoplus_{c \in C'} c(\alpha_\varphi) \leq \bigoplus_{c \in C'} c(\beta_\varphi)$ for $\varphi \in \Gamma^{(\leq)}$, and $\bigoplus_{c \in C'} c(\alpha_\varphi) < \bigoplus_{c \in C'} c(\beta_\varphi)$ for all $\varphi \in \Gamma \cup \mathcal{L}_{<}^{\mathcal{A}}$. Thus $C' \in \bigcap_{\varphi \in \Gamma} \mathcal{C}_\varphi \neq \emptyset$. □

Remember, that $\mathcal{P}^s = \{\{C\} \in \mathcal{P}_{\mathcal{C}} \mid C \subset \mathcal{C}\}$ contains all Pareto models that consist of only a single set. The proof of Proposition 4 directly implies the following equivalence.

Corollary 1. *Let* $\Gamma \subseteq \mathcal{L}^{\mathcal{A}}$. *$\Gamma$ is $\mathcal{P}$-consistent if and only if Γ is $\mathcal{P}^s$-consistent.*

Consider the relation of $\mathcal{P}$ and $\mathcal{P}^s$ for deduction. $\Gamma \vDash_{\mathcal{P}} \varphi$ implies $\Gamma \vDash_{\mathcal{P}^s} \varphi$ because $\mathcal{P}^s \subseteq \mathcal{P}$. However, Example 3 shows the contrary is not true.

To find characterisations for preference deduction for $\mathcal{P}_{\mathcal{C}}$, for a given set $B \subseteq \mathcal{C}$, define $\Gamma_{<B}$ to be the set of statements in Γ that are strictly satisfied by evaluations $B \subseteq \mathcal{C}$, i.e., $\Gamma_{<B} = \{\varphi \in \Gamma \mid \bigoplus_{c \in B} c(\alpha_\varphi) < \bigoplus_{c \in B} c(\beta_\varphi)\}$. Similarly, $\Gamma_{=B} = \{\varphi \in \Gamma \mid \bigoplus_{c \in B} c(\alpha_\varphi) = \bigoplus_{c \in B} c(\beta_\varphi)\}$. Recall, that the non-strict version of preference statements Γ is denoted by $\Gamma^{(\leq)}$. Thus, $\Gamma_{\hookrightarrow B} = (\Gamma \setminus \Gamma_{<B}) \cup \Gamma_{<B}^{(\leq)}$ replaces the preference statements in Γ that are strictly satisfied by B with their non-strict versions.

The following two propositions give characterisations for deduction of non-strict statements and strict statements, respectively. Both propositions can be proven by technical constructions.

Proposition 5. *Let $\Gamma \subseteq \mathcal{L}^{\mathcal{A}}$ be a $\mathcal{P}$-consistent set of preference statements and let $\alpha \leq \beta \notin \Gamma$ be a non-strict statement. $\Gamma \not\vdash_{\mathcal{P}_C} \alpha \leq \beta$ if and only if there exists a set $B \in \bigcap_{\psi \in \Gamma^{(\leq)}} \mathcal{C}_\psi \cap \mathcal{C}_{\alpha > \beta}$ such that $\Gamma_{\hookrightarrow B}$ is $\mathcal{P}_{C \setminus B}$-consistent, i.e., the $(\alpha \leq \beta)$-opposing set B can be extended to a Γ-satisfying Pareto model.*

Proposition 6. *Let $\Gamma \subseteq \mathcal{L}^{\mathcal{A}}$ and let $\alpha < \beta \notin \Gamma$ be a strict statement. $\Gamma \not\vdash_{\mathcal{P}} \alpha < \beta$ if and only if $\Gamma \not\vdash_{\mathcal{P}} \alpha \leq \beta$ or $\bigcap_{\psi \in \Gamma} \mathcal{C}_\psi \cap \mathcal{C}_{\alpha = \beta} \neq \emptyset$.*

Note, that the characterisation for deduction and consistency can be realised as algorithms for $\mathcal{P}$-PCP and $\mathcal{P}$-PDP, but cannot be implemented in polynomial time. In fact, we can prove the following complexity results for PCP and PDP.

Theorem 1. *The $\mathcal{P}$-Preference Consistency Problem is NP-complete.*

Proof. For any given Pareto model we can check in polynomial time if it satisfies all given preference statements. Thus, PCP is in the class NP. We prove NP-completeness by a reduction from SAT. Let $\mathcal{B} = K_1, \ldots, K_m$ be a set of clauses in conjunctive normal form with clauses $K_i = (l_{i,1} \vee \cdots \vee l_{i,k_i})$ for $i = 1, \ldots, m$, where the literals $l_{i,j}$ are chosen from the set of Boolean variables $\mathcal{X} = \{x_1, \ldots, x_n\}$. In the following, we construct an instance of PCP from the SAT instance $\mathcal{B}$. Let $s \in \mathbb{Q}$ with $s > e$ and $\oplus$ be an associative, commutative and strictly monotonic operation with neutral element e. For every Boolean variable x_j, we construct three evaluations: p_j (corresponding to $x_j = 1$), n_j (corresponding to $x_j = e$) and the auxiliary evaluation h_j. The set of evaluations $\mathcal{C} = \{p_j, n_j, h_j \mid j = 1, \ldots, n\}$ has cardinality polynomial in n. We define the function Q that maps the literals involved in $\mathcal{B}$ to the evaluation functions $\mathcal{C}$ by $Q(x_j) = p_j$ and $Q(\neg x_j) = n_j$. Let the set of alternatives be $\mathcal{A} = \{\alpha_i, \beta_i \mid i = 1, \ldots, m\} \cup \{\gamma_j, \delta_j, \epsilon_j, \zeta_j, \eta_j, \theta_j \mid j = 1, \ldots, n\}$. Then the cardinality of $\mathcal{A}$ is polynomial in the given sizes m and n. Let the values of the evaluation functions on the alternatives be given by the following tables. For $i = 1, \ldots, m$ and $j = 1, \ldots, n$,

	$\alpha_i < \beta_i$	
$Q(l)$ with $l \in K_i$	e	s
others	e	e

	$\epsilon_j < \zeta_j$		$\eta_j \leq \theta_j$	
p_j	e	s	s	e
n_j	e	s	s	e
h_j	e	e	e	s
others	e	e	e	e

The set $\Gamma = \{\alpha_i < \beta_i \mid i = 1, \ldots, m\} \cup \{\epsilon_j < \zeta_j, \eta_j \leq \theta_j \mid j = 1, \ldots, n\}$ of preference statements on $\mathcal{A}$ is polynomial in the given sizes m and n.

In the following we prove that there exists a Γ-satisfying Pareto model with evaluations in C if and only if there exists a satisfying truth assignment for $\mathcal{B}$. Because of the equivalence between $\mathcal{P}$- and $\mathcal{P}^s$-consistency stated in Corollary 1, we can restrict the following considerations to Pareto models in $\mathcal{P}^s$.

Suppose there exists a Γ-satisfying Pareto model $M = \{C\}$ with $C \subseteq \mathcal{C}$. In the following, we prove that for each $j = 1, \ldots, n$, the set C contains either p_j or n_j and not both. Suppose for some $j \in \{1, \ldots, n\}$, $p_j \notin C$ and $n_j \notin C$. Then, the $\oplus$-combination of evaluations in C evaluates to e for both ϵ_j and ζ_j. This contradicts $M \vDash \epsilon_j < \zeta_j$. Thus, for all $j = 1, \ldots, n$, either $p_j \in C$ or $n_j \in C$. Now suppose, for some $j \in \{1, \ldots, n\}$, that $h_j \notin C$. Then, C evaluates to be $\geq s$ on η_j and to be e on θ_j. This contradicts $M \vDash \eta_j \leq \theta_j$. Thus, $h_j \in C$ for all $j = 1, \ldots, n$. Suppose, for some $j \in \{1, \ldots, n\}$, both $p_j \in C$ and $n_j \in C$. Because $h_j \in C$, C evaluates to be $s \oplus s (> s)$ on η_j and to be s on θ_j. Again, this contradicts $M \vDash \eta_j \leq \theta_j$. Hence, for each $j = 1, \ldots, n$, M contains either $p_j \in C$ or $n_j \in C$ but not both.

Thus, for a Γ-satisfying model $M \in \mathcal{P}^s$ the assignment A, with $A(l_{i,k}) = 1$ if and only if $Q(l_{i,k}) \in M$, is well defined. Furthermore, we can show that M contains at least one evaluation $Q(l)$ with $l \in K_i$ for every clause with $i = 1, \ldots, m$. Suppose otherwise. Then, $\bigoplus_{c \in C} c(\alpha_i) = e \oplus \cdots \oplus e = \bigoplus_{c \in C} c(\beta_i)$. This is a contradiction to $M \vDash \alpha_i < \beta_i$. Thus, A is a satisfying truth assignment of the SAT instance $\mathcal{B}$.

Conversely, let A be a satisfying truth assignment of the Boolean formula $\mathcal{B}$. Consider the Pareto model $M = \{C\}$ with $h_j \in C$, and $p_j \in C$ if and only if $A(x_j) = 1$, and $n_j \in C$ if and only if $A(x_j) = 0$. We show $M \vDash_{\mathcal{P}} \Gamma$:

- $\alpha_i <_C \beta_i$: Since A satisfies $\mathcal{B}$, there exists $l \in \{l_{i,1}, \ldots, l_{i,k_i}\}$ for every clause K_i with $A(l) = 1$. Thus, $Q(l) \in C$ and $\bigoplus_{c \in C} c(\alpha_i) = e < s \leq \bigoplus_{c \in C} c(\beta_i)$.
- $\epsilon_j <_C \zeta_j$: Every variable x_j is assigned to be true or false. Thus either $p_j \in C$ or $n_j \in C$ (not both), and $\bigoplus_{c \in C} c(\epsilon_j) = e < s = \bigoplus_{c \in C} c(\delta_j)$.
- $\eta_j \leq_C \theta_j$: Either $p_j \in C$ or $n_j \in C$ but not both, and $h_j \in C$. Thus, $\bigoplus_{c \in C} c(\eta_j) = s = \bigoplus_{c \in C} c(\theta_j)$.

Hence, we have shown, that there exists a satisfying truth assignment for $\mathcal{B}$ if and only if there exists a Γ-satisfying Pareto model in $\mathcal{P}_\mathcal{C}^s$, which is if and only if there exists a Γ-satisfying Pareto model in $\mathcal{P}_\mathcal{C}$.   □

Theorem 2. *The $\mathcal{P}$-Preference Deduction Problem is coNP-complete.*

Proof. For any given Pareto model we can check in polynomial time if it satisfies all given preference statements Γ and does not satisfy φ. Thus we can verify in polynomial time that $\Gamma \nvDash \varphi$ for some instance of PDP. Hence, PDP is in the class coNP. We prove coNP-completeness by a reduction from SAT. For a set of clauses $\mathcal{B} = K_1, \ldots, K_m$, consider the preference structure and statements as constructed in the proof of Theorem 1. In the following, we will define a preference statement $\varphi : \rho < \sigma$ such that no Γ-satisfying model satisfies φ. Hence, $\Gamma \vDash_{\mathcal{P}} \varphi$ if and only if Γ is $\mathcal{P}$-inconsistent, which by the previous proof is if and only if $\mathcal{B}$ is not satisfiable. For every evaluation function $c \in \mathcal{C}$ let

$c(\rho) = c(\sigma) = e$. Then every Pareto model M satisfies $M \vDash \rho = \sigma$, because every set in M evaluates to e on both ρ and σ. Thus, $M \nvDash \rho < \sigma$.   □

4   Relation with Other Preference Models

In this section we compare the cautiousness of inference based on Pareto models with inference based on other well-known preference models. Here, we compare the sets of undominated alternatives for the order relations induced by the different preference models. In applications like recommender systems or multi-objective optimisation it can be very helpful to use inferences that keep the number of undominated alternatives small, so that the user is not overwhelmed when she is presented with them. First, we define HCLP models, lexicographic models and weighted average models as in [4,13].

Definition 4 (HCLP Model). *For a preference structure $\langle \mathcal{A}, \mathcal{C}, \oplus \rangle$, an HCLP model H is an ordered partition of a subset of evaluations. More specifically, $H = (C_1, \ldots, C_r)$ with $r \geq 0$ for pairwise disjoint sets C_i such that $\bigcup_{i=1,\ldots,r} C_i \subseteq \mathcal{C}$.*

An HCLP model forms a hierarchy on a subset of evaluation functions. Let $HCLP$ denote the set of all HCLP models. Each HCLP model $H = (C_1, \ldots, C_r)$ induces an order relation on the set of alternatives $\mathcal{A}$ by comparing the combination of evaluations in the sets (by operator $\oplus$) in a lexicographic manner.

- $\alpha <_H \beta$ if there exists $j \in \{1, \ldots, r\}$ such that $\bigoplus_{c \in C_i} c(\alpha) = \bigoplus_{c \in C_i} c(\beta)$ for all $1 \leq i < j$ and $\bigoplus_{c \in C_j} c(\alpha) < \bigoplus_{c \in C_j} c(\beta)$. *(Written $H \vDash_{HCLP} \alpha < \beta$.)*
- $\alpha \leq_H \beta$ if $\bigoplus_{c \in C_i} c(\alpha) = \bigoplus_{c \in C_i} c(\beta)$ for all $1 \leq i \leq r$; or $\alpha <_H \beta$. *(Written $H \vDash_{HCLP} \alpha \leq \beta$.)*
- $\alpha \equiv_H \beta$ if $\alpha \leq_H \beta$ and $\alpha \geq_H \beta$. *(Written $H \vDash_{HCLP} \alpha \equiv \beta$.)*

Definition 5 (Simple Lexicographic Model). *For a preference structure $\langle \mathcal{A}, \mathcal{C}, \oplus \rangle$, a simple lexicographic model or LEX model $L = (c_1, \ldots, c_r)$ is an ordered subset of evaluations $\{c_1, \ldots, c_r\} \subseteq \mathcal{C}$ with $|\{c_1, \ldots, c_r\}| = r \geq 0$.*

LEX models form a special case of HCLP models in which sets are restricted to contain only one evaluation. The order relations $\leq_L$ and $<_L$ induced by a LEX model $L = (c_1, \ldots, c_r)$ are defined analogously. Let LEX denote the set of all simple lexicographic models. Then $LEX \subseteq HCLP$.

Definition 6 (Weighted Average Model). *For a preference structure $\langle \mathcal{A}, \mathcal{C}, \oplus \rangle$, a weighted average model or WA model $\boldsymbol{w}$ is a normalised weights vector $\boldsymbol{w} \in \mathbb{R}^{|\mathcal{C}|}$ such that for each $i \in \{1, \ldots, |\mathcal{C}|\}$, $\boldsymbol{w}_i \geq 0$, and $\sum_{i=1}^{|\mathcal{C}|} \boldsymbol{w}_i = 1$.*

Let WA be the set of all weighted average models. Each $\boldsymbol{w} \in \mathbb{R}^{|\mathcal{C}|}$ induces an order relation on $\mathcal{A}$ by comparing weighted sums of evaluations $\mathcal{C} = \{c_1, \ldots, c_{|\mathcal{C}|}\}$:

- $\alpha \leq_w \beta$ if $\sum_{i=1}^{|C|} w_i c_i(\alpha) \leq \sum_{i=1}^{|C|} w_i c_i(\beta)$. *(Written $w \vDash_{WA} \alpha \leq \beta$.)*
- $\alpha <_w \beta$ if $\sum_{i=1}^{|C|} w_i c_i(\alpha) < \sum_{i=1}^{|C|} w_i c_i(\beta)$. *(Written $w \vDash_{WA} \alpha < \beta$.)*
- $\alpha \equiv_w \beta$ if $\sum_{i=1}^{|C|} w_i c_i(\alpha) = \sum_{i=1}^{|C|} w_i c_i(\beta)$. *(Written $w \vDash_{WA} \alpha \equiv \beta$.)*

For a *-consistent set of strict and non-strict preference statements $\Gamma \subseteq \mathcal{L}^A$ with $* = LEX, WA, HCLP, \mathcal{P}$ or $\mathcal{P}(1)$, we define order relations $<_\Gamma^*$ and $\ll_\Gamma^*$ on the set of alternatives A in the following way. For $\alpha, \beta \in A$, $\alpha <_\Gamma^* \beta$ if and only if $\Gamma \vDash_* \alpha \leq \beta$ and $\Gamma \nvDash_* \beta \leq \alpha$. For $\alpha, \beta \in A$, $\alpha \ll_\Gamma^* \beta$ if and only if $\Gamma \vDash_* \alpha < \beta$. For a set $S \subseteq A$, let $\text{Opt}(S, \prec)$ denote the set of undominated elements in S w.r.t. an irreflexive and acyclic relation $\prec$, i.e., $\text{Opt}(S, \prec)$ is the set of elements $\alpha \in S$ such that for every $\beta \in S$, $\beta \nprec \alpha$. Then $\text{Opt}(S, \prec)$ represents the alternatives that could be optimal for a user under the assumption that the users preference model is an order relation of the form $\prec$. In [4] the following relations were established between weighted average (WA) and lexicographic (LEX) models. Here, $\nsubseteq$ signifies that the set relation $\subseteq$ dos not necessarily hold for every $S \subseteq A$ and $\Gamma \subseteq \mathcal{L}^A$ (but might hold for some). On the other hand $\subseteq$ means that the relation is true for any arbitrary $S \subseteq A$ and $\Gamma \subseteq \mathcal{L}^A$.

$$\text{Opt}(S, <_\Gamma^{WA}) \subseteq \text{Opt}(S, \ll_\Gamma^{WA})$$
$$\nsubseteq \qquad\qquad \cup |$$
$$\text{Opt}(S, <_\Gamma^{LEX}) \subseteq \text{Opt}(S, \ll_\Gamma^{LEX})$$

In the following, we extend these results by:

$$\text{Opt}(S, <_\Gamma^{HCLP}) \subseteq \text{Opt}(S, \ll_\Gamma^{HCLP}) \qquad\qquad \text{Opt}(S, <_\Gamma^{HCLP}) \subseteq \text{Opt}(S, \ll_\Gamma^{HCLP}))$$
$$\text{(II)} \nsubseteq \qquad\qquad \text{(I)} \cup| \qquad\qquad\qquad \text{(VII)} \nsubseteq \qquad\qquad\qquad \text{(IV)} \cup|$$
$$\text{Opt}(S, <_\Gamma^{\mathcal{P}}) \quad \subseteq \text{Opt}(S, \ll_\Gamma^{\mathcal{P}}) \qquad \text{and} \qquad \text{Opt}(S, <_\Gamma^{LEX}) \quad \subseteq \text{Opt}(S, \ll_\Gamma^{LEX})$$
$$\text{(VII)} \nsubseteq \qquad\qquad \text{(III)} \cup| \qquad\qquad\qquad\qquad \text{(VI)} \nsubseteq \qquad\qquad\qquad \text{(V)} \cup|$$
$$\text{Opt}(S, <_\Gamma^{\mathcal{P}(1)}) \quad \subseteq \text{Opt}(S, \ll_\Gamma^{\mathcal{P}(1)}) \qquad\qquad \text{Opt}(S, <_\Gamma^{\mathcal{P}(1)}) \quad \subseteq \text{Opt}(S, \ll_\Gamma^{\mathcal{P}(1)})$$

Note, that the relations $\text{Opt}(S, <_\Gamma^*) \subseteq \text{Opt}(S, \ll_\Gamma^*))$ follow directly from the implication $\Gamma \vDash_* \alpha < \beta \Rightarrow \Gamma \vDash_* \alpha \leq \beta$ and $\Gamma \nvDash_* \beta \leq \alpha$, which is true for any $* = LEX, WA, HCLP, \mathcal{P}$ or $\mathcal{P}(1)$. Furthermore, the relations (III) and (IV) follow directly from the inclusions $\mathcal{P}(1) \subseteq \mathcal{P}$ and $LEX \subseteq HCLP$, respectively. The relations marked with (I) are a consequence of Proposition 7.

Proposition 7. *Let $\Gamma \subseteq \mathcal{L}^A$ and $\varphi \in \mathcal{L}^A$. If $\Gamma \vDash_{HCLP} \varphi$, then $\Gamma \vDash_{\mathcal{P}} \varphi$.*

Proof. Assume that $\Gamma \vDash_{HCLP} \varphi$. Consider a model $M = \{C_1, \dots, C_m\} \in \mathcal{P}$ with $M \vDash_{\mathcal{P}} \Gamma$; we will show that $M \vDash_{\mathcal{P}} \varphi$, thus proving that $\Gamma \vDash_{\mathcal{P}} \varphi$. For any permutation π on the set $\{1, \dots, m\}$, $H_\pi = (C_{\pi(1)}, \dots, C_{\pi(m)})$ is an HCLP model with $H_\pi \vDash_{HCLP} \gamma$ for all $\gamma \in \Gamma$. Since $\Gamma \vDash_{HCLP} \varphi$, $H_\pi \vDash_{HCLP} \varphi$ for all permutations π. Also, in a φ-satisfying HCLP model, the first level C set must satisfy $\bigoplus_{c \in C} c(\alpha_\varphi) \leq \bigoplus_{c \in C} c(\beta_\varphi)$. Thus, for every set $C \in M$, $\bigoplus_{c \in C} c(\alpha_\varphi) \leq \bigoplus_{c \in C} c(\beta_\varphi)$. In case φ is a strict statement, there exists a set $C \in M$ such that $\bigoplus_{c \in C} c(\alpha_\varphi) < \bigoplus_{c \in C} c(\beta_\varphi)$. This implies that $M \vDash_{\mathcal{P}} \varphi$. As we considered an arbitrary Γ- satisfying Pareto model M, we have $\Gamma \vDash_{\mathcal{P}} \varphi$. $\qquad\square$

Analogously, one can prove Proposition 8 which implies relations (V).

Proposition 8. *Let* $\Gamma \subseteq \mathcal{L}^{\mathcal{A}}$ *and* $\varphi \in \mathcal{L}^{\mathcal{A}}$. *If* $\Gamma \vDash_{LEX} \varphi$, *then* $\Gamma \vDash_{\mathcal{P}(1)} \varphi$.

The relations (II) and (VI) are demonstrated in the following example.

Example 5. *Consider the preference structure* $\langle \mathcal{A}, \mathcal{C}, \oplus \rangle$ *with operator* $\oplus$ *as the standard addition on* $\mathbb{Q}^{\geq 0}$. *The table on the right gives the values of the evaluation functions* $\mathcal{C} = \{c_1, c_2\}$ *on alternatives* $\mathcal{A} = \{\alpha, \beta, \gamma\}$. *Let* $S = \mathcal{A}$ *and* $\Gamma = \{\beta < \alpha\}$. *The*

	α	β	γ
c_1	2	1	1
c_2	0	2	3

Γ-satisfying HCLP models are $(\{c_1\})$ *and* $(\{c_1\}, \{c_2\})$. *The only* Γ-*satisfying Pareto model is* $\{\{c_1\}\}$. *Furthermore,* $(\{c_1\}) \vDash_{HCLP} \beta \equiv \gamma$ *and* $\{\{c_1\}\} \vDash_{\mathcal{P}}$ $\beta \equiv \gamma$. *Also,* $(\{c_1\}, \{c_2\}) \vDash_{HCLP} \beta \leq \gamma$ *and* $(\{c_1\}, \{c_2\}) \nvDash_{HCLP} \beta \geq \gamma$. *Thus,* $\Gamma \vDash_{\mathcal{P}} \beta \leq \gamma, \beta \geq \gamma$, *and* $\Gamma \vDash_{HCLP} \beta \leq \gamma$ *and* $\Gamma \nvDash_{HCLP} \beta \geq \gamma$. *Then* $Opt(S, <_{\Gamma}^{\mathcal{P}})$ $= \{\beta, \gamma\} \nsubseteq \{\beta\} = Opt(S, <_{\Gamma}^{HCLP})$. *Note, that the models* $(\{c_1\})$ *and* $(\{c_1\}, \{c_2\})$ *are in particular LEX models and* $\{\{c_1\}\}$ *is in* $\mathcal{P}(1)$. *Thus,* $Opt(S, <_{\Gamma}^{\mathcal{P}(1)}) \nsubseteq$ $Opt(S, <_{\Gamma}^{LEX})$ *holds.*

The relations in (VII) are demonstrated by the following example.

Example 6. *Consider the preference structure* $\langle \mathcal{A}, \mathcal{C}, \oplus \rangle$ *with operator* $\oplus$ *as the standard addition on* $\mathbb{Q}^{\geq 0}$. *The table on the right gives the values of the evaluation functions* $\mathcal{C} = \{c_1, c_2\}$ *on alternatives* $\mathcal{A} = \{\alpha, \beta, \gamma, \delta\}$. *Let* $S = \mathcal{A}$ *and* $\Gamma = \{\beta \leq \alpha, \gamma \leq \beta\}$.

	α	β	γ	δ
c_1	2	0	1	2
c_2	1	2	0	3

The only Γ-*satisfying LEX model is* () *and the only* Γ-*satisfying* $\mathcal{P}(1)$ *model is* {}. *The* Γ-*satisfying HCLP models are* $(\{c_1, c_2\})$ *and* () *and the* Γ-*satisfying* $\mathcal{P}$ *models are* $\{\{c_1, c_2\}\}$ *and* {}. *The empty model entails* $\alpha \equiv \beta \equiv \gamma \equiv \delta$ *for LEX, HCLP,* $\mathcal{P}(1)$ *and* $\mathcal{P}$. *For the HCLP model* $H = (\{c_1, c_2\})$, $\gamma <_H \beta <_H \alpha <_H \delta$. *Similarly, for the Pareto model* $M = \{\{c_1, c_2\}\} \in \mathcal{P}$, $\gamma <_M \beta <_M \alpha <_M \delta$. *Thus,* $Opt(S, <_{\Gamma}^{\mathcal{P}(1)}) = \{\alpha, \beta, \gamma, \delta\} \nsubseteq \{\gamma\} = Opt(S, <_{\Gamma}^{\mathcal{P}})$. *Also,* $Opt(S, <_{\Gamma}^{LEX}) = \{\alpha, \beta, \gamma, \delta\} \nsubseteq \{\gamma\} = Opt(S, <_{\Gamma}^{HCLP})$.

5 Conclusion

We investigated the Preference Deduction Problem and the Preference Consistency Problem based on Pareto models. Here, we developed characterisations for consistency and deduction (strict and non-strict) which allow one to design algorithms for PCP and PDP. However, PCP and PDP are NP-complete and coNP-complete, respectively. In the special case of singleton models, the characterisations of consistency and deduction lead to polynomial algorithms that solve PCP and PDP in $O(|\Gamma||\mathcal{C}|)$ for given preferences Γ and evaluations $\mathcal{C}$. A comparison shows that Pareto models lead to a less cautious form of inference considering the relations $\ll_{\Gamma}^{*}$, which is often desirable. However, the conjunctive definition of Pareto satisfaction can lead to more sets of preference statements being inconsistent, in comparison with other semantics we considered. In future work, we plan to investigate the cautiousness of inference based on Pareto models under relation $<_{\Gamma}^{*}$ experimentally. Here, it is essential to implement good algorithms to solve PDP (and PCP) based on Pareto models in $\mathcal{P}$. Furthermore, we plan to extend our theory to more complex preference languages.

Acknowledgments. This publication has emanated from research conducted with the financial support of Science Foundation Ireland (SFI) under Grant Number SFI/12/RC/2289.

References

1. Abraham, D.J., Cechlárová, K., Manlove, D.F., Mehlhorn, K.: Pareto optimality in house allocation problems. In: Deng, X., Du, D.-Z. (eds.) ISAAC 2005. LNCS, vol. 3827, pp. 1163–1175. Springer, Heidelberg (2005)
2. Borzsonyi, S., Kossmann, D., Stocker, K.: The skyline operator. In: 17th International Conference On Data Engineering, pp. 421–430. IEEE Computer Society, Heidelberg (2001)
3. Bridge, D., Ricci, F.: Supporting product selection with query editing recommendations. In: 1st ACM Conference on Recommender Systems (RecSys 2007), pp. 65–72. ACM Press, Minneapolis (2007)
4. George, A.-M., Razak, A., Wilson, N.: The comparison of multi-objective preference inference based on lexicographic and weighted average models. In: 27th IEEE International Conference on Tools with Artificial Intelligence (ICTAI 2015), pp. 88–95. IEEE Press, Vietri sul Mare (2015)
5. George, A.-M., Wilson, N., O'Sullivan, B.: Towards fast algorithms for the preference consistency problem based on hierarchical models. In: 25th IEEE International Joint Conference on Artificial Intelligence (IJCAI 2016). AAAI Press, New York (2016, to be published)
6. Figueira, J., Greco, S., Ehrgott, M.: Multiple Criteria Decision Analysis: State of the Art Surveys. Springer, London (2005)
7. Maarry, K.E., Lofi, C., Balke, W.-T.: Crowdsourcing for query processing on web data: a case study on the skyline operator. J. Comput. Inf. Technol. (CIT) **23**(1), 43–60 (2015)
8. Marinescu, R., Razak, A., Wilson, N.: Multi-objective constraint optimization with tradeoffs. In: Schulte, C. (ed.) CP 2013. LNCS, vol. 8124, pp. 497–512. Springer, Heidelberg (2013)
9. Trabelsi, W., Wilson, N., Bridge, D., Ricci, F.: Preference dominance reasoning for conversational recommender systems: a comparison between a comparative preferences and a sum of weights approach. Int. J. Artif. Intell. Tools **20**, 591–616 (2011)
10. Wallis, W.D.: The Mathematics of Elections and Voting. Springer, Heidelberg (2014)
11. Wilson, N.: Efficient inference for expressive comparative preference languages. In: Twenty-First International Joint Conference on Artificial Intelligence (IJCAI 2009), pp. 961–966. AAAI Press, Pesadena (2009)
12. Wilson, N.: Preference inference based on lexicographic models. In: 21st European Conference on Artificial Intelligence (ECAI 2014), pp. 921–926. IOS Press, Prague (2014)
13. Wilson, N., George, A.-M., O'Sullivan, B.: Computation and complexity of preference inference based on hierarchical models. In: 24th IEEE International Joint Conference on Artificial Intelligence (IJCAI 2015), pp. 3271–3277. AAAI Press, Buenos Aires (2015)

Persuasion Dialogues via Restricted Interfaces Using Probabilistic Argumentation

Anthony Hunter[✉]

Department of Computer Science, University College London,
Gower Street, London WC1E 6BT, UK
anthony.hunter@ucl.ac.uk

Abstract. For persuasion dialogues between a software system and user, a user should be able to present arguments. Unfortunately, this would involve natural language processing which is not viable for this task in the short-term. A compromise is to allow the system to present potential counterarguments to the user, and the user expresses his/her degree of belief in each of them. In this paper, we present a protocol for persuasion that supports this type of move, and show how the system can use the epistemic approach to probabilistic argumentation to model the user, and thereby optimize the choice of moves.

1 Introduction

Computational models of argument can potentially be used for systems to persuade users to change their behavior (e.g. to eat less, to exercise more, to use less electricity, to vote, to not text while driving, etc.) [14]. A **system** (the *persuader* running for example as an app) enters into a dialogue with a **user** (the *persuadee* using the app) to persuade them to believe a specific argument called the persuasion goal (e.g. eat more fruit because it is healthy for you).

By choosing appropriate arguments to present to the user, the system may raise the user's belief in the persuasion goal. However, for the system, there is a problem of how to get arguments from the user in order to support a fair and frank persuasion dialogue. We assume the system cannot understand arguments presented in natural language given the complexity of processing arguments in free text. Hence, the interface with the user is restricted. Our solution is for the system to give a menu of arguments, and the user presents agreement/disagreement in each argument by giving it a score (as in a Likert scale [20]). This score is in the unit interval and denotes the belief that the user has in the argument (i.e. the degree to which the user thinks the premises are true and the claim follows from the premises).

Example 1. Suppose the system gives argument A in Fig. 1 as its persuasion goal. It is aware of two potential counterarguments B and C. So it presents these in a menu, and asks the user for his/her degree of belief in them. If the user declares belief greater than 0.5 in B (resp. C), then the system presents D (resp. E) with the aim of lowering the user's belief in B (resp. C) and increasing the user's belief in A.

S. Schockaert and P. Senellart (Eds.): SUM 2016, LNAI 9858, pp. 184–198, 2016.
DOI: 10.1007/978-3-319-45856-4_13

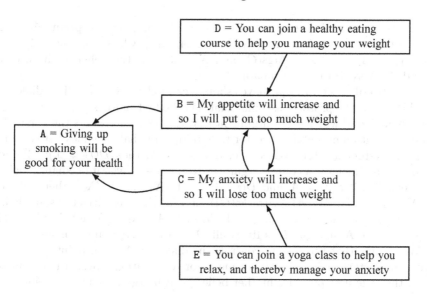

Fig. 1. Example of argument graph for persuasion. It contains the arguments known (but not necessarily believed) by the system. Argument A could be a persuasion goal and so B and C are potential counterarguments for the user.

The above example is a kind of asymmetric dialogue where the moves available to the persuader are different to those available to the persuadee. There is a recent proposal for asymmetric persuasion dialogues with a general definition for probabilistic user models, and a general definition for updating user models in terms of mass redistributions [16]. However, [16] does not consider the following issues: how a menu of potential counterarguments could be presented to the user, how the user could express his/her belief in each of them, or how these moves can be used in a protocol that is fair to the user. We address these issues by making the following contributions in this paper: (1) A dialogue protocol that incorporates the menu move and that is fair to the persuadee; (2) A probabilistic model of the persuadee that can be updated through the dialogue and used by the persuader to predict whether the persuasion is successful; and (3) A method for simulation of the persuadee by the persuader when deciding on which moves to make in the dialogue.

2   Dialogues via Restricted Interfaces

We base our paper on abstract argumentation [6]. We assume our dialogues concern an **argument graph** G where $\mathsf{Args}(G)$ is the set of arguments in G, and $\mathsf{Attacks}(G)$ is the set of attack relations in G. Also $\Gamma \subseteq \mathsf{Args}(G)$ is **conflict-free** iff there is no $A, B \in \Gamma$ s.t. $(A, B) \in \mathsf{Attacks}(G)$. We assume that G contains the arguments known (but not necessarily believed) by the system.

A **dialogue** is a sequence of moves $D = [m_1, \ldots, m_k]$. Equivalently, we use D as a function with an index position i to return the move at that index (i.e. $D(i) = m_i$). A **move** is one of the following: (1) A **posit** A where $A \in \mathsf{Args}(G)$; (2) A **menu** $[A_1/X_1, \ldots, A_n/X_n]$ where for each $A/X \in [A_1/X_1, \ldots, A_n/X_n]$, $A \in \mathsf{Args}(G)$ and $X \in [0,1]$ is the belief of the user in A; and (3) A **system termination** $\perp$.

A **protocol** specifies what moves should/can follow each move in a dialogue. For this paper, the protocol assumes that: (1) the first move is a posit called the **persuasion goal** which is the argument that the persuader wants the persuadee to believe (with a probability greater than 0.5); (2) a dialogue does not continue after the system has terminated (i.e. if $1 \leq i < k$, then $D(i) \neq \perp$); (3) each argument in a menu is a counterargument to the posit given immediately before the menu (i.e. if $D(i) = A$, and $D(i+1) = [A_1/X_1, \ldots, A_n/X_n]$, then for each $A_j/X_j \in D(i+1)$, $(A_j, A) \in \mathsf{Attacks}(G)$); and (4) the user gives the same belief to an argument if it is repeated (i.e. If $\exists i, j$ s.t. $A/X \in D(i)$ and $A/X' \in D(j)$ then $X = X'$). A dialogue D is **finite** iff $D = [m_1, \ldots, m_k]$ and k is finite.

We assume that the system controls the dialogue. At each point in the dialogue, the system makes a posit, or menu, or termination move. If it is a menu move, then the user provides his/her belief in each argument in the menu.

Example 2. For Fig. 1, if the system gives the persuasion goal A, then $[\mathsf{B}/0.9, \mathsf{C}/0.2]$ is a menu move where B and C are from the system, and 0.9 and 0.2 are from the user.

For a dialogue $D = [m_1, \ldots, m_k]$, let $\mathsf{Steps}(D) = \{1, \ldots, k\}$. For dialogues D' and D, the **subsequence relation**, denoted $D' \sqsubseteq D$, holds iff for all $i', j' \in \mathsf{Steps}(D')$, if $i' < j'$, then there are $i, j \in \mathsf{Steps}(D)$ such that $i < j$ and $D'(i') = D(i)$ and $D'(j') = D(j)$. For example, $[[\mathsf{F}/0.9, \mathsf{G}/0.2], \mathsf{D}] \sqsubseteq [\mathsf{A}, [\mathsf{F}/0.9, \mathsf{G}/0.2], \mathsf{C}, \mathsf{D}, \mathsf{E}, \perp]$. Also $D' \sqsubset D$ is defined as $D' \sqsubseteq D$ and not $D \sqsubseteq D'$.

3   Fair Dialogues

In this section, we ensure dialogues are fair by allowing the persuadee to express belief in potential counterarguments.

Definition 1. *For $A, B \in \mathsf{Args}(G)$, A **indirectly attacks** B iff (1) $A \neq B$ and (2) either $(A, B) \in \mathsf{Attacks}(G)$ or there are $(A, A'), (A', A'') \in \mathsf{Attacks}(G)$ s.t. $A \neq A'$ and $A' \neq A''$ and A'' indirectly attacks B.*

Example 3. Let $\rightsquigarrow$ denote the "indirectly attacks" relationship. So for the following graph $\mathsf{A} \rightsquigarrow \mathsf{B}$, $\mathsf{A} \rightsquigarrow \mathsf{D}$, $\mathsf{B} \rightsquigarrow \mathsf{A}$, $\mathsf{B} \rightsquigarrow \mathsf{C}$, $\mathsf{B} \rightsquigarrow \mathsf{E}$, $\mathsf{C} \rightsquigarrow \mathsf{D}$, $\mathsf{C} \rightsquigarrow \mathsf{B}$, $\mathsf{D} \rightsquigarrow \mathsf{A}$, $\mathsf{D} \rightsquigarrow \mathsf{E}$, $\mathsf{D} \rightsquigarrow \mathsf{C}$, $\mathsf{E} \rightsquigarrow \mathsf{B}$, and $\mathsf{E} \rightsquigarrow \mathsf{D}$.

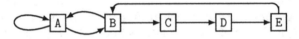

Proposition 1. *Let $X \subseteq \mathsf{Args}(G)$ be s.t. there is no $A \in X$ where $(A, A) \in \mathsf{Attacks}(G)$. X is conflict-free iff for all $A, B \in X$, it is not the case that A indirectly attacks B.*

Definition 2. *For $A, B \in \mathsf{Args}(G)$, A **defends** B iff (1) $A \neq B$ and (2) either there is a (A, C), $(C, B) \in \mathsf{Attacks}(G)$ s.t. $A \neq C$ and $C \neq B$, or there is a C s.t. A defends C and C defends B.*

Proposition 2. *For $B, A \in \mathsf{Args}(G)$, if B indirectly attacks A, then there is a $(B, C) \in \mathsf{Attacks}(G)$ s.t. $C = A$ or C defends A.*

To compose the menus, we assume in Definition 4 that each posit is followed by a menu of arguments that attack the posit according to the argument graph, and that have not already appeared in a menu and indirectly attacked by the posit. As we cover in Sect. 5, we will aim for belief in the posit and disbelief in the counterargument, and so informally, if a posit indirectly attacks a counter-argument in an earlier menu, then we do not need to present it to the user in a menu again.

Definition 3. *For a dialogue D, a graph G, an argument A, and a step i. The **fair attacks**, $\mathsf{FairAttacks}(G, D, A, i)$, is $\{B \mid (B, A) \in \mathsf{Attacks}(G)$ and there is no $j < i$ s.t. $B/Y \in D(j)$ and A indirectly attacks $B\}$.*

Definition 4. *A dialogue D is **fair** for G iff for each i,*

$$\text{if } D(i) = A \text{ and } \mathsf{FairAttacks}(G, D, A, i) \neq \emptyset$$
$$\text{then } D(i + 1) = [B_1/X_1, \ldots, B_n/X_n]$$

where $\mathsf{FairAttacks}(G, D, A, i) = \{B_1, \ldots, B_n\}$.

Example 4. The dialogue $[\mathsf{A}, [\mathsf{B}/0.9], \mathsf{C}, \bot]$ is fair for both the following graphs.

Example 5. For Fig. 1, $[\mathsf{A}, [\mathsf{B}/1, \mathsf{C}/0], \mathsf{D}, \bot]$, $[\mathsf{A}, [\mathsf{B}/0, \mathsf{C}/0.7], \mathsf{E}, \bot]$, $[\mathsf{A}, [\mathsf{B}/0, \mathsf{C}/0], \bot]$, $[\mathsf{A}, [\mathsf{B}/0.9, \mathsf{C}/1], \mathsf{C}, [\mathsf{B}/0.9], \bot]$, and $[\mathsf{A}, [\mathsf{B}/0.9, \mathsf{C}/0.65], \mathsf{D}, \mathsf{E}, \bot]$, are fair.

Example 6. The dialogue $[\mathsf{A}, [\mathsf{B}/0.9, \mathsf{C}/0.7], \mathsf{C}, \bot]$ is fair for the left graph and the dialogues $[\mathsf{A}, [\mathsf{B}/0.5], \bot]$ and $[\mathsf{A}, [\mathsf{B}/1], \mathsf{C}, [\mathsf{A}/0.9], \mathsf{B}, [\mathsf{C}/0.9], \mathsf{A}, [\mathsf{B}/1], \ldots]$ are fair for the right graph.

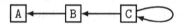

Example 7. For the following graph, C does not indirectly attack C and so the self-attacks causes the fair dialogue $[\mathsf{A}, [\mathsf{B}/1, \mathsf{C}/1], \mathsf{C}, [\mathsf{C}/1], \mathsf{C}, [\mathsf{C}/1], \ldots]$ to be infinite.

An **odd cycle** is a sequence of arguments $A_1, \ldots, A_m$ s.t. each A_{i+1} attacks A_i and A_1 attacks A_m where m is odd.

Proposition 3. *If argument graph G contains no odd cycles, and D is a fair dialogue, then D is finite.*

We can assign responsibility of arguments to the persuadee and persuader as follows.

Definition 5. *Let D be a dialogue, the* **persuader arguments** *are* Persuader $(D) = \{A \mid \exists i \in \text{Steps}(D) \ s.t. \ D(i) = A\}$ *and the* **persuadee arguments***, are* Persuadee$(D) = \{B \mid \exists i \in \text{Steps}(D) \ s.t. \ B/X \in D(i)\}$.

Example 8. For $D = [\text{A}, [\text{B}/0.9], \text{C}, \perp]$, Persuader$(D) = \{\text{A}, \text{C}\}$ and Persuadee $(D) = \{\text{B}\}$.

From the perspective of the user, if the dialogue is fair, then s/he has been able to express his/her belief/disbelief in the potential counterarguments known by the system.

4   Probabilistic User Models

We use the epistemic approach to probabilistic argumentation [1,13,17,25].

Definition 6. *A* **mass distribution** *P over* Args(G) *is such that* $\sum_{\Gamma \subseteq \text{Args}(G)} P(\Gamma) = 1$. *Let* Dist$(G)$ *be the set of mass distributions over G. The* **probability of an argument** *A is* $P(A) = \sum_{\Gamma \subseteq \text{Args}(G) \ s.t. \ A \in \Gamma} P(\Gamma)$.

For a mass distribution P, and $A \in \text{Args}(G)$, $P(A)$ is the belief that an agent has in A (i.e. the degree to which the agent believes the premises and the conclusion drawn from those premises). When $P(A) > 0.5$, then the agent believes the argument to some degree, whereas when $P(A) \leq 0.5$, then the agent disbelieves the argument to some degree.

Definition 7. *The* **epistemic extension** *for mass distribution P is* Extension $(P) = \{A \in \text{Args}(G) \mid P(A) > 0.5\}$.

Example 9. Consider the graph in Fig. 1. If $P(\text{A}) = 0.2$, $P(\text{B}) = 0.9$, $P(\text{C}) = 0.4$, $P(\text{D}) = 0.2$, and $P(\text{E}) = 0.8$, then Extension$(P) = \{\text{B}, \text{E}\}$.

The epistemic approach provides a finer grained assessment of an argument graph than given by Dung's definition of extensions. By adopting constraints on the distribution, the epistemic approach subsumes Dung's approach [25]. However, there is also a need for a non-standard view [17] where we adopt weaker constraints on the distribution. For instance, an important aspect of the epistemic approach is the representation of disbelief in arguments even when they are unattacked. In this case, a key constraint for the non-standard view is the following which ensures that the mass distribution respects the structure of the graph, without forcing an unattacked argument to be believed [13].

Definition 8. *A mass distribution P is* **rational** *for G iff* $\forall (A, B) \in$ Attacks(G), *if $P(A) > 0.5$, then $P(B) \leq 0.5$.*

	A	B	C	D	E	Rational
P_1	0.6	0.9	0.4	0.6	0.7	No
P_2	0.3	0.9	0.3	0.1	0.8	Yes
P_3	0.9	0.1	0.2	0.8	0.2	Yes

Example 10. Examples of mass distribution for Fig. 1.

The system (the persuader) uses a mass distribution as a model of the user (the persuadee). It can update the model at each stage of the dialogue. This is useful for asymmetric dialogues where the user is not allowed to posit arguments/counterarguments. So the only way the user can treat arguments that s/he does not accept is by disbelieving them (and the user model is intended to reflect this). In contrast, in symmetric dialogues, the user can posit counterarguments to an argument that s/he does not accept.

5   Winning Dialogues

In this paper, we consider two mass distributions for a dialogue. The first is the **initial distribution**, denoted P_0, which is the model of the user before the dialogue starts, and the second is the **final distribution**, denoted P_k which is the model of the user once the dialogue of k steps has terminated. In this section, we assume we have the final distribution, and in Sect. 7 we discuss how the final distribution can be obtained from the initial distribution using the moves in the dialogue.

The next definition ensures that every menu item that is changed from believed (when the user presents belief in the menu item) to disbelieved (by the end of the dialogue) has an attacker that is posited later in the dialogue and is believed.

Definition 9. *A dialogue D is* **frank** *for final distribution P_k iff for $1 \leq i \leq k$, for each $B/X \in D(i)$, if $X > 0.5$, and $P_k(B) \leq 0.5$, then there is an index j and argument C such that $i < j$ and $D(j) = C$ and $(C, B) \in$ Attacks(G) and $P_k(C) > 0.5$ and $C \neq B$.*

Example 11. The dialogue $[A, [B/1, C/0.8], D, E, \perp]$ is fair and frank for the following argument graph G and rational final distribution P_k where $P_k(A) = 0.8$, $P_k(B) = 0.2$, $P_k(C) = 0.2$, $P_k(D) = 0.9$, and $P_k(E) = 0.9$.

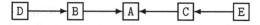

From the perspective of the persuader, if s/he wants to persuade the persuadee of the persuasion goal A, then the aim is for $P_k(A) > 0.5$ where P_k is the final distribution, and so the persuader can regard the dialogue as a winning dialogue, whereas if $P_k(A) \leq 0.5$, then the persuader can regard the dialogue as a losing dialogue. We formalize this next.

Definition 10. *Let P_k be a rational final distribution, and let D be a fair, finite, and frank, dialogue w.r.t. P_k and G s.t. $D(1) = A$ and $D(k) = \perp$. If $P_k(A) > 0.5$, then D is a* **winning dialogue**, *otherwise D is a* **losing dialogue.**

Example 12. For the following argument graph G and rational mass distribution P_k where $P_k(A) = 0.9$, $P_k(B) = 0$, $P_k(C) = 1$, $P_k(D) = 0$, and $P_k(E) = 0.6$.

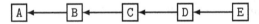

Let $D = [A, [B/0.9], C, [D/0.6], E, \perp]$. So D is fair, finite, and frank for P_k, and D is a winning dialogue. Also $\mathsf{Persuader}(D) = \{A, C, E\}$ and $\mathsf{Persuadee}(D) = \{B, D\}$.

Example 13. For the following argument graph G and rational final distribution P_k where $P_k(A) = 0$, $P_k(B) = 0$, and $P_k(C) = 1$.

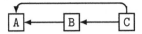

Let $D = [A, [B/0, C/1], C, \perp]$. So D is fair, finite, and frank for P_k, and D is a losing dialogue. Also $\mathsf{Persuader}(D) = \{A, C\}$ and $\mathsf{Persuadee}(D) = \{B, C\}$.

Example 14. For the graph in Fig. 1 and rational distribution P_k where $P_k(A) = 0.7$, $P_k(B) = 0$, $P_k(C) = 0$, $P_k(D) = 1$, and $P_k(E) = 1$. Let $D = [A, [B/0.9, C/0.8], D, E, \perp]$. So D is fair, finite, and frank for P_k, and D is a winning dialogue. Also $\mathsf{Persuader}(D) = \{A, D, E\}$ and $\mathsf{Persuadee}(D) = \{B, C\}$.

We now introduce the notion of minimality of a dialogue to remove superfluous moves.

Definition 11. *Let D be a winning dialogue w.r.t. P_k and G. D is* **minimal** *iff for all $D' \sqsubseteq D$, D' is not a winning dialogue w.r.t. P_k and G.*

Example 15. Fair dialogues for the graph include $D_1 = [A, [B/0.8], C, [E/0.9], F, \perp]$, $D_2 = [A, [B/0.8], D, [F/0.9], \perp]$, and $D_3 = [A, [B/0.8], C, [E/0.9], F, G, \perp]$. Let $P_k(A) = 0.8$, $P_k(B) = 0$, $P_k(C) = 0.8$, $P_k(D) = 0$, $P_k(E) = 0$, $P_k(F) = 0.8$, and $P_k(G) = 0.8$. So D_1 and D_3 are winning. D_2 is not frank and so losing. Also D_1 is minimal but D_3 is not minimal.

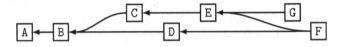

The following results show that minimal winning dialogues are well-behaved in that (1) the persuader arguments are conflict-free, (2) each persuadee argument is either not believed by the persuadee (as indicated in the menu) or is countered by the persuader, (3) the persuader and persuadee arguments are disjoint, and (4) all persuader arguments are believed and no persuadee argument is believed.

Proposition 4. *Let G be an argument graph and P_k be a rational final distribution. If D is a minimal winning dialogue w.r.t. P_k and G, then* Persuader(D) *is conflict-free.*

Proposition 5. *Let G be an argument graph and P_k be a rational final distribution. Also let D be a minimal winning dialogue w.r.t. P_k and G. For all $(B, A) \in$ Attacks(G), if $A \in$ Persuader(D), then either $B/X \in D(i)$ for some i and $X \leq 0.5$ or there is $C \in$ Persuader(D) s.t. $(C, B) \in$ Attacks(G).*

Note, we do not assume that the user is always consistent. For example, in Fig. 1, the final distribution could be s.t. $P_k(\mathrm{B}) = 0.9$ and $P_k(\mathrm{C}) = 0.8$. This would give Extension$(P_k) = \{\mathrm{B,C}\}$ which is not conflict-free. Of course, this would mean that the dialogue is not a winning dialogue for the persuader.

Proposition 6. *Let G be an argument graph and P be a rational final distribution. If D is a minimal winning dialogue w.r.t. P_k and G, then* Persuader$(D) \cap$ Persuadee$(D) = \emptyset$.

Proposition 7. *Let G be an argument graph and P_k be a rational final distribution. If D is a minimal winning dialogue w.r.t. P_k and G, then for all $A \in$ Persuader(D), $P_k(A) > 0.5$ and for all $B \in$ Persuadee(D), $P_k(B) \leq 0.5$.*

The following example shows that a winning dialogue does not necessarily have all its persuader arguments being in the epistemic extension.

Example 16. Consider the following graph with final distribution $P_k(\mathrm{A}) = 1$, $P_k(\mathrm{B}) = 0$, $P_k(\mathrm{C}) = 0$, $P_k(\mathrm{D}) = 1$, and $P_k(\mathrm{E}) = 1$. So Extension$(P_k) = \{\mathrm{A,D,E}\}$. The dialogue $D = [\mathrm{A}, [\mathrm{B}/1], \mathrm{C}, [\mathrm{D}/1], \mathrm{E}, \perp]$ is winning w.r.t. P_k and G. Also Persuader$(D) = \{\mathrm{A,C,E}\}$. So the persuader arguments are not a subset of the epistemic extension. However, $D' = [\mathrm{A}, [\mathrm{B}/1], \mathrm{E}, \perp]$ is a subdialogue where Persuader$(D') \subseteq$ Extension(P_k) and it is winning w.r.t. P_k and G.

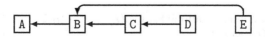

Proposition 8. *If P_k is a rational final distribution, and D is a minimal winning dialogue w.r.t. P_k and G, then* Persuader$(D) \subseteq$ Extension(P_k) *holds.*

So a minimal dialogue uses arguments in the epistemic extension of P_k to present a winning position for the goal.

6 Delineated Subgraphs

The aim of this section is to better understand the proposal so far. For this, we consider properties of the subgraph of the argument graph as delineated by the dialogue.

Definition 12. *Let D be a dialogue and let G' be a subgraph of G. D **delineates** G' iff* $\mathsf{Args}(G') = \{A \mid \exists i \ s.t. \ D(i) = A \ or \ A/X \in D(i)\}$ *and* $\mathsf{Attacks}(G') = \{(A, B) \in \mathsf{Attacks}(G) \mid A, B \in \mathsf{Args}(G')\}$.

Example 17. For the following graph (left), $D_1 = [\mathsf{A}, [\mathsf{B}/1], \mathsf{C}, [\mathsf{B}/1], \mathsf{C}, \ldots]$ delineates the graph (left), whereas $D_2 = [\mathsf{A}, [\mathsf{B}/1], \bot]$ delineates the subgraph (right).

So when a dialogue D delineates a graph G, the nodes in G are exactly the arguments that appear in the posits and menus of D, and the arcs are just the arcs from the argument graph that involve those arguments.

A user declaration is what a user initially believes in an argument in a menu. Only some arguments have a user declaration, and the aim of the dialogue is to change the user's beliefs in some of these user declarations in order to have a winning dialogue.

Definition 13. *For a dialogue D, let* $\mathsf{Declarations}(D) = \{B/X \mid \exists i \ s.t. \ B/X \in D(i)\}$ *be the arguments in a menu, let* $\mathsf{Declared}(D) = \{B \mid B/X \in \mathsf{Declarations}(D)\}$ *and let* $\mathsf{Undeclared}(D) = \{A \in \mathsf{Args}(G) \mid A \notin \mathsf{Declared}(D)\}$.

Example 18. Consider the graph in Fig. 1. For the dialogue $[\mathsf{A}, [\mathsf{B}/0.9, \mathsf{C}/0.1], \mathsf{D}, \bot]$, we get $\mathsf{Declared}(D) = \{\mathsf{B}, \mathsf{C}\}$ and $\mathsf{Undeclared}(D) = \{\mathsf{A}, \mathsf{D}, \mathsf{E}\}$.

The next definition retrieves the belief that the user assigns to each argument in a menu, and assigns belief of 0 to any argument that does not appear in a menu.

Definition 14. *The **declared belief**, denoted Q_D, of the persuadee in dialogue D is*

$$Q_D(B) = \begin{cases} X & \text{for each } B/X \in \mathsf{Declarations}(D) \\ 0 & \text{for each } B \in \mathsf{Undeclared}(D) \end{cases}$$

Example 19. Continuing Example 18, $Q_D(\mathsf{A}) = 0$, $Q_D(\mathsf{B}) = 0.9$, $Q_D(\mathsf{C}) = 0.1$, $Q_D(\mathsf{D}) = 0$, and $Q_D(\mathsf{E}) = 0$.

The following definition captures the subgraph of argument graph G that contains all the relevant arguments given the user beliefs. It is based on a partition of the nodes in the subgraph. One partition denotes the persuader arguments and the other partition denotes the persuadee arguments. Essentially, for each persuader argument in the subgraph, all the attackers of the argument are also in the subgraph, whereas for each persuadee argument in the subgraph, all the attackers of the argument are also in the subgraph, or the persuadee argument is not believed by the persuadee.

Definition 15. *Let Q_D be the declared belief in D. $G' \sqsubseteq G$ is a **good subgraph** of G for D iff there is a partition of $\mathsf{Args}(G')$ into sets Φ and Ψ (i.e. $\Phi \cap \Psi = \emptyset$ and $\Phi \cup \Psi = \mathsf{Args}(G')$), such that the persuasion goal is in Φ, and for each $A \in \Phi \cup \Psi,$*

- if $A \in \Psi$, then $Q_D(A) \leq 0.5$ *or* $\exists (B, A) \in \mathsf{Attacks}(G)$ *s.t.* $(B \in \Phi$ *and* $(B, A) \in \mathsf{Attacks}(G'))$
- if $A \in \Phi$, then $\forall (B, A) \in \mathsf{Attacks}(G)$, $(B \in \Psi$ *and* $(B, A) \in \mathsf{Attacks}(G'))$

We call (Φ, Ψ) *the* **partition** *of the good subgraph.*

So a good subgraph is identified just by the declared beliefs expressed by the user in the menu moves. As shown below, not every fair dialogue has a good subgraph.

Example 20. The dialogue $[A, [B/1, C/1], D, E, \perp]$ is winning for Fig. 1 and the final distribution P_k where $P_k(A) = 1$, $P_k(B) = 0$, $P_k(C) = 0$, $P_k(D) = 1$, and $P_k(E) = 1$. The graph is the good subgraph for D with partition $\Phi = \{A, D, E\}$ and $\Psi = \{B, C\}$.

Example 21. The dialogue $[A, [B/1], C, \perp]$ is winning for the following graph and the final distribution P_k where $P_k(A) = 1$, $P_k(B) = 0$, and $P_k(C) = 1$. The graph is the good subgraph for D with partition $\Phi = \{A, C\}$ and $\Psi = \{B\}$.

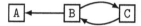

Example 22. Dialogues $[A, [B/1, C/1], C, \perp]$ and $[A, [B/1, C/0], C, \perp]$ are losing for the graph and any final rational distribution. There is no good subgraph for the above dialogues, whereas the dialogue $[A, [B/0.3, C/0.1], \perp]$ is winning for the graph and a good subgraph (which is the graph itself) has the partition $\Phi = \{A\}$ and $\Psi = \{B, C\}$.

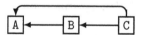

Example 23. $[A, [B/1], C, [A/1], B, [C/1], A, [B/1], \ldots]$ is a losing dialogue for the graph (left), and any rational final distribution. There is no good subgraph for the above dialogue, whereas the dialogue $[A, [B/0], \perp]$ is winning for the graph and its good subgraph (right) has the partition $\Phi = \{A\}$ and $\Psi = \{B\}$.

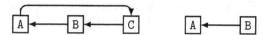

Next we show that the partition of a good subgraph splits the arguments between persuader and persuadee.

Proposition 9. *If D is a winning dialogue w.r.t. P_k and G and (Φ, Ψ) is the partition of the good subgraph of G for D, then $\Phi = \mathsf{Persuader}(D)$ and $\Psi = \mathsf{Persuadee}(D)$.*

The following result shows that if the persuasion goal of dialogue D is believed (according to the final distribution P_k), and G' is a good subgraph of G for D, then G' does not contain any odd cycles.

Proposition 10. *If G' is a good subgraph of G for D, then G' contains no odd cycles.*

We now consider how the declarative notion of a good subgraph corresponds to winning dialogues (and the associated delineated subgraph). We show that we get a good subgraph from a minimal winning dialogue, and then we show that we can construct a winning dialogue from a good subgraph.

Proposition 11. *Let $D(1) = A$. If D is a minimal winning dialogue w.r.t. P_k and G, then there is a G' s.t. G' is a good subgraph of G for D where D delineates G' and P_k is rational for G' and $P_k(A) > 0.5$.*

Proposition 12. *If G' is a good subgraph of G for D, where (Φ, Ψ) is the partition of G', and P_k is a mass distribution s.t. $P_k(B) > 0.5$ for each $B \in \Phi$, and $P_k(C) \leq 0.5$ for each $C \in \Psi$, then there is a dialogue D, where D is a winning dialogue w.r.t. P_k and G, and D delineates G'.*

So the notion of the good subgraph provides a declarative perspective on winning dialogues.

7   Updating Mass

Given an initial distribution P_0, representing the system's model of the user's beliefs at the start of the dialogue, we update the model to give the final distribution P_k. For this, we introduce the notion of an update method which generates a mass distribution P_k from P_0 based on the moves in D.

Definition 16. *Let P_0 be an initial distribution and let D be a dialogue. An* **update function,** *$\mathsf{Update}(P_0, D)$, returns a final distribution P_k such that if $D = [\bot]$, then $P_0 = P_k$.*

There are many possibilities for defining an update function. Here we give a basic update function (below) as an example. It updates the belief in an argument based on the belief in the arguments appearing after it in the dialogue. For $D(i) = A$, belief in the arguments in the menu $D(i+1) = [B_1/X_1, \ldots, B_n/X_n]$ determines the belief in A. Similarly, for $D(i) = [B_1/X_1, \ldots, B_n/X_n]$, and each B_j in the menu, belief in the posits that occur after move $D(i)$ (i.e. moves that occur from $i+1$ to k) determine the belief in B_j.

Definition 17. *For initial distribution P_0 and dialogue D, a* **basic update function** *is $\mathsf{Update}(P_0, D) = P_k$ s.t. for each $A \in \{B \mid \exists i \ s.t. \ D(i) = B \ or \ B/X \in D(i)\}$:*

$$P_k(A) = \begin{cases} 0.2 & \text{if } A \in \mathsf{Persuader}(D) \text{ and } \exists B \in \mathsf{Opp}(D, A) \ s.t. \ P_k(B) > 0.5 \\ 0.2 & \text{if } A \in \mathsf{Persuadee}(D) \text{ and } \exists B \in \mathsf{Pro}(D, A) \ s.t. \ P_k(B) > 0.5 \\ 0.8 & \text{if } A \in \mathsf{Persuader}(D) \text{ and } \forall B \in \mathsf{Opp}(D, A), P_k(B) \leq 0.5 \\ Q_D(A) & \text{if } A \in \mathsf{Persuadee}(D) \text{ and } \forall B \in \mathsf{Pro}(D, A), P_k(B) \leq 0.5 \end{cases}$$

where $\mathsf{Opp}(D, A) = \{B \mid \exists i \ s.t. \ D(i) = A \text{ and } B/X \in D(i+1)\}$ and $\mathsf{Pro}(D, A) = \{B \mid \exists i, j \ s.t. \ i < j \text{ and } A/X \in D(i) \text{ and } D(j) = B \text{ and } (B, A) \in \mathsf{Attacks}(G)\}$.

Example 24. Consider the graph in Fig. 1. For $D = [\text{A}, [\text{B}/0.9, \text{C}/0.4], \text{D}, \perp]$, with $P_0(\text{A}) = 0.1$, $P_0(\text{B}) = 0.7$, $P_0(\text{C}) = 0.5$, $P_0(\text{D}) = 0.1$, and $P_0(\text{E}) = 0.1$. For the basic update function, $\mathsf{Update}(P_0, D) = P_k$ where $P_k(\text{A}) = 0.8$, $P_k(\text{B}) = 0.2$, $P_k(\text{C}) = 0.4$, $P_k(\text{D}) = 0.8$, and $P_k(\text{E}) = 0.1$.

The values 0.2 and 0.8 in the basic update definition are indicative of possible assignments. More sophisticated modelling of users allows for the calculation of the value as a function of the value assigned to the counterarguments.

Proposition 13. *If* $\mathsf{Update}(P_0, D) = P_k$ *is basic, and* D *delineates* G', *then* P_k *is rational for* G'.

There is a range of alternatives to the basic update in [16] that allow for a range of different kinds of user to be modelled. These include options for modelling more credulous and more skeptical users.

8 Using a User Model to Optimize Dialogues

The system wants a final distribution P_k s.t. $P_k(A) > 0.5$ for persuasion goal A. This is done in one of two modes.

In **interaction mode**, the system gives posit and menu moves, and the user gives belief in each argument in each menu (as in Example 24). At the end of the dialogue, the final mass P_k is obtained using an update function, and $P_k(A)$ is used as a prediction of the degree to which the user believes the persuasion goal $D(1) = A$.

In **simulation mode**, the system simulates a dialogue with the user in order to predict the outcome. For this, the initial mass P_0 is used for the user responses (and so P_0 is a proxy for the user answers). If this simulation is run with each possible dialogue, a dialogue can be chosen that maximizes $P_k(A)$ where A is the persuasion goal.

In this section, we focus on simulation mode. For optimization, we consider the fair and finite dialogues for a particular persuasion goal A and initial mass P_0. We denote this set $\mathsf{Fair}(G, A, P_0)$. The set of simulated dialogues is the subset where each user response is specified by the initial distribution. We use the simulated dialogues when we consider what would be the optimal choice of dialogue before undertaking the actual dialogue.

Definition 18. *The set of* **simulated dialogues**, *denoted* $\mathsf{Simulate}(G, A, P_0)$, *is* $\{D \in \mathsf{Fair}(G, A, P_0) \mid$ *for each* i, *if* $B/X \in D(i)$, *then* $P_0(B) = X\}$.

Example 25. Consider Fig. 1 with the initial distribution P_0 where $P_0(\text{A}) = 0.2$, $P_0(\text{B}) = 0.9$, $P_0(\text{C}) = 0.7$, $P_0(\text{D}) = 0.1$, and $P_0(\text{E}) = 0.5$. So the fair dialogue $[\text{A}, [\text{B}/0.9, \text{C}/0.7], \text{D}, \text{E}, \perp]$ is a simulated dialogue.

Definition 19. *For a dialogue* D, *with the initial distribution* P_0, *a basic update function* $\mathsf{Update}(P_0, D) = P_k$, *and persuasion goal* $D(i) = A$, *the* **score function** *is defined as* $\mathsf{Score}(D, P_0) = P_k(A)$.

Example 26. For a basic update function with Example 25, $\mathsf{Score}(D, P_0) = 0.8$.

We define the locally optimal dialogues as dialogues for which all subdialogues have a lower score, and all superdialogues do not have a higher score. So a locally optimal dialogue is minimal in the sense that every move in the dialogue is required in order to get the score, and it is minimal in the sense that adding further moves will not improve the score.

Definition 20. *The* **locally optimal dialogues** *are the dialogues* Local $(G, A, P_0) = \{D \in \mathsf{Simulate}(G, A, P_0) \mid \forall D' \in \mathsf{Simulate}(G, A, P_0),$ *if* $D' \sqsubset D,$ *then* $\mathsf{Score}(D', P_0) < \mathsf{Score}(D, P_0)$ *and if* $D \sqsubset D',$ *then* $\mathsf{Score}(D', P_0) \leq \mathsf{Score}(D, P_0)\}$.

A globally optimal dialogue is a locally optimal dialogue that has the maximum score of locally optimal dialogues.

Definition 21. *The* **globally optimal dialogues** *are the dialogues* Global $(G, A, P_0) = \{D \in \mathsf{Local}(G, A, P_0) \mid \forall D' \in \mathsf{Local}(G, A, P_0)\; \mathsf{Score}(D', P_0) \leq \mathsf{Score}(D, P_0)\}$.

Example 27. For the following graph, let $P_0(\mathsf{A}) = 0.6$, $P_0(\mathsf{B}) = 0.3$, $P_0(\mathsf{C}) = 0.3$, and $P_0(\mathsf{D}) = 0.9$.

The final distribution P_k for each dialogue is given below. So D_1 and D_2 are winning dialogues for P_k, but only D_2 is locally optimal (and therefore globally optimal).

	A	B	C	D
$D_1 = [\bot]$	0.6	0.3	0.3	0.9
$D_2 = [\mathsf{A}, [\mathsf{B}/0.3], \bot]$	0.8	0.3	0.3	0.9

Proposition 14. *If there is a winning dialogue D for G and P_k, where* $\mathsf{Update}(P_0, D) = P_k$, *then there is a $D' \in \mathsf{Global}(G, A, P_0)$ s.t.* $\mathsf{Score}(D', P_0) > 0.5$.

So if there is a winning dialogue, then there is a globally optimal dialogue with the same outcome.

9   Discussion

In this paper, we have made the following contributions: (1) Introduced the menu move to get the user's belief in potential counterarguments; (2) Presented a fair and frank protocol for persuasion dialogues; and (3) Used the user model to optimize the choice of moves in the persuasion dialogues. For this, we have used the epistemic approach to probabilistic argumentation. This contrasts with the constellations approach (e.g. [7,12,19]) which is concerned with the uncertainty about the structure of the graph rather than belief in arguments.

The proposal in this paper relies on a user model. This can be generated by querying the user, or by learning from previous interactions with similar users. Some recent studies indicate the potential viability of an empirical approach [5,24].

Most proposals for dialogical argumentation focus on protocols (e.g. [4,8,21, 22]). Some strategies have been investigated (e.g. [3,9,18,26]) but the important issue of uncertainty is under-developed. A probabilistic model of the opponent has been used in a dialogue strategy allowing the selection of moves for an agent based on what it believes the other agent is aware of [23]. The history of previous dialogues is used to predict the arguments that an opponent might put forward [10]. For modelling dialogues, a probabilistic finite state machine can represent the possible moves that each agent can make in each state of the dialogue [15]. This has been generalized to POMDPs when there is uncertainty about what an opponent is aware of [11]. However, none of these proposals consider the beliefs of the opposing agent or asymmetric dialogues. In [2], a probabilistic model of persuadee beliefs is used by the persuader to optimize choice of beliefs to present, but there is no consideration of how to get beliefs from the persuadee or how to update the model based on the dialogue. Therefore, the proposal in this paper is an important contribution towards the theoretical foundations for using argumentation in apps for helping persuade users to change behaviour (e.g. eat less, exercise more, drive more carefully, etc.).

Acknowledgements. This research was partly funded by EPSRC grant EP/ N008294/1 for the Framework for Computational Persuasion project.

References

1. Baroni, P., Giacomin, M., Vicig, P.: On rationality conditions for epistemic probabilities in abstract argumentation. In: Computational Models of Argument (COMMA 2014), pp. 121–132 (2014)
2. Black, E., Coles, A., Bernardini, S.: Automated planning of simple persuasion dialogues. In: Bulling, N., van der Torre, L., Villata, S., Jamroga, W., Vasconcelos, W. (eds.) CLIMA 2014. LNCS, vol. 8624, pp. 87–104. Springer, Heidelberg (2014)
3. Black, E., Hunter, A.: Reasons and options for updating an opponent model in persuasion dialogues. In: Proceedings of the International Workshop on the Theory and Applications of Formal Argumentation (TAFA 2015) (2015)
4. Caminada, M., Podlaszewski, M.: Grounded semantics as persuasion dialogue. In: Computational Models of Argument (COMMA 2012), pp. 478–485 (2012)
5. Cerutti, F., Tintarev, N., Oren, N.: Formal arguments, preferences, and natural language interfaces to hhuman: an empirical evaluation. In: Proceedings of ECAI 2014, pp. 207–212 (2014)
6. Dung, P.: On the acceptability of arguments and its fundamental role in non-monotonic reasoning, logic programming, and n-person games. Artif. Intell. **77**, 321–357 (1995)

7. Dung, P., Thang, P.: Towards (probabilistic) argumentation for jury-based dispute resolution. In: Computational Models of Argument (COMMA 2010), pp. 171–182. IOS Press (2010)
8. Fan, X., Toni, F.: Assumption-based argumentation dialogues. In: Proceedings of IJCAI 2011, pp. 198–203 (2011)
9. Fan, X., Toni, F.: A general framework for sound assumption-based argumentation dialogues. Artif. Intell. **216**, 20–54 (2014)
10. Hadjinikolis, C., Siantos, Y., Modgil, S., Black, E., McBurney, P.: Opponent modelling in persuasion dialogues. In: Proceedings of IJCAI 2013, pp. 164–170 (2013)
11. Hadoux, E., Beynier, A., Maudet, N., Weng, P., Hunter, A.: Optimization of probabilistic argumentation with Markov decision models. In: Proceedings of IJCAI 2015 (2015)
12. Hunter, A.: Some foundations for probabilistic argumentation. In: Computational Models of Argument (COMMA 2012), pp. 117–128 (2012)
13. Hunter, A.: A probabilistic approach to modelling uncertain logical arguments. Int. J. Approx. Reason. **54**(1), 47–81 (2013)
14. Hunter, A.: Opportunities for argument-centric persuasion in behaviour change. In: Fermé, E., Leite, J. (eds.) JELIA 2014. LNCS, vol. 8761, pp. 48–61. Springer, Heidelberg (2014)
15. Hunter, A.: Probabilistic strategies in dialogical argumentation. In: Straccia, U., Calì, A. (eds.) SUM 2014. LNCS, vol. 8720, pp. 190–202. Springer, Heidelberg (2014)
16. Hunter, A.: Modelling the persuadee in asymmetric argumentation dialogues for persuasion. In: Proceedings of IJCAI 2015 (2015)
17. Hunter, A., Thimm, M.: Probabilistic argumentation with incomplete information. In: Proceedings of ECAI 2014, pp. 1033–1034 (2014)
18. Kontarinis, D., Bonzon, E., Maudet, N., Moraitis, P.: Empirical evaluation of strategies for multiparty argumentative debates. In: Bulling, N., van der Torre, L., Villata, S., Jamroga, W., Vasconcelos, W. (eds.) CLIMA 2014. LNCS, vol. 8624, pp. 105–122. Springer, Heidelberg (2014)
19. Li, H., Oren, N., Norman, T.J.: Probabilistic argumentation frameworks. In: Modgil, S., Oren, N., Toni, F. (eds.) TAFA 2011. LNCS, vol. 7132, pp. 1–16. Springer, Heidelberg (2012)
20. Likert, R.: A technique for the measurement of attitudes. Arch. Psychol. **140**, 1–55 (1932)
21. Prakken, H.: Coherence and flexibility in dialogue games for argumentation. J. Logic Comput. **15**(6), 1009–1040 (2005)
22. Prakken, H.: Formal sytems for persuasion dialogue. Knowl. Eng. Rev. **21**(2), 163–188 (2006)
23. Rienstra, T., Thimm, M., Oren, N.: Opponent models with uncertainty for strategic argumentation. In: Proceedings of IJCAI 2013, pp. 332–338 (2013)
24. Rosenfeld, A., Kraus, S.: Providing arguments in discussions based on the prediction of human argumentative behavior. In: Proceedings of AAAI 2015 (2015)
25. Thimm, M.: A probabilistic semantics for abstract argumentation. In: Proceedings of ECAI 2012, pp. 750–755 (2012)
26. Thimm, M.: Strategic argumentation in multi-agent systems. Kunstliche Intell. **28**(3), 159–168 (2014)

Metric Logic Program Explanations for Complex Separator Functions

Srijan Kumar[1], Edoardo Serra[2], Francesca Spezzano[2(✉)],
and V.S. Subrahmanian[1]

[1] Computer Science Department, University of Maryland, College Park, USA
{srijan,vs}@cs.umd.edu
[2] Computer Science Department, Boise State University, Boise, USA
{edoardoserra,francescaspezzano}@boisestate.edu

Abstract. There are many classifiers that treat entities to be classified as points in a high-dimensional vector space and then compute a
separator S between entities in class +1 from those in class −1. However, such classifiers are usually very hard to explain in plain English to
domain experts. We propose Metric Logic Programs (MLPs) which are a
fragment of constraint logic programs as a new paradigm for explaining
S. We present multiple measures of quality of an MLP and define the
problem of finding an MLP-Explanation of S and show that it - and
various related problems - are NP-hard. We present the MLP_Extract
algorithm to extract MLP explanations for S. We show that while our
algorithms provide more succinct, simpler, and higher fidelity explanations than association rules that are less expressive, our algorithms do
require additional run-time.

1 Introduction

There are many data mining applications in which generating a human-
understandable explanation of why classifications are correct is more important
than making a prediction. We would be unhappy if a car mechanic told us that
the reason we need an expensive repair is because 2 times the reading of sensor
A plus 5 times the cube of sensor reading B exceeds 10. This classifier is highly
accurate, but unintelligible. *The goal of this paper is to generate high-quality,
succinct explanations of separators generated by other predictive algorithms. We
do not make predictions in this paper — we assume predictions are made by a
separator. We wish to come up with good explanations of those separators.* Examples of separators that can be explained using the techniques in this paper include
support vector machines (SVM) and Gaussian process classification (GPC).

Unlike past work seeking to explain separators with association rules [2], we
propose to explain a host of separators with a fragment of Constraint Logic Programming [11] with negation [4]. We introduce *Metric Logic Programs* (MLPs)
in which metric logic rules (ML-rules for short) have three types of constraints
in rule bodies: positive interval constraints, negative interval constraints, and
metric constraints. The heads of ML-rules classify objects into the category +1.

© Springer International Publishing Switzerland 2016
S. Schockaert and P. Senellart (Eds.): SUM 2016, LNAI 9858, pp. 199–213, 2016.
DOI: 10.1007/978-3-319-45856-4_14

This very specific type of rule allows greater expressive power than classical association rules [2]. Moreover, it is easy for humans to understand such rules. We propose, for the first time, an algorithm to extract MLPs that best "match" a given separator function's (such as the separators returned by SVM or GPC) ability to recognize the +1 class. For a given MLP to match a separator ϕ, it must classify all training data instances in the same way as ϕ — moreover, ML-rules must define regions that have a bounded overlap with the region identified as belonging to the -1 class by ϕ. We also require such rules to be simple, having at most a certain body size. The MLP-Explanation (MLP-E) problem is that of finding an MLP of minimal cardinality (i.e. as few rules as possible) subject to the above constraints. We prove that MLP-E is NP-hard and so are several problems associated with it.[1]

We have created an MLP_Extract algorithm to solve the MLP-Explanation problem and tested it against some past work on finding association rules to explain SVM using 7 real-world open-source data sets. Our experiments show that MLP_Extract beats past work handily on the quality of explanations. By using MLPs, MLP_Extract provides significantly smaller rule sets (less than half the size of its nearest competitor), significantly simpler rule bodies (less than half the body size), as well as significantly improved fidelity. Fidelity is the percentage of points on which the extracted MLPs agree with the separator function ϕ that we are trying to explain. This comes, however, at the cost of increased run time of our MLP_Extract algorithm and hence, MLP_Extract should be used when having human intelligible applications is important (e.g. when a company wants to make an expensive change to their production line or when a bank wants to make a big investment in a stock).

Note that we are using a standard classifier (such as SVM or GPC) for predictive purposes, and our MLPs are trying to explain those classifiers to a lay person. The MLPs themselves are not used for prediction. Our work is in the same spirit as abductive inference [10,12] where a set of observations (e.g. the given data) must be explained. In classical abductive LP, the set of observations and a logic program would be augmented with a set of hypothesis so that the LP and hypothesis together entail the observations. In our setting, we still have observations (given data) and a theory (the separator function) and we try to infer an MLP that best explains the separator.

Problem Description. As in classical classification, we assume there is a set of training points $T = \{x_1, \ldots, x_s\}$ where each $x_i \in \mathbb{R}^n$ is an input vector of dimensionality n which has an associated "ground truth" class $y_i \in \{-1, +1\}$. We assume that a separator $\phi : \mathbb{R}^n \to \{-1, +1\}$ has been found and that ϕ *predicts* the class to which x_i belongs. ϕ may be an imperfect predictor, i.e. it may not always be the case that $\forall x_i \in T, \phi(x_i) = y_i$. *Our goal is to find an MLP that best explains the predictor* ϕ. A "best explanation" must be succinct, easily understandable by ordinary humans not versed in classification algorithms, and must closely match the separator ϕ.

---

[1] The proofs of all theorems can be found in the Appendix at the end of the paper.

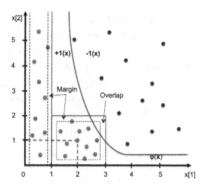

Fig. 1. Geometric representation of the metric logic program in Example 1 for explaining the separator $\phi(\mathbf{x})$.

2 Metric Logic Programs

Let D denote the set $\{1, \ldots, n\}$ of dimensions. Our constants, denoted x (possibly with subscripts) are members of $\mathbb{R}^n$. We use $\mathbf{x}$, possibly with subscripts, to denote variable symbols ranging over points in $\mathbb{R}^n$. $\mathbf{x}[i]$ denotes $\mathbf{x}$'s ith component. As usual [13], a *term* is either a variable symbol or a constant symbol. Our language has just one unary predicate symbol $+1$. If p is a predicate symbol and t is a term, then $p(t)$ is an *atom*. For instance, if $n = 2$, $+1((2, 1))$ is an atom saying that the point $(2, 1)$ belongs to class $+1$. An *atom* is an expression of the form $+1(\mathbf{x})$ and $-1(\mathbf{x})$. We now define constraints.

- If $\mathbf{x}$ is a variable symbol and $l_i, u_i \in \mathbb{R}$, then $l_i \leq \mathbf{x}[i] \leq u_i$ is an *interval constraint*.
- If $\mathbf{x}$ is a variable symbol and $l_i, u_i \in \mathbb{R}$, then $\neg(l_i < \mathbf{x}[i] < u_i)$ is a *negative constraint*.
- If $\mathbf{x}$ is a variable symbol, $z \in T$ is a point, and $d \in \mathbb{R}$, then $IN(\mathbf{x}, z, d)$ is a *metric constraint*.

Intuitively, $IN(\mathbf{x}, z, d)$ holds iff the distance between $\mathbf{x}$ and z is less than or equal to d along each and every dimension. Continuing with our running example, $IN(\mathbf{x}, (2, 1), 1)$ describes the square whose corners are $(1,2)$, $(1,0)$, $(3,0)$ and $(3,2)$. Any point x within this rectangle will satisfy the constraint $IN(\mathbf{x}, (2, 1), 1)$.[2]

If $A(\mathbf{x})$ is an atom and $C_1(\mathbf{x}), \ldots, C_n(\mathbf{x})$ are constraints (of any of the three types listed above), then

$$A(\mathbf{x}) \leftarrow C_1(\mathbf{x}) \wedge \cdots \wedge C_n(\mathbf{x})$$

is a *Metric Logic (ML)* rule. A *Metric Logic Program* (MLP) $\mathcal{M}$ is a finite set of ML-rules.

---

[2] Though metric constraints can be expressed via interval constraints, it would require n interval constraints to express it. This would yield a very long rule body, losing our desire to have succinct rules. We use metric constraints to gain succinctness.

For space reasons, we do not provide a model-theoretic definition of entailment. Informally, $\mathcal{M}$ entails $+1(x)$ iff there exists an ML-rule with $+1(\mathbf{x}) \leftarrow C_1[\mathbf{x}] \wedge \ldots, C_n[\mathbf{x}]$ such that for all $1 \leq i \leq n$, all the constraints $C_i/[\mathbf{x}/x]$ hold where $C_i[\mathbf{x}/x]$ is the result of substituting x for $\mathbf{x}$ in C_i. *Throughout this paper, we assume MLPs are used to classify members of $\mathbb{R}^n$ into the class $+1$. Anything that is not explicitly classified as belonging to class $+1$ is in class -1 (by closed world assumption* [16]*).* Then, we assume that our rules always have the predicate $+1$ (or alternatively -1) in the head.

Example 1. Consider the small MLP $\mathcal{M}_1$ given below.

$$+1(\mathbf{x}) \leftarrow IN(\mathbf{x}, (2,1), 1).$$
$$+1(\mathbf{x}) \leftarrow 0 \leq \mathbf{x}[1] \leq 1.$$

Intuitively, we can see that the atom $+1((2.5, 1.5))$ is entailed by the above program as the first rule is fired when $\mathbf{x} = (2.5, 1.5)$.

Given a set W of points and a ML-rule r, the following definitions specify which points in W are covered by r with a margin $m \geq 0$. The margin is considered to avoid overfiting of rule r with points in W. The program $\mathcal{M}_1$ is visually represented by the two hyper-rectangles to the left of the separator ϕ as shown in Fig. 1.

Definition 1 (Constraint Satisfaction). *Suppose $x' \in \mathbb{R}^n$ is a point, $m > 0$ is a "margin" and C is a constraint. x' satisfies C with margin m iff:*

- *Case $C = (l_i \leq \boldsymbol{x}[i] \leq u_i)$: $l_i + m \leq x'[i] \leq u_i - m$.*
- *Case $C = \neg(l_i < \boldsymbol{x}[i] < u_i)$: $x'[i] \leq l_i - m$ or $u_i + m \leq x'[i]$.*
- *Case $C = IN(\boldsymbol{x}, z, d)$: $\max_{i \in D} |x'[i] - z[i]| \leq d - m$.*

We now define what it means for a rule to "cover" a point $x' \in \mathbb{R}^n$.

Definition 2 (Rule Covering). *Given a point $x' \in \mathbb{R}^n$, an ML-rule r and a margin $m \geq 0$, r covers x' with margin m if x' satisfies each constraint C in body(r) with margin m. The set $cp(W, r, m)$ of covered points is:*

$$cp(W, r, m) = \{x' | x' \in W \wedge x' \text{ is covered by } r \text{ with margin } m\}.$$

Think of W above as referring to all points on the $+1$ side of the separator ϕ. $cp(W, r, m)$ tells us how many points on that side of the separator are covered by ML-rule r with margin m. This is the set of points (on that side of the separator line) that are "covered" by r. The set of points covered by an MLP $\mathcal{M}$ is the union of all points covered by each ML-rule $r \in \mathcal{M}$. We now formally define the entailment.

Definition 3 (Entailment with Margin m). *Given a point $x' \in \mathbb{R}^n$, an MLP $\mathcal{M}$ and a margin $m \geq 0$, we say that the atom $+1(x')$ (resp. $-1(x')$), is entailed by $\mathcal{M}$ with margin m iff there exists a rule $r \in \mathcal{M}$ having the predicate symbol $+1$ (resp. -1) in the head s.t. $x' \in cp(W, r, m)$.*

The previous definition of entailment coincides with this one when $m = 0$.

Example 2. In Fig. 1, let W be everything to the left of ϕ, let $m = 0$, and r be an ML-rule represented by the hyper-rectangle on the right. The portion of points to the left of ϕ covered by this hyper-rectangle is the set $cp(W, r, m)$ (here, r covers 11 points). For the MLP $\mathcal{M}_1$, the union of points in the regions covered by the two hyper-rectangles to the left of ϕ constitute $cp(W, \mathcal{M}_1, m)$ (20 points in total).

The above discussion shows that the body of an ML-rule r uniquely determines a region $Reg(r) \subseteq \mathbb{R}^n$. A separator's goal is to separate $\mathbb{R}^n$ into a part that captures members of the $+1$ class predicted by ϕ and another that captures members of the predicted -1 class. Algorithms like SVM and GPC go to considerable effort to find good separators and use them for good prediction. Our MLPs attempt to explain these separators rather than to use them to predict. So the MLP must not contain rules that span both sides of the separator as this is inconsistent with the separator. This underlies the concept of overlap below.

Example 3. Consider Fig. 1 again. Suppose W is the set of all points to the right of ϕ, and $\mathcal{M}_1$ consists of the two rules of Example 1 to explain the left side of ϕ, represented by the two hyper-rectangles. The portion of points to the right of ϕ which are covered by them represents the level of inconsistency between $\mathcal{M}_1$ and ϕ. *The larger the area of the rectangles in the right side of ϕ is, the more "inconsistent" the ML-rules are in capturing the data on the left side of the separator line.*

We now formally define *overlap* below.

Definition 4 (Overlap). *Given a fixed separator function ϕ and an ML-rule r, the overlap $\mathbf{ov}(r)$ is the fraction of all points $x \in cp(\mathbb{R}^n, r, 0)$ such that $\phi(x) = -1$.*

Intuitively, the overlap of r with ϕ is the fraction of the region covered by r which ϕ states to be in class -1. Intuitively, r misclassifies this region (even if no training points appear in the region, if the separator is a good one, non-training data might fall into these overlapping regions, leading to misclassification error).

From Fig. 1, we see that the overlap of the right hyper-rectangle is greater than the left one (whose overlap is 0). The Average Overlap (AO) of an MLP $\mathcal{M}$ is the average of the overlaps of ML-rules $r \in \mathcal{M}$.

Theorem 1. *Given a rule r, a fixed separator function ϕ, the problem of computing the overlap $\mathbf{ov}(r)$ is $\#P$-hard.*

Recall that proofs of all theorems can be found in the Appendix at the end of the paper.

To mitigate this intractability, we approximately compute $\mathbf{ov}(r)$ using a Monte Carlo algorithm that uniformly samples points covered by r.

We now formally define the MLP-Explanation problem.

Metric Logic Program Explanation (MLP-E) Problem.

INPUT: Training set $T = \{x_1, \ldots, x_s\}$, separator ϕ, integer $r_{max} > 0$, margin $m > 0$.

OUTPUT: An MLP $\mathcal{M}$ s.t. $|P|$ is minimal, subject to:

1. *Each point $x_i \in T$ s.t. $\phi(x_i) = +1$ are covered,* i.e. $\forall x_i \in T$ s.t. $\phi(x_i) = +1$ there is an ML-rule $r \in \mathcal{M}$ s.t. $x_i \in cp(T, r, m)$;
2. *No points $x_i \in T$ s.t. $\phi(x_i) = -1$ is covered,* i.e. $\forall x_i \in T$ s.t. $\phi(x_i) = -1$ there is no ML-rule $r \in \mathcal{M}$ s.t. $x_i \in cp(T, r, m)$;.
3. *Overlap is bounded.* For each $r \in \mathcal{M}$, $\mathbf{ov}(\phi) \leq ov_{max}$ for some constant ov_{max}.
4. *ML-rule size is bounded.* All ML-rules in $\mathcal{M}$ have at most r_{max} constraints.

To best match a separator, we require that ML-rules in $\mathcal{M}$ must exactly match ϕ. Moreover, we require that the ML-rules honor the separation constraint found as much as possible by bounding overlap. We also ensure comprehensibility by requiring that rules have at most r_{max} constraints. Subject to these constraints, we want to find a minimal-sized MLP. Unfortunately, solving the MLP-Explanation problem is intractable.

Theorem 2. *MLP-E is* **NP**-*hard*[3].

To make matters a bit worse, it turns out that finding ML-rules that satisfy just constraints (2), (3), and (4) is NP-hard.

Theorem 3. *Finding an ML-rule that satisfies constraints 2, 3 and 4 of the MLP-E problem and maximizes the number of covered points in a set W is* **NP**-*hard.*

3   The **MLP_Extract** Algorithm

Our MLP_Extract algorithm heuristically solves the MLP-E-problem because of the intractability results in Theorems 2 and 3. Our algorithm is a set-covering approach in which we want to cover all training points predicted by the separator to be in the $+1$ class (the set W) while satisfying the other constraints in the MLP-E problem.

MLP_Extract starts by invoking **MLRuleGenerator** to come up with a list of candidate rules. It then iterates and in each loop, it finds the ML-rule from the candidate set that covers the maximal number of points in the set W. It adds this ML-rule to the result and deletes the covered points from W. This loop ends when $W = \emptyset$.

---

[3] MLP-E may not be in **NP** due to the overlap constraint. After guessing the set E of ML-rules in non-deterministic polynomial time, we need an oracle to check overlap, but this is at least $\#P$-hard by Theorem 1. We leave this as an open problem.

The set $\overline{W}$ of points predicted by ϕ to be in class -1.

The **MLRuleGenerator** considers points to be covered (from W). It shuffles the set W of points, then chooses the first point and tries to generate a rule covering that point and not covering any point in the set $\overline{W}$ of points predicted by ϕ to be in class -1. This rule is generated through invocation of the **MLRuleCreator** algorithm (Algorithm 3) which separately ensures that constraints (2), (3), (4) of the definition of the MLP-E-problem are satisfied. The generated rule is improved to cover more points in W as explained in the next paragraph. The set of ML-rules is iteratively improved to cover remaining points in W by calling **MLRuleCreator**. When all points in W have been processed, the rule produced is returned. Note that because of the shuffle operation (Line 2), **MLRuleGenerator** returns a different set of ML-rules each time it is invoked by MLP_Extract. As this is done nR times (the maximum number of rules that is allowed to explain the points) in lines 3–4 of MLP_Extract, we get nR different sets of ML-rules.

Algorithm 1. MLP_Extract Algorithm

```
 1: procedure RulesResult=MLP_EXTRACT (W, W̄, y)
 2:     Rules = ∅
 3:     for (1 ≤ i ≤ nR) do
 4:         Rules = Rules ∪ MLRuleGenerator(W, W̄, y);
 5:     end for
 6:     RulesResult = ∅
 7:     while (|W| > 0) do
 8:         choose rule ∈ arg max_{rule∈Rules} cp(W, {rule}, m);
 9:         if (|cp(W, {rule}, m)| > 0) then
10:             RulesResult = RulesResult ∪ {rule};
11:             W = W \ cp(W, {rule}, m);
12:             Rules = Rule \ rule;
13:         else
14:             break;
15:         end if
16:     end while
17:     return RulesResult;
18: end procedure
```

The **MLRuleCreator** algorithm finds rules satisfying constraints (2), (3) and (4) of the MLP-E problem. Given a set W of points predicted by the separator to be in the $+1$ class, let $\texttt{Constraints}(W)$ be the set of all possible constraints that can be used to create a rule that covers all points in W. $\texttt{Constraints}(W)$ is the union of three sets, $\texttt{Constraints}_1(W)$, $\texttt{Constraints}_2(W)$ and $\texttt{Constraints}_3(W)$ that are the sets containing interval, negative and metric constraints, respectively. The equations below specifies the definition of each of these sets (see also Example 4), given the margin m.

$$\texttt{Constraints}_1(W) = \Big\{ l_i \leq \mathbf{x}[i] \leq u_i \mid l_i = [(\min_{\mathbf{x} \in W} \mathbf{x}[i]) - m],$$
$$u_i = [(\max_{\mathbf{x} \in W} \mathbf{x}[i] + m)], i \in D \Big\}.$$

$$\texttt{Constraints}_2(W) = \Big\{ \neg(a + m < \mathbf{x}[i] < b - m) \mid i \in D,$$
$$(a, b) \in CI(W, i), b - a > 2m \Big\}.$$
$$\texttt{Constraints}_3(W) = \Big\{ IN(\mathbf{x}, x_p, d) \mid x_p \in W, d = \max_{(l_i \leq \mathbf{x}[i] \leq u_i) \in \texttt{Constraints}_1(W)}$$
$$\max(|\mathbf{x}_p[i] - l_i|, |\mathbf{x}_p[i] - u_i|) \Big\}.$$

We briefly explain these definitions.

(i) $\texttt{Constraints}_1(W)$ is the constraint with the tightest interval that contains all points in W.

(ii) $\texttt{Constraints}_2(W)$ is the set of constraints describing the intervals that do not have any points from $\overline{W}$ in them. Given $i \in D$, $CI(W, i)$ is the set of intervals such that no point in W has its $i - th$ component within the interval. That is, $CI(W, i) = \{(\mathbf{x}_1[i], \mathbf{x}_2[i]) \mid \mathbf{x}_1, \mathbf{x}_2 \in W, \mathbf{x}_1[i] < \mathbf{x}_2[i], \neg\exists \mathbf{x}_3 \in W s.t.\ \mathbf{x}_1[i] < \mathbf{x}_3[i] < \mathbf{x}_2[i]\}$. Observe that each negative constraint referring to the feature i is always within the corresponding interval constraint in $\texttt{Constraints}_1$ for the same feature i.

(iii) $\texttt{Constraints}_3(W)$ is the set of metric constraints with the smallest possible d's and centered at each point $x_p \in W$ that contains all the points in W.

Algorithm 2. Rules Generation Algorithm

```
1:  procedure Rules=MLRULEGENERATOR(W, W̄, y)
2:      shuffle W;
3:      Rules = ∅;
4:      while W ≠ ∅ do
5:          rule = null;
6:          W' = ∅;
7:          W'' = ∅;
8:          while (W ≠ ∅) do
9:              take the first element w in W;
10:             W = W \ {w};
11:             W' = W' ∪ {w};
12:             r =MLRuleCreator(W', W̄, y)
13:             if (r ≠ null) then
14:                 rule = r;
15:             else
16:                 W' = W' \ {w}
17:                 W'' = W'' ∪ {w}
18:             end if
19:         end while
20:         if (rule ≠ null) then
21:             Rules = Rules ∪ {rule};
22:         end if
23:         W = W''
24:     end while
25:     return Rules;
26: end procedure
```

The following example illustrates these concepts.

Example 4. Let $W = \{x_a, x_b, x_c\}$ (cf. Fig. 2). Then, the set of all interval constraints is $\texttt{Constraints}_1(W) = \{a \leq \mathbf{x}[1] \leq b,\ c \leq \mathbf{x}[2] \leq d\}$ (see Fig. 2a). The set containing all possible negative constraints is formed by all intervals depicted

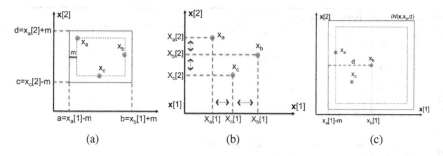

Fig. 2. Illustration of the sets $\texttt{Constraints}_1(W)$, $\texttt{Constraints}_2(W)$ and $\texttt{Constraints}_3$ (W) for $W = \{x_a, x_b, x_c\}$.

with the symbol $\longleftrightarrow$ in Fig. 2b. Thus, $CI(W, 1) = \{(x_a[1], x_c[1]), (x_c[1], x_b[1])\}$, while $CI(W, 2) = \{(x_c[2], x_b[2]), (x_b[2], x_a[2])\}$. Then:

$$\texttt{Constraints}_2(W) = \{ \begin{array}{l} \neg(x_a[1] + m < \mathbf{x}[1] < x_c[1] - m), \\ \neg(x_c[1] + m < \mathbf{x}[1] < x_b[1] - m), \\ \neg(x_c[2] + m < \mathbf{x}[2] < x_b[2] - m), \\ \neg(x_b[2] + m < \mathbf{x}[2] < x_a[2] - m) \end{array} \}$$

where m is the margin. An example of a metric constraint in $\texttt{Constraints}_3(W)$ is shown in Fig. 2c. It is the square centered at x_b and has a side of size $2d$ where $d = (x_b[1] - x_a[1]) + m$. This metric constraint is the set of points x s.t. $IN(\mathbf{x}, x_b, d)$ covers x. Thus, the set $\texttt{Constraints}_3(W)$ contains metric constraints similar to the one above described, one for each point in W.

In addition to covering points in W belonging to the $+1$ class, we want to make sure that the constraints do not cover points in the other class $\bar{y}$, i.e. the class -1. For this, we define a function $notCov(A, \overline{W})$ that returns the set $\overline{W}' \subseteq \overline{W}$ of points not in W that are not covered by constraint A. It is defined as:

- if A is the positive constraint $a \leq \mathbf{x}[i] \leq b$, then $notCov(A, \overline{W}) = \{x \in \overline{W} | (l_i \leq x[i] < a) \vee (b < x[i] \leq u_i)\}$.
- if A is the negative constraint $\neg(a < \mathbf{x}[i] < b)$, then $notCov(A, \overline{W}) = \{x \in \overline{W} | a < x[i] < b\}$.
- if A is a metric constraint $IN(\mathbf{x}, x_p, d)$, then $notCov(A, \overline{W}) = \{x \in \overline{W} | \max_{i \in D} |x_p[i] - x[i]| > d\}$.

The **MLRuleCreator** algorithm (Algorithm 3) takes a set W of points predicted by separator ϕ to be in the $+1$ class, the set $\overline{W}$ of points predicted by ϕ to be in class -1, and the class y as input and outputs an ML-rule that is discovered by the heuristic which (i) covers all the points in W, (ii) does not cover any points in $\overline{W}$, (iii) has an overlap of at most c_{max}, and (iv) has at most r_{max} constraints.

The first step of the algorithm builds $\texttt{Constraints}(W)$ (Line 2). The **greedy-Covering** function then finds a set $B \subseteq \texttt{Constraints}(W)$ of possible constraints. The problem of selecting B is a set covering problem: each constraint A in $\texttt{Constraints}(W)$, if selected as part of the body of an ML-rule, ensures that the points in $not-Cov(A, \overline{W}) \subseteq \overline{W}$ are excluded by the rule. Then this is equivalent to a set covering problem by selecting a set B that does not cover any point in $\overline{W}$. As set covering is

Algorithm 3. Rule Creation Algorithm

```
 1: procedure rule=MLRULECREATOR(W, W̄, y)
 2:     Compute Constraints(W);
 3:     B = greedyCovering(Constraints(W), W̄);
 4:     while |B| ≤ r_max do
 5:         E = computeOverlap(B, nS, y);
 6:         if (|E|/nS ≤ c_max) then
 7:             rule = ⋀_{A∈B} A → y;
 8:             return rule;
 9:         end if
10:         W̄ = W̄ ∪ E;
11:         B = greedyCovering(Constraints(W), W̄);
12:     end while
13:     return null;
14: end procedure

15: procedure B=GREEDYCOVERING(A_W, W̄)
16:     B = ∅;
17:     while (|W̄| > 0) do
18:         choose A ∈ arg max_{A∈A_W} |notCov(A, W̄)|;
19:         B = B ∪ {A};
20:         A_W = A_W \ {A};
21:         W̄ = W̄ \ notCov(A, W̄);
22:     end while
23:     return B;
24: end procedure

25: procedure E=COMPUTEOVERLAP(B, nS, y)
26:     E = ∅;
27:     for (1 ≤ i ≤ nS) do
28:         x =getSample(B);
29:         if (class(x) ≠ y) then
30:             E = E ∪ {x};
31:         end if
32:     end for
33:     return E;
34: end procedure
```

NP-hard, **greedyCovering** computes the greedy $ln(uco)$[4]-approximation of the exact covering, i.e., at each iteration, it computes and adds to B the constraint that covers the maximal number of points in $\overline{W}$ which are not yet covered by any selected constraint, until all undesirable points are uncovered. As a consequence, the size of B and the the number of constraints per rule is minimized.

The second step of Algorithm 3 iteratively improves the set B until its size is at most r, so that the ML-rule defined by the constraints in B has an overlap below ov_{max}. If the size of B is greater than r, the algorithm returns $null$ as there is no ML-rule with at most r constraints which satisfies all the conditions - it covers the points in W, does not cover the points in $\overline{W}$, and has an overlap of at most c_{max}. The overlap is estimated by the **computeOverlap** method by uniformly sampling (see Algorithm 4) nS points in the region covered by the ML-rule described by the constraints in B, and approximating the overlap as the percentage of sampled points E that are classified by the separator ϕ in the class -1. If the overlap is at most ov_{max}, then the ML-rule $+1(\mathbf{x}) \leftarrow \bigwedge_{A∈B} A$ is accepted. Otherwise, the set of sampled points E is used to reduce the overlap of the ML-rule defined by the constraints in B - by adding E to $\overline{W}$ so that in the next iteration these points will not be covered, and, hence, the overlap will decrease.

---

[4] uco is the maximum number of points in $\overline{W}$, over all constraints.

Algorithm 4. Uniform Sampling of a point **x** in the hyper-rectangle defined by B

```
 1: procedure x=GETSAMPLE(B)
 2:     for each i ∈ D do
 3:         x[i] =getCoordinateSample(B, i)
 4:     end for
 5:     return x;
 6: end procedure

 7: procedure a=GETCOORDINATESAMPLE(B, i)
 8:     l = L_i, u = U_i;
 9:     for each (l_j ≤ x[i] ≤ u_j) ∈ B do
10:         l = max(l, l_j);
11:         u = min(u, u_j);
12:     end for
13:     for each (maxDist(x_p, x) ≤ d) ∈ B do
14:         l = max(l, x_p[i] − d);
15:         u = min(u, x_p[i] + d);
16:     end for
17:     Let C be a ordered list containing all negative constraints ¬(l_j < x[i] < u_j) ∈ B;
18:     H = ∅;
19:     for each not(l_j < x[i] < u_j) ∈ C do
20:         H = H ∪ {(l ≤ x[i] ≤ l_j)};
21:         l = u_j;
22:     end for
23:     H = H ∪ {(l ≤ x[i] ≤ u)};
24:     Guess an interval (l_j ≤ x[i] ≤ u_j) ∈ H with a PDF assigning probability values proportion-
           ally to the interval width;
25:     Uniformly guess a number a s.t. l_j ≤ a ≤ u_j;
26:     return a;
27: end procedure
```

4 Experiments

In this section, we compare the performance of MLP_Extract with past attempts to explain SVM separators. There have been several efforts to rules to explain SVM (cf. Sect. 5). We used 7 standard datasets (Pima Indians, Breast Cancer Wisconsin, Dermatology, Heart Diseases, Iris, Ionosphere and German) from the UCI repository for the comparison. We ran all experiments on an Intel Xeon @ 2.3 GHz, 24 GB RAM Linux machine.

We compared our algorithm against techniques that generate association rules (the special case of our framework that only allows interval constraints) - CART, C4.5 and JRipper — both with and without the ALBA dataset generator [14]. We also compared our algorithm with the SQRex-SVM algorithm [3].

The algorithms are compared using standard metrics: (i) Average number of rules, (ii) Average number of antecedents, (iii) Average fidelity, and (iv) Average running time. The fidelity of an MLP is the fraction of training points for which the explanation assigns the same label as the separator ϕ. Formally, given a set of points $T = \{x_1, \ldots, x_s\}$, the separator function ϕ, and its MLP-explanation $\mathcal{M}$, the *fidelity* of $\mathcal{M}$ is:

$$\texttt{fidelity}(\mathcal{M}) = \frac{|\{x_i \mid \mathcal{M} \models +1(x_i) \wedge \phi(x_i) = +1\}|}{|T|}.$$

We experimented with all five possible combinations of constraints in ML-rules. We denote by IL constraints of the form $a \leq x[i] \leq b$, by NL constraints of the form $\neg(a < x[i] < b)$, and by ML metric constraints. Thus, we experimented with our

Table 1. Table showing average results comparing all the algorithms over all the datasets. The shaded rows show the results of our MLP_Extract algorithm with subset of constraints. Values in bold represent the best results for the corresponding evaluation metric.

Algorithm	Avg. # Rules	Avg. # Antd	Avg. Fidelity	Avg. Runtime (sec)
CART	7.29	2.56	85.03	0.49
C4.5	17.99	3.39	61.65	0.38
Jripper	4.40	1.40	85.26	0.16
CART+Alba	10.09	2.86	89.92	0.76
C4.5+Alba	27.29	3.80	86.77	0.50
Jripper+Alba	4.77	1.78	88.35	0.34
Sqrexsvm	16.83	1.53	53.03	**0.06**
MLP_Extract(IL)	7.60	1.90	94.71	3176.36
MLP_Extract(ML)	11.51	**0.69**	94.67	71.25
MLP_Extract(IL+ML)	9.27	2.27	**97.47**	2794.72
MLP_Extract(IL+NL)	6.83	2.13	90.22	3103.54
MLP_Extract(IL+NL+ML)	**2.06**	0.72	95.25	10.60

algorithm by considering the following 5 combinations of constraints: (i) IL, (ii) ML, (iii) IL + ML, (iv) IL + NL, and (v) IL + NL + ML. We set $r_{max} = 4$, $ov_{max} = 10\%$. Table 1 shows the results after 10-fold cross validation on each dataset (90 % training, 10 % validation) in each fold. The measures described above are calculated for each fold and averaged. The table also shows the average running time (in seconds) taken to compute the rules after the SVM is obtained[5]. All our results are statistically valid with $p < 0.002$ in the majority of the cases (paired t-test)[6]. From the table, we can conclude that the MLP_Extract algorithm with IL + NL + ML constraints:

- It produces rules half as many rules as non-MLP_Extract explanations, reflecting a two-fold improvement in simplicity.
- The rules it produces have only half as many constraints as its nearest non-MLP_Extract competitors, again representing a 2-fold increase in simplicity.
- It beats all non-MLP_Extract competitors in terms of fidelity.
- It has larger run-time than past work.

In short, the MLP_Extract algorithm with IL + NL + ML constraints handily beats most competitors on most measures related to the quality of the explanation generated — but it does so at the expense of run-time.

5   Related Work

There has been substantial work in explanation of Support Vector Machines. A good survey on this topic can be found in [3]. Among the algorithms discussed in the survey, the most effective algorithms in terms of comprehensibility and fidelity are: CART [5], C4.5

---

[5] Tables 3–9 in the online Appendix [1] show the results for each data set.

[6] Detailed results are reported in Tables 10–15 in the online Appendix [1].

[15], JRipper [6] and SQRex-SVM [3]. [14] proposed a method named Active Learning Based Approach (ALBA) to incorporate additional data instances close to the decision boundary by using the support vectors. This was shown to improve the fidelity of the generated rules. We therefore compare our algorithm with these works with and without ALBA. In contrast to all of these works, MLP-Explanation uses simple metric logicrules that are not just richer than set of rules with interval constraints only, but is also easy to understand. We show that MLP-Explanation's best algorithm outperforms past work in terms of the quality of the extracted rules when measured by comprehensibility and fidelity, while taking slightly longer time to run.

As described in [8,18], there are other attempts to explain SVMs with ellipsoids and hyper-rectangles, fuzzy rules and distance-based regions, but the comprehensibility of these methods is low. Therefore, we do not compare against these methods.

In addition to SVMs, other classifiers have also been explained such as neural networks [7,17] and random forest.

6   Conclusions

There are numerous applications in which we wish to explain separators (such as SVM and GPC separators) to ordinary users in a simple, easy to understand way. In this paper, we propose Metric Logic Programs that have the following good properties. First, MLPs can succinctly and simply express rules that ordinary users can understand. Our results show that MLPs are both twice as simple and twice as succinct as past work (outside this paper). Second, MLPs have significantly higher fidelity than non-MLP based attempts to explain SVM. They much more accurately represent the predictions made by separators like SVM and GPC than past work. On the flip side, we note that computing MLPs requires more run-time than past work. Hence, it is appropriate to use it in applications where generating a human-intelligible explanation is very important (e.g. when data mining results provide input to decision makers for business and policy applications).

Acknowledgements. Parts of this work were supported by ONR grant N000141612739 and ARO grant W911NF1610342.

Appendix: Proofs

Proof **of Theorem** 1 (*Sketch*). Dyer [9] proved that computing the volume of the polytope $P = \{\mathbf{x} \in \mathbb{R}^n \mid \mathbf{a}^T \mathbf{x} \leq c, 0 \leq \mathbf{x}[i] \leq 1, i = 1, \ldots, n\}$, where $\mathbf{a}$ is a vector of integers greater than 0, is $\#P$-hard. Let us assume to have a hyper-rectangle R where $0 \leq \mathbf{x}[i] \leq 1, \forall i \in D$, and a hyper-plane of the form $\mathbf{w}^T \phi(\mathbf{x}) + b = 0$, where $\mathbf{w} = \mathbf{a}$ and $b = -c - 1$. Since the volume of R is equal to 1, then, computing $\mathbf{ov}(R, y) = \frac{V_{\overline{y}}(R)}{V(R)} = V_{\overline{y}}(R)$ where $V_{\overline{y}}(R)$ represents the volume of $\mathbf{ov}(R, y)$ is the same of computing the volume of the polytope P.

Proof **of Theorem** 2 (*Sketch*). The result is proven with a reduction from the 3-colorability problem, that is proven be **NP**-hard, to a decision version of the MLP-Explanation problem that is the following: verify whether there exists at most k MLRs that satisfy all the four constraints of the MLP-Explanation problem. Given a graph

$G = (V, E)$, the 3-colorability problem consists into verifying whether there exists a color assignment to node s.t. two neighbors node are not colored with the same color.

The reduction is the following. We set (i) $k = 3$, (ii) $n = |V|$, i.e. we have one dimension for each vertex, (iii) $T^y = \{\mathbf{u}_i \in \{0,1\}^n \mid \mathbf{u}_i[i] = 1 \wedge i \in D : (\forall j \in D \wedge j \neq i \Rightarrow \mathbf{u}_i[j] = 0)\}$ to represent all vertices $v_i \in V$, (iv) $T^{\overline{y}} = \{\mathbf{u} \in \{0,1\}^n \mid (v_i, v_j) \in E \wedge \mathbf{u}[i] = 1 \wedge \mathbf{u}[j] = 1 \wedge (\forall h \in D : h \neq i, j \Rightarrow \mathbf{u}[h] = 0)\}$ to represent the set E of edges, and (v) $m = 0$. Because of the first MLP-Explanation problem constraint, and $k = 3$, a node must be covered by at least one rule of the three, so each rule assigns a color to each rule.

For instance, suppose we have in G only two vertices v_1 and v_2 and one edge (v_1, v_2). Then, $T^y = \{[1,0], [0,1]\}$ and $T^{\overline{y}} = \{[1,1]\}$. Considering now the rule $0 \leq \mathbf{x}[1] \leq 1 \wedge 0 \leq \mathbf{x}[2] \leq 1 \rightarrow y$, we have that it covers $T^y \cup T^{\overline{y}}$.

Then, it is not possible that there exist two nodes covered by the same rule that are connected by an edge, otherwise a point in $T^{\overline{y}}$ is covered by the rule. This implies that it is not possible to use the same color to color two nodes connected by an edge.

Note that it is possible that the same node can be colored in two different ways, but to obtain a feasible coloring it is sufficient choosing one of the two color without violate the constraints. It follows that the decision version of the MLP-Explanation problem is at least hard as the 3-colorability, and this means that the MLP-Explanation problem is **NP**-hard.

Proof of **Theorem** 3 (*Sketch*). We prove the theorem via a reduction from maximal independent set problem proven to be **NP**-hard. We recall that, given a graph $G = (V, E)$ the maximal independent set problem consists into find a set of vertices $V' \subseteq V$ s.t. $|V'| \geq k$ and there are no edges in E between any pair of vertices in V'. The reduction is the following. We set (i) $n = |V|$, i.e. we have one dimension for each vertex, (ii) $W = \{\mathbf{u}_i \in \{0,1\}^n \mid \mathbf{u}_i[i] = 1 \wedge i \in D : (\forall j \in D \wedge j \neq i \Rightarrow \mathbf{u}_i[j] = 0)\}$ to represent all vertices $v_i \in V$, (iii) $\overline{W} = \{\mathbf{u} \in \{0,1\}^n \mid (v_i, v_j) \in E \wedge \mathbf{u}[i] = 1 \wedge \mathbf{u}[j] = 1 \wedge (\forall h \in D : h \neq i, j \Rightarrow \mathbf{u}[h] = 0)\}$ to represent the set E of edges, and (iv) $m = 0$. Then, our problem is to find a rule, if there exists, that covers at least k points in W and no point in $\overline{W}$. In this reduction we do not consider the MLP-Explanation problem constraints 2 and 3. Note that if a rule covers two vertices then it automatically cover also the edge between them if it exist. For instance, suppose we have in G only two vertices v_1 and v_2 and one edge (v_1, v_2). Then, $W = \{[1,0], [0,1]\}$ and $\overline{W} = \{[1,1]\}$. Considering now the rule $0 \leq \mathbf{x}[1] \leq 1 \wedge 0 \leq \mathbf{x}[2] \leq 1 \rightarrow y$, we have that it covers $W \cup \overline{W}$. It follows that finding a rule that covers at least k points in W and does not cover any point in $\overline{W}$ is at least hard as the independent set problem.

References

1. Online appendix (2016). https://sites.google.com/site/mlpextraction/
2. Agrawal, R., Imieliński, T., Swami, A.: Mining association rules between sets of items in large databases. SIGMOD Rec. **22**(2), 207–216 (1993)
3. Barakat, N.H., Bradley, A.P.: Rule extraction from support vector machines: a review. Neurocomputing **74**(1–3), 178–190 (2010)
4. Beldiceanu, N., Carlsson, M., Flener, P., Pearson, J.: On the reification of global constraints. Constraints **18**(1), 1–6 (2013)
5. Breiman, L., Friedman, J., Olshen, R., Stone, C.: Classification and Regression Trees. Wadsworth and Brooks, Monterey (1984)

6. Cohen, W.W.: Fast effective rule induction. In: ICML, pp. 115–123 (1995)
7. Craven, M.W., Shavlik, J.W.: Extracting tree-structured representations of trained networks. Adv. Neural Inf. Process. Syst. **8**, 24–30 (1996)
8. Diederich, J. (ed.): Rule Extraction from Support Vector Machines. Studies in Computational Intelligence, vol. 80. Springer, Heidelberg (2008)
9. Dyer, M.E., Frieze, A.M.: On the complexity of computing the volume of a polyhedron. SIAM J. Comput. **17**(5), 967–974 (1988)
10. Eiter, T., Gottlob, G.: The complexity of logic-based abduction. J. ACM (JACM) **42**(1), 3–42 (1995)
11. Jaffar, J., Lassez, J.-L.: Constraint logic programming. In: POPL, pp. 111–119 (1987)
12. Kakas, A.C., Michael, A., Mourlas, C.: ACLP: abductive constraint logic programming. J. Log. Program. **44**(1), 129–177 (2000)
13. Lloyd, J.W.: Foundations of Logic Programming. Springer, New York (1987)
14. Martens, D., Baesens, B., Van Gestel, T.: Decompositional rule extraction from support vector machines by active learning. IEEE Trans. Knowl. Data Eng. **21**(2), 178–191 (2009)
15. Quinlan, J.R.: C4.5: Programs for Machine Learning. Morgan Kaufmann Publishers Inc., Los Altos (1993)
16. Reiter, R.: On closed world data bases. In: Ginsberg, M.L. (ed.) Readings in Non-monotonic Reasoning, pp. 300–310. Kaufmann, Los Altos (1987)
17. Schmitz, G.P., Aldrich, C., Gouws, F.S.: ANN-DT: an algorithm for extraction of decision trees from artificial neural networks. IEEE Trans. Neural Netw. **10**(6), 1392–1401 (1999)
18. Zhu, P., Qinghua, H.: Rule extraction from support vector machines based on consistent region covering reduction. Knowl. Based Syst. **42**, 1–8 (2013)

A Two-Stage Online Approach for Collaborative Multi-agent Planning Under Uncertainty

Iván Palomares[✉], Kim Bauters, Weiru Liu, and Jun Hong

School of Electronics, Electrical Engineering and Computer Science,
Queen's University Belfast, Belfast, Northern Ireland
{i.palomares,k.bauters,w.liu,j.hong}@qub.ac.uk

Abstract. In a team of multiple agents, the pursuance of a common goal is a defining characteristic. Since agents may have different capabilities, and effects of actions may be uncertain, a common goal can generally only be achieved through a careful cooperation between the different agents. In this work, we propose a novel two-stage planner that combines online planning at both team level and individual level through a subgoal delegation scheme. The proposal brings the advantages of online planning approaches to the multi-agent setting. A number of modifications are made to a classical UCT approximate algorithm to (i) adapt it to the application domains considered, (ii) reduce the branching factor in the underlying search process, and (iii) effectively manage uncertain information of action effects by using information fusion mechanisms. The proposed online multi-agent planner reduces the cost of planning and decreases the temporal cost of reaching a goal, while significantly increasing the chance of success of achieving the common goal.

1 Introduction

Planning is an essential component of autonomous agents. It involves the selection of a series of actions to perform to achieve a goal desired by the agent [19]. Such a series of actions is commonly referred to as *a plan*. Ideally, planning algorithms attempt to take all information about the environment into account when coming up with a plan. However, it is often infeasible to (optimally) plan in realistic environments due to their size and the uncertainty of action outcomes [12]. *Multi-agent planning* is a particular branch of planning where there is a collective approach from multiple agents to achieve a goal [18]. In *collaborative* multi-agent planning, a team of agents try to accomplish a task leading to a common goal by combining their capabilities and knowledge [15]. Two main approaches for collaborative multi-agent planning can be distinguished: (i) *centralised*, which involves a planner agent with full knowledge of the environment and the joint task to undertake, and (ii) *distributed* or decentralised [4], in which agents plan individually and coordinate with each other to find a common solution for the planning

---

The original version of this chapter has been revised: In an older version Fig. 6 was represented incorrectly. An erratum to this chapter is available at 10.1007/978-3-319-45856-4_27

S. Schockaert and P. Senellart (Eds.): SUM 2016, LNAI 9858, pp. 214–229, 2016.
DOI: 10.1007/978-3-319-45856-4_15

problem [10,13]. Centralised multi-agent planning is typically the most efficient, but is only feasible if agents do not have private or sensitive information [1].

Collaborative multi-agent planning has been an active subject of research in recent years [2,9,14,16]. However, most of these works focus on *offline planning* rather than *online planning*. Online planning differentiates itself from offline planning by not fully elaborating a plan *before* execution, but instead to interleave planning and execution. To this end, it employs approximate methods such as Monte-Carlo Tree Search (MCTS) [3] to return the next *'good enough'* action rather than a complete series of actions [5]. Online planning approaches have the ability to narrow the scope of the search space, to return "good enough" actions anytime and to efficiently re-plan when an unexpected situation is encountered while acting. So far, online planning has been mainly applied to individual agent planning problems, with only a few proposals for online multi-agent planning presented in [11,20,21]. Wu et al. [20], use Decentralized POMDPs and stage games for planning in ad-hoc teams, without pre-coordination, such that each agent independently plans its next actions under teamwork considerations. The authors also developed in [21] an online planning approach aimed at minimizing inter-agent communication. Paquet et al. [11] presented a method called Real-Time Belief Space Search (RTBSS) for determining the best next action in large real-time environments.

In this paper we focus on problems and application domains characterised by:

- the existence of a fixed team of agents with common goals requiring coordination;
- planning at team level is required to ensure coordination between agents;
- each agent knows the outcome probabilities of its own actions only.

An example of domains under these settings are SCADA supervisory control systems, e.g. for power grid management, or navigation in hazardous environments such as nuclear sites [6]. The scenario utilised to describe our proposal refers to navigation by multiple robots for clearance in a country park. To the best of our knowledge, problems defined under these settings have not been addressed yet in online planning.

To efficiently solve problems in these domains we introduce a novel two-stage online collaborative planner where actions may have stochastic effects. The first stage is a team level centralised planner which plans on an abstract level and delegates subgoals to individual agents. The second stage is an individual level distributed planner where each agent pursues its assigned subgoal. The proposed planner extends the MCTS-based UCT algorithm [8] to (i) collectively plan for the next best subgoals for every agent in the team, and (ii) to individually come up with suitable plans to achieve the assigned subgoals (individual level planning). A fusion approach [22] is introduced in the team planner to combine uncertain information about the effects of actions, which will help to significantly reduce the search space.

To adequately scope our work we furthermore assume the following principles:

Principle 1. Agents act in parallel to achieve a common goal. A team planner agent determines the next subgoal each agent should individually accomplish.

Principle 2. The agents act in a purely collaborative way, i.e. there is no form of competition in terms of distinct, conflict goals amongst agents. Furthermore, agents carry out their actions independently, such that no effects of interfering the actions of the other agents are considered.

Principle 3. No privacy preservation constraints amongst agents are considered.

The rest of the paper is organised as follows. We start off with some preliminaries in Sect. 2. In Sect. 3 the scenario used to illustrate our proposal is introduced. Our novel, two-stage online multi-agent planner is proposed in Sect. 4 and evaluated in Sect. 5, demonstrating its ability to reduce the cost of planning and acting in parallel, as well as increasing the chances of successfully reaching the goal established. Finally, concluding remarks are drawn in Sect. 6.

2   Preliminaries

In offline planning, a complete plan or course of actions to achieve a goal is firstly generated and then executed by the agent. Therefore, when multiple agents are present and there is no need for preserving private individual information, the planning process can be easily centralised even though execution is performed in a distributed fashion [21]. By contrast, online planning interleaves planning with execution: instead of generating the whole plan a priori, online planners return a next *"good-enough"* action to be executed at the current state. When an unexpected outcome is obtained, online planners can immediately pick up on this new information and do not need to plan in advance for all such eventualities. Our work focuses on integrating online planning at team and individual levels by using online team planning as a delegation scheme.

UCT (*Upper Confidence bounds applied to Trees*) [8] is a state-of-the-art *anytime* algorithm that combines MCTS [3] with multi-bandit selection methods [8], and has been utilised for planning in domains pervaded by uncertainty. UCT [5] allows to quickly return a non-trivial decision after performing a series of *rollouts* in which outcomes of actions are sampled based on their probability. A rollout consists in traversing the search tree from the root node to a node representing a terminal state. Every time a node is visited in UCT, the selection of the action to take at its corresponding state is based on all previous rollouts, favouring actions that either produced higher rewards or were rarely visited in previous rollouts. This allows for a balance between exploitation (selecting actions with better reward statistics so far) and exploration (selecting actions that have still been rarely simulated). A *decision node* in UCT represents an environment state. A decision node corresponding to a non-terminal state can be expanded into available actions at that state, leading to child decision nodes for the outcomes of such actions. The root decision node represents the current environment state [5].

In every iteration, UCT applies the following four steps (see Fig. 1): (a) *Selection*: select a child node based on a selection function. (b) *Expansion*: randomly expand the selected node to a new unsampled one. (c) *Rollout*: randomly simulate a playout (e.g. a sequence of selected actions and their outcomes) until

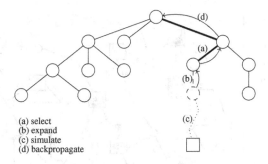

(a) select
(b) expand
(c) simulate
(d) backpropagate

Fig. 1. The four distinct steps in every MCTS iteration.

reaching a terminal state. (d) *Backpropagation*: compute a reward value associated to the terminal state reached, and propagate it back up through the tree to the root node, updating the information for each node in the path.

3   Scenario Overview

The country park scenario serves to illustrate the concepts and ideas presented in this paper. A team of forest management robots (agents) are situated in different locations of a country park, in a region frequently affected by natural disasters such as strong winds and wildfires. After a storm, a number of fallen boulders are detected in locations around the park. The robots, which operate in parallel, must plan and coordinate together to clear the affected locations efficiently. The problem is further complicated by the following factors: (i) the park is organised into a number of locations or *Points of Interest* (PoI) labelled a to n, and a network of hiking trails labelled t_1 to t_{64} connecting the PoIs; (ii) some trails are safer than others due to their width (see Fig. 2). Falling off a trail (e.g. into a cliff, due to a landslide, etc.) permanently disables the robot; and (iii) each robot has different competences and/or physical sizes, therefore the probability of successfully crossing a trail can vary from robot to robot. The robots are fully aware of their current position and the position of the boulders in the scenario. Moreover, robots can communicate with the team planner agent to inform about e.g. reaching a new PoI, clearing a boulder, or falling off a trail.

When applying our framework to this scenario the *high-level team planning* will direct robots to neighbouring[1] PoI on their way to reach a boulder to clear. On the *low-level individual planning* the agents themselves will plan for how to reach that neighbouring PoI given their knowledge of the trails and the likelihood of reaching the PoI in any of the available ways given their capabilities/physical sizes.

---

[1] Neighbouring PoIs are those which can be reached from the current agent position without getting through any other PoI.

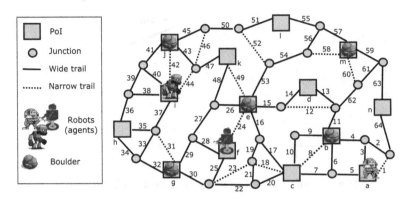

Fig. 2. Country park scenario. PoIs are labeled a to n, and trails (edges) are numbered t_1 to t_{64}

4 Online Collaborative Multi-agent Planner Under Uncertainty

In this section we present an online multi-agent planner for collaborative teams of agents whose actions have stochastic outcomes. The main characteristics of the planner are: (1) two planning stages (team planning and individual planning) are interleaved through a subgoal delegation scheme, (2) online planning is utilised through two extensions of the UCT algorithm adapted to both planning phases, and (3) a number of mechanisms are proposed to deal with uncertain stochastic information effectively, whilst preventing an excessive search space.

4.1 Notation and Basic Concepts

The following notation is introduced to refer to the different elements utilised in the proposed multi-agent planner:

- There exists a set $\mathcal{AG} = \{1, 2, \ldots, n\}$ of *agents*.
- There are n *action libraries* $\mathcal{A}_1, \mathcal{A}_2, \ldots, \mathcal{A}_n$, one for each agent $i \in \mathcal{AG}$. An action library $\mathcal{A}_i = \{a_i^1, \ldots, a_i^m\}$ encompasses a finite set of actions a_i^k, $k = 1, \ldots, m$, that can be performed by the agent, i.e. its capabilities. For simplicity, all agents have access to the same actions (e.g. move forward) but the probabilities of outcomes are distinct for each agent.
- A subgoal library $\mathcal{C} = \{c^1, \ldots, c^u\}$ common to all agents describes the possible subgoals that can be assigned to them. A subgoal is achieved by an agent i by applying (a sequence of) actions from its action library $\mathcal{A}_i$, as explained later.

Action, plan and (sub)goal representation is based on PPDDL (Probabilistic Planning Domain Definition Language) [23], as illustrated in several examples throughout this section. PPDDL is fully supported by implementations of MCTS-based techniques.

The set of all possible environment states is represented as $\mathcal{E}$. An *environment state* is denoted by $\epsilon \in \mathcal{E}$, where ϵ_0 denotes the current state, and $\mathcal{E}_G \subset \mathcal{E}$ is the subset of all possible goal states ϵ_G. Since the team planner agent is responsible for the team planning process, it must be able to formulate environment states at team level. A decision node in the search tree constructed during team planning includes these two elements:

1. Collective information about the current state of *all* agents involved in the team planning process, describing each agent's individual status: in our example the positions of robots in the environment.
2. Other purely environmental information: in our example, the locations of remaining boulders, if any.

Thus, a decision node $N(\epsilon)$ associated to an environment state ϵ, is formalised as a 2-tuple $N(\epsilon) = \langle s(\mathcal{AG}); s(env) \rangle$. The set $s(\mathcal{AG}) = \{s_1, \ldots, s_n\}$ denotes the current state of every agent, and $s(env)$ represents environmental information. Conversely, we refer to states modelled in the individual planning phase performed by agent $i \in \mathcal{AG}$ as *agent states*, $\epsilon^i \in \mathcal{E}^i$. Their associated decision nodes $N(\epsilon^i)$ contain more specific information than the (team level) environment states ϵ introduced above, namely information about i and the environment only. They are formally represented as $N(\epsilon^i) = \langle s_i; s(env) \rangle$. In either case (and as occurs with classic UCT), the root decision node describes the current environment (*resp.* agent) state, ϵ_0 (*resp.* ϵ_0^i).

Example 1. Consider the country park scenario (Sect. 3). Let s_i be the state of agent i. For simplicity, we assume an agent state is solely formed by a predicate of the form, $at(i, L)$, indicating the location L of agent i (which can be either one of the 14 PoIs labeled 'a' to 'n', a junction connecting some of the 64 trails in the park, or the symbol "−" indicating that the agent failed in executing an action and is no longer operating). On the other hand, let $s(env) = \bigwedge_{at(boulder, L)} L$ be the locations of boulders not cleared out yet. A decision node describing this environment state is formalised as follows:

$$N(\epsilon) = \langle \{at(1, a), at(2, f), at(3, i)\}; b \wedge e \wedge g \wedge j \wedge m \rangle$$

with $b \wedge e \wedge g \wedge j \wedge m$ being environmental information (locations of boulders not cleared yet). Suppose that agent 1 plans individually to cross t_5. When reaching the junction connecting t_5, t_6 and t_7 (denoted by $t_{5,6,7}$), its resulting decision node $N(\epsilon^i)$ is:

$$N(\epsilon^1) = \langle at(t_{5,6,7}); b \wedge e \wedge g \wedge j \wedge m \rangle$$

with same environmental information, i.e. no PoIs with boulders have been reached yet.   □

We now introduce the three central concepts in the proposed planner: *primitive action*, *subgoal* and *team action*. These concepts are illustrated in Fig. 3 to facilitate their understanding.

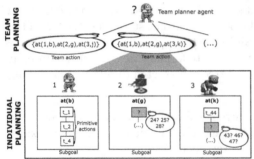

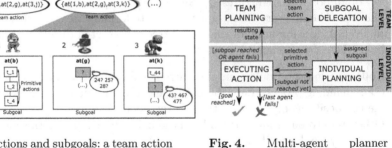

Fig. 3. Actions and subgoals: a team action is associated one or more subgoals, each of which indicates (in our scenario) a target location to be reached e.g. $at(k)$, whereas primitive actions indicate trails to be crossed, e.g. t_44.

Fig. 4. Multi-agent planner scheme: the team planner delegates subgoals to active agents; each agent in turn plans for achieving its subgoal and relegates execution results back to the team planner.

Definition 1. *A primitive action $a_i^k \in \mathcal{A}_i$ can be individually undertaken by agent $i \in \mathcal{AG}$, e.g. t_1 for the action of moving across trail '1'. Primitive actions are evaluated and selected during individual planning.*

Definition 2. *A subgoal $c_i \in \mathcal{C}$ assigned to agent i represents an individual state i should aim for, e.g. $at(a)$, which indicates that i must reach the PoI labeled 'a'. Subgoals are assigned by the team planner agent to every agent in the team.*

Definition 3. *A team action $\tau = \{\sigma_i, i \in pa(\tau)\}$ encompasses a number of subgoals σ_i simultaneously assigned to a team of participating agents $pa(\tau) \subseteq \mathcal{AG}$ (one subgoal per agent) at a given time. Team actions are formulated during team planning, and they involve those agents that need a new subgoal to be pursued at a given state.*

Example 2. Suppose that the following team action is selected as a result of team planning in the country park scenario, $\tau = \{at(1, n), at(2, e), at(3, g)\}$. This means that the subgoal of reaching location 'n', $at(n)$, is delegated to robot 1, the subgoal $at(e)$ is delegated into 2 and the subgoal $at(g)$ is delegated into 3. □

Outcomes of team actions are environment states that result either from the successful accomplishment by every agent of its assigned subgoal, or from one or more agents in $pa(\tau)$ failing to accomplish it (being deemed unavailable hereinafter because e.g. they fell off a trail). In the search tree constructed during team planning, decision nodes (except for $N(\epsilon_0)$) represent outcomes of team actions.

A general scheme of the proposed two-stage multi-agent planner is depicted in Fig. 4 and explained in the following two subsections.

4.2   Team Planning

The team planning process aims at determining the next best team action τ describing the immediate subgoals each agent is assigned. This is not a straightforward task for two reasons: (1) determining the probabilities of occurrence of each available team action requires stochastic information about individual action libraries, and (2) having multiple agents acting in parallel may involve a significant number of possible outcomes for τ.

To cope with these difficulties, we firstly distinguish two distinct types of outcomes for any τ. A *success outcome* occurs when *all* agents in $pa(\tau)$ succeed in achieving their respective subgoals. A special case of a success outcome is when the common goal has been achieved. In such a case the success outcome is also a *goal state*. Whenever we do not have a success outcome, we say that we have an *undesired outcome*. Both goal states and undesired outcomes are regarded as *terminal states*[2].

Based on this distinction, we can now focus on defining a reward-driven online team planner. In particular, we will introduce a method based on uncertain information fusion to estimate rewards of team actions. Next, we describe how the phases of the UCT algorithm are adapted to deal with such team actions. The subsequent individual planning phase (Sect. 4.3) describes how each agent accurately plans to pursue its assigned subgoal, taking account of its probabilities of action outcomes.

Reward Estimation at Team Level. In UCT, a reward function assigns a value to the terminal state encountered at the end of a rollout before it is backpropagated: the greater this value, the more rewarding the outcome is deemed. Below we introduce a collective reward function that allows to preserve a reduced branching factor in the search tree by summarising all possible forms of undesired outcome into one. This general function must be instantiated to suit the specific scenario tackled.

Definition 4. *Let $\mathcal{E}_F (\subset \mathcal{E})$ be a set of all undesired outcomes and $\mathcal{E}_G$ a set of all goal states, as defined in Sect. 4.1. The set of all terminal states is given by $\mathcal{E}_G \cup \mathcal{E}_F = \mathcal{E}_T$, and $\mathcal{E}_{\overline{\tau}} \subset \mathcal{E}_F$ is the set of all the possible undesired outcomes ϵ_F of τ. We propose summarising such outcomes as one in the search tree, therefore $\mathcal{E}_{\overline{\tau}}$ is deemed as a single terminal state hereinafter for the reward computation of undesired outcomes. We define a reward function f as a mapping $f : \mathcal{E}_T \rightarrow [-1, 1] \backslash \{0\}$, with the following properties:*

(i) *$f(\epsilon_G) > 0$, $\forall \epsilon_G \in \mathcal{E}_G$, i.e. arriving at a goal state always produces a positive reward value.*

(ii) *$f(\mathcal{E}_{\overline{\tau}}) < 0$, $\forall \mathcal{E}_{\overline{\tau}} \subset \mathcal{E}_F$, i.e. arriving at any undesired outcome always produces a negative reward value.*

---

[2] Undesired outcomes are considered as terminal states: if an unexpected situation is encountered, the remaining agents start another planning process upon the resulting environment state.

(iii) *Let* $d \in \mathbb{N}$ *be the depth level at which the terminal state is encountered.* *Assume two identical terminal states* ϵ_1, ϵ_2 *can be reached at depth* d_1 *and* d_2 *respectively, with* $d_1 < d_2$. *Then* $f(\epsilon_1) \geq f(\epsilon_2)$.

The computation of $f(\mathcal{E}_{\bar{\tau}}) < 0$ (property (ii)) is based on the aggregation of information related to each form of undesired outcome $\epsilon_F \in \mathcal{E}_{\bar{\tau}}$, as explained below. It follows from property (iii) that similar goal states lead to an equal or higher reward when they are encountered after a lower number of consecutive team actions. Similarly, undesired outcomes are equally or less detrimental when encountered earlier. A discount factor $\delta \in]0, 1[$ can be applied in f to reflect this property.

The reward value for an undesired outcome of τ is defined as follows. Based on each $\epsilon_F \in \mathcal{E}_{\bar{\tau}}$, two indicators $\varphi(\epsilon_F), \gamma(\epsilon_F) \in [0, 1]$ are introduced for *resp.* (i) the number of agents in the team who fail to accomplish their subgoal σ_i in τ, $|fa(\tau)|$, with respect to the total number of participating agents; and (ii) the resulting "distance" to the (closest) goal state. The former is computed as $\varphi(\epsilon_F) = |fa(\tau)|/|pa(\tau)|$, whereas the latter is domain-dependent. For our scenario, it is calculated based on the number of remaining boulders when ϵ_F occurs, i.e. $\gamma(\epsilon_F) = \#remaining/\#boulders$.

In addition, $|\mathcal{E}_{\bar{\tau}}|$ is the total number of possible undesired outcomes ϵ_F of τ. This parameter is calculated in our scenario as $|\mathcal{E}_{\bar{\tau}}| = 2^{|pa(\tau)|} - 1$, because the number of possible outcomes only depends on the (possible subsets of) agents in $pa(\tau)$ which fail in achieving their assigned subgoal. Hence, $f(\mathcal{E}_{\bar{\tau}})$ is defined as follows:

$$f(\mathcal{E}_{\bar{\tau}}) = -\delta^{d-1} \frac{\sum_{\epsilon_F \in \mathcal{E}_{\bar{\tau}}} \mathcal{U}\left(\varphi(\epsilon_F), \gamma(\epsilon_F)\right)}{|\mathcal{E}_{\bar{\tau}}|} \tag{1}$$

with $\mathcal{U} : [0, 1]^2 \to [0, 1]$ a uninorm aggregation function [22], that combines the two indicators φ, γ into a single value (as explained below). The fusion procedure applied in Eq. (1) for reward computation eliminates the need for splitting undesired outcomes into multiple leaf nodes. This significantly simplifies the search tree constructed.

Uninorm aggregation functions are a generalisation of t-norm and t-conorm functions [22] with a neutral element $g \in]0, 1[$, fulfilling the full reinforcement property, i.e. if the two values to aggregate $x, y \in [0, 1]$ are both higher (*resp.* lower) than g, then the aggregated result becomes even higher (*resp.* lower). Conversely, they present a compensating (averaging) behaviour if one of the values is high and the other is low. The reinforcement property is particularly interesting in the application domains considered in this paper to emphasise situations when:

(i) There are few remaining agents, far away from reaching their goal, in which case both φ and γ are high and the aggregated value is reinforced upwards.
(ii) Most agents still remain and they are close to the goal, in which case φ, γ are low and the aggregated value is reinforced downwards.

The use of uninorm functions affects therefore the assessment of single undesired outcomes $\epsilon_F \in \mathcal{E}_{\bar{\tau}}$ in the two cases outlined above. Because of the minus sign in

Eq. (1), in our context $\mathcal{U}$ behaves as a cost function: the higher its value for a given outcome $\epsilon_F \in \mathcal{E}_{\overline{T}}$, the less rewarding this outcome is, hence the lower the resulting $f(\mathcal{E}_{\overline{T}})$ will be. An example of these functions is the cross-ratio uninorm with $g = 0.5$ [7]:

$$
\mathcal{U}(x, y) = \begin{cases} 0 & (x, y) \in \{(0, 1), (1, 0)\}, \\ \dfrac{xy}{xy + (1-x)(1-y)} & \text{otherwise.} \end{cases} \tag{2}
$$

Regarding reward computation for goal states, since we consider problems where all agents share a common goal, the reward function for any $\epsilon_G \in \mathcal{E}_G$ can be simply defined as $f(\epsilon_G) = \delta^{d-1}$, i.e. the sooner the goal is accomplished (lower d), the less resources are consumed by agents to reach it, hence the more beneficial the outcome is.

Example 3. Assume the current state of the environment in the country park scenario is given by $N(\epsilon_0) = \langle \{at(1, n), at(2, k), at(3, -)\}; j \wedge m \rangle$, which means that robots 1 and 2 are active and situated in 'n' and 'k' respectively, whereas 3 already fell off a trail, and the only remaining boulders are located in 'j' and 'm'. One of the available team actions for $pa(\tau) = \{1, 2\}$ is $\tau = \{at(1, m), at(2, j)\}$, whose completion intuitively implies achieving the overall team goal, in which case $d = 1$ and $f(\epsilon_G) = \delta^{d-1} = 1, \forall \delta$. The reward of reaching the undesired outcome is computed based on Eqs. (1) and (2):

$$
f(\mathcal{E}_{\overline{T}}) = -\frac{\mathcal{U}(0.5, 0.33) + \mathcal{U}(0.5, 0.33) + \mathcal{U}(1, 0.66)}{3} = -0.55
$$

$\square$

UCT-based Search Process at Team Level. Assuming that a team action can either lead to a success outcome, or to a(n) (summarised) undesired outcome, the collective search tree structure is adapted as follows: every edge representing a team action leads to a *node pair* formed by the decision nodes associated to the success outcome and the undesired outcome (see Fig. 5). The latter is regarded as a leaf node (terminal state), as explained earlier. If, however, the success outcome of the node pair does not represent a goal state, it can be expanded into a number of next available team actions at that state.

The backpropagation process is now adapted to the proposed node pair structure. We firstly explain how rewards are updated through nodes generated during rollout, up to the last expanded node. Rewards throughout the rollout path cannot be accurately calculated, since a team action τ_j immediately taken at a non-terminal state can eventually lead to different terminal states with varying rewards. Notwithstanding, it is possible to estimate the *"best and worst possible scenario"* that might be encountered at any state in the rollout path. In other words, given a state ϵ in the rollout path, we can estimate the highest (*resp.* lowest) reward that could be eventually achieved after applying a number of team actions posterior to ϵ. Based on this, we propose modeling the reward of a non-terminal state $\epsilon_S \in \mathcal{E} \backslash \mathcal{E}_T$ as an interval, $f(\epsilon_S) = f(\tau_j) = [f(\tau_j)^-, f(\tau_j)^+]$, with $f(\tau_j)^- \in [-1, 0[$ and $f(\tau_j)^+ \in]0, 1]$. Here, τ_j is the (unique) team action generated upon ϵ_S during rollout, therefore the interval-valued reward is easily calculated as:

$$f(\tau_j) = [\min_{\tau_k \dashv \tau_j} f(\mathcal{E}_{\overline{\tau}_k}), f(\epsilon_G)] \tag{3}$$

where $\tau_k \dashv \tau_j$ represents all rollout actions τ_k posterior to τ_j. The shaded area in Fig. 6 illustrates backpropagation through rollout nodes up to $N(\epsilon_1)$.

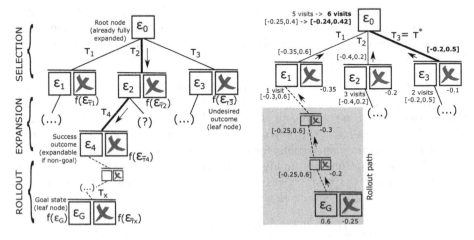

Fig. 5. UCT-based search in team planning

Fig. 6. Team planner backpropagation

Backpropagation between the last expanded node and the root node updates rewards and also increases the visit count for nodes in the path. However, given a node $N(\epsilon'_S)$ resulting from applying τ_j at a previous state ϵ_S, the reward interval backpropagated to $N(\epsilon_S)$ is not necessarily $f(\tau_j)$, but instead that of the most rewarding action available at ϵ_S. It is therefore necessary to compare the interval-valued rewards of all available actions at ϵ_S and backpropagate the highest one. To do this, the method in [17] to calculate the preference degree between intervals of real numbers is utilised:

$$P(\tau_j > \tau_k) = \frac{\max(0, f_j^+ - f_k^-) - \max(0, f_j^- - f_k^+)}{(f_j^+ - f_j^-) + (f_k^+ - f_k^-)} \tag{4}$$

where interval bounds $f(\tau_j)^-$ are denoted as f_j^- for simplicity. This allows to determine the most rewarding available action τ^* at ϵ_S. Rewards $f(\epsilon_S) = [f(\epsilon_S)^-, f(\epsilon_S)^+]$ are then updated based on the number of visits its corresponding node received so far:

$$f(\epsilon_S)^- = \frac{f(\tau^*)^- + \#visits \cdot f(\epsilon_S)^-_{old}}{\#visits + 1} \qquad f(\epsilon_S)^+ = \frac{f(\tau^*)^+ + \#visits \cdot f(\epsilon_S)^+_{old}}{\#visits + 1} \tag{5}$$

In Fig. 6, τ_3 is more rewarding than the team action in the backpropagation path, τ_1. Therefore, rewards in $N(\epsilon_0)$ are updated based on $f(\tau_3) = [-0.2, 0.5]$.

After a number of iterations, the *best* next team action $\tau = \{\sigma_i, i \in pa(\tau)\}$ is returned. The team planner then delegates the subgoal σ_i into each participating agent i, which proceeds to the individual planning phase to pursue the assigned subgoal.

4.3   Individual Planning

The online approach utilised for the individual planning phase is a standard UCT-based approach with multiple reward rollouts at each iteration. We distinguish two types of nodes between which the algorithm alternates during construction of the tree: decision nodes and chance nodes. The latter represent available primitive actions at the state described by their parent decision node. Each chance node has in turn a number of children decision nodes, one for each possible action outcome. The tree structure is represented in Fig. 7.

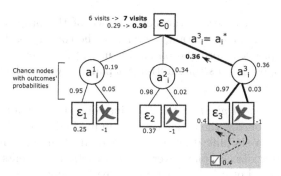

Fig. 7. Individual search tree structure and rollout-backpropagation after expanding into a_i^3

When a decision node $N(\epsilon^i)$ is expanded, a child chance node representing one of the available actions at that state is generated. New decision nodes for the outcomes of the newly generated chance node are also added to the tree. The subsequent rollout phase of UCT is modified so that, at each iteration of the algorithm, a number r of rollouts are carried out for each non-terminal outcome[3]. This allows to quickly obtain accurate reward estimates for the state from which rollouts are being currently performed, as well as thoroughly exploring the different courses of action available from each outcome. Each rollout takes place until a terminal state (either subgoal achievement or failure) is encountered, and it is followed by the backpropagation and cumulation of the reward obtained up to the root node. The reward value of every individual fail state ϵ_F^i is instantiated

---

[3] In the country park scenario, primitive actions have at most one non-terminal outcome, but this could not be the case in other different scenarios with multiple stochastic action outcomes.

as $f(\epsilon^i_F) = -1$, as failing any primitive action in our scenario implies that the agent is no longer available. On the other hand, for an individual (sub)goal state ϵ_G we again have $f(\epsilon^i_G) = \delta^{d-1}$. The reward update process between the last expanded node and the root node is applied differently for each type of node (see Fig. 7):

1. *Chance node*: The reward $f(a^k_i) \in [-1,1]$ of a chance node associated to a^k_i is calculated as the probability-weighted mean of its outcomes' rewards.
2. *Decision node*: Rewards of decision nodes are updated similarly as explained in the team planner, with the only difference that individual rewards of non-terminal states are real values instead of intervals. Assuming that a^*_i is the most rewarding available action at ϵ^i, the reward in $N(\epsilon^i)$ is updated as follows:

$$f(\epsilon^i) = \frac{f(a^*_i) + \#visits \cdot f(\epsilon^i)_{old}}{\#visits + 1} \tag{6}$$

5   Experiments and Results

In this section we demonstrate the performance of the proposed multi-agent planner. Throughout the evaluation, we refer to the country park scenario from Sect. 3, and the problem formulation shown in Fig. 2. To evaluate the performance of our proposed *two-stage* multi-agent planner, we consider the following two baselines:

1. *one-stage multi-agent planner*: this baseline coincides with a fully centralised planner, which controls the actions of each individual agent. We implemented this baseline as a simplification of our proposed planning framework, where the team planner directly plans over primitive actions of agents. Team actions are thus composed of primitive actions instead of subgoals.
2. *multiple agents planning individually*: each agent plans independently and individually for the primitive actions to achieve the overall goal of clearing *all* boulders from PoIs. In this baseline there is no coordination schema amongst agents. To make the baseline more goal-aware, agents do communicate with each other to update their environmental information when necessary, e.g. if a PoI has been cleared.

In the experiment we pit our novel two-stage multi-agent planner against both baselines as discussed above. Each approach is used to solve 100 instances of the park scenario (see Fig. 2). The following metrics are subsequently considered:

(i) *%success*: percentage of executions in which the goal is achieved (higher is better);
(ii) *#actions*: total number of primitive actions undertaken by all agents per execution, before achieving the goal or failing to complete it (lower is better).

The first metric gives an indication of how good each approach is in tackling this particular scenario, whereas the second metric gives an indication of the temporal complexity of the solutions found by each method.

Table 1. Comparison of success rate and average number of primitive actions

	Two-stage	One-stage	Individually
% Success	85	62	52
Avg. # actions	15.96	21.68	34.63

Table 1 summarises the resulting values of each metric for the three planning approaches being compared. Figure 8 depicts the value of #*actions* obtained by the proposed planner for each execution, compared to those obtained by the two baseline planning approaches. Our results show that a team of agents coordinated by the proposed two-stage framework and acting in parallel outperform both baseline approaches, in terms of the temporal cost (number of required primitive actions) to reach the goal (particularly compared to the individual planning baseline); along with a significant increase in the planning robustness, i.e. the chances of successfully reaching the common goal. Based on these results, we conclude that our two-stage online multi-agent planning approach endowed with a subgoal delegation mechanism allows for higher robustness and lower cost in the planning domains under uncertainty considered. Furthermore, in the scenario considered, the inclusion of a subgoal delegation scheme intuitively allows for a significant reduction in search space, compared to planning at team level over primitive actions directly.

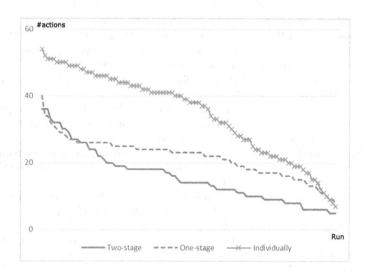

Fig. 8. Comparison of the number of primitive actions (ordered from most to least) undertaken by agents per execution

6 Conclusions

In this paper, we have presented a two-stage online collaborative multi-agent planner for application domains where agent actions have uncertain stochastic effects. The proposed planner interleaves team and individual online planning through a subgoal delegation scheme, and extends state-of-the-art approximate algorithms to suit the characteristics of the planning problems considered. The proposed framework estimates rewards of action outcomes at team level, by using uncertain information fusion procedures, to determine the next best subgoals to be individually pursed by each agent in the team. Future lines of investigation aim at developing data-driven online team planning approaches that enable precise estimations of outcome probabilities of team actions alongside rewards, and the integration of prunning policies in both planning stages.

Acknowledgments. This work has been funded by EPSRC PACES project (Ref: EP/J012149/1).

References

1. Brafman, R., Domshlak, C.: From one to many: planning for loosely coupled multi-agent systems. In: Proceedings of ICAPS 2008 (2008)
2. Brafman, R.I.: A privacy preserving algorithm for multi-agent planning and search. In: Proceedings of IJCAI 2015, pp. 1530–1536 (2015)
3. Browne, C., Powley, E., Whitehouse, D., Lucas, S., Cowling, P.I., Rohlfshagen, P., Tavener, S., Perez, D., Samothrakis, S., Colton, S.: A survey of Monte Carlo tree search methods. IEEE Trans. Comput. Intell. AI Games **4**(1), 1–43 (2012)
4. Durfee, E.: Distributed problem solving and planning. In: Weiss, G. (ed.): A Modern Approach to Distributed Artificial Intelligence (1999)
5. Keller, T., Eyerich, P.: PROST: probabilistic planning based on UCT. In: Proceedings of ICAPS 2012 (2012)
6. Killough, R., Bauters, K., McAreavey, K., Liu, W., Hong, J.: Risk-aware planning in BDI agents. In: Proceedings of the 8th International Conference on Agents and Artificial Intelligence (ICAART 2016) (2016)
7. Klement, E., Mesiar, R., Pap, E.: On the relationship of associative compensatory operators to triangular norms and conorms. Int. J. Uncertainty Fuzziness Knowl.-Based Syst. **04**(02), 129–144 (1996)
8. Kocsis, L., Szepesvári, C.: Bandit based Monte-Carlo planning. In: Fürnkranz, J., Scheffer, T., Spiliopoulou, M. (eds.) ECML 2006. LNCS (LNAI), vol. 4212, pp. 282–293. Springer, Heidelberg (2006)
9. Marcolino, L.S., Matsubara, H.: Multi-agent Monte Carlo Go. In: Proceedings of AAMAS 2011, pp. 21–28. International Foundation for Autonomous Agents and Multiagent Systems (2011)
10. Melo, F.S., Sardinha, A.: Ad hoc teamwork by learning teammates' task. Auton. Agent. Multi-Agent Syst. **30**(2), 175–219 (2015)
11. Paquet, S., Tobin, L., Chaib-Draa, B.: An online POMDP algorithm for complex multiagent environments. In: Proceedings of AAMAS 2005, pp. 970–977 (2005)
12. Russell, S., Norvig, P.: Artificial Intelligence: A Modern Approach. Pearson Education, Upper Saddle River (2009)

13. Semsar-Kazerooni, E., Khorasani, K.: Multi-agent team cooperation: a game theory approach. Automatica **45**(10), 2205–2213 (2009)
14. Smith, R.: Coordination of temporal plans in dynamic environments for mobile agents. Laboratoire d'Informatique de Paris VI (2012)
15. Torreño, A., Onaindia, E., Sapena, O.: FMAP: distributed cooperative multi-agent planning. Appl. Intell. **41**(2), 606–626 (2014)
16. Torreño, A., Sapena, O., Onaindia, E.: Global heuristics for distributed cooperative multi-agent planning. In: 25th International Conference on Automated Planning and Scheduling, ICAPS 2015, pp. 225–233. AAAI Press (2015)
17. Wang, Y., Yang, J., Xu, D.: A preference aggregation method through the estimation of utility intervals. Comput. Oper. Res. **32**, 2027–2049 (2005)
18. de Weerdt, M., Clement, B.: Introduction to planning in multiagent systems. Multiagent Grid Syst. **5**(4), 345–355 (2009)
19. Weld, D.: Recent advances in AI planning. AI Mag. **20**, 93–123 (1999)
20. Wu, F., Zilberstein, S., Chen, X.: Online planning for ad hoc autonomous agent teams. In: Proceedings of IJCAI 2011, pp. 439–445 (2011)
21. Wu, F., Zilberstein, S., Chen, X.: Online planning for multi-agent systems with bounded communication. Artif. Intell. **175**(2), 487–511 (2011)
22. Yager, R., Rybalov, A.: Uninorm aggregation operators. Fuzzy Sets Syst. **80**, 111–120 (1996)
23. Younes, H., Littman, M.: PPDDL1.0: an extension to PDDL for expressing planning domains with probabilistic effects. In: Proceedings of ICAPS 2003 (2003)

∃-ASP for Computing Repairs with Existential Ontologies

Jean-François Baget[1], Zied Bouraoui[2(✉)], Farid Nouioua[3], Odile Papini[3],
Swan Rocher[4], and Eric Würbel[3]

[1] INRIA, Montpellier, France
baget@lirmm.fr
[2] Cardiff University, Cardiff, UK
BouraouiZ@cardiff.ac.uk
[3] Aix-Marseille University, Marseille, France
{farid.nouioua,odile.papini,eric.wurbel}@univ-amu.fr
[4] University of Montpellier, Montpellier, France
rocher@lirmm.fr

Abstract. Repair-based techniques are a standard way of dealing with
inconsistency in the context of ontology-based data access where several
inconsistency-tolerant semantics have been mainly proposed for lightweight description logics. In this paper we present a generic transformation from knowledge bases expressed within existential rules formalism
into an ASP program. We propose different strategies for this transformation, and highlight the ones for which answer sets of the generated
program correspond to various kinds of repairs used in inconsistency-
tolerant inferences.

1 Introduction

Dealing with inconsistency in ontology-based query answering is one of the
challenging problems that received a lot of attention in recent years, (e.g.
[2,7,11,17]). In such a setting, inconsistency problem comes from the data, i.e.
occurs when assertional facts contradict constraints imposed by the ontological knowledge. In case of inconsistency, standard inference is meaningless: All
queries would be positively answered. In this paper we focus on the mainstream
approach that considers that the ontology, built by experts, is correct, and that
only data has to be repaired. Other approaches (e.g. [20]) rely upon the assumption that the database is reliable but the rules are not. The latter assumption
will not be explored in this paper and left for future work.

Many works (e.g. [12,16,18]), basically inspired by the approaches proposed
in database area (e.g. [1,9]) and in propositional logic (e.g. [8]), deal with inconsistency by proposing several inconsistency-tolerant inferences, called *semantics*.
These semantics are based on the notion of assertional base repair which is closely

---

This work was supported by the projects ASPIQ (ANR-12-BS02-0003) and the ERC
Starting Grant 637277.

S. Schockaert and P. Senellart (Eds.): SUM 2016, LNAI 9858, pp. 230–245, 2016.
DOI: 10.1007/978-3-319-45856-4_16

related to the notion of database repair [16] or maximally consistent subbase used in the propositional logic setting. An ABox repair is simply an assertional subbase which is consistent with an ontology. Ontology-based consistent query answering (AR-semantics) [16] comes down first to compute the set of repairs (i.e. all possible maximally consistent subsets of facts consistent with the ontological knowledge) and then to check to which extent a query can be entailed using these repairs. As shown in [10,16], the AR-semantics (also called universal entailment) is a hard task (co-NP complete) for lightweight DLs [16,19]. In fact, inconsistency-tolerant semantics were introduced for the lightweight description logics *DL-Lite* (e.g. [16]), and later extended to other description logics (e.g. [19]) or existential rules (e.g. [17]). In this paper, we use existential rules (e.g. [5]) (also called Datalog $+/-$) as ontology language that generalizes lightweight description logics, such as *DL-Lite* and *EL* by allowing the use of any predicate arity as well as cyclic structures.

Recently the ASP framework [6], a convenient paradigm for knowledge representation and reasoning, especially when information is incomplete, has been enriched in order to deal with existential variables [13]. ∃-ASP is a fragment of ASP that generalises skolemized existential rules. It allows for enriching lightweight description logics with non-monotonic features, and benefits from decidability results obtained for existential rules. ∃-ASP has been naturally implemented on top of the ASP solver ASPeRiX[1], which does not rely on preliminary grounding to compute answer sets [14,15].

The paper first recalls the logical frameworks used in this paper: Existential rules in Sect. 2, ∃-ASP in Sect. 3, and the best known notions of repair in Sect. 4. Our contribution is presented in Sect. 5. We present a generic transformation from knowledge bases expressed within existential rules formalism into an ASP program. We propose different strategies for this transformation, and highlight the ones for which answer sets of the generated program correspond to various kinds of repairs used in inconsistency-tolerant inferences. The sound and complete ∃-ASP algorithm which is central to ASPeRiX computations will be used to prove the one-to-one correspondence between the answer sets of the generated program and the knowledge base repairs.

2   Existential Rules

We consider a *vocabulary* $\mathcal{V}$ consisting of three disjoint sets, the set $\mathcal{P}$ of *predicate names*, the set $\mathcal{F}$ of *function symbols* (each provided with an arity) and the set $\mathcal{C}$ of *constants*. Disjoint with $\mathcal{V}$, we also consider a set $\mathcal{X}$ of *variables*. In what follows, constants will be notated in lowercase and variables in uppercase. The set of *terms* is defined inductively as follows: Constants and variables alike are terms, and if $f \in \mathcal{F}$ is a function symbol of arity k and $t_1, \ldots, t_p$ are terms, then $f(t_1, \ldots, t_p)$ is also a term. An *atom* is an object of form $p(t_1, \ldots, t_k)$, where p is a predicate name of arity k and the t_i are *terms*. An atom is said *basic* when none of its terms involve any function symbol, and is said *grounded* when no

---

[1] Available at http://www.info.univ-angers.fr/pub/claire/asperix/.

variable is used to define any of its terms. A set of atoms is said basic (resp. grounded) when all its atoms are basic (resp. grounded).

Homomorphisms. A *substitution* is a mapping σ from a set of variables to a set of terms. If A is a set of atoms and σ is a substitution, we note $\sigma(A)$ the set of atoms obtained, for each variable x appearing both in an atom of A and the domain of σ, by replacing non-recursively each occurence of x in A by $\sigma(x)$. For example, let $A = \{p(f(X,Y),Z),q(X,a)\}$ and $\sigma : X \mapsto f(X,a), Y \mapsto X$. Then $\sigma(A) = \{p(f(f(X,a),X),Z),q(f(X,a),a)\}$. Let F and Q be two sets of atoms. A *homomorphism* from Q to F is a substitution σ such that $\sigma(Q) \subseteq F$. If we note $\phi(A)$ the first-order logics (FOL) formula obtained by the conjunction of the atoms in A, and $\Phi(A)$ the existential closure of $\phi(A)$, it is well known that $\Phi(F) \models \Phi(Q)$ iff there exists a homomorphism from Q to F. Let σ be a bijective substitution from the variables of F to a fresh set of constants (that appear neither in F nor in Q). The ground set of atoms $\sigma(F)$ is called a *grounding* of F and it holds that $\Phi(F) \models \Phi(Q)$ iff $\Phi(\sigma(F)) \models \Phi(Q)$.

Existential Rules. An *existential rule* is of form $B \to H$ where both the *body* B and the *head* H are sets of *basic* atoms. We often note such a rule $B[\boldsymbol{X},\boldsymbol{Y}] \to H[\boldsymbol{Y},\boldsymbol{Z}]$, where the variables in $\boldsymbol{X}$ are those that appear only in the body, the variables in $\boldsymbol{Y}$ (called the *frontier*) are those that appear both in the body and the head, and those in $\boldsymbol{Z}$ (called *existential variables*) are those that appear only in the head. The FOL formula associated with this existential rule is $\forall \boldsymbol{X} \forall \boldsymbol{Y}(\phi(B) \to (\exists \boldsymbol{Z}\phi(H)))$. For example, the FOL formula associated with $p(X,Y),r(X,Y',a) \to r(Y,Y',Z),p(Z,Z')$ is $\forall X \forall Y \forall Y'(p(X,Y) \wedge r(X,Y',a) \to (\exists Z \exists Z' r(Y,Y',Z) \wedge p(Z,Z')))$. Let $R = B \to H$ be a rule with frontier $\boldsymbol{Y}$ and existential variables $\boldsymbol{Z}$. Let us consider a substitution σ_R that maps each existential variable $Z \in \boldsymbol{Z}$ to a functional term $f_z^R(\boldsymbol{Y})$. Then we say that $sk(R) = B \to \sigma_R(H)$ is a *skolemization* of R. Let R be the rule given in the example, then $sk(R) = p(X,Y),r(X,Y',a) \to r(Y,Y',f_Z^R(Y,Y')),p(f_Z^R(Y,Y'),f_{Z'}^R(Y,Y'))$.

Derivations. Consider now a set of atoms F and a skolemized existential rule $R = B \to H$. We say that R is *applicable* to F when there exists a homomorphism σ from B to F. In that case, the application of R on F according to σ produces a set of atoms $\alpha(F,R,\sigma) = F \cup \sigma(H)$. Note that when F is ground, $\alpha(F,R,\sigma)$ is also ground. Let R be the rule given in the previous example, and $F = p(a,g(b)),r(a,g(b),a)$. The substitution $\sigma : X \mapsto a, Y \mapsto g(b), Y' \mapsto g(b)$ is a homomorphism from B to F and $\alpha(F,R,\sigma) = F \cup \{r(g(b),g(b),f_Z^R(g(b),g(b))),p(f_Z^R(g(b),g(b)),f_{Z'}^R(g(b),g(b)))\}$.

Let F be a set of atoms and $\mathcal{R}$ be a set of rules. A $\mathcal{R}$-*derivation* from F is a (possibly infinite) sequence $F = F_0, F_1, \ldots, F_i, \ldots$ such that, $\forall i > 0$, there exists a rule $R = B \to H \in \mathcal{R}$ and a homomorphism σ from B to F_{i-1} such that $F_i = \alpha(F_{i-1},R,\sigma)$. The *result* of a finite derivation $F_0, \ldots, F_k$ is the set of atoms F_k, when it is infinite we define it as the (infinite) union of all F_i. A derivation is said *full* when, for every rule $R = B \to H \in \mathcal{R}$, for every homomorphism σ from B to its result, there exists some F_i in the derivation such that $F_{i+1} = \alpha(F_i,R,\sigma)$. Any full $\mathcal{R}$-derivation on F produces the same result, and we call that result the $\mathcal{R}$-closure of F and note it $Cl_{\mathcal{R}}(F)$ (or simply $Cl(F)$ when there is no ambiguity on $\mathcal{R}$). When we consider a set $\Pi = F \cup \mathcal{R}$ as a program (as in Sect. 3), we note $Cl(\Pi) = Cl_{\mathcal{R}}(F)$.

Theorem 1. *Let F and Q be two set of atoms, and $\mathcal{R}$ be a set of existential rules. We note F_g a grounding of F and $\mathcal{R}_{sk}$ the skolemization of $\mathcal{R}$. Then $Cl_{\mathcal{R}_{sk}}(F_g)$ is a universal model, i.e., $F, \mathcal{R} \models Q$ iff there is a homomorphism from Q to $Cl_{\mathcal{R}_{sk}}(F_g)$.*

Skolem Chase. Deciding whether or not $F, \mathcal{R} \models Q$ is undecidable. However, for all positive instances of the problem, a homomorphism from Q to $Cl_{\mathcal{R}_{sk}}(F_g)$ can be found after finitely many steps of a breadth first derivation. Such a derivation is called the *skolem chase*. For a more precise relationship between the skolem chase and other chases found in the litterature, the reader can refer to [4]. A lot of work has been devoted to predicting that the chase will stop. Acyclicity conditions on a set of existential rules such as the ones presented in [3] ensure that the closure $Cl_{\mathcal{R}_{sk}}(F_g)$ will be finite.

3 Existential ASP

Syntax. An *existential ASP (∃-ASP) rule* is of form $H \leftarrow B^+, not\, B_1^-, \ldots, not\, B_k^-$ where the *positive body* B^+, the *negative bodies* B^- and the *head* H are sets of basic atoms. Intuitively, such a rule means "if the positive body is verified, and none of the negative bodies are, then we can conclude with the head". To make our definitions easier to read, and without loss of generality (see the safety condition in [13]), we consider that all variables appearing in negative bodies also appear in the positive body. An *∃-ASP program* is a set Π_F of basic atoms and a set $\Pi_{\mathcal{R}}$ of ∃-ASP rules. As for existential rules, we can skolemize ∃-ASP rules respecting the safety condition as follows: The skolemization of the previous rule results in $\sigma(H) \leftarrow B^+, not\, B_1^-, \ldots, not\, B_k^-$, where $\sigma(H) \leftarrow B^+$ is the skolemization of $H \leftarrow B^+$, as defined for existential rules. The skolemization of an ∃-ASP program is defined by the grounding of Π_F and the skolemization of $\Pi_{\mathcal{R}}$. For example, let $r(X, Z) \leftarrow p(X, Y), not\, q(X), not\,(r(Y, a), r(a, b))$ be an existential ASP rule. Its skolemization is $r(X, f_Z^R(X)) \leftarrow p(X, Y), not\, q(X), not(r(Y, a), r(a, b))$.

Note that the skolemization of an existential ASP program (without function symbol) is a standard ASP program with function symbols.

Semantics. In what follows we consider Π an ASP program obtained from a skolemized existential ASP program. Let $\mathcal{C}_{\Pi}$ be the set of constants appearing in Π and $\mathcal{F}_{\Pi}$ be the set of function symbols appearing in Π. The *Herbrand domain* of Π is the minimal set of ground terms $\mathcal{H}_{\Pi}$ such that $\mathcal{C}_{\Pi} \subseteq \mathcal{H}_{\Pi}$ and, if $f \in \mathcal{F}_{\Pi}$ is a function symbol of arity k and $h_1, \ldots, h_k$ are in $\mathcal{H}_{\Pi}$, then $f(h_1, \ldots, h_k)$ is also in $\mathcal{H}_{\Pi}$. If $R = H \leftarrow B^+, not\, B_1^-, \ldots, not\, B_k^-$ is a rule in Π and σ is a substitution from all its variables in to $\mathcal{H}_{\Pi}$, then the rule $\sigma(R) = \sigma(H) \leftarrow \sigma(B^+), not\, \sigma(B_1^-), \ldots, not\, \sigma(B_k^-)$ is a *grounding* of R. The grounding of a program Π is the program obtained from all possible groundings of all rules in Π. Not that the Herbrand domain (and thus the grounding) of a finite Π is infinite as soon as Π contains a constant and a predicate symbol of arity ≥ 1. Let us now consider the grounding Π^G of Π and a (possibly infinite) set of ground atoms E. The *reduct* of Π^G with respect to E, denoted $\Pi^G_{|E}$, is the minimal set that contains all (ground) atoms of Π^G and, for each skolemized $\exists$-ASP rule $R = H \leftarrow B^+, not\, B_1^-, \ldots, not\, B_k^-$ in Π_G, if there is no B_i^- such that $B_i^- \subseteq E$, then $H \leftarrow B^+$ (called the *positive part* of R) is a skolemized existential rule of $\Pi^G_{|E}$.

Finally, E is an *answer set* (stable model) of Π when $E = Cl(\Pi^G_{|E})$. We define the answer sets of an existential ASP program as the answer sets of its skolemization. Note that it is not a neutral choice, for a semantic point of view (see the discussion in [4] where using different chases can lead to different semantics and different answer sets).

Computation. Given an ASP program Π, most solvers rely upon a 2-step algorithm that first compute the grounding Π^G of Π, then use Π_G to build an answer set E (using for instance a SAT solver). However, the grounding becomes infinite as soon as function symbols (such as the ones obtained from our skolemization) are involved. Some solvers can try to extract from the grounding rules that have no chance to be involved in the second step, but doing that optimally would require to compute that second step, making the 2-steps separation useless. On the other hand, the ASP solver ASPeRiX [14,15] does not require grounding to compute answer sets (indeed, using homomorphisms during the computation is equivalent to generate the grounding effectively required at that step of a computation). Since our proofs in Sect. 5 heavily rely upon the soundness and completeness of that algorithm, we explain here its basic version.

In ASPeRiX, given a skolemized existential ASP program Π, a *computation* is an incremental development of a (possibly infinite) binary tree. Each node of this tree contains 3 fields: IN is the set of ground atoms that have been proven in the current branch, OUT is a set of forbidden sets of ground atoms, and MBT (Must Be True) is a set of mandatory disjunctions of sets of ground atoms. Initially, the tree contains a single node, its root, whose IN field contains all ground atoms of Π, and whose fields OUT and MBT are empty. At each step, the computation selects a leaf n of the tree and a rule $R = H \leftarrow B^+, not\, B_1^-, \ldots, not\, B_k^-$ such that there exists a homomorphism σ from B^+ to IN(n) and (R, σ) has not already been evaluated on n nor on any of its ancestors. Now we say that (R, σ) is evaluated on n and there is 3 possible outcomes. **Blocked case:** If there exists a negative body B_i^- in R such that $\sigma(B_i^-) \subseteq$IN(n), meaning that one of the negative bodies appears in IN(n), then this step produces nothing (but marks this evaluation as done). **Positive case:** If $R = H \leftarrow B^+$ contains no negative body, then we update IN(n) with the result of the rule application, and do not change OUT nor MBT. Then IN(n) = α(IN(n), R, σ) =IN(n)$\cup\sigma(H)$. **Choice case:** otherwise we create two children n_1 and n_2 of n. In n_1 we effectively apply the rule and forbid its negative bodies to appear in the final result, in n_2 we must prove that we have the right not to apply it by finding one of the negative bodies in the final result. Then $\text{IN}(n_1) = \alpha(\text{IN}(n), R, \sigma) = \text{IN}(n) \cup \sigma(H)$, $\text{OUT}(n_1)$ is the set of sets of atoms whose elements are those of $\text{OUT}(n)$ and the k sets of atoms $\sigma(B_i^-)$, for $1 \leq i \leq k$, $\text{MBT}(n_1) = \text{MBT}(n)$ and $\text{IN}(n_2) = \text{IN}(n)$, $\text{OUT}(n_2) = \text{OUT}(n)$, and $\text{MBT}(n_2)$ is the set of disjunctions of sets of atoms whose elements are those of $\text{MBT}(n)$ and the disjunction $\vee_{1 \leq i \leq k} \sigma(B_i^-)$.

Consider a (possibly infinite) branch of this tree. Similarly to what was done for derivations, we define the *result* of that branch as the (possibly infinite) union, for all nodes n in that branch, of the $\text{IN}(n)$. When such a branch is finite, its result is $\text{IN}(l)$, where l is the leaf of the branch. A branch is said full when, for every rule R and every homomorphism σ from B^+ to the result of the branch, (R, σ) has been evaluated on some node of the branch. If n is a node of a branch and B is a set of atoms, we say that B satisfies $\text{OUT}(n)$ when, for every set of atoms $O \in \text{OUT}(n)$, $O \not\subseteq B$. In the same way, we say that B satisfies $\text{MBT}(n)$ when, for every disjunction $M_1 \vee \ldots \vee M_k \in \text{MBT}(n)$, there exists a M_i such that $M_i \subseteq B$. A branch is said OUT-*valid* (resp. MBT-*valid*) when its result satisfies $\text{OUT}(n)$ (resp. MBT-(n)) for every node n in the branch. A branch that is both OUT-valid and MBT-valid is said *valid*.

Theorem 2. *Let Π be a skolemized existential ASP program. Then A is an answer set of Π iff A is the result of a full valid branch in the computation of Π.*

Properties. It is first important to note that, when the positive part of rules satisfy the acyclicity conditions presented in [4], then the computation produces a finite tree. In that case, validity of a branch with leaf l admits a simpler characterization: A branch is OUT-valid (resp. MBT-valid) when $\text{IN}(l)$ satisfies $\text{OUT}(l)$ (resp. $\text{MBT}(l)$).

Then we point out the monotonic increase of the field IN: If a node n' is a descendant of a n, then $\text{IN}(n) \subseteq \text{IN}(n')$. It follows that if there is a node n such that $\text{IN}(n)$ does not satisfy $\text{OUT}(n)$, then no branch containing n is OUT-valid, so we can cut the development of the computation tree for node n. Such an optimization is more difficult to achieve using the MBT field, to stop the development of the computation tree for node n, we have to prove that there exists a disjunction $M_1 \vee \ldots \vee M_k \in \text{MBT}(n)$ and a set of atoms M_i that will never be contained in the IN field of any descendant of n. Simple arguments achieve that goal in the ASP programs we generate in Sect. 5.

4 The Notion of Repair

We now recall the definitions of repairs [1,10,16] rephrased within the framework of existential rules. Let $\mathcal{K} = (F, \mathcal{R}, \mathcal{N})$ be a knowledge base where F is a set of ground atoms, $\mathcal{R}$ is a set of existential rules, and $\mathcal{N}$ is a set of negative constraints, *i.e.* a set of rules of form $\bot \leftarrow B$ where B is a set of basic atoms and $\bot$ is the absurd symbol. We say that a set of atoms Y is *consistent* w.r.t. $(\mathcal{R}, \mathcal{N})$ when $(F, \mathcal{R}, \mathcal{N}) \not\models \bot$, *i.e.* when $Cl(Y, \mathcal{R} \cup \mathcal{N})$ does not contain $\bot$. Our knowledge base is thus consistent when F is consistent w.r.t. $(\mathcal{R}, \mathcal{N})$. Different kind of *repairs* can be considered when the knowledge base is inconsistent.

(Standard) repairs: A *repair* of $\mathcal{K}$ is an inclusion-maximal subset F' of F that is consistent w.r.t. $(\mathcal{R}, \mathcal{N})$, and we note $F' \in R(\mathcal{K})$. **Closed repairs**: If X is a set of atoms, we call *ground positive closure* of X and note $g^+Cl(X)$ the restriction of $Cl(X, \mathcal{R})$ to basic ground atoms (whose terms are only constants, and not obtained with function symbols). A *closed repair* of $\mathcal{K}$ is a set of basic ground atoms $F'' = g^+Cl(F')$, where F' is a standard repair of $\mathcal{K}$, and we note $F'' \in CR(\mathcal{K})$. **Repairs of closure**: A *repair of the closure* of $\mathcal{K}$ is a standard repair F' of $(g^+Cl(F, \mathcal{R}), \mathcal{R}, \mathcal{N})$, and we note $F' \in RC(\mathcal{K})$.

Recently a unified framework combining modifiers (way of computing the repairs) and inferences strategies has been proposed for querying ontological knowledge bases represented with existential rules [2]. This framework covers the best known semantics and introduces new ones. The semantics are denoted by $\langle \circ_i, s \rangle$ where $\circ_i$ is a modifier and $s \in \{\forall, \exists, \cap, maj\}$ is an inference strategy. Within this framework $\circ_1$ computes the set of repairs, $\circ_5$ computes the closed repairs and $\circ_7$ computes the repairs of the closure.

5   Computing Repairs with $\exists$-ASP

In this section we describe the transformation from a knowledge base $\mathcal{K}$ into a generic $\exists$-ASP program Π. Though this program computes "repairs" in the broad sense, two configurable modules (namely selection and display) are used to obtain the intended behaviour. In particular, we show that, given specific rules, this program can compute the repairs, the closed repairs or the repairs of the closure of $\mathcal{K}$. This transformation relies upon the following steps: (1) $\mathcal{K}$ is put into its skolemized form, (2) the user selects either the select or the display transformation scheme, (3) the transformation builds the program Π, using an extended vocabulary, (4) we use an ASP solver to compute the answer sets of Π, (5) the restriction of those answer sets to the original vocabulary provides the "repairs".

5.1   Transformation into $\exists$-ASP

Our knowledge base is built upon an original vocabulary $\mathcal{V}$. For every predicate name $p \in \mathcal{V}$, we consider different versions of p that will be used in the extended vocabulary of our $\exists$-ASP program: p_i for initial predicate, p_p for possible predicate, p_n for forbidden predicate, p_c for chosen predicate, p_s for may be selected predicate, p_v for valid predicate, p_g for ground predicate, and p_d for display predicate. If A is a set of atoms built upon the original vocabulary, we note A_x the set of atoms $p_x(t)$ built upon the extended vocabulary where $p(t)$ is an atom of A. The $\exists$-ASP program Π is obtained as follows:

Encoding of Initial Facts: Π contains F_i (every atom of F is considered as an initial fact of the program Π).

Encoding of Positive Closure: For every predicate name in $\mathcal{V}$, we have a rule of form $[P_1:]$ $p_p(X) \leftarrow p_i(X)$, those rules assert that every initial atom is possible; and for every rule $B(X) \rightarrow H(X, Y)$ in $\mathcal{R}_{sk}$, we have a rule of form $[R_1:]$ $H_p(X, Y)$, $fct(Y_1)$, $\cdots$, $fct(Y_k) \leftarrow B_p(X)$ where the Y_i are the functional terms of the head of the skolemized rule, those rules are used to encode the positive closure $Cl(F, \mathcal{R})$ with possible atoms, and to "mark" functional terms. Finally, for every predicate name $p \in \mathcal{V}$, we have a rule of form $[P_2:]$ $p_g(X) \leftarrow p_p(X), not fct(X_1), \cdots not fct(X_k)$ asserting that every possible atom using no functional term is ground.

Selection Strategy: Those configurable rules provide the user strategy to define which atoms (of form p_s) are selectable, *i.e.* can appear or not in the "repairs". We provide here two such strategies: **SEL1** says that every initial atom is selectable. For every predicate name $p \in \mathcal{V}$, we have a rule $[S_1:]$ $p_s(X) \leftarrow p_i(X)$. **SEL2** says that every ground possible atom is selectable. For every predicate name $p \in \mathcal{V}$, we have a rule $[S_2:]$ $p_s(X) \leftarrow p_g(X)$.

Choice Rules: These rules are the core of our program, since they will build all possible subsets of selectable atoms. They say that every atom that is selectable and not forbidden must be chosen. $[P_3:]$ $p_c(X) \leftarrow p_s(X), not p_n(X)$.

Definition of Contexts: For every atom $p(t)$, the atom $p_v(t, c)$ asserts that $p(t)$ is valid in the context c. All chosen atoms are valid in the *base* context. This is encoded, for each predicate name $p \in \mathcal{V}$, by the rule $[P_4:]$ $p_v(X, base) \leftarrow p_c(X)$. An atom $p(t)$ that is not chosen will be valid in its own context, encoded by the term $ctx(p, t)$. This is encoded, for each predicate name $p \in \mathcal{V}$, by the rule $[P_5:]$ $p_v(X, ctx(p, X))$, $context(ctx(p, X)) \leftarrow p_s(X)$, $not p_c(X)$. Finally, we say that every atom valid in the base context is also valid in any other context. For each predicate name $p \in \mathcal{V}$, we have the rule $[P_6:]$ $p_v(X, C) \leftarrow p_v(X, base), context(C)$. The base context encodes the chosen atoms. Every other context encodes the adding of one particular unchosen atom to the already chosen ones. Intuitively, to obtain a repair we will have to prove that the base context is consistent and that all other contexts are not, meaning that the base context is maximal.

Context Closure: Every atom that can be deduced from those valid in a particular context will also be valid in that context. For every skolemized existential rule of the form $B(X) \rightarrow H(X)$, we obtain the rule $[R_2:]$ $H_v(X, C) \leftarrow B_v(X, C)$. Then we say that if a constraint is violated in a given context, then that context is *absurd*. For any constraint in $\mathcal{N}$ of the form $p^1(X_1), \cdots, p^k(X_k) \rightarrow \bot$ we add the rule of form $[C_1:]$ $absurd(C) \leftarrow p_v^1(X_1, C), \cdots, p_v^k(X_k, C)$.

Retropropagation of Absurd Contexts: Finally, we say that if the base context is absurd, then every atom valid in that context is forbidden. For every predicate $p \in \mathcal{V}$, we have the rule $[C_2:]$ $p_n(X) \leftarrow p_c(X), absurd(base)$. For other absurd contexts, only selectable unchosen atoms of that specific context are forbidden. For every predicate $p \in \mathcal{V}$, we have the rule $[C_3:]$ $p_n(X) \leftarrow not p_c(X), p_s(X), p_v(X, C), context(C), absurd(C)$.

Visualization Strategy: Those configurable rules provide the user strategy to define which atoms (of form p_d) are displayable, *i.e.* can appear or not in the visualization of the "repairs". Whatever the strategy chosen, only displayable atoms that are valid in the base context will be displayed (*i.e.* added using the original vocabulary). This is encoded, for each predicate name $p \in \mathcal{V}$, by the rule $[D:]\ p(\boldsymbol{X}) \leftarrow p_d(\boldsymbol{X}), p_v(\boldsymbol{X}, base)$. We provide here two such strategies: **DISP1** says that every initial atom is displayable. For every predicate name $p \in \mathcal{V}$, we have a rule $[V_1:]\ p_d(\boldsymbol{X}) \leftarrow p_i(\boldsymbol{X})$. **DISP2** says that every ground possible atom is displayable. For every predicate name $p \in \mathcal{V}$, we have a rule $[V_2:]\ p_d(\boldsymbol{X}) \leftarrow p_g(\boldsymbol{X})$.

Example 1. Let $\mathcal{K} = (\mathcal{F}, \mathcal{R}, \mathcal{N})$ be a knowledge base such that $F = \{p(a), q(a)\}$, $\mathcal{R}_{sk} = \{p(X) \rightarrow r(X, f(X)), q(X) \rightarrow s(X), r(X, Y) \rightarrow t(X)\}$ and $\mathcal{N} = \{r(X, Y), q(X) \rightarrow \bot\}$. The original vocabulary of $\mathcal{K}$ contains the predicate names $\{p, q, r, t\}$.

The **initial facts** are $p_i(a)$. and $q_i(a)$.

The rules encoding the **positive closure** are those of form P_1 for initialization (we restricted those to the predicates appearing in initial form): $p_p(X) \leftarrow p_i(X)$. and $q_p(X) \leftarrow q_i(X)$., those of form R_1 for propagation: $r_p(X, f(X)), fct(f(X)) \leftarrow p_p(X)$. $s_p(X) \leftarrow q_p(X)$. $t_p(X) \leftarrow r_p(X, Y)$. and those of form P_2 to detect ground atoms: $p_g(X) \leftarrow p_p(X), not\, fct(X)$. $q_g(X) \leftarrow q_p(X), not\, fct(X)$. $r_g(X, Y) \leftarrow r_p(X, Y), not\, fct(X), not\, fct(Y)$. $s_g(X) \leftarrow s_p(X), not\, fct(X)$. $t_g(X) \leftarrow t_p(X),\ not\, fct(X)$.

Two **selection strategies** are possible. With **SEL1** we have: $p_s(X) \leftarrow p_i(X)$. and $q_s(X) \leftarrow q_i(X)$. With **SEL2** we have: $p_s(X) \leftarrow p_g(X)$. $q_s(X) \leftarrow q_g(X)$. $r_s(X, Y) \leftarrow r_g(X, Y)$. $s_s(X) \leftarrow s_g(X)$. and $t_s(X) \leftarrow t_g(X)$.

The **choice rules** are: $p_c(X) \leftarrow p_s(X), not\, p_n(X)$. $q_c(X) \leftarrow q_s(X), not\, q_n(X)$. $r_c(X, Y) \leftarrow r_s(X, Y), not\, r_n(X, Y)$. $s_c(X) \leftarrow s_s(X), not\, s_n(X)$. $t_c(X) \leftarrow t_s(X), not\, t_n(X)$.

For the **definition of contexts**, we have the rules of form P_4 defining the base context: $p_v(X, base) \leftarrow p_c(X)$. $q_v(X, base) \leftarrow q_c(X)$. $r_v(X, Y, base) \leftarrow r_c(X, Y)$. $s_v(X, base) \leftarrow s_c(X)$. $t_v(X, base) \leftarrow t_c(X)$. the rules of form P_5 defining other contexts: $p_v(X, ctx(p, X)), context(ctx(p, X)) \leftarrow p_s(X), not\, p_c(X)$. $q_v(X, ctx(q, X)), context(ctx(q, X)) \leftarrow q_s(X), not\, q_c(X)$. $r_v(X, Y, ctx(r, X, Y)), context(ctx(r, X, Y)) \leftarrow r_s(X, Y), not\, r_c(X, Y)$. $s_v(X, ctx(s, X)), context(ctx(s, X)) \leftarrow s_s(X), not\, s_c(X)$. $t_v(X, ctx(t, X)), context(ctx(t, X)) \leftarrow t_s(X), not\, t_c(X)$. and the rules of form P_6 encoding inheritance of base context: $p_v(X, C) \leftarrow p_v(X, base), context(C)$. $q_v(X, C) \leftarrow q_v(X, base), context(C)$. $r_v(X, Y, C) \leftarrow r_v(X, Y, base), context(C)$. $s_v(X, C) \leftarrow s_v(X, base), context(C)$. $t_v(X, C) \leftarrow t_v(X, base), context(C)$.

The **context closure** will be computed with the rules of form R_2: $r_v(X, f(X), C) \leftarrow p_v(X, C)$. $s_v(X, C) \leftarrow q_v(X, C)$. $t_v(X, C) \leftarrow r_v(X, Y, C)$. and inconsistencies will be detected by the rule of form C_1: $absurd(C) \leftarrow r_v(X, Y, C), q_v(X, C)$.

Retropropagation of absurd contexts is handled by rules of form C_2: $p_n(X) \leftarrow p_c(X), absurd(base)$. $q_n(X) \leftarrow q_c(X), absurd(base)$. $r_n(X, Y) \leftarrow$

$r_c(X,Y), absurd(base).$
$s_n(X) \leftarrow s_c(X), absurd(base).$ $t_n(X) \leftarrow t_c(X), absurd(base).$ and C_3: $p_n(X) \leftarrow$
$not\, p_c(X), p_s(X), p_v(X,C), context(C), absurd(C).$ $q_n(X) \leftarrow not\, q_c(X), q_s(X),$
$q_v(X,C), context(C), absurd(C).$ $r_n(X,Y) \leftarrow not\, r_c(X,Y), r_s(X,Y), r_v(X,Y,$
$C), context(C), absurd(C).$ $s_n(X) \leftarrow not\, s_c(X), s_s(X), s_v(X,C), context(C),$
$absurd(C).$ $t_n(X) \leftarrow not\, t_c(X), t_s(X), t_v(X,C), context(C), absurd(C).$
Finally, **display rules** contain the rules of form D: $p(X) \leftarrow p_d(X), p_v(X, base).$
$q(X) \leftarrow q_d(X), q_v(X, base).$ $r(X,Y) \leftarrow r_d(X,Y), r_v(X,Y, base).$ $s(X) \leftarrow$
$s_d(X), s_v(X, base).$ $t(X) \leftarrow t_d(X), t_v(X, base).$ And the choice of strategy
DISP1 with rules: $p_d(X) \leftarrow p_i(X).$ $q_d(X) \leftarrow q_i(X).$ $r_d(X,Y) \leftarrow r_i(X,Y).$
$s_d(X) \leftarrow s_i(X).$ $t_d(X) \leftarrow t_i(X).$ or of strategy **DISP2** with rules: $p_d(X) \leftarrow$
$p_g(X).$ $q_d(X) \leftarrow p_g(X).$ $r_d(X,Y) \leftarrow r_g(X,Y).$ $s_d(X) \leftarrow s_g(X).$ $t_d(X) \leftarrow t_g(X).$

It is important to note that when the skolem chase halts for the original existential rules KB (such fragments have been studied for instance in [4]) then the Skolem chase also halts on the positive part of the generated ASP program, and thus (see properties in Sect. 3) the ASPeRiX computation generates all answer sets in finite time.

5.2   General Form of the Computation Tree of Π

Let us now examine what is happening during a computation of such a program Π. We first point out that we can evaluate rules in a particular order: (1) the positive closure rules of form P_1, (2) those of form R_1, (3) those of form P_2, (4) the selection rules, (5) the choice rules P_3, (6) the definitions of contexts of form P_4, (7) those of form P_5, (8) those of form P_6, (9) the context closure of form R_2, (10) and those of form C_1, (11) the retropropagation rules C_2 and (12) C_3, and (13) the visualisation rules. Indeed, we can check that, if $i < j$ are two of those steps, no rule evaluated at step j can trigger a new application of a rule that was evaluated at step i. This will not always be the case with any selection rules provided by the user, but this property is satisfied by the strategies **SEL1** and **SEL2** presented here. Among all equivalent computation trees, we will thus consider those that respect that particular order: The *natural* computations of Π.

Proposition 1. *Let $\mathcal{K} = (\mathcal{F}, \mathcal{R}, \mathcal{N})$ be a knowledge base, and let Π be the ∃-ASP program obtained from the above encoding. At the end of Step 3 the natural computation tree corresponding to Π only has one finite branch that could lead to a full valid branch.*

Proof. The computation of Π is a binary tree. Initially the root is s.t $IN(root) = \mathcal{F}_i, OUT(root) = \emptyset, MBT(root) = \emptyset$. After $|\mathcal{F}_i|$ applications of the rule P_1, $IN(root) = \mathcal{F}_i \cup \mathcal{F}_p$, since the rule P_1 is positive (the negative body of P_1 is empty) $OUT(root)$ and $MBT(root)$ are unchanged. (In the following in case of positive rule we do not specify that the fields OUT and MBT do not change.) After a possible infinite number of applications of the rule R_1, $IN(root) = \mathcal{F}_i \cup (Cl(\mathcal{F}, \mathcal{R}))_p \cup \{fct(t), t \notin$ basic terms of $Cl(\mathcal{F})\}$. We develop the computation tree using the rule P_2, starting from the root, for each node n we look for a homomorphism σ in $IN(root)$ s.t $\sigma(X_i){=}t_i$ where t_i is a grounded term. Two cases hold:

- case 1: $\exists t_i$ such that $fct(t_i) \in IN(root)$. This is the blocked case of the computation tree given in Sect. 3. The node is not changed.
- case 2: $\nexists t_i$ such that $fct(t_i) \in IN(root)$. This is the choice case in the computation tree given in Sect. 3. The node n has two children n_1 and n_2 such that $IN(n_1) = IN(n) \cup \{p_g(t_1, \cdots, t_k)\}$, $OUT(n_1) = OUT(n) \cup \{\{fct(t_1)\}$, $\cdots, \{fct(t_k)\}\}$, $MBT(n_1) = MBT(n)$ and $IN(n_2) = IN(n)$, $OUT(n_2) = OUT(n)$, $MBT(n_2) = MBT(n) \cup \{fct(t_1) \vee \cdots \vee fct(t_k)\}$.

Note that we get all $fct(t_i)$ that could be generated and there will be no other way to obtain others. According to the properties in Sect. 3 none of the $fct(t_i)$ in $MBT(n_2)$ can be proved therefore this branch cannot lead to a valid branch. At the end of Step 3, the computation tree only has one branch that could lead to a valid branch and therefore to an anwser set. Since there is a finite number of atoms without function symbol, this only branch is finite and l denotes its leaf and $IN(l) = \mathcal{F}_i \cup (Cl(\mathcal{F}, \mathcal{R}))_p \cup \{fct(t)|$ t is a functional term of $Cl(\mathcal{F}, \mathcal{R})\} \cup (\{a \in Cl(\mathcal{F}, \mathcal{R})|$a is a basic atom$\})_g$, $OUT(l) = \{\{fct(t)\}|$t is a functional term of $Cl(\mathcal{F}, \mathcal{R})\}$ and $MBT(l) = MBT(n)$. As no further development of the computation tree can add any atom with predicate name $fct(t)$, the result of any branch having the node l as ancestor will satisfy $OUT(l)$. Thus, in the following, we will ignore $OUT(l)$.

Example 2. (Example 1, continued) At the end of Step 3 the computation tree has only one branch and l denotes its leaf. We have $IN(l) = \{p_i(a), q_i(a), p_p(a), q_p(a), r_p(a, f(a)), fct(f(a)), s_p(a), t_p(a), p_g(a), q_g(a), s_g(a), t_g(a)\}$, $OUT(l) = \{\{fct(a)\}\}$ and $MBT(l) = \{fct(f(a))\}$. Note that this branch may lead to a full valid branch since $IN(l)$ satisfies $OUT(l)$ and $IN(l)$ satisfies $MBT(l)$.

Proposition 2. *Let $\mathcal{K}{=}(\mathcal{F},\mathcal{R},\mathcal{N})$ be a knowledge base, and let Π be the $\exists$-ASP program obtained from the above encoding. Let X be the finite set of selectable atoms obtained after Step 4. At the end of Step 5 the natural computation tree corresponding to Π has $2^{|X|}$ finite branches (each one determined by the subset Y of the chosen atoms in X).*

Proof. As shown in Proposition 1 the computation tree corresponding to Π obtained at the end of Step 3 only has one finite branch and l denotes its leaf. We start from l where $IN(l)$, $OUT(l)$ and $MBT(l)$ are given at the end of the proof of Proposition 1. Step 4 proposes two strategies for selecting the predicates, in order to handle both cases, we consider the set of atoms X provided by the selection rules and the field IN is updated with X. Thanks to the proposed selection rules X is always finite. The application of the rules P_3 leads to the development of $2^{|X|}$ sub-branches from l, each one encoding a subset $Y \subseteq X$.

The branch associated with Y has a leaf denoted by l_{Y_1} such that $IN(l_{Y_1}) = IN(l) \cup Y$ denoted by $INY1$, $OUT(l_{Y_1}) = OUT(l) \cup \{\{p_n(t) \,|\, p_s(t) \in Y\}\}$ and $MBT(l_{Y_1}) = MBT(l) \cup \{(X \backslash Y)_n\}$.

Proposition 3. Let $\mathcal{K} = (\mathcal{F}, \mathcal{R}, \mathcal{N})$ be a knowledge base, and let Π be the $\exists$-ASP program obtained from the above encoding. Let l_{Y_1} be the leaf of a branch obtained after Step 5 of the natural computation tree. Then l_{Y_1} can lead to at most one valid full branch, which is finite.

Proof. We now consider the development of the computation tree from l_{Y_1}. The application of the rules P_4 introduces the *base* context and since they are positive only the field IN is updated, thus $IN(l_{Y_1}) = INY1 \cup \{p_v(t, base) \,|\, p(t) \in Y\}$. The rules P_5 introduce the contexts different from the *base* context. These are choice rules however like in the case of rules P_2 no other application of rules can generate chosen predicates $(p_c(t))$ therefore there is only one branch that can eventually lead to a valid branch and l_{Y_2} denotes its leaf. Note that is branch is finite because X is finite. Thus $IN(l_{Y_2}) = IN(l_{Y_1}) \cup \{p_v(t, ctx(p, t)) \,|\, p(t) \in X \backslash Y\} \cup \{context(ctx(p, t)), \,|\, p(t) \in X \backslash Y\}$, denoted by $INY2$, the fields OUT and MBT are unchanged. The application of the rules P_6 updates the field IN, thus $IN(l_{Y_2}) = INY2 \cup \{p_v(t, c)) \,|\, p(t) \in Y\}$, denoted by $NY3$, where c is a constant different from *base*. The application of rules R_2 updates the field IN, thus $IN(l_{Y_2}) = INY3 \cup \{p_v(t, base) \,|\, p(t) \in Cl(Y, \mathcal{R})\} \cup \{p_v(t, c) \,|\, c = ctx(q, u), \; c \neq base$ and $p(t) \in Cl(Y \cup \{q(u)\}, \mathcal{R})\}$, denotes $INY4$. The application of the rules C_1 updates the field IN, thus $IN(l_{Y_2}) = INY4 \cup \{absurd(base) \,|\, Cl(Y, \mathcal{R})$ violates a constraint$\} \cup \{absurd(c) \,|\, c = ctx(q, u), \; c \neq base$ and $Cl(Y \cup \{q(u)\}, \mathcal{R})$ violates a constraint$\}$, denoted by $INY5$. The application of the rules C_2 updates the field IN, thus $IN(l_{Y_2}) = INY5 \cup Y_n$ if $Cl(Y, \mathcal{R})$ violates a constraint or $IN(l_{Y_2}) = INY5$ otherwise. The rules C_3 introduce the forbidden predicates These are choice rules however like in the case of rules P_4 no other application of rules can generate chosen predicates $(p_c(t))$ therefore there is only one branch that can eventually lead to a valid branch. l_{Y_3} denotes its leaf. Note that this branch is finite because X is finite. Thus $IN(l_{Y_3}) = IN(l_{Y_2}) \cup \{p_n(t) \,|\, Cl(Y \cup p_c(t), \mathcal{R})$ violates a constraint$\}$ denoted by $INY6$, the fields OUT and MBT are unchanged. Step 13 proposes two strategies for visualizing the predicates, with the strategy **DISP1** the field IN is updated such that $IN(l_{Y_3}) = INY6 \cup \{p_d(t) \,|\, p_i(t) \in \mathcal{F}_i\}$, while with the strategy **DISP2** the field IN is updated such that $IN(l_{Y_3}) = INY6 \cup \{p_d(t) \,|\, p_g(t) \in (Cl(\mathcal{F}, \mathcal{R}))_p\}$. Finally the display rule D updates the field IN, thus $IN(l_{Y_3}) = INY7 \cup \{p(t)\}$ where p is valid in the *base* context and $p_d(t)$ has been selected by a visualization strategy. At the end of Step 13, the branch associated with Y is full. The computation is finite even if its nodes can require an infinite derivation.

5.3 Computation Tree of Π and Repairs

As a preliminary remark, and since all the branches of the computation tree are finite, let us point out that we can thus use the characterization of the validity given in the properties of Sect. 3 using the leaves of that tree. The branch associated with Y is $OUT - valid$ if and only if $IN(l_{Y_3})$ satisfies $OUT(l_{Y_3})$. Moreover, the branch associated with Y is $MBT - valid$ if and only if $IN(l_{Y_3})$ satisfies $MBT(l_{Y_3})$.

Theorem 3. *Let $\mathcal{K}=(\mathcal{F},\mathcal{R},\mathcal{N})$ be a knowledge base. Let Π be the $\exists$-ASP program obtained from $\mathcal{K}$ according to the above encoding. Let Y be a subset of the set of selectable atoms X. The full branch of the computation tree corresponding to Π, associated with Y is valid if and only if Y is a maximal subset of X such that $Cl(Y,\mathcal{R}\cup\mathcal{N}) \not\models \bot$.*

Proof. By hypothesis $Y \subseteq X$, thus by Proposition 3 the computation tree provides a full branch associated with Y and l denotes its leaf. We prove the first the direction by contraposition. If $Cl(Y,\mathcal{R}\cup\mathcal{N}) \models \bot$ then $\exists N \in \mathcal{N}$ such that $Cl(Y,\mathcal{R}) \models \mathcal{N}$ thus $absurd(base) \in IN(l)$, thus $\forall p(t) \in Y$ we have $p_n(t) \in IN(l)$ and $p_n(t) \in OUT(l)$ therefore the branch associated with Y is not $OUT - valid$. Suppose now that $Cl(Y,\mathcal{R}\cup\mathcal{N}) \not\models \bot$ but there exists $p(t) \in X\backslash Y$ s.t $Cl(Y\cup\{p(t)\},\mathcal{R}\cup\mathcal{N}) \not\models \bot$ thus $p_v(t,ctx(p,t)) \in IN(l)$ and we cannot obtain $absurd(ctx(p,t))$. However $p_n(t)$ could only be obtained from $absurd(ctx(p,t))$, $p_n(t) \notin IN(l)$ but since $p(t) \in X\backslash Y$, $p_n(t) \in MBT(l)$ therefore the branch is not MBT-valid.

We now prove the other direction. Let Y be a maximal subset of X such that $Cl(Y,\mathcal{R}\cup\mathcal{N}) \not\models \bot$. Thus $absurd(base) \notin IN(l)$ and $\forall p(t) \in Y$, $p_n(t) \notin IN(l)$. Since $OUT(l) = \{\{p_n(t) \,|\, p(t) \in Y\}\}$ then the branch associated with Y is $OUT - valid$. Y is maximal w. r. t. set inclusion thus $\forall q(u) \in X\backslash Y$ we have $Cl(Y\cup\{q(u)\},\mathcal{R}\cup\mathcal{N}) \models \bot$, thus $absurd(ctx(q,u)) \in IN(l)$, thus $q_n(u) \in IN(l)$ and since $q(u) \in X\backslash Y$ then $q_n(u) \in MBT(l)$ therefore the branch associated with Y is MBT-valid.

We did not discuss yet the effects of the selection and visualization strategies on the results of our program. If we select the atoms with Strategy **SEL1** then X is exactly the set F. If we select the atoms with Strategy **SEL2** then X is exactly the ground closure of F. According to Theorem 3, using Strategy **SEL1** the result of the branch associated with Y is an answer if and only if Y is maximal consistent subset of F while using Strategy **SEL2** the result of the branch associated with Y is an answer if and only if Y is maximal consistent subset of the ground closure of F. When displaying atoms with Strategy **DISP1** the restriction of the answer set associated with a branch Y to the predicates of the original vocabulary is exactly $Cl(Y,\mathcal{R}) \cap F$ while displaying the atoms with Strategy **DISP2** the restriction of the answer set associated with a branch Y to the predicates of the original vocabulary is exactly $Cl(Y,\mathcal{R})$. Let Π be an $\exists$-ASP program obtained from the above encoding. Let AS be an answer set of Π, $\rho(AS)$ denotes the restriction of AS to the original vocabulary $\mathcal{V}$ and $\rho(\Pi) = \{\rho(AS) \,|\, AS \in AS(\Pi)\}$.

Corollary 1. *Let $\mathcal{K} = (\mathcal{F}, \mathcal{R}, \mathcal{N})$ be knowledge base. Let Π_1 be the ∃-ASP program obtained from the above encoding using strategies* **SEL1** *and* **DISP1**. *Then $\rho(\Pi_1)$ is the set of repairs of K. Let Π_5 be the ∃-ASP program obtained from the above encoding using strategies* **SEL1** *and* **DISP2**. *Then $\rho(\Pi_5)$ is the set of closed repairs of K. Let Π_7 be the ∃-ASP program obtained from the above encoding using strategies* **SEL2** *and* **DISP2**. *Then $\rho(\Pi_7)$ is the set of repairs of the closure of K.*

Example 3. The selection strategy **SEL1** allows one to select the predicates in F and provides the set $X = \{p_s(a), q_s(a)\}$. The computation tree develops 4 branches, each one encoding a subset of Y of X. Only two of them are full valid branches. The selection strategy **SEL2** allows one to select the predicates in the grounded closure of F and provides the set $X = \{p_s(a), q_s(a), s_s(a), t_s(a)\}$. The computation tree develops 16 branches, each one encoding a subset of Y of X. Only two of them are full valid branches. The visualization strategy **DISP1** allows one to display valid predicates within the *base* context which belong to F while the visualization strategy **DISP2** allows one to display valid predicates within the *base* context which belong to grounded closure of F. Using strategies **SEL1** and **DISP1** we obtain an ∃-ASP program denoted by Π_1 such that the answer sets restricted to the original vocabulary are $\{p(a)\}$ and $\{q(a)\}$. Note that they correspond to the repairs of $\mathcal{K}$. Using strategies **SEL1** and **DISP2** we obtain an ∃-ASP program denoted by Π_5 s.t the answer sets restricted to the original vocabulary are $\{p(a), t(a)\}$ and $\{q(a), s(a)\}$. Note that they correspond to the closed repairs of $\mathcal{K}$. Using strategies **SEL2** and **DISP1** we obtain an ∃-ASP program denoted by Π_7 s.t the answer sets restricted to the original vocabulary are $\{p(a), s(a), t(a)\}$ and $\{q(a), s(a), t(a)\}$. Note that they correspond to the repairs of the closure of $\mathcal{K}$.

5.4   Other Strategies

We have presented here a generic encoding of a knowledge base $\mathcal{K}$ into an ASP program that computes different kind of repairs of $\mathcal{K}$, according to the different selection rules and display rules we have chosen in that encoding. This generic ASP program could take into account other possible select/display rules to achieve different outcome. For instance, let us consider the following set of rules. **Selection rules**: The user defines all "optional" atoms with rules of form $p_s(\boldsymbol{X}) \leftarrow p_i(\boldsymbol{X}).$, where all atoms of F with predicate name p are optional and $p_s(\boldsymbol{a}) \leftarrow p_i(\boldsymbol{a}).$, where the atom $p(\boldsymbol{a})$ of F is optional and then asserts that every atom of F that is not optional is mandatory. For every predicate name p, there is a rule of form $p_v(\boldsymbol{X}, base) \leftarrow p_i(\boldsymbol{X}), notp_s(\boldsymbol{X})$. **Display rules**: The user can use rules similar to the selection rules to display only optional atoms of F. With such a set of select/display rules, the program Π will admit an answer set only when the subset M of mandatory atoms of F (i.e. those that are not declared optional) is consistent w.r.t. $(\mathcal{R}, \mathcal{N})$, and in that case, if AS is an answer set of Π, $\rho(AS)$ will be an inclusion-maximal subset F' of F such that $M \cup F'$ is consistent w.r.t. $(\mathcal{R}, \mathcal{N})$.

6　Conclusion

This paper presented a generic encoding in $\exists$-ASP of repair-based techniques for inconsistent knowledge bases expressed within the formalism of existential rules. We focused on three kinds of repairs that allow for computing query answering with the following semantics proposed in [2]: $\langle \circ_1, \forall \rangle$ (corresponds to AR-semantics [16]), $\langle \circ_1, \cap \rangle$ (corresponds to IAR-semantics [16]), $\langle \circ_7, \forall \rangle$ (close to CAR-semantics [16]), $\langle \circ_7, \cap \rangle$ (close to ICAR-semantics [16]) and $\langle \circ_5, \cap \rangle$ (corresponds to ICR-semantics [10]). Indeed these semantics can be rephrased in our framework as follows. Let $\mathcal{K}$ be a knowledge base and let q and q_v be first order formulas, where q_v is obtained from q by replacing each predicate $p(t)$ occurring in q by $p_v(t, base)$ we have: (1) $\mathcal{K} \models_{\langle \circ_1, \forall \rangle} q$ iff $\forall AS \in AS(\Pi_1)$, $q_v \in AS$. (2) $\mathcal{K} \models_{\langle \circ_1, \cap \rangle} q$ iff $q_v \in \cap_{AS_i \in AS(\Pi_1)} AS_i$. (3) $\mathcal{K} \models_{\langle \circ_7, \forall \rangle} q$ iff $\forall AS \in AS(\Pi_7)$, $q_v \in AS$. (4): $\mathcal{K} \models_{\langle \circ_7, \cap \rangle} q$ iff $q_v \in \cap_{AS_i \in AS(\Pi_7)} AS_i$. (5): $\mathcal{K} \models_{\langle \circ_5, \cap \rangle} q$ iff $q_v \in \cap_{AS_i \in AS(\Pi_5)} AS_i$.

A future work will be dedicated to the implementation and experimentation of the proposed encoding with $ASPeRiX$ [14]. Another interesting issue is the extension of this encoding to the modifiers proposed within the unified framework for inconsistency-tolerant query answering stemming from the selection modifier based on cardinality.

References

1. Arenas, M., Bertossi, L.E., Chomicki, J.: Consistent query answers in inconsistent databases. In: Proceedings of SIGACT-SIGMOD-SIGART, pp. 68–79 (1999)
2. Baget, J.F., Benferhat, S., Bouraoui, Z., Croitoru, M., Mugnier, M.L., Papini, O., Rocher, S., Tabia, K.: A general modifier-based framework for inconsistency-tolerant query answering. In: Proceedings of KR 2016 (2016)
3. Baget, J., Garreau, F., Mugnier, M., Rocher, S.: Extending acyclicity notions for existential rules. In: Proceedings of ECAI 2014, pp. 39–44 (2014)
4. Baget, J., Garreau, F., Mugnier, M., Rocher, S.: Revisiting chase termination for existential rules and their extension to nonmonotonic negation. In: Proceedings of NMR 2014 (2014)
5. Baget, J., Leclère, M., Mugnier, M., Salvat, E.: On rules with existential variables: walking the decidability line. Artif. Intell. **175**(9–10), 1620–1654 (2011)
6. Baral, C.: Knowledge Representation Reasoning and Declarative Problem Solving. Cambridge University Press, Cambridge (2008)
7. Benferhat, S., Bouraoui, Z., Tabia, K.: How to select one preferred assertional-based repair from inconsistent and prioritized DL-Lite knowledge bases? In: Proceedings of IJCAI 2015, pp. 1450–1456 (2015)
8. Benferhat, S., Dubois, D., Prade, H.: Some syntactic approaches to the handling of inconsistent knowledge bases: a comparative study part 1: the flat case. Stud. Logica **58**(1), 17–45 (1997)
9. Bertossi, L.E.: Database Repairing and Consistent Query Answering. Synthesis Lectures on Data Management. Morgan & Claypool, Los Altos (2011)
10. Bienvenu, M.: On the complexity of consistent query answering in the presence of simple ontologies. In: Proceedings of AAAI 2012 (2012)

11. Bienvenu, M., Bourgaux, C., Goasdoué, F.: Querying inconsistent description logic knowledge bases under preferred repair semantics. In: Proceedings of AAAI 2016 (2016)
12. Bienvenu, M., Rosati, R.: Tractable approximations of consistent query answering for robust ontology-based data access. In: Proceedings of IJCAI 2013 (2013)
13. Garreau, F., Garcia, L., Lefèvre, C., Stéphan, I.: ∃-asp. In: Proceedings of JOWO 2015 (2015)
14. Lefèvre, C., Béatrix, C., Stéphan, I., Garcia, L.: ASPeRIX, a first order forward chaining approach for answer set computing. CoRR (2015, to appear in TPLP). arXiv:1503.07717
15. Lefèvre, C., Nicolas, P.: A first order forward chaining approach for answer set computing. In: Erdem, E., Lin, F., Schaub, T. (eds.) LPNMR 2009. LNCS, vol. 5753, pp. 196–208. Springer, Heidelberg (2009)
16. Lembo, D., Lenzerini, M., Rosati, R., Ruzzi, M., Savo, D.F.: Inconsistency-tolerant query answering in ontology-based data access. J. Web Sem. **33**, 3–29 (2015)
17. Lukasiewicz, T., Martinez, M.V., Pieris, A., Simari, G.I.: From classical to consistent query answering under existential rules. In: Proceedings of AAAI 2015, pp. 1546–1552 (2015)
18. Lukasiewicz, T., Martinez, M.V., Simari, G.I.: Inconsistency handling in datalog+/- ontologies. In: Proceedings of ECAI 2012, pp. 558–563 (2012)
19. Rosati, R.: On the complexity of dealing with inconsistency in description logic ontologies. In: Proceedings of the 22nd International Joint Conference on Artificial Intelligence IJCAI 2011, pp. 1057–1062 (2011)
20. Wan, H., Zhang, H., Xiao, P., Huang, H., Zhang, Y.: Query answering with inconsistent existential rules under stable model semantics. In: Proceedings of AAAI 2016 (2016)

Probabilistic Reasoning in the Description Logic $\mathcal{ALCP}$ with the Principle of Maximum Entropy

Rafael Peñaloza[1(✉)] and Nico Potyka[2]

[1] Free University of Bozen-Bolzano, Bolzano, Italy
rafael.penaloza@unibz.it
[2] University of Osnabrück, Osnabrück, Germany
npotyka@uni-osnabrueck.de

Abstract. A central question for knowledge representation is how to encode and handle uncertain knowledge adequately. We introduce the probabilistic description logic $\mathcal{ALCP}$ that is designed for representing context-dependent knowledge, where the actual context taking place is uncertain. $\mathcal{ALCP}$ allows the expression of logical dependencies on the domain and probabilistic dependencies on the possible contexts. In order to draw probabilistic conclusions, we employ the principle of maximum entropy. We provide reasoning algorithms for this logic, and show that it satisfies several desirable properties of probabilistic logics.

1 Introduction

A fundamental element of any intelligent application is storing and manipulating the knowledge from the application domain. Logic-based knowledge representation languages such as description logics (DLs) [1] provide a clear syntax and unambiguous semantics that guarantee the correctness of the results obtained. However, languages based on classical logic are ill-suited for handling the uncertainty inherent to many application domains. To overcome this limitation, various probabilistic logics have been investigated during the last three decades (e.g., [3,15,20]). In particular, several probabilistic DLs have been developed [18,19]. To handle probabilistic knowledge, many approaches require a complete definition of joint probability distributions (JPD) [5,6,8,16,26]. One approach to avoid a full JPD specification was proposed by Paris [22]: the user gives a partial specification through a set of probabilistic constraints and the partial knowledge is completed by means of the principle of maximum entropy.

In this paper we consider a new probabilistic extension of description logics based on the principle of maximum entropy. In our approach we group different axioms from a knowledge base together into so-called contexts, which are identified by a propositional formula. Intuitively, each context corresponds to a possible situation, in which the associated sub-KB is guaranteed to hold. Uncertainty is associated to the contexts through a set of probabilistic constraints, which are interpreted under the principle of maximum entropy.

To facilitate the understanding of our approach, we focus on the DL $\mathcal{ALC}$ [27] as a prototypical example of a knowledge representation language, and propositional probabilistic constraints as the framework for expressing uncertainty.

© Springer International Publishing Switzerland 2016
S. Schockaert and P. Senellart (Eds.): SUM 2016, LNAI 9858, pp. 246–259, 2016.
DOI: 10.1007/978-3-319-45856-4_17

As reasoning service we consider subsumption relations between concepts given some partial knowledge of the current context. Since the knowledge in a knowledge base is typically incomplete, one cannot expect to obtain a precise probability for a given consequence. Instead, we compute a belief interval that describes all the probability degrees that can be associated to the consequence without contradiction. The lowest bound of the interval corresponds to a sceptical view, considering only the most fundamental models of the knowledge base. The upper bound, in contrast, reflects the credulous belief in which every context that is not explicitly removed is considered. In the worst-case, we get the trivial interval $[0, 1]$, in the best case, we get a point probability where the upper and lower bounds coincide. In some applications, it might be reasonable to consider only one of these bounds. For instance, if the probability interval that a treatment will cause heavy complications is $[0.01, 0.05]$, we might want to use the upper bound 0.05. In contrast, when the probability interval that a treatment will be successful is $[0.7, 0.9]$, we might be more interested in the lower bound 0.7.

The main contributions of this paper are the following:

- we define the new probabilistic description logic $\mathcal{ALCP}$ that allows for a flexible description of axiomatic dependencies, and its reasoning problems (Sect. 3);
- we explain in detail how degrees of belief for the subsumption problem can be computed (Sect. 4); and
- we show that $\mathcal{ALCP}$ satisfies several desirable properties of probabilistic logics (Sect. 5).[1]

2   Maximum Entropy

We start by recalling the basic notions of probabilistic propositional logic and the principle of maximum entropy.

Let $\mathcal{L}$ be a propositional language constructed over a finite signature $\mathsf{sig}(\mathcal{L})$, i.e., a set of propositional variables, in the usual way. An $\mathcal{L}$-interpretation v is a truth assignment of the propositional variables in $\mathsf{sig}(\mathcal{L})$. $Int(\mathcal{L})$ denotes the set of all $\mathcal{L}$-interpretations. Satisfaction of a formula $\phi \in \mathcal{L}$ by an $\mathcal{L}$-interpretation $v \in Int(\mathcal{L})$ (denoted $v \models \phi$) is defined as usual. A probability distribution over $\mathcal{L}$ is a function $P : Int(\mathcal{L}) \to [0, 1]$ where $\sum_{v \in Int(\mathcal{L})} P(v) = 1$. Probability distributions are extended to arbitrary $\mathcal{L}$-formulas ϕ by setting $P(\phi) = \sum_{v \models \phi} P(v)$.

Definition 1 (Probabilistic Constraints, Models). *Given the propositional language $\mathcal{L}$, a* probabilistic constraint *(over $\mathcal{L}$) is an expression of the form*

$$c_0 + \sum_{i=1}^{k} c_i \cdot \mathsf{p}(\phi_i) \geq 0 \tag{1}$$

where $c_0, c_i \in \mathbb{R}$, and $\phi_i \in \mathcal{L}$, $1 \leq i \leq k$. A probability distribution P over $\mathcal{L}$ is a model *of the probabilistic constraint $c_0 + \sum_{i=1}^{k} c_i \cdot \mathsf{p}(\phi_i) \geq 0$ if and only if*

---

[1] The full proofs are available at the technical report [23].

$c_0 + \sum_{i=1}^{k} c_i \cdot P(\phi_i) \geq 0$. *The distribution P is a model of the set of probabilistic constraints $\mathcal{R}$ ($P \models \mathcal{R}$) off it satisfies all the constraints in $\mathcal{R}$. The set of all models of $\mathcal{R}$ is denoted by $Mod(\mathcal{R})$. If $Mod(\mathcal{R}) \neq \emptyset$, we say that $\mathcal{R}$ is consistent.*

Our probabilistic constraints can express the most common types of constraints considered in the literature of probabilistic logics. For instance, probabilistic conditionals $(\psi \mid \phi)[\ell, u]$ are satisfied iff $\ell \cdot P(\phi) \leq P(\psi \wedge \phi) \leq u \cdot P(\phi)$ [17]. That is, the conditional is satisfied iff the conditional probability of ψ given ϕ is between ℓ and u whenever $P(\phi) > 0$. Sometimes $P(\phi) > 0$ is demanded, but strict inequalities are computationally difficult and the semantical differences are negligible in many cases, see [25] for a thorough discussion. These conditions can be expressed in the form (1) as follows

$$\mathsf{p}(\psi \wedge \phi) - \ell \cdot \mathsf{p}(\phi) \geq 0, \qquad and$$
$$u \cdot \mathsf{p}(\phi) - \mathsf{p}(\psi \wedge \phi) \geq 0.$$

Probabilistic constraints can also express more complex restrictions; for example, we can state that the probability that a bird cannot fly is at most one fourth of the probability that a bird flies through the constraint

$$\frac{1}{4}\mathsf{p}(\textsc{bird} \wedge \textsc{flies}) - \mathsf{p}(\textsc{bird} \wedge \neg\textsc{flies}) \geq 0. \tag{2}$$

To improve readability, we will often rewrite constraints in a more compact manner, using conditionals as in the first example, or e.g. rewriting (2) as $\frac{1}{4}\mathsf{p}(\textsc{bird} \wedge \textsc{flies}) \geq \mathsf{p}(\textsc{bird} \wedge \neg\textsc{flies})$.

In general, consistent sets of probabilistic constraints have infinitely many models, and there is no obvious way to distinguish between them. One well-studied approach for dealing with this diversity is to focus on the model that maximizes the entropy

$$H(P) = - \sum_{v \in Int(\mathcal{L})} P(v) \cdot \log P(v).$$

From an information-theoretic point of view, the maximum entropy (ME) distribution can be regarded as the most conservative one in the sense that it minimizes the information-theoretic distance (that is, the KL-divergence) to the uniform distribution among all probability distributions that satisfy our constraints. In particular, if there are no restrictions on the probability distributions considered, then the uniform distribution is the ME distribution, see, e.g., [28] for a more detailed discussion of these issues. A complete characterization of maximum entropy for the purpose of uncertain reasoning can be found in [22].

Definition 2 (ME-Model). *Let $\mathcal{R}$ be a consistent set of probabilistic constraints. The ME-model $P_{\mathcal{R}}^{ME}$ of $\mathcal{R}$ is the unique solution of the maximization problem $\arg\max_{P \models \mathcal{R}} H(P)$.*

Existence and uniqueness of $P_{\mathcal{R}}^{ME}$ follows from the fact that H is strictly concave and continuous, and that the probability distributions that satisfy $\mathcal{R}$ form a compact and convex set. $P_{\mathcal{R}}^{ME}$ is usually computed by deriving an unconstrained optimization problem by means of the Karush-Kuhn-Tucker conditions. The resulting problem can be solved, for instance, by (quasi-)Newton methods with cost $|Int(\mathcal{L})|^3$, see, e.g., [21] for more details on these techniques.

3 The Probabilistic Description Logic $\mathcal{ALCP}$

$\mathcal{ALCP}$ is a probabilistic extension of the classical description logic $\mathcal{ALC}$ capable of expressing complex logical and probabilistic relations. As with classical DLs, the main building blocks in $\mathcal{ALCP}$ are *concepts*. Syntactically, $\mathcal{ALCP}$ concepts are constructed exactly as $\mathcal{ALC}$ concepts. Given two disjoint sets $\mathsf{N_C}$ of *concept names* and $\mathsf{N_R}$ of *role names*, $\mathcal{ALCP}$ concepts are built using the grammar rule $C ::= A \mid \neg C \mid C \sqcap C \mid \exists r.C$, where $A \in \mathsf{N_C}$ and $r \in \mathsf{N_R}$. Note that we can derive disjunction, universal quantification and subsumption from these rules by using logical equivalences like $C_1 \sqcup C_2 \equiv \neg(\neg C_1 \sqcap \neg C_2)$. The knowledge of the application domain is expressed through a finite set of axioms that restrict the way the different concepts and roles may be interpreted. To express both probabilistic and logical relationships, each axiom is annotated with a formula from $\mathcal{L}$ that intuitively expresses the context in which this axiom holds.

Definition 3 (KB). *An $\mathcal{L}$-restricted general concept inclusion ($\mathcal{L}$-GCI) is of the form $\langle C \sqsubseteq D : \kappa \rangle$ where C, D are $\mathcal{ALCP}$ concepts and κ is an $\mathcal{L}$-formula. An $\mathcal{L}$-TBox is a finite set of $\mathcal{L}$-GCIs. An $\mathcal{ALCP}$ knowledge base (KB) over $\mathcal{L}$ is a pair $\mathcal{K} = (\mathcal{R}, \mathcal{T})$ where $\mathcal{R}$ is a set of probabilistic constraints and $\mathcal{T}$ is an $\mathcal{L}$-TBox.*

Example 4. Consider an application modeling beliefs about bacterial and viral infections using the concept names strep (streptococcal infection), bac (bacterial infection), vir (viral infection), inf (infection), and ab (antibiotic); and the role names sf (suffers from), and suc (successful treatment); and the propositional variables RES (antibiotic resistance), and H (heavy use of antibiotics by patient). Define the $\mathcal{L}$-TBox $\mathcal{T}_{\mathsf{exa}}$ containing the $\mathcal{L}$-GCIs

$$\langle \exists \mathsf{sf.bac} \sqsubseteq \exists \mathsf{suc.ab} : \neg\mathrm{RES} \wedge \neg\mathrm{H} \rangle, \quad \langle \exists \mathsf{sf.vir} \sqsubseteq \neg\exists \mathsf{suc.ab} : \top \rangle, \quad \langle \mathsf{strep} \sqsubseteq \mathsf{bac} : \top \rangle,$$
$$\langle \exists \mathsf{sf.bac} \sqsubseteq \neg\exists \mathsf{suc.ab} : \mathrm{RES} \rangle, \qquad\qquad\qquad \langle \mathsf{bac} \sqsubseteq \mathsf{inf} : \top \rangle, \quad \langle \mathsf{vir} \sqsubseteq \mathsf{inf} : \top \rangle,$$

where $\top$ is any $\mathcal{L}$-tautology. For example, the first $\mathcal{L}$-GCI states that a bacterial infection can be treated successfully with antibiotics if no antibiotic resistance is present and there was no heavy use of antibiotics; the second one states that viral infections can never be treated with antibiotics successfully. Consider additionally the set $\mathcal{R}$ containing the probabilistic constraints containing

$$(\mathrm{RES})[0.05], \qquad\qquad (\mathrm{RES} \mid \mathrm{H})[0.8].$$

That is, the probability of an antibiotic resistance is 5 % if no further information is given. If the patient used antibiotics heavily, the probability increases to 80 %.

Notice that the probabilistic constraints, and hence the representation of the uncertainty in the knowledge, refer only to the propositional formulas that label the $\mathcal{L}$-GCIs. In $\mathcal{ALCP}$, the uncertainty of the knowledge is handled through these propositional formulas as explained next.

A possible world interprets both the axiom language (i.e., the concept and role names) and the context language (the propositional variables). Intuitively, it describes a possible context ($\mathcal{L}$-interpretation) together with the relationships between concepts in that situation ($\mathcal{ALC}$-interpretation).

Definition 5 (Possible World). *A possible world is a triple* $\mathcal{I} = (\Delta^{\mathcal{I}}, \cdot^{\mathcal{I}}, v^{\mathcal{I}})$ *where* $\Delta^{\mathcal{I}}$ *is a non-empty set (called the* domain*),* $v^{\mathcal{I}}$ *is an* $\mathcal{L}$-*interpretation, and* $\cdot^{\mathcal{I}}$ *is an interpretation function that maps every concept name* A *to a set* $A^{\mathcal{I}} \subseteq \Delta^{\mathcal{I}}$ *and every role name* r *to a binary relation* $r^{\mathcal{I}} \subseteq \Delta^{\mathcal{I}} \times \Delta^{\mathcal{I}}$.

The interpretation function $\cdot^{\mathcal{I}}$ is extended to complex concepts as usual in DLs by letting $(\neg C)^{\mathcal{I}} := \Delta^{\mathcal{I}} \setminus C^{\mathcal{I}}$; $(\exists r.C)^{\mathcal{I}} := \{d \in \Delta^{\mathcal{I}} \mid \exists e \in \Delta^{\mathcal{I}}.(d, e) \in r^{\mathcal{I}}, e \in C^{\mathcal{I}}\}$; and $(C \sqcap D)^{\mathcal{I}} := C^{\mathcal{I}} \cap D^{\mathcal{I}}$. A possible world is a model of an $\mathcal{L}$-GCI iff it satisfies the description logic constraint of the axiom whenever it satisfies the context.

Definition 6 (Model of TBox). *A possible world* $\mathcal{I} = (\Delta^{\mathcal{I}}, \cdot^{\mathcal{I}}, v^{\mathcal{I}})$ *is a model of the* $\mathcal{L}$-GCI $\langle C \sqsubseteq D : \kappa \rangle$ $(\mathcal{I} \models \langle C \sqsubseteq D : \kappa \rangle)$ *iff (i)* $v^{\mathcal{I}} \not\models \kappa$, *or (ii)* $C^{\mathcal{I}} \subseteq D^{\mathcal{I}}$. *It is a model of the* $\mathcal{L}$-*TBox* $\mathcal{T}$ *iff it is a model of all* $\mathcal{L}$-GCIs in $\mathcal{T}$.

The classical DL $\mathcal{ALC}$ is a special case of $\mathcal{ALCP}$ where all the axioms are annotated with an $\mathcal{L}$-tautology $\top$. To preserve the syntax of classical DLs, we denote such $\mathcal{L}$-GCIs as $C \sqsubseteq D$ instead of $\langle C \sqsubseteq D : \top \rangle$. In this case, the condition (i) from Definition 6 cannot be satisfied, and hence a model is required to satisfy $C^{\mathcal{I}} \subseteq D^{\mathcal{I}}$ for all $\mathcal{L}$-GCIs $C \sqsubseteq D$ in the TBox. For a deeper introduction to classical $\mathcal{ALC}$, see [1].

According to our semantics, we only demand that the $\mathcal{L}$-GCIs are satisfied in some specific contexts. Thus, it is often useful to focus on the classical $\mathcal{ALC}$ TBox that contains the knowledge that holds in a particular situation. For a KB $\mathcal{K} = (\mathcal{R}, \mathcal{T})$ and $v \in Int(\mathcal{L})$, the v-*restricted TBox* is the $\mathcal{ALC}$ TBox

$$\mathcal{T}_v := \{C \sqsubseteq D \mid \langle C \sqsubseteq D : \kappa \rangle \in \mathcal{T}, v \models \kappa\}.$$

The possible world $\mathcal{I}$ satisfies $\mathcal{T}_v$ ($\mathcal{I} \models \mathcal{T}_v$) if for all $\mathcal{L}$-GCIs $C \sqsubseteq D \in \mathcal{T}_v$ it holds that $C^{\mathcal{I}} \subseteq D^{\mathcal{I}}$. In the following, we will often consider *subsumption* and *strong non-subsumption* between concepts w.r.t. a restricted TBox. We say that C is *subsumed* by D w.r.t. $\mathcal{T}_v$ ($\mathcal{T}_v \models C \sqsubseteq D$) if for every $\mathcal{I} \models \mathcal{T}_v$ it holds that $C^{\mathcal{I}} \subseteq D^{\mathcal{I}}$. Dually, C is *strongly non-subsumed* by D w.r.t. $\mathcal{T}_v$ ($\mathcal{T}_v \models C \not\sqsubseteq D$) if for every $\mathcal{I} \models \mathcal{T}_v$, $C^{\mathcal{I}} \not\subseteq D^{\mathcal{I}}$ holds. Notice that strong non-subsumption requires that the inclusion between axioms does not hold in *any* possible world satisfying $\mathcal{T}_v$. Hence, this condition is more strict than just negating the subsumption relation.

We now describe how the probabilistic constraints are handled in our logic. An $\mathcal{ALCP}$-interpretation consists of a finite set of possible worlds and a probability function over these worlds.

Definition 7 ($\mathcal{ALCP}$-Interpretation). *An $\mathcal{ALCP}$-interpretation is a pair of the form $\mathcal{P} = (\mathfrak{I}, P_{\mathfrak{I}})$, where $\mathfrak{I}$ is a non-empty, finite set of possible worlds and $P_{\mathfrak{I}}$ is a probability distribution over $\mathfrak{I}$.*

Each $\mathcal{ALCP}$-interpretation induces a probability distribution over $\mathcal{L}$. The probability of a context can be obtained by adding the probabilities of all possible worlds in which this context holds.

Definition 8 (Distribution Induced by $\mathcal{P}$). *Let $\mathcal{P} = (\mathfrak{I}, P_{\mathfrak{I}})$ be an $\mathcal{ALCP}$-interpretation. The probability distribution $P^{\mathcal{P}} : Int(\mathcal{L}) \to [0,1]$ induced by $\mathcal{P}$ is defined by $P^{\mathcal{P}}(v) := \sum_{\mathcal{I} \in \mathfrak{I}|_v} P_{\mathfrak{I}}(\mathcal{I})$, where $\mathfrak{I}|_v = \{(\Delta^{\mathcal{I}}, \cdot^{\mathcal{I}}, v^{\mathcal{I}}) \in \mathfrak{I} \mid v^{\mathcal{I}} = v\}$.*

As usual, reasoning is restricted to interpretations that satisfy the restrictions imposed by the knowledge base. In our case, we have to demand that the interpretation is consistent with both the classical and the probabilistic part of our knowledge base. That is, we consider only those possible worlds that satisfy both the terminological knowledge ($\mathcal{T}$) and the probabilistic constraints ($\mathcal{R}$).

Definition 9 (Model). *Let $\mathcal{P} = (\mathfrak{I}, P_{\mathfrak{I}})$ be an $\mathcal{ALCP}$-interpretation. $\mathcal{P}$ is consistent with the TBox $\mathcal{T}$ if every $\mathcal{I} \in \mathfrak{I}$ is a model of $\mathcal{T}$. $\mathcal{P}$ is consistent with the set of probabilistic constraints $\mathcal{R}$ iff $P^{\mathcal{P}} \models \mathcal{R}$. The $\mathcal{ALCP}$-interpretation $\mathcal{P}$ is a model of the KB $\mathcal{K} = (\mathcal{R}, \mathcal{T})$ iff it is consistent with both $\mathcal{T}$ and $\mathcal{R}$. As usual, a KB is consistent iff it has a model.*

Notice that $\mathcal{ALCP}$-KBs can express both, logical and probabilistic dependencies between axioms. For instance, two $\mathcal{L}$-GCIs $\langle C_1 \sqsubseteq D_1 : \kappa_1 \rangle$ and $\langle C_2 \sqsubseteq D_2 : \kappa_2 \rangle$ where $\kappa_1 \Rightarrow \kappa_2$ express that whenever the first $\mathcal{L}$-GCI is satisfied, the second one must also hold. Similarly, the probabilistic dependencies between axioms are expressed via the probabilistic constraints of the labeling formulas.

We are interested in computing degrees of belief for subsumption relations between concepts. We define the conditional probability of a subsumption relation given a context with respect to a given $\mathcal{ALCP}$-interpretation following the usual notions of conditioning.

Definition 10 (Probability of Subsumption). *Let C, D be concepts, κ a context and $\mathcal{P}$ an $\mathcal{ALCP}$-interpretation. The conditional probability of $C \sqsubseteq D$ given κ with respect to $\mathcal{P}$ is*

$$Pr_{\mathcal{P}}(C \sqsubseteq D \mid \kappa) := \frac{\sum_{\mathcal{I} \in \mathfrak{I}, \mathcal{I} \models \kappa, \mathcal{I} \models C \sqsubseteq D} P_{\mathfrak{I}}(\mathcal{I})}{\sum_{\mathcal{I} \in \mathfrak{I}, \mathcal{I} \models \kappa} P_{\mathfrak{I}}(\mathcal{I})}. \tag{3}$$

Notice that the denominator in (3) can be rewritten as

$$\sum_{\mathcal{I} \in \mathfrak{I}, \mathcal{I} \models \kappa} P_{\mathfrak{I}}(\mathcal{I}) = \sum_{v \models \kappa} \sum_{\mathcal{I} \in \mathfrak{I}|_v} P_{\mathfrak{I}}(\mathcal{I}) = \sum_{v \models \kappa} P^{\mathcal{P}}(v) = P^{\mathcal{P}}(\kappa).$$

As usual, the conditional probability is only well-defined when $P^{\mathcal{P}}(\kappa) > 0$.

Recall that the set of probabilistic constraints $\mathcal{R}$ may be satisfied by an infinite class of probability distributions. In the spirit of maximum entropy reasoning, we consider only the most conservative ones in the sense that they induce the ME-model $P_{\mathcal{R}}^{ME}$ of $\mathcal{R}$.

Definition 11 (ME-$\mathcal{ALCP}$-Model). *An $\mathcal{ALCP}$-model $\mathcal{P}$ of $\mathcal{K}$ is called an ME-$\mathcal{ALCP}$-model of $\mathcal{K}$ iff $P^{\mathcal{P}} = P^{ME}_{\mathcal{R}}$. The set of all ME-$\mathcal{ALCP}$-models of $\mathcal{K}$ is denoted by $Mod_{ME}(\mathcal{K})$. $\mathcal{K}$ is called* ME-consistent *iff $Mod_{ME}(\mathcal{K}) \neq \emptyset$.*

Note that ME-consistency is a strictly stronger notion of consistency. ME-consistent knowledge bases are always consistent, but the converse does not necessarily hold if the classical TBox obtained from $\mathcal{T}$ by restricting to a context is inconsistent as we show in the following example.

Example 12. Let $\mathsf{sig}(\mathcal{L}) = \{x\}$ and $\mathcal{K} = (\mathcal{R}, \mathcal{T})$ be the KB with $\mathcal{R} = \emptyset$ and $\mathcal{T} = \{\langle A \sqcup \neg A \sqsubseteq A \sqcap \neg A : x \rangle\}$. Since $A \sqcup \neg A \sqsubseteq A \sqcap \neg A$ is contradictorial, each $\mathcal{ALCP}$-model of $\mathcal{K}$ must satisfy $\neg x$. There certainly are such models, but in each such model $\mathcal{P}$, $P^{\mathcal{P}}(x) = 0$. However, since $\mathcal{R} = \emptyset$, we have $P^{ME}_{\mathcal{R}}(x) = 0.5$ and hence $\mathcal{K}$ has no ME-model.

ME-inconsistency rules out some undesired cases in which the whole knowledge base is consistent, but the TBox restricted to some context is inconsistent. The following theorem gives a simple characterization of ME-consistency: to verify ME-consistency of a KB, it suffices to check consistency of the TBoxes induced by the $\mathcal{L}$-interpretations that have positive probability with respect to $P^{ME}_{\mathcal{R}}$. By the properties of the ME distribution, these are the interpretations that are not explicitly restricted to have zero probability through $\mathcal{R}$.

Theorem 13. *The KB $\mathcal{K} = (\mathcal{R}, \mathcal{T})$ is ME-consistent iff for every $v \in Int(\mathcal{L})$ such that $P^{ME}_{\mathcal{R}}(v) > 0$, $\mathcal{T}_v$ is consistent.*

For the rest of this paper we consider only ME-consistent KBs. Hence, whenever we speak of a KB $\mathcal{K}$, we implicitly assume that $\mathcal{K}$ has at least one ME-model.

We are interested in computing the probability of a subsumption relation w.r.t. a given KB $\mathcal{K}$. Notice that, although we consider only one probability distribution $P^{ME}_{\mathcal{R}}$, there can still exist many different ME-models of $\mathcal{K}$, which yield different probabilities for the same subsumption relation. One way to handle this is to consider the smallest and largest probabilities that can be consistently associated to this relation. We call them the *sceptical* and the *creduluos* degrees of belief, respectively.

Definition 14 (Degree of Belief). *Let C, D be $\mathcal{ALCP}$ concepts, κ a context, and $\mathcal{K} = (\mathcal{R}, \mathcal{T})$ an $\mathcal{ALCP}$ KB. The* sceptical degree of belief *of $C \sqsubseteq D$ given κ w.r.t. $\mathcal{K}$ is*

$$\mathcal{B}^s_{\mathcal{K}}(C \sqsubseteq D \mid \kappa) := \inf_{\mathcal{P} \in Mod_{ME}(\mathcal{K})} Pr_{\mathcal{P}}(C \sqsubseteq D \mid \kappa).$$

The credulous degree of belief *of $C \sqsubseteq D$ given κ w.r.t. $\mathcal{K}$ is*

$$\mathcal{B}^c_{\mathcal{K}}(C \sqsubseteq D \mid \kappa) := \sup_{\mathcal{P} \in Mod_{ME}(\mathcal{K})} Pr_{\mathcal{P}}(C \sqsubseteq D \mid \kappa).$$

Example 15. Consider $\mathcal{K}_{\mathsf{exa}}$ from Example 4. If we ask for the degrees of belief that a patient who suffers from an infection can be successfully treated with antibiotics, we obtain

$$\mathcal{B}^{s}_{\mathcal{K}_{exa}}(\exists sf.inf \sqsubseteq \exists suc.ab \mid \top) = 0,$$
$$\mathcal{B}^{c}_{\mathcal{K}_{exa}}(\exists sf.inf \sqsubseteq \exists suc.ab \mid \top) = 1.$$

These bounds are not very informative, but they are perfectly justified by our knowledge base since we do not know anything about the effectiveness of antibiotics with respect to infections in general. However, for a patient who suffers from a streptococcal infection we get

$$\mathcal{B}^{s}_{\mathcal{K}_{exa}}(\exists sf.strep \sqsubseteq \exists suc.ab \mid \top) = 0.9405,$$
$$\mathcal{B}^{c}_{\mathcal{K}_{exa}}(\exists sf.strep \sqsubseteq \exists suc.ab \mid \top) = 0.95.$$

If we know that this patient used antibiotics heavily in the past, then there is nothing in our knowledge base that guarantees the existence of a successful treatment. Hence, the degrees of belief become

$$\mathcal{B}^{s}_{\mathcal{K}_{exa}}(\exists sf.strep \sqsubseteq \exists suc.ab \mid \text{H}) = 0$$
$$\mathcal{B}^{c}_{\mathcal{K}_{exa}}(\exists sf.strep \sqsubseteq \exists suc.ab \mid \text{H}) = 0.2.$$

Our definition of the sceptical degree of belief raises a philosophical question: should there be no difference between the degree of belief 0 and an infinitely small degree of belief? A dual question arises for the credulous degree of belief and the probability 1. However, as we show in the next section, the sceptical and credulous degrees of belief actually correspond to minimum and maximum rather than to infimum and supremum (see Corollary 20) so that these questions become vacuous. From the following theorem we can conclude that every intermediate degree can also be obtained by some model of the KB.

Theorem 16 (Intermediate Value Theorem). *Let $p_1 < p_2$ and $\mathcal{P}_1$ and $\mathcal{P}_2$ be two ME-$\mathcal{ALCP}$-models of the KB $\mathcal{K} = (\mathcal{R}, \mathcal{T})$ such that $Pr_{\mathcal{P}_1}(C \sqsubseteq D \mid \kappa) = p_1$ and $Pr_{\mathcal{P}_2}(C \sqsubseteq D \mid \kappa) = p_2$. Then for each p between p_1 and p_2 there exists an ME-$\mathcal{ALCP}$-model $\mathcal{P}$ of $\mathcal{K}$ such that $Pr_{\mathcal{P}}(C \sqsubseteq D \mid \kappa) = p$*

As we will show in Corollary 20, both the sceptical degree $\mathcal{B}^{s}_{\mathcal{K}}(C \sqsubseteq D \mid \kappa)$ and the credulous degree $\mathcal{B}^{c}_{\mathcal{K}}(C \sqsubseteq D \mid \kappa)$ are in fact witnessed by some ME-models. Therefore it is meaningful to consider the whole interval of beliefs between $\mathcal{B}^{s}_{\mathcal{K}}(C \sqsubseteq D \mid \kappa)$ and $\mathcal{B}^{c}_{\mathcal{K}}(C \sqsubseteq D \mid \kappa)$.

Definition 17 (Belief Interval). *Let C, D be $\mathcal{ALCP}$ concepts, $\kappa \in \mathcal{L}$ a context and $\mathcal{K} = (\mathcal{R}, \mathcal{T})$ a $\mathcal{ALCP}$ KB. The* belief interval *for $C \sqsubseteq D$ w.r.t. $\mathcal{K}$ given κ is*

$$\mathcal{B}_{\mathcal{K}}(C \sqsubseteq D \mid \kappa) := [\mathcal{B}^{s}_{\mathcal{K}}(C \sqsubseteq D \mid \kappa), \mathcal{B}^{c}_{\mathcal{K}}(C \sqsubseteq D \mid \kappa)].$$

4   Computing Beliefs

In this section we show how to compute the belief interval. The first theorem states that the sceptical degreef of belief for a subsumption relation can be computed by adding the probabilities of those $\mathcal{L}$-interpretations w that entail this subsumption in the corresponding restricted TBox $\mathcal{T}_w$.

Theorem 18. *Let $\mathcal{K} = (\mathcal{R}, \mathcal{T})$ be a KB, C, D two concepts, and κ a context such that $P_{\mathcal{R}}^{ME}(\kappa) > 0$. Then*

$$\mathcal{B}_{\mathcal{K}}^{s}(C \sqsubseteq D \mid \kappa) = \frac{\sum_{w \in Int(\mathcal{L}), \mathcal{T}_w \models C \sqsubseteq D, w \models \kappa} P_{\mathcal{R}}^{ME}(w)}{P_{\mathcal{R}}^{ME}(\kappa)}.$$

Dually, the credulous degree of belief for a subsumption relation can be computed by removing all the situations in which this relation cannot possibly hold.

Theorem 19. *Let $\mathcal{K} = (\mathcal{R}, \mathcal{T})$ be a KB, C, D two concepts, and κ a context with $P_{\mathcal{R}}^{ME}(\kappa) > 0$. Then*

$$\mathcal{B}_{\mathcal{K}}^{c}(C \sqsubseteq D \mid \kappa) = 1 - \frac{\sum_{w \in Int(\mathcal{L}), \mathcal{T}_w \models C \not\sqsubseteq D, w \models \kappa} P_{\mathcal{R}}^{ME}(w)}{P_{\mathcal{R}}^{ME}(\kappa)}.$$

To prove these theorems, one can build two models of the KB $\mathcal{K}$, $\mathcal{P}$ and $\mathcal{Q}$ such that $Pr_{\mathcal{P}}(C \sqsubseteq D \mid \kappa)$ and $Pr_{\mathcal{Q}}(C \sqsubseteq D \mid \kappa)$ are those degrees expressed by Theorems 18 and 19, respectively. As a byproduct of these proofs, we obtain that the infimum and supremum that define the sceptical and the credulous degrees of belief actually correspond to minimum and maximum taken by some ME-models, yielding the following corollary.

Corollary 20. *Let $\mathcal{K}$ be an $\mathcal{ALCP}$ KB, C, D be two concepts, and κ be a context. There exist two ME-models $\mathcal{P}, \mathcal{Q}$ of $\mathcal{K}$ with $\mathcal{B}_{\mathcal{K}}^{s}(C \sqsubseteq D \mid \kappa) = Pr_{\mathcal{P}}(C \sqsubseteq D \mid \kappa)$ and $\mathcal{B}_{\mathcal{K}}^{c}(C \sqsubseteq D \mid \kappa) = Pr_{\mathcal{Q}}(C \sqsubseteq D \mid \kappa)$.*

The direct consequence of Theorems 18 and 19 is that if we want to compute the belief interval for $C \sqsubseteq D$ given some context, it suffices to identify all $\mathcal{L}$-interpretations whose induced (classical) TBoxes entail the subsumption relation $C \sqsubseteq D$ (for the sceptical belief) or the strong non-subsumption $C \not\sqsubseteq D$ (for credulous belief). Recall that every set of propositional interpretations can be represented by a propositional formula. This motivates the following definition.

Definition 21 (Consequence Formula). *An $\mathcal{L}$-formula ϕ is a consequence formula for $C \sqsubseteq D$ (respectively $C \not\sqsubseteq D$) w.r.t. the $\mathcal{L}$-TBox $\mathcal{T}$ if for every $w \in Int(\mathcal{L})$ it holds that $w \models \phi$ iff $\mathcal{T}_w \models C \sqsubseteq D$ (respectively $\mathcal{T}_w \models C \not\sqsubseteq D$).*

If we are able to compute these consequence formulas, then the computation of the belief interval can be reduced to the evaluation of the probability of these formulas w.r.t. the ME-distribution satisfying $\mathcal{R}$.

Theorem 22. *Let $\mathcal{K} = (\mathcal{R}, \mathcal{T})$ be an $\mathcal{ALCP}$ KB, ϕ and ψ be consequence formulas for $C \sqsubseteq D$ and $C \not\sqsubseteq D$ w.r.t. $\mathcal{T}$, respectively, and κ a context. Then $\mathcal{B}_{\mathcal{K}}^{s}(C \sqsubseteq D \mid \kappa) = P_{\mathcal{R}}^{ME}(\phi \mid \kappa)$ and $\mathcal{B}_{\mathcal{K}}^{c}(C \sqsubseteq D \mid \kappa) = 1 - P_{\mathcal{R}}^{ME}(\psi \mid \kappa)$.*

Example 23. In our running example, one can see that a consequence formula for $\exists sf.strep \sqsubseteq \exists suc.ab$ is $\neg RES \wedge \neg H$. Indeed, in order to deduce this consequence it is necessary to satisfy the first axiom of $\mathcal{T}_{exa}$, which is only guaranteed in the

---

Algorithm 1. Computing degrees of belief

Input: KB $\mathcal{K} = (\mathcal{R}, \mathcal{T})$, concepts C, D, context κ
Output: Belief degrees $\left(\mathcal{B}^s_{\mathcal{K}}(C \sqsubseteq D | \kappa), \mathcal{B}^c_{\mathcal{K}}(C \sqsubseteq D | \kappa)\right)$
  $\ell_s \leftarrow 0; \ell_c \leftarrow 0$
  for all $v \in Int(\mathcal{L})$ **do**
    if $v \models \kappa$ **then**
      if $\mathcal{T}_v \models C \sqsubseteq D$ **then**
        $\ell_s \leftarrow \ell_s + P^{ME}_{\mathcal{R}}(v)$
      else if $\mathcal{T}_v \models C \not\sqsubseteq D$ **then**
        $\ell_c \leftarrow \ell_c + P^{ME}_{\mathcal{R}}(v)$
  return $\left(\ell_s / P^{ME}_{\mathcal{R}}(\kappa), 1 - \ell_c / P^{ME}_{\mathcal{R}}(\kappa)\right)$

---

context $\neg\text{RES} \wedge \neg\text{H}$. Similarly, RES is a consequence formula for $\exists\text{sf.strep} \not\sqsubseteq \exists\text{suc.ab}$. Knowing both the consequence formulas and the ME-model, we can deduce

$$\mathcal{B}^s_{\mathcal{K}_{\text{exa}}}(\exists\text{sf.strep} \sqsubseteq \exists\text{suc.ab} \mid \top) = P^{ME}_{\mathcal{R}}(\neg\text{RES} \wedge \neg\text{H}) = 0.9405, \text{ and}$$

$$\mathcal{B}^c_{\mathcal{K}_{\text{exa}}}(\exists\text{sf.strep} \sqsubseteq \exists\text{suc.ab} \mid \text{H}) = 1 - P^{ME}_{\mathcal{R}}(\text{RES} \mid \text{H}) = 0.2.$$

In particular, Theorem 22 implies that the belief interval can be computed in two phases. The first phase uses purely logical reasoning to compute the consequence formulas, while the second phase applies probabilistic inferences to compute the degrees of belief from these formulas. We now briefly explain how the consequence formulas can be computed.

Notice first that subsumption and non-subsumption are monotonic consequences in the sense of [2]; that is, if an $\mathcal{ALC}$ TBox $\mathcal{T}$ entails the subsumption $C \sqsubseteq D$, then every superset of $\mathcal{T}$ also entails this consequence. Similarly, adding more axioms to a TBox entailing $C \not\sqsubseteq D$ does not remove this entailment. Moreover, the set of all $\mathcal{L}$-formulas (modulo logical equivalence) forms a distributive lattice ordered by generality, in which $\mathcal{L}$-interpretations are all the join prime elements. Thus, the consequence formulas from Definition 21 are in fact the so-called *boundaries* from [2]. Hence, they can be computed using any of the known boundary computation approaches.

Assuming that the number of contexts is small in comparison to the size of the TBox, it is better to compute the degrees of belief through a more direct approach following Theorems 18 and 19. In order to compute $\mathcal{B}^s_{\mathcal{K}}(C \sqsubseteq D \mid \kappa)$ and $\mathcal{B}^c_{\mathcal{K}}(C \sqsubseteq D \mid \kappa)$, it suffices to enumerate all interpretations $v \in Int(\mathcal{L})$ and check whether $\mathcal{T}_v \models C \sqsubseteq D$ or $\mathcal{T}_v \models C \not\sqsubseteq D$, and $v \models \kappa$, or not (see Algorithm 1). This approach requires $2^{|\text{sig}(\mathcal{L})|}$ calls to a standard $\mathcal{ALC}$ reasoner, and each of these calls runs in exponential time on $|\mathcal{T}|$ [9]. Notice that this algorithm has an *anytime* behaviour: it is possible to stop its execution at any moment and obtain an approximation of the belief interval. Moreover, the longer the algorithm runs, the better this approximation becomes. Thus, this method is adequate for a system where finding good approximations efficiently may be more important than computing the precise answers.

5   Properties

We now investigate some properties of probabilistic logics [22]. First we show that $\mathcal{ALCP}$ is *language and representation invariant*. Invariance is meant with respect to logical objects. Language invariance means that just extending the language without changing the knowledge base should not affect reasoning results. Representation invariance means that equivalent knowledge bases should yield equal inference results. Notice that different notions of *representation dependence* exist in the literature. For instance, in [11] a very different notion is considered, where the language and the knowledge base are changed simultaneously. This case is not covered by our notion of representation invariance. $\mathcal{ALCP}$ also satisfies an *independence* property; i.e., reasoning results about a part of the language are not changed, when we add knowledge about an independent part of the language. Finally, $\mathcal{ALCP}$ is *continuous* in the sense that minor changes in the probabilistic knowledge expressed by a knowledge base cannot induce major changes in the reasoning results.

Theorem 24 (Representation Invariance). *Let $\mathcal{K}_i = (\mathcal{R}_i, \mathcal{T}_i)$, $i \in \{1,2\}$, be two KBs such that $Mod(\mathcal{R}_1) = Mod(\mathcal{R}_2)$ and $Mod(\mathcal{T}_1) = Mod(\mathcal{T}_2)$. Then for all concepts C, D and contexts $\kappa \in \mathcal{L}$, $\mathcal{B}_{\mathcal{K}_1}(C \sqsubseteq D \mid \kappa) = \mathcal{B}_{\mathcal{K}_2}(C \sqsubseteq D \mid \kappa)$.*

$\mathcal{ALCP}$ is not only representation invariant, but also language invariant. This property is of computational interest, in particular in combination with independence, that we investigate subsequently. To illustrate this, suppose that we added knowledge about bone fractures in our medical example, which is independent of the knowledge about infections. Independence guarantees that we can ignore the knowledge about infections when answering queries about bone fractures. In this way, we can decrease the size of the knowledge base. Language invariance guarantees that we can also ignore the concepts, relations and propositional variables related to the infection domain. Thus, we can decrease the size of the language. Exploiting both properties, the size of the computational problems can sometimes be decreased significantly.

Theorem 25 (Language Invariance). *Let $\mathcal{K}_1, \mathcal{K}_2$ be KBs over $\mathcal{L}^1, \mathsf{N}_\mathsf{C}^1, \mathsf{N}_\mathsf{R}^1$ and $\mathcal{L}^2, \mathsf{N}_\mathsf{C}^2, \mathsf{N}_\mathsf{R}^2$, respectively. If $\mathcal{K}_1 = \mathcal{K}_2$, $\mathcal{L}^1 \subseteq \mathcal{L}^2$, $\mathsf{N}_\mathsf{C}^1 \subseteq \mathsf{N}_\mathsf{C}^2$ and $\mathsf{N}_\mathsf{R}^1 \subseteq \mathsf{N}_\mathsf{R}^2$, then for all concepts $C, D \in \mathsf{N}_\mathsf{C}^1$ and contexts $\kappa \in \mathcal{L}^1$, it holds that*

$$\mathcal{B}_{\mathcal{K}_1}(C \sqsubseteq D \mid \kappa) = \mathcal{B}_{\mathcal{K}_2}(C \sqsubseteq D \mid \kappa).$$

For an $\mathcal{L}$-TBox $\mathcal{T}$, we define the *signature* of $\mathcal{T}$ to be the set $\mathsf{sig}(\mathcal{T})$ of all concept names and role names appearing in $\mathcal{T}$. Likewise, $\mathsf{sig}(\mathcal{R})$ is the set of all propositional variables appearing in $\mathcal{R}$. The signature of a KB $\mathcal{K} = (\mathcal{R}, \mathcal{T})$ is $\mathsf{sig}(\mathcal{K}) := \mathsf{sig}(\mathcal{R}) \cup \mathsf{sig}(\mathcal{T})$.

Theorem 26 (Independence). *Let $\mathcal{K}_1, \mathcal{K}_2$ be s.t. $\mathsf{sig}(\mathcal{K}_1) \cap \mathsf{sig}(\mathcal{K}_2) = \emptyset$, C, D be two concepts, and κ a context where $(\mathsf{sig}(C) \cup \mathsf{sig}(D) \cup \mathsf{sig}(\kappa)) \cap \mathsf{sig}(\mathcal{K}_2) = \emptyset$. Then $\mathcal{B}(C \sqsubseteq_{\mathcal{K}_1} D \mid \kappa) = \mathcal{B}(C \sqsubseteq_{\mathcal{K}_1 \cup \mathcal{K}_2} D \mid \kappa)$.*

To conclude, we consider continuity. One important practical feature of continuous probabilistic logics is that they guarantee a numerically stable behaviour. That is, minor rounding errors due to floating-point arithmetic will not result in major errors in the computed probabilities. As demonstrated by Paris in [22], measuring the difference between probabilistic knowledge bases is subtle and is best addressed by comparing knowledge bases extensionally; i.e., with respect to their model sets. To this end, Paris considered the Blaschke metric. Formally, the *Blaschke distance* $\|S_1, S_2\|_B$ between two convex sets S_1, S_2 is defined by

$$\inf\{\delta \in \mathbb{R} \mid \forall P_1 \in S_1 \exists P_2 \in S_2 : \|P_1, P_2\|_2 \leq \delta \ and$$
$$\forall P_2 \in S_2 \exists P_1 \in S_1 : \|P_2, P_1\|_2 \leq \delta\}$$

Intuitively, $\|S_1, S_2\|_B$ is the smallest real number d such that for each distribution in one of the sets, there is a probability distribution in the other that has distance at most d to the former. We say that a sequence of knowledge bases $(\mathcal{K}_i)$ converges to a knowledge base $\mathcal{K}$ iff the classical part of each $\mathcal{K}_i$ is equivalent to the classical part of $\mathcal{K}$ and the probabilistic part converges to the probabilistic part of $\mathcal{K}$. Our reasoning approach behaves indeed continuously with respect to this metric.

Theorem 27 (Continuity). *Let* $(\mathcal{K}_i)$ *be a convergent sequence of KBs with limit* $\mathcal{K}$ *and* $\mathcal{B}_{\mathcal{K}_i}(C \sqsubseteq D \mid \kappa) = [\ell_i, u_i]$. *If* $\mathcal{B}_{\mathcal{K}}(C \sqsubseteq D \mid \kappa) = [\ell, u]$, *then* (l_i) *converges to* ℓ *and* (u_i) *converges to* u *(with respect to the usual topology on* $\mathbb{R}$*).*

6   Related Work

Relational probabilistic logical approaches can be roughly divided into those that consider probability distributions over the domain, those that consider probability distributions over possible worlds and those that combine both ideas [10]. Our framework belongs to the second group. Maximum entropy reasoning in propositional probabilistic logics has been discussed extensively, e.g., in [13,22], and various extensions to first-order languages have been considered in recent years [3,4,14,15]. In these works, the domain is restricted to a finite number of constants or bounded in the limit. We circumvent the need to do so by combining a classical first-order logic with unbounded domain with a probabilistic logic with fixed domain.

Many probabilistic DLs have also been considered in the last decades [16, 18,19]. Our approach is closest to Bayesian DLs [5,6] and DISPONTE [26]. The greatest difference with the former lies in the fact that $\mathcal{ALCP}$ KBs do not require a complete specification of the probability distribution, but only a set of probabilistic constraints. Moreover, the previous formalisms consider only the sceptical degree of belief, while we are interested in the full belief interval. In contrast to DISPONTE, $\mathcal{ALCP}$ is capable of expressing both, logical and probabilistic dependencies between the axioms in a KB; in addition, DISPONTE requires all uncertainty degrees to be assigned as mutually independent point probabilities, while $\mathcal{ALCP}$ allows for a more flexible specification.

7   Conclusions

We have introduced the probabilistic DL $\mathcal{ALCP}$, which extends the classical DL $\mathcal{ALC}$ with the capability of expressing and reasoning about uncertain contextual knowledge defined through the principle of maximum entropy. Effective reasoning methods were developed using the decoupling between the logical and the probabilistic components of $\mathcal{ALCP}$ KBs. We also studied the properties of this logic in relation to other probabilistic logics.

We plan to extend this work in several directions. First, instead of considering the ME-model, we could reason over all probability distributions that satisfy our probabilistic constraints similar to [12,17,20]. This will result in larger belief intervals in general. A smaller interval is preferable since it corresponds to a more precise degree of belief. However, when using all probability distributions the size of the interval can be a good indicator for the variation of the possible beliefs in our query with respect to the knowledge base.

In some applications it is also useful to allow more expressive propositional or relational context languages like those proposed in [4,7,15,24]. Similarly, we can consider other DLs for our concept language. Indeed, $\mathcal{ALC}$ was chosen as a prototypical DL for studying the basic properties of our framework. Including additional constructors into the formalism should be relatively simple. In contrast, considering other reasoning problems beyond subsumption is less straightforward. Recall, for instance, that if an $\mathcal{ALCP}$ KB $\mathcal{K}$ contains an inconsistent context with positive probability, then $\mathcal{K}$ has no models. It is thus unclear how to handle the probability of consistency of a KB.

Practical reasoning with $\mathcal{ALCP}$ can be currently performed by combining existing ME-reasoners[2] with any $\mathcal{ALC}$-reasoner[3] according to Algorithm 1. Clearly, such an approach can still be further optimized. We are working on combining the classical and probabilistic reasoning parts in more sophisticated ways.

References

1. Baader, F., Calvanese, D., McGuinness, D.L., Nardi, D., Patel-Schneider, P.F. (eds.): The Description Logic Handbook: Theory, Implementation, and Applications, 2nd edn. Cambridge University Press, Cambridge (2007)
2. Baader, F., Knechtel, M., Peñaloza, R.: Context-dependent views to axioms and consequences of semantic web ontologies. J. Web Semant. **12–13**, 22–40 (2012)
3. Barnett, O., Paris, J.B.: Maximum entropy inference with quantified knowledge. Log. J. IGPL **16**(1), 85–98 (2008)
4. Beierle, C., Kern-Isberner, G., Finthammer, M., Potyka, N.: Extending and completing probabilistic knowledge and beliefs without bias. KI **29**(3), 255–262 (2015)
5. Ceylan, I.I., Rafael, P.: The Bayesian description logic $\mathcal{BEL}$. In: Demri, S., Kapur, D., Weidenbach, C. (eds.) IJCAR 2014. LNCS, vol. 8562, pp. 480–494. Springer, Switzerland (2014)

---

[2] https://www.fernuni-hagen.de/wbs/research/log4kr/.
[3] http://owl.cs.manchester.ac.uk/tools/list-of-reasoners/.

6. d'Amato, C., Fanizzi, N., Lukasiewicz, T.: Tractable reasoning with Bayesian description logics. In: Greco, S., Lukasiewicz, T. (eds.) SUM 2008. LNCS (LNAI), vol. 5291, pp. 146–159. Springer, Heidelberg (2008)
7. De Bona, G., Cozman, F.G., Finger, M.: Towards classifying propositional probabilistic logics. J. Appl. Log. **12**(3), 349–368 (2014)
8. Domingos, P.M., Lowd, D.: Markov Logic: An Interface Layer for Artificial Intelligence. Synthesis Lectures on Artificial Intelligence and Machine Learning. Morgan & Claypool Publishers, Los Altos (2009)
9. Donini, F.M., Massacci, F.: ExpTime tableaux for $\mathcal{ALC}$. Artif. Intell. **124**(1), 87–138 (2000)
10. Halpern, J.Y.: An analysis of first-order logics of probability. Artif. Intell. **46**, 311–350 (1990)
11. Halpern, J.Y., Koller, D.: Representation dependence in probabilistic inference. JAIR **21**, 319–356 (2004)
12. Hansen, P., Perron, S.: Merging the local and global approaches to probabilistic satisfiability. Int. J. Approx. Reason. **47**(2), 125–140 (2008)
13. Kern-Isberner, G.: Conditionals in Nonmonotonic Reasoning and Belief Revision: Considering Conditionals as Agents. LNCS (LNAI), vol. 2087. Springer, Heidelberg (2001)
14. Kern-Isberner, G., Thimm, M.: Novel semantical approaches to relational probabilistic conditionals. In: Proceedings of KR 2010, pp. 382–391. AAAI Press (2010)
15. Kern-Isberner, G., Lukasiewicz, T.: Combining probabilistic logic programming with the power of maximum entropy. Artif. Intell. **157**(1–2), 139–202 (2004)
16. Klinov, P., Parsia, B.: A hybrid method for probabilistic satisfiability. In: Bjørner, N., Sofronie-Stokkermans, V. (eds.) CADE 2011. LNCS, vol. 6803, pp. 354–368. Springer, Heidelberg (2011)
17. Lukasiewicz, T.: Probabilistic deduction with conditional constraints over basic events. JAIR **10**, 380–391 (1999)
18. Lukasiewicz, T., Straccia, U.: Managing uncertainty and vagueness in description logics for the semantic web. J. Web Semant. **6**(4), 291–308 (2008)
19. Lutz, C., Schröder, L.: Probabilistic description logics for subjective uncertainty. In: Proceedings of KR 2010. AAAI Press (2010)
20. Nilsson, N.J.: Probabilistic logic. Artif. Intell. **28**, 71–88 (1986)
21. Nocedal, J., Wright, S.J.: Numerical Optimization, 2nd edn. Springer, Berlin (2006)
22. Paris, J.: The Uncertain Reasoner's Companion - A Mathematical Perspective. Cambridge University Press, Cambridge (1994)
23. Peñaloza, R., Potyka, N.: Probabilistic reasoning in the description logic ALCP with the principle of maximum entropy (full version). CoRR abs/1606.09521 (2016). http://arXiv.org/abs/1606.09521
24. Potyka, N.: Reasoning over linear probabilistic knowledge bases with priorities. In: Beierle, C., Dekhtyar, A. (eds.) SUM 2015. LNCS, vol. 9310, pp. 121–136. Springer, Heidelberg (2015)
25. Potyka, N.: Relationships between semantics for relational probabilistic conditional logics. In: Computational Models of Rationality, Essays dedicated to Gabriele Kern-Isberner, pp. 332–347. College Publications (2016)
26. Riguzzi, F., Bellodi, E., Lamma, E., Zese, R.: Epistemic and statistical probabilistic ontologies. In: Proceedings of URSW 2012, vol. 900, pp. 3–14. CEUR-WS (2012)
27. Schmidt-Schauß, M., Smolka, G.: Attributive concept descriptions with complements. Artif. Intell. **48**(1), 1–26 (1991)
28. Yeung, R.W.: Information Theory and Network Coding. Springer Science & Business Media, Berlin (2008)

Fuzzy Quantified Structural Queries to Fuzzy Graph Databases

Olivier Pivert$^{(\boxtimes)}$, Olfa Slama, and Virginie Thion

University of Rennes 1 – Irisa, Lannion, France
{olivier.pivert,olfa.slama,virginie.thion}@irisa.fr

Abstract. This paper deals with *fuzzy quantified queries* in a graph database context. We study a particular type of structural quantified query and show how it can be expressed in the language FUDGE that we previously proposed. A processing strategy based on a compilation mechanism that derives regular (nonfuzzy) queries for accessing the relevant data is also described.

Keywords: Graph databases · Fuzzy quantified queries

1 Introduction

Even though the concept of a graph database is not exactly new [2], it is only recently that the database community has started to show a strong interest in it, due in particular to the rise of linked data on the Web and the profusion of domains where networked objects have to be handled: social networks, genomics, cartographic databases, etc.

Simultaneously, the need for flexible querying has been acknowledged by database researchers, and many approaches to relational database preference queries have been proposed in the last decade, see e.g. [14]. However, the pioneering work in this domain dates back to the 70's and is based on fuzzy set theory [15]. Since then, much effort has been made to come up with expressive and efficient flexible querying tools based on fuzzy logic, see e.g. [9]. In particular, *fuzzy quantified queries* have proved useful in a relational database context for expressing different types of imprecise information needs [4]. In a graph database context, such queries have an even higher potential since they can exploit the *structure* of the graph, beside the attribute values attached to the nodes or edges. Nevertheless, only one approach from the literature, described in [5], considered *fuzzy quantified queries* so far, and only in a limited way. In the present paper, we intend to integrate *fuzzy quantified queries* in a framework that we defined previously in [10,11].

The remainder of the paper is organized as follows. Section 2 presents the different elements that constitute the context of the work. Section 3 is a refresher about fuzzy quantified statements. Section 4 discusses related work. In Sect. 5, we consider a specific type of fuzzy quantified structural query, we propose a syntactic format for expressing it in the FUDGE language defined in [10], and

© Springer International Publishing Switzerland 2016
S. Schockaert and P. Senellart (Eds.): SUM 2016, LNAI 9858, pp. 260–273, 2016.
DOI: 10.1007/978-3-319-45856-4_18

we describe its interpretation. Section 6 deals with query processing. Finally, Sect. 7 recalls the main contributions and outlines research perspectives.

2   Background Notions

In this section, we recall important notions about graph databases, fuzzy graph theory, fuzzy graph databases, and the query language FUDGE.

2.1   Graph Databases

A graph database management system enables managing data for which the structure of the schema is modeled as a graph (nodes are entities and edges are relations between entities), and data is handled through graph-oriented operations and type constructors. Different models of graph databases have been proposed in the literature (see [2] for an overview), including the *attributed graph* (aka. *property graph*) aimed to model a network of entities with embedded data. In this model, nodes and edges may contain data in *attributes* (aka. *properties*).

2.2   Fuzzy Graphs

A *graph* G is a pair (V, R), where V is a set and R is a relation on V. The elements of V (resp. R) correspond to the vertices (resp. edges) of the graph. Similarly, any fuzzy relation ρ on a set V can be regarded as defining a weighted graph, or fuzzy graph [13], where the edge $(x, y) \in V \times V$ has weight or strength $\rho(x, y) \in [0, 1]$.

An important operation on fuzzy relations is composition. Assume ρ_1 and ρ_2 are two fuzzy relations on V. Thus, composition $\rho = \rho_1 \circ \rho_2$ is also a fuzzy relation on V s.t. $\rho(x, z) = \max_y \min(\rho_1(x, y), \rho_2(y, z))$. The composition operation can be shown to be associative: $(\rho_1 \circ \rho_2) \circ \rho_3 = \rho_1 \circ (\rho_2 \circ \rho_3)$. The associativity property allows us to use the notation $\rho^k = \rho \circ \rho \circ \ldots \circ \rho$ for the composition of ρ with itself $k - 1$ times. In addition, following [16], we define ρ^0 to be s.t. $\rho^0(x, y) = 0, \forall(x, y)$.

Useful notions related to fuzzy graphs are those of strength and length of a path. Their definition, drawn from [13], is given hereafter.

Strength of a path. — A path p in G is a sequence $x_0 \rightarrow x_1 \rightarrow \ldots \rightarrow x_n$ $(n \geq 0)$ such that $\rho(x_{i-1}, x_i) > 0, 1 \leq i \leq n$ and where n is the number of links in the path. The *strength* of the path is defined as

$$ST(p) = \min_{i=1..n} \rho(x_{i-1}, x_i). \tag{1}$$

In other words, the strength of a path is defined to be the weight of the weakest edge of the path. Two nodes for which there exists a path p with $ST(p) > 0$ between them are called *connected*. We call p a cycle if $n \geq 2$ and $x_0 = x_n$. It is possible to show that $\rho^k(x, y)$ is the strength of the strongest path from x to y

containing at most k links. Thus, the strength of the strongest path joining any two vertices x and y (using any number of links) may be denoted by $\rho^\infty(x, y)$.

Length and *distance.* — The *length* of a path $p = x_0 \to x_1 \to \ldots \to x_n$ in the sense of ρ is defined as follows:

$$Length(p) = \sum_{i=1}^{n} \frac{1}{\rho(x_{i-1}, x_i)}. \tag{2}$$

Clearly $Length(p) \geq n$ (it is equal to n if ρ is Boolean, i.e., if G is a nonfuzzy graph). We can then define the *distance* between two nodes x and y in G as

$$Distance(x, y) = \min_{all\ paths\ x\ to\ y} Length(p). \tag{3}$$

It is the length of the shortest path from x to y. It can be shown that *Distance* is a metric [13], i.e., $Distance(x, x) = 0$, $Distance(x, y) = Distance(y, x)$, and $Distance(x, z) \leq Distance(x, y) + Distance(y, z)\ \forall z$.

2.3   Fuzzy Graph Databases

We are interested in fuzzy graph databases where nodes and edges can carry data (e.g. key-value pairs in attributed graphs). So, we consider an extension of the notion of a *fuzzy graph*: the *fuzzy data graph* as defined in [11].

Definition 1 (Fuzzy data graph). *Let E be a set of labels. A fuzzy data graph G is a quadruple (V, R, κ, ζ), where V is a finite set of nodes (each node n is identified by n.id), $R = \bigcup_{e \in E} \{\rho_e : V \times V \to [0, 1]\}$ is a set of labeled fuzzy edges between nodes of V, and κ (resp. ζ) is a function assigning a (possibly structured) value to nodes (resp. edges) of G.*

In the following, a *graph database* is meant to be a fuzzy data graph. Figure 1 is an example of a fuzzy data graph in which the degree associated with A -contributor-> B is the proportion of journal papers co-written by A and B, over the total number of journal papers written by B. The degree associated with J -domain-> D is the extent to which the journal J belongs to the research domain D.

Nodes are assumed to be typed. If n is a node of V, then $Type(n)$ denotes its type. In Fig. 1, the nodes IJWS12, IJAR14, IJIS16, IJIS10 and IJUFK15 are of type *journal*, the nodes IJWS12-p, IJAR14-p, IJIS16-p, IJIS10-p, IJIS10-p1 and IJUFK15-p of type *paper*, and the nodes Andreas, Peter, Maria, Claudio, Michel, Bazil and Susan are of type *author*, the nodes named Database are of type *domain* and the other nodes are of type *impact_factor*. For nodes of type *journal, paper, author* and *domain*, a property, called *name*, contains the identifier of the node and for nodes of type *impact_factor*, a property, called *value*, contains the value of the node. In Fig. 1, the value of the property *name* or *value* for a node appears inside the node.

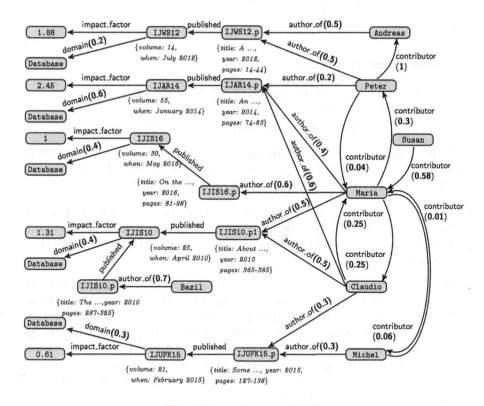

Fig. 1. Fuzzy data graph $\mathcal{DB}$

2.4 The FUDGE Query Language

FUDGE, based on the algebra described in [10], is an extension of the Cypher language [8], used in the Neo4j graph DBMS [1]. These languages are based on graph pattern matching, meaning that a query Q over a fuzzy data graph $\mathcal{DB}$ defines a graph pattern and answers to Q are its isomorphic subgraphs that can be found in $\mathcal{DB}$. More concretely, a pattern has the form of a subgraph where variables can occur. An answer maps the variables in elements of $\mathcal{DB}$.

A fuzzy graph pattern expressed à la Cypher consists of a set of expressions `(n1:Type1)-[exp]->(n2:Type2)` or `(n1:Type1)-[e:label]->(n2:Type2)` where n1 and n2 are node variables, e is an edge variable, label is a label of E, exp is a fuzzy regular expression, and Type1 and Type2 are node types. Such an expression denotes a path satisfying a fuzzy regular expression exp (that is *simple* in the second form e) going from a node of type Type1 to a node of type Type2. All its arguments are optional, so the simplest form of an expression is `()-[]->()` denoting a path made of two nodes connected by any edge. Conditions on attributes are expressed on nodes and edges variables in a WHERE clause.

Example 1. We denote by $\mathcal{P}$ the fuzzy graph pattern:

```
1   MATCH
2     (au2)-[:contributor+]->(au1:author),
3     (au1)-[:author_of]->(ar1:paper), (ar1)-[:published]->(j1),
4     (au1)-[:author_of]->(ar2:paper), (ar2)-[:published]->(j2)
5   WHERE j1.name="IJWS12"
```

Listing 1.1. Pattern expressed *à la Cypher*

This pattern "models" information concerning authors (au2) who have, among their close contributors, an author (au1) who published a paper (ar1) in IJWS12 and also published a paper (ar2) in a journal (j2).   ◇

Let us illustrate the way a selection query can be expressed in FUDGE, that embarks fuzzy preferences over the data and the structure specified in the graph pattern. Given a graph database $\mathcal{DB}$, a selection query expressed in FUDGE is composed of:

1. A list of DEFINE clauses for fuzzy term declarations. If a fuzzy term fterm corresponds to a trapezoidal function defined by the quadruple (A-a, A, B and B+b), then the clause has the form DEFINE fterm AS (A-a,A,B,B+b). If fterm is a decreasing function, then the clause has the form DEFINEDESC fterm AS (δ, γ) meaning that the support of the term is $[0, \gamma]$ and its core $[0, \delta]$ (there is the corresponding DEFINEASC clause for increasing functions).
2. A MATCH clause, which has the form MATCH pattern WHERE conditions that expresses the fuzzy graph pattern.

Example 2. Listing 1.2 is an example of a FUDGE query.

```
1   DEFINEDESC short AS (3,5), DEFINEASC high AS (0.5,2) IN
2   MATCH
3     (au2)-[(contributor+)|Length IS short]->(au1:author),
4     (au1)-[:author_of]->(ar1:paper), (ar1)-[:published]->(j1),
5     (au1)-[:author_of]->(ar2:paper), (ar2)-[:published]->(j2),
6     (j2)-[:impact_factor]->(i)
7   WHERE j1.name="IJWS12" AND i.value IS high
```

Listing 1.2. A FUDGE query

This pattern "models" information concerning authors (au2) who have, among their close contributors (connected by a short path — Length IS short — made of contributor edges), an author (au1) who published a paper (ar1) in IJWS12 and also published a paper (ar2) in a journal (j2) which has a *high* impact factor (i.value IS high). The fuzzy terms *short* and *high* are defined on line 1.   ◇

3   Refresher on Fuzzy Quantified Statements

In this section, we recall important notions about fuzzy quantifiers and present one of the approaches that have been proposed in the literature for interpreting fuzzy quantified statements.

3.1   Fuzzy Quantifiers

Zadeh [17] distinguishes between absolute and relative fuzzy quantifiers. Absolute quantifiers refer to a number while relative ones refer to a proportion. Quantifiers may also be increasing, as "at least half", or decreasing, as "at most three". An absolute quantifier Q is represented by a function μ_Q from an integer range to $[0, 1]$ whereas a relative quantifier is a mapping μ_Q from $[0, 1]$ to $[0, 1]$. In both cases, the value $\mu_Q(j)$ is defined as the truth value of the statement "$Q\,X$ are A" when exactly j elements from X fully satisfy A (whereas it is assumed that A is fully unsatisfied for the other elements). Figure 2 gives two examples of monotonous decreasing and increasing quantifiers respectively.

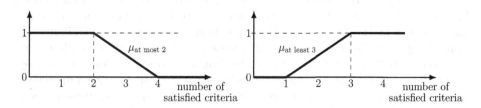

Fig. 2. Quantifiers "at most 2" (left) and "at least 3" (right)

Calculating the truth degree of the statement "$Q X$ are A" raises the problem of determining the cardinality of the set of elements from X which satisfy A. If A is a Boolean predicate, this cardinality is a precise integer (k), and then, the truth value of "$Q X$ are A" is $\mu_Q(k)$. If A is a fuzzy predicate, this cardinality cannot be established precisely and then, computing the quantification corresponds to establishing the value of function μ_Q for an imprecise argument.

3.2   Zadeh's Interpretation

Let X be the usual (crisp) set $\{x_1, x_2, \ldots, x_n\}$. Zadeh [17] defines the cardinality of the set of elements of X which satisfy A, denoted by $\Sigma count(A)$, as:

$$\Sigma count(A) = \sum_{i=1}^{n} \mu_A(x_i) \tag{4}$$

The truth degree of the statement "$Q\,X$ are A" is then given by

$$\mu(Q\,X\ are\ A) = \begin{cases} \mu_Q(\Sigma count(A)) & \text{(absolute)}, \\ \mu_Q\left(\dfrac{\Sigma count(A)}{n}\right) & \text{(relative)} \end{cases} \tag{5}$$

where n denotes the cardinality of X.

As for quantified statements of the form "$Q\,B\,X$ are A" (with Q relative), their interpretation is as follows:

$$\mu(Q\,B\,X\,are\,A) = \mu_Q\left(\frac{\Sigma count(A \cap B)}{\Sigma count(B)}\right) = \mu_Q\left(\frac{\sum_{x \in X} \top(\mu_A(x),\,\mu_B(x))}{\sum_{x \in X} \mu_B(x)}\right) \quad (6)$$

where $\top$ denotes a triangular norm (for instance the minimum).

4   Related Work

Fuzzy quantified queries have been thoroughly studied in a relational database context, see e.g. [4,7] where they serve to express conditions about data *values*. In a graph database context, a new dimension can be exploited that concerns the *structure* of the graph. In [16], Yager briefly mentions the possibility of using *fuzzy quantified queries* in a social network database context, such as the question of whether "*most* of the people residing in *western* countries have *strong* connections with each other" and suggests to interpret it using an OWA operator. However, the author does not propose any formal language for expressing such queries.

A first attempt to extend Cypher with *fuzzy quantified queries* — in the context of a *regular* (crisp) graph database — is described in [5,6]. In [5], the authors take as an example a graph database representing hotels and their customers and consider the following fuzzy quantified query:

```
1  MATCH (c1:customer)-[:knows**almost3]->(c2:customer) RETURN c1,c2
```

looking for pairs of customers linked through *almost 3* hops. The syntax ** is used for indicating what the authors call a *fuzzy linker*. However, the interpretation of such queries is not formally given. The authors give a second example that involves the fuzzy concept *popular* applied to hotels. They assume that a hotel is popular if a large proportion of customers visited it. First, they consider a crisp interpretation of this concept (*large* being seen as equivalent to *at least* n) and recall how the corresponding query can be expressed in Cypher:

```
1  MATCH (c:customer)-[:visit]->(h:hotel) WITH h, count(*) AS cpt
2  WHERE cpt > n - 1 RETURN h
```

Then, the authors switch to a fuzzy interpretation of the term *popular* and propose the expression:

```
1  MATCH (c:customer)-[:visit]->(h:hotel) WITH h, count(*) AS cpt
2  WHERE popular(cpt) > 0 RETURN h
```

In [6], the same authors propose an approach aimed to summarize a (crisp) graph database by means of fuzzy quantified statements of the form $Q\,X$ *are* A, in the same spirit as what Rasmussen and Yager did for relational databases [12]. Again, they consider that the degree of truth of such a statement is obtained by a sigma-count (according to Zadeh's interpretation) and show how the corresponding queries can be expressed in Cypher. More precisely, given a graph database

G and a summary $S = a-[r]->b$, Q, the authors consider two degrees of truth of S in G defined by $truth_1(S) = \mu_Q\left(count(distinct\ S)/count(distinct\ a)\right)$ and $truth_2(S) = \mu_Q\left(count(distinct\ S)/count(distinct\ a-[r]->(?))\right)$. They illustrate these notions using a database representing students who rent or own a house or an apartment. The degree of truth (in the sense of the second formula above) of the summary "$S = student-[rent]->apartment,\ most$" — meaning "most of the students rent an apartment" (as opposed to a house) — is given by the membership degree to the fuzzy quantifier $most$ of the ratio: (number of times a relationship of type $rents$ appears between a student and an apartment) over (number of relations of type $rents$ starting from a $student$ node).

A limitation of this approach is that only the quantifier is fuzzy (whereas in general, in a fuzzy quantified statement of the form "$Q\ B\ X$ are A", the predicates A and B may be fuzzy too).

5   Fuzzy Quantified Queries in the FUDGE Language

In the following, we consider *fuzzy quantified queries* involving fuzzy predicates (beside the quantifier) over *fuzzy* graph databases. The fuzzy quantified statements considered are of the form "Q nodes, that are connected according to a certain pattern to a node x, satisfy a fuzzy condition φ". An example of such a statement is: "*most* of the papers of which x is a *main* author, have been published in a *renowned* database journal".

This type of statement rewrites "$Q\ Y_{P(x)}$ are φ" where the quantifier Q is represented by a fuzzy set and denotes either a relative quantifier (e.g., most) or an absolute one (e.g., at least three), $Y_{P(x)}$ designates the fuzzy set of nodes connected, according to the pattern $P(x)$, to a node x in the graph, and φ, is represented also by a fuzzy set and denotes fuzzy (possibly compound) conditions. In a general setting, we have a statement of the form "$Q\ B\ X$ are A" where B is the fuzzy condition "to be connected (according to the pattern $P(x)$) to a node x", X is the set of nodes in the graph, and A is the fuzzy condition φ. In the particular case where the graph is crisp, we get a statement of the form "$Q\ X$ are A" where the referential X is the (crisp) set of nodes connected to x.

Example 3. The query that consists in finding "*most* of the papers of which x is a *main* author, have been published in a *renowned* database journal" may be expressed in FUDGE as follows:

```
1  DEFINEQRELATIVEASC most AS (0.3,0.8),
2  DEFINEASC strong AS (0,1), DEFINEASC high AS (0.5,2) IN
3  MATCH
4     (x:author)-[author_of|ST IS strong]->(p:paper),
5     (p:paper)-[:published]->(j:journal)-[:impact_factor]->(i:impact_factor),
6     (j:journal)-[:domain]->(d)
7  WITH x HAVING most(p) ARE (i.value IS high AND d.name="database")
8  RETURN x
```

where the DEFINEQRELATIVEASC clause defines the fuzzy relative increasing quantifier *most* of Fig. 3(c), and the next DEFINEASC clauses define the ascending fuzzy terms *strong* and *high* of Fig. 3(d) and (a).

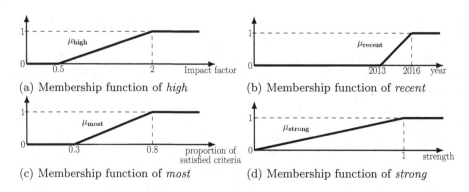

Fig. 3. Membership functions

We now consider a slightly more complex version of the above example by adding a fuzzy condition on the papers' publication date: "*most* of the recent papers written by an important author x have been published in a *renowned* database journal". The syntactic form of this query, denoted by $Q_{mostAuthors}$ in the following, is given in Listing 1.3.   ◇

```
1   DEFINEQRELATIVEASC most AS (0.3,0.8), DEFINEASC recent AS (2013,2016),
2   DEFINEASC strong AS (0,1), DEFINEASC high AS (0.5,2) IN
3   MATCH
4     (x:author)-[author_of|ST IS strong]->(p:paper),
5     (p:paper)-[:published]->(j:journal)-[:impact_factor]->(i:impact_factor),
6     (j:journal)-[:domain]->(d)
7   WHERE p.year IS recent
8   WITH x HAVING most(p) ARE (i.value IS high AND d.name="database")
9   RETURN X
```

Listing 1.3. Syntax of the fuzzy quantified query $Q_{mostAuthors}$

The general syntactic form of *fuzzy quantified queries* is given in the Listing 1.4.

```
1   DEFINE... IN
2   MATCH P(x,y) WHERE fc₁(y)
3   WITH x HAVING Quant(y) ARE fc₂
4   RETURN X
```

Listing 1.4. Syntax of a fuzzy quantified query

It contains a list of DEFINE clauses for the fuzzy quantifiers and the fuzzy terms declarations, a MATCH clause for fuzzy graph pattern selection, a WHERE clause for expressing the (possibly fuzzy) conditions on values, a HAVING clause for the fuzzy quantified statement definition, and a RETURN clause for specifying which elements should be returned in the resultset. P(x,y) denotes the fuzzy graph pattern involving the nodes x and y. fc_1 and fc_2 are fuzzy conditions.

Interpretation: From a conceptual point of view, its interpretation involves three derived queries (hereafter, the DEFINE clauses are been omitted for the sake of simplicity). The first one, Q_1 (given in Listing 1.5), aims to retrieve the elements matching the variable x, for which we will then need to calculate a satisfaction degree. Query Q_1 is obtained by removing the WITH and HAVING clauses from the initial query (one may also remove some useless parts of P(x,y), as illustrated in Example 4 below).

```
1   MATCH P(x,y) WHERE fc₁(y)
2   RETURN x
```

Listing 1.5. Derived query Q_1

The second derived query, denoted by $Q_2(e)$ (given in Listing 1.6), where e is an element returned by Q_1, is obtained by removing the WITH and HAVING clauses from the initial query, integrating the fuzzy condition fc_2 and the condition x.name=e in the WHERE clause and adding the clause RETURN y. According to the semantics of a FUDGE query, its result, denoted by $A_{Q_2(x)}$, is a set of elements $\{(\mu_1/y_1), ..., (\mu_n/y_n)\}$, where μ_i is the satisfaction degree associated with the element y_i.

```
1   MATCH P(x,y) WHERE fc₁(y) AND fc₂ AND x.name=e
2   RETURN y
```

Listing 1.6. Derived queries $Q_2(e)$ for each e retrieved by Q_1

The third derived query, denoted by $Q_3(e)$ (given in Listing 1.7), is the initial fuzzy query from the MATCH to the WHERE clause, adding the condition x.name=e in the WHERE clause and the clause RETURN y as follows:

```
1   MATCH P(x,y) WHERE fc₁(y) AND x.name=e
2   RETURN y
```

Listing 1.7. Derived queries $Q_3(e)$ for each e retrieved by Q_1

The result of this query, denoted by $A_{Q_3(x)}$, takes the form of a set of elements $\{(\mu'_1/y_1), ..., (\mu'_m/y_m)\}$, where μ'_i is the satisfaction degree associated with element y_i. Note that Q_3 only differs from Q_2 by its WHERE clause.

In accordance with the semantics of the projection, if the same value of y_i appears in several instances in the resultset of $Q_2(x)$ or $Q_3(x)$, duplicates are eliminated and the final degree associated with y_i in $A_{Q_2(x)}$ and $A_{Q_3(x)}$ is equal to the maximum degree associated with these occurrences.

Then, the results of the initial fuzzy relative quantified query Q (involving the fuzzy quantifier $\mathcal{Q}$) are results of the query Q_1 derived from Q, and the final satisfaction degree associated with each element e of these results is

$$\mu(e) = \mu_{\mathcal{Q}} \left(\frac{\sum_{(\mu_i/y_i) \in A_{Q_2(e)}} \mu_i}{\sum_{(\mu'_i/y_i) \in A_{Q_3(e)}} \mu'_i} \right) \tag{7}$$

In case of a fuzzy absolute quantified query, the final satisfaction degree associated with each element e is $\mu(e) = \mu_Q\left(\sum_{(\mu_i/y_i)\in A_{Q_2(e)}} \mu_i\right)$.

Example 4. Let us consider the query $Q_{mostAuthors}$ of Listing 1.3. We evaluate this query according to the fuzzy data graph $\mathcal{DB}$ of Fig. 1. In order to interpret $Q_{mostAuthors}$, we first evaluate the following query Q_1, derived from $Q_{mostAuthors}$, that retrieves "the authors (x) who highly contributed to at least one recent paper (p) published in a journal".

```
1  MATCH (x:author)-[author_of|ST IS strong]->(p:paper),
2    (p:paper)-[:published]->(j:journal)
3  WHERE p.year IS recent
4  RETURN x
```

Listing 1.8. Query Q_1 derived from $Q_{mostAuthors}$

Q_1 returns four results $X = \{$Peter, Maria, Claudio, Michel$\}$. The authors Andreas, Susan and Bazil do not belong to the resultset of Q_1 because Susan has not written a journal paper yet and Andreas and Bazil do not have a recent paper.

For each element x from the resultset X of Q_1, we process two queries $Q_2(x)$ and $Q_3(x)$. The query $Q_2(x)$, derived from $Q_{mostAuthors}$, aims to retrieve "the recent papers of which x is a *main* author, that have been published in a *renowned* database journal". For instance, for the element Maria, the query $Q_2(Maria)$ is expressed as follows:

```
1  MATCH (x:author)-[author_of|ST IS strong]->(p:paper),
2    (p:paper)-[:published]->(j:journal)-[:impact_factor]->(i:impact_factor),
3    (j:journal)-[:domain]->(d)
4  WHERE p.year IS recent AND i.value IS high
5    AND d.name="database" AND x.name="Maria"
6  RETURN p
```

Listing 1.9. Query $Q_2(Maria)$ derived from $Q_{mostAuthors}$

For a given x, we get a list of papers with their respective satisfaction degrees: $\mu(p) = \min(\mu_{strong}(\rho_{author}(x,p)), \mu_{recent}(p), \mu_{high}(i))$. For the running example, we then have $A_{Q_2(Peter)} = \{(\min(0.5, 0, 0.92)/$IJWS12_p$), (\min(0.2, 0.33, 1)/$IJAR14_p$)\} = \{(0/$IJWS12_p$), (0.2/$IJAR14_p$)\}$, $A_{Q_2(Maria)} = \{(0.33/$IJAR14_p$), (0.33/$IJIS16_p$), (0/IJIS10_p1)\}$, $A_{Q_2(Claudio)} = \{(0.33/$IJAR14_p$), (0/$IJIS10_p1$), (0.07/$IJUFK15_p$)\}$, $A_{Q_2(Michel)} = \{(0.07/$IJUFK15_p$)\}$.

Query $Q_3(x)$, derived from $Q_{mostAuthors}$, aims to retrieve "the recent papers of which x is a *main* author, that have been published in a journal". For instance, for the element Maria, the query $Q_3(Maria)$ is expressed as follows:

```
1  MATCH (x:author)-[author_of|ST IS strong]->(p:paper),
2    (p:paper)-[:published]->(j:journal)-[:impact_factor]->(i:impact_factor),
3    (j:journal)-[:domain]->(d)
4  WHERE p.year IS recent AND x.name="Maria"
5  RETURN p
```

Listing 1.10. Query $Q_3(Maria)$ derived from $Q_{mostAuthors}$

For a given x, we get a set of papers written by x satisfying the conditions of query $Q_3(x)$ with their respective satisfaction degrees as follows: $\mu(p) = min(\mu_{strong}(\rho_{author}(x,p)), \mu_{recent}(p))$. For the running example, we then have $A_{Q_3(Peter)} = \{(0/\text{IJWS12\_p}), (0.2/\text{IJAR14\_p})\}$, $A_{Q_3(Maria)} = \{(0.33/\text{IJAR14\_p}),$ $(0.6/\text{IJIS16\_p}), (0/\text{IJIS10\_p1})\}$, $A_{Q_3(Claudio)} = \{(0.33/\text{IJAR14\_p}), (0/\text{IJIS10\_p1}),$ $(0.3/\text{IJUFK15\_p})\}$, $A_{Q_3(Michel)} = \{(0.3/\text{IJUFK15\_p})\}$.

Lastly, the final result of the query $Q_{mostAuthors}$ evaluated on $\mathcal{DB}$, given by Formula 7, is $\{\mu(Peter) = \mu_{most}(\frac{0.2}{0.2}) = 1,\ \mu(Maria) = \mu_{most}(\frac{0.66}{0.93}) = 0.82,$ $\mu(Claudio) = \mu_{most}(\frac{0.4}{0.63}) = 0.67,\ \mu(Michel) = \mu_{most}(\frac{0.07}{0.3}) = 0\}$.   ◇

6 About Query Processing

The evaluation strategy we propose for these queries consists of a software add-on layer over the *Neo4j* graph DBMS. This software, called SUGAR, efficiently evaluates FUDGE queries that contain fuzzy preferences, but its initial version, described in [10,11], does not support fuzzy quantified statements. We now consider the implementation of this functionality, based on the theoretical foundations defined in the previous section. The SUGAR software implements two modules, which interact with the embedded Neo4j crisp engine (see Fig. 4): *The Transcriptor module*, aimed to translate a FUDGE query requested by a user into a (crisp) cypher one (using the derivation principle presented in [9] in the context of relational databases), which is then sent to the crisp Neo4j engine, and *The Score Calculator module*, which calculates the satisfaction degree associated with each answer returned by the crisp engine, and ranks the answers.

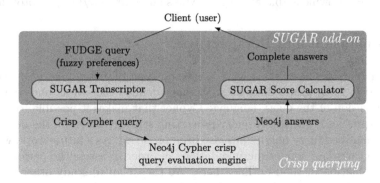

Fig. 4. SUGAR software architecture

The main process in our work is the quantified statement evaluation step which is described in Algorithm 1. For quantified queries of the type introduced in the previous section (i.e. using relative quantifiers), the principle is to first evaluate the fuzzy query Q_1. For each tuple x from the resulset of Q_1, we evaluate with SUGAR the fuzzy queries $Q_2(x)$ and $Q_3(x)$. The final satisfaction degree is given by Formula 7 according to $Q_2(x)$ and $Q_3(x)$ resultsets. Finally, we get as an output answers ranked by decreasing order of the satisfaction degree.

Algorithm 1. Algorithm for the evaluation of a fuzzy quantified query

---

Input : A query Q containing a fuzzy quantifier $Quant$
Output: Results X of Q with associated satisfaction degrees $\{\mu(x) | x \in X\}$

1 **begin**
2   Derive queries Q_1, Q_2 and Q_3 from Q;
3   X=evaluate(Q_1);
4   **foreach** *element x from the result of X* **do**
5   evaluate($Q_2(x)$);
6   evaluate($Q_3(x)$);
7        $\mu(x) = \mu_{Quant}(\mu_{A_{Q2(x)}}(y)/\mu_{A_{Q3(x)}}(y))$;
8   Rank answers of X by decreasing satisfaction degree (μ)

For a given x, queries $Q_2(x)$ and $Q_3(e)$ embed the same graph pattern (they only differ by their WHERE clause that is more restrictive for Q_2). This means that these queries could be processed together at evaluation time. Then one can see on Algorithm 1 that evaluating a fuzzy quantified query implies processing $x + 1$ FUDGE queries where x is the number of elements that match the pattern declared in the MATCH clause of the initial query (without the quantified statement). The cost of the evaluation of a graph pattern query depends on the form of its pattern [3] and it has already been showed in [10] that a FUDGE query does not significantly increase the cost with respect to a crisp query in the case of selection graph pattern queries.

As a proof-of-concept of the proposed approach, the FUDGE prototype is available and downloadable at http://www-shaman.irisa.fr/fudge-prototype/.

7   Conclusion and Perspectives

In this paper, we have dealt with a specific type of *fuzzy quantified queries*, addressed to fuzzy graph databases. We have defined the syntax and semantics of an extension of the query language Cypher that makes it possible to express and interpret such queries. A query processing strategy based on the derivation of non-quantified fuzzy queries has also been proposed. As a future work, we first intend to carry out some experimentations in order to assess the performances of the evaluation method outlined here. We then plan to study other types of fuzzy quantified queries. An example of a fuzzy quantified statement that is out of the scope of the present approach is "find the authors x that had a paper published in *most* of the *renowned* database journals". More generally, it would be interesting to study fuzzy quantified queries that aim to find the nodes x such that x is connected (by a path) to $\mathcal{Q}$ nodes reachable by a given pattern and satisfying a given condition C.

Acknowledgement. This work has been partially funded by the French DGE (Direction Générale des Entreprises) under the project ODIN.

References

1. Neo4j web site. www.neo4j.org
2. Angles, R., Gutierrez, C.: Survey of graph database models. ACM Comput. Surv. **40**(1), 1–39 (2008)
3. Barceló, P., Libkin, L., Reutter, J.L.: Querying regular graph patterns. J. ACM **61**(1), 8:1–8:54 (2014)
4. Bosc, P., Liétard, L., Pivert, O.: Quantified statements and database fuzzy querying. In: Bosc, P., Kacprzyk, J. (eds.) Fuzziness in Database Management Systems, pp. 275–308. Physica Verlag, Heidelberg (1995)
5. Castelltort, A., Laurent, A.: Fuzzy queries over noSQL graph databases: perspectives for extending the cypher language. In: Laurent, A., Strauss, O., Bouchon-Meunier, B., Yager, R.R. (eds.) IPMU 2014, Part III. CCIS, vol. 444, pp. 384–395. Springer, Heidelberg (2014)
6. Castelltort, A., Laurent, A.: Extracting fuzzy summaries from NoSQL graph databases. In: Andreasen, T., et al. (eds.) FQAS'15. AISC, vol. 400, pp. 189–200. Springer, Switzerland (2015)
7. Kacprzyk, J., Zadrożny, S., Ziółkowski, A.: FQUERY III +: a "human-consistent" database querying system based on fuzzy logic with linguistic quantifiers. Inf. Syst. **14**(6), 443–453 (1989)
8. Neo Technology: The Neo4j Manual v2.0.0, part III (2013)
9. Pivert, O., Bosc, P.: Fuzzy Preference Queries to Relational Databases. Imperial College Press, London (2012)
10. Pivert, O., Smits, G., Thion, V.: Expression and efficient processing of fuzzy queries in a graph database context. In: Proceedings of the 24th IEEE International Conference on Fuzzy Systems (Fuzz-IEEE 2015), Istanbul, Turkey (2015)
11. Pivert, O., Thion, V., Jaudoin, H., Smits, G.: On a fuzzy algebra for querying graph databases. In: Proceedings of the IEEE International Conference on Tools with Artificial Intelligence (ICTAI 2014), pp. 748–755, Limassol, Cyprus (2014)
12. Rasmussen, D., Yager, R.R.: Summary SQL - a fuzzy tool for data mining. Intell. Data Anal. **1**(1–4), 49–58 (1997)
13. Rosenfeld, A.: Fuzzy graphs. In: Fuzzy Sets and their Applications to Cognitive and Decision Processes, pp. 77–97. Academic Press, London (1975)
14. Stefanidis, K., Koutrika, G., Pitoura, E.: A survey on representation, composition and application of preferences in database systems. ACM Trans. Database Syst. **36**(3), 19 (2011). http://doi.acm.org/10.1145/2000824.2000829
15. Tahani, V.: A conceptual framework for fuzzy query processing - a step toward very intelligent database systems. Inf. Process. Manag. **13**(5), 289–303 (1977)
16. Yager, R.R.: Social network database querying based on computing with words. In: Pivert, O., Zadrożny, S. (eds.) Flexible Approaches in Data, Information and Knowledge Management. SCI, vol. 497, pp. 241–257. Springer, Switzerland (2013)
17. Zadeh, L.A.: A computational approach to fuzzy quantifiers in natural languages. Computi. Math. Appl. **9**, 149–183 (1983)

Reasoning with Data - A New Challenge for AI?

Henri Prade[1,2(✉)]

[1] IRIT, Université Paul Sabatier, 118 route de Narbonne,
31062 Toulouse Cedex 09, France
prade@irit.fr
[2] QCIS, University of Technology, Sydney, Australia

Abstract. Artificial intelligence (AI) traditionally deals with knowledge rather than with data (with the noticeable exception of machine learning). The term "knowledge" refers here to information with a generic flavor, while "data" refers to information pertaining to (collections of) particular cases. The formalization of reasoning patterns with data has been much less studied until now than knowledge representation and its application to knowledge-based systems and reasoning, possibly in presence of imperfect information. Data are positive in nature by manifesting the possibility of what is observed or reported, and contrast with knowledge that delimit the extent of what is potentially possible by specifying what is impossible. Reasoning from knowledge and data goes much beyond the application of knowledge to data as in expert systems. Besides, the idea of similarity naturally applies to data and gives birth to specific forms of reasoning such as case-based reasoning, case-based decision, or even case-based argumentation, interpolation, extrapolation, and analogical reasoning. Moreover, the analysis, the interpretation of data sets raise original reasoning problems for making sense of data. This article is a manifesto in favor of the study of types of reasoning which have been somewhat neglected in AI, by showing that AI should contribute to (knowledge) and data sciences, not only in the machine learning and in the data mining areas.

Keywords: Knowledge · Data · Bipolarity · Similarity · Possibility theory

1 Introduction

Historically, knowledge representation and reasoning have played a central role in artificial intelligence (AI). AI has been more a "knowledge science" than a "data science" until now. This does not mean that AI fully ignores data. Certainly not. Machine learning, which has recently become the most prominent part of AI, works with data, and is extensively used for inducing knowledge from data. Note that in this paper we use the term "knowledge" for referring to information having a *generic* flavor, while "data" pertains to collections of *particular* cases or instances.

Originally, knowledge was mainly supposed to be provided by experts. Expert systems, which were popular from the mid-seventies to the mid-nineties of the

© Springer International Publishing Switzerland 2016
S. Schockaert and P. Senellart (Eds.): SUM 2016, LNAI 9858, pp. 274–288, 2016.
DOI: 10.1007/978-3-319-45856-4_19

last century, are prototypical illustrations of this state of facts. However, the idea of extracting knowledge from data has been there for a long time as well. This is especially the case with numerical methods such as Bayesian nets, fuzzy rules-based systems, or neural nets. Besides, data mining methods look for pieces of knowledge of interest including association rules that may have not been thought of before.

The aim of this paper is neither to survey methods that extract knowledge from data, nor to discuss machine learning, but rather to provide a structured overview of problems and approaches where data are directly involved in reasoning processes. Note that in this paper we use the phrase "reasoning with data", which may cover indifferently "reasoning about data", or "reasoning from data". Obviously, expert systems by operating the separation of the knowledge base from the factual part of the information pertaining to the case at end, were dealing with data. But these data, called facts there, were used in isolation and were specific of the case at hand to which the generic knowledge had to be applied. The factual base was gathering only facts pertaining to a single case at once, so it was not really a data base (which usually gathers data pertaining to collections of different cases). This remark applies as well to abductive reasoning in diagnosis, where symptoms are facts pertaining to a given situation.

As in knowledge-based systems, description logics also separate knowledge (in a "TBox") and data (in a "ABox", which is not restricted to a single case) [2]. Then they confront knowledge and data, but do not reason from data alone. In that respect, case-based reasoning by working from a repertory of cases, shows that AI has considered the problem of reasoning from data (more precisely from tuples of data, called cases) for a long time.

Interestingly enough, research on case-based reasoning has remained apart from the main knowledge representation and reasoning trend, and has been much less oriented towards formal theoretical studies. Indeed "reasoning with data" could not benefit much of the tradition of mathematical reasoning and mathematical logic interested in the deduction of universal theorems, while applied mathematics applies generic equations to (numerical) data, as it was the case for knowledge-based systems (up to the problem of handling exceptions and uncertainty, not much encountered in mathematics).

Reasoning with data, which certainly includes case-based reasoning, is however potentially much larger, as we are trying to suggest in this paper. Moreover, reasoning with data and reasoning with knowledge are not necessarily topics that should be considered separately. Indeed reasoning from both knowledge and data may be worth doing. This is already the case in machine learning, where background knowledge, when available, is jointly used with data, or in case-based reasoning where domain knowledge may be taken into account, but not so much in deductive reasoning.

Knowledge and data are of different nature, and are not subject to have exactly the same kinds of defects, even if knowledge may be incomplete or pervaded with uncertainty, and data may be missing or suspect. Indeed knowledge may be inconsistent, or may be incoherent with respect to potential data, while data can be accumulated without inconsistency, nor redundancy. Data cannot be inconsistent by themselves, but only with respect to integrity constraints. Still some discrepancy may exist between data, which is a matter of (dis)similarity, and may then suggest outliers among data (if the reliability of the data is not fully guaranteed). But this differs from logical inconsistency between pieces of knowledge.

Moreover, as just mentioned, the notion of similarity makes sense for data, and is often instrumental when reasoning with data, while knowledge is more concerned with subsumption. Besides, it is worth mentioning that data, even if there is a massive amount of them, may be scarce in some areas where we would need to have more information.

In fact, data are a positive form of information, while knowledge has rather a negative flavor. Indeed knowledge restricts possible worlds, and thus implicitly states what worlds are *impossible*. The more knowledge you have, the greater the restriction on the remaining possible worlds, and the closer the information is to be complete about the world of interest, provided that the knowledge you have remains consistent. This contrasts with data that by nature are diverse, but should be regarded as positive information expressing that some worlds are *really possible*, since they are observed, or reported (assuming that the sources are reliable).

The paper is a kind of manifesto[1] in favor of more unified thinking and researches on the diverse forms of use of data in reasoning, possibly jointly with knowledge. The rest of the paper is structured as follows. The next section recalls how the idea of bipolarity, which distinguishes between positive and negative information may provide a setting for reasoning with data, in a coherent manner with respect to knowledge-based reasoning. Section 3 deals with similarity-based reasoning, including case-based reasoning, case-based decision, analogical reasoning, interpolation and extrapolation; it also points out the role of data in argumentation. Section 4 surveys issues related to the need of making sense of data, of reasoning about data, rather than reasoning from data, as in the two previous sections.

2   Reasoning with Data vs. Reasoning with Knowledge: A Bipolar Issue

Pieces of knowledge are generally understood as constraints[2] on sets of possible worlds. "Humans are mortal" means that it is impossible to find a human who is not mortal. Thus generic information, generally referred to as knowledge, may be viewed as *negative*, in the sense that what is really stated is an *impossibility*, which by complementation defines a set of worlds that are not impossible, i.e. that are *potentially* possible. Generic knowledge may have exceptions, and thus

---

[1] A preliminary version of this paper exists in French [41].

[2] Such a view is sometime termed as being "intensional"; see Pearl [38] who opposes it, in the case of rules, to "extensional" approaches where a (decision) rule would then express the license (rather than the obligation) to do something.

the information is pervaded with uncertainty. In such a case, the situation is basically the same, but impossibility is no longer fully strong. "Generally birds fly" is to be understood as it is rather impossible, but maybe not completely impossible to find birds that cannot fly. The more knowledge we have, the more restricted the remaining set of possible worlds, by effect of the conjunctive combination of such *restrictive* pieces of information.

By contrast, if we consider the piece of data "Mary is 111 years old", it is both a fact about Mary, and the indication that it is *possible for sure* (guaranteed possible) to live until 111 years, as long we regard the information as reliable. This type of information, based on observed, or reported cases, is not of the same nature as the claim that according to our understanding of our biological nature, it would be impossible to live more than 150 years in any case, where here living until 140 years remains just a potential possibility, as long as no case is reported. Observed facts give birth to what may be termed *positive* information. Positive information can be accumulated without any risk of inconsistency. For instance, if you want to know the price for a house having some specificities to let at a given time period, you may look to list of offers, select the ones that correspond to what you are looking for, and from them gather a collection of prices that can be regarded as possible for sure. But this does not mean that any other price would be impossible.

Possibility theory [19] (but also evidence theory [23], particular modal logics [15]) are suitable frameworks for representing both positive and negative information. Indeed the representation capabilities of possibilistic logic that extends classical logic by associating formulas with certainty levels, can be enlarged into a bipolar possibilistic setting [4,15]. It allows the separate representation of both negative and positive information taken in the following sense. Negative information reflects what is not (fully) impossible and remains potentially possible. It induces (prioritized) constraints on where the real world is (when expressing knowledge), which can be encoded by necessity-based possibilistic logic formulas. Positive information expressing what is actually possible, is encoded by another type of formula based on a set function called guaranteed (or actual) possibility measure (which is to be distinguished from "standard" possibility measures that rather express potential possibility (as a matter of consistency with the available information). This bipolar setting is thus of interest for representing both knowledge and reported data.

Positive information can be represented by formulas denoted $[\varphi, d]$, which expresses the constraint $\Delta(\varphi) \geq d$, where Δ denotes a measure of strong (actual) possibility [19] defined from a possibility distribution δ by $\Delta(\varphi) = \min_{\omega \models \varphi} \delta(\omega)$. Thus, the piece of positive information $[\varphi, d]$ expresses that any model of φ is at least possible with degree d (d reflects the minimal confidence in the reported observations gathered in the models of φ). More generally, let $D = \{[\varphi_j, d_j] \mid j = 1, \cdots, k\}$ be a positive possibilistic logic base. Its semantics is given by the possibility distribution

$$\delta_D(\omega) = \max_{j=1,\cdots,k} \delta_{[\varphi_j, d_j]}(\omega)$$

with $\delta_{[\varphi_j, d_j]}(\omega) = 0$ if $\omega \models \neg\varphi_j$, and $\delta_{[\varphi_j, d_j]}(\omega) = d_j$ if $\omega \models \varphi_j$. As can be seen, δ_D is obtained as the max-based *disjunctive* combination of the representation of each formula in D. This is in agreement with the idea that observations accumulate and are never in conflict with each other.

This contrasts with a standard possibilistic logic base $K = \{(\psi_i, c_i)\}_{i=1,\cdots,m}$, which is associated with the possibility distribution π_K representing the weighted set of models of K:

$$\pi_K(\omega) = \min_{i=1,\cdots,m} \max(\mu_{||\psi_i||}(\omega), 1 - c_i)$$

where an interpretation ω is all the less possible as it falsifies a formula ψ_i having a higher level of certainty c_i ($\mu_{||\psi_i||}$ is the characteristic function of the set of models of ψ_i). Each formula (ψ_i, c_i) corresponds to the semantic constraint $N(\psi_i) \geq c_i$, where N is a necessity measure, associated with a measure of (weak) possibility Π. Namely, we have $N(\psi) = 1 - \Pi(\neg\psi)$. Thus, the formula (ψ_i, c_i) expressed that the interpretations outside $||\psi_i||$ have a level of possibility upper bounded by $1 - c_i$, and are somewhat impossible (when ψ_i is fully certain, $c_i = 1$, and the possibility of any $\omega \notin ||\psi_i||$ is 0, which means full impossibility).

A positive possibilistic knowledge base $D = \{[\varphi_j, d_j] | j = 1, k\}$ is inconsistent with a negative possibilistic knowledge base $K = \{(\varphi_i, a_i) | i = 1, m\}$ as soon as the following fuzzy set inclusion is violated:

$$\forall\omega, \ \delta_D(\omega) \leq \pi_K(\omega).$$

This violation occurs when something is observed or reported, while one is somewhat certain that the opposite should be true. Then a revision should take place by either questioning the generic knowledge represented by K, or what is reported, which is represented by D.

Reasoning with both negative and positive information is clearly an issue of interest, since one may have information of both type in the same time. For instance consider, a second-hand car; there may exist some rules stating that for a car of some trade mark having some mileage, the price should be in some range, but one may also have examples of similar cars recently sold. See [15,51] for general settings allowing us to reason with knowledge and data in the same time. It is also worth mentioning that the setting of version space learning is bipolar in nature, since counter-examples play the role of negative information (counter-examples are by nature associated with the negation of generic rules), and examples are positive information [45].

3   Similarity-Based Forms of Reasoning

Similarity plays an important role when dealing with data. Two obvious examples are clustering data in unsupervised learning, and k-nearest neighbors methods in classification. Another example is provided by fuzzy rules in rule-based fuzzy controllers, where a rule is of the form "if the observed output x is in A, the command y should be chosen in B", and A and B are fuzzy sets [32][3]. These fuzzy sets, which have unimodal membership functions, may be understood as expressing closeness to the mode of the membership function. If a (resp. b) is the unique value having a membership grade to A (resp. B) equal to 1, then the rule means "the closer x is to a, the closer y is to b". This a gradual rule [6,18]. This is the basis for an *interpolation* mechanism [39], as soon as we have a second rule "the closer x is to a', the closer y is to b'", and an input $x = a_0$, such that $a_0 \in [a, a']$. This can be also related to the representation of co-variations [46].

3.1   Case-Based Reasoning

Case-based reasoning (CBR) is the main form of reasoning with data studied in AI. An attempt at formalizing it has been proposed in the setting of fuzzy sets and possibility theory [29]. Viewing a case as a pair (<situation>, <associated result>), it relies on the modeling of a CBR principle that relates the similarity of situations to the similarity of associated results. Let us state the idea more formally. Let $\mathcal{C}$ be a repertory of n cases $c_i = (s_i, r_i)$ with $i = 1, ..., n$, where $s_i \in \mathcal{S}$ (resp. $r_i \in \mathcal{R}$) denotes a situation (resp. a result). Let S and R be two graded similarity relations (assumed to be reflexive and symmetrical) defined on $\mathcal{S} \times \mathcal{S}$ and $\mathcal{R} \times \mathcal{R}$ respectively, where $S(s, s') \in [0, 1]$ and $R(r, r') \in [0, 1]$. Let us assume that we use a CBR principle based on the gradual rule "the more similar s_0 to s_i, the more similar r_0 to r_i" [1], where s_0 denotes the situation under consideration, and r_0 the unknown associated result. Then, it leads to the following expression for the fuzzy set $\widetilde{r}_0$ of possible values for the unknown value y of r_0:

$$\widetilde{r}_0(y) = \min_{(s_j, r_j) \in \mathcal{C}} S(s_0, s_j) \rightarrow R(y, r_j) \tag{1}$$

where $\rightarrow$ denotes Gödel implication $a \rightarrow b = 1$ if $a \leq b$ and $a \rightarrow b = b$ if $a > b$. It is worth noticing that the above expression underlies an *interpolation* mechanism. For instance, if a second hand car s_0 is identical to two other cars s and s', except that its mileage is between the ones of s and s', then the estimated price r_0 will be between r and r', and may be quite precise due to the min-based combination in (1). Thus, the estimation of r_0 is not just based on the closest similar case, but takes advantage of the "position" of s_0 among the s_i's such as $(s_i, r_i) \in \mathcal{C}$. In order to ensure the normalization of the fuzzy set $\widetilde{r}_0$ in (1), it is necessary for the repertory of cases to be "consistent" with the CBR principle used (see [13] for details), which means, informally speaking, that *the cases in the repertory* should themselves obey the principle "the more similar two case situations, the more similar the case results". In particular, letting $s_0 = s_i$, if we want to ensure $\widetilde{r}_i(r_i) = 1$ (i.e., one retrieves the case (s_i, r_i) as a solution) for any i, we should have $\forall i \; \forall j \; S(s_i, s_j) \leq R(r_i, r_j)$.

---

[3] Strictly speaking, such a rule was usually modeled as meaning "if x is in A, then y *can* be chosen in B", implicitly taking the view that it was reflecting commands already observed as being successful, and thus echoing positive information, or "extensional" rules [38]; see footnote 2.

If, on the contrary, there exist i and j such that $S(s_i, s_j) > R(r_i, r_j)$, i.e., the situations are more similar than the results, then another *weaker* CBR principle should be used. Namely, the fuzzy CBR principle reads "the more similar s_0 to s_i, the more *possible* the similarity r_0 and r_i", and then we obtain [16]

$$\tilde{r}_0(y) = \max_{(s_j, r_j) \in \mathcal{C}} \min(S(s_0, s_j), R(y, r_j)) \tag{2}$$

As can be seen, we now take the *union* (rather than the intersection) of the fuzzy sets of values close to the r_i's weighted by the similarity of s_0 with s_i, for all $(s_j, r_j) \in \mathcal{C}$. For instance, if a second hand car s_0 is quite similar to two other cars s and s', thus themselves quite similar, but having quite different prices r and r', then the estimated price r_0 will be the union of the fuzzy sets of values that are close to r or close to r' (the union may be replaced here by the convex hull, for taking into account that here the price domain is a continuum). Generally speaking, the result may be quite imprecise due to the max-based combination in (2). Still, it is a weighted union of all the possibilities that are supported by known cases. Note also that (2) is fully in the spirit of reasoning with data as discussed in the previous section: each result of a reported case is all the more guaranteed to be possible as the case is similar to the situation at hand, and all these conclusions are combined disjunctively.

One might also think of using a fuzzy rule of the form "the more similar s_0 to s_i, the more *certain* the similarity r_0 and r_i", leading to an expression similar to (1) where Gödel implication is replaced by Dienes implication (i.e., $a \rightarrow b = \max(1 - a, b)$). However, such a rule would be less appropriate here, even if it leaves room for exceptions, since we observe that $\tilde{r}_i(r_i) = 1$ holds for any i, only if $\forall i \, \forall j \, S(s_i, s_j) > 0 \Rightarrow R(r_i, r_j) = 1$, which is a condition stronger than the one for (1) with Gödel implication.

A thorough study of the formalization of CBR principles linking the similarity of solutions to the one of problems is presented in the research monograph [29].

3.2   Case-Based Decision

This approach can be readily extended to *case-based decision*, where we have a repertory $\mathcal{D}$ of experienced decisions under the form of cases $c_i = (s_i, d, r_i)$, which means that decision d in situation s_i has led to result r_i (it is assumed that r_i is uniquely determined by s_i and d). Classical expected utility is then changed into $U(d) = \frac{\Sigma_{(s_i, d, r_i) \in \mathcal{D}} S(s_0, s_i) \cdot u(r_i)}{\Sigma_{(s_i, d, r_i) \in \mathcal{D}} S(s_0, s_i)}$, where u is a utility function, here supposed to be valued in $[0, 1]$ [28]. Besides, counterparts to (1) and (2) are

$$U_*(d) = \min_{(s_i, d, r_i) \in \mathcal{D}} S(s_0, s_i) \rightarrow u(r_i)$$

and

$$U^*(d) = \max_{(s_i, d, r_i) \in \mathcal{D}} \min(S(s_0, s_i), u(r_i)).$$

$U_*(d)$ is a pessimistic qualitative utility that expresses that a decision d is all the better as the fuzzy set of results associated with situations similar to s_0 where decision d was experienced is included in the fuzzy set of good results. When $\rightarrow$ is Dienes implication, $U_*(d) = 1$ only if the result obtained with decision d in any known situation somewhat similar to s_0 was fully satisfactory. $U^*(d)$ is an optimistic qualitative utility since it expresses that a decision d is all the better as it was already successfully experienced in a situation similar to s_0. See [14] for postulate-based justifications. Another idea would be to use the approach of the previous subsection for estimating the more or less possible results of each decision, and then to compute the possible values of the utility function for each of them, which would then lead to compare fuzzy utilities.

A situation s is usually described by means of several features, i.e., $s = (s^1, ..., s^m)$. Then the evaluation of the similarity between two situations s and $s' = (s'^1, ..., s'^m)$ amounts to estimating the similarity according to each feature k according to a similarity relation S^k, and to combine these partial similarities using some aggregation operator agg, namely $S(s, s') = agg_{k=1,...,m} S^k(s^k, s'^k)$. A classical choice for agg is the conjunction operator min, which retains the smallest similarity value as the global evaluation. But one may also think, for instance, of using some weighted aggregation if all the features have not the same importance. See [12] for a detailed example (with min).

Besides, the approach can be extended to prediction about some imprecisely or fuzzily specified cases (e.g., one has to estimate the price of a car with precisely specified features except that the horse power is between 90 and 110). A further generalization is necessary in order to accommodate incompletely specified cases in the repertory. See [16] for these extensions in the case of possibility rules (thus corresponding to (2)), and [31] for the discussion of several other generalizations (including the discounting of untypical cases and the flexible handling and adequate adaptation of different similarity relations, which provides a way of incorporating domain-specific (expert) knowledge). A comparative discussion with instance-based learning algorithms, a form of transduction, is in [30]. Applications to flexible querying [9], including examples (and counter-examples)-based querying[4], and to recommendation systems [17] have been also proposed.

Lastly, one may think of cases that provide an argumentative support in favor of a claim as positive examples of it, or more strongly of cases used as a counter-example to a rule used in an argument; see a brief outline of this idea in [40], when discussing an argumentative view of case-based decision.

3.3 Analogical Reasoning

The notion of similarity is as essential to CBR as it is to the idea of analogy, and in particular, to analogical proportions. The core idea underlying analogical proportions comes from the numerical field where proportions express an equality of ratios, e.g. $\frac{1}{2} = \frac{5}{10}$, which could be read "1 is to 2 as 5 is to 10". It is also

---

[4] An item is all the more a solution as it resembles to some example(s) in all important aspects, and is dissimilar from all counter-examples in some important aspect(s).

agreed that "read is to reader as lecture is to lecturer" is a natural language analogical proportion, and the notation *read : reader :: lecture : lecturer* is then preferred. More generally, an analogical proportion is an expression usually denoted $a : b :: c : d$ involving 4 terms a, b, c, d, which reads "a is to b as c is to d". It clearly involves comparisons between the pairs (a, b) and (c, d). Recent works have led to a logical formalization of analogical proportions, where similarities/dissimilarities existing between a and b are equated to similarities/dissimilarities existing between c and d.

Let us assume that the items a, b, c, d represent sets of binary features belonging to an universe U (i.e. an item is then viewed as the set of binary features in U that it satisfies). Then, the dissimilarity between a and b can be appreciated in terms of $a \cap \overline{b}$ and/or $\overline{a} \cap b$, where $\overline{a}$ denotes the complement of a in U, while the similarity is estimated by means of $a \cap b$ and/or of $\overline{a} \cap \overline{b}$. Then, an analogical proportion between subsets is formally defined as [35]:

$$a \cap \overline{b} = c \cap \overline{d} \text{ and } \overline{a} \cap b = \overline{c} \cap d$$

This expresses that "a differs from b as c differs from d" and that "b differs from a as d differs from c". It can be viewed as the expression of a co-variation. It has an easy counterpart in Boolean logic, where a, b, c, d now denote simple Boolean variables. In this logical setting, "are equated to" translates into "are equivalent to" ($\equiv$), $\overline{a}$ is now the negation of a, and $\cap$ is changed into a conjunction ($\wedge$), and we get the logical condition expressing that 4 Boolean variables make an analogical proportion:

$$(a \wedge \overline{b} \equiv c \wedge \overline{d}) \wedge (\overline{a} \wedge b \equiv \overline{c} \wedge d)$$

It is logically equivalent to the following condition that expresses that the pairs made by the extremes and the means, namely (a, d) and (b, c), are (positively and negatively) similar [35]:

$$(a \wedge d \equiv b \wedge c) \wedge (\overline{a} \wedge \overline{d} \equiv \overline{b} \wedge \overline{c}).$$

An analogical proportion is then a Boolean formula. It takes the truth value "1" only for any of the 6 following patterns for *abcd*: $1111, 0000, 1100, 0011, 1010, 0101$. For the 10 other lines of its truth table, it is false (i.e., equal to 0). As expected, it satisfies the following remarkable properties:

$$a : b :: a : b \text{ (reflexivity)},$$
$$\text{(and thus } a : a :: a : a \text{ (identity))};$$
$$a : b :: c : d \Rightarrow c : d :: a : b \text{ (symmetry)};$$
$$a : b :: c : d \Rightarrow a : c :: b : d \text{ (central permutation)}.$$

Another worth noticing property [42] is the fact that the analogical proportion remains true for the negation of the Boolean variables. It expresses that the result does not depend on a positive or a negative[5] encoding of the features:

---

[5] The use of these words here just refers to the application of a negation, and should not be confused with their use in other parts of the paper.

$$a : b :: c : d \Rightarrow \overline{a} : \overline{b} :: \overline{c} : \overline{d} \text{ (code independency)}.$$

Finally, analogical proportions satisfy a unique solution property, which means that, 3 Boolean values a, b, c being given, when we have to find a fourth one x such that $a : b :: c : x$ holds, we have either no solution (as in the cases of $011x$ or $100x$), or a unique one (as, e.g., in the case of $110x$). More formally, the analogical equation $a : b :: c : x$ is solvable iff $((a \equiv b) \vee (a \equiv c)) = 1$. In that case, the unique solution x is $a \equiv (b \equiv c)$ [35]. This allows us to deal with Boolean analogical proportions in a simple way.

The basic idea underlying the analogical proportion-based inference is as follows: *if there is a proportion that holds between the first p components of four vectors, then this proportion should hold for the last remaining components as well.* This inference principle [50] can be formally stated as below:

$$\frac{\forall i \in \{1, ..., p\}, \quad a_i : b_i :: c_i : d_i \text{ holds}}{\forall j \in \{p + 1, ..., n\}, \quad a_j : b_j :: c_j : d_j \text{ holds}}$$

This is a generalized form of analogical reasoning, where we transfer knowledge from some components of our vectors to their remaining components.

It is worth pointing out that properties such as *full identity* or *code independency* are especially relevant in that perspective. Indeed, it is expected that in the case where d is such that it exists a case a in the repertory with $\forall i \in \{1, ..., p\}, d_i = a_i$, then $a_i : a_i :: a_i : d_i$ holds. Thus, the approach includes the extreme particular case where we have to classify (or to predict components of) an item whose representation (in the input space) is completely similar to the one of a completely known item. The code independency property, which expresses independence with respect to the encoding, seems also very desirable since it ensures that whatever the convention used for the positive or the negative encodings of the value of each feature and of the class, one shall obtain the same result for features in $\{p + 1, ..., n\}$. Then analogical reasoning amounts to finding completely informed triples suitable for inferring the missing value(s) of an incompletely informed item as in the following example. In case of the existence of several possible triples leading to possibly distinct plausible conclusions, a voting procedure may be used, as in case-based reasoning.

Let us consider for instance a database of homes to let, containing houses (1) and flats (0), which are well equipped or not (1/0), which are cheap or expensive (1/0), where you have to pay a tax or not (1/0). Then a house, well equipped, expensive and taxable is represented by the vector $a = (1, 1, 0, 1)$. Having 2 other cases $b = (1, 0, 1, 1)$, $c = (0, 1, 0, 1)$, we can predict the price and taxation status of a new case d which is a flat not well equipped, i.e. $d = (0, 0, x, y)$ where 2 values are unknown. Applying the above approach, and noticing that an analogical proportion $a : b :: c : d$ holds for the 2 first components of each vector, we "infer" that such a proportion should hold for the 2 last components as well, yielding $x = 1$ and $y = 1$ (i.e. cheap and taxable).

This approach, using Boolean analogical proportions, has been extended to numerical features using multiple-valued connectives [43]. It has been successfully applied to classification problems [3, 34, 44], where the attribute to be predicted is the class of the new item. Analogical proportions may be also applied to interpolation and extrapolation reasoning between if-then rules [10, 48, 49], but this is beyond their direct application to data.

4   Making Sense of Data

Making sense of data may cover a large range of situations where we reason about data. By reasoning about data, we mean reasoning from a (possibly dynamic) set of data, without the purpose of drawing a conclusion on a particular attribute in a given situation, as in deductive, abductive, case-based, or analogical reasoning. The issue is then to understand the whole set of data in a way or another. Reasoning about data covers a variety of problems as briefly reviewed now.

A first class of problems is when receiving a flux of information to figure out what is going on. We are close to the recognition of temporal scenarii [52]. We may need to identify what causes what (see, e.g., [7]). In such problems, we have to check if data fits with knowledge describing an abnormal, or the normal course of things.

Another important class of problems deals with the structuring of the data. We may start from a table of data, as in formal concept analysis [25], where a formal context R indicates what Boolean attribute(s) is/are true for a given object. Then, a formal concept is a maximal pair (X, Y), such as $X \times Y \subseteq R$ where X is a set of objects and Y is a set of properties; each object in X has all properties in Y, and each property in Y is possessed by all objects in X. A formal context is associated with a lattice of formal concepts, from which association rules can be extracted [24, 36]. This is the theoretical basis for data mining.

Interestingly enough, the operator which is at the basis of the definition of formal concepts is analogous to the guaranteed possibility measure mentioned in Sect. 2; indeed, in a formal concept (X, Y), the properties in Y are guaranteed for any object in X. Note also that $(x, y) \in R$ is understood here as a positive fact, while $(x', y') \notin R$ is not viewed as a negative fact, it rather means that the piece of information $(x', y') \in R$ is not available (at least if there is no closed world assumption underlying the formal context R). Moreover, other possibility theory operators have been imported in formal concept analysis, and enables us to consider other forms of reasoning, still to be investigated in detail, including case-based reasoning, see [20]. Moreover, formal concept analysis can be related [21] to other theoretical frameworks such as rough sets [37] or extensional fuzzy sets, in the general setting of granular computing [53], where the idea of clustering is implicitly at work. Closely related is the summarization of data which exploits ideas of similarity and clustering (e.g., [5, 27, 33]).

Classification or estimation methods are usually black box devices. They may be learnt from data. It is clearly of interest to lay bare the contents of these black boxes in understandable terms. There have been a number of attempts in that directions; let us mention a few examples like a non-monotonic inference view [26] or a fuzzy rule-based interpretation [8] of neural nets, or more recently a weighted logic view of Sugeno integrals [22] laying bare the rules underlying the global estimation.

5 Concluding Remarks

Taking machine learning and data mining apart, reasoning with data has remained confined in few specialized works (at least if we restrict ourselves to formalized approaches), or in particular areas such as fuzzy logic, or rough sets [37]. This overview has emphasized two important points: (i) data and knowledge being of different nature, they should be handled differently, and handling both knowledge and data requires a bipolar setting; (ii) similarity (and dissimilarity) play an important role when reasoning with data.

It becomes timely to recognize reasoning with data as a general research trend in AI, to identify all the facets and issues raised by the handling of data in various forms of reasoning, and to develop a unified view of these problems. It may also contribute to a better interfacing between reasoning and learning research areas [11,33,47].

References

1. Arrazola, I., Plainfossé, A., Prade, H., Testemale, C.: Extrapolation of fuzzy values from incomplete data bases. Inf. Syst. **14**(6), 487–492 (1989)
2. Baader, F., Horrocks, I., Sattler, U.: Description logics. In: van Harmelen, F., Lifschitz, V., Porter, B. (eds.) Handbook of Knowledge Representation, chapter 3, pp. 135–180. Elsevier (2007)
3. Bayoudh, S., Miclet, L., Delhay, A.: Learning by analogy: a classification rule for binary and nominal data. In: Proceedings of International Conference on Artificial Intelligence (IJCAI 2007), pp. 678–683 (2007)
4. Benferhat, S., Dubois, D., Kaci, S., Prade, H.: Modeling positive and negative information in possibility theory. Int. J. Intell. Syst. **23**, 1094–1118 (2008)
5. Bosc, P., Dubois, D., Pivert, O., Prade, H., De Calmès, M.: Fuzzy summarization of data using fuzzy cardinalities. In: Proceedings of 9th International Conference Information Processing and Management of Uncertainty in Knowledge-Based Systems (IPMU 2002), Annecy, pp. 1553–1559, 1–5 July 2002
6. Bouchon-Meunier, B., Laurent, A., Lesot, M.-J., Rifqi, M.: Strengthening fuzzy gradual rules through "all the more" clauses. In: Proceedings of IEEE International Conference on Fuzzy Systems (Fuzz-IEEE 2010), Barcelona, July 2010
7. Chassy, P., de Calmès, M., Prade, H.: Making sense as a process emerging from perception-memory interaction: a model. Int. J. Intell. Syst. **27**, 757–775 (2012)
8. d'Alché-Buc, F., Andrés, V., Nadal, J.-P.: Rule extraction with fuzzy neural network. Int. J. Neural Syst. **5**(1), 1–11 (1994)
9. De Calmès, M., Dubois, D., Hüllermeier, E., Prade, H., Sédes, F.: Flexibility, fuzzy case-based evaluation in querying: an illustration in an experimental setting. Int. J. Uncertain. Fuzziness Knowl. Based Syst. **11**(1), 43–66 (2003)
10. Derrac, J., Schockaert, S.: Inducing semantic relations from conceptual spaces: a data-driven approach to plausible reasoning. Artif. Intell. **228**, 66–94 (2015)
11. Domingos, P., Kok, S., Lowd, D., Poon, H., Richardson, M., Singla, P.: Markov logic. In: Raedt, L., Frasconi, P., Kersting, K., Muggleton, S.H. (eds.) Probabilistic Inductive Logic Programming. LNCS (LNAI), vol. 4911, pp. 92–117. Springer, Heidelberg (2008)

12. Dubois, D., Esteva, F., Garcia, P., Godo, L., López de Mántaras, R., Prade, H.: Fuzzy modelling of case-based reasoning and decision. In: Leake, D.B., Plaza, E. (eds.) ICCBR 1997. LNCS, vol. 1266, pp. 599–610. Springer, Heidelberg (1997)

13. Dubois, D., Esteva, F., Garcia, P., Godo, L., López de Mántaras, R., Prade, H.: Fuzzy set modelling in case-based reasoning. Int. J. Intell. Syst. **13**, 345–373 (1998)

14. Dubois, D., Godo, L., Prade, H., Zapico, A.: On the possibilistic decision model: from decision under uncertainty to case-based decision. Int. J. Uncertain. Fuzziness Knowl. Based Syst. **7**(6), 631–670 (1999)

15. Dubois, D., Hajek, P., Prade, H.: Knowledge-driven versus data-driven logics. J. Log. Lang. Inf. **9**, 65–89 (2000)

16. Dubois, D., Hüllermeier, E., Prade, H.: Fuzzy set-based methods in instance-based reasoning. IEEE Trans. Fuzzy Syst. **10**(3), 322–332 (2002)

17. Dubois, D., Hüllermeier, E., Prade, H.: Fuzzy methods for case-based recommendation and decision support. J. Intell. Inf. Syst. **27**, 95–115 (2006)

18. Dubois, D., Prade, H.: Gradual inference rules in approximate reasoning. Inf. Sci. **61**(1–2), 103–122 (1992)

19. Dubois, D., Prade, H., Possibility theory: qualitative and quantitative aspects. In: Gabbay, D., Smets, P. (eds.) Quantified Representation of Uncertainty and Imprecision. Handbook of Defeasible Reasoning and Uncertainty Management Systems Series, vol. 1, pp. 169–226. Kluwer Academic Publishers (1998) .

20. Dubois, D., Prade, H.: Possibility theory and formal concept analysis: characterizing independent sub-contexts and handling approximations. Fuzzy Sets Syst. **196**, 4–16 (2012)

21. Dubois, D., Prade, H.: Bridging gaps between several forms of granular computing. Granul. Comput. **1**(2), 115–126 (2016)

22. Dubois, D., Prade, H., Rico, A.: The logical encoding of Sugeno integrals. Fuzzy Sets Syst. **241**, 61–75 (2014)

23. Dubois, D., Prade, H., Smets, P.: "Not impossible" vs. "guaranteed possible" in fusion and revision. In: Benferhat, S., Besnard, P. (eds.) ECSQARU 2001. LNCS (LNAI), vol. 2143, pp. 522–531. Springer, Heidelberg (2001)

24. Duquenne, V., Guigues, J.-L.: Famille minimale d'implications informatives résultant d'un tableau de données binaires. Math. Sci. Hum. **24**(95), 5–18 (1986)

25. Ganter, B., Wille, R.: Formal Concept Analysis. Springer, New York (1999)

26. Gärdenfors, P.: Nonmonotonic inference, expectations, and neural networks. In: Kruse, R., Siegel, P. (eds.) Symbolic and Quantitative Approaches to Uncertainty. LNCS, vol. 548, pp. 12–27. Springer, Heidelberg (1991)

27. Gaume, B., Navarro, E., Prade, H.: Clustering bipartite graphs in terms of approximate formal concepts and sub-contexts. Int. J. Comput. Intell. Syst. **6**(6), 1125–1142 (2013)

28. Gilboa, I., Schmeidler, D.: Case-based decision theory. Q. J. Econ. **110**, 605–639 (1995)

29. Hüllermeier, E.: Case-Based Approximate Reasoning. Theory and Decision Library. Springer, New York (2007)

30. Hüllermeier, E., Dubois, D., Prade, H.: Model adaptation in possibilistic instance-based reasoning. IEEE Trans. Fuzzy Syst. **10**(3), 333–339 (2002)

31. Hüllermeier, E., Dubois, D., Prade, H.: Knowledge-based extrapolation of cases: a possibilistic approach. In: Bouchon-Meunier, B., Gutiérrez-Ríos, J., Magdalena, L., Yager, R.R. (eds.) Technologies for Constructing Intelligent Systems 1, pp. 377–390. Springer, Heidelberg (2002)

32. Mamdani, E.H., Assilian, S.: An experiment in linguistic synthesis with a fuzzy logic controller. Int. J. Man Mach. Stud. **7**, 1–13 (1975)

33. Memory, A., Kimmig, A., Bach, S.H., Raschid, L., Getoor, L.: Graph summarization in annotated data using probabilistic soft logic. In: Bobillo, F., et al. (eds.) Proceedings of 8th International Workshop on Uncertainty Reasoning for the Semantic Web (URSW 2012), Boston, November 2011, vol. 900, pp. 75–86. CEUR Workshop Proceedings (2012)
34. Miclet, L., Bayoudh, S., Delhay, A.: Analogical dissimilarity: definition, algorithms and two experiments in machine learning. J. Artif. Intell. Res. (JAIR) **32**, 793–824 (2008)
35. Miclet, L., Prade, H.: Handling analogical proportions in classical logic and fuzzy logics settings. In: Sossai, C., Chemello, G. (eds.) ECSQARU 2009. LNCS, vol. 5590, pp. 638–650. Springer, Heidelberg (2009)
36. Pasquier, N., Bastide, Y., Taouil, R., Lakhal, L.: Efficient mining of association rules using closed itemset lattices. Inf. Syst. **24**(1), 25–46 (1999)
37. Pawlak, Z.: Rough Sets: Theoretical Aspects of Reasoning About Data. Kluwer Academic Publishers, Dordrecht (1991)
38. Pearl, J.: Probabilistic Reasoning in Intelligent Systems: Networks of Plausible Inference. Morgan Kaufmann Publishers, San Mateo (1988)
39. Perfilieva, I., Dubois, D., Prade, H., Esteva, F., Godo, L., Hodáková, P.: Interpolation of fuzzy data: analytical approach and overview. Fuzzy Sets Syst. **192**, 134–158 (2012)
40. Prade, H.: Qualitative evaluation of decisions in an argumentative manner - a general discussion in a unified setting. In: Proceedings of 4th Conference of the European Society for Fuzzy Logic and Technology (EUSFLAT-LFA 2005 Joint Conference), Barcelona, 7–9 September, pp. 1003–1008 (2005)
41. Prade, H.: Raisonner avec des données. Un nouveau chantier pour l'IA? Actes 10èmes Jour. Intellig. Artif. Fondamentale (JIAF), Montpellier, 15–17 June 2016. https://www.supagro.fr/jfpc_jiaf_2016/Articles.IAF.2016/Actes.IAF.2016.pdf
42. Prade, H., Richard, G.: From analogical proportion to logical proportions. Log. Univers. **7**(4), 441–505 (2013)
43. Prade, H., Richard, G.: Analogical proportions and multiple-valued logics. In: van der Gaag, L.C. (ed.) ECSQARU 2013. LNCS, vol. 7958, pp. 497–509. Springer, Heidelberg (2013)
44. Prade, H., Richard, G., Yao, B.: Enforcing regularity by means of analogy-related proportions - a new approach to classification. Int. J. Comput. Inf. Syst. Ind. Manag. Appl. **4**, 648–658 (2012)
45. Prade, H., Serrurier, M.: Bipolar version space learning. Int. J. Intell. Syst. **23**(10), 1135–1152 (2008)
46. Raccah, P.Y. (ed.): Topoï et Gestion des Connaissances. Masson, Paris (1996)
47. Russell, S.J.: Unifying logic and probability. Commun. ACM **58**(7), 88–97 (2015)
48. Schockaert, S., Prade, H.: Interpolation and extrapolation in conceptual spaces: a case study in the music domain. In: Rudolph, S., Gutierrez, C. (eds.) RR 2011. LNCS, vol. 6902, pp. 217–231. Springer, Heidelberg (2011)
49. Schockaert, S., Prade, H.: Completing symbolic rule bases using betweenness and analogical proportion. In: Prade, H., Richard, G. (eds.) Computational Approaches to Analogical Reasoning: Current Trends, pp. 195–215. Springer, Heidelberg (2014)
50. Stroppa, N., Yvon, F.: Analogical learning and formal proportions: definitions and methodological issues. Technical report, ENST D-2005-004, Paris, June 2005
51. Ughetto, L., Dubois, D., Prade, H.: Implicative and conjunctive fuzzy rules - a tool for reasoning from knowledge and examples. In: Proceedings of 15th National Conference in Artificial Intelligence (AAAI 1999), Orlando, pp. 214–219, July 1999

52. Vu, V.-T., Brémond, F., Thonnat, M.: Automatic video interpretation: a novel algorithm for temporal scenario recognition. In: Gottlob, G., Walsh, T. (eds.) Proceedings of 18th International Joint Conference Artificial Intelligence (IJCAI 2003), Acapulco, 9–15 August, pp. 1295–1302 (2003)
53. Zadeh, L.A.: Toward a theory of fuzzy information granulation and its centrality in human reasoning and fuzzy logic. Fuzzy Sets Syst. **90**, 111–128 (1997)

Probabilistic Spatial Reasoning in Constraint Logic Programming

Carl Schultz[1,3]($\boxtimes$), Mehul Bhatt[2,3], and Jakob Suchan[2,3]

[1] University of Münster, Münster, Germany
schultzc@uni-muenster.de
[2] University of Bremen, Bremen, Germany
[3] The DesignSpace Group, Bremen, Germany

Abstract. In this paper we present a novel framework and full implementation of probabilistic spatial reasoning within a Logic Programming context. The crux of our approach is extending Probabilistic Logic Programming (based on distribution semantics) to support reasoning over spatial variables via Constraint Logic Programming. Spatial reasoning is formulated as a numerical optimisation problem, and we implement our approach within ProbLog 1. We demonstrate a range of powerful features beyond what is currently provided by existing probabilistic and spatial reasoning tools.

Keywords: Probabilistic Logic Programming · Constraint Logic Programming · Declarative spatial reasoning

1 Introduction

The research field of declarative spatial reasoning focuses on extending Knowledge Representation and Reasoning frameworks to natively support variables that range over spatial domains (such as Constraint Logic Programming [3] and Answer Set Programming Modulo Theories [23]). The aim is to provide a high-level logic programming language for seamlessly reasoning about both conceptual, domain specific knowledge and spatial constraints between objects.

However, in many application scenarios spatial information is only available with a degree of uncertainty. For example, spatial relations that have been determined to hold between objects may come from image recognition software that is prone to various segmentation errors. Extensions to Logic Programming for supporting probabilistic reasoning such as ProbLog provide a natural interface for expressing such information.

For a simple example, let circles C_1, C_2, C_3 have the following qualitative spatial relations: (a) C_1 is inside C_2 and touching its boundary (i.e. it is a *tangential proper part* (tpp)) with probability 0.7; (b) C_1 is inside C_2 and *not* touching its boundary (i.e. it is a *non-tangential proper part* (ntpp)) with probability 0.3; (c) C_2 is external to C_3 and touching its boundary (i.e. it is *externally connected* (ec)) with probability 0.8. Circles C_1, C_2, C_3 could be spatial representations of

© Springer International Publishing Switzerland 2016
S. Schockaert and P. Senellart (Eds.): SUM 2016, LNAI 9858, pp. 289–302, 2016.
DOI: 10.1007/978-3-319-45856-4_20

cells $(cell_1, cell_2, cell_3)$ in a histopathology application that have been automatically recognised from an image of a stained tissue section:

```
0.8 :: image_data(relation(ec),   id(cell2), id(cell3)).
%% mutually exclusive options for the relation between cell1 and cell2
0.7 :: image_data(relation(tpp),  id(cell1), id(cell2)) ;
0.3 :: image_data(relation(ntpp), id(cell1), id(cell2)).
%% no information available about the relation between cell1 and cell3
image_data(_, id(cell1), id(cell3)).

spatial_relation(Relation, Id1, Id2) :-
  image_data(Relation, Id1, Id2),
  spatial_representation(Id1, Shape1),
  spatial_representation(Id2, Shape2),
  topology(Relation, Shape1, Shape2).
```

We can then formulate a query that asks what topological relations may hold between cells C_1 and C_3, and what the probabilities are of the logic programs in which those relations are consistent:

```
?- topology(Relation),
|    Query = (spatial_relation(_, cell1, cell2),
|             spatial_relation(_, cell2, cell3)),
|             spatial_relation(Relation, cell1, cell3)),
|    problog_exact(Query, Prob, _), Prob > 0.
Relation = dc, Prob = 0.8;
Relation = ec, Prob = 0.56;
false.
```

The spatial reasoning component has determined that only two topological relations are possible: C_1 is *disconnected* from C_3 (dc) or C_1 is *externally connected* to C_3 (ec). The probabilistic reasoning component has determined the exact probabilities of each set of facts. The meaning is that there is a 0.8 probability (resp. 0.56) that C_1, C_3 can be arranged to be *dc* (resp. *ec*) without violating any other constraints, i.e. the probabilities refer to the *consistency* of the relations.[1] As an integrated system these components provide a powerful framework for expressing complex probabilistic models that involve spatial clauses in a high-level manner.

In this paper we develop foundations for a probabilistic declarative spatial reasoning system within Constraint Logic Programming. Building on our previous work, we target a specific class of *qualitative* spatial constraints that we formulate in the framework of *numerical optimisation*, including: contact, incidence, orientation, relative size. We make the following novel contributions:

- We show how mixed numerical-qualitative spatial reasoning, along with soft constraints, can be naturally specified in our spatial reasoning framework due to the formulation as a numerical optimisation problem (Sect. 3);

---

[1] Importantly, observe that the probabilities do not state that the *dc* relation *holds* with probability 0.8; this cannot be the case as *dc* and *ec* are mutually exclusive, and yet the probabilities 0.8 and 0.56 sum to more than 1. Such an inference would require information about the spatial distribution of the objects which has not been given in the problem description.

- We integrate spatial reasoning (based on numerical optimisation) within the framework of probabilistic logic programming based on Sato's distribution semantics (Sect. 4);
- We define probabilistic extensions of three fundamental spatial reasoning tasks: consistency, configuration generation, and interactive geometry (Sect. 4).

2 Preliminaries: Probabilistic Logic Programming

We build on the probabilistic logic programming theory used in the original ProbLog [8], which, along with other prominent approaches, is based on Sato's distribution semantics [18]. We emphasise that our approach is not directly dependent on ProbLog specifically; we have opted to build on the ProbLog framework[2] as it provides efficient and sound inference procedures for computing success probabilities of probabilistic logic programming queries. Our approach for integrating spatial reasoning can be similarly employed in other probabilistic logic programming frameworks.

Prolog [22]. We assume basic familiarity with first-order logic. A *term* is either a variable, constant, or a structure $f(t_1, \ldots, t_n)$ with functor f applied to terms $t_1, \ldots, t_n$. An *atom* $p(t_1, \ldots, t_n)$ is a predicate p of arity n with terms $t_1, \ldots, t_n$. A Prolog program L_P consists of a finite set of universally quantified *rules* of the form $h \leftarrow b_1, \ldots, b_n$ such that h is an atom, and the expression $b_1, \ldots, b_n$ is a conjunction of atoms (i.e. rules are Horn clauses). Prolog *facts* are rules of the form $h \leftarrow \top$. A *query* is a conjunction of atoms $b_1, \ldots, b_n$. A ground term is a term with no variables. The Herbrand universe U of L_P is the set of ground terms that can be made from the constants and function symbols of L_P. Let q be a query, then $q\theta$ is a conjunction of ground atoms resulting from an assignment θ of all variables in q to values from U. A query is a logical consequence of L_P if there exists an assignment θ such that $(L_P \models q\theta)$.

Distribution Semantics [18]. Let $L_T = \{f_1, \ldots, f_n\}$ be a set of facts and let L_P be a set of facts and rules (i.e. L_P is a Prolog program). Moreover, the *disjoint condition* between L_T and L_P holds: no atom in L_T unifies with a rule in L_P. A joint distribution can be given to the set of facts in L_T, resulting in $T = \{p_1 : f_1, \ldots, p_n : f_n\}$, where p_i is a probability and f_i is a ground Prolog fact. T defines a probability distribution over subsets of logic programs $L_T \cup L_P$ as follows. Let $L \subseteq L_T$, then the probability of this program L given T is [8]:

$$P(L|T) = \Big(\prod_{f_i \in L} p_i \Big) \cdot \Big(\prod_{f_i \in L_T \setminus L} 1 - p_i \Big)$$

We will henceforth refer to $(T \cup L_P)$ as a ProbLog program [8]. Given query q and ProbLog program $(T \cup L_P)$, the *success probability* $P(q|(T, L_P))$ of q is defined as follows [8]:

---

[2] Specifically, we have used the original ProbLog 1 implemented in Yap Prolog v6.3.4 with the default ProbLog algorithm flags and settings when consulted.

$$P(q|(L, L_P)) = \begin{cases} 1 & \exists \theta ((L \cup L_P) \models q\theta) \\ 0 & \text{otherwise} \end{cases}$$

$$P(q, L|(T, L_P)) = P(q|(L, L_P)) \cdot P(L|T)$$

$$P(q|(T, L_P)) = \sum_{M \subseteq L_T} P(q, M|(T, L_P))$$

Informally, the success probability of q is the sum of the probabilities of all logic programs (that are subsets of the given ProbLog program) in which q can be proven.

ProbLog supports annotated disjunctions to model mutually exclusive options of the form $\{p'_1 : f'_1, ..., p'_n : f'_n\}$ such that $p'_1 + \cdots + p'_n \leq 1$ interpreted as only one f'_i being true in a given logic program according to the assigned probabilities p'_i (we use the encodings presented in [12] Chap. 3.3).

3   Spatial Representation and Reasoning

The qualitative spatial domain (QS) that we focus on in our formal framework consists of the following ontology.

Spatial Domains. Domain entities in QS include *points, line segments, circles, simple polygons,* and *egg-yolk regions*. While our method is applicable to a wide range of 2D and 3D spatial objects and qualitative relations, for brevity and clarity we primarily focus on a 2D spatial domain. Our method is readily applicable to other 2D and 3D spatial domains and qualitative relations, for example, as defined in [3,4,16]:

- a *point* is a pair of reals x, y,
- a *line segment* is a pair of end points p_1, p_2 ($p_1 \neq p_2$),
- a *circle* is a centre point p and a real radius r ($0 < r$),
- an *egg yolk* region[3] is defined by a circular upper and lower approximation c^+, c^- such that c^- is a *proper part* of c^+,
- a *simple polygon* is defined by a list of n vertices (points) $p_1, \ldots, p_n$ (spatially ordered counter-clockwise) such that the boundary is non-self-intersecting, i.e., there does not exist a polygon boundary edge between vertices p_i, p_{i+1} that intersects some other edge p_j, p_{j+1} for all $1 \leq i < j < n$ and $i + 1 < j$.

A spatial *object* $o \in O$ is a variable associated with a spatial domain D (e.g. the domain of 2D points). An *instance* of an object $i \in D$ is an element from the domain. Given $O = \{o_1, \ldots, o_n\}$, and domains $D_1, \ldots, D_n$ such that o_i is

---

[3] We employ the egg-yolk method of modelling regions with indeterminante boundaries [6] to characterise a class of regions (including polygons) that satisfies topological and relative orientation relations [19]. Each egg-yolk region is an equivalence class for all regions that are contained within the upper approximation (the *egg white*), and completely contain the lower approximations (the *egg yolk*).

associated with domain D_i, then a *configuration* of objects ψ is a one-to-one mapping between object variables and instances from the domain, $\psi(o_i) \in D_i$.

For example, a variable o_1 is associated with the domain D_1 of 2D points. The point $(0,1)$ is an instance of D_1. A configuration is defined that maps o_1 to $(0,1)$ i.e. $\psi(o_1) = (0,1)$.

Spatial Relations. Let $D_1, \ldots, D_n$ be spatial domains. A spatial relation r of arity n $(0 < n)$ is defined as:

$$r \subseteq D_1 \times \cdots \times D_n$$

That is, each spatial relation is an equivalence class of instances of spatial objects. Given a set of objects O, a relation r of arity n can be asserted as a constraint that must hold between objects $o_1, \ldots, o_n \in O$, denoted $r_{1,\ldots,n}$. The constraint $r_{1,\ldots,n}$ is satisfied by configuration ψ if $\big(\psi(o_1), \ldots, \psi(o_n)\big) \in r$.

For example, if dc is a topological relation *disconnected*, and O is a set of polygon objects, then $dc_{4,9}$ is the constraint that polygons $o_4, o_9 \in O$ are disconnected.

We define the following spatial relations in $\mathcal{QS}$. We have selected this candidate set of relations as (a) they have been studied extensively within artificial intelligence [1,14,15], and (b) they demonstrate a range of spatial aspects. The set of supported relations is readily extensible within our framework.

Mereotopology. Part-whole and contact relations between regions [17]: *disconnected (dc), externally connected (ec), partially overlapping (po), tangential proper-part (tpp), non-tangential proper part (ntpp), equal (eq), discrete from (dr)* defined as *dc* or *ec*, and *proper part (pp)* defined as *tpp* or *ntpp*.

Relative Orientation. Left, right, collinear, in front, behind orientation relations of *points* and *regions* with respect to *line segments*, and *parallel, perpendicular* relations between *line segments*.

Incidence. Interior, on boundary, exterior incidence relations between *points* and *regions*.

Size. Smaller, equisized, larger size relations between *regions*.

Spatial Reasoning Tasks. In the following tasks the input is a set of objects O and a set of qualitative spatial relations R between those objects.

Consistency. Determine whether there exists a configuration ψ of O that satisfies all relation constraints in R. Such a configuration is called a *consistent configuration*.

Generating configurations. Return a consistent configuration ψ of O.

Interactive geometry. Given (a possibly inconsistent) configuration ψ, and an object $o \in O$, return a consistent configuration ψ' such that $\psi(o) = \psi'(o)$.

Intuitively, interactive geometry allows a user to "move", "resize" or otherwise manipulate object instances in a configuration. The spatial solver automatically updates the other object instances so that the given spatial relations are maintained at all times.

3.1 Formulating Spatial Semantics as Numerical Optimisation

One approach for formalising the semantics of spatial reasoning is by *analytic geometry*, i.e. to encode qualitative spatial relations as systems of polynomial equations and inequalities. The task of determining whether a set of spatial relations is consistent is then equivalent to determining whether the set of polynomial constraints are satisfiable. We have previously shown how all relations in $\mathcal{QS}$ (as described above) can be expressed as polynomial constraints [3, 23].

Numerical Optimisation. Let $X = (x_1, \ldots, x_n)$ be a vector of n real variables (encoding object parameters) over m polynomial equation constraints (encoding qualitative spatial relations): $f_i(x_1, \ldots, x_n) = 0$ for $1 \leq i \leq m$. Numerical optimisation is used to solve the system of constraints by applying an optimisation function such as the sum of squares [10]:

$$\sigma(X) = \sum_{i=1}^{m} f_i(X)^2$$

Iterative methods for solving systems of polynomial constraints generate sequences of approximate solutions that aim to converge on a solution. Many specialised global and local optimisation algorithms have been developed e.g. low storage BFGS [5].

Proposition 1. *Spatial reasoning based on numerical optimisation supports the required tasks of (1) consistency, (2) configuration generation, and (3) interactive geometry.*

(1) A system of polynomial constraints over variables X is satisfiable when the sum of squares is minimised, $\sigma(X) = 0$. When such a minimum is found then the corresponding spatial constraint problem is consistent. (2) The real values assigned to variables X that minimise the sum of squares are retrieved from the numerical optimisation algorithm. These values correspond to a consistent configuration of spatial objects. (3) Variables in X can be marked as immutable so that their currently assigned value will not be changed by the numerical optimisation algorithm. Interactive geometry is formalised in numerical optimisation by modifying a variable value $x \in X$ (e.g. representing moving a geometric point by clicking and dragging the point in a GUI), marking the variable as immutable, running the numerical optimisation algorithm to find values that minimise the polynomial constraints.

Proposition 2. *Spatial reasoning based on numerical optimisation is (1) sound when consistency is determined by the algorithm, and (2) incomplete when inconsistency is determined by the algorithm.*

(1) By definition, spatial consistency requires that at least one configuration ψ exists that satisfies all constraints R simultaneously. Assume a numerical optimisation algorithm finds a global minimum $\sigma(X) = 0$. Then it has produced values for X that are interpreted as a spatially consistent configuration. Therefore, at

least one consistent configuration necessarily exists when $\sigma(X) = 0$ (i.e. the values that globally minimised σ). (2) There is no guarantee of convergence of numerical optimisation methods in general, and thus consistent spatial problems may not be determined to be consistent.

With respect to inconsistency, it is standard within geometric constraint solving to define thresholds that define the global minimum, and an upper limit of the number of iterations [10]. Thus, in the case when an inconsistency is reported, there is considerable scope in adapting the numerical optimisation framework to suit the needs of the current application task. For instance, we routinely combine numerical optimisation with other analytic approaches, primarily Satisfiability Modulo Theories (SMT) solvers such as z3 [7]. Such systems are both sound and complete but have highly prohibitive computational complexity, i.e. $O(2^{2^n})$ (see [2] for details). We use this to identify inconsistent triples of objects (i.e. path consistency) when numerical optimisation fails.

3.2 Soft Constraints

Constraints f_i can be separated into strict constraints F' and soft constraints F. The numerical optimisation procedure is executed as usual by minimising $\sigma(X)$ at each iteration, however consistency now only relies on the strict set of constraints being satisfied, i.e.

$$\sigma'(X) = \sum_{f' \in F'} f'(X)^2$$

The procedure is terminated when $\sigma'(X) = 0$. Thus, the algorithm attempts to minimise soft constraints, but this is no longer a criterion for spatial consistency.

4 Probabilistic Spatial Reasoning in Constraint Logic Programming

In this section we integrate spatial reasoning (based on numerical optimisation) within the probabilistic logic programming framework via Constraint Logic Programming (CLP)[13].

CLP(ProbLog + $\mathcal{QS}$). A term in standard probabilistic logic programming is either a variable, constant, or a functor applied to terms. We extend this so that a term can also be *spatial variable* o ranging over a spatial domain D as defined in Sect. 3. All permitted spatial domains are uncountably infinite,[4] and thus logic programs defined with such terms are no longer restricted to the Herbrand universe [13].

Let r be a *spatial constraint* (i.e. a primitive constraint [13]) defined over spatial variables. The set of permitted functor symbols corresponding to spatial

---

[4] To clarify, there are an infinite number of 2D points defined by two real coordinates, and so the spatial domain of 2D points is infinite in size. Similarly the domains of lines, circles, egg-yolk regions, and polygons are infinite.

constraints are specified in Sect. 3 (e.g. *dc*, *ec*, etc.). Each spatial constraint is defined as a particular system of polynomial constraints over spatial object parameters.[5] A spatial constraint $r_{o_1,...,o_n}$ with arity n is solvable over spatial variables $o_1, ..., o_n$ if the corresponding numerical optimisation problem can be globally minimised, $\sigma(X) = 0$, as defined in Sect. 3.1. We extend the definition of a rule to [13]:

$$h \leftarrow \alpha_1, ..., \alpha_k$$

where α_i is either a spatial constraint or an atom. We denote a set of such rules as $L_{P_{QS}}$. Similarly, queries take the form $\alpha_1, ..., \alpha_k$. Given spatial domains $D_1, ..., D_m$, and query q, then $q\theta_{QS}$ is a conjunction of atoms resulting from an assignment of all variables in q to values from $(U \cup \bigcup_{i=1}^{m} D_i)$. A query is a logical consequence of $L_{P_{QS}}$ if $\exists \theta_{QS}(L_{P_{QS}} \models q\theta_{QS})$.

We refer to a probabilistic logic program extended to spatial variables and constraints as CLP(ProbLog + QS). A CLP(ProbLog + QS) program consists of:

- a set of facts, each labelled with a probability $T = \{p_1 : f_1, ..., p_n : f_n\}$
- a set of rules $L_{P_{QS}}$ of the form $h \leftarrow \alpha_1, ..., \alpha_k$

The disjoint condition holds between $L_T, L_{P_{QS}}$, where $L_T = \{f_1, ..., f_n\}$. Given query q and CLP(ProbLog + QS) program $(T \cup L_{P_{QS}})$, the *success probability* $P(q|(T, L_{P_{QS}}))$ of q is defined as the usual success probability of a probabilistic logic program (based on distribution semantics) with θ_{QS} replacing θ.

That is, the success probability of a query in CLP(ProbLog + QS) is the probability that it has a *spatially consistent* proof given the distribution defined by T. Standard spatial reasoning tasks are extended according to the distribution of logic programs defined by T:

Probabilistic Consistency. Determine the probability that there exists a configuration ψ of O that satisfies all relation constraints in R in a randomly sampled logic program.

Probabilistic Configuration. Return a consistent configuration ψ of O in a randomly sampled logic program with at least probability p.

Probabilistic Interactive Geometry. Given (a possibly inconsistent) configuration ψ, and an object $o \in O$, return a consistent configuration ψ' such that $\psi(o) = \psi'(o)$ in a randomly sampled logic program with at least probability p.

Implementation. The probabilistic spatial constraint system is implemented using native CLP language features within ProbLog 1 (and thus can seamlessly be utilised in any such similar probabilistic logic programming framework), which is implemented in Yap; we are using Yap version 6.3.4. Spatial constraints are maintained in plain CLP via attributed variables. The current consistent configuration is also maintained via variable attributes. When a new spatial constraint is introduced or two spatial variables are unified then consistency of the spatial

---

[5] For brevity we do not list all of the spatial constraint definitions here, and instead we refer readers to [3, 23].

constraint store is evaluated by an external call to a numerical optimisation solver. Importantly, the use of the external solver is stateless, i.e. all spatial constraints are maintained on the Prolog side. This guarantees that the integration with the external solver does not interfere with the SLD resolution procedure (which is the procedure used to prove queries in Prolog), i.e. the system is equivalent to a plain CLP program with a stateless spatial reasoning "oracle" that provides semantics for determining whether a given spatial constraint store is consistent. We refer readers to [21] for further details on implementing spatial reasoning in CLP.

5   Illustrative Examples and Evaluation

We have fully implemented our probabilistic spatial reasoning framework. In this section we demonstrate applicability on problems from spatial Q/A. CLP(ProbLog + $\mathcal{QS}$) is implemented in Yap, and we have integrated the geometric constraint solver FreeCAD.[6]

Probabilistic Spatial Composition. (Figure 1(a)) Let c_1, c_2, c_3 be circles with the following relations: *tpp* (tangential proper part) holds between c_1, c_2 with probability 0.7; *ntpp* (non-tangential proper part) holds between c_1, c_2 with probability 0.3; *ec* (external contact) holds between c_1, c_2 with probability 0.8. What topological relations can possibly hold between c_1, c_3, and what are the respective probabilities of each possible relation?

```
0.7 :: relation(tpp,  c1, c2); 0.3 :: relation(ntpp, c1, c2).
0.8 :: relation(ec,   c2, c3).
object(id(c1), type(circle)).
object(id(c3), type(circle)).
object(id(c2), type(circle)).

?- topology(Relation),
|   Query = (relation(_,c1,c2),
|            relation(_,c2,c3),
|            relation(Relation,c1,c3)),
|   problog_exact(Query,Prob,_), Prob > 0.
Relation = dc, Prob = 0.8;
Relation = ec, Prob = 0.56;
false.
```

CLP(ProbLog + $\mathcal{QS}$) determines that the only possible relations between $c1, c3$ are (see Fig. 1(b) and (c)):

1. *ec* with probability 0.56, which occurs when $c1, c2$ are *tpp* and $c2, c3$ are *ec*, i.e. $P(ec(c1, c3)) = P(tpp(c1, c2)) \cdot P(ec(c2, c3)) = 0.7 \cdot 0.8 = 0.56$.
2. *dc* with probability 0.8, which occurs when $c2, c3$ are *ec*, and $c1, c2$ are either *tpp* or *ntpp*. The probability that $c1, c2$ are either *tpp* or *ntpp* is calculated as an annotated disjunction, $P(tpp(c1, c2)) + P(ntpp(c1, c2)) = 0.7 + 0.3 = 1.0$. Therefore, $P(dc(c1, c3)) = P(ec(c2, c3)) \cdot (P(tpp(c1, c2)) + P(ntpp(c1, c2))) = 0.8 \cdot 1.0 = 0.8$.

---

[6] www.freecadweb.org.

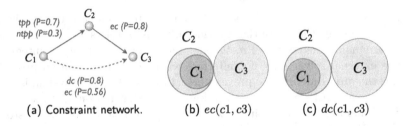

Fig. 1. Probabilistic Spatial Composition.

Notice that we deliberately did not consider the probability that $\neg ec(c_2, c_3)$ (although we could do so with a second annotated disjunction); i.e. we are only interested in logic programs in which $ec(c_2, c_3)$ is provable, a fact which has probability 0.8 in our scenario. This demonstrates that we are not restricted to modelling jointly-exhaustive pairwise disjoint sets of spatial relations.

Next we add the constraint that the centres of c_1, c_2, c_3 are not collinear.

```
| Query = (relation(not_collinear, centre(c1), centre(c2), centre(c3)),
| ...
```

CLP(ProbLog + $\mathcal{QS}$) correctly infers that the ec relation can not hold between c_1, c_3 if the centres of all three circles are not collinear.

Growing Bacteria Colonies. Let $b_1, \ldots, b_5$ be five bacterial colonies been cultivated in a petri dish. Over time each colony grows until it comes in contact with another colony, at which point growth is interrupted due to competition of resources. Colonies are spatially represented as circles. After some weeks in a given laboratory experiment, each pair of colonies either have no contact (spatially *disconnected*) or are in conflict (spatially *externally connected*) with probabilities 0.8 and 0.2 respectively.

In the first experiment three of the colonies are *seeded* in specific locations: the centres of b_1, b_2, b_3 are $(0,0), (35, 82), (2, 133)$ respectively.

```
colony(id(b1)). colony(id(b2)). colony(id(b3)).
0.8 :: bacteria(no_contact, id(I), id(J)) ;
0.2 :: bacteria(in_conflict, id(I), id(J)) :- colony(id(I)), colony(id(J)).
```

```
colony_relation(no_contact, Id1, Id2) :-
  shape(Id1, Shape1), shape(Id2, Shape2),
  bacteria(no_contact, Id1, Id2), topology(dc, Shape1, Shape2).
colony_relation(in_conflict, Id1, Id2) :-
  shape(Id1, Shape1), shape(Id2, Shape2),
  bacteria(in_conflict, Id1, Id2), topology(ec, Shape1, Shape2).
```

```
colonies([R12,R13,R23]) :- colony_relation(R12, id(b1), id(b2)), ...
```

We pose the following queries:

```
%% all colonies are in conflict
?- Query = (colonies(Relations), forall(member(R, Relations), R=in_conflict)),
|  prob_exact(Query, Prob, _).
Prob = 0.008
%% all colonies have unrestricted growth
?- Query = (colonies(Relations), forall(member(R, Relations), R=no_contact)),
|  problog_exact(Query, Prob, _).
Prob = 0.512
%% some colonies are in conflict
?- Query = (colonies(Relations), member(in_conflict, Relations)),
|  problog_exact(Query, Prob, _).
Prob = 0.488
```

There is a 0.4 probability that any given pair of colonies are the same bacteria species with comparable resources and will grow at precisely the same rate. This corresponds to colonies being of *equal size*.

```
%% all colonies are the same species
?- Query = (colonies(_,Species), forall(member(S, Species), S=same_species)),
|  problog_exact(Query, Prob, _).
Prob = 0.04096
%% all colonies are the same species and in conflict
?- Query = (colonies(Relations,Species),
|              forall(member(R, Relations), R=in_conflict)),
|              forall(member(S, Species),   S=same_species)),
|  problog_exact(Query, Prob, _).
Prob = 0.0
```

CLP(ProbLog + $\mathcal{QS}$) correctly determines that all colonies being of the same species and in conflict is spatially impossible given the initial seeded positions. In the final experiment two additional bacteria $b4, b5$ are introduced at unspecified locations. CLP(ProbLog + $\mathcal{QS}$) correctly determines that it is also spatially impossible that all colonies are in conflict regardless of their species, as five circles can not be mutually externally connected in the plane.

```
%% all colonies are in conflict
?- Query = (colonies(Relations,_), forall(member(R, Relations), R=in_conflict)),
|  problog_exact(Query, Prob, _).
Prob = 0.0
```

Evaluating Runtime. As an indication of the practicality of our approach with respect to runtime we have executed the following tests. We emphasise that our focus in this paper is on the integration of spatial reasoning within a probabilistic logic programming framework, and not on evaluating and optimising runtime efficiency of spatial solving; we anticipate that runtimes of the spatial solving component can be significantly improved by utilising optimisations e.g. presented in [20]. Experiments were run on a Mac OSX 10.8.5 with 2.6 GHz Intel Core i7. Due to the heuristic nature of optimisation algorithms, we are currently conducting more comprehensive experiments with statistical analysis of runtimes based on a wider range of inputs; the runtimes below are only based on a single run of each test.

The first test is a set of relations $r(c_i, c_{i+1})$, such that c_i, c_{i+1} are circles, for $1 \leq i < N$. Running the test, for example, with $N = 11$ and $r = ntpp$, takes

0.095 s; $r = ec$ takes 0.363 s; $r = dc$ takes 0.014 s; $r = tpp$ takes 0.704 s; $r = po$ takes 0.006 s. In all cases a consistent configuration is generated.

In the second test we have $N = 10$ circles such that each pair c_i, c_{i+1} ($1 \leq i < N$) can take one of two mutually exclusive relations: $ec(c_i, c_{i+1})$ with probability 0.8, and $dr(c_i, c_{i+1})$ with probability 0.2. We execute a query asking for the exact probability that some relation holds between each pair c_i, c_{i+1}, causing ProbLog to consider all combinations of possible relations. There are $N - 1 = 9$ relations, and each relation can select one of two options giving $2^9 = 512$ combinations, i.e. spatial problems to solve. This takes 263.73 s, or approximately 0.5 s per spatial problem.

The final test focuses on interactive geometry: we simulate the scenario where an image is segmented and processed, giving a set of circles that are initially arranged in a $N \times N$ grid such that they are all disconnected. For this test we select $N = 5$ giving $5 \times 5 = 25$ circles - all circles can be moved and resized, i.e. the problem contains 75 spatial parameters. Two (arbitrary) circles e.g. c_8, c_{11} need to be modified to become *partially overlapping* $po(c_8, c_{11})$ (while still be discrete from all other circles). All other pairs of circles are *discrete*: $dr(c_i, c_j)$ for all $1 \leq i < j \leq 25$ except when ($i = 8 \wedge i = 11$). The spatial problem for the *po* case is solved in 4.02 s.

6   Conclusions and Related Work

We have presented a framework and full implementation in CLP(ProbLog + $\mathcal{QS}$) that integrates spatial reasoning with probabilistic logic programming. Our method facilitates efficient high-level reasoning about both probabilistic facts, domain-specific knowledge and spatial constraints in a seamless manner.

Within the fields of Artificial Intelligence and Knowledge Representation and Reasoning, a variety of frameworks have been developed that formalise notions of *space*, and spatial relations between objects. Diverse frameworks include: (a) geometric reasoning and constructive solid geometry [14]; (b) relational algebraic semantics of 'qualitative spatial calculi' [15]; and (c) axiomatic frameworks of mereotopology and mereogeometry [1].

However, the distinction with our research here, and what we argue is lacking within the KR community, is a systematic formal account and computational characterisation of such spatial theories as a KR language —e.g., *suited for declarative modelling, commonsense inference and query*. In this paper we emphasise the power of such a research agenda, as our approach leverages from the strengths of both extensive research in probabilistic logic programming and spatial reasoning.

Table 1 compares the capabilities of CLP(ProbLog + $\mathcal{QS}$) with other prominent spatial reasoning systems, and the original ProbLog system. GQR [9] is a binary constraint calculi reasoner. Spatial reasoning with GQR has a number of key limitations: numerical information cannot be incorporated, and reasoning is not complete i.e. it only guarantees path-consistency [15]. The SMT solver z3 [7] is not integrated within a logic programming framework, and is not capable of

Table 1. Feature comparison with other prominent reasoning systems.

Property	GQR	z3	ProbLog	CLP(QS)	ASPMT(QS)	CLP(ProbLog + QS)
Rule-Based Reasoning	-	-	✓	✓	✓	✓
Probabilistic Reasoning	-	-	✓	-	-	✓
Mixed Numerical-Qualitative Reasoning	-	✓	-	✓	✓	✓
Spatial Consistency	✓	✓	-	✓	✓	✓
Complete for Consistency	-	✓	-	-	✓	-
Spatial Quantification	-	✓	-	✓	✓	✓
Interactive Geometry	-	-	-	✓	-	✓

facilitating interactive geometry. CLP(QS) is our extension of Constraint Logic Programming to spatial variables [3]; the distinction in this paper is that we have integrated core spatial reasoning components of CLP(QS) into a probabilistic logic programming framework. ASPMT(QS) [23] is our extension of Answer Set Programming Modulo Theories to support spatial variables; as this system utilises SMT solving for spatial reasoning, it is also not capable of interactive geometry nor probabilistic reasoning. CLP(ProbLog + QS) is the only system capable of probabilistic spatial reasoning within a KR context.

Girlea and Amir [11] present an approach and algorithm for probabilistic inference with region connection calculus relations. The key distinctions with our work are that we propose a fundamentally different mechanism for spatial reasoning based on numerical optimisation, and we integrate spatial reasoning within probabilistic logic programming to support application specific rules and background knowledge. In a topic related to interactive geometry, Wallgrün [24] presents an approach for adjusting polygonal data to satisfy specified qualitative spatial relations, based on mixed-integer programming. An interesting direction for future research is determining how such a method could be incorporated into a probabilistic logic programming framework.

References

1. Aiello, M., Pratt-Hartmann, I.E., van Johan Benthem, F.A.K.: Handbook of Spatial Logics. Springer, Secaucus (2007)
2. Arnon, D.S., Collins, G.E., McCallum, S.: Cylindrical algebraic decomposition I: the basic algorithm. SIAM J. Comput. **13**(4), 865–877 (1984)
3. Bhatt, M., Lee, J.H., Schultz, C.: CLP(QS): a declarative spatial reasoning framework. In: Egenhofer, M., Giudice, N., Moratz, R., Worboys, M. (eds.) COSIT 2011. LNCS, vol. 6899, pp. 210–230. Springer, Heidelberg (2011)
4. Bouhineau, D.: Solving geometrical constraint systems using CLP based on linear constraint solver. In: Calmet, J., Campbell, J.A., Pfalzgraf, J. (eds.) AISMC-3. LNCS, vol. 1138, pp. 274–288. Springer, Heidelberg (1996)
5. Byrd, R.H., Lu, P., Nocedal, J., Zhu, C.: A limited memory algorithm for bound constrained optimization. SIAM J. Sci. Comput. **16**(5), 1190–1208 (1995)
6. Cohn, A.G., Gotts, N.M.: The 'egg-yolk' representation of regions with indeterminate boundaries. Geogr. Objects Indeterminate Boundaries **2**, 171–187 (1996)

7. de Moura, L., Bjørner, N.S.: Z3: an efficient SMT solver. In: Ramakrishnan, C.R., Rehof, J. (eds.) TACAS 2008. LNCS, vol. 4963, pp. 337–340. Springer, Heidelberg (2008)

8. De Raedt, L., Kimmig, A., Toivonen, H.: Problog: a probabilistic prolog and its application in link discovery. In: IJCAI, vol. 7, pp. 2462–2467 (2007)

9. Gantner, Z., Westphal, M., Wölfl, S.: GQR-A fast reasoner for binary qualitative constraint calculi. In: Proceedings of AAAI, vol. 8 (2008)

10. Ge, J.-X., Chou, S.-C., Gao, X.-S.: Geometric constraint satisfaction using optimization methods. Comput. Aided Des. **31**(14), 867–879 (1999)

11. Girlea, C., Amir, E.: Probabilistic region connection calculus. In: Workshop on Spatio-temporal Dynamics, Co-located at the European Conference on Artifcial Intelligence (ECAI 2012), pp. 62–67 (2012)

12. Gutmann, B.: On continuous distributions and parameter estimation in probabilistic logic programs. Ph.D. dissertation, Ph. D thesis, KULeuven (2011)

13. Jaffar, J., Michaylov, S., Stuckey, P.J., Yap, R.H.C.: The CLP (R) language and system. ACM Trans. Program. Lang. Syst. (TOPLAS) **14**(3), 339–395 (1992)

14. Kapur, D., Mundy, J.L. (eds.): Geometric Reasoning. MIT Press, Cambridge (1988)

15. Ligozat, G.: Qualitative Spatial and Temporal Reasoning. Wiley-ISTE, London (2011)

16. Pesant, G., Boyer, M.: Reasoning about solids using constraint logic programming. J. Autom. Reason. **22**(3), 241–262 (1999)

17. Randell, D.A., Cui, Z., Cohn, A.G.: A spatial logic based on regions and connection. KR **92**, 165–176 (1992)

18. Sato, T.: A statistical learning method for logic programs with distribution semantics. In: The 12th International Conference on Logic Programming (ICLP 1995) (1995)

19. Schultz, C., Bhatt, M.: Encoding relative orientation and mereotopology relations with geometric constraints in CLP(QS). In: 1st Workshop on Logics for Qualitative Modelling and Reasoning (LQMR 2015), Lodz, Poland, September 2015

20. Schultz, C., Bhatt, M.: Spatial symmetry driven pruning strategies for efficient declarative spatial reasoning. In: Fabrikant, S.I., Raubal, M., Bertolotto, M., Davies, C., Freundschuh, S., Bell, S. (eds.) COSIT 2015. LNCS, vol. 9368, pp. 331–353. Springer, Heidelberg (2015). doi:10.1007/978-3-319-23374-1_16

21. Schultz, C., Bhatt, M.: A numerical optimisation based characterisation of spatial reasoning. In: Alferes, J.J., Bertossi, L., Governatori, G., Fodor, P., Roman, D. (eds.) RuleML 2016. LNCS, vol. 9718, pp. 199–207. Springer, Heidelberg (2016). doi:10.1007/978-3-319-42019-6_13

22. Van Gelder, A., Ross, K.A., Schlipf, J.S.: The well-founded semantics for general logic programs. J. ACM (JACM) **38**(3), 619–649 (1991)

23. Wałęga, P.A., Bhatt, M., Schultz, C.: ASPMT(QS): non-monotonic spatial reasoning with answer set programming modulo theories. In: Calimeri, F., Ianni, G., Truszczynski, M. (eds.) LPNMR 2015. LNCS, vol. 9345, pp. 488–501. Springer, Heidelberg (2015)

24. Wallgrün, J.O.: Exploiting qualitative spatial reasoning for topological adjustment of spatial data. In: Proceedings of the 20th International Conference on Advances in Geographic Information Systems, pp. 229–238. ACM (2012)

ChoiceGAPs: Competitive Diffusion as a Massive Multi-player Game in Social Networks

Edoardo Serra[1], Francesca Spezzano[1(✉)], and V.S. Subrahmanian[2]

[1] Computer Science Department, Boise State University, Boise, USA
{edoardoserra,francescaspezzano}@boisestate.edu
[2] Computer Science Department, University of Maryland, College Park, USA
vs@cs.umd.edu

Abstract. We consider the problem of modeling competitive diffusion in real world social networks via the notion of ChoiceGAPs which combine choice logic programs and Generalized Annotated Programs. We assume that each vertex in a social network is a player in a multi-player game (with a huge number of players) — the choice part of the ChoiceGAPs describes utilities of players for acting in various ways based on utilities of their neighbors in those and other situations. We define multi-player Nash equilibrium for such programs — but because they require some conditions that are hard to satisfy in the real world, we introduce the new model-theoretic concept of strong equilibrium. We show that strong equilibria can capture all Nash equilibria. We prove a host of complexity (intractability) results for checking existence of strong equilibria and identify a class of ChoiceGAPs for which strong equilibria can be polynomially computed. We perform experiments on a real-world Facebook data set surrounding the 2013 Italian election and show that our algorithms have good predictive accuracy with an Area Under a ROC Curve that, on average, is over 0.76.

1 Introduction

The need to understand and predict the results of diffusion in social networks has taken on great importance in recent years. Most past work assumes a non-competitive scenario in which we model diffusion of one phenomenon at a time. However, in the real world, multiple competing phenomena are often diffusing concurrently. For instance, the "likes" for a political candidate A and a competing candidate B might be mutually exclusive — a person may support at most one of them. Likewise, two competing marketing campaigns, one each for the iOS and Android platforms, may garner "likes" from supporters of each but it is unlikely that they will both get "likes" from the same person. In a similar vein, various "issues" may have supporters - for instance, in the US, there are "pro" and "anti" abortion supporters, "pro" and "anti" immigration supporters, etc. In all these cases, people typically choose at most one of these *positions*.

In this paper, we present the ChoiceGAP framework using which we can model competing diffusive processes via a mix of generalized annotated programs (GAPs) [14] and Choice Logic Programs [17]. The use of GAPs to model

S. Schockaert and P. Senellart (Eds.): SUM 2016, LNAI 9858, pp. 303–319, 2016.
DOI: 10.1007/978-3-319-45856-4_21

diffusion processes was already proposed in [6,19] — there, the authors show how many well-known diffusion models can be expressed as GAPs.[1] [19] assumes only one diffusive process is occurring at a time and there is no competition going on. [6] presents first steps toward modeling competitive diffusion but does so by identifying one solution of a convex set of constraints. They do not present complexity results, nor do they present accuracy results based on real data, and their framework usually takes hours to compute.

After introducing the syntax and semantics of ChoiceGAPs in Sect. 2, we define in Sect. 3 the notion of strong equilibrium which represents the solution concept of our game and present complexity results about the existence of strong equilibria and about the entailment problem. When members of a social network can choose at most one of n different competing positions, we first use n different diffusion models, each capturing how support for each of the competing positions spreads through a social network. Each vertex in the social network can be considered to be a player in the game with one of $n + 1$ choices to make. He can either choose one of the competing positions or he can choose none – he can never choose more than one. The players' utility (for a given course of action, e.g. being pro-Obamacare) is defined by a choice rule that uses inputs from the n different GAPs. We can think of the spread of support for a political candidate in a social network as a "game" in which an equilibrium represents a stable adoption of positions by the members of the social network. Section 4 formally defines our game and compares "strong" and "Nash" [16] equilibria. Unfortunately, Nash equilibria require assumptions that are unrealistic in real world social networks. We show that every game (in our sense) can be expressed using a ChoiceGAP in such a way that strong equilibria capture Nash equilibria without inheriting any of the disadvantages. Because the entailment problem is intractable, we identify a class of ChoiceGAPs called "Vertex Independent Choice" (or VIC) programs and show that for a class of these called VIC_2 programs, we can both find a strong equilibrium (and they are guaranteed to exist) and solve the entailment problem in PTIME (all proofs are in Appendix C [1]). Section 6 describes experiments we have carried out pertaining to a real competitive situation during the 2013 Italian election using data gathered from Facebook. Depending upon the settings used in our algorithms, our experiments show that our algorithms achieve an average Area Under ROC Curve of 0.762, showing good predictive accuracy.

2 Choice GAPs

In this section, we formally define a social network (SN) and introduce the *Choice Generalized Annotated Program* (ChoiceGAP) paradigm.

---

[1] Specifically, [19] shows that ChoiceGAPs can express cascade models such as [8] used to model the spread of "favorites" in Flickr, tipping models such as the Jackson-Yariv model of product adoption in economics [12], the SIR and the SIS models of disease spread [2,11], as well as homophilic models such as those involving mobile phone usage [4].

Social Network Formalization. We assume the existence of two arbitrary but fixed disjoint sets VP, EP of *vertex* and *edge predicate symbols* respectively. Each vertex predicate symbol has arity 1 and each edge predicate symbol has arity 2.

Definition 1. *A social network is a 4-tuple* $(\mathsf{V}, \mathsf{E}, l_{vert}, w)$ *where:*

1. V *is a finite set whose elements are called* vertices.
2. $\mathsf{E} \subseteq \mathsf{V} \times \mathsf{V} \times EP$ *is a finite set of* labeled edges.
3. $l_{vert} : \mathsf{V} \to 2^{VP}$ *is a function, called the vertex labeling function.*
4. $w : E \to [0,1]$ *is a function assigning a weight to each edge.* □

Syntax of Choice GAPs (ChoiceGAPs). A ChoiceGAP consists of two parts: (1) an "annotation" language and (2) a logical language that is connected to the annotation language via certain shared syntactic elements.

Let AVar be a set of symbols (called "annotated variable symbols") ranging over the unit real interval $[0,1]$ and let $\mathcal{F}$ be a set of symbols (called "annotation function symbols"), each with an associated arity.

Definition 2 (Annotation). *Annotations are inductively defined as follows: (1) Any member of* $[0,1] \cup$ AVar *is an annotation. (2) If* $f \in \mathcal{F}$ *is an n-ary annotation function symbol and* $t_1, \ldots, t_n$ *are annotations, then* $f(t_1, \ldots, t_n)$ *is an annotation*[2]. □

We define a separate logical language whose constants are members of V and whose predicate symbols consist of $VP \cup EP$. We also assume the existence of a set $\mathcal{V}$ of variables ranging over the constants (vertices). No function symbols are present. Terms and atoms are defined in the usual way (cf. [Lloyd 1987]). If $A = p(t_1, \ldots, t_n)$ is an atom and $p \in VP$ (resp. $p \in EP$), then A is called a vertex (resp. edge) atom.

Definition 3 (Annotated Atom/GAP-Rule/GAP). *If A is an atom and μ is an annotation, then $A : \mu$ is an annotated atom. If A is a vertex (resp. edge) atom, then $A : \mu$ is also called a vertex (resp. edge) annotated atom. If $A_0 : f(\mu_1, \ldots, \mu_n)$, $A_1 : \mu_1, \ldots$, $A_n : \mu_n$ are annotated atoms, then $A_0 : f(\mu_1, \ldots, \mu_n) \leftarrow A_1 : \mu_1, \ldots, A_n : \mu_n$ is an annotated rule.[3] When $n = 0$, the above rule is called a* fact. *A generalized annotated program (GAP) is a finite set of annotated rules. An annotated atom (resp. a rule, a GAP) is ground iff there are no occurrence of variables from either* AVar *or* V *in it.* □

Every social network $SN = (\mathsf{V}, \mathsf{E}, l_{vert}, w)$ can be represented by the set of GAP-rules (actually facts) $\Pi_{SN} = \{q(v) : 1 \leftarrow \mid v \in \mathsf{V} \land q \in l_{vert}(v)\} \cup \{ep(v_1, v_2) :$

---

[2] As in the case of Generalized Annotated Programs [14], note that each annotation function symbol f of arity i denotes some fixed pre-theoretically defined function from $[0,1]^i$ to $[0,1]$.

[3] We refer to $A_0 : f(\mu_1, \ldots, \mu_n)$ as the *head* of the rule, and to $A_1 : \mu_1, \ldots, A_n : \mu_n$ as the *body* of the rule.

$w((\langle v_1, v_2, ep \rangle)) \leftarrow | \langle v_1, v_2, ep \rangle \in \mathbf{E}\}$. To construct a GAP from a social network SN, we look at each vertex v and each property q. If v has property q, then $q(v){:}1{\leftarrow}$ is inserted into Π_{SN}. Likewise, we look at each edge $(v_1, v_2) \in \mathbf{E}$. If this edge has weight w and edge property ep, then we insert the fact $ep(v_1, v_2){:}w{\leftarrow}$ into Π_{SN}.

ChoiceGAPs extend GAPs by adding a single rule called a *Vertex Choice (VC) Rule* inspired by the *choice* construct for classical Datalog [17]. Every ChoiceGAP consists of a GAP together with a single vertex choice rule.

Definition 4 (Vertex Choice (VC) Rule). *Suppose* $\{a_1, \ldots, a_m\}$ *and* $\{b_1, \ldots, b_m\}$ *are two ordered sets of vertex predicate symbols. Then* $b_1(X), \ldots, b_m(X) \hookleftarrow a_1(X), \ldots, a_m(X)$ *is a* vertex choice (VC) *rule of size* m *for the vertex* X. *A VC-rule is ground iff there are no occurrence of variables from* $\mathcal{V}$ *in it.* □

The body indicates the possible choices for a vertex, while the head contains the possible decisions. Note that edge predicate symbols cannot appear anywhere inside a VC-rule. Moreover, usually, only conflicting predicate symbols occur within a VC-rule and usually the predicate symbol b_i is the decision predicate corresponding to a utility predicate a_i. VC-rules do not contain any annotations.

Definition 5 (Choice GAP). *A* Choice GAP *(ChoiceGAP)* Π *is a finite set of annotated rules plus a single vertex choice rule.* □

Semantics of ChoiceGAP. We are now ready to define the semantics of Choice-GAPs. Given a ChoiceGAP Π, let $\texttt{atoms}$ denote the set of all ground atoms of Π.

Definition 6 (Interpretation). *Given a ChoiceGAP* Π, *an interpretation* I *for* Π *is any mapping* $I : \texttt{atoms} \to [0, 1]$ *of ground atoms to real numbers in* $[0, 1]$. □

Thus, an interpretation merely assigns a certainty value to each ground atom in $\texttt{atoms}$. The set $\mathcal{I}$ of all interpretations can be partially ordered via the ordering $\preceq$ defined as follows: $I_1 \preceq I_2$ iff for all ground atoms A, $I_1(A) \leq I_2(A)$. $\mathcal{I}$ forms a complete lattice under the $\preceq$ ordering. Given two interpretations I_1 and I_2, we define their intersection $I_1 \cap I_2$ as the interpretation $(I_1 \cap I_2)$ such that $(I_1 \cap I_2)(A) = \min(I_1(A), I_2(A))$ for all $A \in \texttt{atoms}$. Similarly, the union $I_1 \cup I_2$ of interpretations I_1 and I_2 is the interpretation $I_1 \cup I_2$ such that $(I_1 \cup I_2)(A) = \max(I_1(A), I_2(A))$ for all $A \in \texttt{atoms}$. We are now ready to define satisfaction.

Definition 7 (Satisfaction). *Let* I *be an interpretation.*

- *I satisfies a ground annotated atom* $A : \mu$, *denoted* $I \models A : \mu$, *iff* $I(A) \geq \mu$.
- *I satisfies a ground ChoiceGAP annotated rule* r *of the form* $A_0 : \mu_0 \leftarrow A_1 : \mu_1, \ldots, A_n : \mu_n$, *denoted* $I \models r$, *iff* $I(A_0) \geq \mu_0$ *or for some* $i \in \{1, \ldots, n\}$, $I \not\models A_i : \mu_i$.
- *I satisfies a ground VC-rule* r *of the form* $B_1, \ldots, B_m \hookleftarrow A_1, \ldots, A_m$, *denoted* $I \models r$, *iff* $\exists i \in \{1, \ldots, m\}$ *such that* $I(B_i) = I(A_i)$ *and* $\forall j \in \{1, \ldots, m\}, j \neq i$, $I(B_j) = 0$.

- *I satisfies a non-ground GAP/VC rule iff it satisfies all ground instances of it.*
- *I satisfies a **ChoiceGAP** Π (or is a model of Π) iff I satisfies all rules in Π.*

$\square$

A key part of this definition is the satisfaction of VC-rules. For I to satisfy a VC-rule r of the form shown above, there must exist exactly one pair (A_i, B_i) such that $I(A_i) = I(B_i) \geq 0$. For all other pairs (A_j, B_j), we have $I(A_j) = I(B_j) = 0$. We now provide a simple example.

Example 1. Consider a social network SN and two diffusion models DM_1 and DM_2 relating to diffusion about the tendency to buy ASUS computers versus buying Macs. For this toy example which will be used throughout the paper, we assume these are the only two options of computers to buy (the same reasoning works if there are n different computers to buy). We assume there are two vertices $1, 2$ and a friend edge from 1 to 2.

$$SN = friend(1,2) : 1 \leftarrow$$

$$DM_1 = \begin{cases} buyAsus^U(1) : 0.6 \leftarrow \\ buyAsus^U(Y) : \mu \leftarrow friend(X,Y) : 1, buyAsus^D(X) : \mu \end{cases}$$

$$DM_2 = \begin{cases} buyMac^U(1) : 0.3 \leftarrow \\ buyMac^U(Y) : \mu \leftarrow friend(X,Y) : 1, buyMac^D(X) : \mu \end{cases}$$

Suppose we have the vertex choice rule

$$r : buyMac^D(X), buyAsus^D(X) \leftrightarrow buyMac^U(X), buyAsus^U(X)$$

For each conflicting vertex predicate vp, we introduce a "utility"predicate vp^U and a "decision" predicate vp^D. The former contains the utility value of the corresponding choice, while the latter represents the vertex's actual choice.

Consider the two interpretations I_1 and I_2 shown below.

	$buyAsus^U(1)$	$buyAsus^D(1)$	$buyAsus^U(2)$	$buyAsus^D(2)$	$buyMac^U(1)$	$buyMac^D(1)$	$buyMac^U(2)$	$buyMac^D(2)$
I_1	0.6	0.6	0.6	0.6	0.3	0.0	0.3	0.0
I_2	0.6	0.6	0.6	0.0	0.3	0.0	0.7	0.7

Consider the situation of vertex 1. Interpretation I_1 assigns: (i) 0.6 to all ground atoms $buyAsus^D(1), buyAsus^U(1), buyAsus^D(2), buyAsus^U(2)$, (ii) 0.3 to $buyMac^U(1)$, (iii) 0 to $buyMac^D(1)$, (iv) 0.3 to $buyMac^U(2)$, and (v) 0 to $buyMac^D(2)$.

*We see that I_1 satisfies all the diffusion rules as well as the one VC-rule. Consider the ground instance of this VC-rule with $X = 1$. Exactly one of the two head decision atoms, $buyAsus^D(1)$ has a value greater than 0 (0.6) and this coincides with the value assigned by I_1 to $buyAsus^U(1)$. Likewise, when we consider the ground instance with $X = 2$, we see the same thing. Thus, I_1 is a model of the **ChoiceGAP** program $\Pi = SN \cup DM_1 \cup DM_2 \cup \{r\}$. Similarly, we can also establish that I_2 is also a model of Π.*

3   Coherent Models and Strong Equilibria

Though I_2 is a model of Π in the above example, it assigns overly high utilities. For instance, consider the second rule of DM_2 with the substitution $\theta = \{X = 1, Y = 2\}$. We know that for the ground atom $buyMac^D(1)$ in the body of this rule after θ is applied to it, $I_2(buyMac^D(1)) = 0$. But the head of this rule under substitution θ, which is the atom $buyMac^U(2)$ is assigned a utility of 0.7 instead of the 0 that is the minimum needed for this rule to be satisfied. In order to address this, we define the concept of a *coherent* model.

Definition 8 (Coherence Transformation). *Suppose Π is a ChoiceGAP, $r \in$ ground(Π) is an instance of the single VC-rule in Π, and I an interpretation. Suppose r has the form $B_1(v), \ldots, B_m(v) \hookleftarrow A_1(v), \ldots, A_m(v)$ The coherence-transform of r is the set $coh(r, I) = \{B_i(v) : \mu \leftarrow A_i(v) : \mu \mid I(A_i(v)) > 0$ and $I(A_i(v)) = I(B_i(v))\}$. Note that this set can be empty.*

The coherence transform *of Π w.r.t. I is simply the GAP ground($\Pi^{non\text{-}vc}$) $\cup$ $\bigcup_{\substack{r \in ground(\Pi) \wedge \\ r \text{ is a VC-rule}}} coh(r, I)$, where $\Pi^{non\text{-}vc}$ is the set of all non-VC rules in Π.*

Thus, the coherence transform of Π w.r.t. I simply looks at ground VC-rules in *ground(Π)*. If there is a ground atom $A_i(v)$ in the body of the rule such that $I(A_i(v)) > 0$ and $I(A_i(v)) = I(B_i(v))$, then we include the GAP rule $B_i(v) : I(B_i(v)) \leftarrow A_i(v) : I(B_i(v))$ in coh(Π, I) — otherwise we just get rid of the rule. All non-VC rules of Π are included in coh(Π, I). Thus, coh(Π, I) *is always a GAP which, by* [14], *is guaranteed to have a unique minimal model.* We use $\mathcal{MM}(\Pi)$ to denote the minimum model of a GAP Π. We can now define coherent models.

Definition 9 (Coherent Model). *Let Π be a ChoiceGAP and let M be a model for Π. M is a* coherent model *for Π iff it is the minimum model of the GAP coh(Π, M).*   □

We now present a quick example of coherent models.

Example 2. We show that the model I_1 from Example 1 is a coherent model for the following *ChoiceGAP Π*:

$$\Pi = \begin{cases} friend(1,2) : 1 & \leftarrow \\ buyAsus^U(1) : 0.6 & \leftarrow \\ buyAsus^U(Y) : \mu & \leftarrow friend(X,Y) : 1, buyAsus^D(X) : \mu \\ buyMac^U(1) : 0.3 & \leftarrow \\ buyMac^U(Y) : \mu & \leftarrow friend(X,Y) : 1, buyMac^D(X) : \mu \\ buyMac^D(X), buyAsus^D(X) \hookleftarrow buyMac^U(X), buyAsus^U(X) \end{cases}$$

Let r be the single VC-rule in Π. By grounding Π we obtain

$$ground(\Pi) = \begin{cases} friend(1,2) : 1 & \leftarrow \\ buyAsus^U(1) : 0.6 & \leftarrow \\ buyAsus^U(2) : 0.6 & \leftarrow friend(1,2) : 1, buyAsus^D(1) : 0.6 \\ buyMac^U(1) : 0.3 & \leftarrow \\ buyMac^D(1), buyAsus^D(1) \hookleftarrow buyMac^U(1), buyAsus^U(1) \\ buyMac^D(2), buyAsus^D(2) \hookleftarrow buyMac^U(2), buyAsus^U(2) \end{cases}$$

Consider each of the two ground VC-rules above. For the first VC-rule, we see that $I_1(buyMac^D(1)) \neq I_1(buyMac^U(1))$ and $I_1(buyAsus^D(1)) = I_1(buyAsus^U(1))$ = 0.6 > 0. Hence, the rule $buyAsus^D(1) : 0.6 \leftarrow buyAsus^U(1) : 0.6$ belongs to the set $coh(r, I_1)$, and gets added to the coherent transform of Π w.r.t. I_1, denoted by Π' in the following. Likewise, with the second VC-rule, we know that $I_1(buyMac^D(2)) = I_1(buyMac^U(2)) = 0$, and $I_1(buyAsus^D(2)) = I_1(buyAsus^U(2))$ = 0.6 > 0 and so we add the GAP rule $buyAsus^D(2) : 0.6 \leftarrow buyAsus^U(2) : 0.6$ to Π'. The final GAP Π' that we get is the same as ground(Π) but where the two vertex choice rules are replaced as discussed above. It is easy to see that I_1 is the minimal model of Π'. Hence, I_1 is a coherent model of Π.

We now introduce the concept of Strong equilibrium.

Definition 10 (Strong Equilibrium). *A coherent model I is a Strong equilibrium for a ChoiceGAP Π iff for each ground vertex choice rule of the form $B_1, \ldots, B_m \leftarrow A_1, \ldots, A_m$ it is the case that $\sum_{i=1}^{m} I(B_i) = \max(I(A_1), \ldots, I(A_m))$.* □

Recall that by the definition of VC-rule satisfaction, there exists only one B_i such that $I(B_i) \geq 0$, while, for all other B_j, for $j \neq i$, $I(B_j) = 0$. Thus, a Strong equilibrium is a coherent model where each choice coincides with the maximum annotation value, taken as a measure of utility, in the VC-rule body. We use SE(Π) to denote the set of all strong equilibria of a ChoiceGAP Π.

Example 3. The coherent model I_1 from Examples 1 and 2 is a Strong equilibrium because (i) $I_1(buyAsus^D(1)) + I_1(buyMac^D(1)) = 0.6 + 0.0 = \max(I_1(buyAsus^U(1)), I_1(buyMac^U(1))) = \max(0.6, 0.3) = 0.6$, and (ii) $I_1(buyAsus^D(2)) + I_1(buyMac^D(2)) = 0.6 + 0.0 = \max(I_1(buyAsus^U(2)), I_1(buyMac^U(2))) = \max(0.6, 0.3) = 0.6$.

We are now ready to define when a ChoiceGAP entails an annotated atom.

Definition 11 (Entailment). *A ChoiceGAP Π entails a ground annotated atom AA, denoted $\Pi \models AA$, iff every Strong equilibrium of Π satisfies AA.* □

ChoiceGAP Complexity. In this section, we study the computational complexity of various problems related to strong equilibria. Our first complexity result shows that determining existence of strong equilibria is an NP-complete problem.

Theorem 1 (Strong Equilibria Existence Complexity). *Given a Choice-GAP Π as input, the problem of deciding whether Π has a Strong equilibrium is NP-complete under data and combined complexity.* □

A major problem occurs when multiple strong equilibria exist. In this case, a player who computes all of these strong equilibria may not know which strong equilibria the other players might act in accordance with. Thus, he may wish to know if a particular action he is considering is true in all strong equilibria. This problem too is intractable.

Theorem 2 (Entailment). *Given a ChoiceGAP program Π and a ground annotated atom AA as input, the problem of deciding whether $\Pi \models AA$ is coNP-complete under data and combined complexity.* □

4   ChoiceGAPs : A Game Perspective

Let Π be a ChoiceGAP, SN be a social network, and let n be the number of vertices in SN. Each vertex v is considered to be a player $\mathcal{P}_v$. We use Γ_Π to denote the set of all players in Π. In this section, we first describe the concept of a state (which basically is a mapping of players to actions, specifying the action the player takes). We develop a formal definition of a Nash equilibrium for the resulting game, as well as a relationship between states and strong equilibria for the game. Each player $\mathcal{P}_v \in \Gamma_\Pi$ has a the same set of actions (or strategies) $Q = \{1, \ldots, m\}$ where m is the size of the vertex choice rule in Π. These are the m competing choices the player can make (e.g. buying an Asus vs. buying a Mac). A *state* S for a ChoiceGAP Π represents a choice for each player $\mathcal{P}_v$ and it is defined as a mapping $S : \Gamma_\Pi \to Q$. Given a ChoiceGAP Π and a state S for Π, we define the notion of an *induced ground GAP Π_S*.

Definition 12 (Induced Ground GAP Π_S). *Suppose Π is a ChoiceGAP and S is a state for Π. We define a GAP Π_S that can be obtained from Π and S as follows: (1) replace each ground VC-rule $r : b_1(v), \ldots, b_m(v) \hookleftarrow a_1(v), \ldots, a_m(v)$ in ground (Π), with the ground annotated rule $b_i(v) : X \leftarrow a_i(v) : X$ where $i = S(\mathcal{P}_v)$. (2) All non-VC rules in Π are also in Π_S.*

Intuitively, when considering the ground instance r of a VC-rule in Π and a state S, exactly one of the $b_i(v)$'s can be true in the state as a vertex v can make exactly one choice. This choice is the $i = S(\mathcal{P}_v)$.

Proposition 3 *Let Π be a ChoiceGAPsuch that every predicate appearing in the head of the VC-rule does not appear in the head of a GAP rule, and let S be a state. Then, the minimal model of Π_S is a coherent model for Π.*

Given a state S, each player has a *utility value* for each of its actions. The utility $u(S, \mathcal{P}_v, i)$ of the player $\mathcal{P}_v$ performing the action $i \in Q$ in the state S is given by the value assumed by the atom $a_i(v)$ in the interpretation $\mathcal{MM}(\Pi_S)$, i.e. we set $u(S, \mathcal{P}_v, i) = \mathcal{MM}(\Pi_S)(a_i(v))$, where $a_i(x)$ is the i'th atom in the body of the VC-rule. This value is the likelihood of the player performing action $i \in Q$ according to the GAP Π_S. We assume that each player is a rational agent, i.e. he is motivated by maximizing his own payoff.

Definition 13 (State Representation of Strong Equilibria). *A state S represents a Strong equilibrium for Π iff, for all players $\mathcal{P}_v \in \Gamma_\Pi$, $u(S, \mathcal{P}_v, S(\mathcal{P}_v)) \geq u(S, \mathcal{P}_v, i)$, for each action $i \in Q$.*

Intuitively, a state is a choice of actions, one for each player. In contrast, strong equilibria, as defined in the previous section, is a coherent model of a ChoiceGAP that satisfies certain equilibrium conditions. The above definition specifies the relationship between states and strong equilibria so we can refer to the actions taken in a strong equilibrium as a state and vice versa. Note that the set $\{\mathcal{MM}(\Pi_S) \mid S \text{ is a state}\}$ contains all strong equilibria for Π - but not all its members are necessarily strong equilibria.

Nash Equilibrium vs. Strong Equilibrium. A Nash equilibrium is a state where no player has anything to gain by unilaterally changing his own action. In order to define Nash equilibria, we first define the utility $\hat{u}(S, \mathcal{P}_v)$ of a state S for a player $\mathcal{P}_v$ as follows: $\hat{u}(S, \mathcal{P}_v) = u(S, \mathcal{P}_v, S(\mathcal{P}_v))$. This definition says the utility of the state S for player $\mathcal{P}_v$ is simply the utility of the action $S(\mathcal{P}_v)$ that he takes in that state.

Definition 14 (Nash Equilibrium). *Let Π be a ChoiceGAP and S a state. $\mathcal{MM}(\Pi_S)$ is a Nash equilibrium for Π iff, for each player $\mathcal{P}_v$, $\hat{u}(S, \mathcal{P}_v) \geq \hat{u}(S', \mathcal{P}_v)$ for each S' such that $S(\mathcal{P}_{v'}) = S'(\mathcal{P}_{v'})$ if $v' \neq v$, and $S(\mathcal{P}_{v'}) \neq S'(\mathcal{P}_{v'})$ if $v' = v$.* □

Intuitively, $\mathcal{MM}(\Pi_S)$ is a Nash equilibrium if all players have no utility benefit in moving in other states. Thus, if one player tries to perform an action different from that in a Nash equilibrium (trying to raise his own utility), this would imply a reduced utility for some other player, who may then try to perform some other action, leading to an unstable situation. The above definition of classical Nash equilibrium applied to competitive diffusion in SNs assumes that each player has common knowledge about: (1) the whole structure of the social network (and every vertex in it), (2) for all players, how they think (diffusion model mechanism for each vertex), and (3) the strategies adopted by each other player. All these assumptions are needed to compute the utility $\hat{u}(S', p)$ — unfortunately, they are too strong for a real-world social network context. In most real-world social networks, we have information on our neighbors but not on others. Likewise, we are not privy to the strategies of the players and how they make decisions. Fortunately, our notion of strong equilibrium works without all these assumptions and, as stated in the following theorem, it is able to capture all Nash equilibria as well.

A *generic game* G is a triple $G = (\hat{P}, \hat{Q}, \hat{U})$ where (i) $\hat{P}$ is the set of players $\{p_1, \ldots, p_n\}$, (ii) $\hat{Q} = \{q_1, \ldots, q_m\}$ is the set of actions (the same for each player), and (iii) $\hat{U} = \{\hat{u}_1, \ldots, \hat{u}_n\}$ is the set of utility functions $\hat{u}_i : \hat{Q}^n \to \Re$, one for each player.

Theorem 4 NASH EQUILIBRIA CAN BE CAPTURED BY STRONG EQUILIBRIA OF CHOICEGAPs. *For every generic game $G = (\hat{P}, \hat{Q}, \hat{U})$, there exists a Choice-GAP Π such that the strong equilibria of Π coincide with the Nash equilibria of G.*

Apt and Simon [3] define a social network game where all users of the social network must choose one product from among a set of products and their utilities depend on the choices of their neighbors. We show in the online Appendix A [1] that their game can be expressed with our framework, i.e. here exists a Choice-GAP Π s.t. the strong equilibria of Π coincide with the Nash equilibria of their game. As a consequence, we can provide a *new* special case of their game (i.e. when only two products are considered as choices) where a Nash equilibrium always exists and can be computed in PTIME.

5   Vertex Independent Choice Programs

As strong equilibria may not exist for all ChoiceGAPs we will define a class
of programs called *vertex independent choice (VIC) programs* and denoted by
VIC_2, for which a Strong equilibrium always exists when the size of the vertex
choice rule is 2.

Definition 15 (Dependency Graph). *Suppose Π is a ChoiceGAP. The
dependency graph $\mathcal{G}(\Pi)$ associated with Π has the set VP of vertex predicates as
the set of vertices. The set E of edges is defined as follows: $(p_2, p_1) \in E$ iff (1)
there is a ChoiceGAP rule r with p_2 appearing in body(r) and p_1 in head(r), or
(2) in the vertex choice rule $r : B_1, \ldots, B_m \hookleftarrow A_1, \ldots, A_m$ there is an $1 \leq i \leq m$
such that p_2 appears in A_i and p_1 appears in B_i.*

We are now ready to define a VIC program.

Definition 16 (Vertex Independent Choice (VIC) Program). *A Choice-
GAP Π is said to be* Vertex Independent Choice (VIC) *if (1) every predicate
symbol appearing in the head of the VC-rule in Π does not appear in the head of
a GAP rule, and (2) Suppose $B_1, \ldots, B_m \hookleftarrow A_1, \ldots, A_m \in \Pi$ and p_1 appears in
B_j and p_2 appears in A_i and $i \neq j$. Then there is no path from p_1 to p_2 in the
dependency graph $\mathcal{G}(\Pi)$.*

*A VIC-program is said to be a VIC_m program when its VC-rule has the form
$B_1, \ldots, B_m \hookleftarrow A_1, \ldots, A_m$.*

Intuitively, the VIC condition requires that the choice of a vertex is completely independent, because (1) it cannot be forced by factors other than the
diffusion process, and (2) it is not influenced by conflicting atoms.

Given a VIC_m program Π containing the vertex choice rule $b_1(X), \ldots, b_m(X)$
$\hookleftarrow a_1(X), \ldots, a_m(X)$, and having dependency graph $\mathcal{G}(\Pi)$, we define m sets of
predicates $Pred_\Pi^1, \ldots, Pred_\Pi^m$ of Π, such that each set $Pred_\Pi^i$ contains all the
predicates obtained by a reverse visit (i.e. with each edge inverted, e.g. edge
(a, b) is considered as (b, a)) of $\mathcal{G}(\Pi)$ starting from the predicate b_i. Moreover,
given a state S, we can divide the induced ground VIC program Π_S into m
independent programs $\Pi_S^1, \ldots, \Pi_S^m$, where each Π_S^m contains all rules from Π_S
involving only predicates from $Pred_{\Pi_S}^i$.

The following result shows some properties of VIC programs.

Proposition 5. *Given two states S_1 and S_2 of a VIC program Π, where S_2
only differs from S_1 in the choice of player p, i.e. $S_1(p') = S_2(p')$ if $p' \neq p$, and
$S_1(p') \neq S_2(p')$ if $p' = p$, then for each player $\hat{p} \in \Gamma_\Pi$ the following statements
hold:*

1. $u(S_1, \hat{p}, S_1(p)) \geq u(S_2, \hat{p}, S_1(p))$.
2. $u(S_1, \hat{p}, S_2(p)) \leq u(S_2, \hat{p}, S_2(p))$.
3. $\forall j \in Q \setminus \{S_1(p), S_2(p)\} : \quad u(S_1, \hat{p}, j) = u(S_2, \hat{p}, j)$. $\qquad\qquad\square$

Example 4 below shows that VIC programs are not guaranteed to have strong equilibria.

Example 4. Consider the following VIC program where the size of vertex choice rule is 3:

$$g^U(1) : 0.4 \leftarrow \qquad r^U(2) : 0.4 \leftarrow \qquad b^U(3) : 0.4 \leftarrow$$

$$b^U(1) : 1.0 \leftarrow b^D(3) : 0.2$$
$$g^U(2) : 1.0 \leftarrow g^D(1) : 0.2$$
$$r^U(3) : 1.0 \leftarrow r^D(2) : 0.2$$

$$g^D(X), r^D(X), b^D(X) \hookleftarrow g^U(X), r^U(X), b^U(X)$$

This program does not have any Strong equilibrium. Moreover, observe that if we remove any one of the facts, three strong equilibria exist.

The following result shows that the problem of checking existence of a strong equilibrium for VIC_3 programs is NP-hard.

Theorem 6 (Existence of Strong Equilibrium for VIC_3 Programs).
*Given a VIC ChoiceGAP program Π where the size of vertex choice rule is 3, the problem of deciding whether Π has a Strong equilibrium is still **NP**-hard under data and combined complexity.* □

The following result shows that for VIC programs, all Nash equilibria are strong equilibria, but the converse is not necessarily true.

Theorem 7. *Let Π be a VIC program. Then every Nash equilibrium is a Strong equilibrium for Π, but in general a Strong equilibrium for Π may not be a Nash equilibrium.* □

VIC_2 Programs. Fortunately, VIC_2 programs have two nice properties. First, they are guaranteed to have a strong equilibrium. And second, the problem of finding a strong equilibrium can be solved in polynomial time. Algorithm 1 shows how to find such a strong equilibrium. We use the concept of state defined in Sect. 4. We start (line 2) by creating an initial state where all players take action 1 (of the two actions 1, 2 supported by the VIC_2 program). Recall that for each player $\mathcal{P}_v$, we have only two choices in VIC_2 programs, i.e. $Q(\mathcal{P}_v) = \{1, 2\}$. If this state is not a strong equilibrium, we identify all players for which a higher utility is obtained by performing action 2 (lines $3-7$) and if this is the case, we set their action appropriately. Finally (line 8), we return the minimal model of the induced ground GAP Π_S (see Definition 12). Observe that a different Strong equilibrium can be found by inverting action 1 with 2 and vice versa.

Theorem 8. *Algorithm 1 runs in **PTIME** and returns a Strong equilibrium (that always exists).* □

Algorithm 1. Algorithm finding a Strong equilibrium.

1: **procedure** $findSE$(ChoiceGAP VIC_2 program Π)
2:     Let S be a state s.t. $S(\mathcal{P}_v) = 1$ for all players $\mathcal{P}_v \in \Gamma_\Pi$;
3:     **while** (S does not represent a Strong equilibrium for Π) **do**
4:         **for all** (players $\mathcal{P}_v$ s.t. $u(S, \mathcal{P}_v, 1) < u(S, \mathcal{P}_v, 2)$) **do**
5:             Set $S(\mathcal{P}_v) = 2$;
6:         **end for**
7:     **end while**
8: **return** $\mathcal{MM}(\Pi_S)$
9: **end procedure**

From the set of all ground atoms of a VIC_2 program Π, we can define two partial interpretations: $\mathcal{MM}(\Pi_S^1)$ is the interpretation for all atoms in $\mathcal{MM}(\Pi_S)$ referring to action 1 — $\mathcal{MM}(\Pi_S^2)$ is the interpretation for all atoms in $\mathcal{MM}(\Pi_S)$ referring to action 2. Let S_{12} (S_{21}) be the state identifying the Strong equilibrium computed by Algorithm 1 (resp. by inverting the action 1 with 2 and vice versa). The following result shows certain relationships about the utilities returned by the different minimal models of GAPs depending upon our choice of S.

Theorem 9 (Maximal and Minimal Models). *Suppose Π is a VIC_2 program. For each state S identifying a Strong equilibrium the following statements hold:* $\mathcal{MM}(\Pi_{S_{12}}^2) \preceq \mathcal{MM}(\Pi_S^2) \preceq \mathcal{MM}(\Pi_{S_{21}}^2)$ *and* $\mathcal{MM}(\Pi_{S_{21}}^1) \preceq \mathcal{MM}(\Pi_S^1) \preceq \mathcal{MM}(\Pi_{S_{12}}^1)$.

The following result shows that checking whether an action is true in all strong equilibria is polynomially solvable in the case of VIC_2 programs.

Proposition 10 (Entailment in VIC_2). *Given a VIC_2 program Π and a ground annotated atom AA, the problem of deciding whether $\Pi \models AA$ is in* **PTIME** *under data and combined complexity.* $\square$

6   Experiments

We ran experiments to check the scalability and accuracy of our framework in predicting real-world election outcomes by considering Facebook discussions surrounding the latest Italian general election (2013). All experiments were run on an Intel I7 2.70 GHz machine with 8 GB RAM.

Dataset. We used a dataset extracted from Facebook containing information about Italian Facebook users and their Facebook friends, together with all Facebook pages that each user likes. For each Facebook *like* we store the page url, name and type (e.g. Actor/Director, Public Figure, Community, Political Organization, etc.). The dataset contains about $65\,K$ users, $84\,K$ friendship relations, and $520\,K$ likes. As our dataset was extracted after the elections, it contains a lot of user preferences about the political parties and/or politicians involved in the electoral competition, expressed in terms of likes of pages maintained by political parties and/or politicians. There were three main political alliances involved in the election competition, denoted by p_1, p_2 and p_3.

For each user u in our Facebook dataset and for each party p_i who participated in the elections, we assigned a confidence value $\rho(u, p_i) \in [0, 1]$, $1 \le i \le 3$ and $\sum_{i=1}^{3} \rho(u, p_i) = 1$, that expresses how much the user u likes the party p, as follows. First of all, we classified the Facebook pages of type Political Organization or Politician contained in the dataset (1002 pages) into three categories, p_1, p_2 and p_3, according to the content of the page. Second, for each user u and for each party p_i, we computed the value $\rho(u, p_i) = \frac{\#likes(u,p_i)}{\sum_{i=1}^{3} \#likes(u,p_i)}$, where $\#likes(u, p_i)$ is the number of Facebook pages of type p_i user u likes. Finally, we classified a user u as *supporter* of the party p_i, if p_i corresponds to the maximum coefficient $\rho(u, p_i)$.

In our experiments we considered 4 competitions, namely (C1) p_2 vs. p_3, (C2) p_2 and p_3 vs. p_1, (C3) p_2 vs. p_1, and (C4) p_3 vs. p_1. For each competition, we constructed 20 (training set, validation set) pairs of data to use in the experiments. We did this as follows: given the set U of users having at least one *like* to a page of type Political Organization or Politician (a total of 1 439 users), and a value $\delta \in [0, 100]$, we randomly select $\delta\%$ of the users in U to be part of the training set, while the remaining $(1 - \delta)\%$ of users are part of the validation set. We used 20, 30, 40, 50, 60, 70 and 80 as values for δ. Of course, our algorithm is then executed over the whole network (65 K users).

Diffusion Models. We used three different diffusion models in our experiments. The first diffusion model is a kind of cascade model in which the likelihood of a vertex adopting a political preference is the average of the likelihoods of its friends adopting that position:

$$model_1 : \begin{array}{l} choice1(v) : \frac{1}{|nbr(v)|} \sum_{u \in nbr(v)} \mu_u \leftarrow \bigwedge_{u \in nbr(v)} choice1(u) : \mu_u. \\ choice2(v) : \frac{1}{|nbr(v)|} \sum_{u \in nbr(v)} \mu_u \leftarrow \bigwedge_{u \in nbr(v)} choice2(u) : \mu_u. \end{array}$$

Due to lack of space we report the other two diffusion models (including a tipping model [9,18]) in the Online Appendix B [1]. For each competition-diffusion model pair, we computed the maximal model (M_1) and the minimal model (M_2) using Algorithm 1. We assigned real utility values to users in the training set, while users in the validation set were assigned a 0 utility value (because we will use our model to predict which of the two political orientations these users prefer). The real utility values are computed by taking into account the values $\rho(u, p_i)$. For instance, for the second competition the utility of vertex u for p_2 and p_3 is $u_1(u) = \frac{\rho(u,p_2)+\rho(u,p_3)}{\rho(u,p_1)+\rho(u,p_2)+\rho(u,p_3)}$, while the utility of u for p_1 is $u_2(u) = \frac{\rho(u,p_1)}{\rho(u,p_1)+\rho(u,p_2)+\rho(u,p_3)}$.

Area Under the ROC Curve. To evaluate our model, we built a threshold classifier by using bounds over the vertices' utility values returned by the models M_1 and M_2 (details are reported in Appendix B [1]). We computed the ROC curve by varying the threshold τ, and used the Area Under the ROC curve (AUROC) to measure the accuracy of our model. A receiver operating characteristic (ROC) curve plots false positive rates on the x-axis and true-positive rates on the y-axis. The AUROC is the area under the resulting curve. Figure 1 (left) shows a graph of the average AUROC as we vary the size of the training set from 20 % of the overall data set to 80 % in steps of 10 %. For each value of this size, we randomly selected a data set of that size from our Facebook data in 20 ways. Then, as mentioned above, another 4500 combinations of parameters were considered, making a total of 90,000 experimental settings for each data set size. We have a total of 8 data set sizes, making 720 K runs in all in our experiments. For each data set size, Fig. 1 (left) shows the average AUROC we derived. We see that on average, the AUROC varies between 0.75 and 0.78 which is quite a narrow band. Recall that an AUROC of 0.5 denotes random guessing and hence these AUROCs show strong predictive power. Moreover, the predictive power seems relatively flat as we vary the size of the training set from 20 % to 80 %, varying by just about 3 percentage points overall, which indicates that we can get good predictive accuracy even without large training sets. Figure 1 (right) shows the standard deviation of the AUROCs we obtained. We see the important trend that the standard deviation stays small, under 0.05, even as the size of the training set varies from 20 % to 80 %. Table 1 in [1] reports the maximum AUROC we obtained for each competition. With the exception of competition C1, the AUROC is over 0.88 for competitions C2 and C3, and over 0.75 for C4.

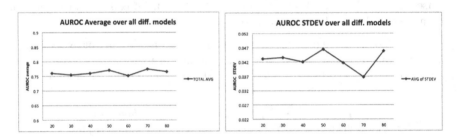

Fig. 1. On y-axis average AUROC (left) and standard deviation of AUROC (right) as we vary the size of the training set (x-axis) from 20 % to 80 % of the entire Facebook data set.

7 Related Work

To the best of our knowledge, this paper presents the *first* game-theoretic framework for competitive diffusion which scales to large social networks and which has been proven to have high accuracy. Many works have addressed the problem of competitive diffusion through social networks but with a perspective different from our work. [5,7,10] extended the "influence maximization problem" [13] to a competitive scenario. In this setting, the players are entities outside the social network (and not the network users) that try to diffuse new technologies, rumors, etc. [7,10] allow one competitor to actively maximize the diffusion of a property against competing static ones. In our work, all competitors are active at the same time. The diffusion model that is typically used is an extension of the independent cascade model which has the sub-modular property. In [5] all players are active and their move consists in choosing an initial set of seeds to maximize their influence on the network. They prove this game has mixed-strategy Nash Equilibria (but not pure ones). [15] addresses the problem as a 2-player-game where the players are the competitors or rumors. The first player starts by choosing its set of seeds, then the second player makes his choice of different seeds. The payoff of a player is computed after the diffusion (propagated with specific models) has terminated and equals the number of vertices that believes in the rumor corresponding to the player. They show that computing the optimal strategy for both players is NP-complete, as well as determining an approximated solution for the first player. *In contrast to all the above efforts, our framework allows more than two competitors, allows vertices and edges to have property labels, and, in addition, our framework of ChoiceGAPs allows us to express a huge variety of diffusion models whereas these other papers focus on just one type of diffusion model. Moreover, we do not require diffusion models having the submodularity property. Also, our algorithm is scalable and performs well in practice.*

[6] presented a logic-based competitive diffusion model in which they induced a probability distribution over the space of models of a annotated logic program and hypothesized that the most likely "model" was the one that was likely to happen in practice. This one model of the annotated logic program was used to make forecasts (e.g. if the model said more people would adopt choice 1 instead of choice 2, then that is what would happen). However, no accuracy results were presented. One flaw with this is that it is possible that the most probable model has probability 5 % and suggests that more people would adopt choice 1, while the remaining models (carrying 95 % probability of occurring) suggest they would adopt choice 2. Moreover, even on networks of under 10 K vertices, the algorithm took many, many hours to compute. In contrast, the results of this paper show far greater scalability as well as strong accuracy results.

This paper builds upon our previous work [19] leveraging a GAPs [14] framework for diffusion in networks. However, [19] differs in several key aspects: it does not consider competitive diffusion models (then GAPs are not combined with choice logic programs), and addresses a different problem, i.e. determining which vertices in the network will cause a property to spread to a maximal extend (w.r.t. a complex aggregate). The problem considered here is determine how competing properties will diffuse.

8   Conclusions

In real-world social networks, multiple diffusive phenomena are competing for the attention of the same individual. In this paper, we take the problem of competing diffusions "head on". Using the general framework of ChoiceGAPs, we build a game-theoretic framework in which every social network user is considered to be a player — thus the resulting game consists of a very large number of players. We show that certain models of the resulting logic programs can be thought of as "strong equilibria" models having very nice properties, similar to Nash equilibria (whose direct use would require making some unrealistic assumptions). We prove that the entailment problem is coNP-complete for a general ChoiceGAP and we identify a tractable class of ChoiceGAPs called VIC_2 programs where a strong equilibrium always exists and the entailment is in PTIME. We tested our framework on the real-world competitive diffusion situation of the 2013 Italian election on a data set we extracted from Facebook. We show that our framework works well in practice and can predict the number of those who like various political parties with an AUROC of 0.76 on average across all experiments.

Acknowledgements. Parts of this work were supported by ARO grant W911NF1610342.

References

1. Online appendix (2016). https://sites.google.com/site/choicegap
2. Anderson, R.M., May, R.M.: Population biology of infectious diseases: part I. Nature **280**(5721), 361 (1979)
3. Apt, K.R., Simon, S.: Social network games with obligatory product selection. In: GandALF, pp. 180–193 (2013)
4. Aral, S., Muchnik, L., Sundararajan, A.: Distinguishing influence-based contagion from homophily-driven diffusion in dynamic networks. Proc. Nat. Acad. Sci. (PNAS) **106**(51), 21544–21549 (2009)
5. Bharathi, S., Kempe, D., Salek, M.: Competitive influence maximization in social networks. In: Deng, X., Graham, F.C. (eds.) WINE 2007. LNCS, vol. 4858, pp. 306–311. Springer, Heidelberg (2007)
6. Broecheler, M., Shakarian, P., Subrahmanian, V.S.: A scalable framework for modeling competitive diffusion in social networks. In: SocialCom/PASSAT, pp. 295–302 (2010)
7. Carnes, T., Nagarajan, C., Wild, S.M., van Zuylen, A.: Maximizing influence in a competitive social network: a follower's perspective. In: ICEC 2007, pp. 351–360 (2007)
8. Cha, M., Mislove, A., Gummadi, P.K.: A measurement-driven analysis of information propagation in the flickr social network. In: Proceedings of the International World Wide Web Conference, pp. 721–730 (2009)
9. Granovetter, M.S.: The strength of weak ties. Am. J. Sociol. **78**(6), 1360–1380 (1973)
10. He, X., Song, G., Chen, W., Jiang, Q.: Influence blocking maximization in social networks under the competitive linear threshold model. In: SDM, p. 463 (2012)
11. Hethcote, H.W.: Qualitative analyses of communicable disease models. Math. Biosci. **28**(3–4), 335–356 (1976)
12. Jackson, M., Yariv, L.: Diffusion on social networks. Economie Publique **16**, 69–82 (2005)
13. Kempe, D., Kleinberg, J., Tardos, E.: Maximizing the spread of influence through a social network. In: KDD, pp. 137–146 (2003)
14. Kifer, M., Subrahmanian, V.: Theory of generalized annotated logic programming and its applications. J. Log. Program. **12**(3&4), 335–367 (1992)
15. Kostka, J., Oswald, Y.A., Wattenhofer, R.: Word of mouth: rumor dissemination in social networks. In: Shvartsman, A.A., Felber, P. (eds.) SIROCCO 2008. LNCS, vol. 5058, pp. 185–196. Springer, Heidelberg (2008)

16. Nash, J.F.: Equilibrium points in n-person games. Proc. Nat. Acad. Sci. USA **36**(1), 48–49 (1950)

17. Saccà, D., Zaniolo, C.: Stable models and non-determinism in logic programs with negation. In: PODS, pp. 205–217 (1990)

18. Schelling, T.C.: Micromotives and Macrobehavior. W.W. Norton and Co., New York (1978)

19. Shakarian, P., Broecheler, M., Subrahmanian, V.S., Molinaro, C.: Using generalized annotated programs to solve social network diffusion optimization problems. In: ACM Transactions on Computational Logic (2012)

Short Papers

Challenges for Efficient Query Evaluation on Structured Probabilistic Data

Antoine Amarilli[1], Silviu Maniu[2(✉)], and Mikaël Monet[1]

[1] Télécom ParisTech, Université Paris-Saclay, Paris, France
[2] LRI, Université Paris-Sud, Université Paris-Saclay, Orsay, France
silviu.maniu@lri.fr

Abstract. Query answering over probabilistic data is an important task but is generally intractable. However, a new approach for this problem has recently been proposed, based on *structural decompositions* of input databases, following, e.g., tree decompositions. This paper presents a vision for a database management system for probabilistic data built following this structural approach. We review our existing and ongoing work on this topic and highlight many theoretical and practical challenges that remain to be addressed.

1 Introduction

To have an accurate description of the real world, it is often necessary to associate probabilities to our observations. For instance, experimental and scientific data may be inherently uncertain, because, e.g., of imperfect sensor precision, harmful interferences, or incorrect modelling. Even when crisp data can be obtained, it can still be the case that we do not trust who retrieved it or how it came to us. The notion of *probabilistic databases* has been introduced to capture this uncertainty, reason over it, and query it: these databases are augmented with probability information to describe how uncertain each data item is. Given a probabilistic database D and a query q, the *probabilistic query evaluation problem* (PQE) asks for the probability that the query q holds on D. Unfortunately, even on the simplest probabilistic database models, PQE is generally intractable [14].

One possibility to work around this intractability is to use approximate approaches, such as Monte Carlo sampling on the data instances. A different direction was recently explored in [2], namely, restricting the kind of *input instances* that we allow, in what we call the *structural approach*. It is shown in [2] that the data complexity of PQE is linear if the instances have *bounded treewidth*, i.e., they can be structurally decomposed in a tree-like structure where each node must contain at most k elements, for a fixed parameter k. Moreover, in [3], it is shown that bounding the instance treewidth is *necessary* to ensure the tractability of PQE, because some queries are hard on *any* unbounded-treewidth instance family (under some conditions). Hence, bounded-treewidth methods seem to be the right way to make PQE tractable by the structural approach.

S. Schockaert and P. Senellart (Eds.): SUM 2016, LNAI 9858, pp. 323–330, 2016.
DOI: 10.1007/978-3-319-45856-4_22

These theoretical works, however, left open the question of practical applicability: many challenges must still be addressed to implement a practical system using these techniques. First, obtaining an optimal decomposition of an arbitrary instance is NP-hard [5]. Second, the complexity is only polynomial in the *data*, with the query and parameter being fixed; this hides a constant which can be exponential in the width k and non-elementary in the query q. Third, we do not know which real datasets can indeed be decomposed, at least partially, with a small k.

This paper thus presents our vision of a database management system based on the structural approach, and gives an overview of the research directions, both theoretical and practical, which we intend to address to this end.

2   Probabilistic Query Evaluation: A Structural Approach

We first review our *structural* approach [2] for probabilistic query evaluation (PQE). The approach is illustrated in Fig. 1.

The approach applies to *tuple-independent (TID) instances* (but generalizes to more expressive models [1]). Formally, a TID instance I is a relational database D where each tuple $t \in D$ has some probability p_t. The TID I represents a probability distribution over the subinstances $D' \subseteq D$ (subsets of facts): following the independence assumption, the probability of D' is $\prod_{t \in D'} p_t \times \prod_{t \in D \setminus D'} (1 - p_t)$.

We study the *probabilistic query evaluation* (PQE) problem: given a *Boolean query* q and TID instance I, determine the probability that q holds on I, i.e., the total probability of the subinstances of I that satisfy q. We refer to the *combined complexity* of PQE when I and q are given as input; we refer to *data complexity* when I is the input and q is fixed.

The first step of the structural approach (Sect. 3) is to translate the query q to a formalism that can be efficiently evaluated. In the approach of [2],

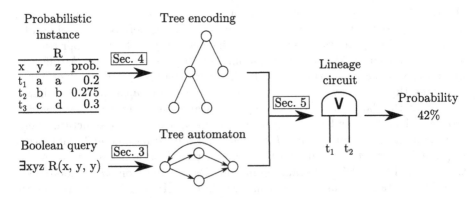

Fig. 1. Overview of the structural approach for PQE

following [13], the query is compiled to a *tree automaton*, i.e., a finite-state automaton over trees [12]. The approach works for expressive queries written in *monadic second-order logic*, which covers in particular first-order logic and (unions of) conjunctive queries. This translation of the query is independent from the instance, so does not affect data complexity; however, it depends on a *parameter k* of the instance, to be defined soon. Intuitively, the automaton represents an algorithm to evaluate the query on suitable instances.

The second step (Sect. 4) applies to the instance I, and computes a *structural decomposition* of it. In [2], we compute a *tree decomposition* [10,11], equivalent to junction trees in graphical models [19], and then a *tree encoding* over a finite alphabet: the results of [3] show that tree decompositions are essentially the only possible way to make PQE tractable. The *parameter k* measures how well I could be decomposed: in our case, k is the *treewidth*, measuring how close I is to a tree. By *treelike* instances, we mean instances whose treewidth is bounded by a constant.

The third step (Sect. 5) is to compute a *lineage* of the query q on the instance I, i.e., compute an object that represents concisely the subinstances of I that satisfy q. This object can be used for PQE, as what we want to compute is precisely the total probability of this set of subinstances. Specifically, we compute a *Boolean lineage circuit* of the tree automaton for the query over the tree encoding of the instance, according to the construction of [2]. This step is purely symbolic and does not perform any numerical probability computation.

The fourth and last step is to evaluate efficiently the probability of the query from this lineage representation, by computing the probability that the circuit is true. This task cannot be performed efficiently on arbitrary Boolean circuits, but it is feasible in our context, for two independent reasons [2,3]. First, this circuit can also be tree decomposed, which allows us to apply a message-passing algorithm [19] for efficient probability computation. Second, in the case where we made the query automaton *deterministic* [12], the circuit is actually a d-DNNF [15], for which probabilistic query evaluation is tractable.

3   Efficient Compilation to Expressive Automata

Compiling the query to an automaton following the structural approach of [2], by applying [13], is generally non-elementary in the query. This section presents our main ideas to address this problem: we intend to restrict to *tractable query fragments*, and to use *more expressive automata targets* to compile the query more efficiently. These challenges are not specific to PQE; the next section presents the lineage computation tasks, which are specific to PQE.

Efficient Compilation. Of course, we cannot hope to compile all *Monadic Second Order* logic (MSO) to automata efficiently, or even all *conjunctive queries* (CQs). Indeed, efficient compilation to automata implies that non-probabilistic query evaluation is also tractable in combined complexity on treelike instances;

however, CQs are already hard to evaluate in this sense (even on fixed instances). Hence, we can only hope to compile *restricted* query languages efficiently.

Many fragments are known from earlier work to enjoy efficient combined query evaluation. In the database context, for instance, *acyclic CQs* can be evaluated in polynomial combined complexity [23]. This generalizes to first-order logical sentences that can be written with at most k variables, i.e., FO^k [17]. However, it also generalizes to the *guarded fragment* (GF) [4], whose combined complexity is also PTIME, and where better bounds can be derived if we know the instance treewidth [9]. The tractability of GF, however, does not capture other interesting query classes: reachability queries, and more generally *two-way regular path queries* (2RPQs) and variants thereof [6], as well as Monadic Datalog as in [16].

Our first task would thus be to develop an expressive query language that captures GF, 2RPQs, and Monadic Datalog. Ideally this fragment should be *parameterized*, i.e., all CQs or all FO queries q could be expressible in the fragment, up to increasing some parameter k_q, with the compilation being PTIME for fixed k_q but intractable in k_q. We would then develop an efficient algorithm to compile such queries to automata that check them on bounded-treewidth instances, for fixed values of the query parameter k_q and of the treewidth. Our ongoing work in this direction investigates very recent extensions of GF with negation and fixpoints [7,8], for which compilation to automata was studied as a tool for logical satisfiability. We believe that these results, suitably extended and adapted to query evaluation, can yield to bounded-treewidth automaton compilation methods that covers the query classes that we mentioned.

Expressive Automata Targets. The efficient compilation of queries to automata is made easier by allowing more expressive automaton classes as the target language. In [2], we used *bottom-up tree automata*, which process the tree decomposition of the instance from the leaves to the root. Our idea is to move to more expressive representations, namely, *two-way alternating automata* [12]. These automata can navigate through the tree in every direction (including already visited parts), and thus can be more concise. The notion of *alternation* allows automata to change states based on complex Boolean formulae on the neighboring states, which also helps for concision. Indeed, the expressive languages of [7] are compiled to two-way alternating parity automata, which further use a parity acceptance condition on infinite runs, to evaluate fixpoints.

To make automaton compilation more efficient, another idea is to compile queries to automata with a concise implicit representation. In particular, we can use automata with a *structured* state space: the states are tuples of Boolean values, and the transition function can be written concisely for each coordinate of the tuple as a function of the tuples of child states. It may be possible to capture the tractability of query evaluation for 2RPQs via automaton methods, structuring the state space to memorize separately the regular sublanguages of paths between node pairs.

4   Obtaining Tree Decompositions

Estimating Treewidth. As we have mentioned, computing the treewidth of an instance directly is an NP-hard problem. Hence, a practical system using the structural approach must compute tree decompositions more efficiently, even if this limits us to non-optimal decompositions. We intend to experiment with two main kinds of methods to obtain tree decompositions efficiently: *separator-based* algorithms, which recursively divide the instance based on various heuristics; and *elimination ordering* algorithms, where the nodes in the graph are ordered using some measure and eliminated one by one from the graph [10]. To estimate the quality of our decompositions, we can also estimate *lower bounds* on the instance treewidth: for instance via graph degeneracy or average degree [11].

Query-Specific Decompositions. In some cases, knowledge about the query can help us to obtain better tree decompositions of the instance. A trivial situation is when we know that the query is only on a subset of the database relations: we can then ignore the others when decomposing. More subtly, if we know that specific *joins* are not made by the query, then we may be able to rewrite the instance accordingly, and lower the treewidth. For instance, if no R- and S-atoms share a variable in the query, then the instance $\{R(a,b), S(b,c)\}$ can be rewritten to $\{R(a,b), S(b',c)\}$, which may lower the treewidth by disconnecting elements. We do not understand this process yet in the general case, but we believe that a theory of lineage-preserving instance rewritings for a given query (or query class) can be developed, using the notion of *instance unfoldings* introduced in [3].

5   Tractable Lineage Targets

Once we have compiled the query to an automaton and decomposed the instance to a tree encoding, our goal is to compute a *lineage representation* of the automaton on the encoding, namely, a representation of the subinstances where the query holds, which we will build as a Boolean circuit. We can then use this to perform PQE, by computing the probability of the query as that of the lineage. In so doing, we need to rely on the fact that the lineage is in a class of circuits for which probability can be efficiently computed.

To this end, a first step towards a practical system is to adapt the methods of [2] to the expressive automaton classes that are needed for efficient query compilation. We believe that this is possible, but with a twist: because two-way automata can navigate a tree in every direction, they may go back from where they came, thus resulting in cyclic runs. Therefore, it seems that the natural lineages that we would obtain for alternating two-way automata are *cyclic Boolean circuits*, which we call *Boolean cycluits*. A semantics for such circuits would need to be defined based on the semantics of automaton runs and reachable states: we believe that the evaluation could follow least fixed-point semantics, and be performed in linear time.

Second, we would need to perform efficient probability computation on these cycluits. One first way to address this would be to eliminate cycles and transform them to tractable classes of Boolean circuits (e.g., d-DNNFs), which we believe can be done assuming bounds on the treewidth of the cycluits. Alternatively, we can apply message passing methods directly on the cycluits [19]; or we can try to rewrite the automaton to produce acyclic circuits or even d-DNNFs directly. All these methods would be generally intractable in the query, which is unsurprising: indeed, PQE is often intractable even for languages with tractable combined complexity, and efficient compilation to automata. It would be interesting, however, to identify islands of tractability; and, in intractable cases, to benchmark the previously mentioned approaches and see which ones perform best in practice.

Another important direction for a practical system is to be able to evaluate queries on instances where facts are not independent, i.e., go beyond the TID formalism. For instance, facts could be present or absent according to a complex lineage, like the cc-instances of [1]. In this context, new methods can be efficient. For instance, if the number of probabilistic events is small, performing *Shannon expansions* on some well-chosen events may make large parts of the instance deterministic, making the query easier to evaluate on these parts.

6   Practical Matters

We now review possible approaches and directions to implement and evaluate the structural approach for PQE on real-world datasets.

Results on Treelike Instances. In [21], the structural approach has been compared with one of the existing probabilistic data management systems, namely MayBMS [18]. The instances considered have been randomly generated to have low treewidth ($\leqslant 7$). The results show that an implementation of the structural approach can perform query evaluation faster than the exact methods of MayBMS, in cases where there are many matches and many correlations between them. Indeed, MayBMS does not take advantage of the fact that the instances are treelike. However, in this work, the queries were compiled to automata by hand rather than automatically, and there was no study of practical datasets.

Practical Datasets and Partial Decompositions. A first question is to extend this study to practical datasets, and to investigate whether such datasets have low treewidth, or whether we can use approximate decompositions or reasonably low treewidth. Our preliminary results suggest that some datasets have high treewidth, but others, in particular transportation networks, have treewidth much smaller than their size. For instance, the OpenStreetMaps graph of Paris has over 4 million nodes and 5 million edges, but we estimated its treewidth to be $\leqslant 521$. We do not know yet of a theoretical reason explaining why transportation networks generally exhibit this property.

However, this bound is still too large to be practical. One way to work around this problem is thus to compute a *partial decomposition* [22] of the instance, i.e., a tree decomposition of a part of the instance whose width is at most k, with k fixed. This results in a structure formed of a forest of instances with treewidth $\leqslant k$, called the *tentacles*, that interface with a *core*, i.e., the remaining facts, whose treewidth is too high and that cannot be decomposed. Our preliminary experiments have shown that, for some transportation networks, a partial decomposition for $k = 10$ results in a core instance whose size is about 10 % of the original instance.

This decrease in the size of the core, in turn, can potentially have an immediate effect in the processing of queries. Preliminary results [20] have shown that using partial decompositions of fixed treewidth for probabilistic reachability queries, in conjunction with sampling in the core graph, can make query processing up to 5 times faster.

Tentacle Summarization. An important problem when computing probabilities on partial decompositions is the interface between the tentacles and the core, i.e., we must find a way to *summarize* the tentacles in the core when applying sampling to the core. As the tentacles are treelike, we can efficiently compute probabilities and lineages in them: the goal of summarization is to eliminate the tentacles and replace them by *summary* facts that are added to the core. In the case of simple queries, such as reachability queries, the summary facts can have the same semantics as in the original instance, but this does not seem to generalize to arbitrary queries: it may even be the case that some queries cannot be rewritten to the summary facts while remaining in the same language.

Having summarized the tentacles, we may also answer queries approximately via *sampling*, using the (exact) tentacle summaries added to the core: as the instance is now smaller, this process can be performed faster.

References

1. Amarilli, A.: Leveraging the structure of uncertain data. Ph.D. thesis, Télécom ParisTech (2016). 2016-ENST-0021
2. Amarilli, A., Bourhis, P., Senellart, P.: Provenance circuits for trees and treelike instances. In: Halldórsson, M.M., Iwama, K., Kobayashi, N., Speckmann, B. (eds.) ICALP 2015. LNCS, vol. 9135, pp. 56–68. Springer, Heidelberg (2015)
3. Amarilli, A., Bourhis, P., Senellart, P.: Tractable lineages on treelike instances: limits and extensions. In: Proceedings of PODS (2016, to appear)
4. Andréka, H., Németi, I., van Benthem, J.: Modal languages and bounded fragments of predicate logic. J. Philos. Log. **27**(3), 217–274 (1998)
5. Arnborg, S., Corneil, D.G., Proskurowski, A.: Complexity of finding embeddings in a k-tree. SIAM J. Algebr. Discret. Methods **8**(2), 277–284 (1987)
6. Barceló Baeza, P.: Querying graph databases. In: Proceedings of PODS (2013)
7. Benedikt, M., Bourhis, P., Vanden Boom, M.: A step up in expressiveness of decidable fixpoint logics. In: Proceedings of LICS (2016, to appear)

8. Benedikt, M., Ten Cate, B., Colcombet, T., Boom, M.V.: The complexity of bound-edness for guarded logics. In: Proceedings of LICS (2015)
9. Berwanger, D., Grädel, E.: Games and model checking for guarded logics. In: Nieuwenhuis, R., Voronkov, A. (eds.) LPAR 2001. LNCS (LNAI), vol. 2250, p. 70. Springer, Heidelberg (2001)
10. Bodlaender, H.L., Koster, A.: Treewidth computations I. Upper bounds. Inf. Comput. **208**(3), 259–275 (2010)
11. Bodlaender, H.L., Koster, A.: Treewidth computations II. Lower bounds. Inf. Comput. **209**(7), 1103–1119 (2011)
12. Comon, H., Dauchet, M., Gilleron, R., Löding, C., Jacquemard, F., Lugiez, D., Tison, S., Tommasi, M.: Tree automata: techniques and applications (2007)
13. Courcelle, B.: The monadic second-order logic of graphs. I. Recognizable sets of finite graphs. Inf. Comput. **85**(1), 12–75 (1990)
14. Dalvi, N., Suciu, D.: Efficient query evaluation on probabilistic databases. VLDBJ **16**(4), 523–544 (2007)
15. Darwiche, A.: On the tractable counting of theory models and its application to truth maintenance and belief revision. J. Appl. Non-Class. Log. **11**(1–2), 11–34 (2001)
16. Gottlob, G., Pichler, R., Wei, F.: Monadic datalog over finite structures of bounded treewidth. TOCL **12**(1), 3 (2010)
17. Grädel, E., Otto, M.: On logics with two variables. TCS **224**(1), 73–113 (1999)
18. Huang, J., Antova, L., Koch, C., Olteanu, D.: MayBMS: a probabilistic database management system. In: Proceedings of SIGMOD (2009)
19. Lauritzen, S.L., Spiegelhalter, D.J.: Local computations with probabilities on graphical structures and their application to expert systems. JRSS Ser. B **50**, 157–224 (1988)
20. Maniu, S., Cheng, R., Senellart, P.: ProbTree: a query-efficient representation of probabilistic graphs. In: Proceedings of BUDA (2014)
21. Monet, M.: Probabilistic evaluation of expressive queries on bounded-treewidth instances. In: Proceedings of Ph.D. Symposium of SIGMOD/PODS. ACM (2016, to appear)
22. Wei, F.: TEDI: efficient shortest path query answering on graphs. In: Proceedings of SIGMOD (2010)
23. Yannakakis, M.: Algorithms for acyclic database schemes. In: Proceedings of VLDB (1981)

Forgetting-Based Inconsistency Measure

Philippe Besnard[(✉)]

IRIT, CNRS, Université Paul Sabatier,
118 route de Narbonne, F-31062 Toulouse Cedex, France
besnard@irit.fr

Abstract. We propose to apply a variant of forgetting, a simple method to restore consistency, in order to get a new inconsistency measure from the following intuitive idea: How much effort is needed to restore consistency of a knowledge base is presumably indicative of how inconsistent the knowledge base is. We discuss properties of the inconsistency measure obtained, in particular in the face of well-known postulates for inconsistency measures. We also mention in what sense this new measure does not fall into the dichotomy of inconsistency measures proposed in the literature: alphabet-based approaches vs formula-based approaches.

1 Introduction

Inconsistency measures have gained much interest recently (Ammoura et al. 2015; Grant and Hunter 2013; Hunter et al. 2014; Jabbour et al. 2015, 2016; Liu and Mu 2016; McAreavey et al. 2014; Mu et al. 2012; Mu 2015; Thimm 2013, 2016a, 2016b; Thimm and Wallner 2016; Xiao and Ma 2012). An inconsistency measure ascribes a quantity to a logical knowledge base, a quantity which is meant to tell how inconsistent the knowledge base is. Here, we apply forgetting (Lin and Reiter 1994), a well-known method to restore consistency (Lang and Marquis 2002), in order to get a new inconsistency measure from the following idea: How much effort is needed to restore consistency of a knowledge base is presumably indicative of how inconsistent the knowledge base is.

1.1 Formal Preliminaries

By a knowledge base, we mean a finite multiset of formulas of propositional logic. We use $\neg$, $\wedge$, $\vee$ to denote the usual Boolean connectives: negation, conjunction, disjunction. We use Greek letters $\varphi, \psi, \ldots$, whether indexed or not, to denote formulas of propositional logic. We use capital Greek letters $\Delta, \Gamma, \ldots$ to denote knowledge bases (i.e., multisets of formulas of propositional logic, as just said). We use κ (which is introduced in Definition 1) to denote forgetting: Intuitively, κ "forgets" occurrences of a propositional variable.

© Springer International Publishing Switzerland 2016
S. Schockaert and P. Senellart (Eds.): SUM 2016, LNAI 9858, pp. 331–337, 2016.
DOI: 10.1007/978-3-319-45856-4_23

2   An Inconsistency Measure

We consider formulas labelled with superscripts denoting occurrences of atoms. Every formula φ in which an unlabelled atom v occurs $k > 0$ times is identified as $\varphi(v^1, \ldots, v^k)$ where v^i denotes the ith unlabelled occurrence of v in φ.[1]

Example. The unlabelled formula $a \wedge b \wedge \neg b$ is identified with the labelled formula $a^1 \wedge b^1 \wedge \neg b^2$.

Accordingly, given the list of propositional variables $\mathcal{P} = v_1, v_2, \ldots$ define the set of atom occurrences as

$$\mathcal{A} \stackrel{\text{def}}{=} \bigcup_{v \in \mathcal{P}} \{v^1, v^2, \ldots\}$$

Importantly, v^i is identified with v^j for all purposes (e.g., consistency issues) except for purposes of occurrences of atoms. In particular, a Boolean combination of labelled formulas may display multiple copies of the same atom occurrence e.g., $(a^1 \wedge b^1 \wedge \neg b^2) \,\big|\, b^1 \to \top, \bot$ (see below) is $(a^1 \wedge \top \wedge \neg b^2) \vee (a^1 \wedge \bot \wedge \neg b^2)$.

Notation. The symbol $\to$ is used for substitution as follows.

$$\varphi \left| \begin{array}{l} v_1^{i_1} \to \psi_1 \\ \vdots \\ v_k^{i_h} \to \psi_h \end{array} \right.$$

denotes the formula resulting from φ by replacing simultaneously each atom occurrence $v_j^{i_j}$ by ψ_j (informally speaking, an atom occurrence refers either to an unlabelled occurrence of the atom or to a labelled version of the atom). The abbreviation

$$\overset{m}{\underset{1}{\bigvee}} \varphi \,\big|\, v^i \to \psi_1, \ldots, \psi_m$$

is used to denote the disjunction whose each disjunct is the formula obtained from φ by replacing v^i by one of $\psi_1, \ldots, \psi_m$ in turn.

Example. Taking φ to be $a^1 \wedge b^1 \wedge \neg b^2 \wedge (b^3 \vee \neg(a^1 \wedge b^1))$, the substitution of b^1 by $\top$ in φ is denoted by $\varphi \,|\, (b^1 \to \top)$, yielding $a^1 \wedge \top \wedge \neg b^2 \wedge (b^3 \vee \neg(a^1 \wedge \top))$. That is, *all* occurrences of b^1 in φ are replaced by occurrences of $\top$. Also, $\bigvee \varphi \,|\, b^1 \to \top, \bot$ denotes $[a^1 \wedge \top \wedge \neg b^2 \wedge (b^3 \vee \neg(a^1 \wedge \top))] \vee [a^1 \wedge \bot \wedge \neg b^2 \wedge (b^3 \vee \neg(a^1 \wedge \bot))]$.

Definition 1. $\kappa_{i,v}.\varphi$ *is the labelled formula obtained from the labelled formula[2] φ by replacing the atom occurrences v^i in φ, first by $\top$, second by $\bot$, taking the disjunction thereof. In symbols,*

$$\kappa_{i,v}.\varphi \stackrel{\text{def}}{=} \varphi(v^1, \ldots, v^{i-1}, \top, v^{i+1}, \ldots, v^k) \vee \varphi(v^1, \ldots, v^{i-1}, \bot, v^{i+1}, \ldots, v^k)$$

---

[1] As to labelling, logical constants $\top$ and $\bot$ are not considered atoms: A formula in which either occurs is regarded as labelled if all other atoms in it are superscripted.

[2] That is, if φ is unlabelled, it is identified with $\varphi(v_1^1, \ldots, v_1^{i_1}, \ldots, v_p^1, \ldots, v_p^{i_p})$ where $v_1, \ldots, v_p$ are all the propositional variables in φ.

For clarity, let us stress that $\kappa_{i,v}.\varphi$ is a labelled formula hence $\kappa_{j,u}.(\kappa_{i,v}.\varphi)$ is such that $\kappa_{j,u}$ introduces no superscript (but it duplicates superscripted atoms).

Lemma 1.   *Using the substitution notation,*

$$\kappa_{i_1,v_1}.\kappa_{i_2,v_2}.\cdots.\kappa_{i_h,v_h}.\varphi = \bigvee_1^{2^h} \varphi \begin{vmatrix} v_1^{i_1}\to\top,\bot \\ \vdots \\ v_h^{i_h}\to\top,\bot \end{vmatrix}$$

In previous work (Lin and Reiter 1994; Lang and Marquis 2002; Lang et al. 2003) about forgetting, it is shown that consistency can be recovered if enough atoms are forgotten. It is of interest to characterize which *occurrences* of atoms are enough to consider if consistency is to be recovered.

Definition 2.   *Define $\sigma(\varphi)$ as the set of multisets of atom occurrences whose forgetting is enough to turn φ into a consistent formula, in symbols,*

$$\sigma(\varphi) \stackrel{def}{=} \{A \subseteq \mathcal{A} \mid \exists h \exists v_1^{i_1}..v_h^{i_h}, A = \{v_1^{i_1},\ldots,v_h^{i_h}\}, \kappa_{i_1,v_1}.\kappa_{i_2,v_2}.\cdots.\kappa_{i_h,v_h}.\varphi \not\vdash \bot\}.$$

Then, the inconsistency number of φ is intuitively the minimum number n of (iterated) applications of κ operators such that $\kappa_{i_1,v_1}.\kappa_{i_2,v_2}.\cdots.\kappa_{i_h,v_h}.\varphi \not\vdash \bot$ i.e. such that φ is turned into a consistent formula.

Definition 3.   *The inconsistency number of Γ is $n(\Gamma)$, defined as*

$$n(\Gamma) \stackrel{def}{=} \min_{A\in\sigma(\wedge\Gamma)} |A|$$

Reminder. Before turning to the examples, it is important to repeat that v^i is identified with v^j for most purposes, including consistency issues. For instance, in Example 2, $(\top \wedge a^2) \wedge (\neg a^3 \wedge \neg a^4)$ is inconsistent because it is identified with $(\top \wedge a^i) \wedge (\neg a^i \wedge \neg a^i)$ which is inconsistent, whatever i.

Example 1. Let $\Gamma_1 = \{a \vee a, \neg a \vee \neg a\}$. Then, $\bigwedge \Gamma_1 = (a^1 \vee a^2) \wedge (\neg a^3 \vee \neg a^4)$. $\{a^1\} \in \sigma(\Gamma_1)$ since $\kappa_{1,a}.\bigwedge \Gamma_1$ is $[(\top \vee a^2) \wedge (\neg a^3 \vee \neg a^4)] \vee [(\bot \vee a^2) \wedge (\neg a^3 \vee \neg a^4)]$ which is consistent. Hence $n(\Gamma_1) = 1$.

Example 2. Let $\Gamma_2 = \{a \wedge a, \neg a \wedge \neg a\}$. Hence, $\bigwedge \Gamma_2 = (a^1 \wedge a^2) \wedge (\neg a^3 \wedge \neg a^4)$. It does not matter whether considering a^1 instead of a^2 and a^3 instead of a^4. $\kappa_{1,a}.\bigwedge \Gamma_2$ is $[(\top \wedge a^2) \wedge (\neg a^3 \wedge \neg a^4)] \vee [(\bot \wedge a^2) \wedge (\neg a^3 \wedge \neg a^4)]$ which is inconsistent. $\kappa_{3,a}.\kappa_{1,a}.\bigwedge \Gamma_2$ is $[(\top \wedge a^2) \wedge (\neg\top \wedge \neg a^4)] \vee [(\bot \wedge a^2) \wedge (\neg\top \wedge \neg a^4)] \vee [(\top \wedge a^2) \wedge (\neg\bot \wedge \neg a^4)] \vee [(\bot \wedge a^2) \wedge (\neg\bot \wedge \neg a^4)]$ i.e. $[\bot \vee \bot] \vee [\bot \vee \bot]$ which is inconsistent (and so is $\kappa_{4,a}.\kappa_{1,a}.\bigwedge \Gamma_2$). However, $\kappa_{2,a}.\kappa_{1,a}.\bigwedge \Gamma_2$ is $[(\top \wedge \top) \wedge (\neg a^3 \wedge \neg a^4)] \vee [(\bot \wedge \top) \wedge (\neg a^3 \wedge \neg a^4)] \vee [(\top \wedge \bot) \wedge (\neg a^3 \wedge \neg a^4)] \vee [(\bot \wedge \bot) \wedge (\neg a^3 \wedge \neg a^4)]$ i.e. $[(\neg a^3 \wedge \neg a^4) \vee \bot] \vee [\bot \vee \bot]$, it is consistent. Hence, $n(\Gamma_2) = 2$.

Keep in mind that n refers to the *minimum* amount of forgetting needed to restore consistency. E.g., each of the knowledge bases Γ below satisfies $n(\Gamma) = 1$.

$$\{a, \neg a\}$$
$$\{a \wedge a, \neg a\}$$
$$\{a \vee b, a \vee \neg b, \neg a \vee b, \neg a \vee \neg b\}$$

3   How Inconsistent About v?

Besides determining how inconsistent Γ is, it would be interesting to determine how inconsistent Γ is *about* some v.

Definition 4. $n|_v(\Gamma) \stackrel{\text{def}}{=} \min_{A \in \sigma(\wedge \Gamma)} | A \cap \{v\}_\omega |$

Notation. $\{v\}_\omega$ denotes the multiset consisting of countably many copies of v.

Example 3. Let $\Gamma_3 = \{(a \wedge \neg a) \vee (b \wedge \neg b)\}$. Therefore, $\{b^1\} \in \sigma(\Gamma_3)$ because $\kappa_{1,b} \cdot \wedge \Gamma_3$ is $[(a^1 \wedge \neg a^2) \vee (\top \wedge \neg b^2)] \vee [(a^1 \wedge \neg a^2) \vee (\bot \wedge \neg b^2)]$ which is consistent. Hence, $n|_a(\Gamma_3) = 0$ due to $\{b^1\} \cap \{a\}_\omega$ being empty. Similarly, $n|_b(\Gamma_3) = 0$. However, $n(\Gamma_3) = 1$.

Comment. The reader may be unhappy that $n|_v(\Gamma) = 0$ captures both the case that v is involved in no contradiction in Γ and the case (as in Example 3) that v is involved in a contradiction together with at least another atom. There are many ways to change Definition 4, e.g. by considering some liability function l (with the constraint $l_{v,\sigma}(\Gamma) > 1$) so as to alternatively define $n|_v$ as follows:

$$n|_v(\Gamma) = \begin{cases} 0 & \text{if } A \cap \{v\}_\omega = \emptyset \text{ for all } A \in \sigma(\wedge \Gamma) \\ \min_{A \in \sigma(\wedge \Gamma)} | A \cap \{v\}_\omega | & \text{if } A \cap \{v\}_\omega \neq \emptyset \text{ for all } A \in \sigma(\wedge \Gamma) \\ 1/l_{v,\sigma}(\Gamma) & \text{otherwise} \end{cases}$$

Anyway, knowledge bases can be compared in the following way: Γ is at least as v-*inconsistent* as Γ' iff $n|_v(\Gamma) \geq n|_v(\Gamma')$.

Lemma 2.   *If $n(\Gamma) \geq n(\Gamma')$ then there exists an atom v such that Γ is at least as v-inconsistent as Γ'.*

Lemma 3.   *$n(\Gamma) \geq n(\Gamma')$ if for every v, Γ is at least as v-inconsistent as Γ'.*

It is also possible to compare the involvement of atoms in the conflicts of a knowledge base. Therefore, if atoms can be mapped to topics, such a measure $n|_v$ would permit to judge whether a topic gives rise to more severe conflicts than some other topic, or to judge whether the overall inconsistency degree of the knowledge base amounts to the inconsistency degree ascribed to such and such topic. (Please keep in mind that "severe" only refers to intensity, there can be a severe conflict about a topic of little importance.)

4   Postulates for Inconsistency Measures

We now turn to examining what postulates are satisfied by our inconsistency measure n. In this respect, a useful lemma is the following one.

Lemma 4.   *For all $j \geq h$, if $\kappa_{i_1,v_1} \cdot \cdots \cdot \kappa_{i_h,v_h} \cdot \varphi \not\vdash \bot$ then $\kappa_{i_1,v_1} \cdot \cdots \cdot \kappa_{i_j,v_j} \cdot \varphi \not\vdash \bot$. If $\varphi \not\vdash \bot$ then for all $j \geq 0$, $\kappa_{i_1,v_1} \cdot \cdots \cdot \kappa_{i_j,v_j} \cdot \varphi \not\vdash \bot$ (hence $2^{\mathcal{A}} \subseteq \sigma(\varphi)$ for $\varphi \not\vdash \bot$).*

We begin with considering postulates proposed in Hunter and Konieczny (2010), expressed using I to denote an arbitrary inconsistency measure.

- $I(\Gamma) = 0$ iff $\Gamma \nvdash \bot$ *(Consistency Null)*
- $I(\Gamma \cup \Gamma') \geq I(\Gamma)$ *(Monotony)*
- If φ is free[3] for Γ then $I(\Gamma \cup \{\varphi\}) = I(\Gamma)$ *(Free Formula Independence)*

It happens that our inconsistency measure n satisfies the postulates above. However, n fails the following postulate, also due to (Hunter and Konieczny 2010).

- If $\varphi \vdash \psi$ and $\varphi \nvdash \bot$ then $I(\Gamma \cup \{\varphi\}) \geq I(\Gamma \cup \{\psi\})$ *(Dominance)*

Example 4. Let $\Gamma = \{\neg a \wedge \neg a \wedge \neg a\}$. Take $\varphi = a$ and $\psi = a \wedge a \wedge a$. Then, $n(\Gamma \cup \{\varphi\}) = 1$ but $n(\Gamma \cup \{\psi\}) = 3$.

Failure of (Dominance) entails failure wrt the postulate (Besnard 2014) below

- if $\Gamma' \nvdash \bot$ and $\Gamma' \equiv \Gamma''$ then $I(\Gamma \cup \Gamma') = I(\Gamma \cup \Gamma'')$ *(Exchange)*

Furthermore, our inconsistency measure n satisfies the following postulate, introduced in Besnard (2014).

- if $\sigma\Gamma = \Gamma'$ and $\sigma'\Gamma' = \Gamma$ for some substitutions σ and σ' then $I(\Gamma) = I(\Gamma')$ *(Variant Equality)*

Keeping in mind that Γ denotes a multiset of formulas, it is easy to check that n satisfies the next postulate also introduced in Besnard (2014).

- $I(\Gamma \cup \{\varphi, \psi\}) = I(\Gamma \cup \{\varphi \wedge \psi\})$ *(Adjunction Invariancy)*

Since n satisfies both (Monotony) and (Adjunction Invariancy), it satisfies

- $I(\Gamma \cup \{\varphi \wedge \psi\}) \geq I(\Gamma \cup \{\varphi\})$ *(Conjunction Dominance)*

Similarly, an easy consequence of (Free Formula Independence) is

- $I(\Gamma \cup \{\top\}) = I(\Gamma)$ *(Tautology Independence)*

which our inconsistency measure n satisfies as well as the related postulate (Besnard 2014) below

- if $\varphi \equiv \top$ then $I(\Gamma \cup \{\varphi \wedge \psi\}) = I(\Gamma \cup \{\psi\})$ *($\top$-conjunct Independence)*

---

[3] A formula φ is free for Γ iff $\Delta \cup \{\varphi\} \vdash \bot$ for no consistent subset Δ of Γ.

5 Conclusion

The inconsistency measure introduced in this paper shows two main distinctive features. First, it deals with multisets of formulas. Second, it breaks the dichotomy suggested in Hunter and Konieczny (2010) which splits the universe of inconsistency measures into two categories: inconsistency measures based on minimal inconsistent subsets and inconsistency measures based on the alphabet (i.e., what atoms are involved in conflicts). Indeed, Example 4 is such that the inconsistency value differs in two cases with isomorphic sets of minimal inconsistent subsets and also differs in two cases where the alphabet consists of one propositional symbol.

Acknowledgements. The author is grateful to the reviewers for both useful comments on this paper and insightful suggestions about this topic.

References

Ammoura, M., Raddaoui, B., Salhi, Y., Oukacha, B.: On measuring inconsistency using maximal consistent sets. In: Destercke, S., Denoeux, T. (eds.) ECSQARU 2015. LNCS, vol. 9161, pp. 267–276. Springer, Switzerland (2015)

Besnard, P.: Remedying inconsistent sets of premises. Approx. Reason. **45**(2), 308–320 (2007)

Besnard, P.: Revisiting postulates for inconsistency measures. In: Fermé, E., Leite, J. (eds.) JELIA 2014. LNCS, vol. 8761, pp. 383–396. Springer, Heidelberg (2014)

Grant, J., Hunter, A.: Distance-based measures of inconsistency. In: van der Gaag, L.C. (ed.) ECSQARU 2013. LNCS, vol. 7958, pp. 230–241. Springer, Heidelberg (2013)

Hunter, A., Konieczny, S.: On the measure of conflicts: Shapley inconsistency values. Artif. Intell. **174**(14), 1007–1026 (2010)

Hunter, A., Parsons, S., Wooldridge, M.: Measuring inconsistency in multi-agent systems. Künstliche Intelligenz **28**(3), 169–178 (2014)

Jabbour, S., Ma, Y., Raddaoui, B., Sais, L., Salhi, Y.: A MIS partition based framework for measuring inconsistency. In: Proceedings of the 15th Conference on Principles of Knowledge Representation and Reasoning (KR 2016), pp. 84–93. AAAI Press (2016)

Jabbour, S., Raddaoui, B., Sais, L.: Inconsistency-based ranking of knowledge bases. In: Proceedings of the 7th International Conference on Agents and Artificial Intelligence (ICAART 2015), vol. 2, pp. 414–419. SciTePress (2015)

Lang, J., Marquis, P.: Resolving inconsistencies by variable forgetting. In: Proceedings of the 8th Conference on Principles of Knowledge Representation and Reasoning (KR 2002), pp. 239–250. Morgan Kaufmann (2002)

Lang, J., Liberatore, P., Marquis, P.: Propositional independence: formula-variable independence and forgetting. J. Artif. Intell. Res. **18**, 391–443 (2003)

Lin, F.: On strongest necessary and weakest sufficient conditions. Artif. Intell. **128**(1–2), 143–159 (2001)

Lin, F., Reiter, R.: Forget it! In: Proceedings of the AAAI Fall Symposium on Relevance, pp. 154–159 (1994)

Liu, W., Mu, K.: Editors of special issue on theories of inconsistency measures and their applications. Approx. Reason. (2016, to appear)

McAreavey, K., Liu, W., Miller, P.: Computational approaches to finding and measuring inconsistency in arbitrary knowledge bases. Approx. Reason. **55**, 1659–1693 (2014)

Kedian, M.: Responsability for inconsistency. Approx. Reason. **61**, 43–60 (2015)

Kedian, M., Liu, W., Jin, Z.: Measuring the blame of a formula for inconsistent prioritized knowledge bases. Logic Comput. **22**(3), 481–516 (2012)

Su, K., Lv, G., Zhang, Y.: Reasoning about knowledge by variable forgetting. In: Proceedings of the 9th Conference on Principles of Knowledge Representation and Reasoning (KR 2004), pp. 576–586. Morgan Kaufmann (2004)

Thimm, M.: Inconsistency measures for probabilistic logics. Artif. Intell. **197**, 1–24 (2013)

Thimm, M.: On the expressivity of inconsistency measures. Artif. Intell. **234**, 120–151 (2016)

Thimm, M.: Stream-based inconsistency measurement. Approx. Reason. **68**, 68–87 (2016)

Thimm, M., Wallner, J.P.: Some complexity results on inconsistency measurement. In Proceedings of the 15th Conference on Principles of Knowledge Representation and Reasoning (KR 2016), pp. 114–124. AAAI Press (2016)

Xiao, G., Ma, Y.: Inconsistency measurement based on variables in minimal unsatisfiable subsets. In: Proceedings of the 20th European Conference on Artificial Intelligence (ECAI 2012), pp. 864–869. IOS Press (2012)

A Possibilistic Multivariate Fuzzy c-Means Clustering Algorithm

Ludmila Himmelspach[(⊠)] and Stefan Conrad

Institute of Computer Science, Heinrich-Heine-Universität Düsseldorf,
40225 Düsseldorf, Germany
{himmelspach,conrad}@cs.uni-duesseldorf.de

Abstract. In this paper, we present a new *possibilistic multivariate fuzzy c-means* (PMFCM) clustering algorithm. PMFCM is a combination of multivariate fuzzy c-means (MFCM) and possibilistic fuzzy c-means (PFCM) that produces membership degrees of data objects to each cluster according to each feature and typicality values of data objects to each cluster. In this way, PMFCM produces a multivariate partitioning of a data set detecting clusters with unevenly distributed data over different features. It also reduces the influence of noise and outliers to computation of cluster centers.

Keywords: Fuzzy clustering · c-Means models · Possibilistic clustering · Multivariate memberships

1 Introduction

Clustering is an unsupervised learning technique for identifying groups of similar data objects within a data set. It is used in many fields, including image processing, bioinformatics, text mining where high dimensional data objects have to be grouped. Clustering high dimensional data bears several challenges that can be explained on the example of text clustering where a document is represented by a vector of *tf-idf*s of terms in the collection [1]. Due to the documents related to several topics, there are usually overlapping clusters in the data set. Depending on the range of topics, only few feature values in data vectors are significantly greater than zero. This implies that only few dimensions determine clusters. The information about the belonging of data objects to clusters in each dimension might be of great use. Finally, documents in the collection that do not belong to any cluster have to be recognized as noise and outliers. In this paper, we propose a new objective function based possibilistic multivariate fuzzy clustering algorithm that aims at satisfying these requirements.

The rest of the paper is organized as follows: in Sect. 2 we give a short overview over the different fuzzy clustering algorithms that we used as a basis for our approach. The possibilistic multivariate fuzzy c-means algorithm is presented in Sect. 3. The evaluation results of our method and the comparison with the basic approach are presented in Sect. 4. Section 5 closes the paper with a short summary and the discussion of future research.

© Springer International Publishing Switzerland 2016
S. Schockaert and P. Senellart (Eds.): SUM 2016, LNAI 9858, pp. 338–344, 2016.
DOI: 10.1007/978-3-319-45856-4_24

2 Related Works

The first problem described in introduction can be solved by using the *fuzzy c-means* (FCM) [2] clustering algorithm that assigns each data object to each cluster with a membership degree. The objective function of the fuzzy c-means algorithm is defined as follows:

$$J_m(U, V; X) = \sum_{k=1}^{n} \sum_{i=1}^{c} u_{ik}^m d^2(v_i, x_k), \qquad (1)$$

where c is the number of clusters, $u_{ik} \in [0, 1]$ is the membership degree of data object x_k to cluster i, $m > 1$ is the fuzzification parameter, $d(v_i, x_k)$ is the distance between cluster center v_i and data object x_k. The objective function of FCM has to be minimized under constraint (2) to obtain a good partitioning of the data set.

$$\sum_{i=1}^{c} u_{ik} = 1 \ \ \forall k \in \{1, ..., n\} \ \text{and} \ \sum_{k=1}^{n} u_{ik} > 0 \ \ \forall i \in \{1, ..., c\}. \qquad (2)$$

FCM is able to model the soft transitions between clusters. The information about the clustering structure, especially about the overlaps between clusters can be derived from the partitioning results.

The problem about FCM is that due to constraint (2) it assigns outliers and noise points to clusters in the same way as data objects within clusters. On the one hand, the information about whether a data object is a typical representative of the data structure or whether it is an outlier or noise point cannot be derived from the membership degrees. On the other hand, the outliers affect the computation of cluster centers. This problem can be solved by using the *possibilistic fuzzy c-means* (PFCM) [3] clustering algorithm that additionally produces the typicality values of data objects to clusters which express a relative degree of typicality of a data object to the overall structure of data. The objective function of PFCM is defined as follows:

$$J_{m,\eta}(U, T, V; X) = \sum_{k=1}^{n} \sum_{i=1}^{c} (a u_{ik}^m + b t_{ik}^\eta) d^2(v_i, x_k) + \sum_{i=1}^{c} \gamma_i \sum_{k=1}^{n} (1 - t_{ik})^\eta, \qquad (3)$$

where $t_{ik} \leq 1$ is the typicality value of data object x_k to cluster i, $m > 0$ and $\eta > 0$ are user defined constants. The first term in the objective function of PFCM has the same meaning as in FCM, where constants $a > 0$ and $b > 0$ control the relative influence of fuzzy memberships and typicality values. The second term ensures that the typicality values are determined as large as possible. The second summand is weighted by the parameter $\gamma_i > 0$ that the authors in [4] recommend to choose by computing:

$$\gamma_i = K \frac{\sum_{k=1}^{n} u_{ik}^m d^2(v_i, x_k)}{\sum_{k=1}^{n} u_{ik}^m} \quad 1 \leq i \leq c, \qquad (4)$$

where the $\{u_{ik}\}$ are the terminal membership degrees computed by FCM and $K > 0$ (usually $K = 1$). The objective function of PFCM has to be minimized under constraint (2) and $\sum_{k=1}^{n} t_{ik} > 0$, $\forall i \in \{1, ..., c\}$.

The possibilistic fuzzy c-means algorithm solves the first and the third problems described above but it assumes that all features are equally important for all clusters. Since few features usually determine particular clusters in high dimensional data sets, using either the attribute weighting fuzzy clustering algorithm [5] or the *multivariate fuzzy c-means* (MFCM) [6] method might be a better choice in such domains. We abstain from using the subspace clustering algorithms because they determine clusters in subspaces disregarding values of data objects in other features. In our case we aim for finding clusters where data objects have similar values in all features. Since MFCM produces the membership degrees of data objects to each cluster according to each feature which is beneficial for subsequent use of clustering results, we use it as a basis for our approach. The objective function of MFCM is defined as follows:

$$J_m(U, V; X) = \sum_{k=1}^{n} \sum_{i=1}^{c} \sum_{j=1}^{p} u_{ikj}^m (v_{ij} - x_{kj})^2, \tag{5}$$

where p is the number of features and $u_{ikj} \in [0, 1]$ is the membership degree of data object x_k to cluster i on feature j. Similarly to FCM, the objective function of MFCM has to be minimized under constraint (6).

$$\sum_{i=1}^{c} \sum_{j=1}^{p} u_{ikj} = 1 \;\; \forall k \in \{1, ..., n\} \text{ and } \sum_{j=1}^{p} \sum_{k=1}^{n} u_{ikj} > 0 \;\; \forall i \in \{1, ..., c\}. \tag{6}$$

In order to obtain the membership degrees of data objects to clusters, the authors propose to sum up the multivariate membership degrees over the dimensions [6]. Like FCM, its multivariate version does not recognize outliers and noise points as such assigning them to clusters in the same way as data objects within clusters.

3   A Possibilistic Multivariate Fuzzy c-Means Clustering Algorithm

The possibilistic FCM algorithm simultaneously produces membership degrees and the typicality values of data objects to clusters which makes it possible to derive the information about the overlaps between clusters and the noise points from the partitioning results. Unfortunately, it does not provide the information about the dimensions in which clusters overlap. This information might be valuable for subsequent use. Therefore, in our new approach called *possibilistic multivariate fuzzy c-means* (PMFCM) we combine the ideas of PFCM and MFCM algorithms. We define the objective function of PMFCM as follows:

$$J_{m,\eta}(U, T, V; X) = \sum_{k=1}^{n} \sum_{i=1}^{c} \sum_{j=1}^{p} (a u_{ikj}^m + b t_{ik}^\eta)(v_{ij} - x_{kj})^2 + p \sum_{i=1}^{c} \gamma_i \sum_{k=1}^{n} (1 - t_{ik})^\eta. \tag{7}$$

In (7) the typicality values of data objects to clusters are included in the weighting of the dimension-wise distances between data objects and cluster centers. We do not compute the typicality values of data objects to clusters at each feature because we consider the noise points as data objects that have a large overall distance (here, the Euclidean distance) to cluster centers. Unlike MFCM, we do not constrain the sum over all clusters and variables to a particular data object to be 1. In order to keep the equal weighting of distances by the membership degrees and the typicality values, we only constrain the sum over all clusters to a particular data object in each feature to be 1. Thus, the objective function of PMFCM has to be minimized under constraint (8).

$$\sum_{i=1}^{c} u_{ikj} = 1 \ \forall k, j \ \wedge \ \sum_{k=1}^{n} u_{ikj} > 0 \ \forall i, j \ \wedge \ \sum_{k=1}^{n} t_{ik} > 0 \ \forall i. \tag{8}$$

In PMFCM, the membership degrees, the typicality values, and the cluster centers are updated according to formulae (9), (10), and (11).

$$u_{ikj} = \frac{1}{\sum_{l=1}^{c} \left(\frac{(x_{kj} - v_{ij})^2}{(x_{kj} - v_{lj})^2} \right)^{\frac{1}{m-1}}} \qquad 1 \le i \le c, \ 1 \le k \le n, \ 1 \le j \le p. \tag{9}$$

$$t_{ik} = \frac{1}{1 + \left(\frac{b \sum_{j=1}^{p} (x_{kj} - v_{ij})^2}{\gamma_i p} \right)^{\frac{1}{\eta - 1}}} \qquad 1 \le i \le c, \ 1 \le k \le n. \tag{10}$$

$$v_{ij} = \frac{\sum_{k=1}^{n} (au_{ikj}^m + bt_{ik}^\eta) x_{kj}}{\sum_{k=1}^{n} (au_{ikj}^m + bt_{ik}^\eta)} \qquad 1 \le i \le c, \ 1 \le j \le p. \tag{11}$$

The membership degrees of data objects to clusters can be computed in our model as the average of the multivariate membership degrees over all variables, $u_{ik} = \frac{1}{p} \sum_{j=1}^{p} u_{ikj}$.

The working principle of PMFCM is basically the same as of PFCM. So, due to the lack of space we omit the details and refer to [3]. As in [4] we also recommend using terminal outputs of FCM for the initialization of our algorithm.

4   Data Experiments

The proposed algorithm PMFCM is tested on artificial data in order to examine its ability to correctly determine the centers of clusters that have different extends in different dimensions in presence of noise and outliers. Unfortunately, we could not test its ability to distinguish between the data objects belonging to clusters and the noise points because the transitions between the data objects on the border of clusters and noise points are rather soft. Therefore, we could not find any meaningful threshold for typicality values to differentiate between cluster objects and noise.

Figure 1(a) shows the data set *4-clusters* with 1245 data objects unequally distributed on one spherical cluster and three clusters that have a low variance in one dimension. The sum of the distances between the means of clusters in this data set is 31.5785. We generated the data set *4-clusters-noise* by adding 150 noise points to the data set *4-clusters*. The data set *4-clusters-noise* is depicted in Figure 1(b).

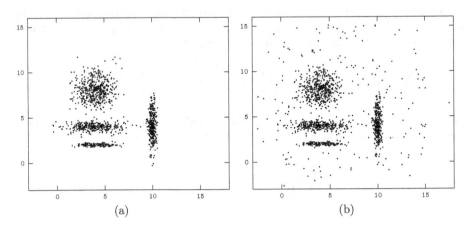

(a)   (b)

Fig. 1. Test data: (a) 4-clusters, (b) 4-clusters-noise.

Table 1 shows the comparison results between the algorithms MFCM and PMFCM for $a = 0.5$ and different values of b on the data set with four clusters without noise. We computed the Frobenius distance d_{orig} between the original means of clusters and the cluster centers produced by the clustering algorithms. We also computed the sum of the distances between the cluster centers d_{means} produced by the clustering algorithms. For a small values of b our approach produced less accurate cluster prototypes than MFCM. It determined cluster centers too close to each other, while MFCM produced cluster centers that were farther from each other than the original means of clusters. However, our approach produced much more accurate cluster centers for $b = 12$ than MFCM. With the increasing weight of the typicality values, our algorithm produced cluster centers that were slightly farther from each other than the original means of clusters. Unfortunately, we did not manage to find the golden mean where the sum of

Table 1. Comparison between MFCM and PMFCM on data set *4-clusters*.

	MFCM: $m = 2$	PMFCM: $m = 2$, $\eta = 2$ $a = 0.5$, $b = 4$	PMFCM: $m = 2$, $\eta = 2$ $a = 0.5$, $b = 12$	PMFCM: $m = 2$, $\eta = 2$ $a = 0.5$, $b = 20$
d_{orig}	2.49	2.92	1.12	1.17
d_{means}	33.73	27.87	31.52	31.65

the distances between the cluster centers produced by PMFCM corresponded to the sum of the distances between the original means of clusters in order to test whether or not our algorithm could produce the cluster centers which met the original means of clusters.

Table 2 shows the comparison results between MFCM and our algorithm on the data set *4-clusters-noise*. Unsurprisingly, the MFCM algorithm produced less accurate cluster centers than on the data set *4-clusters*. This is due to the fact that MFCM does not deemphasize the noise points while clustering. Consequently, it adjusted the cluster centers according to the distribution of all data objects in the data set. In contrast, PMFCM did not sustain a loss of performance in comparison to the data set without noise points. The fact that our approach produced more accurate cluster centers than on the data set *4-clusters* is due to the presence of noise points located close to the cluster borders. Apparently, such noise points advantageously completed the clusters so that PMFCM was able to produce more accurate cluster centers. As on the data set *4-clusters*, PMFCM produced cluster centers farther from each other with the increasing b and achieved the best results for $a = 0.5$ and $b = 12$.

Table 2. Comparison between MFCM and PMFCM on data set *4-clusters-noise*.

	MFCM: $m = 2$	PMFCM: $m = 2$, $\eta = 2$ $a = 0.5$, $b = 4$	PMFCM: $m = 2$, $\eta = 2$ $a = 0.5$, $b = 12$	PMFCM: $m = 2$, $\eta = 2$ $a = 0.5$, $b = 20$
d_{orig}	8.82	2.43	0.93	0.94
d_{means}	41.14	27.38	31.27	31.89

5   Conclusion and Future Works

In this paper, we proposed a possibilistic multivariate fuzzy c-means (PMFCM) algorithm that produces a multivariate partitioning of a data set detecting clusters with unevenly distributed data over different features in presence of noise points and outliers. In experiments, we showed that our algorithm is able to produce more accurate cluster centers than the MFCM algorithm on data sets with and without noise. Like the PFCM algorithm, the performance of the proposed method depends on the choice of the parameters that control the influence of the membership degrees and the typicality values. Therefore, in the future we plan to adapt MFCM to other possibilistic clustering models to test if the role of the right choice of user defined parameters can be minimized. Furthermore, we aim to apply our method for the text clustering to find out whether the subsequent text retrieval can be improved by the multivariate membership degrees. In this context it would be very helpful to find a heuristic for a distinction between the data objects belonging to clusters and noise points.

References

1. Sparck Jones, K.: A statistical interpretation of term specificity and its application in retrieval. J. Document. **28**(1), 11–21 (1972)
2. Bezdek, J.C.: Pattern Recognition with Fuzzy Objective Function Algorithms. Kluwer Academic Publishers, Norwell (1981)
3. Pal, N.R., Pal, K., Keller, J.M., Bezdek, J.C.: A possibilistic fuzzy c-means clustering algorithm. IEEE Trans. Fuzzy Syst. **13**(4), 517–530 (2005)
4. Krishnapuram, R., Keller, J.M.: A possibilistic approach to clustering. IEEE Trans. Fuzzy Syst. **1**(2), 98–110 (1993)
5. Keller, A., Klawonn, F.: Fuzzy clustering with weighting of data variables. Int. J. Uncertainty Fuzziness Knowl.-Based Syst. **8**(6), 735–746 (2000)
6. Pimentel, B.A., de Souza, R.M.C.R.: A multivariate fuzzy c-means method. Appl. Soft Comput. **13**(4), 1592–1607 (2013)

A Measure of Referential Success Based on Alpha-Cuts

Nicolás Marín, Gustavo Rivas-Gervilla, and Daniel Sánchez[✉]

Department of Computer Science and A.I.,
University of Granada, 18071 Granada, Spain
{nicm,daniel}@decsai.ugr.es, g.r.gervilla@gmail.com

Abstract. In this paper we propose a measure of the referential success of a referring expression, defined by a collection of fuzzy properties, with respect to a certain object. The measure yields the degree to which the object is univocally identified by the referring expression among a collection of objects in a certain context. We consider the alpha-cuts of the fuzzy subset of objects that satisfy the referring expression as crisp versions of the problem, and we obtain the final measure by measuring the subset of levels in $[0,1]$ where the referring expression has referential success in the crisp sense.

Keywords: Referring expression generation · Referential success · Linguistic descriptions of data · Fuzzy properties

1 Introduction

Data-to-text systems, originated in the natural language generation area [1], aim at *generating linguistic descriptions of data* (GLiDD), that is, generating texts expressing the relevant information in a dataset for specific purposes. This problem has been also dealt with by researchers in the fuzzy sets community, mostly under the name of *linguistic summarization*, since fuzzy sets are specially well suited for filling the semantic gap between data and natural language. However, in linguistic summarization, a query is usually employed on the data, providing as result a single (usually quantified) statement, whilst linguistic description of data does not consider a particular query, and the description is comprised of a collection of statements obtained after a search procedure, among other differences [2].

One of the most relevant tasks in GLiDD is that of *referring expression generation* (REG) [3,4]. Given a dataset containing objects and their properties, a referring expression is a collection of properties that are put together with the communicative purpose of uniquely identifying a certain object in the dataset. When a referring expression re univocally identifies an object o, we say that re *has referential success* regarding o.

When objects satisfy properties to a certain degree, for instance when properties are fuzzy, the referential success is also a matter of degree. This problem

© Springer International Publishing Switzerland 2016
S. Schockaert and P. Senellart (Eds.): SUM 2016, LNAI 9858, pp. 345–351, 2016.
DOI: 10.1007/978-3-319-45856-4_25

is presented in [5] and it is studied with more depth in relation to measures of specificity of fuzzy sets in [6]. Some related work is much earlier, see [7] for the generation of discriminating descriptions of objects, and [8] for the related problem of querying by examples and counter-examples, the latter with the difference that one does not necessarily point to a unique object. Given a referring expression re comprised of a collection of fuzzy properties, and a certain object o to be referred to, the measures proposed in these papers yield a degree of referential success of re with respect to o as a value in $[0, 1]$.

In this paper we show how a measure of referential success of a referring expression re with fuzzy properties can be defined on the basis of α-cuts of the fuzzy subset of objects that satisfy re. Specifically, it is defined as the measure of the subset of levels in $[0,1]$ where, in the corresponding α-cuts, the referring expression have referential success in the usual crisp sense.

2   Referential Success and Fuzziness

Let P be a set of properties, O a set of objects, and $re = \{p_1, ..., p_n\} \subseteq P$ a referring expression. As we have previously mentioned, for a referring expression to have referential success, it must not only describe the object that is intended to be identified, but it should not describe any other.

This concept, in conventional approaches to the referring expression generation problem, becomes a matter of compliance with the following restriction:

$$\bigcap_{p_i \in re} [\![p_i]\!] = \{o\} \tag{1}$$

where, for each property $p \in P$, $[\![p]\!] \subseteq O$ denotes the set of objects that accomplish property p, and o is the object the referring expression intends to point to.

However, in many cases, the management of referring expressions in relation to a given object of the context under study does not perfectly fit into a bi-valuated framework. In many domains of application, some of these properties have a gradual compliance with the objects under study, and this fact has an impact on how to handle referring expressions. For example, in the case of images, many of the concepts that can be used to describe an object within a scene have the mentioned fuzziness. Consider, for example, properties like color, shape, or position. Many of these concepts are gradual in nature: when is an object considered to be red?, when do we say that it is triangular?, or, when is it located on the top left of the image?

The fuzzy set theory allows us to handle the problem of representation and manipulation of such properties, that can be employed in referring expressions. In this sense, if we consider that $p(o)$ is the degree of compliance of object o with property p, then the accuracy of a referring expression $re = \{p_1, ..., p_n\}$ can be calculated as follows [5]:

$$acc_{re}(o) = \bigotimes_{i=1}^{n} p_i(o)$$ (2)

where $\otimes$ is a t-norm. In this paper we shall consider the minimum as t-norm, and the results we show in the following are valid for this particular case.

This expression induces the appearance of a fuzzy set of objects associated with each reference expression re, namely, the set of referred objects defined by the following membership function:

$$O_{re}(o) = acc_{re}(o), \forall o \in O$$ (3)

where O is the set of all objects in the context under study.

This set is fuzzy and can be simply understood as the information that the expression brings about which object in the context is the object referred to by the expression. In this fuzzy environment, the calculation of the referential success of a given referring expression has to be adapted because it also becomes a gradual concept. This problem is presented in [5] and it is studied with more depth in relation to measures of specificity of fuzzy sets in [6].

In this latter work, three properties that a referential success measure must satisfy are proposed:

Property 1. $rs(re, o) = 1$ iff $O_{re} = \{o\}$.

Property 2. If $O_{re}(o) = 0$ then $rs(re, o) = 0$.

Property 3. If $O_{re}(o_i) \leq O_{re'}(o_i) \ \forall o_i \in O \backslash \{o\}$ and $O_{re}(o) \geq O_{re'}(o)$ then $rs(re, o) \geq rs(re', o)$.

This set of properties is rather general and opens the possibility of defining a broad range of measures. As an example, Eq. (4) defines a family of referential success measures that fulfills these properties [5] (additional families can be found in [6]):

$$rs(re, o_i) = O_{re}(o_i) \otimes \left(\bigotimes_{o_j \in O \wedge j \neq i} \neg(O_{re}(o_j)) \right)$$ (4)

where $\otimes$ is a t-norm and $\neg$ is a fuzzy negation.

These measures can be the basis, not only for validating referring expressions, but also for the development of heuristics which aid to guide the operation of algorithms for the automatic generation of such expressions.

3   Analyzing Referential Success on α-cuts

The REG problem can be addressed by means of optimization algorithms that search the space of referring expressions induced by a collection of properties, looking for the referring expression which optimizes a measure of referential success. In this sense, measures as those discussed in the previous section are a good tool for building systems for generating referring expressions. Such algorithms are well known in the field of soft computing.

In the field of conventional natural language generation systems, there are well known algorithms and techniques for generating such expressions [3, 4]. One way to reuse all the know-how involving these classic approaches to the REG problem with fuzzy properties is to establish mechanisms that permit to adapt these yet developed algorithms and techniques in the fuzzy case.

The simplest way to do that is to fix a compliance threshold that discriminates which properties hold for every object. Given a fuzzy set F and a threshold $\alpha \in [0, 1]$, the set of objects in F with degree at least α is a crisp set called the α-cut of F. This is a conventional way to filter the graded results in a wide range of applications of fuzzy logic as in the case of fuzzy rules systems or in the area of flexible querying, to cite only a couple of well known examples. As we will see, depending on the considered threshold, different referring expressions arise; the analysis of this fact along interval [0,1] lead us to an alternative measure of referential success.

3.1   Some Definitions

Once a threshold α is considered, the set of objects that accomplish each property above this threshold is crisp.

Definition 1. *Let $re = \{p_1, ..., p_n\}$ be a referring expression with p_i fuzzy properties and let α be a value in [0,1]. For each property p_i, the set of objects that accomplish the property with at least level α, denoted $[\![p_i]\!]_\alpha$, is the α-cut of $O_{\{p_i\}}$.*

According to this definition, we can adapt the crisp definition of referential success for a given referring expression and threshold.

Definition 2. *Let $re = \{p_1, ..., p_n\}$ be a referring expression conformed by fuzzy properties, α a value in [0,1], and a given object o in the context under study. We say that re has referential success at level α and for object o if and only if:*

$$\bigcap_{p_i \in re} [\![p_i]\!]_\alpha = \{o\} \tag{5}$$

On the basis of these definitions, we can define the validity set associated to a referring expression as follows:

Definition 3. *Let $re = \{p_1, ..., p_n\}$ be a referring expression conformed by fuzzy properties and a given object o in the context under study. The validity set of re for object o is the set of α-values where the referring expression has referential success, that is:*

$$V_{re}^o = \left\{ \alpha \mid \bigcap_{p_i \in re} [\![p_i]\!]_\alpha = \{o\} \right\} \tag{6}$$

Let us introduce the following proposition:

Proposition 1. *If $V_{re}^o \neq \emptyset$, then V_{re}^o is an interval.*

Proof. Since the intersection in Eq. (6) is performed on α-cuts of the same level, it is immediate that

$$\bigcap_{p_i \in re} [\![p_i]\!]_\alpha = (O_{re})_\alpha \qquad (7)$$

where $(O_{re})_\alpha$ is the α-cut of O_{re} with the accuracy defining O_{re} in Eq. (3) calculated using the minimum as t-norm in Eq. (3). Since α-cuts are nested so that $\alpha > \beta$ implies $(O_{re})_\alpha \subseteq (O_{re})_\beta$, it is not possible to find $1 \geq \alpha > \beta > \delta \geq 0$ such that $(O_{re})_\alpha = (O_{re})_\delta = \{o\}$ and $(O_{re})_\beta \neq \{o\}$. Hence, when it is not empty, V_{re}^o is an interval.

3.2 The Measure

That is, roughly speaking, each referring expression such that $V_{re}^o \neq \emptyset$ begins to have referential success at a certain value $\alpha_1 \in [0,1]$ and stops having referential success at another (lower or equal) $\alpha_2 \in [0,1]$, with

$$\alpha_1 = \sup(V_{re}^o) \qquad (8)$$
$$\alpha_2 = \inf(V_{re}^o) \qquad (9)$$

where $\sup(A)$ and $\inf(A)$ stand, respectively, for the supremum and the infimum of the set A.

Proposition 2. *Let re be a referring expression with fuzzy properties and O_{re} the fuzzy subset of objects satisfying re. Let $O = \{o_1, o_2, \ldots, o_m\}$ with $m \geq 2$ such that $O_{re}(o_i) \geq O_{re}(o_{i+1}) \; \forall 1 \leq i < m$. Let $o \in O$ and $V_{re}^o \neq \emptyset$. Then*

1. $o = o_1$
2. $\alpha_1 = O_{re}(o) > O_{re}(o_2) = \alpha_2$

Proof. Under the conditions,

- If $o \neq o_1$ or $O_{re}(o_1) = O_{re}(o_2)$ then there is no $\alpha \in [0,1]$ such that $(O_{re})_\alpha = \{o\}$, and hence $V_{re}^o = \emptyset$ (contradiction). Hence, $o = o_1$ and $O_{re}(o_1) > O_{re}(o_2)$.
- For $\alpha > O_{re}(o)$ it is $(O_{re})_\alpha = \emptyset$. For $O_{re}(o) \geq \alpha > O_{re}(o_2)$ it is $(O_{re})_\alpha = \{o\}$. For $O_{re}(o_2) > \alpha$ it is $\{o, o_2\} \subseteq (O_{re})_\alpha$ and hence $(O_{re})_\alpha \neq \{o\}$. Hence, $V_{re}^o = \{\alpha \in [0,1] \mid O_{re}(o) \geq \alpha > O_{re}(o_2)\}$ and hence $\alpha_1 = O_{re}(o) > O_{re}(o_2) = \alpha_2$.

Thus, the greater the value of α_1, the greater the accuracy of the expression for object o. The lower the value of α_2, the lower the accuracy of the expression for objects different than o. According to this, we can define the following measure of referential success for a referring expression re regarding object o:

$$rs(re, o) = \begin{cases} \alpha_1(\alpha_1 - \alpha_2), & V_{re}^o \neq \emptyset \\ 0, & \text{otherwise} \end{cases} \qquad (10)$$

Let us show that this measure satisfies the required properties for a measure of referential success:

Proposition 3. *Equation (10) satisfy Properties 1, 2 and 3 for measures of referential success.*

Proof. We have three properties:

1. $rs(re, o) = 1$ iff $\alpha_1 = 1$ and $\alpha_2 = 0$ and $V_{re}^o \neq \emptyset$ iff $(O_{re})_\alpha = \{o\} \; \forall \alpha \in (0, 1]$ iff $O_{re} = \{o\}$.
2. If $O_{re}(o) = 0$ then $o \notin (O_{re})_\alpha \; \forall \alpha \in (0, 1]$ and we have two cases:
   - If $O = \{o\}$ then $V_{re}^o = \{0\}$ and $\alpha_1 = \alpha_2 = 0$, hence $rs(re, o) = 0$.
   - If $\{o\} \subsetneq O$ then $V_{re}^o = \emptyset$, and hence $rs(re, o) = 0$.
3. Let $O_{re}(o_i) \leq O_{re'}(o_i) \; \forall o_i \in O \backslash \{o\}$ and $O_{re}(o) \geq O_{re'}(o)$. Let $O = \{o_1, o_2, \ldots, o_m\}$ with $m \geq 2$ such that $O_{re}(o_i) \geq O_{re}(o_{i+1}) \; \forall 1 \leq i < m$ and $O = \{o'_1, o'_2, \ldots, o'_m\}$ such that $O_{re}(o'_i) \geq O_{re}(o'_{i+1}) \; \forall 1 \leq i < m$. We have two cases:
   - If $V_{re'}^o = \emptyset$ or $V_{re'}^o = \{0\}$ then $rs(re', o) = 0$ and $rs(re, o) \geq rs(re', o)$.
   - If $\{0\} \neq V_{re'}^o \neq \emptyset$ then by Proposition 2 we have $o = o'_1$ and $\alpha'_1 = O_{re'}(o) > O_{re'}(o'_2) = \alpha'_2$. By the conditions of the third property it is immediate that $o = o_1 = o'_1$ and

$$O_{re}(o) = \alpha_1 \geq \alpha'_1 = O_{re'}(o) > O_{re'}(o'_2) = \alpha'_2 \geq \alpha_2 = O_{re}(o_2)$$

and hence

$$rs(re, o) = \alpha_1(\alpha_1 - \alpha_2) > \alpha'_1(\alpha'_1 - \alpha'_2) = rs(re', o)$$

4   Conclusions

We have proposed a measure of referential success for referring expressions with fuzzy properties. The motivation behind this measure is the use of work by α-cuts in adapting to the fuzzy case existing crisp REG algorithms [3,4]. The application of the measure for such purpose will be an object of a future paper. The proposed measure can be considered as part of the quality assessment model for linguistic description of data [2,9,10]. Also future work will be the application of the resulting algorithm in the linguistic description of data, particularly on digital images [11] and time series data [2,12–16]. Finally, we will consider results using other t-norms in the definition of accuracy, that will require redefining the set V_{re}^o of Eq. (6).

Acknowledgments. This work has been partially supported by the Spanish Ministry of Economy and Competitiveness and the European Regional Development Fund (FEDER) under project TIN2014-58227-P.

References

1. Reiter, E.: An architecture for data-to-text systems. In: Proceedings of the Eleventh European Workshop on Natural Language Generation, ENLG 2007, pp. 97–104 (2007)
2. Marín, N., Sánchez, D.: On generating linguistic descriptions of time series. Fuzzy Sets Syst. **285**, 6–30 (2016)
3. Krahmer, E., van Deemter, K.: Computational generation of referring expressions: a survey. Comput. Linguist. **38**(1), 173–218 (2012)
4. van Deemter, K., Gatt, A., van der Sluis, I., Power, R.: Generation of referring expressions: assessing the incremental algorithm. Cogn. Sci. **36**(5), 799–836 (2012)
5. Gatt, A., Marín, N., Portet, F., Sánchez, D.: The role of graduality for referring expression generation in visual scenes. In: Carvalho, J.P., Lesot, M.-J., Kaymak, U., Vieira, S., Bouchon-Meunier, B., Yager, R.R. (eds.) IPMU 2016. CCIS, vol. 610, pp. 191–203. Springer, Heidelberg (2016). doi:10.1007/978-3-319-40596-4_17
6. Marín, N., Rivas-Gervilla, G., Sánchez, D.: Using specificity to measure referential success in referring expressions with fuzzy properties. In: IEEE International Conference on Fuzzy Systems, FUZZ-IEEE (2016)
7. Farreny, H., Prade, H.: On the best way of designating objects in sentence generation. Kybernetes **13**(1), 43–46 (1984)
8. De Calmès, M., Dubois, D., Hullermeier, E., Prade, H., Sedes, F.: Flexibility and fuzzy case-based evaluation in querying: an illustration in an experimental setting. Int. J. Uncertain Fuzziness Knowl.-Based Syst. **11**(1), 43–66 (2003)
9. Castillo-Ortega, R., Marín, N., Sánchez, D., Tettamanzi, A.G.B.: Quality assessment in linguistic summaries of data. In: Greco, S., Bouchon-Meunier, B., Coletti, G., Fedrizzi, M., Matarazzo, B., Yager, R.R. (eds.) IPMU 2012, Part II. CCIS, vol. 298, pp. 285–294. Springer, Heidelberg (2012)
10. Bugarín, A., Marín, N., Sánchez, D., Triviño, G.: Aspects of quality evaluation in linguistic descriptions of data. In: 2015 IEEE International Conference on Fuzzy Systems, FUZZ-IEEE 2015, Istanbul, Turkey, 2–5 August 2015, pp. 1–8 (2015)
11. Castillo-Ortega, R., Chamorro-Martínez, J., Marín, N., Sánchez, D., Soto-Hidalgo, J.M.: Describing images via linguistic features and hierarchical segmentation. In: Proceedings of the IEEE International Conference on Fuzzy Systems, FUZZ-IEEE 2010, Barcelona, Spain, 18–23, pp. 1–8 (2010)
12. Ramos-Soto, A., Bugarín, A., Barro, S.: On the role of linguistic descriptions of data in the building of natural language generation systems. Fuzzy Sets Syst. **285**, 31–51 (2016)
13. Castillo-Ortega, R., Marín, N., Sánchez, D.: Linguistic query answering on data cubes with time dimension. Int. J. Intell. Syst. **26**(10), 1002–1021 (2011)
14. Castillo-Ortega, R., Marín, N., Sánchez, D.: A fuzzy approach to the linguistic summarization of time series. Multiple-Valued Logic Soft Comput. **17**(2–3), 157–182 (2011)
15. Castillo-Ortega, R., Marín, N., Sánchez, D., Tettamanzi, A.: A multi-objective memetic algorithm for the linguistic summarization of time series. In: 13th Annual Genetic and Evolutionary Computation Conference, GECCO, pp. 171–172 (2011)
16. Kacprzyk, J., Zadrozny, S.: Computing with words is an implementable paradigm: fuzzy queries, linguistic data summaries, and natural-language generation. IEEE Trans. Fuzzy Syst. **18**(3), 461–472 (2010)

Graded Justification of Arguments via Internal and External Endogenous Features

Francesco Santini[✉]

Dipartimento di Matematica e Informatica, University of Perugia, Perugia, Italy
francesco.santini@dmi.unipg.it

Abstract. We propose a framework to compute a graded justification of arguments and a ranking of them. The framework is based on two different features that can be directly extracted from an Argumentation Framework (endogenously). Hence, the suggested approach does not consider any side-information on arguments or attacks, e.g., in the form of preferences. The two features are derived from *(i)* allowing a number of attacks inside an extension, and *(ii)* computing how well such an extension can defend its arguments (the difference between the number of attacks and counter-attacks). The ranking of arguments is provided by computing their justification status w.r.t the semantics redefined through *i* and *ii*.

1 Introduction and Related Work

Argumentation is based on the exchange and valuation of interacting arguments, followed by the selection of the most acceptable of them (for example, in order to take a decision). The original notion of defence is very simple: if argument a attacks argument b, and c attacks a, then c defends b. Defining the properties of an argumentation semantics [9] amounts to specifying the criteria for deriving a set of subsets of arguments (i.e., *extensions*) from an *Abstract Argumentation Framework* (*AAF*), which is defined by a set of arguments and an attack relationship, i.e., $\langle \mathscr{A}_{rgs}, R \rangle$. On the basis of such extensions, a justification status can be assigned to each argument; in particular, an argument is considered as justified, w.r.t. a given semantics, if it belongs to all its extensions [14].

In the following, for "graduality" we refer to the concept expressed in [8]: a partitioning of the set of arguments into more than the two usual subsets of "selected" and "non-selected" arguments (as in classical semantics [9]), in order to represent different levels of increasing preference. To be more precise, we refer to approach described the seminal work of Pollock [14], where different degrees of justification are computed in order to define a strength level for each argument.

To key-idea behind this paper is to extract information from an AAF, taking inspiration from [12]. Such information, both in [12] and here, is used to differentiate the same classical semantics [9] (e.g., admissible) according to different strength levels, thus obtaining graded semantics. From graded semantics we then derive a notion of graded justification for arguments, leading to a more fine-grained notion than what provided by non-graded approaches, as also advanced

© Springer International Publishing Switzerland 2016
S. Schockaert and P. Senellart (Eds.): SUM 2016, LNAI 9858, pp. 352–359, 2016.
DOI: 10.1007/978-3-319-45856-4_26

in [16]. Reaching such enrichment in the definition of argument justification is the ultimate aim of this paper.

As in [12], we consider a feature that concerns a strength level related to defence, that is a score that relates the arguments inside and outside an extension. In addition, we extract one more feature that concerns only the arguments inside an extension. As in [5] we suppose to being capable to allow some attacks in an extension (differently from [5], here attacks are not weighted). The basic idea is that an argument that is justified when allowing a lower amount of inconsistency is stronger than an argument justified when tolerating a higher number of internal attacks. Even this feature can be directly extracted from a plain AAF, and it directly derives from the structure of a given extension.

The paper is structured as follows: after summarising the preliminary information on Abstract Argumentation systems (Sect. 2), we introduce the suggested approach (Sect. 3) and an example to show how it works in practice. A final section wraps up the paper with related work from the literature, conclusions, and future work (Sect. 4).

2 Background

In this section we briefly summarise the background information related to classical Abstract Argumentation Frameworks (AAFs) [9].

Definition 1 (AAF). *An Abstract Argumentation Framework (AAF) is a pair $\langle \mathscr{A}_{rgs}, R \rangle$ of a set A of arguments and a binary relation $R \subseteq \mathscr{A}_{rgs} \times A$, called the attack relation. $\forall a, b \in \mathscr{A}_{rgs}$, aRb (or, $a \rightarrowtail b$) means that a attacks b. An AAF may be represented by a directed graph whose nodes are arguments and edges represent the attack relation. A set of arguments $\mathscr{E} \subseteq \mathscr{A}_{rgs}$ attacks an argument a, i.e., $\mathscr{E} \rightarrowtail a$, if a is attacked by an argument of $\mathscr{E}$, i.e., $\exists b \in \mathscr{E}.b \rightarrowtail a$.*

Definition 2 (Defence). *Given $F = \langle \mathscr{A}_{rgs}, R \rangle$, an argument $a \in \mathscr{A}_{rgs}$ is defended (in F) by a set $\mathscr{E} \subseteq \mathscr{A}_{rgs}$ if for each $b \in \mathscr{A}_{rgs}$, such that $b \rightarrowtail a$, then $\mathscr{E} \rightarrowtail b$ holds.*

The "acceptability" of an argument can be defined under different semantics σ which characterise a collective "acceptability" for arguments. In Definition 3 we only report the original semantics given by Dung [9]: $\sigma = \{cf, adm, com, prf, stb, gde\}$, which stand for conflict-free, admissible, complete, preferred, stable, and grounded semantics.

Definition 3 (Semantics [9]). *Let $F = \langle \mathscr{A}_{rgs}, R \rangle$ be an AAF. A set $\mathscr{E} \subseteq \mathscr{A}_{rgs}$ is conflict-free, denoted $\mathscr{E} \in cf(F)$, iff there is no $a, b \in \mathscr{E}$, such that $a \rightarrowtail b \in R$. For $\mathscr{E} \in cf(F)$, it holds that (i) $\mathscr{E} \in adm(F)$, if each $a \in \mathscr{E}$ is defended by $\mathscr{E}$; (ii) $\mathscr{E} \in com(F)$, if $\mathscr{E} \in adm(F)$ and for each $a \in A$ defended by $\mathscr{E}$, $a \in \mathscr{E}$ holds; (iii) $\mathscr{E} \in prf(F)$, if $\mathscr{E} \in adm(F)$ and there is no $\mathscr{C} \in adm(F)$ with $\mathscr{E} \subset \mathscr{C}$; (iv) $\mathscr{E} \in stb(F)$, if for each $a \in \mathscr{A}_{rgs} \backslash \mathscr{E}$, $\mathscr{E} \rightarrowtail a$; (v) $\mathscr{E} = gde(F)$ if $\mathscr{E} \in com(F)$ and there is no $\mathscr{C} \in com(F)$ with $\mathscr{C} \subset \mathscr{E}$.*

At a first level, the justification state of an argument can be conceived in terms of its extension membership: accepted (if it belongs to every extension), rejected (if it does not belong to any extension), or undecided, if it is in some extensions and not in others.

Definition 4 (Argument Justification [15]). *Given any of the semantics σ in Definition 3 and a framework F, an argument a is* (i) *justified iff $\forall \mathscr{E} \in \sigma(F), a \in \mathscr{E}$,* (ii) *$a$ is defensible if $\exists \mathscr{E} \in \sigma(F), a \in \mathscr{E}$ and a is not justified,* (iii) *a is overruled iff $\nexists \mathscr{E} \in \sigma(F), a \in \mathscr{E}$.*

Example 1. Consider $F = \langle \mathscr{A}_{rgs}, R \rangle$ in Fig. 1, with $\mathscr{A}_{rgs} = \{a, b, c, d, e\}$ and $R = \{a \rightarrowtail b, c \rightarrowtail b, c \rightarrowtail d, d \rightarrowtail c, d \rightarrowtail e, e \rightarrowtail e\}$. In F we have $adm(F) = \{\emptyset, \{a\}, \{c\}, \{d\}, \{a, c\}, \{a, d\}\}$, $com(F) = \{\{a\}, \{a, c\}, \{a, d\}\}$, $prf(F) = \{\{a, d\}, \{a, c\}\}$, $stb(F) = \{\{a, d\}\}$, and $gde(F) = \{a\}$. Hence, argument a is sceptically accepted in $com(F)$, $prf(F)$ and $stb(F)$, while it is only credulously accepted in $adm(F)$.

Fig. 1. An example of AAF.

3   Graded Justification

The two principles in [12] are, *(i)* having fewer attackers is better than having more, and *(ii)* having more defenders is better than having fewer. The result is the definition of a graded defence $d_{m,n}(\mathscr{E})$, which defines different levels of defence-strength: if $d_{m,n}(\mathscr{E})$ holds, $\mathscr{E}$ is a set of arguments for which each $a \in \mathscr{E}$ does not have at least m attackers that are not counter-attacked by at least n arguments in $\mathscr{E}$. Hence, if both $m \leq s$ and $t \leq n$, being mn-defended is preferable over being st-defended. From this defence, the authors accordingly define graded semantics (e.g., mn-complete), and, w.r.t. these semantics, they define graded justification of arguments in the same way as in Definition 4.

We propose two different features instead. The basic idea behind the first one is that, if we tolerate a given amount of conflict inside an extension, then some arguments may become "more justifiable": e.g., an overruled argument may become defensible because some attacks are now tolerated. While in [5] this amount corresponds to the sum of weights associated with attacks, here it is just the number of attacks between any two arguments in $\mathscr{E}$. The second feature concerns a strength level w.r.t the arguments outside an extension $\mathscr{E}$ (specular to the first feature). It is composed by two parts: the fist one counts the number of outward attacks (w.r.t. $\mathscr{E}$) from arguments that are not attacked (this is not considered in [12]), while the second one counts the number of counter-attacks in $\mathscr{E}$. In Definition 5 we compute such two features (*Internal* and *External*):

Definition 5. *Given a AAF* $= \langle \mathscr{A}_{rgs}, R \rangle$ *and a subset of arguments* $\mathscr{E} \subseteq \mathscr{A}_{rgs}$, *we define the following two functions:*

- *$I : (\mathscr{A}_{rgs}, \mathscr{E}) \rightarrow \mathbb{N}$ returns the number of attacks in* $\mathscr{E}$: $\sum\limits_{a,b \in \mathscr{E}} (a \rightarrowtail b)$
- *$E : (\mathscr{A}_{rgs}, \mathscr{E}) \rightarrow \mathbb{N}$ returns the number of attacked arguments from all un- attacked ones in* $\mathscr{E}$, *plus the number of counter-attacks from* $\mathscr{E}$:

$$-\Big(\sum_{a \in \mathscr{E},\, b,c \notin \mathscr{E},\, \nexists b.b \rightarrowtail a} (a \rightarrowtail c) \;+\; \sum_{a,c \in \mathscr{E},\, b \notin \mathscr{E},\, \exists b.b \rightarrowtail a} (c \rightarrowtail b) \Big)$$

In Definition 6 we redefine the notion of conflict-free semantics as $\bar{\alpha}$-conflict-free semantics: a number of attacks up to a maximum of $\bar{\alpha}$ can be present in $\mathscr{E}$. Such inconsistency budget has been already considered in other works, as [5,10], even if for different purposes (e.g., to find more than one grounded extension in [10]).

Definition 6 ($\bar{\alpha}$-Conflict-Free Semantics). *Given an AAF* $= \langle \mathscr{A}_{rgs}, R \rangle$, *a subset of arguments* $\mathscr{E} \subseteq \mathscr{A}_{rgs}$ *is* $\bar{\alpha}$-*conflict-free iff* $I(\mathscr{A}_{rgs}, \mathscr{E}) \leq \bar{\alpha}$.

Now we define $\bar{\gamma}$-defence, which extends Dung's defence by counting if the total number of counter-attacks is greater than the total number of attacks:

Definition 7 ($\bar{\gamma}$-Defence). *Given an AAF* $= \langle \mathscr{A}_{rgs}, R \rangle$ *and a set of arguments* $\mathscr{E} \subseteq \mathscr{A}_{rgs}$, *then* $\bar{\gamma}$-*defends* $b \in \mathscr{E}$ *iff* $E(\mathscr{A}_{rgs}, \mathscr{E}) \leq \bar{\gamma}$.

The notion of $\bar{\gamma}$-defence brings to the definition of the first semantics in Definition 3 that takes advantage of the notion of defence, that is the $\bar{\alpha}^{\bar{\gamma}}$-admissible semantics:

Definition 8 ($\bar{\alpha}^{\bar{\gamma}}$-Admissible Semantics). *Given an AAF* $= \langle \mathscr{A}_{rgs}, R \rangle$, *an* $\bar{\alpha}$-*conflict-free set* $\mathscr{E} \subseteq \mathscr{A}_{rgs}$ *is* $\bar{\alpha}^{\bar{\gamma}}$-*admissible iff it is classically admissible according to [9] (see Definition 3) and* $D(\mathscr{A}_{rgs}, \mathscr{E}) \leq \bar{\gamma}$.

As an example, w.r.t Fig. 1, $\{d, e\}$ is 2^{-1}-admissible, while $\{d\}$ is 0^{-2}-admissible. For the sake of presentation, in this work we do not extend the other semantics in Definition 3.

Both $\bar{\alpha}$ and $\bar{\gamma}$ represent a degree of "goodness" for each $\bar{\alpha}^{\bar{\gamma}}$-admissible semantics: if $\bar{\alpha}$ and/or $\bar{\gamma}$ are increased, than strength-level of the corresponding semantics decreases:

Proposition 1. *Given* $\bar{\alpha}_1 \leq \bar{\alpha}_2$ *and* $\bar{\gamma}_1 \leq \bar{\gamma}_2$, *if* $\mathscr{E}$ *is* $\bar{\alpha}_2^{\bar{\gamma}_2}$-*admissible then it is also* $\bar{\alpha}_1^{\bar{\gamma}_1}$-*admissible.*

In the following definition we rephrase the three-level classification in Definition 4 by considering $\bar{\alpha}^{\bar{\gamma}}$-admissible semantics.

Definition 9 ($\bar{\alpha}^{\bar{\gamma}}$-Justification). *Given* $F = \langle \mathscr{A}_{rgs}, R \rangle$, *and* $\mathscr{E}_{adm_{\bar{\alpha}^{\bar{\gamma}}}}(F)$ *the set of all the* $\bar{\alpha}^{\bar{\gamma}}$-*admissible extensions. An argument* $a \in \mathscr{A}_{rgs}$ *is*

- $\bar{\alpha}^{\bar{\gamma}}$-*justified if and only if* $\forall \mathscr{E} \in \mathscr{E}_{adm_{\bar{\alpha}^{\bar{\gamma}}}}(F)$, $a \in \mathscr{E}$;

- $\bar{\alpha}^{\bar{\gamma}}$-*defensible if and only if a is not $\bar{\alpha}^{\bar{\gamma}}$-justified but $\exists \mathscr{E} \in \mathscr{E}_{adm_{\bar{\alpha}^{\bar{\gamma}}}}(F)$, $a \in \mathscr{E}$;*
- $\bar{\alpha}^{\bar{\gamma}}$-*overruled if and only if $\forall \mathscr{E} \in \mathscr{E}_{adm_{\bar{\alpha}^{\bar{\gamma}}}}(F)$, $a \notin \mathscr{E}$.*

Using Proposition 1, we show what happens to $\mathscr{E}_{adm_{\bar{\alpha}^{\bar{\gamma}}}}(F)$ when $\bar{\alpha}$ and $\bar{\gamma}$ change:

Proposition 2. *Given $F = \langle \mathscr{A}_{rgs}, R \rangle$, $\bar{\alpha}_1 < \bar{\alpha}_2$ and $\bar{\gamma}_1 < \bar{\gamma}_2$, then $\mathscr{E}_{cf_{\bar{\alpha}_1 \bar{\gamma}_1}}(F) \subseteq \mathscr{E}_{cf_{\bar{\alpha}_2 \bar{\gamma}_2}}(F)$ and $\mathscr{E}_{adm_{\bar{\alpha}_1 \bar{\gamma}_1}}(F) \subseteq \mathscr{E}_{adm_{\bar{\alpha}_2 \bar{\gamma}_2}}(F)$.*

We have now all the ingredients to let justification become graded. For instance, if argument a is justified in $\mathscr{E}_{adm_{\bar{\alpha}_1 \bar{\gamma}_1}}(F)$, while argument b is only justified in $\mathscr{E}_{adm_{\bar{\alpha}_2 \bar{\gamma}_2}}(F)$ but not justified in $\mathscr{E}_{adm_{\bar{\alpha}_1 \bar{\gamma}_1}}(F)$, then a is preferred w.r.t. b.

From Proposition 2 we relate how the justification of a changes by increasing $\bar{\alpha}$ and $\bar{\gamma}$:

Proposition 3. *For $\bar{\alpha}_1 < \bar{\alpha}_2$, $\bar{\gamma}_1 \leq \bar{\gamma}_2$, $a \in \mathscr{A}_{rgs}$, the three justification statuses in Definition 4 (justified/defensible/overruled), and considering the $\bar{\alpha}^{\bar{\gamma}}$-admissible semantics, we have:*

- *If a is $\bar{\alpha}_1^{\bar{\gamma}_1}$-defensible then a cannot be $\bar{\alpha}_2^{\bar{\gamma}_2}$-justified.*
- *If a is $\bar{\alpha}_1^{\bar{\gamma}_1}$-overruled then a cannot be $\bar{\alpha}_2^{\bar{\gamma}_2}$-justified.*
- *If a is $\bar{\alpha}_1^{\bar{\gamma}_1}$-defensible or $\bar{\alpha}_1^{\bar{\gamma}_1}$-justified, then it cannot be $\bar{\alpha}_2^{\bar{\gamma}_2}$-overruled.*

While only justified (resp. defeasible) arguments can be considered as "stronger" than defensible ones (resp. overruled), we can exploit α and γ to have a more refined ranking. We define a partial order among arguments as stated by the rules in Definition 10.

Definition 10 (Ranking of Arguments). *Given $\bar{\alpha}_1 < \bar{\alpha}_2$, $\bar{\gamma}_1 < \bar{\gamma}_2$, $a, b \in \mathscr{A}_{rgs}$, and a given the $\bar{\alpha}^{\bar{\gamma}}$-admissible semantics, then all arguments are incomparable except:*

- *if a is $\bar{\alpha}_1^{\bar{\gamma}_1}$-justified and b is $\bar{\alpha}_1^{\bar{\gamma}_1}$-defensible, then a is strictly stronger than b (i.e., $a \succ b$);*
- *if a is $\bar{\alpha}_1^{\bar{\gamma}_1}$-defensible and b is $\bar{\alpha}_1^{\bar{\gamma}_1}$-overruled, then a is strictly stronger than b (i.e., $a \succ b$);*
- *if a, b are $\bar{\alpha}_1^{\bar{\gamma}_1}$-justified, but only a is $\bar{\alpha}_2^{\bar{\gamma}_2}$-justified, then a is strictly stronger than b (i.e., $a \succ b$);*
- *if a, b are $\bar{\alpha}_2^{\bar{\gamma}_2}$-defensible, but only a is $\bar{\alpha}_1^{\bar{\gamma}_1}$-defensible while b is $\bar{\alpha}_1^{\bar{\gamma}_1}$-overruled, then a is strictly stronger than b (i.e., $a \succ b$).*

Example 2. To show how the proposed ranking can be extracted, we consider the AAF in Fig. 2 and the $\bar{\alpha}^{\bar{\gamma}}$-admissible semantics. In the following, we highlight in bold the first time an argument appears in the set of extensions, i.e., the first time it is at least defensible. By not allowing any internal attack and not considering the second feature (i.e., $0^{-\infty}$-admissible semantics) we obtain $\{\emptyset, \{\mathbf{e}\}, \{\mathbf{d}\}, \{d, e\}\}$. By allowing one attack instead (i.e., $1^{-\infty}$-admissible) we obtain: $\{\emptyset, \{e\}, \{d\}, \{\mathbf{c}, d\}, \{\mathbf{b}, d\}, \{d, e\}, \{c, d, e\}, \{b, d, e\}\}$. Finally, by admitting two attacks (i.e., $2^{-\infty}$-admissible) we let also argument a appear: $\{\emptyset, \{e\}, \{d\}, \{c, d\}, \{d, e\}, \{c, d, e\}, \{b, d\}, \{b, d, e\}, \{b, c, d\}, \{b, c, d, e\}, \{\mathbf{a}, d, e\}\}$.

According to the ranking defined in Sect. 3, the result is that $d, e \succ b, c \succ a$. From this example, we define a more refined ranking of arguments w.r.t. just computing Dung's admissible extensions, which are $\{\emptyset, \{e\}, \{d\}, \{d, e\}\}$. From this set we can only say that arguments e and d are defensible, but no information is given about b and a. If we compute the stable semantics (the strictest one [9]), the only result $\{d, e\}$ adds no info.

However, by using the second feature we can directly compare also d and e: $E(\mathscr{A}_{rgs}, \{e\}) = -1$, $E(\{d\}) = -3$, and $E(\mathscr{A}_{rgs}, \{d, e\}) = -4$. According to the ranking in Definition 1 (item 3), $d \succ e$ because both arguments are 0^{-4}-justified, but only d is 0^{-3}-justified , while e is only 0^{-1}-justified. Note that comparing d and e is not possible in [12], since $d_{m,n}(\mathscr{E})$ does not consider un-attacked arguments. It may be reasonable to prefer a more aggressive argument, since it rules out more arguments, following the principle behind the preferred/stable semantics (see also Sect. 4 for possible refinements in this sense).

Arguments b and c are incomparable, by looking at the current ranking $d \succ e \succ b, c \succ a$. Therefore we exploit E: $\{b, d\}$ is 1^{-4}-defensible, while $\{c, d\}$ is only 1^{-3}-defensible: hence $b \succ c$, according to Definition 10. b is preferred w.r.t. c because the conflict with d (present in both cases) is tolerated in $\{b, d\}$ with the purpose to better defend b from a, with two counter-attacks. Hence, the final ranking is $d \succ e \succ b \succ c \succ a$.

The procedure followed in Example 2 can be generalised to an algorithm, as proposed in Fig. 3, in order to avoid enumerating all the extensions for any couple $\langle \bar{\alpha}, \bar{\gamma} \rangle$.

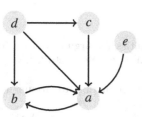

Fig. 2. The AAF used in Example 2.

Algorithm 1 Graded Ranking

Require: $F = \langle \mathscr{A}_{rgs}, R \rangle$
$S_{\bar{\alpha}} = \emptyset, \bar{\alpha} = 0, \gamma_0 = -|R| - |\mathscr{A}_{rgs}|$
repeat
$\quad S_{\bar{\alpha}} = S_{\bar{\alpha}} \cup \mathscr{E}_{adm_{\bar{\alpha}\bar{\gamma}}}(F)$
$\quad \bar{\alpha} = \bar{\alpha} + 1$
until (All $a \in \mathscr{A}_{rgs}$ appear in $S_{\bar{\alpha}}$ or $\bar{\alpha} = |R|$)
$Rk = $ rank $\mathscr{A}_{rgs}$ using Def. 10 over $S_{\bar{\alpha}}$
for all (incomparable $a, b, \ldots \in Rk$ with same $\bar{\alpha}_0$) **do**
$\quad \bar{\gamma} = \gamma_0, S_{\bar{\gamma}} = \emptyset$
$\quad$ **repeat**
$\quad\quad S_{\bar{\gamma}} = S_{\bar{\gamma}} \cup \mathscr{E}_{adm_{\bar{\alpha}_0 \bar{\gamma}}}(F)$
$\quad\quad \bar{\gamma} = \bar{\gamma} + 1$
$\quad$ **until** (All $a \in \mathscr{E}_{adm_{\bar{\alpha}\bar{\gamma}}}(F)$ appear in $S_{\bar{\gamma}}$ or $\bar{\gamma} = 0$)
$\quad Rk_{\bar{\gamma}} = $ rank incomparable $a, b, \ldots \in Rk$ with same
$\quad \bar{\alpha}$ using Def. 10 over $S_{\bar{\gamma}}$
$\quad$ Update Rk with $Rk_{\bar{\gamma}}$
end for
Ensure: Rk is a ranking of $\mathscr{A}_{rgs}$ according to Def. 10

Fig. 3. How to find graded ranking.

4 Related Work and Conclusion

We have introduced a framework where to rank arguments according to graded justification, with the final aim to extend [14]. We use the principles that, *(i)* the more an extension breaks Dung's conflict-freeness, the more it is weaker, and *(ii)* the more it counter-attacks outside arguments and defends its arguments, the more it is stronger. We relax conflict-freeness in order to get more information from the AAF structure, and to strictly rank more arguments than in [14].

Some previous work aimed at defining different levels of acceptability for arguments [1–3,8,11,16]. Such levels can be obtained by attaching numerical scores between 0 and 1 to each argument, or by ranking arguments over an ordinal scale. One distinct but still related work is [13]: there the objective is not to question the classical binary framework for inference, where an argument is inferred or not, but to define inference relations allowing to infer more arguments than sceptical inference.

However, differently from [3,8,16] for instance, we grade the justification status of arguments through a generalisation of the body of notions used in Dung's theory, such as defence/acceptability and extensions. The proposed approach is similar to [12], but here we can also rank not-attacked arguments. The idea to apply relaxation [5] to compute graded justification is novel; moreover, we propose an algorithm to avoid the computation of all the extensions for any couple $\langle \bar{\alpha}, \bar{\gamma} \rangle$.

For a recent comparison of ranking-based semantics for Abstract Argumentation, the interested reader can refer to [7].

All the exploited features can be directly extracted from the AAF structure itself (endogenously). In the future more features can be elicited and composed with the ones used in this work: for instance, the defence in [12] could represent a further criterion. Other features may come from Graph Theory: for instance, the cluster coefficient of $\mathscr{E}$ can be used together with $\bar{\alpha}$, in order to weigh the distribution of internal attacks of an extension, besides its number as in this paper.

The presented framework can be extended to *Weighted AAFs* [4,10] by considering the weights associated with attacks instead of the number of attacks, or to coalition-based partitioning of arguments [6].

References

1. Amgoud, L., Ben-Naim, J.: Ranking-based semantics for argumentation frameworks. In: Liu, W., Subrahmanian, V.S., Wijsen, J. (eds.) SUM 2013. LNCS, vol. 8078, pp. 134–147. Springer, Heidelberg (2013)
2. Baroni, P., Caminada, M., Giacomin, M.: An introduction to argumentation semantics. Knowl. Eng. Rev. **26**(4), 365–410 (2011)
3. Besnard, P., Hunter, A.: A logic-based theory of deductive arguments. Artif. Intell. **128**(1–2), 203–235 (2001)

4. Bistarelli, S., Rossi, F., Santini, F.: A collective defence against grouped attacks for weighted abstract argumentation frameworks. In: Proceedings of the Twenty-Ninth International Florida Artificial Intelligence Research Society Conference, FLAIRS, pp. 638–643. AAAI Press (2016)
5. Bistarelli, S., Santini, F.: A common computational framework for semiring-based argumentation systems. In: 19th European Conference on Artificial Intelligence, ECAI 2010. FAIA, vol. 215, pp. 131–136. IOS Press (2010)
6. Bistarelli, S., Santini, F.: Coalitions of arguments: an approach with constraint programming. Fundam. Inform. **124**(4), 383–401 (2013)
7. Bonzon, E., Delobelle, J., Konieczny, S., Maudet, N.: A comparative study of ranking-based semantics for abstract argumentation. In: Proceedings of the Thirtieth AAAI Conference on Artificial Intelligence, pp. 914–920. AAAI Press (2016)
8. Cayrol, C., Lagasquie-Schiex, M.: Graduality in argumentation. J. Artif. Intell. Res. (JAIR) **23**, 245–297 (2005)
9. Dung, P.M.: On the acceptability of arguments and its fundamental role in nonmonotonic reasoning, logic programming and n-person games. Artif. Intell. **77**(2), 321–357 (1995)
10. Dunne, P.E., Hunter, A., McBurney, P., Parsons, S., Wooldridge, M.: Weighted argument systems: basic definitions, algorithms, and complexity results. Artif. Intell. **175**(2), 457–486 (2011)
11. Dvořák, W.: On the complexity of computing the justification status of an argument. In: Modgil, S., Oren, N., Toni, F. (eds.) TAFA 2011. LNCS, vol. 7132, pp. 32–49. Springer, Heidelberg (2012)
12. Grossi, D., Modgil, S.: On the graded acceptability of arguments. In: Proceedings of the Twenty-Fourth International Joint Conference on Artificial Intelligence, IJCAI, pp. 868–874. AAAI Press (2015)
13. Konieczny, S., Marquis, P., Vesic, S.: On supported inference and extension selection in abstract argumentation frameworks. In: Destercke, S., Denoeux, T. (eds.) Symbolic and Quantitative Approaches to Reasoning with Uncertainty. LNCS, vol. 9161, pp. 49–59. Springer, Heidelberg (2015)
14. Pollock, J.L.: How to reason defeasibly. Artif. Intell. **57**(1), 1–42 (1992)
15. Prakken, H., Vreeswijk, G.: Logics for defeasible argumentation. In: Gabbay, D.M., Guenthner, F. (eds.) Handbook of Philosophical Logic, vol. 4, pp. 219–318. Springer, Heidelberg (2002)
16. Wu, Y., Caminada, M.: A labelling-based justification status of arguments. Stud. Logic **3**(4), 12–29 (2010)

Erratum to: A Two-Stage Online Approach for Collaborative Multi-agent Planning Under Uncertainty

Iván Palomares[✉], Kim Bauters, Weiru Liu, and Jun Hong

School of Electronics, Electrical Engineering and Computer Science,
Queen's University Belfast, Belfast, Northern Ireland
{i.palomares, k.bauters, w.liu, j.hong}@qub.ac.uk

Erratum to:
Chapter 15 in: S. Schockaert and P. Senellart (Eds.)
Scalable Uncertainty Management
DOI: 10.1007/978-3-319-45856-4_15

In an older version of the paper starting on p. 214 of the SUM proceedings (LNCS 9858), Fig. 6 was represented incorrectly. This has been corrected.

The updated original online version for this chapter can be found at 10.1007/978-3-319-45856-4_15

Author Index

Printed in the United States
By Bookmasters